Windows System Programming
Fourth Edition

Windows System Programming
Fourth Edition

Johnson M. Hart

♦♦Addison-Wesley

Upper Saddle River, NJ • Boston • Indianapolis • San Francisco
New York • Toronto • Montreal • London • Munich • Paris • Madrid
Capetown • Sydney • Tokyo • Singapore • Mexico City

Many of the designations used by manufacturers and sellers to distinguish their products are claimed as trademarks. Where those designations appear in this book, and the publisher was aware of a trademark claim, the designations have been printed in initial capital letters or in all capitals.

The author and publisher have taken care in the preparation of this book, but make no expressed or implied warranty of any kind and assume no responsibility for errors or omissions. No liability is assumed for incidental or consequential damages in connection with or arising out of the use of the information or programs contained herein.

The publisher offers excellent discounts on this book when ordered in quantity for bulk purchases or special sales, which may include electronic versions and/or custom covers and content particular to your business, training goals, marketing focus, and branding interests. For more information, please contact:

U.S. Corporate and Government Sales
(800) 382-3419
corpsales@pearsontechgroup.com

For sales outside of the U.S., please contact:

International Sales
international@pearsoned.com

Visit us on the Web: informit.com/aw

Library of Congress Cataloging-in-Publication Data
Hart, Johnson M.
  Windows system programming / Johnson M. Hart.
    p. cm.
  Includes bibliographical references and index.
  ISBN 978-0-321-65774-9 (hardback : alk. paper)
  1. Application software—Development. 2. Microsoft Windows (Computer file). 3. Application program interfaces (Computer software). I. Title.

  QA76.76.A65H373 2010
  005.3—dc22

                                                    2009046939

ISBN-13: 978-0-321-65774-9
ISBN-10:   0-321-65774-8
Text printed in the United States on recycled paper at Courier in Westford, Massachusetts.
First printing, February 2010

To Andrew and William

Contents

Figures

Tables

Programs

Program Runs

Preface

This book describes application development using the Microsoft Windows Application Programming Interface (API), concentrating on the core system services, including the file system, process and thread management, interprocess communication, network programming, and synchronization. The examples concentrate on realistic scenarios, and in many cases they're based on real applications I've encountered in practice.

The Win32/Win64 API, or the Windows API, is supported by Microsoft's family of 32-bit and 64-bit operating systems; versions currently supported and widely used include Windows 7, XP, Vista, Server 2003, Server 2008, and CE. Older Windows family members include Windows 2000, NT, Me, 98, and 95; these systems are obsolete, but many topics in this book still apply to these older systems.

The Windows API is an important factor for application development, frequently replacing the POSIX API (supported by UNIX and Linux) as the preferred API for applications targeted at desktop, server, and embedded systems now and for the indefinite future. Many programmers, regardless of experience level, need to learn the Windows API quickly, and this book is designed for them to do so.

Objectives and Approach

The objectives I've set for the book are to explain what Windows is, show how to use it in realistic situations, and do so as quickly as possible without burdening you with unnecessary detail. This book is not a reference guide, but it explains the central features of the most important functions and shows how to use them together in practical programming situations. Equipped with this knowledge, you will be able to use the comprehensive Microsoft reference documentation to explore details, advanced options, and the more obscure functions as requirements or interests dictate. I have found the Windows API easy to learn using this approach and have greatly enjoyed developing Windows programs, despite occasional frustration. This enthusiasm will show through at times, as it should. This does not mean that I feel that Windows is necessarily better than other operating system (OS) APIs, but it certainly has many attractive features and improves significantly with each major new release.

Many Windows books spend a great deal of time explaining how processes, virtual memory, interprocess communication, and preemptive scheduling work without showing how to use them in realistic situations. A programmer experienced in UNIX, Linux, IBM MVS, or another OS will be familiar with these concepts and will be impatient to find out how they are implemented in Windows. Most Windows books also spend a great deal of space on the important topic of user interface programming. This book intentionally avoids the user interface, beyond discussing simple character-based console I/O, in the interest of concentrating on the important core features.

I've taken the point of view that Windows is just an OS API, providing a well-understood set of features. Many programmers, regardless of experience level, need to learn Windows quickly. Furthermore, understanding the Windows API is invaluable background for programmers developing for the Microsoft .NET Framework.

The Windows systems, when compared with other systems, have good, bad, and average features and quality. Recent releases (Windows 7, Vista, Server 2008) provide new features, such as condition variables, that both improve performance and simplify programming. The purpose of this book is to show how to use those features efficiently and in realistic situations to develop practical, high-quality, and high-performance applications.

Audience

I've enjoyed receiving valuable input, ideas, and feedback from readers in all areas of the target audience, which includes:

- Anyone who wants to learn about Windows application development quickly, regardless of previous experience.

- Programmers and software engineers who want to port existing Linux or UNIX (the POSIX API) applications to Windows. Frequently, the source code must continue to support POSIX; that is, source code portability is a requirement. The book frequently compares Windows, POSIX, and standard C library functions and programming models.

- Developers starting new projects who are not constrained by the need to port existing code. Many aspects of program design and implementation are covered, and Windows functions are used to create useful applications and to solve common programming problems.

- Application architects and designers who need to understand Windows capabilities and principles.

- Programmers using COM and the .NET Framework, who will find much of the information here helpful in understanding topics such as dynamic link libraries (DLLs), thread usage and models, interfaces, and synchronization.

- Computer science students at the upper-class undergraduate or beginning graduate level in courses covering systems programming or application development. This book will also be useful to those who are learning multithreaded programming or need to build networked applications. This book would be a useful complementary text to a classic book such as *Advanced Programming in the UNIX Environment* (by W. Richard Stevens and Stephen A. Rago) so that students could compare Windows and UNIX. Students in OS courses will find this book to be a useful supplement because it illustrates how a commercially important OS provides essential functionality.

The only other assumption, implicit in all the others, is a knowledge of C or C++ programming.

Windows Progress Since the Previous Editions

The first edition of this book, titled *Win32 System Programming,* was published in 1997 and was updated with the second edition (2000) and the third edition (2004). Much has changed, and much has stayed the same since these previous editions, and Windows has been part of ongoing, rapid progress in computing technology. The outstanding factors to me that explain the fourth edition changes are the following:

- The Windows API is extremely stable. Programs written in 1997 continue to run on the latest Windows releases, and Windows skills learned now or even years ago will be valuable for decades to come.

- Nonetheless, the API has expanded, and there are new features and functions that are useful and sometimes mandatory. Three examples of many that come to mind and have been important in my work are (1) the ability to work easily with large files and large, 64-bit address spaces, (2) thread pools, and (3) the new condition variables that efficiently solve an important synchronization problem.

- Windows scales from phones to handheld and embedded devices to laptops and desktop systems and up to the largest servers.

- Windows has grown and scaled from the modest resources required in 1997 (16MB of RAM and 250MB of free disk space!) to operate efficiently on systems orders of magnitude larger and faster but often cheaper.

- 64-bit systems, multicore processors, and large file systems are common, and our application programs must be able to exploit these systems. Frequently, the programs must also continue to run on 32-bit systems.

Changes in the Fourth Edition

This fourth edition presents extensive new material along with updates and reorganization to keep up with recent progress and:

- Covers important new features in Windows 7, Vista, and Server 2008.

- Demonstrates example program operation and performance with screenshots.

- Describes and illustrates techniques to assure that relevant applications scale to run on 64-bit systems and can use large files. Enhancements throughout the book address this issue.

- Eliminates discussion of Windows 95, 98, and Me (the "Windows 9x" family), as well as NT and other obsolete systems. Program examples freely exploit features supported only in current Windows versions.

- Provides enhanced coverage of threads, synchronization, and parallelism, including performance, scalability, and reliability considerations.

- Emphasizes the important role and new features of Windows servers running high-performance, scalable, multithreaded applications.

- Studies performance implications of different program designs, especially in file access and multithreaded applications with synchronization and parallel programs running on multicore systems.

- Addresses source code portability to assure operation on Windows, Linux, and UNIX systems. Appendix B is enhanced from the previous versions to help those who need to build code, usually for server applications, that will run on multiple target platforms.

- Incorporates large quantities of excellent reader and reviewer feedback to fix defects, improve explanations, improve the organization, and address numerous details, large and small.

Organization

Chapters are organized topically so that the features required in even a single-threaded application are covered first, followed by process and thread management features, and finally network programming in a multithreaded environment. This organization allows you to advance logically from file systems to memory management and file mapping, and then to processes, threads, and synchronization, followed by interprocess and network communication and security. This organization also allows the examples to evolve in a natural way, much as a developer might create a simple prototype and then add additional capability. The advanced features, such as asynchronous I/O and security, appear last.

Within each chapter, after introducing the functionality area, such as process management or memory-mapped files, we discuss important Windows functions and their relationships in detail. Illustrative examples follow. Within the text, only essential program segments are listed; complete projects, programs, include files, utility functions, and documentation are on the book's Web site (www.jmhartsoftware.com). Throughout, we identify those features supported only by current Windows versions. Each chapter suggests related additional reading and gives some exercises. Many exercises address interesting and important issues that did not fit within the normal text, and others suggest ways for you to explore advanced or specialized topics.

Chapter 1 is a high-level introduction to the Windows OS family and Windows. A simple example program shows the basic elements of Windows programming style and lays the foundation for more advanced Windows features. Win64 compatibility issues are introduced in Chapter 1 and are included throughout the book.

Chapters 2 and 3 deal with file systems, console I/O, file locking, and directory management. Unicode, the extended character set used by Windows, is also introduced in Chapter 2. Examples include sequential and direct file processing, directory traversal, and management. Chapter 3 ends with a discussion of registry management programming, which is analogous in many ways to file and directory management.

Chapter 4 introduces Windows exception handling, including Structured Exception Handling (SEH), which is used extensively throughout the book. By introducing it early, we can use SEH throughout and simplify some programming tasks and improve quality. Vectored exception handling is also described.

Chapter 5 treats Windows memory management and shows how to use memory-mapped files both to simplify programming and to improve performance. This chapter also covers DLLs. An example compares memory-mapped file access performance and scalability to normal file I/O on both 32-bit and 64-bit systems.

Chapter 6 introduces Windows processes, process management, and simple process synchronization. Chapter 7 then describes thread management in similar terms and introduces parallelism to exploit multiprocessor systems. Examples in each chapter show the many benefits of using threads and processes, including program simplicity and performance.

Chapters 8, 9, and 10 give an extended, in-depth treatment of Windows thread synchronization, thread pools, and performance considerations. These topics are complex, and the chapters use extended examples and well-understood models to help you obtain the programming and performance benefits of threads while avoiding the numerous pitfalls. New material covers new functionality along with performance and scalability issues, which are important when building server-based applications, including those that will run on multiprocessor systems.

Chapters 11 and 12 are concerned with interprocess and interthread communication and networking. Chapter 11 concentrates on the features that are properly part of Windows—namely, anonymous pipes, named pipes, and mailslots. Chapter 12 discusses Windows Sockets, which allow interoperability with non-Windows systems using industry-standard protocols, primarily TCP/IP. Windows Sockets, while not strictly part of the Windows API, provide for network and Internet communication and interoperability, and the subject matter is consistent with the rest of the book. A multithreaded client/server system illustrates how to use interprocess communication along with threads.

Chapter 13 describes how Windows allows server applications, such as the ones created in Chapters 11 and 12, to be converted to Windows Services that can be managed as background servers. Some small programming changes will turn the servers into services.

Chapter 14 shows how to perform asynchronous I/O using overlapped I/O with events and completion routines. You can achieve much the same thing with threads, so examples compare the different solutions for simplicity and performance. In particular, as of Windows Vista, completion routines provide very good performance. The closely related I/O completion ports are useful for some scalable multithreaded servers, so this feature is illustrated with the server programs from earlier chapters. The final topic is waitable timers, which require concepts introduced earlier in the chapter.

Chapter 15 briefly explains Windows object security, showing, in an example, how to emulate UNIX-style file permissions. Additional examples shows how to secure processes, threads, and named pipes. Security upgrades can then be applied to the earlier examples as appropriate.

There are three appendixes. Appendix A describes the example code that you can download from the book's Web site (www.jmhartsoftware.com). Appendix B shows how to create source code that can also be built to run on POSIX (Linux and UNIX) systems; this requirement is common with server applications and organizations that need to support systems other than just Windows. Appendix C compares the performance of alternative implementations of some of the text examples so that you can gauge the trade-offs between Windows features, both basic and advanced.

UNIX and C Library Notes and Tables

Within the text at appropriate points, we contrast Windows style and functionality with the comparable POSIX (UNIX and Linux) and ANSI Standard C library features. Appendix B reviews source code portability and also contains a table listing these comparable functions. This information is included for two principal reasons:

- Many people are familiar with UNIX or Linux and are interested in the comparisons between the two systems. If you don't have a UNIX/Linux background, feel free to skip those paragraphs in the text, which are indented and set in a smaller font.

- Source code portability is important to many developers and organizations.

Examples

The examples are designed to:

- Illustrate common, representative, and useful applications of the Windows functions.

- Correspond to real programming situations encountered in program development, consulting, and training. Some of my clients and course participants have used the code examples as the bases for their own systems. During consulting activities, I frequently encounter code that is similar to that used in the examples, and on several occasions I have seen code taken directly or modified from previous editions. (Feel free to do so yourself; an acknowledgment in your documentation would be greatly appreciated.) Frequently, this code occurs as part of COM, .NET, or C++ objects. The examples, subject to time and space constraints, are "real-world" examples and solve "real-world" problems.

- Emphasize how the functions actually behave and interact, which is not always as you might first expect after reading the documentation. Throughout this book, the text and the examples concentrate on interactions between functions rather than on the functions themselves.

- Grow and expand, both adding new capability to a previous solution in a natural manner and exploring alternative implementation techniques.

- Implement UNIX/Linux commands, such as `ls`, `touch`, `chmod`, and `sort`, showing the Windows functions in a familiar context while creating a useful set of utilities.[1] Different implementations of the same command also give us

---

[1] Several commercial and open source products provide complete sets of UNIX/Linux utilities; there is no intent to supplement them. These examples, although useful, are primarily intended to illustrate Windows usage. Anyone unfamiliar with UNIX or Linux should not, however, have any difficulty understanding the programs or their functionality.

an easy way to compare performance benefits available with advanced Windows features. Appendix C contains the performance test results.

Examples in the early chapters are usually short, but the later chapters present longer examples when appropriate.

Exercises at the end of each chapter suggest alternative designs, subjects for investigation, and additional functionality that is important but beyond the book's scope. Some exercises are easy, and a few are very challenging. Frequently, clearly labeled defective solutions are provided, because fixing the bugs is an excellent way to sharpen skills.

All examples have been debugged and tested under Windows 7, Vista, Server 2008, XP, and earlier systems. Testing included 32-bit and 64-bit versions. All programs were also tested on both single-processor and multiprocessor systems using as many as 16 processors. The client/server applications have been tested using multiple clients simultaneously interacting with a server. Nonetheless, there is no guarantee or assurance of program correctness, completeness, or fitness for any purpose. Undoubtedly, even the simplest examples contain defects or will fail under some conditions; such is the fate of nearly all software. I will, however, gratefully appreciate any messages regarding program defects—and, better still, fixes, and I'll post this information on the book's Web site so that everyone will benefit.

The Web Site

The book's Web site (www.jmhartsoftware.com) contains a downloadable *Examples* file with complete code and projects for all the book's examples, a number of exercise solutions, alternative implementations, instructions, and performance evaluation tests. This material will be updated periodically to include new material and corrections.

The Web site also contains book errata, along with additional examples, reader contributions, additional explanations, and much more. The site also contains PowerPoint slides that can be used for noncommercial instructional purposes. I've used these slides numerous times in professional training courses, and they are also suitable for college courses.

The material will be updated as required when defects are fixed and as new input is received. If you encounter any difficulties with the programs or any material in the book, check these locations first because there may already be a fix or explanation. If that does not answer your question, feel free to send e-mail to jmh_assoc@hotmail.com or jmhart62@gmail.com.

Acknowledgments

Numerous people have provided assistance, advice, and encouragement during the fourth edition's preparation, and readers have provided many important ideas and corrections. The Web site acknowledges the significant contributions that have found their way into the fourth edition, and the first three editions acknowledge earlier valuable contributions. See the Web site for a complete list.

Three reviewers deserve the highest possible praise and thanks for their incisive comments, patience, excellent suggestions, and deep expertise. Chris Sells, Jason Beres, and especially Raymond Chen made contributions that improved the book immeasurably. To the best of my ability, I've revised the text to address their points and invaluable input.

Numerous friends and colleagues also deserve a note of special thanks; I've learned a lot from them over the years, and many of their ideas have found their way into the book in one way or another. They've also been generous in providing access to test systems. In particular, I'd like to thank my friends at Sierra Atlantic, Cilk Arts (now part of Intel), Vault USA, and Rimes Technologies.

Anne H. Smith, the compositor, used her skill, persistence, and patience to prepare this new edition for publication; the book simply would not have been possible without her assistance. Anne and her husband, Kerry, also have generously tested the sample programs on their equipment.

The staff at Addison-Wesley exhibited the professionalism and expertise that make an author's work a pleasure. Joan Murray, the editor, and Karen Gettman, the editor-in-chief, worked with the project from the beginning making sure that no barriers got in the way and assuring that hardly any schedules slipped. Olivia Basegio, the editorial assistant, managed the process throughout, and John Fuller and Elizabeth Ryan from production made the production process seem almost simple. Anna Popick, the project editor, guided the final editing steps and schedule. Carol Lallier and Lori Newhouse, the copy editor and proofreader, made valuable contributions to the book's readability and consistency.

Johnson (John) M. Hart
jmhart62@gmail.com
December, 2009

About the Author

Johnson (John) M. Hart is a consultant in the fields of Microsoft Windows and .NET application development, open systems computing, technical training and writing, and software engineering. He has more than twenty-five years of experience as a software engineer, manager, engineering director, and senior technology consultant at Cilk Arts, Inc., Sierra Atlantic, Hewlett-Packard, and Apollo Computer. John also develops and delivers professional training courses in Windows, UNIX, and Linux and was a computer science professor at the University of Kentucky for nine years. He is the author of technical, trade, and academic articles and books including the first, second, and third editions of *Windows System Programming*.

1 | Getting Started with Windows

Chapter 1 introduces the Microsoft Windows operating system (OS) family and the Windows Application Programming Interface (API) that all family members support. It also briefly describes the 32-bit (Win32) and 64-bit (Win64) API differences and portability issues, and, going forward, we mention Win32 and Win64 only when there is an important distinction.[1] The context will help to distinguish between Windows as an OS and Windows as the API for application development.

The Windows API, like any other OS API, has its own set of conventions and programming techniques, which are driven by the Windows philosophy. A simple file copy example introduces the Windows programming style, and this same style applies to file management, process and memory management, and advanced features such as thread synchronization. In order to contrast Windows with more familiar programming styles, there is a Standard C library version of the first example.

The first step is to review the basic features that any modern OS must provide and, from there, to learn how to use these features in Windows.

Operating System Essentials

Windows makes core OS features available on systems as diverse as cell phones, handheld devices, laptop PCs, and enterprise servers. Considering the most important resources that a modern OS manages helps to explain the Windows API.

- **Memory.** The OS manages a large, flat, virtual memory address space and transparently moves information between physical memory and disk and other secondary storage.

---

[1] Be aware that Microsoft often uses the term "Win32" generically for unmanaged code; all our code is unmanaged and does not use .NET's Common Language Runtime (CLR).

- **File systems**. The OS manages a hierarchical, named file space and provides both direct and sequential access as well as directory and file management.

- **Processors**. The OS must efficiently allocate computational tasks to processors, and multiple processors are increasingly common on even the smallest computers.

- **Resource naming and location**. File naming allows for long, descriptive names, and the naming scheme is extended to objects such as devices, synchronization, and interprocess communication objects. The OS also locates and manages access to named objects.

- **Multitasking**. The OS must manage processes, threads, and other units of independent, asynchronous execution. Tasks can be preempted and scheduled according to dynamically calculated priorities.

- **Communication and synchronization**. The OS manages task-to-task communication and synchronization within single computers as well as communication between networked computers and with the Internet.

- **Security and protection**. The OS provides flexible mechanisms to protect resources from unauthorized and accidental access and corruption.

The Microsoft Windows API supports all these OS features and more and makes them available on a range of Windows versions.

Windows Evolution

Several Windows versions support the Windows API. The multiple distinct Windows versions can be confusing, but from the programmer's perspective, they are similar. In particular, they all support subsets of the *identical* Windows API. Programs developed for one system can, with considerable ease, run on another, resulting in source and, in most cases, binary portability.

New Windows versions have added small amounts of new API functionality, although the API has been remarkably stable since the beginning. Major themes in Windows evolution include the following.

- **Scalability**. Newer versions run on a wider range of computers, up to enterprise servers with multiple processors and large memories and storage systems.

- **Performance**. Newer Windows versions contain internal improvements and some new API features that improve performance.

- **Integration**. Each new release integrates additional technology, such as multimedia, wireless networking, Web Services, .NET, and plug-and-play capability. This technology is, in general, out of scope for this book.

- **Ease of use**. Improved graphical desktop appearance and ease of use are readily apparent with each release.

- **Enhanced API**. Important API enhancements have been added over time. The API is the central topic of this book.

Windows Versions

Windows, in an evolving series of versions, has been in use since 1993. The following versions are important to developers at publication time.

- **Windows 7** was released in October 2009, shortly before this book's publication.

- **Windows Vista** is targeted at the individual user. Most commercial PCs sold since 2007, including desktops, laptops, and notebooks, came with an appropriate version of Windows Vista preinstalled.

- **Windows XP** is Vista's predecessor and is still very popular.

- **Windows Server 2008** is targeted at enterprise and server applications, and it was preceded by **Windows Server 2003**. Computers running Windows Server 2008 frequently exploit multicore technology with multiple independent processors. 64-bit applications are common on Windows Server 2008 computers.

- **Windows 2000** is still in use, although Microsoft will retire support in mid-2010.

- **Windows CE** is a specialized Window version targeted at smaller computers, such as phones, palmtops, and embedded processors, and it provides large subsets of Windows features.

Obsolete Previous Windows Versions

Earlier Windows versions are rare and generally not supported, but they are summarized here to give some historical perspective. While there are numerous exceptions, especially in the later chapters, many examples in this book will operate on these systems, although there are no guarantees.

- **Windows NT** 3.1, 3.5, 3.51, and 4.0 date back to 1993. NT was originally targeted at servers and professional users, with Windows 9x (see the next bullet) sold for personal and office use. Windows 2000 was the successor. The NT kernel is the foundation for the current Windows kernel, even though the term "Windows NT" is obsolete.

- **Windows 95**, **Windows 98**, and **Windows Me** (collectively, **Windows 9x**) were primarily desktop and laptop OSs lacking, among other things, the NT security features. Windows XP replaced these Windows versions.

Further back, Windows 3.1, a 16-bit OS, was dominant on personal computers before the Windows 95 introduction, and its graphical user interface (GUI) was a predecessor to the modern Windows GUI. The API, however, did not support many essential OS features, such as true multitasking; memory management of a large, flat address space; and security.

Going further back to the early 1980s, it is possible to identify DOS as the original "IBM PC" OS. DOS had only a simple command line interface, but the Windows command shell still supports DOS commands. In fact, most of the book's examples are command line programs, so you can run them under the command shell; that is, the Windows cmd program.

Windows NT5 and NT6

Windows 2000, XP, and Server 2003 use Windows NT kernel Version 5, although the minor version (the "x" in 5.x) varies. For example, Windows XP uses kernel Version NT 5.1.2600 ("2600" is the build number). Since the API features depend on the kernel version, it is convenient to use the term "NT5" to refer to these three Windows versions, even though Microsoft no longer uses the term "Windows NT."

The NT6 kernel is the base for Windows 7 (6.1), Vista (6.0), and Server 2008 (6.1 for R2; 6.0 otherwise), and the term "NT6" denotes these three Windows versions.

While many programs will run on earlier versions, in general, we will assume NT5 and NT6, which will allow us to exploit some advanced features. Since some important features are available only in NT6, sample programs test the Windows version number and terminate with an error message if they cannot run on the host computer.

The Microsoft Developer's Network (MSDN) API documentation (www.msdn.microsoft.com) states the version requirements. Check the documentation if there is any doubt about an API function's operation on a particular Windows version. The documentation will name the specific Windows version requirements, such as Windows Vista or Windows Server 2008, whereas we'll frequently state the same requirement as NT6.

Processor Support

Windows can support different underlying processor and computer architectures and has a Hardware Abstraction Layer (HAL) to enable porting to different processor architectures, although this is not a direct concern for the application developer.

Windows runs primarily on the Intel x86 processor family, including the x86-64 (or just x64) 64-bit extension, and compatible Advanced Micro Devices (AMD) processors. Although less common, several Windows server versions run on the Intel Itanium IA-64, a 64-bit architecture radically different from the classic x86 architecture.

The Windows Market Role

Windows is hardly unique in its ability to provide essential functionality on several platforms. After all, numerous proprietary and open OSs have these features, and UNIX[2] and Linux have long been available on a wide range of computers. There are, however, significant advantages, both business and technical, to using Windows and to developing Windows applications.

- Windows dominates the market, especially on the desktop, and has done so for many years with no change in sight.[3] Therefore, Windows applications have a large target market, numbering in the tens of millions and dwarfing other desktop systems, including UNIX, Linux, and Macintosh.

- The market dominance of the Windows OSs means that applications and software development and integration tools are widely and inexpensively available for Windows.

- Windows supports multiprocessor computers. Windows is not confined to the desktop; it can support departmental and enterprise servers and high-performance workstations.[4]

---

[2] UNIX comments always apply to Linux as well as to any other system that supports the POSIX API.

[3] Linux is occasionally mentioned as a threat to Windows dominance, primarily as a server but also for personal applications. While extremely interesting, speculation regarding future developments, much less the comparative merits of Linux and Windows, is out of scope for this book.

[4] The range of Windows host computers can be appreciated by considering that many programs in this book have been tested on computers spanning from an obsolete 486 computer with 16MB of RAM to a 16-processor, 16GB RAM, 2.4GHz enterprise server.

- Windows applications can use a GUI familiar to tens of millions of users, and many Windows applications are customized or "localized" for the language and user interface requirements of users throughout the world.

- Most OSs, other than UNIX, Linux, and Windows, are proprietary to systems from a single vendor.

- The Windows OSs have many features not available in standard UNIX, although they may be available in some UNIX implementations. Thread pools and Windows Services are two examples.

In summary, Windows provides modern OS functionality and can run applications ranging from word processors and e-mail to enterprise integration systems and large database servers. Furthermore, Windows platforms scale from small devices to the desktop and the enterprise. Decisions to develop Windows applications are driven by both technical features and business requirements.

Windows, Standards, and Open Systems

This book is about developing applications using the Windows API. For a programmer coming from UNIX and open systems, it is natural to ask, "Is Windows open?" "Is Windows an industry standard?" "Is Windows just another proprietary API?" The answers depend very much on the definitions of *open*, *industry standard*, and *proprietary*, as well as on the benefits expected from open systems.

The Windows API is totally different from the POSIX standard API supported by Linux and UNIX. Windows does not conform to the X/Open standard or any other open industry standards formulated by standards bodies or industry consortia.

Windows is controlled by one vendor. Although Microsoft solicits industry input and feedback, it remains the sole arbiter and implementor. This means that the user receives many of the benefits that open standards are intended to provide as well as other advantages.

- Uniform implementations reach the market quickly.

- There are no vendor-specific, nonstandard extensions, although the small differences among the various Windows platforms can be important.

- One vendor has defined and implemented competent OS products with all the required operating system features. Applications developers add value at a higher level.

- The underlying hardware platform is open. Developers can select from numerous platform vendors.

Arguments will continue to rage about whether this situation is beneficial or harmful to users and the computer industry as a whole. This book neither enters nor settles the argument; it is merely intended to help application developers use Windows to solve their problems.

Nonetheless, Windows does support many essential standards. For example, Windows supports the Standard C and C++ libraries and a wide array of open interoperability standards. Thus, Windows Sockets provide a standard networked programming interface for access to TCP/IP and other networking protocols, allowing Internet access and interoperability with non-Windows computers. The same is true with Remote Procedure Calls (RPCs).[5] Diverse computers can communicate with high-level database management system (DBMS) protocols using Structured Query Language (SQL). Finally, Internet support with Web and other servers is part of the total Windows offering. Windows supports the key standards, such as TCP/IP, and many valuable options, including X Windows clients and servers, are available at reasonable cost, or even as open source, in an active market of Windows solution suppliers.

In summary, Windows supports the essential interoperability standards, and while the core API is proprietary, it is available cost-effectively on a wide variety of computers.

Windows Principles

It is helpful to keep in mind some basic Windows principles. The Windows API is different in many ways, both large and small, from other APIs such as the POSIX API. Although Windows is not inherently difficult, it requires its own coding style and technique.

Here are some of the major Windows characteristics, which will become much more familiar as you read through the book.

- Many system resources are represented as a *kernel object* identified and referenced by a *handle*. These handles are somewhat comparable to UNIX file descriptors and process IDs.[6] Several important objects are not kernel objects and will be identified differently.

---

[5] Windows Sockets and RPCs are not properly part of Windows, but sockets are described in this book because they relate directly to the general subject matter and approach.

[6] These handles are similar to but not the same as the HWND and HDC handles used in Windows GUI programming. Also, Windows does have a process ID, but it is not used the way a UNIX process ID is used.

- Kernel objects must be manipulated by Windows APIs. There are no "back doors." This arrangement is consistent with the data abstraction principles of object-oriented programming, although Windows is not object oriented.

- Objects include files, processes, threads, pipes for interprocess communication, memory mapping, events, and many more. Objects have security attributes.

- Windows is a rich and flexible interface. First, it contains many functions that perform the same or similar operations; in particular, convenience functions combine common sequences of function calls into one function (`CopyFile` is one such convenience function and is the basis of an example later in this chapter). Second, a given function often has numerous parameters and flags, but you can normally ignore most of them. This book concentrates on the most important functions and options rather than being encyclopedic.

- Windows offers numerous synchronization and communication mechanisms tailored for different requirements.

- The Windows thread is the basic unit of execution. A process can contain one or more threads.

- Windows function names are long and descriptive. The following function names illustrate function name conventions as well as Windows' variety:

  `WaitForSingleObject`

  `WaitForSingleObjectEx`

  `WaitForMultipleObjects`

  `WaitNamedPipe`

  In addition to these features, there are a few conventions for type names.

- The names for predefined data types, required by the API, are in uppercase and are also descriptive. The following typical types occur frequently:

  `BOOL` (defined as a 32-bit object for storing a single logical value)

  `HANDLE` (a handle for a kernel object)

  `DWORD` (the ubiquitous 32-bit unsigned integer)

  `LPTSTR` (a string pointer)

  `LPSECURITY_ATTRIBUTES`

  We'll introduce these and many other data types as required.

- The predefined types avoid the * operator and make distinctions such as differentiating `LPTSTR` (defined as `TCHAR *`) from `LPCTSTR` (defined as `const TCHAR *`). *Note:* `TCHAR` may be a normal `char` or a 2-byte `wchar_t`.

- Variable names, at least in function prototypes, also have conventions. For example, `lpszFileName` might be a "long pointer to a zero-terminated string" representing a file name. This is the so-called Hungarian notation, which this book does not generally use for program variables. Similarly, `dwAccess` is a double word (32 bits) containing file access flags; "dw" denotes a double word.

Note: It is informative to look at the system include files where the functions, constants, flags, error codes, and so on are defined. Many interesting files, such as the following, are part of the Microsoft Visual Studio C++ environment and are normally installed in an include directory along with Visual Studio:

`windows.h` (this file brings in all the others)

`winnt.h`

`winbase.h`

Finally, even though the original Windows API (Win32) was created from scratch, it was designed to be backward-compatible with the Windows 3.1 Win16 API. This has several lingering and annoying effects, even though backward compatibility ceased to be an issue long ago.

- There are anachronisms in types, such as `LPTSTR` and `LPDWORD`, which refer to the "long pointer" that is simply a 32-bit or 64-bit pointer. There is no need for any other pointer type. At other times, the "long" is omitted, and `LPVOID` and `PVOID` are equivalent.[7]

- "`WIN32`" sometimes appears in macro names, such as `WIN32_FIND_DATA`, even though the macro is also used with Win64.

- The former requirement, no longer relevant, for backward compatibility means that numerous 16-bit functions are never used in this book, even though they might seem important. `OpenFile` is such a function; always use `CreateFile` to open an existing file.

---

[7] The include files contain types, such as `PVOID`, without the prefix, but the examples conform to the usage in many other books and the Microsoft documentation.

UNIX and Linux programmers will find some interesting differences in Windows. For example, Windows HANDLEs are "opaque." They are not integers allocated in sequential order. Thus, the fact that 0, 1, and 2 are special file descriptor values, which is important to some UNIX programs, has no analogy in Windows.

Many of the distinctions between, say, UNIX process IDs and file descriptors go away. Windows uses HANDLEs to reference both processes and open files, as well as other kernel objects. While Windows does have a process ID, it is used differently than a UNIX process ID. Many important functions treat file, process, event, pipe, and other handles identically.

UNIX programmers familiar with short, lowercase function and parameter names will need to adjust to the more verbose Windows style.

Critical distinctions are made with such familiar concepts as processes. Windows processes do not, for example, have parent-child relationships, although Windows processes can be organized into job objects.

Finally, Windows text files represent the end-of-line sequence with **CR—LF** rather than with **LF** as in UNIX.

32-bit and 64-bit Source Code Portability

Example source code can be built as both 32-bit and 64-bit executable versions (32-bit executables run on 64-bit computers but cannot exploit the larger address spaces). The essential differences between versions are the pointer variable size and the virtual address space size.

Most of the differences, from a programming point of view, concern the size of pointers and careful avoidance of any assumption that a pointer and an integer (LONG, DWORD, and so on) are of the same length.

Chapter 5 shows additional differences where it is important to use Windows functions that support 64-bit addresses.

With a little care, you will find that it is fairly simple to ensure that your programs will run under either Win32 or Win64. The program examples, both in the book and on the Web site (see the "What You Need to Use This Book" section below), are portable and have been tested on 64-bit computers. There are separate projects for building the 32-bit and 64-bit versions from the same source code.

The Standard C Library: When to Use It for File Processing

Despite the unique Windows features, it is still possible to achieve most file processing (the subject of Chapters 2 and 3) by using the familiar C programming language and its ANSI Standard C library, which are layered on the Windows API.

The C library (the adjectives ANSI and Standard are often omitted) also contains numerous indispensable functions that do not correspond to Windows system calls, such as functions defined in `string.h`, `stdlib.h`, `signal.h`, formatted I/O functions, and character I/O functions. Other functions, however, correspond closely to system calls, such as the `fopen` and `fread` functions in `stdio.h`.

When is the C library adequate, and when is it necessary to use native Windows file management system calls? This same question could be asked about using C++ I/O streams or the system I/O provided within .NET. There is no easy answer, but portability to non-Windows platforms is a consideration in favor of non-Windows functions if an application needs only file processing and not, for example, process management. However, many programmers have formulated guidelines as to when the C library is or is not adequate, and these same guidelines should apply to Windows. In addition, given the increased power, performance potential, and flexibility provided by Windows, it is often convenient or even necessary to go beyond the C library, as we will see starting as early as Chapter 2. Windows file processing features not available with the C library include file locking, memory mapping (required for memory sharing and performance), asynchronous I/O, random access to very long files (more than 4GB in length), and interprocess communication.

The C library file management functions are often adequate for simple programs. With the C library, it is possible to write portable applications without learning Windows, but options are limited. For example, Chapter 5 exploits memory-mapped files for performance and programming convenience, and this functionality is not included in the C library.

What You Need to Use This Book

Here is what you need to build and run the examples in this chapter and the rest of the book.

First, of course, it is helpful to bring your knowledge of applications development; knowledge of C programming is assumed.

Why Use C? Why Not C++?

The examples all use the C language, and, as necessary, use Microsoft extensions. The API is defined in C syntax, and C++ programmers will have no difficulty using the API or extending the C examples. Furthermore, for a variety of reasons, large amounts of legacy and some new code is written in C. Using C also makes the examples accessible to novice as well as intermediate and advanced programmers, all of whom will find portions of the book to be useful.

At times, this choice results in code that is more awkward than one might wish, and the code may strike some readers as a bit backward. For example, variables declarations occur at the start of program blocks rather than at the point of first use, and comments use the /* . . . */ syntax.

Using the Examples

Before you use the examples, however, you will need some basic hardware and software.

- A computer running Windows.[8]

- A C/C++ compiler and development system, such as Microsoft Visual Studio 2005 or 2008.[9] Other vendors also supply development systems, and although none have been tested with the examples, several readers have mentioned using other development systems successfully with only minor adjustments. *Note:* We concentrate on developing Windows console applications and will not truly exploit Microsoft Visual Studio's full powers.

- Enough RAM and disk space for program development. Nearly any commercially available computer will have more than enough memory, disk space, and processing power to run all the example programs and the development system, but check the requirements for the development system.[10]

- The on-line Microsoft Developer's Network (MSDN) documentation, such as that provided with Microsoft Visual Studio. It may be helpful to install this documentation on your disk because you will access it frequently, but you can easily access the information on the MSDN Web site.

- Download the *"Examples"* file, WSP4_Examples.zip, from the book's Web site (www.jmhartsoftware.com). Unzip the file and read ReadMe.txt. *Examples* (the name used from now on) contains source code, Visual Studio projects, executables, and everything else you need to build and run the examples in this book.

---

[8] I've tested Windows 7, Windows Vista, Windows XP, Windows Server 2003, and Windows Server 2008.

[9] At the time of writing, Visual Studio 2010 is in beta test. I've tested several examples with VS 2010 and experienced no conversion difficulties.

[10] The rapid pace of improvements in cost and performance is illustrated by recalling that in 1997 the first edition of this book specified, without embarrassment or apology, 16MB of RAM and 256MB of disk space. This fourth edition is being written on a laptop costing less than $800, with more than 100 times the RAM (the RAM space exceeds the previously required disk space), 300 times the disk space, and a processor running 50 times as fast as the one used when starting the first edition on a $2,500 PC.

Example: A Simple Sequential File Copy

The following sections show short example programs implementing a simple sequential file copy program in three different ways:

1. Using the Standard C library

2. Using Windows

3. Using a single Windows convenience function, `CopyFile`

In addition to showing contrasting programming models, these examples show the capabilities and limitations of the C library and Windows. Alternative implementations will enhance the program to improve performance and increase flexibility.

Sequential file processing is the simplest, most common, and most essential capability of any file system, and nearly any large program processes at least some files sequentially. Therefore, a simple file processing program is a good way to introduce Windows and its conventions.

File copying, often with updating, and the merging of sorted files are common forms of sequential processing. Compilers and text processing tools are examples of other applications that access files sequentially.

Although sequential file processing is conceptually simple, efficient processing that attains optimal speed can be much more difficult to achieve. It can require overlapped I/O, memory mapping, threads, or other techniques.

Simple file copying is not very interesting by itself, but comparing programs gives us a quick way to contrast different systems and to introduce Windows. The following examples implement a limited version of the UNIX `cp` command, copying one file to another, where the file names are specified on the command line. Error checking is minimal, and existing files are simply overwritten. Subsequent Windows implementations of this and other programs will address these and other shortcomings.

File Copying with the Standard C Library

As illustrated in `cpC` (Program 1–1), the Standard C library supports stream `FILE` I/O objects that are similar to, although not as general as, the Windows `HANDLE` objects shown in `cpW` (Program 1–2). This program *does not* use the Windows API directly, but Microsoft's C Library implementation does use the API directly.

Program 1–1 `cpC`: File Copying with the C Library

```
/* Chapter 1. cpC. Basic file copy program.
   C library Implementation. */
```

```c
/* cpC file1 file2: Copy file1 to file2. */

#include <stdio.h>
#include <errno.h>
#define BUF_SIZE 256

int main(int argc, char *argv[])
{
    FILE *inFile, *outFile;
    char rec[BUF_SIZE];
    size_t bytesIn, bytesOut;

    if (argc != 3) {
        printf("Usage: cp file1 file2\n");
        return 1;
    }

    inFile = fopen(argv[1], "rb");
    if (inFile == NULL) {
        perror(argv[1]);
        return 2;
    }

    outFile = fopen(argv[2], "wb");
    if (outFile == NULL) {
        perror(argv[2]);
        return 3;
    }

    /* Process the input file a record at a time. */
    while ((bytesIn = fread(rec, 1, BUF_SIZE, inFile)) > 0) {
        bytesOut = fwrite(rec, 1, bytesIn, outFile);
        if (bytesOut != bytesIn) {
            perror("Fatal write error.");
            return 4;
        }
    }

    fclose(inFile);
    fclose(outFile);
    return 0;
}
```

Run 1–1 is a screenshot of cpC execution with a short test.

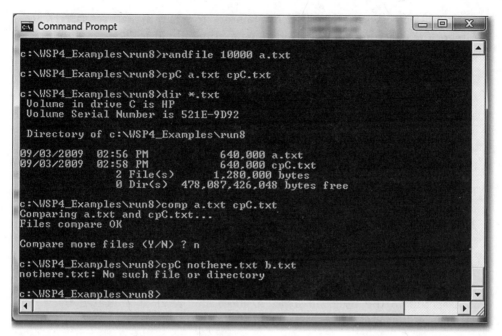

```
c:\WSP4_Examples\run8>randfile 10000 a.txt

c:\WSP4_Examples\run8>cpC a.txt cpC.txt

c:\WSP4_Examples\run8>dir *.txt
 Volume in drive C is HP
 Volume Serial Number is 521E-9D92

 Directory of c:\WSP4_Examples\run8

09/03/2009  02:56 PM           640,000 a.txt
09/03/2009  02:58 PM           640,000 cpC.txt
               2 File(s)      1,280,000 bytes
               0 Dir(s)  478,087,426,048 bytes free

c:\WSP4_Examples\run8>comp a.txt cpC.txt
Comparing a.txt and cpC.txt...
Files compare OK

Compare more files (Y/N) ? n

c:\WSP4_Examples\run8>cpC nothere.txt b.txt
nothere.txt: No such file or directory

c:\WSP4_Examples\run8>
```

Run 1–1   cpC: Execution and Test

- The working directory is set to the directory run8 in the *Examples* directory (see the "Using the Examples" section above). This directory contains the 32-bit programs built with Visual Studio 2008, and we use this directory for nearly all the example program screen shots.

- We need a text file for the test, and the randfile program generates a text file with 64-byte records with some random content. In this case, the output file is a.txt with 10,000 records. We use randfile frequently, and it's available in the *Examples* if you're curious about its operation.

- The second line in the screenshot shows cpC execution.

- The next commands show all the text files and compares them to be sure that the copy was correct. Note that the time stamps are different on the two files.

- The final line shows the error message if you try to copy a file that does not exist.

This simple example clearly illustrates some common programming assumptions and conventions that do not always apply with Windows.

1. Open file objects are identified by pointers to `FILE` structures (UNIX uses integer file descriptors). `NULL` indicates an invalid value. The pointers are, in effect, a form of handle to the open file object.

2. The call to `fopen` specifies whether the file is to be treated as a text file or a binary file. Text files contain system-specific character sequences to indicate situations such as an end of line. On many systems, including Windows, I/O operations on a text file convert between the end-of-line character sequence and the null character that C interprets as the end of a string. In the example, both files are opened in binary mode.

3. Errors are diagnosed with `perror`, which, in turn, accesses the global variable `errno` to obtain information about the function call failure. Alternatively, the `ferror` function could be used to return an error code that is associated with the `FILE` rather than the system.

4. The `fread` and `fwrite` functions directly return the number of objects processed rather than return the value in an argument, and this arrangement is essential to the program logic. A successful read is indicated by a non-negative value, and 0 indicates an end of file.

5. The `fclose` function applies only to `FILE` objects (a similar statement applies to UNIX file descriptors).

6. The I/O is synchronous so that the program must wait for the I/O operation to complete before proceeding.

7. The C library `printf` I/O function is useful for error messages and occurs even in the initial Windows example.

The C library implementation has the advantage of portability to UNIX, Windows, and other systems that support ANSI C. Furthermore, as shown in Appendix C, C library performance for sequential I/O is competitive with alternative implementations. Nonetheless, programs are still constrained to synchronous I/O operations, although this constraint will be lifted somewhat when using Windows threads (starting in Chapter 7).

C library file processing programs, like their UNIX equivalents, are able to perform random access file operations (using `fseek` or, in the case of text files, `fsetpos` and `fgetpos`), but that is the limit of sophistication of Standard C library file I/O. *Note:* Microsoft C++ does provide nonstandard extensions that support, for example, file locking. Finally, the C library cannot control file security.

In summary, if simple synchronous file or console I/O is all that is needed, then use the C library to write portable programs that will run under Windows.

File Copying with Windows

cpW (Program 1–2) shows the same program using the Windows API, and the same basic techniques, style, and conventions are used throughout this book.

Program 1–2 cpW: File Copying with Windows, First Implementation

```
/* Chapter 1. cpW. Basic file copy program. Windows Implementation. */
/* cpW file1 file2: Copy file1 to file2. */

#include <windows.h>
#include <stdio.h>
#define BUF_SIZE 256
int main(int argc, LPTSTR argv[])
{
    HANDLE hIn, hOut;
    DWORD nIn, nOut;
    CHAR buffer[BUF_SIZE];

    if (argc != 3) {
        printf("Usage: cp file1 file2\n");
        return 1;
    }

    hIn = CreateFile(argv[1], GENERIC_READ, FILE_SHARE_READ, NULL,
            OPEN_EXISTING, FILE_ATTRIBUTE_NORMAL, NULL);
    if (hIn == INVALID_HANDLE_VALUE) {
        printf("Cannot open input file. Error: %x\n", GetLastError());
        return 2;
    }

    hOut = CreateFile(argv[2], GENERIC_WRITE, 0, NULL,
            CREATE_ALWAYS, FILE_ATTRIBUTE_NORMAL, NULL);
    if (hOut == INVALID_HANDLE_VALUE) {
        printf("Cannot open output file. Error: %x\n",
                GetLastError());
        return 3;
    }

    while (ReadFile(hIn, buffer, BUF_SIZE, &nIn, NULL) && nIn > 0) {
        WriteFile(hOut, buffer, nIn, &nOut, NULL);
        if (nIn != nOut) {
            printf("Fatal write error: %x\n", GetLastError());
            return 4;
        }
    }
    CloseHandle(hIn); CloseHandle(hOut);
    return 0;
}
```

```
c:\WSP4_Examples\run8>cpW a.txt cpW.txt

c:\WSP4_Examples\run8>dir *.txt
 Volume in drive C is HP
 Volume Serial Number is 521E-9D92

 Directory of c:\WSP4_Examples\run8

09/03/2009  02:56 PM           640,000 a.txt
09/03/2009  02:59 PM           640,000 cpW.txt
               2 File(s)      1,280,000 bytes
               0 Dir(s)   478,087,307,264 bytes free

c:\WSP4_Examples\run8>comp a.txt cpW.txt
Comparing a.txt and cpW.txt...
Files compare OK

Compare more files (Y/N) ? n

c:\WSP4_Examples\run8>cpW nothere.txt b.txt
Cannot open input file. Error: 2

c:\WSP4_Examples\run8>
```

Run 1–2   cpW: Execution and Test

Run 1–2 shows cpW execution, showing the same information as Run 1–1. All text files other than a.txt were removed before the run.

This simple example illustrates some Windows programming features that Chapter 2 will start to explain in detail.

1. windows.h is always necessary and contains all Windows function definitions and data types.

2. Although there are some important exceptions, most Windows objects in this book are identified by variables of type HANDLE, and a single generic Close-Handle function applies to most objects.

3. Close all open handles when they are no longer required so as to free resources. However, the handles will be closed automatically by Windows when a process exits, and Windows will destroy an object and free its resources, as appropriate, if there are no remaining handles referring to the object. (*Note:* Closing the handle does not destroy the file.)

4. Windows defines numerous symbolic constants and flags. Their names are usually quite long and often describe their purposes. INVALID_HANDLE_VALUE and GENERIC_READ are typical.

5. Functions such as ReadFile and WriteFile return BOOL values, which you can use in logical expressions, rather than byte counts, which are arguments. This alters the loop logic slightly.[11] The end of file is detected by a zero byte count and is not a failure.

6. System error codes, as DWORDs, can be obtained immediately after a failed system call through GetLastError. Program 2–1 shows how to obtain Windows-generated textual error messages.

7. Windows has a powerful security system, described in Chapter 15. The output file in this example is owned by the user and will be secured with the user's default settings.

8. Functions such as CreateFile have a rich set of options, and the example uses default values.

File Copying with a Windows Convenience Function

Windows has a number of convenience functions that combine several functions to perform a common task. These convenience functions can also improve performance in some cases (see Appendix C). CopyFile, for example, greatly simplifies the file copy program, cpCF (Program 1–3). Among other things, there is no need to be concerned with the appropriate buffer size, which was arbitrarily 256 in the two preceding programs. Furthermore, CopyFile copies file metadata (such as time stamps) that will not be preserved by the other two programs.

Program 1–3 cpCF: File Copying with a Windows Convenience Function

```
/* Chapter 1. cpCF. Basic file copy program. Windows implementation
   using CopyFile for convenience and improved performance. */
/* cpCF file1 file2: Copy file1 to file2. */

#include <windows.h>
#include <stdio.h>

int main(int argc, LPTSTR argv[])
{
    if (argc != 3) {
        printf("Usage: cpCF file1 file2\n");
        return 1;
    }
```

---

[11] Notice that the loop logic depends on ANSI C's left-to-right evaluation of logical "and" (&&) and logical "or" (| |) operations.

```
    if (!CopyFile(argv[1], argv[2], FALSE)) {
        printf("CopyFile Error: %x\n", GetLastError());
        return 2;
    }
    return 0;
}
```

Run 1–3 shows the cpCF test; notice that CopyFile preserves the file time and other attributes of the original file. The previous two copy programs changed the file time.

Also notice the timep program, which shows the execution time for a program; timep implementation is described in Chapter 6, but it's helpful to use it now. In this example, a.txt is small, and the execution time is minimal and not measured precisely. However, you can easily create larger files with randfile.

Summary

The introductory examples, three simple file copy programs, illustrate many differences between C library and Windows programs. Appendix C shows some of the performance differences among the various implementations. The Windows exam-

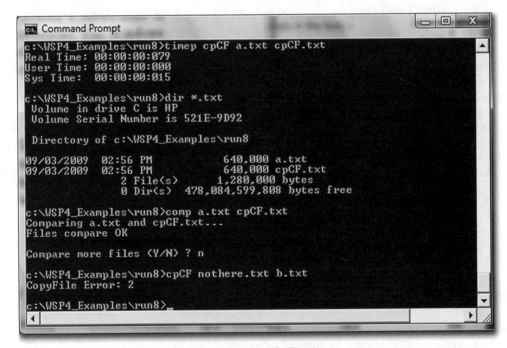

```
c:\WSP4_Examples\run8>timep cpCF a.txt cpCF.txt
Real Time: 00:00:00:079
User Time: 00:00:00:000
Sys Time:  00:00:00:015

c:\WSP4_Examples\run8>dir *.txt
 Volume in drive C is HP
 Volume Serial Number is 521E-9D92

 Directory of c:\WSP4_Examples\run8

09/03/2009  02:56 PM           640,000 a.txt
09/03/2009  02:56 PM           640,000 cpCF.txt
               2 File(s)      1,280,000 bytes
               0 Dir(s)   478,084,599,808 bytes free

c:\WSP4_Examples\run8>comp a.txt cpCF.txt
Comparing a.txt and cpCF.txt...
Files compare OK

Compare more files (Y/N) ? n

c:\WSP4_Examples\run8>cpCF nothere.txt b.txt
CopyFile Error: 2

c:\WSP4_Examples\run8>
```

Run 1–3   cpCF: Execution and Test, with Timing

ples clearly illustrate Windows programming style and conventions but only hint at the functionality available to Windows programmers.

Looking Ahead

Chapters 2 and 3 take a much more extensive look at I/O and the file system. Topics include console I/O, ASCII and Unicode character processing, file and directory management, file attributes, and advanced options, as well as registry programming. These two chapters develop the basic techniques and lay the groundwork for the rest of the book.

Additional Reading

Publication information about the following books is listed in the bibliography.

Windows API

Windows via C / C+ by Jeffrey Richter and Christophe Nasarre, covers Windows programming with significant overlap with this book.

The hypertext on-line MSDN help available with Microsoft Visual C++ documents every function, and the same information is available from the Microsoft home page, www.msdn.microsoft.com, which also contains numerous technical papers covering different Windows subjects. Start with MSDN and search for any topic of interest. You'll find a variety of function descriptions, coding examples, white papers, and other useful information.

Windows History

See Raymond Chen's *The Old New Thing: Practical Development Throughout the Evolution of Windows* for a fascinating insider's look at Windows development with explanations of why many Windows features were designed as they are.

Windows NT Architecture

Windows Internals: Including Windows Server 2008 and Windows Vista, by Mark Russinovich, David Solomon, and Alex Ionescu, is for the reader who wants to know more about Windows design objectives or who wants to understand the underlying architecture and implementation. The book discusses objects, processes, threads, virtual memory, the kernel, and I/O subsystems. You may want to refer to *Windows Internals* as you read this book. Also note the earlier books by these authors and Helen Custer that preceded this book and provide important historical insight into Windows evolution.

UNIX

Advanced Programming in the UNIX Environment, by W. Richard Stevens and Stephen A. Rago, discusses UNIX in much the same terms in which this book discusses Windows. This remains the standard reference on UNIX features and offers a convenient working definition of what UNIX, as well as Linux, provides. This book also contrasts C library file I/O with UNIX I/O, and this discussion is relevant to Windows.

If you are interested in OS comparisons and an in-depth UNIX discussion, *The Art of UNIX Programming*, by Eric S. Raymond, is fascinating reading, although many Windows users may find the discussion slightly biased.

Windows GUI Programming

Windows user interfaces are not covered here. See Brent Rector and Joseph M. Newcomer, *Win32 Programming*, and Charles Petzold, *Programming Windows, Fifth Edition*.

Operating Systems Theory

There are many good texts on general OS theory. *Modern Operating Systems,* by Andrew S. Tanenbaum, is one of the more popular.

The ANSI Standard C Library

The Standard C Library, by P. J. Plauger, is a comprehensive guide. For a quick overview, *The C Programming Language*, by Brian W. Kernighan and Dennis M. Ritchie, lists and explains the complete library, and this book remains the classic book on C. These books can be used to help decide whether the C library is adequate for your file processing requirements.

Windows CE

SAMS Teach Yourself Windows CE Programming in 24 Hours, by Jason P. Nottingham, Steven Makofsky, and Andrew Tucker, is recommended for those who wish to apply the material in this book to Windows CE.

Exercises

1–1. Compile, build, and execute the three file copy programs. Other possibilities include using UNIX compatibility libraries, including the Microsoft Visual C++ library (a program using this library is included in *Examples*). *Note:* All source code is in the *Examples* file, along with documentation to describe how to build and run the programs using Microsoft Visual Studio.

1–2. Become familiar with a development environment, such as Microsoft Visual Studio 2005 or 2008. In particular, learn how to build console applications. Also experiment with the debugger on the programs in this chapter. *Examples* will get you started, and you will find extensive information on the Microsoft MSDN site and with the development environment's documentation.

1–3. Windows uses the carriage return–line feed (CR–LF) sequence to denote an end of line. Determine the effect on Program 1–1 if the input file is opened in binary mode and the output file in text mode, and conversely. What is the effect under UNIX or some other system?

1–4. Time the file copy programs using large files. Use timep to time program execution and use randfile, or any other technique, to generate large files. Obtain data for as many of the combinations as possible and compare the results. Needless to say, performance depends on numerous factors, but by keeping other system parameters the same, it is possible to get helpful comparisons between the implementations. *Suggestion:* Tabulate the results in a spreadsheet to facilitate analysis. Chapter 6 contains a program, timep, for timing program execution, and the executable, timep.exe, is in the *Examples* file *run* directories. Appendix C gives some experimental results.

CHAPTER

2 | Using the Windows File System and Character I/O

The file system and simple terminal I/O are often the first OS features that the developer encounters. Early PC OSs such as MS-DOS did little more than manage files and terminal (or *console*) I/O, and these resources are also central features of nearly every OS.

Files are essential for the long-term storage of data and programs. Files are also the simplest form of program-to-program communication. Furthermore, many aspects of the file system model apply to interprocess and network communication.

The file copy programs in Chapter 1 introduced the four essential file processing functions:

```
CreateFile          WriteFile

ReadFile            CloseHandle
```

This chapter explains these and related functions and also describes character processing and console I/O functions in detail. First, we say a few words about the various file systems available and their principal characteristics. In the process, we'll see how to use Unicode wide characters for internationalization. The chapter includes an introduction to Windows file and directory management.

The Windows File Systems

Windows natively supports four file systems on directly attached devices, but only the first is important throughout the book, as it is Microsoft's primary, full-functionality file system. In addition, file systems are supported on devices such as USB drives. The file system choice on a disk volume or partition is specified when the volume is formatted.

1. The *NT* file system (NTFS) is Microsoft's modern file system that supports long file names, security, fault tolerance, encryption, compression, extended attributes, and very large files[1] and volumes. Note that diskettes, which are now rare, do not support NTFS.

2. The *File Allocation Table* (FAT and FAT32) file systems are rare on current systems and descend from the original MS-DOS and Windows 3.1 FAT (or FAT16) file systems. FAT32 supported larger disk drives and other enhancements, and the term FAT will refer to both versions. FAT does not support Windows security, among other limitations. FAT is the only supported file system for floppy disks and is often the file system on memory cards.

3. The *CD-ROM* file system (CDFS), as the name implies, is for accessing information provided on CD-ROMs. CDFS is compliant with the ISO 9660 standard.

4. The *Universal Disk Format* (UDF), an industry standard, supports DVD drives and will ultimately supplant CDFS. Windows Vista uses the term *Live File System* (LFS) as an enhancement that allows you to add new files and hide, but not actually delete, files.

Windows provides both client and server support for distributed file systems, such as the Networked File System (NFS) and Common Internet File System (CIFS). Windows Server 2003 and 2008 provide extensive support for storage area networks (SANs) and emerging storage technologies. Windows also allows custom file system development.

The file system API accesses all the file systems in the same way, sometimes with limitations. For example, only NTFS supports security. This chapter and the next point out features unique to NTFS as appropriate, but, in general, assume NTFS.

---

[1] "Very large" and "huge" are relative terms that we'll use to describe a file longer than 4GB, which means that you need to use 64-bit integers to specify the file length and positions in the file.

File Naming

Windows supports hierarchical file naming, but there are a few subtle distinctions for the UNIX user and basic rules for everyone.

- The full pathname of a disk file starts with a drive name, such as `A:` or `C:`. The `A:` and `B:` drives are normally diskette drives, and `C:`, `D:`, and so on are hard disks, DVDs, and other directly attached devices. Network drives are usually designated by letters that fall later in the alphabet, such as `H:` and `K:`.

- Alternatively, a full pathname, or Universal Naming Convention (UNC), can start with a double backslash (`\\`), indicating the global root, followed by a server name and a *share name* to indicate a path on a network file server. The first part of the pathname, then, is `\\servername\sharename`.

- The pathname *separator* is the backslash (`\`), although the forward slash (`/`) works in `CreateFile` and other low-level API pathname parameters. This may be more convenient for C/C++ programmers, although it's best simply to use backslashes to avoid possible incompatibility.

- Directory and file names cannot contain any ASCII characters with a value in the range 1–31 or any of these characters:

  `<  >  :  "  |  ?  *  \  /`

  These characters have meaning on command lines, and their occurrences in file names would complicate command line parsing. Names can contain blanks. However, when using file names with blanks on a command line, put each file name in quotes so that the name is not interpreted as naming two distinct files.

- Directory and file names are *case-insensitive*, but they are also *case-retaining*, so that if the creation name is `MyFile`, the file name will show up as it was created, but the file can also be accessed with the name `myFILE`.

- Normally, file and directory names used as API function arguments can be as many as 255 characters long, and pathnames are limited to `MAX_PATH` characters (currently 260). You can also specify very long names with an escape sequence, which we'll describe later.

- A period (`.`) separates a file's name from its extension, and extensions (usually two to four characters after the rightmost period in the file name) conventionally indicate the file's type. Thus, `cci.EXE` would be an executable file, and `cci.C` would be a C language source file. File names can contain multiple periods.

A single period (.) and two periods (..), as directory names, indicate the current directory and its parent, respectively.

With this introduction, it is now time to learn more about the Windows functions introduced in Chapter 1.

Opening, Reading, Writing, and Closing Files

The first Windows function described in detail is CreateFile, which opens existing files and creates new ones. This and other functions are described first by showing the function prototype and then by describing the parameters and function operation.

Creating and Opening Files

This is the first Windows function, so we'll describe it in detail; later descriptions will frequently be much more streamlined as the Windows conventions become more familiar. This approach will help users understand the basic concepts and use the functions without getting bogged down in details that are available on MSDN.

Furthermore, CreateFile is complex with numerous advanced options not described here; we'll generally mention the more important options and sometimes give very brief descriptions of other options that are used in later chapters and examples.

Chapter 1's introductory Windows cpW program (Program 1–2) shows a simple use of CreateFile in which there are two calls that rely on default values for most of the parameters shown here.

```
HANDLE CreateFile (
    LPCTSTR lpName,
    DWORD dwAccess,
    DWORD dwShareMode,
    LPSECURITY_ATTRIBUTES lpSecurityAttributes,
    DWORD dwCreate,
    DWORD dwAttrsAndFlags,
    HANDLE hTemplateFile)

Return: A HANDLE to an open file object, or
    INVALID_HANDLE_VALUE in case of failure.
```

Parameters

The parameter names illustrate some Windows conventions that were introduced in Chapter 1. The prefix dw describes DWORD (32 bits, unsigned) options containing flags or numerical values. lpsz (long pointer to a zero-terminated string), or, more simply, lp, is for pathnames and other strings, although the Microsoft documentation is not entirely consistent. At times, you need to use common sense or read the documentation carefully to determine the correct data types.

lpName is a pointer to the null-terminated string that names the file, pipe, or other named object to open or create. The pathname is normally limited to MAX_PATH (260) characters, but you can circumvent this restriction by prefixing the pathname with \\?\ and using Unicode characters and strings.[2] This technique allows functions requiring pathname arguments to use names as long as 32K characters. The prefix is not part of the name. Finally, the LPCTSTR data type is explained in an upcoming section that also describes generic characters and strings; just regard it as a string data type for now.

dwAccess specifies the read and write access, using GENERIC_READ and GENERIC_WRITE. Flag values such as READ and WRITE do not exist. The GENERIC_ prefix may seem redundant, but it is necessary to conform with the macro names in the Windows header file, winnt.h. Numerous other constant names may seem longer than necessary, but the long names are easily readable and avoid name collisions with other macros.

These values can be combined with a bit-wise "or" operator (|), so to open a file for read and write access:

```
GENERIC_READ | GENERIC_WRITE
```

dwShareMode is a bit-wise "or" combination of:

- 0—The file cannot be shared. Furthermore, not even this process can open a second HANDLE on this file.

- FILE_SHARE_READ—Other processes, including the one making this call, can open this file for concurrent read access.

- FILE_SHARE_WRITE—This allows concurrent writing to the file.

When relevant to proper program operation, the programmer must take care to prevent concurrent updates to the same file location by using locks or other mechanisms. Chapter 3 covers this in more detail.

---

[2] Please see the "Interlude: Unicode and Generic Characters" section later in this chapter for more information.

lpSecurityAttributes points to a SECURITY_ATTRIBUTES structure. Use NULL values with CreateFile and all other functions for now; security is treated in Chapter 15.

dwCreate specifies whether to create a new file, overwrite an existing file, and so on.

- CREATE_NEW—Create a new file. Fail if the specified file already exists.

- CREATE_ALWAYS—Create a new file, or overwrite the file if it already exists.

- OPEN_EXISTING—Open an existing file or fail if the file does not exist.

- OPEN_ALWAYS—Open the file, creating it if it does not exist.

- TRUNCATE_EXISTING—Set the file length to zero. dwCreate must specify at least GENERIC_WRITE access. Destroy all contents if the specified file exists. Fail if the file does not exist.

dwAttrsAndFlags specifies file attributes and flags. There are 32 flags and attributes. Attributes are characteristics of the file, as opposed to the open HANDLE, and these flags are ignored when an existing file is opened. Here are some of the more important attribute and flag values.

- FILE_ATTRIBUTE_NORMAL—This attribute can be used only when no other attributes are set (flags can be set, however).

- FILE_ATTRIBUTE_READONLY—Applications can neither write to nor delete the file.

- FILE_FLAG_DELETE_ON_CLOSE—This is useful for temporary files. Windows deletes the file when the last open HANDLE is closed.

- FILE_FLAG_OVERLAPPED—This attribute flag is important for asynchronous I/O (see Chapter 14).

Several additional flags also specify how a file is processed and help the Windows implementation optimize performance and file integrity.

- FILE_FLAG_RANDOM_ACCESS—The file is intended for random access, and Windows will attempt to optimize file caching.

- FILE_FLAG_SEQUENTIAL_SCAN—The file is for sequential access, and Windows will optimize caching accordingly. These last two access modes are not enforced and are hints to the Windows cache manager. Accessing a file in a manner inconsistent with these access modes may degrade performance.

- FILE_FLAG_WRITE_THROUGH and FILE_FLAG_NO_BUFFERING are two examples of advanced flags that are useful in some advanced applications.

hTemplateFile is the HANDLE of an open GENERIC_READ file that specifies extended attributes to apply to a newly created file, ignoring dwAttrsAndFlags. Normally, this parameter is NULL. Windows ignores hTemplateFile when an existing file is opened. This parameter can be used to set the attributes of a new file to be the same as those of an existing file.

The two CreateFile instances in cpW (Program 1–2) use default values extensively and are as simple as possible but still appropriate for the task. It could be beneficial to use FILE_FLAG_SEQUENTIAL_SCAN in both cases. (Exercise 2–3 explores this option, and Appendix C shows the performance results.)

Notice that if the file share attributes and security permit it, there can be numerous open handles on a given file. The open handles can be owned by the same process or by different processes. (Chapter 6 describes process management.)

Windows Vista and later versions provide the ReOpenFile function, which returns a new handle with different flags, access rights, and so on, assuming there are no conflicts with existing handles to the same file. ReOpenFile allows you to have different handles for different situations and protect against accidental misuse. For example, a function that updates a shared file could use a handle with read-write access, whereas other functions would use a read-only handle.

Closing Files

Windows has a single all-purpose CloseHandle function to close and invalidate kernel handles[3] and to release system resources. Use this function to close nearly all HANDLE objects; exceptions are noted. Closing a handle also decrements the object's handle reference count so that nonpersistent objects such as temporary files and events can be deleted. Windows will close all open handles on exit, but it is still good practice for programs to close their handles before terminating.

Closing an invalid handle or closing the same handle twice will cause an exception when running under a debugger (Chapter 4 discusses exceptions and exception handling). It is not necessary or appropriate to close the standard device handles, which are discussed in the "Standard Devices and Console I/O" section.

```
BOOL CloseHandle (HANDLE hObject)

Return: TRUE if the function succeeds; FALSE otherwise.
```

---

[3] It is convenient to use the term "handle," and the context should make it clear that we mean a Windows HANDLE.

The comparable UNIX functions are different in a number of ways. The UNIX open function returns an integer file descriptor rather than a handle, and it specifies access, sharing, create options, attributes, and flags in the single integer oflag parameter. The options overlap, with Windows providing a richer set.

There is no UNIX equivalent to dwShareMode. UNIX files are always shareable.

Both systems use security information when creating a new file. In UNIX, the mode argument specifies the familiar user, group, and other file permissions.

close is comparable to CloseHandle, but it is not general purpose.

The C library stdio.h functions use FILE objects, which are comparable to handles (for disk files, terminals, tapes, and other devices) connected to streams. The fopen mode parameter specifies whether the file data is to be treated as binary or text. There is a set of options for read-only, update, append at the end, and so on. freopen allows FILE reuse without closing it first. The Standard C library cannot set security permissions.

fclose closes a FILE. Most stdio FILE-related functions have the f prefix.

Reading Files

```
BOOL ReadFile (
    HANDLE hFile,
    LPVOID lpBuffer,
    DWORD nNumberOfBytesToRead,
    LPDWORD lpNumberOfBytesRead,
    LPOVERLAPPED lpOverlapped)

Return: TRUE if the read succeeds (even if no bytes were read due
    to an attempt to read past the end of file).
```

Assume, until Chapter 14, that the file handle does *not* have the FILE_FLAG-_OVERLAPPED option set in dwAttrsAndFlags. ReadFile, then, starts at the current file position (for the handle) and advances the position by the number of bytes transferred.

The function fails, returning FALSE, if the handle or any other parameters are invalid or if the read operation fails for any reason. The function does not fail if the file handle is positioned at the end of file; instead, the number of bytes read (*lpNumberOfBytesRead) is set to 0.

Parameters

Because of the long variable names and the natural arrangement of the parameters, they are largely self-explanatory. Nonetheless, here are some brief explanations.

hFile is a file handle with FILE_READ_DATA access, a subset of GENERIC-_READ access. lpBuffer points to the memory buffer to receive the input data. nNumberOfBytesToRead is the number of bytes to read from the file.

lpNumberOfBytesRead points to the actual number of bytes read by the ReadFile call. This value can be zero if the handle is positioned at the end of file or there is an error, and message-mode named pipes (Chapter 11) allow a zero-length message.

lpOverlapped points to an OVERLAPPED structure (Chapters 3 and 14). Use NULL for the time being.

Writing Files

```
BOOL WriteFile (
    HANDLE hFile,
    LPCVOID lpBuffer,
    DWORD nNumberOfBytesToWrite,
    LPDWORD lpNumberOfBytesWritten,
    LPOVERLAPPED lpOverlapped)
```

Return: TRUE if the function succeeds; FALSE otherwise.

The parameters are familiar by now. Notice that a successful write does not ensure that the data actually is written through to the disk unless FILE_FLAG_WRITE_THROUGH is specified with CreateFile. If the HANDLE position plus the write byte count exceed the current file length, Windows will extend the file length.

UNIX read and write are the comparable functions, and the programmer supplies a file descriptor, buffer, and byte count. The functions return the number of bytes actually transferred. A value of 0 on read indicates the end of file; −1 indicates an error. Windows, by contrast, requires a separate transfer count and returns Boolean values to indicate success or failure.

The functions in both systems are general purpose and can read from files, terminals, tapes, pipes, and so on.

The Standard C library `fread` and `fwrite` binary I/O functions use object size and object count rather than a single byte count as in UNIX and Windows. A short transfer could be caused by either an end of file or an error; test explicitly with `ferror` or `feof`. The library provides a full set of text-oriented functions, such as `fgetc` and `fputc`, that do not exist outside the C library in either OS.

Interlude: Unicode and Generic Characters

Before proceeding, we explain briefly how Windows processes characters and differentiates between 8- and 16-bit characters and generic characters. The topic is a large one and beyond the book's scope, so we only provide the minimum detail required.

Windows supports standard 8-bit characters (type `char` or `CHAR`) and wide 16-bit characters (`WCHAR`, which is defined to be the C `wchar_t` type). The Microsoft documentation refers to the 8-bit character set as ANSI, but it is actually a misnomer. For convenience, we use the term "ASCII," which also is not totally accurate.[4]

The wide character support that Windows provides using the Unicode UTF-16 encoding is capable of representing symbols and letters in all major languages, including English, French, Spanish, German, Japanese, and Chinese.

Here are the normal steps for writing a generic Windows application that can be built to use either Unicode or 8-bit ASCII characters.

1. Define all characters and strings using the generic types `TCHAR`, `LPTSTR`, and `LPCTSTR`.

2. Include the definitions `#define UNICODE` and `#define _UNICODE` in all source modules to get Unicode wide characters (ANSI C `wchar_t`); otherwise, with `UNICODE` and `_UNICODE` undefined, `TCHAR` will be equivalent to `CHAR` (ANSI C `char`). The definition must precede the `#include <windows.h>` statement and is frequently defined on the compiler command line, the Visual Studio project properties, or the project's `stdafx.h` file. The first preprocessor variable controls the Windows function definitions, and the second variable controls the C library.

3. Byte buffer lengths—as used, for example, in `ReadFile`—can be calculated using `sizeof (TCHAR)`.

---

[4] The distinctions and details are technical but can be critical in some situations. ASCII codes only go to 127. There are different ASNI code pages, which are configurable from the Control Panel. Use your favorite search engine or search MSDN with a phrase such as "Windows code page 1252" to obtain more information.

4. Use the collection of generic C library string and character I/O functions in tchar.h. Representative functions are _fgettc, _itot (for itoa), _stprintf (for sprintf), _tcscpy (for strcpy), _ttoi, _totupper, _totlower, and _ftprintf.[5] See MSDN for a complete and extensive list. All these definitions depend on _UNICODE. This collection is not complete. memchr is an example of a function without a wide character implementation. New versions are provided in the *Examples* file as required.

5. Constant strings should be in one of three forms. Use these conventions for single characters as well. The first two forms are ANSI C; the third—the _T macro (equivalently, TEXT and _TEXT)—is supplied with the Microsoft C compiler.

   ```
   "This string uses 8-bit characters"

   L"This string uses 16-bit characters"

   _T("This string uses generic text characters")
   ```

6. Include tchar.h after windows.h to get required definitions for text macros and generic C library functions.

Windows uses Unicode 16-bit characters throughout, and NTFS file names and pathnames are represented internally in Unicode. If the UNICODE macro is defined, wide character strings are required by Windows calls; otherwise, 8-bit character strings are converted to wide characters. Some Windows API functions only support Unicode, and this policy is expected to continue with new functions.

All future program examples will use TCHAR instead of the normal char for characters and character strings unless there is a clear reason to deal with individual 8-bit characters. Similarly, the type LPTSTR indicates a pointer to a generic string, and LPCTSTR indicates, in addition, a constant string. At times, this choice will add some clutter to the programs, but it is the only choice that allows the flexibility necessary to develop and test applications in either Unicode or 8-bit character form so that the program can be easily converted to Unicode at a later date. Furthermore, this choice is consistent with common, if not universal, industry practice.

It is worthwhile to examine the system include files to see how TCHAR and the system function interfaces are defined and how they depend on whether or not UNICODE and _UNICODE are defined. A typical entry is of the following form:

---

[5] The underscore character (_) indicates that a function or keyword is provided by Microsoft C, and the letters t and T denote a generic text character. Other development systems provide similar capability but may use different names or keywords.

```
#ifdef UNICODE
#define TCHAR WCHAR
#else
#define TCHAR CHAR
#endif
```

Alternative Generic String Processing Functions

String comparisons can use `lstrcmp` and `lstrcmpi` rather than the generic `_tcscmp` and `_tcscmpi` to account for the specific language and region, or *locale*, at run time and also to perform *word* rather than *string* comparisons. String comparisons simply compare the numerical values of the characters, whereas word comparisons consider locale-specific word order. The two methods can give opposite results for string pairs such as *coop/co-op* and *were/we're*.

There is also a group of Windows functions for dealing with Unicode characters and strings. These functions handle locale characteristics transparently. Typical functions are `CharUpper`, which can operate on strings as well as individual characters, and `IsCharAlphaNumeric`. Other string functions include `CompareString` (which is locale-specific). The generic C library functions (e.g., `_tprintf`) and the Windows functions will both appear in upcoming examples to demonstrate their use. Examples in later chapters will rely mostly on the generic C library for character and string manipulation, as the C Library has the required functionality, the Windows functions do not add value, and readers will be familiar with the C Library.

The Generic Main Function

Replace the C main function, with its argument list (`argv[]`), with the macro `_tmain`. The macro expands to either `main` or `wmain` depending on the `_UNICODE` definition. The `_tmain` definition is in `tchar.h`, which must be included after `windows.h`. A typical main program heading, then, would look like this:

```
#include <windows.h>
#include <tchar.h>
int _tmain(int argc, LPTSTR argv[])
{
    ...
}
```

The Microsoft C `_tmain` function also supports a third parameter for environment strings. This nonstandard extension is also common in UNIX.

Function Definitions

A function such as `CreateFile` is defined through a preprocessor macro as `CreateFileA` when `UNICODE` is not defined and as `CreateFileW` when `UNICODE` is defined. The definitions also describe the string parameters as 8-bit or wide character strings. Consequently, compilers will report a source code error, such as an illegal parameter to `CreateFile`, as an error in the use of `CreateFileA` or `CreateFileW`.

Unicode Strategies

A programmer starting a Windows project, either to develop new code or to enhance or port existing code, can select from four strategies, based on project requirements.

1. **8-bit only**. Ignore Unicode and continue to use the `char` (or `CHAR`) data type and the Standard C library for functions such as `printf`, `atoi`, and `strcmp`.

2. **8-bit or Unicode with generic code**. Follow the earlier guidelines for generic code. The example programs generally use this strategy with the Unicode macros undefined to produce 8-bit code.

3. **Unicode only**. Follow the generic guidelines, but define the two preprocessor variables. Alternatively, use wide characters and the wide character functions exclusively.

4. **Unicode and 8-bit**. The program includes both Unicode and ASCII code and decides at run time which code to execute, based on a run-time switch or other factors.

As mentioned previously, writing generic code, while requiring extra effort and creating awkward-looking code, allows the programmer to maintain maximum flexibility. However, Unicode only (Strategy 3) is increasingly common, especially with applications requiring a graphical user interface.

`ReportError` (Program 2–1) shows how to specify the language for error messages.

The POSIX XPG4 internationalization standard is considerably different from Unicode. Among other things, characters can be represented by 4 bytes, 2 bytes, or 1 byte, depending on the context, locale, and so on.

Microsoft C implements the Standard C library functions, and there are generic versions. Thus, there is a `_tsetlocale` function in `wchar.h`. Windows uses Unicode characters.

Example: Error Processing

cpW, Program 1–2, showed some rudimentary error processing, obtaining the DWORD error number with the GetLastError function. A function call, rather than a global error number, such as the UNIX errno, ensures that system errors are unique to the threads (Chapter 7) that share data storage.

The function FormatMessage turns the message number into a meaningful message, in English or one of many other languages, returning the message length.

ReportError, Program 2–1, shows a useful general-purpose error-processing function, ReportError, which is similar to the C library perror and to err_sys, err_ret, and other functions. ReportError prints a message specified in the first argument and will terminate with an exit code or return, depending on the value of the second argument. The third argument determines whether the system error message should be displayed.

Notice the arguments to FormatMessage. The value returned by Get-LastError is used as one parameter, and a flag indicates that the message is to be generated by the system. The generated message is stored in a buffer allocated by the function, and the address is returned in a parameter. There are several other parameters with default values. The language for the message can be set at either compile time or run time. This information is sufficient for our needs, but MSDN supplies complete details.

ReportError can simplify error processing, and nearly all subsequent examples use it. Chapter 4 extends ReportError to generate exceptions.

Program 2–1 introduces the include file Everything.h. As the name implies, this file includes windows.h, Environment.h, which has the UNICODE definition, and other include files.[6] It also defines commonly used functions, such as ReportError itself. All subsequent examples will use this single include file, which is in the *Examples* code.

Notice the call to the function LocalFree near the end of the program, as required by FormatMessage (see MSDN). This function is explained in Chapter 5. Previous book editions erroneously used GlobalFree.

See Run 2–2 for sample ReportError output from a complete program, and many other screenshots throughout the book show ReportError output.

---

[6] "Everything" is an exaggeration, of course, but it's everything we need for most examples, and it's used in nearly all examples. Additional special-purpose include files are introduced in later chapters.

Program 2–1   ReportError: Reporting System Call Errors
___

```
#include "Everything.h"

VOID ReportError(LPCTSTR userMessage, DWORD exitCode,
                BOOL printErrorMessage)
/* General-purpose function for reporting system errors.
   Obtain the error number and convert it to the system error message.
   Display this information and the user-specified message to the
   standard error device, using the generic function _ftprintf.
   userMessage: Message to be displayed to standard error device.
   exitCode: 0 - Return.
           > 0 - ExitProcess with this code.
   printErrorMessage:Display the last system error message if set. */
{
    DWORD eMsgLen, errNum = GetLastError();
    LPTSTR lpvSysMsg;

    _ftprintf(stderr, _T("%s\n"), userMessage);
    if (printErrorMessage) {
       eMsgLen = FormatMessage(
              FORMAT_MESSAGE_ALLOCATE_BUFFER |
                FORMAT_MESSAGE_FROM_SYSTEM,
              NULL, errNum,
              MAKELANGID(LANG_NEUTRAL, SUBLANG_DEFAULT),
              (LPTSTR)&lpvSysMsg, 0, NULL);
       if (eMsgLen > 0) {
          _ftprintf(stderr, "%s\n", lpvSysMsg);
       } else {
          _ftprintf(stderr, _T("Last Error Number; %d.\n"), errNum);
       }
       if (lpvSysMsg != NULL) LocalFree(lpvSysMsg); /* See Ch 5. */
    }

    if (exitCode > 0)
       ExitProcess(exitCode);
    return;
}
```
___

Standard Devices

Like UNIX, a Windows process has three standard devices for input, output, and error reporting. UNIX uses well-known values for the file descriptors (0, 1, and 2), but Windows requires HANDLEs and provides a function to obtain them for the standard devices.

```
HANDLE GetStdHandle (DWORD nStdHandle)
```

Return: A valid handle if the function succeeds;
    `INVALID_HANDLE_VALUE` otherwise.

Parameters

`nStdHandle` must have one of these values:

- `STD_INPUT_HANDLE`

- `STD_OUTPUT_HANDLE`

- `STD_ERROR_HANDLE`

The standard device assignments are normally the console and the keyboard. Standard I/O can be redirected.

`GetStdHandle` does not create a new or duplicate handle on a standard device. Successive calls in the process with the same device argument return the same handle value. Closing a standard device handle makes the device unavailable for future use within the process. For this reason, the examples often obtain a standard device handle but do not close it.

Chapter 7's `grepMT` example and Chapter 11's `pipe` example illustrate `GetStdHandle` usage.

```
BOOL SetStdHandle (
    DWORD nStdHandle,
    HANDLE hHandle)
```

Return: `TRUE` or `FALSE` indicating success or failure.

Parameters

In `SetStdHandle`, `nStdHandle` has the same enumerated values as in `GetStdHandle`. `hHandle` specifies an open file that is to be the standard device.

There are two reserved pathnames for console input (the keyboard) and console output: `"CONIN$"` and `"CONOUT$"`. Initially, standard input, output, and error are assigned to the console. It is possible to use the console regardless of any redirection to these standard devices; just use `CreateFile` to open handles to `"CONIN$"` or `"CONOUT$"`. The "Console I/O" section at the end of this chapter covers the subject.

UNIX standard I/O redirection is considerably different (see Stevens and Rago [pp. 61–64]).

The first method is indirect and relies on the fact that the dup function returns the lowest numbered available file descriptor. Suppose you wish to reassign standard input (file descriptor 0) to an open file description, fd_redirect. The first method is:

```
close(STDIN_FILENO);

dup(fd_redirect);
```

The second method uses dup2, and the third uses F_DUPFD on the cryptic and overloaded fcntl function.

Example: Copying Multiple Files to Standard Output

cat, the next example (Program 2–2), illustrates standard I/O and extensive error checking as well as user interaction. This program is a limited implementation of the UNIX cat command, which copies one or more specified files—or standard input if no files are specified—to standard output.

Program 2–2 includes complete error handling. Future program listings omit most error checking for brevity, but the *Examples* contain the complete programs with extensive error checking and documentation. Also, notice the Options function, which is called at the start of the program. This function, included in the *Examples* file and used throughout the book, evaluates command line option flags and returns the argv index of the first file name. Use Options in much the same way as getopt is used in many UNIX programs.

Program 2–2   cat: File Concatenation to Standard Output

```
/* Chapter 2. cat. */
/* cat [options] [files] Only the -s option, which suppresses error
   reporting if one of the files does not exist. */

#include "Everything.h"
#define BUF_SIZE 0x200

static VOID CatFile(HANDLE, HANDLE);
int _tmain(int argc, LPTSTR argv[])
{
    HANDLE hInFile, hStdIn = GetStdHandle(STD_INPUT_HANDLE);
    HANDLE hStdOut = GetStdHandle(STD_OUTPUT_HANDLE);
    BOOL dashS;
    int iArg, iFirstFile;
```

```
    /* dashS will be set only if "-s" is on the command line. */
    /* iFirstFile is the argv[] index of the first input file. */
    iFirstFile = Options(argc, argv, _T("s"), &dashS, NULL);
    if (iFirstFile == argc) { /* No input files in arg list. */
                              /* Use standard input. */
        CatFile(hStdIn, hStdOut);
        return 0;
    }

    /* Process each input files. */
    for (iArg = iFirstFile; iArg < argc; iArg++) {
        hInFile = CreateFile(argv[iArg], GENERIC_READ,
                0, NULL, OPEN_EXISTING, FILE_ATTRIBUTE_NORMAL, NULL);
        if (hInFile == INVALID_HANDLE_VALUE) {
            if (!dashS) ReportError(_T("Error: File does not exist."),
                        0, TRUE);
        } else {
            CatFile(hInFile, hStdOut);
            if (GetLastError() != 0 && !dashS)
                ReportError(_T("Cat Error."), 0, TRUE);
            CloseHandle(hInFile);
        }
    }
    return 0;
}

/* Function that does the work:
/* read input data and copy it to standard output. */
static VOID CatFile(HANDLE hInFile, HANDLE hOutFile)
{
    DWORD nIn, nOut;
    BYTE buffer[BUF_SIZE];
    while (ReadFile(hInFile, buffer, BUF_SIZE, &nIn, NULL)
            && (nIn != 0)
            && WriteFile(hOutFile, buffer, nIn, &nOut, NULL));
    return;
}
```

Run 2–2 shows cat output with and without errors. The error output occurs when a file name does not exist. The output also shows the text that the randfile program generates; randfile is convenient for these examples, as it quickly generates text files of nearly any size. Also, notice that the records can be sorted on the first 8 characters, which will be convenient for examples in later chapters. The "x" character at the end of each line is a visual cue and has no other meaning.

Finally, Run 2–2 shows cat displaying individual file names; this feature is not part of Program 2–2 but was added temporarily to help clarify Run 2–2.

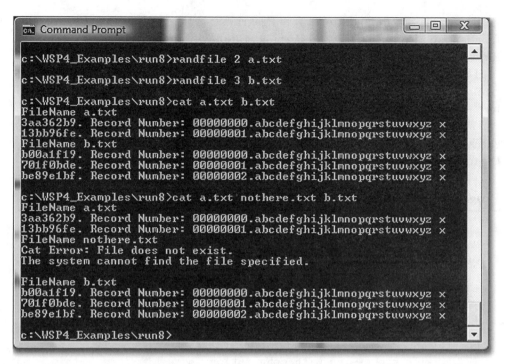

```
c:\WSP4_Examples\run8>randfile 2 a.txt

c:\WSP4_Examples\run8>randfile 3 b.txt

c:\WSP4_Examples\run8>cat a.txt b.txt
FileName a.txt
3aa362b9. Record Number: 00000000.abcdefghijklmnopqrstuvwxyz x
13bb96fe. Record Number: 00000001.abcdefghijklmnopqrstuvwxyz x
FileName b.txt
b00a1f19. Record Number: 00000000.abcdefghijklmnopqrstuvwxyz x
701f0bde. Record Number: 00000001.abcdefghijklmnopqrstuvwxyz x
be89e1bf. Record Number: 00000002.abcdefghijklmnopqrstuvwxyz x

c:\WSP4_Examples\run8>cat a.txt nothere.txt b.txt
FileName a.txt
3aa362b9. Record Number: 00000000.abcdefghijklmnopqrstuvwxyz x
13bb96fe. Record Number: 00000001.abcdefghijklmnopqrstuvwxyz x
FileName nothere.txt
Cat Error: File does not exist.
The system cannot find the file specified.

FileName b.txt
b00a1f19. Record Number: 00000000.abcdefghijklmnopqrstuvwxyz x
701f0bde. Record Number: 00000001.abcdefghijklmnopqrstuvwxyz x
be89e1bf. Record Number: 00000002.abcdefghijklmnopqrstuvwxyz x

c:\WSP4_Examples\run8>
```

Run 2–2   `cat`: Results, with `ReportError` Output

Example: Simple File Encryption

File copying is familiar by now, so Program 2–3 also converts a file byte-by-byte so that there is computation as well as file I/O. The conversion is a modified "Caesar cipher," which adds a fixed number to each byte (a Web search will provide extensive background information). The program also includes some error reporting. It is similar to Program 1–3 (`cpCF`), replacing the final call to `CopyFile` with a new function that performs the file I/O and the byte addition.

The shift number, along with the input and output file, are command line parameters. The program adds the shift to each byte modulo 256, which means that the encrypted file may contain unprintable characters. Furthermore, end of line, end of string, and other control characters are changed. A true Caesar cipher only shifts the letters; this implementation shifts all bytes. You can decrypt the file by subtracting the original shift from 256 or by using a negative shift.

This program, while simple, is a good base for numerous variations later in the book that use threads, asynchronous I/O, and other file processing techniques.

Program 2–4, immediately after Program 2–3, shows the actual conversion function, and Run 2–3 shows program operation with encryption, decryption, and file comparison using the Windows FC command.

Comment: Note that the full *Examples* code uses the Microsoft C Library function, _taccess, to determine if the file exists. The code comments describe two alternative techniques.

Warning: Future program listings after Program 2–3 omit most, or all, error checking in order to streamline the presentation and concentrate on the logic. Use the full *Examples* code if you want to copy any of the examples.

Program 2–3   cci: File Encryption with Error Reporting

```
/* Chapter 2. cci Version 1. Modified Caesar cipher */
/* Main program, which can be linked to different implementations */
/* of the cci_f function. */

/* cci shift file1 file2
 *     shift is the integer added mod 256 to each byte.
 * Otherwise, this program is like cp and cpCF. */

/* This program illustrates:
 *     1. File processing with converstion.
 *     2. Boilerplate code to process the command line.
 */

#include "Everything.h"
#include <io.h>

BOOL cci_f(LPCTSTR, LPCTSTR, DWORD);

int _tmain(int argc, LPTSTR argv[])
{
    if (argc != 4)
        ReportError (_T("Usage: cci shift file1 file2"), 1, FALSE);

    if (!cci_f(argv[2], argv[3], atoi(argv[1])))
        ReportError(_T("Encryption failed."), 4, TRUE);

    return 0;
}
```

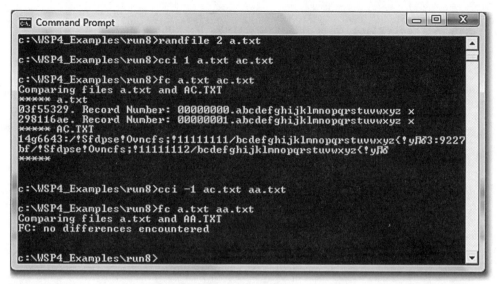

Run 2–3 cci: Caesar Cipher Run and Test

Program 2–4 is the conversion function cci_f called by Program 2–3; later, we'll have several variations of this function.

Program 2–4 cci_f: File Conversion Function

```
/* Chapter 2. Simple cci_f (modified Caesar cipher) implementation */
#include "Everything.h"

#define BUF_SIZE 256

BOOL cci_f(LPCTSTR fIn, LPCTSTR fOut, DWORD shift)

/* Simplified Caesar cipher implementation
 *     fIn:   Source file pathname
 *     fOut:  Destination file pathname
 *     shift: Numerical shift
 * Behavior is modeled after CopyFile */
{
    HANDLE hIn, hOut;
    DWORD nIn, nOut, iCopy;
    CHAR aBuffer[BUF_SIZE], ccBuffer[BUF_SIZE];
    BOOL writeOK = TRUE;

    hIn = CreateFile(fIn, GENERIC_READ, 0, NULL, OPEN_EXISTING,
        FILE_ATTRIBUTE_NORMAL, NULL);
    if (hIn == INVALID_HANDLE_VALUE) return FALSE;
```

```
hOut = CreateFile(fOut, GENERIC_WRITE, 0, NULL, CREATE_ALWAYS,
    FILE_ATTRIBUTE_NORMAL, NULL);
if (hOut == INVALID_HANDLE_VALUE) return FALSE;

while (ReadFile(hIn, aBuffer, BUF_SIZE, &nIn, NULL) &&
        nIn > 0 && writeOK) {
    for (iCopy = 0; iCopy < nIn; iCopy++)
        ccBuffer[iCopy] = (aBuffer[iCopy] + shift) % 256;
    writeOK = WriteFile(hOut, ccBuffer, nIn, &nOut, NULL);
}

CloseHandle(hIn);
CloseHandle(hOut);

return writeOK;
}
```

Performance

Appendix C shows that the performance of the file conversion program can be improved by using such techniques as providing a larger buffer and by specifying FILE_FLAG_SEQUENTIAL_SCAN with CreateFile. Later chapters show more advanced techniques to enhance this simple program.

File and Directory Management

This section introduces the basic functions for file and directory management.

File Management

Windows provides a number of file management functions, which are generally straightforward. The functions described here delete, copy, and rename files. There is also a function to create temporary file names.

File Deletion

You can delete a file by specifying the file name and calling the DeleteFile function. Recall that all absolute pathnames start with a drive letter or a server name.

```
BOOL DeleteFile (LPCTSTR lpFileName)
```

Copying a File

Copy an entire file using a single function, CopyFile, which was introduced in Chapter 1's cpCF (Program 1–3) example.

```
BOOL CopyFile (
    LPCTSTR lpExistingFileName,
    LPCTSTR lpNewFileName,
    BOOL fFailIfExists)
```

CopyFile copies the named existing file and assigns the specified new name to the copy. If a file with the new name already exists, it will be replaced only if fFailIfExists is FALSE. CopyFile also copies file metadata, such as creation time.

Hard and Symbolic Links

Create a hard link between two files with the CreateHardLink function, which is similar to a UNIX hard link. With a hard link, a file can have two separate names. Note that there is only one file, so a change to the file will be available regardless of the name used to open the file.

```
BOOL CreateHardLink (
    LPCTSTR lpFileName,
    LPCTSTR lpExistingFileName,
    BOOL lpSecurityAttributes)
```

The first two arguments, while in the opposite order, are used as in Copy-File. The two file names, the new name and the existing name, must occur in the same file system volume, but they can be in different directories. The security attributes, if any, apply to the new file name.

Windows Vista and other NT6 systems support a similar symbolic link function, but there is no symbolic link in earlier Windows systems.

```
BOOL CreateSymbolicLink (
    LPTSTR lpSymlinkFileName,
    LPTSTR lpTargetFileName,
    DWORD dwFlags)
```

`lpSymlinkFileName` is the symbolic link that is created to `lpTargetFile-Name`. Set `dwFlags` to 0 if the target is a file, and set it to `SYMBOLIC_LINK-_FLAG_DIRECTORY` if it is a directory. `lpTargetFileName` is treated as an absolute link if there is a device name associated with it. See MSDN for detailed information about absolute and relative links.

Renaming and Moving Files

There is a pair of functions to rename, or "move," a file. These functions also work for directories, whereas `DeleteFile` and `CopyFile` are restricted to files.

```
BOOL MoveFile (
    LPCTSTR lpExistingFileName,
    LPCTSTR lpNewFileName)

BOOL MoveFileEx (
    LPCTSTR lpExistingFileName,
    LPCTSTR lpNewFileName,
    DWORD dwFlags)
```

`MoveFile` fails if the new file already exists; use `MoveFileEx` to overwrite existing files.

Note: The `Ex` suffix is common and represents an extended version of an existing function in order to provide additional functionality. Many extended functions are not supported in earlier Windows versions.

The `MoveFile` and `MoveFileEx` parameters, especially the flags, are sufficiently complex to require additional explanation:

`lpExistingFileName` specifies the name of the existing file *or* directory.

`lpNewFileName` specifies the new file or directory name, which cannot already exist in the case of `MoveFile`. A new file can be on a different file system or drive, but new directories must be on the same drive. If `NULL`, the existing file is deleted. Wildcards are not allowed in file or directory names. Specify the actual name.

`dwFlags` specifies options as follows:

- MOVEFILE_REPLACE_EXISTING—Use this option to replace an existing file.

- MOVEFILE_WRITE_THROUGH—Use this option to ensure that the function does not return until the copied file is flushed through to the disk.

- MOVEFILE_COPY_ALLOWED—When the new file is on a different volume, the move is achieved with a CopyFile followed by a DeleteFile. You cannot move a file to a different volume without using this flag, and moving a file to the same volume just involves renaming without copying the file data, which is fast compared to a full copy.

- MOVEFILE_DELAY_UNTIL_REBOOT—This flag, which cannot be used in conjunction with MOVEFILE_COPY_ALLOWED, is restricted to administrators and ensures that the file move does not take effect until Windows restarts. Also, if the new file name is null, the existing file will be deleted when Windows restarts.

UNIX pathnames do not include a drive or server name; the slash indicates the system root. The Microsoft C library file functions also support drive names as required by the underlying Windows file naming.

UNIX does not have a function to copy files directly. Instead, you must write a small program or call system( ) to execute the cp command.

unlink is the UNIX equivalent of DeleteFile except that unlink can also delete directories.

rename and remove are in the C library, and rename will fail when attempting to move a file to an existing file name or a directory to a non-empty directory.

Directory Management

Creating or deleting a directory involves a pair of simple functions.

```
BOOL CreateDirectory (
    LPCTSTR lpPathName,
    LPSECURITY_ATTRIBUTES lpSecurityAttributes)

BOOL RemoveDirectory (LPCTSTR lpPathName)
```

lpPathName points to a null-terminated string with the name of the directory that is to be created or deleted. The security attributes, as with other functions, should be NULL for the time being; Chapter 15 describes file and object security. Only an empty directory can be removed.

A process has a current, or working, directory, just as in UNIX. Furthermore, each individual drive keeps a working directory. Programs can both get and set the current directory. The first function sets the directory.

```
BOOL SetCurrentDirectory (LPCTSTR lpPathName)
```

lpPathName is the path to the new current directory. It can be a relative path or a fully qualified path starting with either a drive letter and colon, such as D:, or a UNC name (such as \\ACCTG_SERVER\PUBLIC).

If the directory path is simply a drive name (such as A: or C:), the working directory becomes the working directory on the specified drive. For example, if the working directories are set in the sequence

```
C:\MSDEV
INCLUDE
A:\MEMOS\TODO
C:
```

then the resulting working directory will be

```
C:\MSDEV\INCLUDE
```

The next function returns the fully qualified pathname into a specified buffer.

```
DWORD GetCurrentDirectory (DWORD cchCurDir,
    LPTSTR lpCurDir)
```

Return: The string length of the pathname, or the required buffer size (in characters including the terminating character) if the buffer is not large enough; zero if the function fails.

cchCurDir is the character (not byte; the ccb prefix denotes byte length) length of the buffer for the directory name. The length must allow for the terminating null character. lpCurDir points to the buffer to receive the pathname string.

Notice that if the buffer is too small for the pathname, the return value tells how large the buffer should be. Therefore, the test for function failure should test both for zero and for the result being larger than the cchCurDir argument.

This method of returning strings and their lengths is common in Windows and must be handled carefully. Program 2–6 illustrates a typical code fragment that performs the logic. Similar logic occurs in other examples. The method is not always consistent, however. Some functions return a Boolean, and the length parameter is used twice; it is set with the length of the buffer before the call, and the function changes the value. `LookupAccountName` in Chapter 15 is one of more complex functions in terms of returning results.

An alternative approach, illustrated with the `GetFileSecurity` function in Program 15–4, is to make two function calls with a buffer memory allocation in between. The first call gets the string length, which is used in the memory allocation. The second call gets the actual string. The simplest approach in this case is to allocate a string holding `MAX_PATH` characters.

Examples Using File and Directory Management Functions

pwd (Program 2–6) uses `GetCurrentDirectory`. Example programs in Chapter 3 and elsewhere use other file and directory management functions.

Console I/O

Console I/O can be performed with `ReadFile` and `WriteFile`, but it is simpler to use the specific console I/O functions, `ReadConsole` and `WriteConsole`. The principal advantages are that these functions process generic characters (`TCHAR`) rather than bytes, and they also process characters according to the console mode, which is set with the `SetConsoleMode` function.

```
BOOL SetConsoleMode (
    HANDLE hConsoleHandle,
    DWORD dwMode)
```

Return: `TRUE` if and only if the function succeeds.

Parameters

hConsoleHandle identifies a console input or screen buffer, which must have `GENERIC_WRITE` access even if it is an input-only device.

dwMode specifies how characters are processed. Each flag name indicates whether the flag applies to console input or output. Five commonly used flags, listed here, control behavior; they are all enabled by default.

- ENABLE_LINE_INPUT—Specify that ReadConsole returns when it encounters a carriage return character.

- ENABLE_ECHO_INPUT—Echo characters to the screen as they are read.

- ENABLE_PROCESSED_INPUT—Process backspace, carriage return, and line feed characters.

- ENABLE_PROCESSED_OUTPUT—Process backspace, tab, bell, carriage return, and line feed characters.

- ENABLE_WRAP_AT_EOL_OUTPUT—Enable line wrap for both normal and echoed output.

If SetConsoleMode fails, the mode is unchanged and the function returns FALSE. GetLastError returns the error code number.

The ReadConsole and WriteConsole functions are similar to ReadFile and WriteFile.

```
BOOL ReadConsole (HANDLE hConsoleInput,
    LPVOID lpBuffer,
    DWORD cchToRead,
    LPDWORD lpcchRead,
    LPVOID lpReserved)

Return: TRUE if and only if the read succeeds.
```

The parameters are nearly the same as with ReadFile. The two length parameters are in terms of generic characters rather than bytes, and lpReserved must be NULL. Never use any of the reserved fields that occur in this and other functions. WriteConsole is now self-explanatory. The next example (Program 2–5) shows how to use ReadConsole and WriteConsole with generic strings and how to take advantage of the console mode.

A process can have only one console at a time. Applications such as the ones developed so far are normally initialized with a console. In many cases, such as a server or GUI application, however, you may need a console to display status or debugging information. There are two simple parameterless functions for this purpose.

```
BOOL FreeConsole (VOID)

BOOL AllocConsole (VOID)
```

FreeConsole detaches a process from its console. Calling AllocConsole then creates a new one associated with the process's standard input, output, and error handles. AllocConsole will fail if the process already has a console; to avoid this problem, precede the call with FreeConsole.

Note: Windows GUI applications do not have a default console and must allocate one before using functions such as WriteConsole or printf to display on a console. It's also possible that server processes may not have a console. Chapter 6 shows how to create a process without a console.

There are numerous other console I/O functions for specifying cursor position, screen attributes (such as color), and so on. This book's approach is to use only those functions needed to get the examples to work and not to wander further than necessary into user interfaces. It is easy to learn additional functions from the MSDN reference material after you see the examples.

For historical reasons, Windows does not support character-oriented terminals in the way that UNIX does, and not all the UNIX terminal functionality is replicated by Windows. For example, UNIX provides functions for setting baud rates and line control functions. Stevens and Rago dedicate a chapter to UNIX terminal I/O (Chapter 11) and one to pseudo terminals (Chapter 19).

Serious Windows user interfaces are, of course, graphical, with mouse as well as keyboard input. The GUI is outside the scope of this book, but everything we discuss works within a GUI application.

Example: Printing and Prompting

The ConsolePrompt function, which appears in PrintMsg (Program 2–5), is a useful utility that prompts the user with a specified message and then returns the user's response. There is an option to suppress the response echo. The function uses the console I/O functions and generic characters. PrintStrings and PrintMsg are the other entries in this module; they can use any handle but are normally used with standard output or error handles. The first function allows a variable-length argument list, whereas the second one allows just one string and is for convenience only. PrintStrings uses the va_start, va_arg, and va_end functions in the Standard C library to process the variable-length argument list.

Example programs will use these functions and the generic C library functions as convenient.

See Run 2–6 after Program 2–6 for sample outputs. Chapters 11 and 15 have examples using `ConsolePrompt`.

Program 2–5   `PrintMsg`: Console Prompt and Print Utility Functions

```
/* PrintMsg.c: ConsolePrompt, PrintStrings, PrintMsg */

#include "Environment.h" /* #define or #undef UNICODE here. */
#include <windows.h>
#include <stdarg.h>

BOOL PrintStrings(HANDLE hOut, ...)
/* Write the messages to the output handle. */
{
    DWORD msgLen, count;
    LPCTSTR pMsg;
    va_list pMsgList; /* Current message string. */
    va_start(pMsgList, hOut); /* Start processing messages. */
    while ((pMsg = va_arg(pMsgList, LPCTSTR)) != NULL) {
        msgLen = _tcslen(pMsg);
            /* WriteConsole succeeds only for console handles. */
        if (!WriteConsole(hOut, pMsg, msgLen, &count, NULL)
                /* Call WriteFile only if WriteConsole fails. */
            && !WriteFile(hOut, pMsg, msgLen * sizeof(TCHAR),
                &count, NULL))
        va_end(pMsgList);
        return FALSE;
    }
    va_end(pMsgList);
    return TRUE;
}

BOOL PrintMsg(HANDLE hOut, LPCTSTR pMsg)
/* Single message version of PrintStrings. */
{
    return PrintStrings(hOut, pMsg, NULL);
}

BOOL ConsolePrompt(LPCTSTR pPromptMsg, LPTSTR pResponse,
        DWORD maxChar, BOOL echo)
/* Prompt the user at the console and get a response
   which can be up to maxChar generic characters. */
{
    HANDLE hIn, hOut;
    DWORD charIn, echoFlag;
    BOOL success;

    hIn = CreateFile(_T("CONIN$"), GENERIC_READ | GENERIC_WRITE, 0,
            NULL, OPEN_ALWAYS, FILE_ATTRIBUTE_NORMAL, NULL);
```

```
    hOut = CreateFile(_T("CONOUT$"), GENERIC_WRITE, 0,
            NULL, OPEN_ALWAYS, FILE_ATTRIBUTE_NORMAL, NULL);

    echoFlag = echo ? ENABLE_ECHO_INPUT : 0;
    success =
            SetConsoleMode(hIn, ENABLE_LINE_INPUT |
                echoFlag | ENABLE_PROCESSED_INPUT)
            && SetConsoleMode(hOut,
                ENABLE_WRAP_AT_EOL_OUTPUT | ENABLE_PROCESSED_OUTPUT)
            && PrintStrings(hOut, pPromptMsg, NULL)
            && ReadConsole(hIn, pResponse, maxChar - 2, &charIn, NULL);

    /* Replace the CR-LF by the null character. */
    if (success)
        pResponse[charIn - 2] = '\0';
    else
        ReportError(_T("ConsolePrompt failure."), 0, TRUE);

    CloseHandle(hIn);
    CloseHandle(hOut);
    return success;
}
```

Notice that `ConsolePrompt` returns a Boolean success indicator. Further-more, `GetLastError` will return the error from the function that failed, but it's important to call `ReportError`, and hence `GetLastError`, before the `Close-Handle` calls.

Also, `ReadConsole` returns a carriage return and line feed, so the last step is to insert a null character in the proper location over the carriage return. The call-ing program must provide the `maxChar` parameter to prevent buffer overflow.

Example: Printing the Current Directory

pwd (Program 2–6) implements a version of the UNIX command pwd. The `MAX_PATH` value specifies the buffer size, but there is an error test to illustrate `GetCurrentDirectory`.

Program 2–6   pwd: Printing the Current Directory

```
/* Chapter 2. pwd. */
/* pwd: Print the current directory. */
/* This program illustrates:
    1. Windows GetCurrentDirectory
    2. Testing the length of a returned string */
```

```
#include "Everything.h"

#define DIRNAME_LEN (MAX_PATH + 2)

int _tmain(int argc, LPTSTR argv[])
{
   /* Buffer to receive current directory allows for the CR,
      LF at the end of the longest possible path. */
   TCHAR pwdBuffer[DIRNAME_LEN];
   DWORD lenCurDir;

   lenCurDir = GetCurrentDirectory(DIRNAME_LEN, pwdBuffer);
   if (lenCurDir == 0)
      ReportError(_T("Failure getting pathname."), 1, TRUE);
   if (lenCurDir > DIRNAME_LEN)
      ReportError(_T("Pathname is too long."), 2, FALSE);

   PrintMsg(GetStdHandle(STD_OUTPUT_HANDLE), pwdBuffer);
   return 0;
}
```

Run 2–6, shows the results, which appear on a single line. The Windows Command Prompt produces the first and last lines, whereas pwd produces the middle line.

Run 2–6   pwd: Determining the Current Directory

Summary

Windows supports a complete set of functions for processing and managing files and directories, along with character processing functions. In addition, you can write portable, generic applications that can be built for either ASCII or Unicode operation.

The Windows functions resemble their UNIX and C library counterparts in many ways, but the differences are also apparent. Appendix B discusses portable coding techniques. Appendix B also has a table showing the Windows, UNIX, and C library functions, noting how they correspond and pointing out some of the significant differences.

Looking Ahead

The next step, in Chapter 3, is to discuss direct file access and to learn how to deal with file and directory attributes such as file length and time stamps. Chapter 3 also shows how to process directories and ends with a discussion of the registry management API, which is similar to the directory management API.

Additional Reading

NTFS and Windows Storage

Inside Windows Storage, by Dilip Naik, is a comprehensive discussion of the complete range of Windows storage options including directly attached and network attached storage. Recent developments, enhancements, and performance improvements, along with internal implementation details, are all described.

Inside the Windows NT File System, by Helen Custer, and *Windows NT File System Internals,* by Rajeev Nagar, are additional references, as is the previously mentioned *Windows Internals: Including Windows Server 2008 and Windows Vista.*

Unicode

Developing International Software, by Dr. International (that's the name on the book), shows how to use Unicode in practice, with guidelines, international standards, and culture-specific issues.

UNIX

Stevens and Rado cover UNIX files and directories in Chapters 3 and 4 and terminal I/O in Chapter 11.

UNIX in a Nutshell, by Arnold Robbins et al., is a useful quick reference on the UNIX commands.

Exercises

2–1. Write a short program to test the generic versions of `printf` and `scanf`.

2–2. Modify the `CatFile` function in `cat` (Program 2–2) so that it uses `WriteConsole` rather than `WriteFile` when the standard output handle is associated with a console.

2–3. `CreateFile` allows you to specify file access characteristics so as to enhance performance. `FILE_FLAG_SEQUENTIAL_SCAN` is an example. Use this flag in `cci_f` (Program 2–4) and determine whether there is a performance improvement for large files, including files larger than 4GB. Also try `FILE_FLAG_NO_BUFFERING` after reading the MSDN `CreateFile` documentation carefully. Appendix C shows results on several Windows versions and computers.

2–4. Run `cci` (Program 2–3) with and without `UNICODE` defined. What is the effect, if any?

2–5. Compare the information provided by `perror` (in the C library) and `ReportError` for common errors such as opening a nonexistent file.

2–6. Test the `ConsolePrompt` (Program 2–5) function's suppression of keyboard echo by using it to ask the user to enter and confirm a password.

2–7. Determine what happens when performing console output with a mixture of generic C library and Windows `WriteFile` or `WriteConsole` calls. What is the explanation?

2–8. Write a program that sorts an array of Unicode strings. Determine the difference between the word and string sorts by using `lstrcmp` and `_tcscmp`. Does `lstrlen` produce different results from those of `_tcslen`? The remarks under the `CompareString` function entry in the Microsoft online help are useful.

2–9. Appendix C provides performance data for file copying and `cci` conversion using different program implementations. Investigate performance with the test programs on computers available to you. Also, if possible, investigate performance using networked file systems, SANs, and so on, to understand the impact of various storage architectures when performing sequential file access.

CHAPTER

3 | Advanced File and Directory Processing, and the Registry

File systems provide more than sequential processing; they must also provide random access, file locking, directory processing, and file attribute management. Starting with random file access, which is required by database, file management, and many other applications, this chapter shows how to access files randomly at any location and shows how to use Windows 64-bit file pointers to access files larger than 4GB.

The next step is to show how to scan directory contents and how to manage and interpret file attributes, such as time stamps, access, and size. Finally, file locking protects files from concurrent modification by more than one process (Chapter 6) or thread (Chapter 7).

The final topic is the Windows registry, a centralized database that contains configuration information for applications and for Windows itself. Registry access functions and program structure are similar to the file and directory management functions, as shown by the final program example, so this short topic is at the chapter's end rather than in a separate chapter.

The 64-Bit File System

The Windows NTFS supports 64-bit file addresses so that files can, in principle, be as long as 2^{64} bytes. The 2^{32}-byte length limit of older 32-bit file systems, such as FAT, constrains file lengths to 4GB (4×10^9 bytes). This limit is a serious constraint for numerous applications, including large database and multimedia systems, so any complete modern OS must support much larger files.

Files larger than 4GB are sometimes called *very large* or *huge* files, although huge files have become so common that we'll simply assume that any file could be huge and program accordingly.

Needless to say, some applications will never need huge files, so, for many programmers, 32-bit file addresses will be adequate. It is, however, a good idea to start working with 64-bit addresses from the beginning of a new development project, given the rapid pace of technical change and disk capacity growth,[1] cost improvements, and application requirements.

Win32, despite the 64-bit file addresses and the support for huge files, is still a 32-bit OS API because of its 32-bit memory addressing. Win32 addressing limitations are not a concern until Chapter 5.

File Pointers

Windows, just like UNIX, the C library, and nearly every other OS, maintains a *file pointer* with each open file handle, indicating the current byte location in the file. The next `WriteFile` or `ReadFile` operation will start transferring data sequentially to or from that location and increment the file pointer by the number of bytes transferred. Opening the file with `CreateFile` sets the pointer to zero, indicating the start of the file, and the handle's pointer is advanced with each successive read or write. The crucial operation required for random file access is the ability to set the file pointer to an arbitrary value, using `SetFilePointer` and `SetFilePointerEx`.

The first function, `SetFilePointer`, is obsolete, as the handling of 64-bit file pointers is clumsy. `SetFilePointerEx`, one of a number of "extended"[2] functions, is the correct choice, as it uses 64-bit pointers naturally. Nonetheless, we describe both functions here because `SetFilePointer` is still common. In the future, if the extended function is supported in NT5 and is actually superior, we mention the nonextended function only in passing.

`SetFilePointer` shows, for the first time, how Windows handles addresses in large files. The techniques are not always pretty, and `SetFilePointer` is easiest to use with small files.

---

[1] Even inexpensive laptop computers contain 80GB or more of disk capacity, so "huge" files larger than 4GB are possible and sometimes necessary, even on small computers.

[2] The extended functions have an "Ex" suffix and, as would be expected, provide additional functionality. There is no consistency among the extended functions in terms of the nature of the new features or parameter usage. For example, `MoveFileEx` (Chapter 2) adds a new flag input parameter, while `SetFilePointerEx` has a `LARGE_INTEGER` input and output parameters. The registry functions (end of this chapter) have additional extended functions.

```
DWORD SetFilePointer (
    HANDLE hFile,
    LONG lDistanceToMove,
    PLONG lpDistanceToMoveHigh,
    DWORD dwMoveMethod)
```

Return: The low-order DWORD (unsigned) of the new file pointer.
The high-order portion of the new file pointer goes to the
DWORD indicated by lpDistanceToMoveHigh (if non-NULL).
In case of error, the return value is 0xFFFFFFFF.

Parameters

hFile is the handle of an open file with read or write access (or both).

lDistanceToMove is the 32-bit LONG *signed* distance to move or *unsigned* file position, depending on the value of dwMoveMethod.

lpDistanceToMoveHigh points to the high-order portion of the move distance. If this value is NULL, the function can operate only on files whose length is limited to $2^{32}-2$. This parameter is also used to receive the high-order return value of the file pointer.[3] The low-order portion is the function's return value.

dwMoveMethod specifies one of three move modes.

- FILE_BEGIN: Position the file pointer from the start of the file, interpreting DistanceToMove as *unsigned*.

- FILE_CURRENT: Move the pointer forward or backward from the current position, interpreting DistanceToMove as *signed*. Positive is forward.

- FILE_END: Position the pointer backward or forward from the end of the file.

You can obtain the file length by specifying a zero-length move from the end of file, although the file pointer is changed as a side effect.

The method of representing 64-bit file positions causes complexities because the function return can represent both a file position and an error code. For example, suppose that the actual position is location $2^{32}-1$ (that is, 0xFFFFFFFF) and that the call also specifies the high-order move distance. Invoke GetLastError to

---

[3] Windows is not consistent, as can be seen by comparing SetFilePointer with GetCurrentDirectory. In some cases, there are distinct input and output parameters.

determine whether the return value is a valid file position or whether the function failed, in which case the return value would not be NO_ERROR. This explains why file lengths are limited to $2^{32}-2$ when the high-order component is omitted.

Another confusing factor is that the high- and low-order components are separated and treated differently. The low-order address is treated as a call by value and returned by the function, whereas the high-order address is a call by reference and is both input and output. SetFilePointerEx is much easier to use, but, first, we need to describe Windows 64-bit arithmetic.

---

lseek (in UNIX) and fseek (in the C library) are similar to SetFilePointerEx. Both systems also advance the file position during read and write operations.

64-Bit Arithmetic

It is not difficult to perform the 64-bit file pointer arithmetic, and our example programs use the Windows LARGE_INTEGER 64-bit data type, which is a union of a LONGLONG (called QuadPart) and two 32-bit quantities (LowPart, a DWORD, and HighPart, a LONG). LONGLONG supports all the arithmetic operations. There is also a ULONGLONG data type, which is unsigned. The guidelines for using LARGE_INTEGER data are:

- SetFilePointerEx and other functions require LARGE_INTEGER parameters.

- Perform arithmetic on the QuadPart component of a LARGE_INTEGER value.

- Use the LowPart and HighPart components as required; this is illustrated in an upcoming example.

SetFilePointerEx

SetFilePointerEx is straightforward, requiring a LARGE_INTEGER input for the requested position and a LARGE_INTEGER output for the actual position. The return result is a Boolean to indicate success or failure.

```
BOOL SetFilePointerEx (
    HANDLE hFile,
    LARGE_INTERGER liDistanceToMove,
    PLARGE_INTEGER lpNewFilePointer,
    DWORD dwMoveMethod)
```

lpNewFilePointer can be NULL, in which case, the new file pointer is not returned. dwMoveMethod has the same values as for SetFilePointer.

Specifying File Position with an Overlapped Structure

Windows provides another way to specify the read/write file position. Recall that the final parameter to both ReadFile and WriteFile is the address of an overlapped structure, and this value has always been NULL in the previous examples. Two members of this structure are Offset and OffsetHigh. You can set the appropriate values in an overlapped structure, and the I/O operation can start at the specified location. The file pointer is changed to point past the last byte transferred, but the overlapped structure values do not change. The overlapped structure also has a handle member used for asynchronous overlapped I/O (Chapter 14), hEvent, that must be NULL for now.

Caution: Even though this example uses an overlapped structure, this is not overlapped I/O, which is covered in Chapter 14.

The overlapped structure is especially convenient when updating a file record, as the following code fragment illustrates; otherwise, separate SetFilePointerEx calls would be required before the ReadFile and WriteFile calls. The hEvent field is the last of five fields, as shown in the initialization statement. The LARGE_INTEGER data type represents the file position.

```
OVERLAPPED ov = { 0, 0, 0, 0, NULL };
RECORD r; /* Definition not shown
    but it includes the refCount field. */
LONGLONG n;
LARGE_INTEGER filePos;
DWORD nRead, nWrite;
...
/* Update the reference count in the nth record. */
filePos.QuadPart = n * sizeof(RECORD);
ov.Offset = filePos.LowPart;
ov.OffsetHigh = filePos.HighPart;
ReadFile(hFile, r, sizeof(RECORD), &nRead, &ov);
r.refCount++; /* Update the record. */
. . .
WriteFile(hFile, r, sizeof(RECORD), &nWrite, &ov);
```

If the file handle was created with the FILE_FLAG_NO_BUFFERING CreateFile flag, then both the file position and the record size (byte count) must be multiples of the disk volume's sector size. Obtain physical disk information, including sector size, with GetDiskFreeSpace.

Note: You can append to the end of the file without knowing the file length. Just specify 0xFFFFFFFF on both Offset and OffsetHigh before performing the write.

Overlapped structures are used again later in this chapter to specify file lock regions and in Chapter 14 for asynchronous I/O and random file access.

Getting the File Size

Determine a file's size by positioning 0 bytes from the end and using the file pointer value returned by SetFilePointerEx. Alternatively, you can use a specific function, GetFileSizeEx, for this purpose. GetFileSizeEx, like SetFilePointerEx, returns the 64-bit value as a LARGE_INTEGER.

```
BOOL GetFileSizeEx (
    HANDLE hFile,
    PLARGE_INTEGER lpFileSize)

Return: The file size is in *lpFileSize. A false return indicates
    an error; check GetLastError.
```

GetFileSize (now obsolete) and GetFileSizeEx require that the file have an open handle. It is also possible to obtain the length by name. GetCompressed-FileSize returns the size of the compressed file, and FindFirstFile, discussed in the upcoming "File Attributes and Directory Processing" section, gives the exact size of a named file.

Setting the File Size, File Initialization, and Sparse Files

The SetEndOfFileEx function resizes the file using the current value of the file pointer to determine the length. A file can be extended or truncated. With extension, the contents of the extended region are not defined. The file will actually consume the disk space and user space quotas unless the file is a sparse file. Files can also be compressed to consume less space. Exercise 3–1 explores this topic.

SetEndOfFileEx sets the physical end of file beyond the current "logical" end. The file's *tail,* which is the portion between the logical and physical ends, contains no valid data. You can shorten the tail by writing data past the logical end.

With sparse files, disk space is consumed only as data is written. A file, directory, or volume can be specified to be sparse by the administrator. Also, the

DeviceIoControl function can use the FSCTL_SET_SPARSE flag to specify that an existing file is sparse. Program 3–1 illustrates a situation where a sparse file can be used conveniently. SetFileValidData does not apply to sparse files.

NTFS files and file tails are initialized to zeros for security.

Notice that the SetEndOfFileEx call is not the only way to extend a file. You can also extend a file using many successive write operations, but this will result in more fragmented file allocation; SetEndOfFile allows the OS to allocate larger contiguous disk units.

Example: Random Record Updates

Program 3–1, RecordAccess, maintains a fixed-size file of fixed-size records. The file header contains the number of nonempty records in the file along with the file record capacity. The user can interactively read, write (update), and delete records, which contain time stamps, a text string, and a count to indicate how many times the record has been modified. A simple and realistic extension would be to add a key to the record structure and locate records in the file by applying a hash function to the key value.

The program demonstrates file positioning to a specified record and shows how to perform 64-bit arithmetic using the Windows LARGE_INTEGER data type. One error check is included to illustrate file pointer logic. This design also illustrates file pointers, multiple overlapped structures, and file updating with 64-bit file positions.

The total number of records in the file is specified on the command line; a large number will create a very large or even huge file, as the record size is about 300 bytes. Some simple experiments will quickly show that large files should be sparse; otherwise, the entire file must be allocated and initialized on the disk, which could consume considerable time and disk space. While not shown in the Program 3–1 listing, the program contains optional code to create a sparse file. That code will not function on systems that do not support sparse files, such as Windows XP Home Edition.

The *Examples* file (on the book's Web site) provides three related programs: tail.c is another example of random file access; getn.c is a simpler version of RecordAccess that can only read records; and cciMT (included with the programs for Chapter 14 in *Examples*, although not in the text) also illustrates random file access.

Note: Program 3–1 uses the SYSTEMTIME data type and the GetSystemTime function. While we have not discussed these, the usage is straightforward.

Program 3-1   RecordAccess: Direct File Access

```
/* Chapter 3. RecordAccess. */
/* Usage: RecordAccess FileName [nrec]
    If nrec is omitted, FileName must already exist.
    If nrec > 0, FileName is recreated (destroying any existing file)
        and the program exits, having created an empty file.
    If the number of records is large, a sparse file is recommended.
*/
/* This program illustrates:
    1. Random file access.
    2. LARGE_INTEGER arithmetic and using 64-bit file positions.
    3. Record update in place.
    4. File initialization to 0
*/

#include "Everything.h"
#define STRING_SIZE 256
typedef struct _RECORD { /* File record structure */
    DWORD       referenceCount;  /* 0 means an empty record */
    SYSTEMTIME  recordCreationTime;
    SYSTEMTIME  recordLastRefernceTime;
    SYSTEMTIME  recordUpdateTime;
    TCHAR       dataString[STRING_SIZE];
} RECORD;
typedef struct _HEADER { /* File header descriptor */
    DWORD       numRecords;
    DWORD       numNonEmptyRecords;
} HEADER;

int _tmain(int argc, char * argv[])
{
    HANDLE hFile;
    LARGE_INTEGER curPtr;
    DWORD openOption, nXfer, recNo;
    RECORD record;
    TCHAR string[STRING_SIZE], command, extra;
    OVERLAPPED ov = {0, 0, 0, 0, NULL}, ovZero = {0, 0, 0, 0, NULL};
    HEADER header = {0, 0};
    SYSTEMTIME currentTime;
    BOOLEAN headerChange, recordChange;

    openOption = ((argc > 2 && atoi(argv[2]) <= 0) || argc <= 2) ?
            OPEN_EXISTING : CREATE_ALWAYS;
    hFile = CreateFile(argv[1], GENERIC_READ | GENERIC_WRITE,
        0, NULL, openOption, FILE_FLAG_RANDOM_ACCESS, NULL);

    if (argc >= 3 && atoi(argv[2]) > 0)  {
        /* Write the header and pre-size the new file) */
```

```
        header.numRecords = atoi(argv[2]);
        WriteFile(hFile, &header, sizeof(header), &nXfer, &ovZero);
        curPtr.QuadPart = (LONGLONG)sizeof(RECORD) * atoi(argv[2]) +
                        sizeof(HEADER);
        SetFilePointerEx(hFile, curPtr, NULL, FILE_BEGIN);
        SetEndOfFile(hFile);
        return 0;
    }

    /* Read file header: find number of records & non-empty records */
    ReadFile(hFile, &header, sizeof(HEADER), &nXfer, &ovZero);

    /* Prompt the user to read or write a numbered record */
    while (TRUE) {
        headerChange = FALSE; recordChange = FALSE;
        _tprintf(_T("Enter r(ead)/w(rite)/d(elete)/qu(it) Rec#\n"));
        _tscanf(_T("%c%u%c"), &command, &recNo, &extra);
        if (command == 'q') break;
        if (recNo >= header.numRecords) {
            _tprintf(_T("Record Number is too large. Try again.\n"));
            continue;
        }
        curPtr.QuadPart = (LONGLONG)recNo *
            sizeof(RECORD) + sizeof(HEADER);
        ov.Offset = curPtr.LowPart;
        ov.OffsetHigh = curPtr.HighPart;
        ReadFile(hFile, &record, sizeof(RECORD), &nXfer, &ov);
        GetSystemTime(&currentTime); /* To update record time fields */
        record.recordLastRefernceTime = currentTime;
        if (command == 'r' || command == 'd') { /* Report contents */
            if (record.referenceCount == 0) {
                _tprintf(_T("Record Number %d is empty.\n"), recNo);
                continue;
            } else {
                _tprintf(_T("Record Number %d. Reference Count: %d \n"),
                    recNo, record.referenceCount);
                _tprintf(_T("Data: %s\n"), record.dataString);
                /* Exercise: Display times. See Program 3-2 */
            }
            if (command == 'd') { /* Delete the record */
                record.referenceCount = 0;
                header.numNonEmptyRecords--;
                headerChange = TRUE;
                recordChange = TRUE;
            }
        } else if (command == 'w') { /* Write record; first time? */
            _tprintf(_T("Enter new data string for the record.\n)");
            _fgetts(string, sizeof(string), stdin);
            /* Don't use _getts(potential buffer overflow) */
            string[_tcslen(string)-1] = _T('\0'); // remove newline
```

```
            if (record.referenceCount == 0) {
                record.recordCreationTime = currentTime;
                header.numNonEmptyRecords++;
                headerChange = TRUE;
            }
            record.recordUpdateTime = currentTime;
            record.referenceCount++;
            strncpy(record.dataString, string, STRING_SIZE-1);
            recordChange = TRUE;
        } else {
            _tprintf(_T("Command must be r, w, or d. Try again.\n"));
        }

        /* Update record in place if any contents have changed. */
        if (recordChange)
            WriteFile(hFile, &record, sizeof(RECORD), &nXfer, &ov):
        /* Update the number of non-empty records if required */
        if (headerChange)
            WriteFile(hFile, &header, sizeof(header), &nXfer, &ovZero);
    }

    _tprintf(_T("Computed number of non-empty records is: %d\n"),
        header.numNonEmptyRecords);
    ReadFile(hFile, &header, sizeof(HEADER), &nXfer, &ovZero);
    _tprintf(_T("File %s has %d non-empty records.\nCapacity: %d\n"),
        argv[1], header.numNonEmptyRecords, header.numRecords);

    CloseHandle(hFile);
    return 0;
}
```

Run 3–1 shows RecordAccess working with a 6GB file (20 million records). There are write, read, update, and delete operations. The DIR command at the end shows the file size. The file is not sparse, and writing record number 19,000,000 required about two minutes on the test machine. During this time period, the Windows Resource Monitor showed high disk utilization.

Note: The output messages shown in Program 3–1 were shortened and are not exactly the same as those in the Run 3–1 screenshot.

Caution: If you run this program on your computer, do not create such a large number of records unless you have sufficient free disk space. Initially, it's safer to use just a few hundred records until you are confident that the program is operating correctly. Furthermore, while Run 3–1 worked well on a desktop system with plentiful memory and disk storage, it hung on a laptop. Laptop operation was successful, however, with a 600MB file (2 million records).

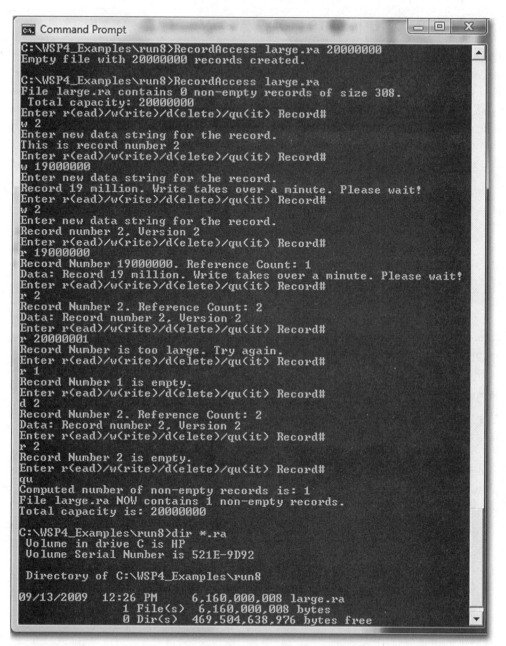

```
Command Prompt                                                    _ □ X

C:\WSP4_Examples\run8>RecordAccess large.ra 20000000
Empty file with 20000000 records created.

C:\WSP4_Examples\run8>RecordAccess large.ra
File large.ra contains 0 non-empty records of size 308.
 Total capacity: 20000000
Enter r(ead)/w(rite)/d(elete)/qu(it) Record#
w 2
Enter new data string for the record.
This is record number 2
Enter r(ead)/w(rite)/d(elete)/qu(it) Record#
w 19000000
Enter new data string for the record.
Record 19 million. Write takes over a minute. Please wait!
Enter r(ead)/w(rite)/d(elete)/qu(it) Record#
w 2
Enter new data string for the record.
Record number 2, Version 2
Enter r(ead)/w(rite)/d(elete)/qu(it) Record#
r 19000000
Record Number 19000000. Reference Count: 1
Data: Record 19 million. Write takes over a minute. Please wait!
Enter r(ead)/w(rite)/d(elete)/qu(it) Record#
r 2
Record Number 2. Reference Count: 2
Data: Record number 2, Version 2
Enter r(ead)/w(rite)/d(elete)/qu(it) Record#
r 20000001
Record Number is too large. Try again.
Enter r(ead)/w(rite)/d(elete)/qu(it) Record#
r 1
Record Number 1 is empty.
Enter r(ead)/w(rite)/d(elete)/qu(it) Record#
d 2
Record Number 2. Reference Count: 2
Data: Record number 2, Version 2
Enter r(ead)/w(rite)/d(elete)/qu(it) Record#
r 2
Record Number 2 is empty.
Enter r(ead)/w(rite)/d(elete)/qu(it) Record#
qu
Computed number of non-empty records is: 1
File large.ra NOW contains 1 non-empty records.
Total capacity is: 20000000

C:\WSP4_Examples\run8>dir *.ra
 Volume in drive C is HP
 Volume Serial Number is 521E-9D92

 Directory of C:\WSP4_Examples\run8

09/13/2009  12:26 PM     6,160,000,008 large.ra
               1 File(s)  6,160,000,008 bytes
               0 Dir(s)   469,504,638,976 bytes free
```

Run 3–1   RecordAccess: Writing, Reading, and Deleting Records

File Attributes and Directory Processing

This section shows how to search a directory for files and other directories that satisfy a specified name pattern and, at the same time, obtain file attributes. Searches require a *search handle* provided by FindFirstFile. Obtain specific files with FindNextFile, and terminate the search with FindClose. There is also an extended version, FindFirstFileEx, which has more search options, such as allowing for case sensitivity. An exercise suggests exploring the extended function.

```
HANDLE FindFirstFile (
   LPCTSTR lpFileName,
   LPWIN32_FIND_DATA lpffd)

Return: A search handle. INVALID_HANDLE_VALUE indicates
   failure.
```

FindFirstFile examines both subdirectory and file names, looking for a name match. The returned HANDLE is for use in subsequent searches. Note that it is not a kernel handle.

Parameters

lpFileName points to a directory or pathname that can contain wildcard characters (? and *). Search for a single specific file by omitting wildcard characters.

lpffd points to a WIN32_FIND_DATA structure (the "WIN32" part of the name is misleading, as this can be used on 64-bit computers) that contains information about the first file or directory to satisfy the search criteria, if any are found.

WIN32_FIND_DATA has the following structure:

```
typedef struct_WIN32_FIND_DATA {
   DWORD dwFileAttributes;
   FILETIME ftCreationTime;
   FILETIME ftLastAccessTime;
   FILETIME ftLastWriteTime;
   DWORD nFileSizeHigh;
   DWORD nFileSizeLow;
   DWORD dwReserved0;
   DWORD dwReserved1;
   TCHAR cFileName[MAX_PATH];
   TCHAR cAlternateFileName[14];
} WIN32_FIND_DATA;
```

Test dwFileAttributes for the values described with CreateFile along with some additional values, such as FILE_ATTRIBUTE_SPARSE_FILE and FILE-_ATTRIBUTE_ENCRYPTED, which CreateFile does not set. The three file times (creation, last access, and last write) are described in an upcoming section. The file size fields, giving the current file length, are self-explanatory. cFileName is not the pathname; it is the file name by itself. cAlternateFileName is the DOS 8.3 (including the period) version of the file name; this information is rarely used and is appropriate only to determine how a file would be named on an old FAT16 file system.

Frequently, the requirement is to scan a directory for files that satisfy a name pattern containing ? and * wildcard characters. To do this, use the search handle obtained from FindFirstFile, which retains information about the search name, and call FindNextFile.

```
BOOL FindNextFile (
    HANDLE hFindFile,
    LPWIN32_FIND_DATA lpffd)
```

FindNextFile will return FALSE in case of invalid arguments or if no more matching files are found, in which case GetLastError will return ERROR_NO_MORE_FILES.

When the search is complete, close the search handle. Do not use CloseHandle. Closing a search handle will cause an exception. Instead, use the following:

```
BOOL FindClose (HANDLE hFindFile)
```

The function GetFileInformationByHandle obtains the same information for a specific file, specified by an open file handle. It also returns a field, nNumberOfLinks, which indicates the number of hard links set by CreateHardLink; this value is one when the file is first created, is increased by one for each CreateHardLink call targeting the file, and is decreased by one when either a hard link name or the original name is deleted.

The FindNextFile method of wildcard expansion is necessary even in programs executed from the MS-DOS prompt because the DOS shell does not expand wildcards.

Pathnames

You can obtain a file's full pathname using `GetFullPathName`. `GetShortPath-Name` returns the name in DOS 8.3 format, assuming that the volume supports short names.

NT 5.1 introduced `SetFileShortName`, which allows you to change the existing short name of a file or directory. This can be convenient because the existing short names are often difficult to interpret.

Other Methods of Obtaining File and Directory Attributes

The `FindFirstFile` and `FindNextFile` functions can obtain the following file attribute information: attribute flags, three time stamps, and file size. There are several other related functions, including one to set attributes, and they can deal directly with the open file handle rather than scan a directory or use a file name. Three such functions, `GetFileSize`, `GetFileSizeEx`, and `SetEndOfFile`, were described earlier in this chapter.

Distinct functions are used to obtain the other attributes. For example, to obtain the time stamps of an open file, use the `GetFileTime` function.

```
BOOL GetFileTime (
    HANDLE hFile,
    LPFILETIME lpftCreation,
    LPFILETIME lpftLastAccess,
    LPFILETIME lpftLastWrite)
```

The file times here and in the `WIN32_FIND_DATA` structure are 64-bit unsigned integers giving elapsed 100-nanosecond units (10^7 units per second) from a base time (January 1, 1601), expressed as Universal Coordinated Time (UTC).[4] There are several convenient functions for dealing with times.

- `FileTimeToSystemTime` (not described here; see MSDN or Program 3–2) breaks the file time into individual units ranging from years down to seconds and milliseconds. These units are suitable, for example, when displaying or printing times.

---

[4] Do not, however, expect to get 100-nanosecond precision; precision will vary depending on hardware characteristics.

- `SystemTimeToFileTime` reverses the process, converting time expressed in these individual units to a file time.

- `CompareFileTime` determines whether one file time is less than (–1), equal to (0), or greater than (+1) another.

- Change the time stamps with `SetFileTime`; use `NULL` for times that are not to be changed. NTFS supports all three file times, but the FAT gives an accurate result only for the last access time.

- `FileTimeToLocalFileTime` and `LocalFileTimeToFileTime` convert between UTC and the local time.

`GetFileType`, not described in detail here, distinguishes among disk files, character files (actually, devices such as printers and consoles), and pipes (see Chapter 11). The file, again, is specified with a handle.

The function `GetFileAttributes` uses the file or directory name, and it returns just the `dwFileAttributes` information.

```
DWORD GetFileAttributes (LPCTSTR lpFileName)

Return: The file attributes, or INVALID_FILE_ATTRIBUTES in
       case of failure.
```

The attributes can be tested for appropriate combinations of several mask values. Some attributes, such as the temporary file attribute, are originally set with `CreateFile`. The attribute values include the following:

- `FILE_ATTRIBUTE_DIRECTORY`

- `FILE_ATTRIBUTE_NORMAL`

- `FILE_ATTRIBUTE_READONLY`

- `FILE_ATTRIBUTE_TEMPORARY`

Be certain to test the return value for failure (`INVALID_FILE_ATTRIBUTES`, which is `0xFFFFFFFF`) before trying to determine the attributes. This value would make it appear as if all values were set.

The function `SetFileAttributes` changes these attributes in a named file.

opendir, readdir, and closedir in UNIX correspond to the three Find functions. The function stat obtains file size and times, in addition to owning user and group information that relates to UNIX security. fstat and lstat are variations. These functions can also obtain type information. utime sets file times in UNIX. There is no UNIX equivalent to the temporary file attribute.

Temporary File Names

The next function creates names for temporary files. The name can be in any specified directory and must be unique.

GetTempFileName gives a unique file name, with the .tmp suffix, in a specified directory and optionally creates the file. This function is used extensively in later examples (Program 6–1, Program 7–1, and elsewhere).

```
UINT GetTempFileName (
    LPCTSTR lpPathName,
    LPCTSTR lpPrefixString,
    UINT uUnique,
    LPTSTR lpTempFileName)
```

Return: A unique numeric value used to create the file name. This will be uUnique if uUnique is nonzero. On failure, the return value is zero.

Parameters

lpPathName is the directory for the temporary file. "." is a typical value specifying the current directory. Alternatively, use GetTempPath, a Windows function not described here, to give the name of a directory dedicated to temporary files.

lpPrefixString is the prefix of the temporary name. You can only use 8-bit ASCII characters. uUnique is normally zero so that the function will generate a unique four-digit suffix and will create the file. If this value is nonzero, the file is not created; do that with CreateFile, possibly using FILE_FLAG_DELETE_ON_CLOSE.

lpTempFileName points to the buffer that receives the temporary file name. The buffer's byte length should be at least the same value as MAX_PATH. The resulting pathname is a concatenation of the path, the prefix, the four-digit hex number, and the .tmp suffix.

Example: Listing File Attributes

It is now time to illustrate the file and directory management functions. Program 3–2, lsW, shows a limited version of the UNIX ls directory listing command, which is similar to the Windows DIR command. lsW can show file modification times and the file size, although this version gives only the low order of the file size.

The program scans the directory for files that satisfy the search pattern. For each file located, the program shows the file name and, if the -l option is specified, the file attributes. This program illustrates many, but not all, Windows directory management functions.

The bulk of Program 3–2 is concerned with directory traversal. Notice that each directory is traversed twice—once to process files and again to process subdirectories—in order to support the -R recursive option.

Program 3–2, as listed here, will properly carry out a command with a relative pathname such as:

```
lsW -R include\*.h
```

It will not work properly, however, with an absolute pathname such as:

```
lsW -R C:\Projects\ls\Debug\*.obj
```

because the program, as listed, depends on setting the directory relative to the current directory. The complete solution (in *Examples*) analyzes pathnames and will also carry out the second command.

An exercise suggests modifying this program to remove the SetCurrent-Directory calls so as to avoid the risk of program failures leaving you in an unexpected state.

Program 3–2   lsW: File Listing and Directory Traversal

```
/* Chapter 3. lsW file list command */
/* lsW [options] [files] */

#include "Everything.h"

BOOL TraverseDirectory(LPCTSTR, DWORD, LPBOOL);
DWORD FileType(LPWIN32_FIND_DATA);
BOOL ProcessItem(LPWIN32_FIND_DATA, DWORD, LPBOOL);

int _tmain(int argc, LPTSTR argv[])
{
    BOOL flags[MAX_OPTIONS], ok = TRUE;
    TCHAR pathName[MAX_PATH + 1], currPath[MAX_PATH + 1];
```

```
    LPTSTR pSlash, pFileName;
    int i, fileIndex;

    fileIndex = Options(
            argc, argv, _T("Rl"), &flags[0], &flags[1], NULL);

    /* "Parse" the search pattern into "parent" and file name. */
    GetCurrentDirectory(MAX_PATH, currPath); /* Save current path. */
    if (argc < fileIndex + 1)
        ok = TraverseDirectory(_T("*"), MAX_OPTIONS, flags);
    else for (i = fileIndex; i < argc; i++) {
        _tcscpy(pathName, argv[i]);
        _tcscpy(tempPath, argv[i]);

        /* Find the rightmost slash, if any.
            Set the path and use the rest as the file name. */
        pSlash = _tstrrchr(tempPath, '\\');
        if (pSlash != NULL) {
            *pSlash = '\0';
            _tcscat(tempPath, _T("\\"));
            SetCurrentDirectory(tempPath); /* Now restore pathName. */
            pSlash = _tstrrchr(pathName, '\\');
            pFileName = pSlash + 1;
        } else pFileName = pathName;
        ok = TraverseDirectory(pFileName, MAX_OPTIONS, flags) && ok;
        SetCurrentDirectory(currPath); /* Restore working directory. */
    }
}

static BOOL TraverseDirectory(LPCTSTR pathName, DWORD numFlags,
        LPBOOL flags)

/* Traverse a directory; perform ProcessItem for every match. */
/* pathName: Relative or absolute pathname to traverse. */
{
    HANDLE searchHandle;
    WIN32_FIND_DATA findData;
    BOOL recursive = flags[0];
    DWORD fType, iPass;
    TCHAR currPath[MAX_PATH + 1];

    GetCurrentDirectory(MAX_PATH, currPath);

    for (iPass = 1; iPass <= 2; iPass++) {
        /* Pass 1: List files. */
        /* Pass 2: Traverse directories (if -R specified). */
        searchHandle = FindFirstFile(pathName, &findData);
        do {
            fType = FileType(&findData); /* File or directory? */
            if (iPass == 1) /* List name and attributes. */
```

```
            ProcessItem(&findData, MAX_OPTIONS, flags);
        if (fType == TYPE_DIR && iPass == 2 && recursive) {
            /* Process a subdirectory. */
            _tprintf(_T("\n%s\\%s:"), currPath, findData.cFileName);
            /* Prepare to traverse a directory. */
            SetCurrentDirectory(findData.cFileName);
            TraverseDirectory(_T("*"), numFlags, flags);
            SetCurrentDirectory(_T(".."));
        }
    } while (FindNextFile(searchHandle, &findData));
    FindClose(searchHandle);
    }
    return TRUE;
}

static BOOL ProcessItem(LPWIN32_FIND_DATA pFileData,
        DWORD numFlags, LPBOOL flags)
/* List file or directory attributes. */
{
    const TCHAR fileTypeChar[] = {' ', 'd'};
    DWORD fType = FileType(pFileData);
    BOOL Long = flags[1];
    SYSTEMTIME lastWrite;

    if (fType != TYPE_FILE && fType != TYPE_DIR) return FALSE;

    _tprintf(_T("\n"));
    if (Long) { /* Was "-l" option used on the command line? */
        _tprintf(_T("%c"), fileTypeChar[fType - 1]);
        _tprintf(_T("%10d"), pFileData->nFileSizeLow);
        FileTimeToSystemTime(&(pFileData->ftLastWriteTime),
            &lastWrite);
        _tprintf(_T(" %02d/%02d/%04d %02d:%02d:%02d"),
            lastWrite.wMonth, lastWrite.wDay,
            lastWrite.wYear, lastWrite.wHour,
            lastWrite.wMinute, lastWrite.wSecond);
    }
    _tprintf(_T(" %s"), pFileData->cFileName);
    return TRUE;
}

static DWORD FileType(LPWIN32_FIND_DATA pFileData)
/* Types supported - TYPE_FILE: file; TYPE_DIR: directory;
   TYPE_DOT:  . or .. directory */
{
    BOOL isDir;
    DWORD fType;
    fType = TYPE_FILE;
    isDir = (pFileData->dwFileAttributes &
            FILE_ATTRIBUTE_DIRECTORY) != 0;
```

```
    if (isDir)
        if (lstrcmp(pFileData->cFileName, _T(".")) == 0
                || lstrcmp(pFileData->cFileName, _T("..")) == 0)
            fType = TYPE_DOT;
        else fType = TYPE_DIR;
    return fType;
}
```

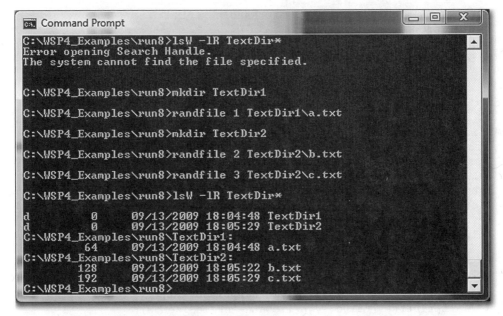

Run 3–2   `lsW`: Listing Files and Directories

Example: Setting File Times

Program 3–3 implements the UNIX touch command, which changes file access and modifies times to the current value of the system time. Exercise 3–12 enhances touch so that the new file time is a command line option, as with the actual UNIX command.

The program uses `GetSystemTimeAsFileTime`, which is more convenient than calling `GetSystemTime` (used in Program 3–1) followed by `SystemTimeToFileTime`. See MSDN for more information, although these functions are straightforward.

Run 3–3 shows touch operation, changing the time of an existing file and creating a new file.

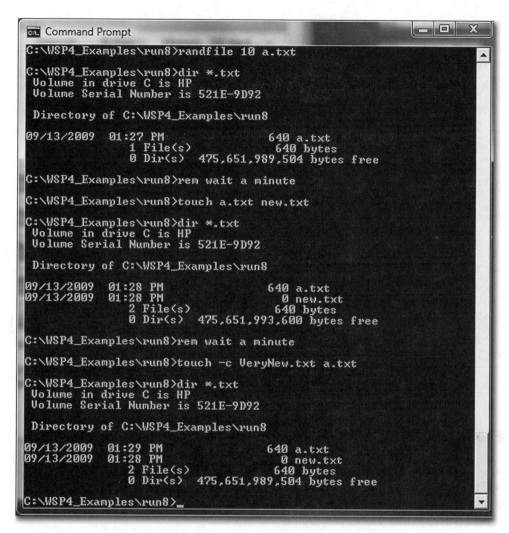

Run 3-3   touch: Changing File Time and Creating New Files

Program 3-3   touch: Setting File Times

```
/* Chapter 3. touch command. */
/* touch [options] files */
#include "Everything.h"

int _tmain(int argc, LPTSTR argv[])
{
    FILETIME newFileTime;
    LPFILETIME pAccessTime = NULL, pModifyTime = NULL;
```

```
    HANDLE hFile;
    BOOL setAccessTime, setModTime, NotCreateNew, maFlag;
    DWORD createFlag;
    int i, fileIndex;

    fileIndex = Options(argc, argv, _T("amc"),
            &setAccessTime, &setModTime, &NotCreateNew, NULL);

    maFlag = setAccessTime || setModTime;
    createFlag = NotCreateNew ? OPEN_EXISTING : OPEN_ALWAYS;

    for (i = fileIndex; i < argc; i++) {
        hFile = CreateFile(argv[i], GENERIC_READ | GENERIC_WRITE, 0,
                NULL, createFlag, FILE_ATTRIBUTE_NORMAL, NULL);
        /* Get current system time and convert to a file time.
           Do not change the create time. */
        GetSystemTimeAsFileTime(&newFileTime);
        if (setAccessTime || !maFlag) pAccessTime = &newFileTime;
        if (setModTime || !maFlag) pModifyTime = &newFileTime;
        SetFileTime(hFile, NULL, pAccessTime, pModifyTime);
        CloseHandle(hFile);
    }
    return 0;
}
```

File Processing Strategies

An early decision in any Windows development or porting project is to select whether to perform file processing with the C library or with the Windows functions. This is not an either/or decision because the functions can be mixed (with caution) even when you're processing the same file.

The C library offers several distinct advantages, including the following.

- The code will be portable to non-Windows systems.

- Convenient line- and character-oriented functions that do not have direct Windows equivalents simplify string processing.

- C library functions are generally higher level and easier to use than Windows functions.

- The line and stream character-oriented functions can easily be changed to generic calls, although the portability advantage will be lost.

Nonetheless, there are some limitations to the C library. Here are some examples.

- The C library cannot manage or traverse directories, and it cannot obtain or set most file attributes.

- The C library uses 32-bit file position in the `fseek` function, although Windows does provide a proprietary `_fseeki64` function. Thus, while it can read huge files sequentially, it is not possible to position arbitrarily in a huge file, as is required, for instance, by Program 3–1.

- Advanced features such as file security, memory-mapped files, file locking, asynchronous I/O, and interprocess communication are not available with the C library. Some of the advanced features provide performance benefits, as shown in Chapter 5 and Appendix C.

Another possibility is to port existing UNIX code using a compatibility library. Microsoft C provides a limited compatibility library with many, but not all, UNIX functions. The Microsoft UNIX library includes I/O functions, but most process management and other functions are omitted. Functions are named with an underscore prefix—for example, `_read`, `_write`, `_stat`, and so on.

Decisions regarding the use and mix of C library, compatibility libraries, and the Windows API should be driven by project requirements. Many of the Windows advantages are shown in the following chapters, and the performance figures in Appendix C are useful when performance is a factor.

File Locking

An important issue in any computer running multiple processes is coordination and synchronization of access to shared objects, such as files.

Windows can lock files, in whole or in part, so that no other process (running program) or thread within the process can access the locked file region. File locks can be read-only (shared) or read-write (exclusive). Most importantly, the locks belong to the process. Any attempt to access part of a file (using `ReadFile` or `WriteFile`) in violation of an existing lock will fail because the locks are mandatory at the process level. Any attempt to obtain a conflicting lock will also fail even if the process already owns the lock. File locking is a limited form of synchronization between concurrent processes and threads; synchronization is covered in much more general terms starting in Chapter 8.

The most general function is `LockFileEx`, and there is a less general function, `LockFile`.

`LockFileEx` is a member of the *extended* I/O class of functions, and the overlapped structure, used earlier to specify file position to `ReadFile` and `WriteFile`, is necessary to specify the 64-bit file position and range of the file region to be locked.

```
BOOL LockFileEx (
    HANDLE hFile,
    DWORD dwFlags,
    DWORD dwReserved,
    DWORD nNumberOfBytesToLockLow,
    DWORD nNumberOfBytesToLockHigh,
    LPOVERLAPPED lpOverlapped)
```

`LockFileEx` locks a byte range in an open file for either shared (multiple readers) or exclusive (one reader-writer) access.

Parameters

`hFile` is the handle of an open file. The handle must have at least `GENERIC_READ`.

`dwFlags` determines the lock mode and whether to wait for the lock to become available.

`LOCKFILE_EXCLUSIVE_LOCK`, if set, indicates a request for an exclusive, read-write lock. Otherwise, it requests a shared (read-only) lock.

`LOCKFILE_FAIL_IMMEDIATELY`, if set, specifies that the function should return immediately with `FALSE` if the lock cannot be acquired. Otherwise, the call blocks until the lock becomes available.

`dwReserved` must be 0. The two parameters with the length of the byte range are self-explanatory.

`lpOverlapped` points to an `OVERLAPPED` data structure containing the start of the byte range. The overlapped structure contains three data members that must be set (the others are ignored); the first two determine the start location for the locked region.

- `DWORD Offset` (this is the correct name; not `OffsetLow`).

- `DWORD OffsetHigh`.

- `HANDLE hEvent` should be set to 0.

A file lock is removed using a corresponding `UnlockFileEx` call; all the same parameters are used except `dwFlags`.

```
BOOL UnlockFileEx (
    HANDLE hFile,
    DWORD dwReserved,
    DWORD nNumberOfBytesToLockLow,
    DWORD nNumberOfBytesToLockHigh,
    LPOVERLAPPED lpOverlapped)
```

You should consider several factors when using file locks.

- The unlock must use exactly the same range as a preceding lock. It is not possible, for example, to combine two previous lock ranges or unlock a portion of a locked range. An attempt to unlock a region that does not correspond exactly with an existing lock will fail; the function returns **FALSE** and the system error message indicates that the lock does not exist.

- Locks cannot overlap existing locked regions in a file if a conflict would result.

- It is possible to lock beyond the range of a file's length. This approach could be useful when a process or thread extends a file.

- Locks are not inherited by a newly created process.

- The lock and unlock calls require that you specify the lock range start and size as separate 32-bit integers. There is no way to specify these values directly with **LARGE_INTEGER** values as there is with **SetFilePointerEx**.

Table 3–1 shows the lock logic when all *or* part of a range already has a lock. This logic applies even if the lock is owned by the same process that is making the new request.

Table 3–1   Lock Request Logic

	Requested Lock Type	
Existing Lock	**Shared Lock**	**Exclusive Lock**
None	Granted	Granted
Shared lock (one or more)	Granted	Refused
Exclusive lock	Refused	Refused

Table 3–2 shows the logic when a process attempts a read or write operation on a file region with one or more locks, owned by a separate process, on all or part of the read-write region. A failed read or write may take the form of a partially completed operation if only a portion of the read or write record is locked.

Table 3–2 Locks and I/O Operation

	I/O Operation	
Existing Lock	**Read**	**Write**
None	Succeeds	Succeeds
Shared lock (one or more)	Succeeds. It is not necessary for the calling process to own a lock on the file region.	Fails
Exclusive lock	Succeeds if the calling process owns the lock. Fails otherwise.	Succeeds if the calling process owns the lock. Fails otherwise.

Read and write operations are normally in the form of `ReadFile` and `WriteFile` calls or their extended versions, `ReadFileEx` and `WriteFileEx` (Chapter 14). Diagnosing a read or write failure requires calling `GetLastError`.

Accessing memory mapped to a file is another form of file I/O: see Chapter 5. Lock conflicts are not detected at the time of memory reference; rather, they are detected at the time that the `MapViewOfFileEx` function is called. This function makes a part of the file available to the process, so the lock must be checked at that time.

The `LockFile` function is a legacy, limited, special case and is a form of advisory locking. Only exclusive access is available, and `LockFile` returns immediately. That is, `LockFile` does not block. Test the return value to determine whether you obtained the lock.

Releasing File Locks

Every successful `LockFileEx` call must be followed by a single matching call to `UnlockFileEx` (the same is true for `LockFile` and `UnlockFile`). If a program fails to release a lock or holds the lock longer than necessary, other programs may not be able to proceed, or, at the very least, their performance will be negatively impacted. Therefore, programs should be carefully designed and implemented so that locks are released as soon as possible, and logic that might cause the program to skip the unlock should be avoided. Chapter 8 discusses this same issue with regard to mutex and `CRITICAL_SECTION` locks.

Termination handlers (Chapter 4) are a useful way to ensure that the unlock is performed.

Lock Logic Consequences

Although the file lock logic in Tables 3–1 and 3–2 is natural, it has consequences that may be unexpected and cause unintended program defects. Here are some examples.

- Suppose that process A and process B periodically obtain shared locks on a file, and process C blocks when attempting to gain an exclusive lock on the same file after process A gets its shared lock. Process B may now gain its shared lock even though C is still blocked, and C will remain blocked even after A releases the lock. C will remain blocked until all processes release their shared locks even if they obtained them after C blocked. In this scenario, it is possible that C will be blocked forever even though all the other processes manage their shared locks properly.

- Assume that process A has a shared lock on the file and that process B attempts to read the file without obtaining a shared lock first. The read will still succeed even though the reading process does not own any lock on the file because the read operation does not conflict with the existing shared lock.

- These statements apply both to entire files and to file regions.

- File locking can produce deadlocks in the same way as with mutual exclusion locks (see Chapter 8 for more on deadlocks and their prevention).

- A read or write may be able to complete a portion of its request before encountering a conflicting lock. The read or write will return FALSE, and the byte transfer count will be less than the number requested.

Using File Locks

File locking examples are deferred until Chapter 6, which covers process management. Programs 6–4, 6–5, and 6–6 use locks to ensure that only one process at a time can modify a file.

UNIX has *advisory* file locking; an attempt to obtain a lock may fail (the logic is the same as in Table 3–1), but the process can still perform the I/O. Therefore, UNIX can achieve locking between cooperating processes, but any other process can violate the protocol.

To obtain an advisory lock, use options to the fcntl function. The commands (the second parameter) are F_SETLK, F_SETLKW (to wait), and F_GETLK. An additional block data structure contains a lock type that is one of F_RDLCK, F_WRLCK, or F_UNLCK and the range.

Mandatory locking is also available in some UNIX systems using a file's set-group-ID and group-execute, both using chmod.

UNIX file locking behavior differs in many ways. For example, locks are inherited through an exec call.

The C library does not support locking, although Visual C++ does supply non-standard locking extensions.

The Registry

The registry is a centralized, hierarchical database for application and system configuration information. Access to the registry is through *registry keys*, which are analogous to file system directories. A key can contain other keys or key/value pairs, where the key/value pairs are analogous to directory names and file names. Each value under a key has a name, and for each key/value pair, corresponding data can be accessed and modified.

The user or administrator can view and edit the registry contents through the registry editor, using the REGEDIT command. Alternatively, programs can manage the registry through the registry API functions described in this section.

Note: Registry programming is discussed here due to its similarity to file processing and its importance in some, but not all, applications. The example will be a straightforward modification of the lsW example. This section could, however, be a separate short chapter. *Therefore, if you are not concerned with registry programming, skip this section.*

The registry contains information such as the following and is stored hierarchically in key/value pairs.

- Windows version number, build number, and registered user. However, programs usually access this information through the Windows API, as we do in Chapter 6 (the version program, available in the *Examples*).

- Similar information for every properly installed application.

- Information about the computer's processor type, number of processors, memory, and so on.

- User-specific information, such as the home directory and application preferences.

- Security information such as user account names.

- Installed services (Chapter 13).

- Mappings from file name extensions to executable programs. These mappings are used by the user interface shell when the user clicks on a file icon. For example, the `.doc` and `.docx` extensions might be mapped to Microsoft Word.

UNIX systems store similar information in the `/etc` directory and files in the user's home directory. The registry centralizes all this information in a uniform way. In addition, the registry can be secured using the security features described in Chapter 15.

The registry management API is described here, but the detailed contents and meaning of the various registry entries are beyond the book's scope. Nonetheless, Figure 3–1 shows a typical view from the registry editor and gives an idea of the registry structure and contents.

Figure 3–1 The Registry Editor

The specific information regarding the host machine's processor is on the right side. The bottom of the left side shows that numerous keys contain information about the software applications on the host computer. Notice that every key must have a default value, which is listed before any of the other key/value pairs.

Registry implementation, including registry data storage and retrieval, is also beyond the book's scope; see the reference information at the end of the chapter.

Registry Keys

Figure 3–1 shows the analogy between file system directories and registry keys. Each key can contain other keys or a sequence of values associated with a key. Whereas a file system is accessed through pathnames, the registry is accessed through keys and value names. Several predefined keys serve as entry points into the registry.

1. HKEY_LOCAL_MACHINE stores physical information about the machine, along with information about installed software. Installed software information is generally created in subkeys of the form SOFTWARE\CompanyName\ ProductName\Version.

2. HKEY_USERS defines user configuration information.

3. HKEY_CURRENT_CONFIG contains current settings, such as display resolution and fonts.

4. HKEY_CLASSES_ROOT contains subordinate entries to define mappings from file extensions to classes and to applications used by the shell to access objects with the specified extension. All the keys necessary for Microsoft's Component Object Model (COM) are also subordinate to this key.

5. HKEY_CURRENT_USER contains user-specific information, including environment variables, printers, and application preferences that apply to the current user.

Registry Management

Registry management functions can query and modify key/value pairs and data and also create new subkeys and key/value pairs. Key handles of type HKEY are used both to specify a key and to obtain new keys.[5] Values are typed; there are several types to select from, such as strings, double words, and expandable strings whose parameters can be replaced with environment variables.

---

[5] It would be more convenient and consistent if the HANDLE type were used for registry management. There are several other exceptions to standard Windows practice that are based on Windows history.

Key Management

Key management functions allow you to open named keys, enumerate subkeys of an open key, and create new keys.

RegOpenKeyEx

The first function, `RegOpenKeyEx`, opens a named subkey. Starting from one of the predefined reserved key handles, you can traverse the registry and obtain a handle to any subordinate key.

```
LONG RegOpenKeyEx (
    HKEY hKey,
    LPCTSTR lpSubKey,
    DWORD ulOptions,
    REGSAM samDesired,
    PHKEY phkResult)
```

The parameters for this first function are explained individually. For later functions, as the conventions become familiar, it is sometimes sufficient to survey them quickly.

hKey identifies a currently open key or one of the predefined reserved key handles. phkResult points to a variable of type HKEY that is to receive the handle to the newly opened key.

lpSubKey is the subkey name you want to open. The subkey name can be a path, such as `Microsoft\WindowsNT\CurrentVersion`. A NULL subkey name causes a new, duplicate key for hKey to be opened.

ulOptions is reserved and must be 0.

samDesired is the access mask describing the security for the new key. Access constants include KEY_ALL_ACCESS, KEY_WRITE, KEY_QUERY_VALUE, and KEY_ENUMERATE_SUBKEYS.

The return is normally ERROR_SUCCESS. Any other result indicates an error. Close an open key handle with RegCloseKey, which takes the handle as its single parameter.

RegEnumKeyEx

RegEnumKeyEx enumerates subkey names of an open registry key, much as FindFirstFile and FindNextFile enumerate directory contents. This function retrieves the key name, class string (rarely used), and time of last modification.

```
LONG RegEnumKeyEx (
    HKEY hKey,
    DWORD dwIndex,
    LPTSTR lpName,
    LPDWORD lpcbName,
    LPDWORD lpReserved,
    LPTSTR lpClass,
    LPDWORD lpcbClass
    PFILETIME lpftLastWriteTime)
```

dwIndex should be 0 on the first call and then should be incremented on each subsequent call. The value name and its size, along with the class string and its size, are returned. Note that there are two count parameters, lpcbName (the subkey name) and lpcbClass, which are used for both input and output for buffer size. This behavior is familiar from GetCurrentDirectory (Chapter 2), and we'll see it again with RegEnumValue. lpClass and lpcbClass are, however, rarely used and should almost always be NULL.

The function returns ERROR_SUCCESS or an error number.

RegCreateKeyEx

You can also create new keys using RegCreateKeyEx. Keys can be given security attributes in the same way as with directories and files (Chapter 15).

```
LONG RegCreateKeyEx (
    HKEY hKey,
    LPCTSTR lpSubKey,
    DWORD Reserved,
    LPTSTR lpClass,
    DWORD dwOptions,
    REGSAM samDesired,
    LPSECURITY_ATTRIBUTES lpSecurityAttributes,
    PHKEY phkResult,
    LPDWORD lpdwDisposition)
```

The individual parameters are as follows:

- lpSubKey is the name of the new subkey under the open key indicated by the handle hKey.

- `lpClass` is a user-defined class type for the key. Use `NULL`, as recommended by MSDN.

- The `dwOptions` flag is usually 0 (or, equivalently, `REG_OPTION_NON_VOLATILE`, the default). Another, mutually exclusive value is `REG_OPTION_VOLATILE`. Nonvolatile registry information is stored in a file and preserved when Windows restarts. Volatile registry keys are kept in memory and will not be restored.

- `samDesired` is the same as for `RegOpenKeyEx`.

- `lpSecurityAttributes` can be `NULL` or can point to a security attribute. The rights can be selected from the same values as those used with `sam-Desired`.

- `lpdwDisposition` points to a `DWORD` that indicates whether the key already existed (`REG_OPENED_EXISTING_KEY`) or was created (`REG_CREATED_NEW-_KEY`).

To delete a key, use `RegDeleteKey`. The two parameters are an open key handle and a subkey name.

Value and Data Management

These functions allow you to get and set the data corresponding to a value name.

RegEnumValue

`RegEnumValue` enumerates the value names and corresponding data for a specified open key. Specify an `Index`, originally 0, which is incremented in subsequent calls. On return, you get the string with the value name as well as its size. You also get the data and its type and size.

```
LONG RegEnumValue (
    HKEY hKey,
    DWORD dwIndex,
    LPTSTR lpValueName,
    LPDWORD lpcbValueName,
    LPDWORD lpReserved,
    LPDWORD lpType,
    LPBYTE lpData,
    LPDWORD lpcbData)
```

The data is returned in the buffer indicated by `lpData`. The result size can be found from `lpcbData`.

The data type, pointed to by `lpType`, has numerous possibilities, including `REG_BINARY`, `REG_DWORD`, `REG_SZ` (a string), and `REG_EXPAND_SZ` (an expandable string with parameters replaced by environment variables). See MSDN for a list of all the data types.

Test the function's return result to determine whether you have enumerated all the keys. The result will be `ERROR_SUCCESS` if you have found a valid key.

`RegQueryValueEx` is similar except that you specify a value name rather than an index. If you know the value names, you can use this function. If you do not know the names, you can scan with `RegEnumValue`.

RegSetValueEx

Set the data corresponding to a named value within an open key using `RegSet-ValueEx`, supplying the key, value name, data type, and data.

```
LONG RegSetValueEx (
    HKEY hKey,
    LPCTSTR lpValueName,
    DWORD Reserved,
    DWORD dwType,
    CONST BYTE * lpData,
    CONST cbData)
```

Finally, delete named values using the function `RegDeleteValue`. There are just two parameters: an open registry key and the value name, just as in the first two `RegSetValueEx` parameters.

Example: Listing Registry Keys and Contents

Program 3–4, `lsReg`, is a modification of Program 3–2 (`lsW`, the file and directory listing program); it processes registry keys and key/value pairs rather than directories and files.

Program 3–4   `lsReg`: Listing Registry Keys and Contents

```
/* Chapter 3. lsReg: Registry list command. Adapted from Prog. 3-2. */
/* lsReg [options] SubKey */
```

```
#include "Everything.h"

BOOL TraverseRegistry(HKEY, LPTSTR, LPTSTR, LPBOOL);
BOOL DisplayPair(LPTSTR, DWORD, LPBYTE, DWORD, LPBOOL);
BOOL DisplaySubKey(LPTSTR, LPTSTR, PFILETIME, LPBOOL);

int _tmain(int argc, LPTSTR argv[])
{
    BOOL flags[2], ok = TRUE;
    TCHAR keyName[MAX_PATH+1];
    LPTSTR pScan;
    DWORD i, keyIndex;
    HKEY hKey, hNextKey;

    /* Tables of predefined key names and keys */
    LPTSTR PreDefKeyNames[] = {
        _T("HKEY_LOCAL_MACHINE"), _T("HKEY_CLASSES_ROOT"),
        _T("HKEY_CURRENT_USER"), _T("HKEY_CURRENT_CONFIG"), NULL };


HKEY PreDefKeys[] = {
        HKEY_LOCAL_MACHINE, HKEY_CLASSES_ROOT,
        HKEY_CURRENT_USER, HKEY_CURRENT_CONFIG };

    keyIndex = Options(
            argc, argv, _T("Rl"), &flags[0], &flags[1], NULL);

    /* "Parse" the search pattern into "key"and "subkey". */
    pScan = argv[keyIndex];
    for (i = 0; *pScan != _T('\\') && *pScan != _T('\0')
            && i < MAX_PATH; pScan++, i++)
                keyName[i] = *pScan;
    keyName[i] = _T('\0');
    if (*pScan == _T('\\')) pScan++;

    /* Translate predefined key name to an HKEY */
    for (i = 0; PreDefKeyNames[i] != NULL &&
            _tcscmp(PreDefKeyNames[i], keyName) != 0; i++) ;
    hKey = PreDefKeys[i];
    RegOpenKeyEx(hKey, pScan, 0, KEY_READ, &hNextKey);
    hKey = hNextKey;

    ok = TraverseRegistry(hKey, argv[keyIndex], NULL, flags);
    RegCloseKey(hKey);
    return ok ? 0 : 1;
}

BOOL TraverseRegistry(HKEY hKey, LPTSTR fullKeyName, LPTSTR subKey,
                    LPBOOL flags)
/* Traverse registry key and subkeys if the -R option is set. */
```

```
{
    HKEY hSubKey;
    BOOL recursive = flags[0];
    LONG result;
    DWORD valueType, index;
    DWORD numSubKeys, maxSubKeyLen, numValues, maxValueNameLen,
            maxValueLen;
    DWORD subKeyNameLen, valueNameLen, valueLen;
    FILETIME lastWriteTime;
    LPTSTR subKeyName, valueName;
    LPBYTE value;
    TCHAR fullSubKeyName[MAX_PATH+1];

    /* Open the key handle. */
    RegOpenKeyEx(hKey, subKey, 0, KEY_READ, &hSubKey);

    /*  Find max size info regarding the key and allocate storage */
    RegQueryInfoKey(hSubKey, NULL, NULL, NULL,
        &numSubKeys, &maxSubKeyLen, NULL, &numValues, &maxValueNameLen,
        &maxValueLen, NULL, &lastWriteTime);
    subKeyName = malloc(TSIZE * (maxSubKeyLen+1));
    valueName  = malloc(TSIZE * (maxValueNameLen+1));
    value      = malloc(maxValueLen);         /* size in bytes */

    /*  First pass for key-value pairs. */
    /*  Assumption: No one edits the registry under this subkey */
    /*  during this loop. Doing so could change add new values */
    for (index = 0; index < numValues; index++) {
        valueNameLen = maxValueNameLen + 1; /* Don't forget to set */
        valueLen     = maxValueLen + 1;     /* these values */
        result = RegEnumValue(hSubKey, index, valueName,
                &valueNameLen, NULL,
                &valueType, value, &valueLen);
        if (result == ERROR_SUCCESS && GetLastError() == 0)
            DisplayPair(valueName, valueType, value, valueLen, flags);
    }

    /* Second pass for subkeys. */
    for (index = 0; index < numSubKeys; index++) {
        subKeyNameLen = maxSubKeyLen + 1;
        result = RegEnumKeyEx(hSubKey, index, subKeyName,
                &subKeyNameLen, NULL, NULL, NULL, &lastWriteTime);
        if (GetLastError() == 0) {
            DisplaySubKey(fullKeyName, subKeyName,
                &lastWriteTime, flags);
            /*  Display subkey components if -R is specified */
            if (recursive) {
                _stprintf(fullSubKeyName, _T("%s\\%s"), fullKeyName,
                    subKeyName);
                TraverseRegistry(hSubKey, fullSubKeyName,
```

```
                    subKeyName, flags);
            }
        }
    }

    _tprintf(_T("\n"));
    free(subKeyName); free(valueName); free(value);
    RegCloseKey(hSubKey);
    return TRUE;
}

BOOL DisplayPair(LPTSTR valueName, DWORD valueType,
                    LPBYTE value, DWORD valueLen, LPBOOL flags)
/* Function to display key-value pairs. */
{

    LPBYTE pV = value;
    DWORD i;

    _tprintf(_T("\n%s = "), valueName);

    switch (valueType) {
    case REG_FULL_RESOURCE_DESCRIPTOR: /* 9: hardware description */
    case REG_BINARY: /*  3: Binary data in any form. */
        for (i = 0; i < valueLen; i++, pV++)
            _tprintf(_T(" %x"), *pV);
        break;
    case REG_DWORD: /* 4: A 32-bit number. */
        _tprintf(_T("%x"), (DWORD)*value);
        break;

    case REG_EXPAND_SZ: /* 2: null-terminated unexpanded string */
    case REG_MULTI_SZ: /* 7: An array of null-terminated strings */
    case REG_SZ: /* 1: A null-terminated string. */
        _tprintf(_T("%s"), (LPTSTR)value);
        break;
    /* ... Several other types */
    }

    return TRUE;
}

BOOL DisplaySubKey(LPTSTR keyName, LPTSTR subKeyName,
        PFILETIME pLastWrite, LPBOOL flags)
{
    BOOL longList = flags[1];
    SYSTEMTIME sysLastWrite;

    _tprintf(_T("\n%s"), keyName);
    if (_tcslen(subKeyName) > 0) _tprintf(_T("\\%s "), subKeyName);
```

```
if (longList) {
    FileTimeToSystemTime(pLastWrite, &sysLastWrite);
    _tprintf(_T("%02d/%02d/%04d %02d:%02d:%02d"),
            sysLastWrite.wMonth, sysLastWrite.wDay,
            sysLastWrite.wYear, sysLastWrite.wHour,
            sysLastWrite.wMinute, sysLastWrite.wSecond);
}
return TRUE;
}
```

Run 3–4 shows lsReg operation, including using the –l option. The –R option also works, but examples require a lot of vertical space and are omitted.

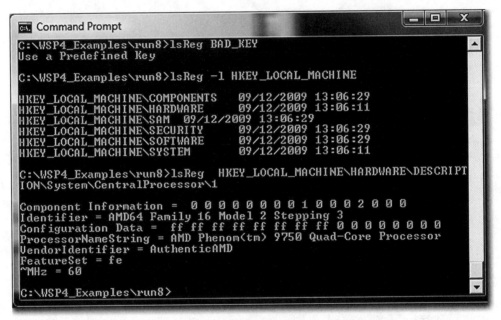

Run 3–4   lsReg: Listing Registry Keys, Values, and Data

Summary

Chapters 2 and 3 described all the important basic functions for dealing with files, directories, and console I/O. Numerous examples show how to use these functions in building typical applications. The registry is managed in much the same way as the file system, as the final example shows.

Later chapters will deal with advanced I/O, such as asynchronous operations and memory mapping.

Looking Ahead

Chapter 4, Exception Handling, simplifies error and exception handling and extends the ReportError function to handle arbitrary exceptions.

Additional Reading

See Jerry Honeycutt's *Microsoft Windows Registry Guide* for information on registry programming and registry usage.

Exercises

3–1. Use the GetDiskFreeSpaceEx function to determine how the different Windows versions allocate file space sparsely. For instance, create a new file, set the file pointer to a large value, set the file size, and investigate the free space using GetDiskFreeSpaceEx. The same Windows function can also be used to determine how the disk is configured into sectors and clusters. Determine whether the newly allocated file space is initialized. FreeSpace.c, provided in the *Examples* file, is the solution. Compare the results for NT5 and NT6. It is also interesting to investigate how to make a file be sparse.

3–2. What happens if you attempt to set a file's length to a size larger than the disk? Does Windows fail gracefully?

3–3. Modify the tail.c program provided in the *Examples* file so that it does not use SetFilePointer; use overlapped structures. Also be sure that it works properly with files larger than 4GB.

3–4. Examine the "number of links" field obtained using the function GetFileInformationByHandle. Is its value always 1? Do the link counts appear to count hard links and links from parent directories and subdirectories? Does Windows open the directory as a file to get a handle before using this function? What about the shortcuts supported by the user interface?

3–5. Program 3–2 (lsW) checks for "." and ".." to detect the names of the current and parent directories. What happens if there are actual files with these names? Can files have these names?

3–6. Does Program 3–2 list local times or UCT? If necessary, modify the program to give the results in local time.

3–7. Enhance Program 3–2 (lsW) so that it also lists the "." and ".." (current and parent) directories (the complete program is in the *Examples* file). Also, add options to display the file creation and last access times along with the last write time.

3–8. Further enhance Program 3–2 (`lsW`) to remove all uses of `SetCurrent-Directory`. This function is undesirable because an exception or other fault could leave you in an expected working directory.

3–9. Create a file deletion command, `rm`, by modifying the `ProcessItem` function in Program 3–2. A solution is in the *Examples* file.

3–10. Enhance the file copy command, `cpW`, from Chapter 1 so that it will copy files to a target directory. Further extensions allow for recursive copying (`-r` option) and for preserving the modification time of the copied files (`-p` option). Implementing the recursive copy option will require that you create new directories.

3–11. Write an `mv` command, similar to the UNIX command of the same name, which will move a complete directory. One significant consideration is whether the target is on a different drive from that of the source file or directory. If it is, copy the file(s); otherwise, use `MoveFileEx`.

3–12. Enhance Program 3–3 (`touch`) so that the new file time is specified on the command line. The UNIX command allows the time stamp to appear (optionally) after the normal options and before the file names. The format for the time is `MMddhhmm[yy]`, where the uppercase `MM` is the month and `mm` is for minutes.

3–13. Program 3–1 (`RecordAccess`) is written to work with large NTFS file systems. If you have sufficient free disk space, test this program with a huge file (length greater than 4GB, and considerably larger if possible); see Run 3–2. Verify that the 64-bit arithmetic is correct. It is not recommended that you perform this exercise on a network drive without permission from the network administrator. Don't forget to delete the test file on completion; disk space is cheap, but not so cheap that you want to leave orphaned huge files.

3–14. Write a program that locks a specified file and holds the lock for a long period of time (you may find the `Sleep` function useful). While the lock is held, try to access the file (use a text file) with an editor. What happens? Is the file properly locked? Alternatively, write a program that will prompt the user to specify a lock on a test file. Two instances of the program can be run in separate windows to verify that file locking works as described. `TestLock.c` in the *Examples* file is a solution to this exercise.

3–15. Investigate the Windows file time representation in `FILETIME`. It uses 64 bits to count the elapsed number of 100-nanosecond units from January 1,

1601. When will the time expire? When will the UNIX file time representation expire?

3–16. Write an interactive utility that will prompt the user for a registry key name and a value name. Display the current value and prompt the user for a new value. The utility could use command prompt cd and dir commands to illustrate the similarities (and differences) between the registry and file systems.

3–17. This chapter, along with most other chapters, describes the most important functions. There are often other functions that may be useful. The MSDN pages for each function provide links to related functions. Examine several, such as FindFirstFileEx, FindFirstFileTransacted, ReplaceFile, SearchPath, and WriteFileGather. Some of these functions are not available in all Windows versions.

CHAPTER

4 | Exception Handling

Windows Structured Exception Handling (SEH) is the principal focus of this chapter, which also describes console control handlers and vectored exception handling.

SEH provides a robust mechanism that allows applications to respond to unexpected asynchronous events, such as addressing exceptions, arithmetic faults, and system errors. SEH also allows a program to exit from anywhere in a code block and automatically perform programmer-specified processing and error recovery. SEH ensures that the program will be able to free resources and perform other cleanup processing before the block, thread, or process terminates either under program control or because of an unexpected exception. Furthermore, SEH can be added easily to existing code, often simplifying program logic.

SEH will prove to be useful in the examples and also will allow extension of the ReportError error-processing function from Chapter 2. SEH is usually confined to C programs. C++, C#, and other languages have very similar mechanisms, however, and these mechanisms build on the SEH facilities presented here.

Console control handlers, also described in this chapter, allow a program to detect external signals such as a Ctrl-C from the console or the user logging off or shutting down the system. These signals also provide a limited form of process-to-process signaling.

The final topic is vectored exception handling. This feature allows the user to specify functions to be executed directly when an exception occurs, and the functions are executed before SEH is invoked.

Exceptions and Their Handlers

Without some form of exception handling, an unintended program exception, such as dereferencing a NULL pointer or division by zero, will terminate a program immediately without performing normal termination processing, such as deleting temporary files. SEH allows specification of a code block, or *exception handler*, which can delete the temporary files, perform other termination operations, and analyze and log the exception. In general, exception handlers can perform any required cleanup operations before leaving the code block.

Normally, an exception indicates a fatal error with no recovery, and the thread (Chapter 7), or even the entire process, should terminate after the handler reports the exception. Do not expect to be able to resume execution from the point where the exception occurs. Nonetheless, we will show an example (Program 4–2) where a program can continue execution.

SEH is supported through a combination of Windows functions, compiler-supported language extensions, and run-time support. The exact language support may vary; the examples here were all developed for Microsoft C.

Try and Except Blocks

The first step in using SEH is to determine which code blocks to monitor and provide them with exception handlers, as described next. It is possible to monitor an entire function or to have separate exception handlers for different code blocks and functions.

A code block is a good candidate for an exception handler in situations that include the following, and catching these exceptions allows you to detect bugs and avoid potentially serious problems.

- Detectable errors, including system call errors, might occur, and you need to recover from the error rather than terminate the program.

- There is a possibility of dereferencing pointers that have not been properly initialized or computed.

- There is array manipulation, and it is possible for array indices to go out of bounds.

- The code performs floating-point arithmetic, and there is concern with zero divides, imprecise results, and overflows.

- The code calls a function that might generate an exception intentionally, because the function arguments are not correct, or for some other occurrence.

SEH uses "try" and "except" blocks. In the examples in this chapter and throughout the book, once you have decided to monitor a block, create the try and except blocks as follows:

```
__try {
    /* Block of monitored code */
}
__except (filter_expression) {
    /* Exception handling block */
}
```

Note that __try and __except are keywords that the C compiler recognizes; however, they are not part of standard C.

The try block is part of normal application code. If an exception occurs in the block, the OS transfers control to the exception handler, which is the code in the block associated with the __except clause. The value of the *filter_expression* determines the actions that follow.

The exception could occur within a block embedded in the try block, in which case the run-time support "unwinds" the stack to find the exception handler and then gives control to the handler. The same thing happens when an exception occurs within a function called within a try block if the function does not have an appropriate exception handler.

For the x86 architecture, Figure 4–1 shows how an exception handler is located on the stack when an exception occurs. Once the exception handler block completes, control passes to the next statement after the exception block unless there is some other control flow statement in the handler. Note that SEH on some other architectures uses a more efficient static registration process (out of scope for this discussion) to achieve a similar result.

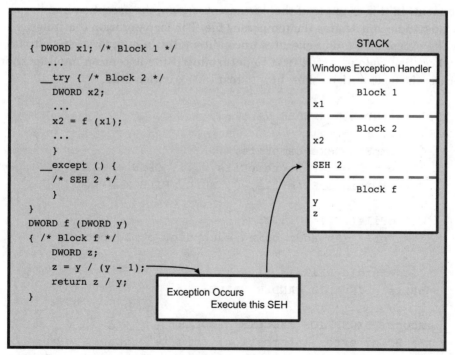

Figure 4–1   SEH, Blocks, and Functions

Filter Expressions and Their Values

The *filter_expression* in the __except clause is evaluated immediately after the exception occurs. The expression is usually a literal constant, a call to a *filter function*, or a conditional expression. In all cases, the expression should return one of three values.

1. EXCEPTION_EXECUTE_HANDLER—Windows executes the except block as shown in Figure 4–1 (also see Program 4–1).

2. EXCEPTION_CONTINUE_SEARCH—Windows ignores the exception handler and searches for an exception handler in the enclosing block, continuing until it finds a handler.

3. EXCEPTION_CONTINUE_EXECUTION—Windows immediately returns control to the point at which the exception occurred. It is not possible to continue after some exceptions, and inadvisable in most other cases, and another exception is generated immediately if the program attempts to do so.

Here is a simple example using an exception handler to delete a temporary file if an exception occurs in the loop body. Notice you can apply the __try clause to any block, including the block associated with a while, if, or other flow control statement. In this example, if there is any exception, the exception handler closes the file handle and deletes the temporary file. The loop iteration continues.

The exception handler executes unconditionally. In many realistic situations, the exception code is tested first to determine if the exception handler should execute; the next sections show how to test the exception code.

```
hFile = INVALID_HANDLE_VALUE;
while (...) __try {
   GetTempFileName(tempFile, ...);
   hFile = CreateFile(tempFile, ..., OPEN_ALWAYS, ...);
   SetFilePointerEx(hFile, 0, NULL, FILE_END);
   ...
   WriteFile(hFile, ...);
   i = *p; /* An addressing exception could occur. */
   ...
   CloseHandle(hFile);
   hFile = INVALID_HANDLE_VALUE;
}
__except (EXCEPTION_EXECUTE_HANDLER) {
   /* Print error information; this is probably a bug */
   if (INVALID_HANDLE_VALUE != hFile) CloseHandle(hFile);
```

```
    hFile = INVALID_HANDLE_VALUE;
    DeleteFile(tempFile);
    /* The loop will now execute the next iteration .*/
}
/* Control passes here after normal loop termination.
   The file handle is always closed and the temp file
   will not exist if there was an exception. */
```

The logic of this code fragment is as follows.

- Each loop iteration writes data to a temporary file associated with the iteration. An enhancement would append an identifier to the temporary file name.

- If an exception occurs in any loop iteration, all data accumulated in the temporary file is deleted, and the next iteration, if any, starts to accumulate data in a new temporary file with a new name. You need to create a new name so that another process does not get the temporary name after the deletion.

- The example shows just one location where an exception could occur, although the exception could occur anywhere within the loop body.

- The file handle is assured of being closed when exiting the loop or starting a new loop iteration.

- If an exception occurs, there is almost certainly a program bug. Program 4–4 shows how to analyze an address exception. Nonetheless, this code fragment allows the loop to continue, although it might be better to consider this a fatal error and terminate the program.

Exception Codes

The __except block or the filter expression can determine the exact exception using this function:

```
DWORD GetExceptionCode (VOID)
```

You must get the exception code immediately after an exception. Therefore, the filter function itself cannot call GetExceptionCode (the compiler enforces this restriction). A common usage is to invoke it in the filter expression, as in the following example, where the exception code is the argument to a user-supplied filter function.

```
__except (MyFilter(GetExceptionCode())) {
}
```

In this situation, the filter function determines and returns the filter expression value, which must be one of the three values enumerated earlier. The function can use the exception code to determine the function value; for example, the filter may decide to pass floating-point exceptions to an outer handler (by returning EXCEPTION_CONTINUE_SEARCH) and to handle a memory access violation in the current handler (by returning EXCEPTION_EXECUTE_HANDLER).

GetExceptionCode can return a large number of possible exception code values, and the codes are in several categories.

- Program violations such as the following:

  - EXCEPTION_ACCESS_VIOLATION—An attempt to read, write, or execute a virtual address for which the process does not have access.

  - EXCEPTION_DATATYPE_MISALIGNMENT—Many processors insist, for example, that DWORDs be aligned on 4-byte boundaries.

  - EXCEPTION_NONCONTINUABLE_EXECUTION—The filter expression was EXCEPTION_CONTINUE_EXECUTION, but it is not possible to continue after the exception that occurred.

- Exceptions raised by the memory allocation functions—HeapAlloc and HeapCreate—if they use the HEAP_GENERATE_EXCEPTIONS flag (see Chapter 5). The value will be either STATUS_NO_MEMORY or EXCEPTION_ACCESS_VIOLATION.

- A user-defined exception code generated by the RaiseException function; see the User-Generated Exceptions subsection.

- A large variety of arithmetic (especially floating-point) codes such as EXCEPTION_INT_DIVIDE_BY_ZERO and EXCEPTION_FLT_OVERFLOW.

- Exceptions used by debuggers, such as EXCEPTION_BREAKPOINT and EXCEPTION_SINGLE_STEP.

GetExceptionInformation is an alternative function, callable only from within the filter expression, which returns additional information, some of which is processor-specific. Program 4–3 uses GetExceptionInformation.

```
LPEXCEPTION_POINTERS GetExceptionInformation (VOID)
```

The `EXCEPTION_POINTERS` structure contains both processor-specific and processor-independent information organized into two other structures, an exception record and a context record.

```
typedef struct _EXCEPTION_POINTERS {
    PEXCEPTION_RECORD ExceptionRecord;
    PCONTEXT ContextRecord;
} EXCEPTION_POINTERS;
```

`EXCEPTION_RECORD` contains a member for the `ExceptionCode` with the same set of values as returned by `GetExceptionCode`. The `ExceptionFlags` member of the `EXCEPTION_RECORD` is either 0 or `EXCEPTION_NONCONTINUABLE`, which allows the filter function to determine that it should not attempt to continue execution. Other data members include a virtual memory address, `ExceptionAddress`, and a parameter array, `ExceptionInformation`.

In the case of `EXCEPTION_ACCESS_VIOLATION` or `EXCEPTION_IN_PAGE-_VIOLATION`, the first element indicates whether the violation was a memory write (1), read (0), or execute (8). The second element is the virtual memory address. The third array element specifies the `NSTATUS` code that caused the exception.

The execute error (code 8) is a Data Execution Prevention (DEP) error, which indicates an attempt to execute data that is not intended to be code, such as data on the heap. This feature is supported as of XP SP2; see MSDN for more information.

`ContextRecord`, the second `EXCEPTION_POINTERS` member, contains processor-specific information, including the address where the exception occurred. There are different structures for each type of processor, and the structure can be found in <winnt.h>.

Summary: Exception Handling Sequence

Figure 4–2 shows the sequence of events that takes place when an exception occurs. The code is on the left side, and the circled numbers on the right show the steps carried out by the language run-time support. The steps are as follows.

1. The exception occurs, in this case a division by zero.

2. Control transfers to the exception handler, where the filter expression is evaluated. `GetExceptionCode` is called first, and its return value is the argument to the function `Filter`.

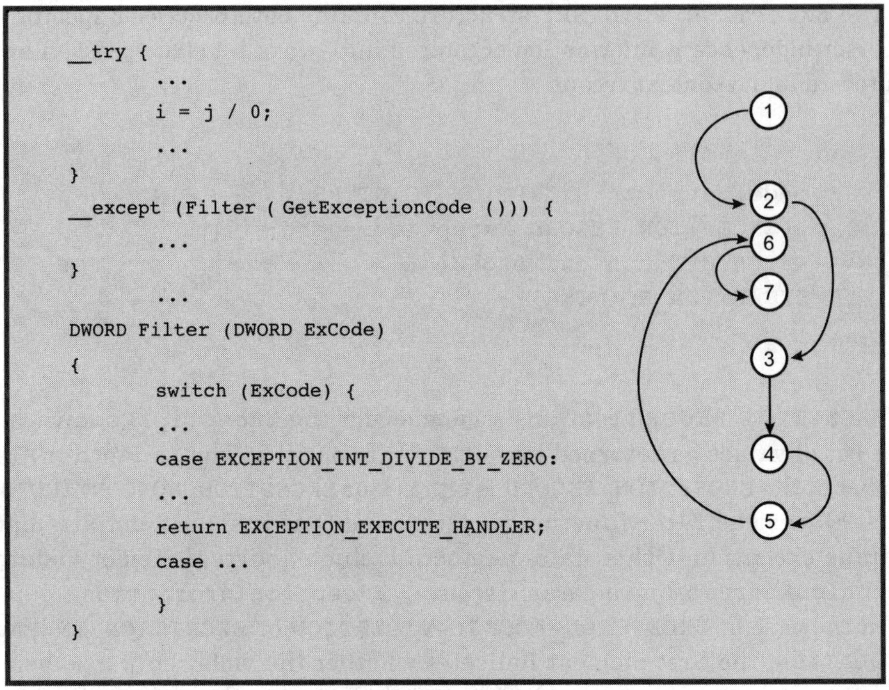

```
    __try {
        ...
        i = j / 0;
        ...
    }
    __except (Filter ( GetExceptionCode ())) {
        ...
    }
        ...
    DWORD Filter (DWORD ExCode)
    {
        switch (ExCode) {
        ...
        case EXCEPTION_INT_DIVIDE_BY_ZERO:
        ...
        return EXCEPTION_EXECUTE_HANDLER;
        case ...
        }
    }
```

Figure 4-2   Exception Handling Sequence

3. The filter function bases its actions on the exception code value.

4. The exception code is `EXCEPTION_INT_DIVIDE_BY_ZERO` in this case.

5. The filter function determines that the exception handler should be executed, so the return value is `EXCEPTION_EXECUTE_HANDLER`.

6. The exception handler, which is the code associated with the `__except` clause, executes.

7. Control passes out of the try-except block.

Floating-Point Exceptions

Readers not interested in floating-point arithmetic may wish to skip this section.

There are seven distinct floating-point exception codes. These exceptions are disabled initially and will not occur without first setting the processor-independent floating-point mask with the `_controlfp` function. Alternatively, enable floating-point exceptions with the /fp:except compiler flag (you can also specify this from Visual Studio).

There are specific exceptions for underflow, overflow, division by zero, inexact results, and so on, as shown in a later code fragment. Turn the mask bit *off* to enable the particular exception.

```
DWORD _controlfp (DWORD new, DWORD mask)
```

The new value of the floating-point mask is determined by its current value (current_mask) and the two arguments as follows:

```
(current_mask & ~mask) | (new & mask)
```

The function sets the bits specified by new that are enabled by mask. All bits *not* in mask are unaltered. The floating-point mask also controls processor precision, rounding, and infinity values, which should not be modified (these topics are out-of-scope).

The return value is the updated setting. Thus, if both argument values are 0, the value is unchanged, and the return value is the current mask setting, which can be used later to restore the mask. On the other hand, if mask is 0xFFFFFFFF, then the register is set to new, so that, for example, an old value can be restored.

Normally, to enable the floating-point exceptions, use the floating-point exception mask value, MCW_EM, as shown in the following example. Notice that when a floating-point exception is processed, the exception must be cleared using the _clearfp function.

```
#include <float.h>
DWORD fpOld, fpNew; /* Old and new mask values. */
   ...
fpOld = _controlfp(0, 0); /* Saved old mask. */
/* Specify six exceptions to be enabled. */
   fpNew = fpOld & ~(EM_OVERFLOW | EM_UNDERFLOW
   | EM_INEXACT | EM_ZERODIVIDE | EM_DENORMAL | EM_INVALID);
/* Set new control mask. MCW_EM combines the six
   exceptions in the previous statement. */
_controlfp(fpNew, MCW_EM);
while (...) __try { /* Perform FP calculations. */
   ... /* An FP exception could occur here. */
}
```

```
    __except (EXCEPTION_EXECUTE_HANDLER) {
        ... /* Analyze and log the FP exception. */
        _clearfp(); /* Clear the exception. */
        _controlfp(fpOld, 0xFFFFFFFF); /* Restore mask. */
        /* Don't continue execution. */
    }
```

This example enables all possible floating-point exceptions except for the floating-point stack overflow, EXCEPTION_FLT_STACK_CHECK. Alternatively, enable specific exceptions by using only selected exception masks, such as EM_OVERFLOW. Program 4–3 uses similar code in the context of a larger example.

Errors and Exceptions

An error can be thought of as a situation that could occur occasionally and synchronously at known locations. System call errors, for example, should be detected and reported immediately by logic in the code. Thus, programmers normally include an explicit test to see, for instance, whether a file read operation has failed. Chapter 2's ReportError function can diagnose and respond to errors.

An exception, on the other hand, could occur nearly anywhere, and it is not possible or practical to test for an exception. Division by zero and memory access violations are examples. Exceptions are asynchronous.

Nonetheless, the distinction is sometimes blurred. Windows will, optionally, generate exceptions during memory allocation using the HeapAlloc and HeapCreate functions if memory is insufficient (see Chapter 5). Programs can also raise their own exceptions with programmer-defined exception codes using the RaiseException function, as described next.

Exception handlers provide a convenient mechanism for exiting from inner blocks or functions under program control without resorting to a goto, longjmp, or some other control logic to transfer control; Program 4–2 illustrates this. This capability is particularly important if the block has accessed resources, such as open files, memory, or synchronization objects, because the handler can release them.

User-generated exceptions provide one of the few cases where it is possible or desirable to continue execution at the exception point rather than terminate the program, thread, or the block or function. However, use caution when continuing execution from the exception point.

Finally, a program can restore system state, such as the floating-point mask, on exiting from a block. Some examples use handlers in this way.

User-Generated Exceptions

You can raise an exception at any point during program execution using the `RaiseException` function. In this way, your program can detect an error and treat it as an exception.

```
VOID RaiseException (
    DWORD dwExceptionCode,
    DWORD dwExceptionFlags,
    DWORD nNumberOfArguments,
    CONST DWORD *lpArguments)
```

Parameters

`dwExceptionCode` is the user-defined code. Do not use bit 28, which is reserved and Windows clears. The error code is encoded in bits 27–0 (that is, all except the most significant hex digit). Set bit 29 to indicate a "customer" (not Microsoft) exception. Bits 31–30 encode the severity as follows, where the resulting lead exception code hex digit is shown with bit 29 set.

- 0—Success (lead exception code hex digit is 2).

- 1—Informational (lead exception code hex digit is 6).

- 2—Warning (lead exception code hex digit is A).

- 3—Error (lead exception code hex digit is E).

`dwExceptionFlags` is normally 0, but setting the value to `EXCEPTION_NONCONTINUABLE` indicates that the filter expression should not generate `EXCEPTION_CONTINUE_EXECUTION`; doing so will cause an immediate `EXCEPTION_NONCONTINUABLE_EXCEPTION` exception.

`lpArguments`, if not `NULL`, points to an array of size `nNumberOfArguments` (the third parameter) containing values to be passed to the filter expression. The values can be interpreted as pointers and are 32 (Win32) or 64 (Win64) bits long, `EXCEPTION_MAXIMUM_PARAMETERS` (15) is the maximum number of parameters that can be passed. Use `GetExceptionInformation` to access this structure.

Note that it is not possible to raise an exception in another process or even another thread in your process. Under very limited circumstances, however, console control handlers, described at the end of this chapter and in Chapter 6, can raise exceptions in a different process.

Example: Treating Errors as Exceptions

Previous examples use `ReportError` to process system call and other errors. The function terminates the process when the programmer indicates that the error is fatal. This approach, however, prevents an orderly shutdown, and it also prevents program continuation after recovering from an error. For example, the program may have created temporary files that should be deleted, or the program may simply proceed to do other work after abandoning the failed task. `ReportError` has other limitations, including the following.

- A fatal error shuts down the entire process when only a single thread (Chapter 7) should terminate.

- You may wish to continue program execution rather than terminate the process.

- Synchronization resources (Chapter 8), such as events or semaphores, will not be released in many circumstances.

Open handles will be closed by a terminating process, but not by a terminating thread. It is necessary to address this and other deficiencies.

The solution is to write a new function that invokes `ReportError` (Chapter 2) with a nonfatal code in order to generate the error message. Next, on a fatal error, it will raise an exception. Windows will use an exception handler from the calling try block, so the exception may not actually be fatal if the handler allows the program to recover and resume. Essentially, `ReportException` augments normal defensive programming techniques, previously limited to `ReportError`. Once a problem is detected, the exception handler allows the program to recover and continue after the error. Program 4–2 illustrates this capability.

Program 4–1 shows the function. It is in the same source module as `Report-Error`, so the definitions and include files are omitted.

Program 4–1   `ReportException`: Exception Reporting Function

```
/* ReportError extension to generate a nonfatal user-exception code. */

VOID ReportException(LPCTSTR userMessage, DWORD exceptionCode)
{
    ReportError(userMessage, 0, TRUE);
    if (exceptionCode != 0) /* If fatal, raise an exception. */
        RaiseException(
            (0x0FFFFFFF & exceptionCode) | 0xE0000000, 0, 0, NULL);
    return;
}
```

`ReportException` is used in Program 4–2 and elsewhere.

The UNIX signal model is significantly different from SEH. Signals can be missed or ignored, and the flow is different. Nonetheless, there are points of comparison.

UNIX signal handling is largely supported through the C library, which is also available in a limited implementation under Windows. In many cases, Windows programs can use console control handlers, which are described near the end of this chapter, in place of signals.

Some signals correspond to Windows exceptions.

Here is the limited signal-to-exception correspondence:

- `SIGILL`—`EXCEPTION_PRIV_INSTRUCTION` or `EXCEPTION_ILLEGAL_INSTRUCTION`

- `SIGSEGV`—`EXCEPTION_ACCESS_VIOLATION`

- `SIGFPE`—Seven distinct floating-point exceptions, such as `EXCEPTION_FLT_DIVIDE_BY_ZERO`

- `SIGUSR1` and `SIGUSR2`—User-defined exceptions

The C library `raise` function corresponds to `RaiseException`.

Windows will not generate `SIGILL`, `SIGSEGV`, or `SIGTERM`, although `raise` can generate one of them. Windows does not support `SIGINT`.

The UNIX `kill` function (`kill` is not in the Standard C library), which can send a signal to another process, is comparable to the Windows function `Generate-ConsoleCtrlEvent` (Chapter 6). In the limited case of `SIGKILL`, there is no corresponding exception, but Windows has `TerminateProcess` and `TerminateThread`, allowing one process (or thread) to "kill" another, although these functions should be used with care (see Chapters 6 and 7).

Termination Handlers

A termination handler serves much the same purpose as an exception handler, but it is executed when a thread leaves a block as a result of normal program flow as well as when an exception occurs. On the other hand, a termination handler cannot diagnose an exception.

Construct a termination handler using the `__finally` keyword in a try-finally statement. The structure is the same as for a try-except statement, but there is no filter expression. Termination handlers, like exception handlers, are a convenient way to close handles, release resources, restore masks, and otherwise restore the process to a known state when leaving a block. For example, a program may execute `return` statements in the middle of a block, and the termination handler can perform the cleanup work. In this way, there is no need to include the cleanup code in the code block itself, nor is there a need for goto or other control flow statements to reach the cleanup code.

Here is the try-finally form, and Program 4–2 illustrates the usage.

```
__try {
    /* Code block. */
}
__finally {
    /* Termination handler (finally block). */
}
```

Leaving the Try Block

The termination handler is executed whenever the control flow leaves the try block for any of the following reasons:

- Reaching the end of the try block and "falling through" to the termination handler

- Execution of one of the following statements in such a way as to leave the block:

    ```
    return
    break
    goto[1]
    longjmp
    continue
    __leave[2]
    ```

- An exception

Abnormal Termination

Termination for any reason other than reaching the end of the try block and falling through or performing a __leave statement is considered an abnormal termi-

---

[1] It may be a matter of taste, either individual or organizational, but many programmers never use the goto statement and try to avoid break, except with the switch statement and sometimes in loops, and with continue. Reasonable people continue to differ on this subject. The termination and exception handlers can perform many of the tasks that you might want to perform with a goto to a labeled statement.

[2] This statement is specific to the Microsoft C compiler and is an efficient way to leave a try-finally block without an abnormal termination.

nation. The effect of __leave is to transfer to the end of the __try block and fall through. Within the termination handler, use this function to determine how the try block terminated.

```
BOOL AbnormalTermination (VOID)
```

The return value will be TRUE for an abnormal termination or FALSE for a normal termination.

Note: The termination would be abnormal even if, for example, a return statement were the last statement in the try block.

Executing and Leaving the Termination Handler

The termination handler, or __finally block, is executed in the context of the block or function that it monitors. Control can pass from the end of the termination handler to the next statement. Alternatively, the termination handler can execute a flow control statement (return, break, continue, goto, longjmp, or __leave). Leaving the handler because of an exception is another possibility.

Combining Finally and Except Blocks

A single try block must have a single finally or except block; it cannot have both, even though it might be convenient. Therefore, the following code would cause a compile error.

```
__try {
    /* Block of monitored code. */
}
__except (filter_expression) {
    /* Except block. */
}
__finally {
    /* Do not do this! It will not compile. */
}
```

It is possible, however, to embed one block within another, a technique that is frequently useful. The following code is valid and ensures that the temporary file is deleted if the loop exits under program control or because of an exception. This technique is also useful to ensure that file locks are released. There is also an inner try-except block with some floating-point processing.

```
__try { /* Outer try-except block. */
    while (...) __try { /* Inner try-finally block. */
        hFile = CreateFile(tempFile, ...);
        if (...) __try { /* Inner try-except block. */
            /* Enable FP exceptions. Perform computations. */
            ...
        }
        __except (fp-filter-expression) {
            ... /* Process FP exception. */ _clearfp();
        }
        ... /* Non-FP processing. /*
    }
    __finally { /* End of while loop. */
    /* Executed on EVERY loop iteration. */
        CloseHandle(hFile); DeleteFile(tempFile);
    }
}
__except (filter-expression) {
    /* Exception handler. */
}
```

Global and Local Unwinds

Exceptions and abnormal terminations will cause a *global stack unwind* to search for a handler, as in Figure 4–1. For example, suppose an exception occurs in the monitored block of the example at the end of the preceding section before the floating-point exceptions are enabled. The termination handler will be executed first, followed by the exception handler at the end. There might be numerous termination handlers on the stack before the exception handler is located.

Recall that the stack structure is dynamic, as shown in Figure 4–1, and that it contains, among other things, the exception and termination handlers. The contents at any time depend on:

- The *static* structure of the program's blocks

- The *dynamic* structure of the program as reflected in the sequence of open function calls

Termination Handlers: Process and Thread Termination

Termination handlers do not execute if a process or thread terminates, whether the process or thread terminates itself by using ExitProcess or ExitThread, or whether the termination is external, caused by a call to TerminateProcess or TerminateThread from elsewhere. Therefore, a process or thread should not execute one of these functions inside a try-except or try-finally block.

Notice also that the C library exit function or a return from a main function will exit the process.

SEH and C++ Exception Handling

C++ exception handling uses the keywords catch and throw and is implemented using SEH. Nonetheless, C++ exception handling and SEH are distinct. They should be mixed with care, or not at all, because the user-written and C++-generated exception handlers may interfere with expected operation. For example, an __except handler may be on the stack and catch a C++ exception so that the C++ handler will never receive the exception. The converse is also possible, with a C++ handler catching, for example, an SEH exception generated with RaiseException. The Microsoft documentation recommends that Windows exception handlers not be used in C++ programs at all but instead that C++ exception handling be used exclusively.

Normally, a Windows exception or termination handler will not call destructors to destroy C++ object instances. However, the /EHa compiler flag (setable from Visual Studio) allows C++ exception handling to include asynchronous exceptions and "unwind" (destroy) C++ objects.

Example: Using Termination Handlers to Improve Program Quality

Termination and exception handlers allow you to make your program more robust by both simplifying recovery from errors and exceptions and helping to ensure that resources and file locks are freed at critical junctures.

Program 4–2, toupper, illustrates these points, using ideas from the preceding code fragments. toupper processes multiple files, as specified on the command line, rewriting them so that all letters are in uppercase. Converted files are named by prefixing UC_ to the original file name, and the program "specification" states that an existing file should not be overridden. File conversion is performed in memory, so there is a large buffer (sufficient for the entire file) allocated for each file. There are multiple possible failure points for each processed file, but the program must defend against all such errors and then recover and attempt to process all the remaining files named on the command line. Program 4–2 achieves this without resorting to the elaborate control flow methods that would be necessary without SEH.

Note that this program depends on file sizes, so it will not work on objects for which GetFileSizeEx fails, such as a named pipe (Chapter 11). Furthermore, it fails for large text files longer than 4GB.

The code in the *Examples* file has more extensive comments.

Program 4–2 toupper: File Processing with Error and Exception Recovery

```
/* Chapter 4. toupper command. */
/* Convert one or more files, changing all letters to uppercase.
   The output file will be the same name as the input file, except
   a UC_ prefix will be attached to the file name. */

#include "Everything.h"

int _tmain(DWORD argc, LPTSTR argv[])
{
    HANDLE hIn = INVALID_HANDLE_VALUE, hOut = INVALID_HANDLE_VALUE;
    DWORD nXfer, iFile, j;
    CHAR outFileName[256] = "", *pBuffer = NULL;
    OVERLAPPED ov = { 0, 0, 0, 0, NULL};
    LARGE_INTEGER fSize;

    /* Process all files on the command line. */
    for (iFile = 1; iFile < argc; iFile++) __try { /* Exceptn block */
        /* All file handles are invalid, pBuffer == NULL, and
           outFileName is empty. This is assured by the handlers */
        if (_tcslen(argv[iFile]) > 250)
            ReportException(_T("The file name is too long."), 1);
        _stprintf(outFileName, "UC_%s", argv[iFile]);

        __try { /* Inner try-finally block */
            hIn = CreateFile(argv[iFile], GENERIC_READ,
                0, NULL, OPEN_EXISTING, 0, NULL);
            if (hIn == INVALID_HANDLE_VALUE)
                ReportException(argv[iFile], 1);

            if (!GetFileSizeEx(hIn, &fSize) || fSize.HighPart > 0)
                ReportException(_T("This file is too large."), 1);

            hOut = CreateFile(outFileName,
                GENERIC_READ | GENERIC_WRITE,
                0, NULL, CREATE_NEW, 0, NULL);
            if (hOut == INVALID_HANDLE_VALUE)
                ReportException(outFileName, 1);

            /* Allocate memory for the file contents */
```

```
            pBuffer = malloc(fSize.LowPart);
            if (pBuffer == NULL)
                ReportException(_T("Memory allocation error"), 1);

            /* Read the data, convert it, and write to the output file */
            /* Free all resources on completion; process next file */

            if (!ReadFile(hIn, pBuffer, fSize.LowPart, &nXfer, NULL)
                    || (nXfer != fSize.LowPart))
                ReportException(_T("ReadFile error"), 1);

            for (j = 0; j < fSize.LowPart; j++) /* Convert data */
                if (isalpha(pBuffer[j])) pBuffer[j] =
                    toupper(pBuffer[j]);

            if (!WriteFile(hOut, pBuffer, fSize.LowPart, &nXfer, NULL)
                    || (nXfer != fSize.LowPart))
                ReportException(_T("WriteFile error"), 1);

        } __finally { /* File handles are always closed */
            /* memory freed, and handles and pointer reinitialized. */
            if (pBuffer != NULL) free(pBuffer); pBuffer = NULL;
            if (hIn  != INVALID_HANDLE_VALUE) {
                CloseHandle(hIn);
                hIn  = INVALID_HANDLE_VALUE;
            }
            if (hOut != INVALID_HANDLE_VALUE) {
                CloseHandle(hOut);
                hOut = INVALID_HANDLE_VALUE;
            }
            _tcscpy(outFileName, _T(""));
        }
    } /* End of main file processing loop and try block. */
    /* This exception handler applies to the loop body */

    __except (EXCEPTION_EXECUTE_HANDLER) {
        _tprintf(_T("Error processing file %s\n"), argv[iFile]);
        DeleteFile(outFileName);
    }
    _tprintf(_T("All files converted, except as noted above\n"));
    return 0;
}
```

Run 4–2 shows toupper operation. Originally, there are two text files, a.txt and b.txt. The cat program (Program 2–2) displays the contents of these two files; you could also use the Windows type command. toupper converts these two files, continuing after failing to find b.txt. Finally, cat displays the two converted files, UC_a.txt and UC_c.txt.

```
Command Prompt
C:\WSP4_Examples\run8>dir *.txt
 Volume in drive C is HP
 Volume Serial Number is 521E-9D92

 Directory of C:\WSP4_Examples\run8

09/20/2009  08:52 AM                56 a.txt
09/20/2009  08:53 AM                30 c.txt
               2 File(s)            86 bytes
               0 Dir(s)    452,872,916,992 bytes free

C:\WSP4_Examples\run8>cat a.txt c.txt
FileName a.txt
This is the first TEst fIle
this IS the secOND line
FileName c.txt
2nd file with just one line

C:\WSP4_Examples\run8>toupper a.txt b.txt c.txt
b.txt
The system cannot find the file specified.

Error occured processing file b.txt
All files converted, except as noted above

C:\WSP4_Examples\run8>dir *.txt
 Volume in drive C is HP
 Volume Serial Number is 521E-9D92

 Directory of C:\WSP4_Examples\run8

09/20/2009  08:52 AM                56 a.txt
09/20/2009  08:53 AM                30 c.txt
09/20/2009  08:54 AM                56 UC_a.txt
09/20/2009  08:54 AM                30 UC_c.txt
               4 File(s)           172 bytes
               0 Dir(s)    452,872,904,704 bytes free

C:\WSP4_Examples\run8>cat UC_a.txt UC_c.txt
FileName UC_a.txt
THIS IS THE FIRST TEST FILE
THIS IS THE SECOND LINE
FileName UC_c.txt
2ND FILE WITH JUST ONE LINE
C:\WSP4_Examples\run8>
```

Run 4–2 toupper: Converting Text Files to Uppercase

Example: Using a Filter Function

Program 4–3 is a skeleton program that illustrates exception and termination handling with a filter function. This example prompts the user to specify the exception type and then proceeds to generate an exception. The filter function disposes of the different exception types in various ways; the selections here are arbitrary and intended simply to illustrate the possibilities. In particular, the program diagnoses memory access violations, giving the virtual address of the reference.

The __finally block restores the state of the floating-point mask. Restoring state, as done here, is not important when the process is about to terminate, but it is important later when a thread is terminated. In general, a process should still restore system resources by, for example, deleting temporary files and releasing synchronization resources (Chapter 8) and file locks (Chapters 3 and 6). Program 4–4 shows the filter function.

This example does not illustrate memory allocation exceptions; they will be used starting in Chapter 5.

Run 4–4, after the filter function (Program 4–4) shows the program operation.

Program 4–3 Exception: Processing Exceptions and Termination

```
#include "Everything.h"
#include <float.h>

DWORD Filter(LPEXCEPTION_POINTERS, LPDWORD);
double x = 1.0, y = 0.0;

int _tmain(int argc, LPTSTR argv[])
{
    DWORD eCategory, i = 0, ix, iy = 0;
    LPDWORD pNull = NULL;
    BOOL done = FALSE;
    DWORD fpOld, fpNew;
    fpOld = _controlfp(0, 0); /* Save old control mask. */
                    /* Enable floating-point exceptions. */
    fpNew = fpOld & ~(EM_OVERFLOW | EM_UNDERFLOW | EM_INEXACT
            | EM_ZERODIVIDE | EM_DENORMAL | EM_INVALID);
    _controlfp(fpNew, MCW_EM);

    while (!done) __try { /* Try-finally. */
        _tprintf(_T("Enter exception type: "));
        _tprintf(_T
            (" 1: Mem, 2: Int, 3: Flt 4: User 5: __leave "));
        _tscanf(_T("%d"), &i);
        __try { /* Try-except block. */
            switch (i) {
            case 1: /* Memory reference. */
                ix = *pNull; *pNull = 5; break;
            case 2: /* Integer arithmetic. */
                ix = ix / iy; break;
            case 3: /* Floating-point exception. */
                x = x / y;
                _tprintf(_T("x = %20e\n"), x); break;
            case 4: /* User-generated exception. */
                ReportException(_T("User exception"), 1); break;
            case 5: /* Use the _leave statement to terminate. */
```

```
            __leave;
        default: done = TRUE;
        }
} /* End of inner __try. */

    __except (Filter(GetExceptionInformation(), &eCategory))
    {
        switch (eCategory) {
            case 0:
                _tprintf(_T("Unknown Exception\n")); break;
            case 1:
                _tprintf(_T("Memory Ref Exception\n")); continue;
            case 2:
                _tprintf(_T("Integer Exception\n")); break;
            case 3:
                _tprintf(_T("Floating-Point Exception\n"));
                _clearfp(); break;
            case 10:
                _tprintf(_T("User Exception\n")); break;
            default:
                _tprintf( _T("Unknown Exception\n")); break;
        } /* End of switch statement. */

        _tprintf(_T("End of handler\n"));
    } /* End of try-except block. */
} /* End of While loop -- the termination handler is below. */

    __finally { /* This is part of the while loop. */
        _tprintf(_T("Abnormal Termination?: %d\n"),
            AbnormalTermination());
    }
    _controlfp(fpOld, 0xFFFFFFFF); /* Restore old FP mask.*/
    return 0;
}
```

Program 4–4 shows the filter function used in Program 4–3. This function simply checks and categorizes the various possible exception code values. The code in the *Examples* file checks every possible value; here the function tests only for a few that are relevant to the test program.

Program 4–4 Filter: Exception Filtering

```
static DWORD Filter(LPEXCEPTION_POINTERS pExP, LPDWORD eCategory)
/* Categorize the exception and decide action. */
{
    DWORD exCode, readWrite, virtAddr;
    exCode = pExP->ExceptionRecord->ExceptionCode;
    _tprintf(_T("Filter. exCode: %x\n"), exCode);
    if ((0x20000000 & exCode) != 0) { /* User exception. */
        *eCategory = 10;
        return EXCEPTION_EXECUTE_HANDLER;
    }

    switch (exCode) {
        case EXCEPTION_ACCESS_VIOLATION:
            readWrite = /* Was it a read, write, execute? */
                    pExP->ExceptionRecord->ExceptionInformation[0];
            virtAddr = /* Virtual address of the violation. */
                    pExP->ExceptionRecord->ExceptionInformation[1];
            _tprintf(
            _T("Access Violation. Read/Write/Exec: %d. Address: %x\n"),
                    readWrite, virtAddr);
            *eCategory = 1;
            return EXCEPTION_EXECUTE_HANDLER;
        case EXCEPTION_INT_DIVIDE_BY_ZERO:
        case EXCEPTION_INT_OVERFLOW:
            *eCategory = 2;
            return EXCEPTION_EXECUTE_HANDLER;
        case EXCEPTION_FLT_DIVIDE_BY_ZERO:
        case EXCEPTION_FLT_OVERFLOW:
            _tprintf(_T("Flt Exception - large result.\n"));
            *eCategory = 3;
            _clearfp();
            return EXCEPTION_EXECUTE_HANDLER;

        default:
            *eCategory = 0;
            return EXCEPTION_CONTINUE_SEARCH;
    }
}
```

```
C:\WSP4_Examples\run8>Excption
Enter exception type:
1: Mem, 2: Int, 3: Flt 4: User 5: _leave 6: return
1
Filter. ExCode: c0000005
Access Violation. Read/Write: 0. Address: 0
Memory ref exception.
End of handler.
Abnormal Termination?: 1
Enter exception type:
1: Mem, 2: Int, 3: Flt 4: User 5: _leave 6: return
2
Filter. ExCode: c0000094
Integer arithmetic exception.
End of handler.
Abnormal Termination?: 1
Enter exception type:
1: Mem, 2: Int, 3: Flt 4: User 5: _leave 6: return
3
x =          1.#INF00e+000
Abnormal Termination?: 1
Enter exception type:
1: Mem, 2: Int, 3: Flt 4: User 5: _leave 6: return
4
Raising user exception.

The operation completed successfully.

Filter. ExCode: e0000001
User generated exception.
End of handler.
Abnormal Termination?: 1
Enter exception type:
1: Mem, 2: Int, 3: Flt 4: User 5: _leave 6: return
5
Abnormal Termination?: 1

C:\WSP4_Examples\run8>Excption
Enter exception type:
1: Mem, 2: Int, 3: Flt 4: User 5: _leave 6: return
6
Abnormal Termination?: 0

C:\WSP4_Examples\run8>
```

Run 4–4 Filter: Exception Filtering

Console Control Handlers

Exception handlers can respond to a variety of asynchronous events, but they do not detect situations such as the user logging off or entering a Ctrl-C from the keyboard to stop a program. Use console control handlers to detect such events.

The function SetConsoleCtrlHandler allows one or more specified functions to be executed on receipt of a Ctrl-C, Ctrl-break, or one of three other console-related signals. The GenerateConsoleCtrlEvent function, described in

Chapter 6, also generates these signals, and the signals can be sent to other processes that are sharing the same console. The handlers are user-specified Boolean functions that take a DWORD argument identifying the signal.

Multiple handlers can be associated with a signal, and handlers can be removed as well as added. Here is the function to add or delete a handler.

```
BOOL SetConsoleCtrlHandler (
    PHANDLER_ROUTINE HandlerRoutine,
    BOOL Add)
```

The handler routine is added if the Add flag is TRUE; otherwise, it is deleted from the list of console control routines. Notice that the signal is not specified. The handler must test to see which signal was received.

The handler routine returns a Boolean value and takes a single DWORD parameter that identifies the signal. The *HandlerRoutine* in the definition is a placeholder; the programmer specifies the name.

Here are some other considerations when using console control handlers.

- If the *HandlerRoutine* parameter is NULL and Add is TRUE, Ctrl-C signals will be ignored.

- The ENABLE_PROCESSED_INPUT flag on SetConsoleMode (Chapter 2) will cause Ctrl-C to be treated as keyboard input rather than as a signal.

- The handler routine actually executes as an *independent thread* (see Chapter 7) within the process. The normal program will continue to operate, as shown in the next example.

- Raising an exception in the handler *will not* cause an exception in the thread that was interrupted because exceptions apply to threads, not to an entire process. If you wish to communicate with the interrupted thread, use a variable, as in the next example, or a synchronization method (Chapter 8).

There is one other important distinction between exceptions and signals. A signal applies to the entire process, whereas an exception applies only to the thread executing the code where the exception occurs.

```
BOOL HandlerRoutine (DWORD dwCtrlType)
```

dwCtrlType identifies the signal (or *event*) and can take on one of the following five values.

1. CTRL_C_EVENT indicates that the Ctrl-C sequence was entered from the keyboard.

2. CTRL_CLOSE_EVENT indicates that the console window is being closed.

3. CTRL_BREAK_EVENT indicates the Ctrl-break signal.

4. CTRL_LOGOFF_EVENT indicates that the user is logging off.

5. CTRL_SHUTDOWN_EVENT indicates that Windows is shutting down.

The signal handler can perform cleanup operations just as an exception or termination handler would. The signal handler can return TRUE to indicate that the function handled the signal. If the signal handler returns FALSE, the next handler function in the list is executed. The signal handlers are executed in the reverse order from the way they were set, so that the most recently set handler is executed first and the system handler is executed last.

Example: A Console Control Handler

Program 4–5 loops forever, calling the self-explanatory Beep function every 5 seconds. The user can terminate the program with a Ctrl-C or by closing the console. The handler routine will put out a message, wait 10 seconds, and, it would appear, return TRUE, terminating the program. The main program, however, detects the exitFlag flag and stops the process. This illustrates the concurrent operation of the handler routine; note that the timing of the signal determines the extent of the signal handler's output. Examples in later chapters also use console control handlers.

Note the use of WINAPI; this macro is for user functions passed as arguments to Windows functions to assure the proper calling conventions. It is defined in the Platform SDK header file windef.h.

Program 4–5　Ctrlc: Signal Handling Program

```
/* Chapter 4. Ctrlc.c */
/* Catch console events. */

#include "Everything.h"

static BOOL WINAPI Handler(DWORD cntrlEvent);
static BOOL exitFlag = FALSE;
```

```
int _tmain(int argc, LPTSTR argv[])

/* Beep periodically until signaled to stop. */
{
    /* Add an event handler. */
    SetConsoleCtrlHandler(Handler, TRUE);

    while (!exitFlag) {
        Sleep(5000); /* Beep every 5 seconds. */
        Beep(1000 /* Frequency. */, 250 /* Duration. */);
    }
    _tprintf(_T("Stopping the program as requested.\n"));
    return 0;
}

BOOL WINAPI Handler(DWORD cntrlEvent)
{
    exitFlag = TRUE;

    switch (cntrlEvent) {
        /* Timing determines if you see the second handler message. */
        case CTRL_C_EVENT:
            _tprintf(_T("Ctrl-C. Leaving in <= 5 seconds.\n"));
            exitFlag = TRUE;
            Sleep(4000); /* Decrease to get a different effect */
            _tprintf(_T("Leaving handler in 1 second or less.\n"));
            return TRUE; /* TRUE indicates the signal was handled. */
        case CTRL_CLOSE_EVENT:
            _tprintf(_T("Close event. Leaving in <= 5 seconds.\n"));
            exitFlag = TRUE;
            Sleep(4000); /* Decrease to get a different effect */
            _tprintf(_T("Leaving handler in <= 1 second.\n"));
            return TRUE; /* Try returning FALSE. Any difference? */
        default:
            _tprintf(_T("Event: %d. Leaving in <= 5 seconds.\n"),
                cntrlEvent);
            exitFlag = TRUE;
            Sleep(4000); /* Decrease to get a different effect */
            _tprintf(_T("Leaving handler in <= 1 second.\n"));
            return TRUE; /* TRUE indicates the signal was handled. */
    }
}
```

There's very little to show with this program, as we can't show the sound effects. Nonetheless, Run 4–5 shows the command window where I typed Ctrl-C after about 11 seconds.

Run 4–5   `Ctrlc`: Interrupting Program Execution from the Console

Vectored Exception Handling

Exception handling functions can be directly associated with exceptions, just as console control handlers can be associated with console control events. When an exception occurs, the *vectored exception handlers* are called first, before the system unwinds the stack to look for structured exception handlers. No keywords, such as __try and __catch, are required.

Vectored exception handling (VEH) management is similar to console control handler management, although the details are different. Add, or "register," a handler using AddVectoredExceptionHandler.

```
PVOID WINAPI AddVectoredExceptionHandler (
    ULONG FirstHandler,
    PVECTORED_EXCEPTION_HANDLER VectoredHandler)
```

Handlers can be chained, so the FirstHandler parameter specifies that the handler should either be the first one called when the exception occurs (nonzero value) or the last one called (zero value). Subsequent AddVectoredException-Handler calls can update the order. For example, if two handlers are added, both with a zero FirstHandler value, the handlers will be called in the order in which they were added.

The return value is a handler to the exception handler (NULL indicates failure). This handle is the sole parameter to RemoveVectoredExceptionHandler, which returns a non-NULL value if it succeeds.

The successful return value is a pointer to the exception handler, that is, *VectoredHandler*. A NULL return value indicates failure.

VectoredHandler is a pointer to the handler function of the form:

```
LONG WINAPI VectoredHandler (PEXCEPTION_POINTERS
    ExceptionInfo)
```

PEXCEPTION_POINTERS is the address of an EXCEPTION_POINTERS structure with processor-specific and general information. This is the same structure
returned by GetExceptionInformation and used in Program 4–4.

A VEH handler function should be fast so that the exception handler will be
reached quickly. In particular, the handler should never access a synchronization
object that might block the thread, such as a mutex (see Chapter 8). In most cases,
the VEH simply accesses the exception structure, performs some minimal
processing (such as setting a flag), and returns. There are two possible return
values, both of which are familiar from the SEH discussion.

1. EXCEPTION_CONTINUE_EXECUTION—No more handlers are executed, SEH is
   not performed, and control is returned to the point where the exception
   occurred. As with SEH, this may not always be possible or advisable.

2. EXCEPTION_CONTINUE_SEARCH—The next VEH handler, if any, is executed.
   If there are no additional handlers, the stack is unwound to search for SEH
   handlers.

Exercise 4–9 asks you to add VEH to Programs 4–3 and 4–4.

Summary

Windows SEH provides a robust mechanism for C programs to respond to and
recover from exceptions and errors. Exception handling is efficient and can result
in more understandable, maintainable, and safer code, making it an essential aid
to defensive programming and higher-quality programs. Similar concepts are
implemented in most languages and OSs, although the Windows solution allows
you to analyze the exact cause of an exception.

Console control handlers can respond to external events that do not generate
exceptions. VEH is a newer feature that allows functions to be executed before
SEH processing occurs. VEH is similar to conventional interrupt handling.

Looking Ahead

`ReportException` and exception and termination handlers are used as convenient in subsequent examples. Chapter 5 covers memory management, and in the process, SEH is used to detect memory allocation errors.

Exercises

4–1. Extend Program 4–2 so that every call to `ReportException` contains sufficient information so that the exception handler can report precisely what error occurred and also the output file. Further enhance the program so that it can work with $CONIN and pipes (Chapter 11).

4–2. Extend Program 4–3 by generating memory access violations, such as array index out of bounds and arithmetic faults and other types of floating-point exceptions not illustrated in Program 4–3.

4–3. Augment Program 4–3 so as to print the value of the floating-point mask after enabling the exceptions. Are all the exceptions actually enabled? Explain the results.

4–4. What values do you get after a floating-point exception, such as division by zero? Can you set the result in the filter function as Program 4–3 attempts to do?

4–5. What happens in Program 4–3 if you do not clear the floating-point exception? Explain the results. *Hint:* Request an additional exception after the floating-point exception.

4–6. Extend Program 4–5 so that the handler routine raises an exception rather than returning. Explain the results.

4–7. Extend Program 4–5 so that it can handle shutdown and log-off signals.

4–8. Confirm through experiment that Program 4–5's handler routine executes concurrently with the main program.

4–9. Enhance Programs 4–3 and 4–4. Specifically, handle floating-point and arithmetic exceptions before invoking SEH.

5 | Memory Management, Memory- Mapped Files, and DLLs

Most programs require some form of dynamic memory management. This need arises whenever there is a need to create data structures whose size or number is not known at program build time. Search trees, symbol tables, and linked lists are common examples of dynamic data structures where the program creates new instances at run time.

Windows provides flexible mechanisms for managing a program's dynamic memory. Windows also provides memory-mapped files to associate a process's address space directly with a file, allowing the OS to manage all data movement between the file and memory so that the programmer never needs to deal with `ReadFile`, `WriteFile`, `SetFilePointer`, or the other file I/O functions. With memory-mapped files, the program can maintain dynamic data structures conveniently in permanent files, and memory-based algorithms can process file data. What is more, memory mapping can significantly speed up file processing, and it provides a mechanism for memory sharing between processes.

Dynamic link libraries (DLLs) are an essential special case of file mapping and shared memory in which files (primarily read-only code files) are mapped into the process address space for execution.

This chapter describes the Windows memory management and file mapping functions, illustrates their use and performance advantages with several examples, and describes both implicitly and explicitly linked DLLs.

Windows Memory Management Architecture

Win32 (the distinction between Win32 and Win64 is important here) is an API for the Windows 32-bit OS family. The "32-bitness" manifests itself in memory addresses, and pointers (`LPCTSTR`, `LPDWORD`, and so on) are 4-byte (32-bit) objects. The Win64 API provides a much larger virtual address space with 8-byte, 64-bit pointers and is a natural evolution of Win32. Nonetheless, use care to ensure that your applications can be targeted at both platforms; the examples have all been tested on both 64-bit and 32-bit systems, and 32-bit and 64-bit executables are available in the *Examples* file. With the example programs, there are comments about changes that were required to support Win64.

Every Windows process, then, has its own private virtual address space of either 4GB (2^{32} bytes) or 16EB (16 exabytes or 2^{64} bytes[1]). Win32 makes at least half of this (2–3GB; 3GB must be enabled at boot time) available to a process. The remainder of the virtual address space is allocated to shared data and code, system code, drivers, and so on.

The details of these memory allocations, although interesting, are not important here. From the programmer's perspective, the OS provides a large address space for code, data, and other resources. This chapter concentrates on exploiting Windows memory management without being concerned with OS implementation. Nonetheless, a very short overview follows.

Memory Management Overview

The OS manages all the details of mapping virtual to physical memory and the mechanics of page swapping, demand paging, and the like. This subject is discussed thoroughly in OS texts. Here's a brief summary.

- The computer has a relatively small amount of physical memory; 1GB is the practical minimum for 32-bit Windows XP, and much larger physical memories are typical.[2]

- Every process—and there may be several user and system processes—has its own virtual address space, which may be much larger than the physical memory available. For example, the virtual address space of a 4GB process is two

---

[1] Current systems cannot provide the full 2^{64}-byte virtual address space. 2^{44} bytes (16 terabytes) is a common processor limit at this time. This limit is certain to increase over time.

[2] Memory prices continue to decline, and "typical" memory sizes keep increasing, so it is difficult to define typical memory size. At the time of publication, even the most inexpensive systems contain 2GB, which is sufficient for Windows XP, Vista, and 7. Windows Server systems generally contain much more memory.

times larger than 2GB of physical memory, and there may be many such processes running concurrently.

- The OS maps virtual addresses to physical addresses.

- Most virtual pages will not be in physical memory, so the OS responds to *page faults* (references to pages not in memory) and loads the data from disk, either from the system swap file or from a normal file. Page faults, while transparent to the programmer, have a significant impact on performance, and programs should be designed to minimize faults. Again, many OS texts treat this important subject, which is beyond the scope of this book.

Figure 5–1 shows the Windows memory management API layered on the Virtual Memory Manager. The Virtual Memory Windows API (`VirtualAlloc`, `VirtualFree`, `VirtualLock`, `VirtualUnlock`, and so on) deals with whole pages. The Windows Heap API manages memory in user-defined units.

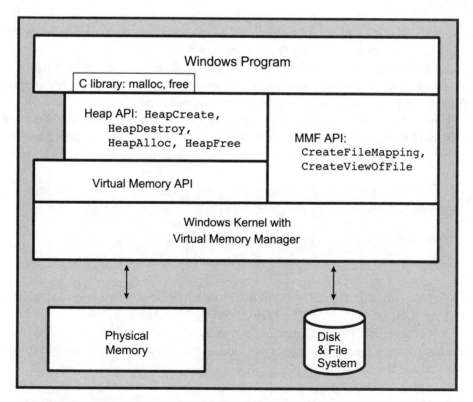

Figure 5–1   Windows Memory Management Architecture

The layout of the virtual memory address space is not shown because it is not directly relevant to the API, and the layout could change in the future. The Microsoft documentation provides this information.

Nonetheless, many programmers want to know more about their environment. To start to explore the memory structure, invoke the following.

```
VOID GetSystemInfo (LPSYSTEM_INFO lpSystemInfo)
```

The parameter is the address of a `PSYSTEM_INFO` structure containing information on the system's page size, allocation granularity, and the application's physical memory address. You can run the `version` program in the *Examples* file to see the results on your computer, and an exercise (with a screenshot) suggests an enhancement.

Heaps

Windows maintains pools of memory in *heaps*. A process can contain several heaps, and you allocate memory from these heaps.

One heap is often sufficient, but there are good reasons, explained below, for multiple heaps. If a single heap is sufficient, just use the C library memory management functions (`malloc`, `free`, `calloc`, `realloc`).

Heaps are Windows objects; therefore, they have handles. However, heaps are not kernel objects. The heap handle is necessary when you're allocating memory. Each process has its own default heap, and the next function obtains its handle.

```
HANDLE GetProcessHeap (VOID)
```

Return: The handle for the process's heap; `NULL` on failure.

Notice that `NULL` is the return value to indicate failure rather than `INVALID_HANDLE_VALUE`, which is returned by `CreateFile`.

A program can also create distinct heaps. It is convenient at times to have separate heaps for allocation of separate data structures. The benefits of separate heaps include the following.

- **Fairness**. If threads allocate memory solely from a unique heap assigned to the thread, then no single thread can obtain more memory than is allocated to its heap. In particular, a memory leak defect, caused by a program neglecting to free data elements that are no longer needed, will affect only one thread of a process.[3]

- **Multithreaded performance**. By giving each thread its own heap, contention between threads is reduced, which can substantially improve performance. See Chapter 9.

- **Allocation efficiency**. Allocation of fixed-size data elements within a small heap can be more efficient than allocating elements of many different sizes in a single large heap. Fragmentation is also reduced. Furthermore, giving each thread a unique heap for storage used only within the thread simplifies synchronization, resulting in additional efficiencies.

- **Deallocation efficiency**. An entire heap and all the data structures it contains can be freed with a single function call. This call will also free any leaked memory allocations in the heap.

- **Locality of reference efficiency**. Maintaining a data structure in a small heap ensures that the elements will be confined to a relatively small number of pages, potentially reducing page faults as the data structure elements are processed.

The value of these advantages varies depending on the application, and many programmers use only the process heap and the C library. Such a choice, however, prevents the program from exploiting the exception generating capability of the Windows memory management functions (described along with the functions). In any case, the next two functions create and destroy heaps.[4]

Creating a Heap

Use `HeapCreate` to create a new heap, specifying the initial heap size.

The initial heap size, which can be zero and is always rounded up to a multiple of the page size, determines how much physical storage (in a *paging file*) is *committed* to the heap (that is, the required space is allocated from the heap) initially, rather than on demand as memory is allocated from the heap. As a program exceeds the initial size, additional pages are committed automatically up to the maximum size. Because the paging file is a limited resource, deferring commitment is a good practice unless it is known ahead of time how large the

---

[3] Chapter 7 introduces threads.

[4] In general, create objects of type X with the `CreateX` system call. `HeapCreate` is an exception to this pattern.

heap will become. `dwMaximumSize`, if nonzero, determines the heap's maximum size as it expands dynamically. The process heap will also grow dynamically.

```
HANDLE HeapCreate (
    DWORD flOptions,
    SIZE_T dwInitialSize,
    SIZE_T dwMaximumSize)
```

Return: A heap handle, or `NULL` on failure.

The two size fields are of type `SIZE_T` rather than `DWORD`. `SIZE_T` is defined to be either a 32-bit or 64-bit unsigned integer, depending on compiler flags (`_WIN32` and `_WIN64`). `SIZE_T` helps to enable source code portability to both Win32 and Win64. `SIZE_T` variables can span the entire range of a 32- or 64-bit pointers. `SSIZE_T` is the signed version but is not used here.

`flOptions` is a combination of three flags.

- `HEAP_GENERATE_EXCEPTIONS`—With this option, failed allocations generate an exception for SEH processing (see Chapter 4). `HeapCreate` itself will not cause an exception; rather, functions such as `HeapAlloc`, which are explained shortly, cause an exception on failure if this flag is set. There is more discussion after the memory management function descriptions.

- `HEAP_NO_SERIALIZE`—Set this flag under certain circumstances to get a small performance improvement; there is additional discussion after the memory management function descriptions.

- `HEAP_CREATE_ENABLE_EXECUTE`—This is an out-of-scope advanced feature that allows you to specify that code can be executed from this heap. Normally, if the system has been configured to enforce data execution prevention (DEP), any attempt to execute code in the heap will generate an exception with code `STATUS_ACCESS_VIOLATION`, partially providing security from code that attempts to exploit buffer overruns.

There are several other important points regarding `dwMaximumSize`.

- If `dwMaximumSize` is nonzero, the virtual address space is allocated accordingly, even though it may not be committed in its entirety. This is the maximum size of the heap, which is said to be *nongrowable*. This option limits a heap's size, perhaps to gain the fairness advantage cited previously.

- If, on the other hand, `dwMaximumSize` is 0, then the heap is *growable* beyond the initial size. The limit is determined by the available virtual address space not currently allocated to other heaps and swap file space.

Note that heaps do not have security attributes because they are not kernel objects; they are memory blocks managed by the heap functions. File mapping objects, described later in the chapter, can be secured (Chapter 15).

To destroy an entire heap, use `HeapDestroy`. `CloseHandle` is not appropriate because heaps are not kernel objects.

```
BOOL HeapDestroy (HANDLE hHeap)
```

`hHeap` should specify a heap generated by `HeapCreate`. Be careful not to destroy the process's heap (the one obtained from `GetProcessHeap`). Destroying a heap frees the virtual memory space and physical storage in the paging file. Naturally, well-designed programs should destroy heaps that are no longer needed.

Destroying a heap is also a quick way to free data structures without traversing them to delete one element at a time, although C++ object instances will not be destroyed inasmuch as their destructors are not called. Heap destruction has three benefits.

1. There is no need to write the data structure traversal code.

2. There is no need to deallocate each individual element.

3. The system does not spend time maintaining the heap since all data structure elements are deallocated with a single call.

The C library uses only a single heap. There is, therefore, nothing similar to Windows heap handles.

The UNIX `sbrk` function can increase a process's address space, but it is not a general-purpose memory manager.

UNIX does not generate signals when memory allocation fails; the programmer must explicitly test the returned pointer.

Managing Heap Memory

The heap management functions allocate and free memory blocks.

HeapAlloc

Obtain memory blocks from a heap by specifying the heap's handle, the block size, and several flags.

```
LPVOID HeapAlloc (
    HANDLE hHeap,
    DWORD dwFlags,
    SIZE_T dwBytes)
```

Return: A pointer to the allocated memory block, or NULL on failure (unless exception generation is specified).

Parameters

hHeap is the heap handle for the heap in which the memory block is to be allocated. This handle should come from either GetProcessHeap or HeapCreate.

dwFlags is a combination of three flags:

- HEAP_GENERATE_EXCEPTIONS and HEAP_NO_SERIALIZE—These flags have the same meaning as for HeapCreate. The first flag is ignored if it was set with the heap's HeapCreate function and enables exceptions for the specific HeapAlloc call, even if HEAP_GENERATE_EXCEPTIONS was not specified by HeapCreate. The second flag should not be used when allocating within the process heap, and there is more information at the end of this section.

- HEAP_ZERO_MEMORY—This flag specifies that the allocated memory will be initialized to 0; otherwise, the memory contents are not specified.

dwBytes is the size of the block of memory to allocate. For nongrowable heaps, this is limited to 0x7FFF8 (approximately 0.5MB). This block size limit applies even to Win64 and to very large heaps.

The return value from a successful HeapAlloc call is an LPVOID pointer, which is either 32 or 64 bits, depending on the build option.

Note: Once HeapAlloc returns a pointer, use the pointer in the normal way; there is no need to make reference to its heap.

Heap Management Failure

The HeapAlloc has a different failure behavior than other functions we've used.

- Function failure causes an exception when using `HEAP_GENERATE_EXCEPTIONS`. The exception code is either `STATUS_NO_MEMORY` or `STATUS_ACCESS-_VIOLATION`.

- Without `HEAP_GENERATE_EXCEPTIONS`, `HeapAlloc` returns a `NULL` pointer.

- In either case, you cannot use `GetLastError` for error information, and hence you cannot use this book's `ReportError` function to produce a text error message.

HeapFree

Deallocating memory from a heap is simple.

```
BOOL HeapFree (
    HANDLE hHeap,
    DWORD dwFlags,
    LPVOID lpMem)
```

`dwFlags` should be 0 or `HEAP_NO_SERIALIZE` (see the end of the section). `lpMem` should be a value returned by `HeapAlloc` or `HeapReAlloc` (described next), and, of course, `hHeap` should be the heap from which `lpMem` was allocated.

A `FALSE` return value indicates a failure, and you can use `GetLastError`, which does not work with `HeapAlloc`. `HEAP_GENERATE_EXCEPTIONS` does not apply to `HeapFree`.

HeapReAlloc

Memory blocks can be reallocated to change their size. Allocation failure behavior is the same as with `HeapAlloc`.

```
LPVOID HeapReAlloc (
    HANDLE hHeap,
    DWORD dwFlags,
    LPVOID lpMem,
    SIZE_T dwBytes)
```

Return: A pointer to the reallocated block. Failure returns `NULL` or causes an exception.

Parameters

The first parameter, hHeap, is the same heap used with the HeapAlloc call that returned the lpMem value (the third parameter). dwFlags specifies some essential control options.

- HEAP_GENERATE_EXCEPTIONS and HEAP_NO_SERIALIZE—These flags are the same as for HeapAlloc.

- HEAP_ZERO_MEMORY—Only newly allocated memory (when dwBytes is larger than the original block) is initialized. The original block contents are not modified.

- HEAP_REALLOC_IN_PLACE_ONLY—This flag specifies that the block cannot be moved. When you're increasing a block's size, the new memory must be allocated at the address immediately after the existing block.

lpMem specifies the existing block in hHeap to be reallocated.

dwBytes is the new block size, which can be larger or smaller than the existing size, but, as with HeapAlloc, it must be less than 0x7FFF8.

It is possible that the returned pointer is the same as lpMem. If, on the other hand, a block is moved (permit this by omitting the HEAP_REALLOC_IN_PLACE-_ONLY flag), the returned value might be different. Be careful to update any references to the block. The data in the block is unchanged, regardless of whether or not it is moved; however, some data will be lost if the block size is reduced.

HeapSize

Determine the size of an allocated block by calling HeapSize with the heap handle and block pointer. This function could have been named HeapGetBlockSize because it does not obtain the heap size. The value will be greater than or equal to the size used with HeapAlloc or HeapReAlloc.

```
SIZE_T HeapSize (
    HANDLE hHeap,
    DWORD dwFlags,
    LPCVOID lpMem)

Return: The size of the block, or zero on failure.
```

The only possible dwFlags value is HEAP_NO_SERIALIZE.

The error return value is (SIZE_T)-1. You cannot use GetLastError to find extended error information.

More about the Serialization and Exceptions Flags

The heap management functions use two unique flags, HEAP_NO_SERIALIZE and HEAP_GENERATE_EXCEPTIONS, that need additional explanation.

The *HEAP_NO_SERIALIZE* Flag

The functions HeapCreate, HeapAlloc, and HeapReAlloc can specify the HEAP_NO_SERIALIZE flag. There can be a small performance gain with this flag because the functions do not provide mutual exclusion to threads accessing the heap. Some simple tests that do nothing except allocate memory blocks measured a performance improvement of about 16 percent. This flag is safe in a few situations, such as the following.

- The program does not use threads (Chapter 7), or, more accurately, the process (Chapter 6) has only a single thread. All examples in this chapter use the flag.

- Each thread has its own heap or set of heaps, and no other thread accesses those heaps.

- The program has its own mutual exclusion mechanism (Chapter 8) to prevent concurrent access to a heap by several threads using HeapAlloc and HeapReAlloc.

The *HEAP_GENERATE_EXCEPTIONS* Flag

Forcing exceptions when memory allocation fails avoids the need for error tests after each allocation. Furthermore, the exception or termination handler can clean up memory that did get allocated. This technique is used in some examples.

Two exception codes are possible.

1. STATUS_NO_MEMORY indicates that the system could not create a block of the requested size. Causes can include fragmented memory, a nongrowable heap that has reached its limit, or even exhaustion of all memory with growable heaps.

2. STATUS_ACCESS_VIOLATION indicates that the specified heap has been corrupted. For example, a program may have written memory beyond the bounds of an allocated block.

Setting Heap Information

`HeapSetInformation` allows you to enable the "low-fragmentation" heap (LFH) on NT5 (Windows XP and Server 2003) computers; the LFH is the default on NT6. This is a simple function; see MSDN for an example. The LFH can help program performance when allocating and deallocating small memory blocks with different sizes.

`HeapSetInformation` also allows you to enable the "terminate on corruption" feature. Windows terminates the process if it detects an error in the heap; such an error could occur, for example, if you wrote past the bounds of an array allocated on the heap.

Use `HeapQueryInformation` to determine if the LFH is enabled for the heap. You can also determine if the heap supports look-aside lists (see MSDN).

Other Heap Functions

`HeapCompact`, despite the name, does not compact the heap. However, it does return the size of the largest committed free block in the heap. `HeapValidate` attempts to detect heap corruption. `HeapWalk` enumerates the blocks in a heap, and `GetProcessHeaps` obtains all the heap handles that are valid in a process.

`HeapLock` and `HeapUnlock` allow a thread to serialize heap access, as described in Chapter 8.

Some functions, such as `GlobalAlloc` and `LocalAlloc`, were used for compatibility with 16-bit systems and for functions inherited from 16-bit Windows. These functions are mentioned first as a reminder that some functions continue to be supported even though they are not always relevant and you should use the heap functions. However, there are cases where MSDN states that you need to use these functions, and memory must be freed with the function corresponding to its allocator. For instance, use `LocalFree` with `FormatMessage` (see Program 2–1, `ReportError`). In general, if a function allocates memory, read MSDN to determine the correct free function, although `FormatMessage` is the only such function used in this book.

Summary: Heap Management

The normal process for using heaps is straightforward.

1. Get a heap handle with either `CreateHeap` or `GetProcessHeap`.

2. Allocate blocks within the heap using `HeapAlloc`.

3. Optionally, free some or all of the individual blocks with `HeapFree`.

4. Destroy the heap and close the handle with `HeapDestroy`.

5. The C run-time library (`malloc`, `free`, etc.) are frequently adequate. However, memory allocated with the C library must be freed with the C library. You cannot assume that the C library uses the process heap.

Figure 5–2 and Program 5–1 illustrate this process.

Normally, programmers use the C library `<stdlib.h>` memory management functions and can continue to do so if separate heaps or exception generation are not needed. `malloc` is then logically equivalent to `HeapAlloc` using the process heap, `realloc` to `HeapReAlloc`, and `free` to `HeapFree`. `calloc` allocates and initializes objects, and `HeapAlloc` can easily emulate this behavior. There is no C library equivalent to `HeapSize`.

Example: Sorting Files with a Binary Search Tree

A search tree is a common dynamic data structure requiring memory management. Search trees are a convenient way to maintain collections of records, and they have the additional advantage of allowing efficient sequential traversal.

Program 5–1 implements a sort (`sortBT`, a limited version of the UNIX `sort` command) by creating a binary search tree using two heaps. The keys go into the *node heap*, which represents the search tree. Each node contains left and right pointers, a key, and a pointer to the data record in the *data heap*. The complete record, a line of text from the input file, goes into the data heap. Notice that the node heap consists of fixed-size blocks, whereas the data heap contains strings with different lengths. Finally, tree traversal displays the sorted file.

This example arbitrarily uses the first 8 bytes of a string as the key rather than using the complete string. Two other sort implementations in this chapter (Programs 5–4 and 5–5) sort files.

Figure 5–2 shows the sequence of operations for creating heaps and allocating blocks. The program code on the right is *pseudocode* in that only the essential function calls and arguments are shown. The virtual address space on the left shows the three heaps along with some allocated blocks in each. The figure differs slightly from the program in that the root of the tree is allocated in the process heap in the figure but not in Program 5–1. Finally, the figure is not drawn to scale.

Note: The actual locations of the heaps and the blocks within the heaps depend on the Windows implementation and on the process's history of previous memory use, including heap expansion beyond the original size. Furthermore, a growable heap may not occupy contiguous address space after it grows beyond the originally committed size. The best programming practice is to make no assumptions; just use the memory management functions as specified.

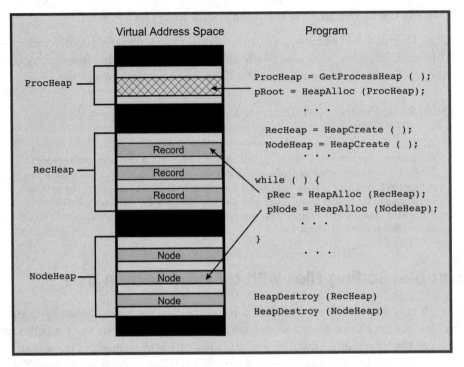

Figure 5–2 Memory Management in Multiple Heaps

Program 5–1 illustrates some techniques that simplify the program and would not be possible with the C library alone or with the process heap.

- The node elements are fixed size and go in a heap of their own, whereas the varying-length data element records are in a separate heap.

- The program prepares to sort the next file by destroying the two heaps rather than freeing individual elements.

- Allocation errors are processed as exceptions so that it is not necessary to test for NULL pointers.

An implementation such as Program 5–1 is limited to smaller files when using Windows because the complete file and a copy of the keys must reside in virtual memory. The absolute upper limit of the file length is determined by the available virtual address space (3GB at most for Win32; the practical limit is less). With Win64, you will probably not hit a practical limit.

Program 5–1 calls several tree management functions: `FillTree`, `InsertTree`, `Scan`, and `KeyCompare`. They are shown in Program 5–2. See Run 5–2, after Program 5–2, for a `sortBT` run example.

This program uses heap exceptions and user-generated exceptions for file open errors. An alternative would be to use `ReportError`, eliminate use of the `HEAP_GENERATE_EXCEPTIONS` flag, and test directly for memory allocation errors.

Program 5–1   `sortBT`: Sorting with a Binary Search Tree

```
/* Chapter 5. sortBT command. Binary Tree version. */
#include "Everything.h"
#define KEY_SIZE 8
typedef struct _TREENODE {/* Tree node structure definition. */
    struct _TREENODE *Left, *Right;
    TCHAR key[KEY_SIZE];
    LPTSTR pData;
} TREENODE, *LPTNODE, **LPPTNODE;
#define NODE_SIZE sizeof (TREENODE)
#define NODE_HEAP_ISIZE 0x8000
#define DATA_HEAP_ISIZE 0x8000
#define MAX_DATA_LEN 0x1000
#define TKEY_SIZE KEY_SIZE * sizeof (TCHAR)
#define STATUS_FILE_ERROR 0xE0000001 /* Customer exception */

LPTNODE FillTree (HANDLE, HANDLE, HANDLE);
BOOL Scan (LPTNODE);
int KeyCompare (LPCTSTR, LPCTSTR), iFile;

BOOL InsertTree (LPPTNODE, LPTNODE);

int _tmain (int argc, LPTSTR argv[])
{
    HANDLE hIn = INVALID_HANDLE_VALUE, hNode = NULL, hData = NULL;
    LPTNODE pRoot;
    CHAR errorMessage[256];
    int iFirstFile = Options (argc, argv, _T ("n"), &noPrint, NULL);
                /* Process all files on the command line. */

    for (iFile = iFirstFile; iFile < argc; iFile++) __try {
        /* Open the input file. */
        hIn = CreateFile (argv[iFile], GENERIC_READ, 0, NULL,
                OPEN_EXISTING, 0, NULL);
        if (hIn == INVALID_HANDLE_VALUE)
            RaiseException (STATUS_FILE_ERROR, 0, 0, NULL);

        __try {
            /* Allocate the two growable heaps. */
            hNode = HeapCreate (
```

```
                   HEAP_GENERATE_EXCEPTIONS | HEAP_NO_SERIALIZE,
                   NODE_HEAP_ISIZE, 0);
               hData = HeapCreate (
                   HEAP_GENERATE_EXCEPTIONS | HEAP_NO_SERIALIZE,
                   DATA_HEAP_ISIZE, 0);

               /* Process the input file, creating the tree. */
               pRoot = FillTree (hIn, hNode, hData);

               /* Display the tree in key order. */
               _tprintf (_T ("Sorted file: %s\n"), argv[iFile]);
               Scan (pRoot);

           } __finally { /* Heaps and file handles are always closed. */

               /* Destroy the two heaps and data structures. */
               if (hNode != NULL) HeapDestroy (hNode);
               if (hNode != NULL) HeapDestroy (hData);
               hNode = NULL; hData = NULL;
               if (hIn != INVALID_HANDLE_VALUE) CloseHandle (hIn);
               hIn = INVALID_HANDLE_VALUE;
           }
       } /* End of main file processing loop and try block. */

       /* Handle the expected exceptions - file error or out of memory. */
       __except ( (GetExceptionCode() == STATUS_FILE_ERROR ||
                   GetExceptionCode() == STATUS_NO_MEMORY)
                ? EXCEPTION_EXECUTE_HANDLER : EXCEPTION_CONTINUE_SEARCH)
       {
           _stprintf (errorMessage, _T ("\n%s %s"),
               _T ("sortBT error on file:"), argv[iFile]);
           ReportError (errorMessage, 0, TRUE);
       }
       return 0;
   }
```

Program 5–2 shows the functions that actually implement the search tree algorithms. FillTree, the first function, allocates memory in the two heaps. Key-Compare, the second function, is used in several other programs in this chapter. Notice that these functions are called by Program 5–1 and use the completion and exception handlers in that program. Thus, a memory allocation error would be handled by the main program, and the program would continue to process the next file.

Program 5–2 FillTree: Tree Management Functions

```
LPTNODE FillTree (HANDLE hIn, HANDLE hNode, HANDLE hData)

/* Fill the tree; Use the calling program's exception handler. */
{
    LPTNODE pRoot = NULL, pNode;
    DWORD nRead, i;
    BOOL atCR;
    TCHAR dataHold[MAX_DATA_LEN];
    LPTSTR pString;

    while (TRUE) {
        /* Allocate and initialize a new tree node. */
        pNode = HeapAlloc (hNode, HEAP_ZERO_MEMORY, NODE_SIZE);
        /* Read the key from the next file record. */
        if (!ReadFile (hIn, pNode->key, TKEY_SIZE,
                &nRead, NULL) || nRead != TKEY_SIZE)
            return pRoot;

        atCR = FALSE; /* Read data until end of line. */
        for (i = 0; i < MAX_DATA_LEN; i++) {
            ReadFile (hIn, &dataHold[i], TSIZE, &nRead, NULL);
            if (atCR && dataHold[i] == LF) break;
            atCR = (dataHold[i] == CR);
        }
        dataHold[i - 1] = '\0';

        /* Combine Key and Data -- Insert in tree. */
        pString = HeapAlloc (hData, HEAP_ZERO_MEMORY,
                (SIZE_T)(KEY_SIZE + _tcslen (dataHold) + 1) * TSIZE);
        memcpy (pString, pNode->key, TKEY_SIZE);
        pString[KEY_SIZE] = '\0';
        _tcscat (pString, dataHold);
        pNode->pData = pString;
        InsertTree (&pRoot, pNode);
    } /* End of while (TRUE) loop. */
    return NULL; /* Failure */
}

BOOL InsertTree (LPPTNODE ppRoot, LPTNODE pNode)
/* Add a single node, with data, to the tree. */
{
    if (*ppRoot == NULL) {
        *ppRoot = pNode;
        return TRUE;
    }
    if (KeyCompare (pNode->key, (*ppRoot)->key) < 0)
        InsertTree (&((*ppRoot)->Left), pNode);
```

```
    else
        InsertTree (&((*ppRoot)->Right), pNode);
}

static int KeyCompare (LPCTSTR pKey1, LPCTSTR pKey2)

/* Compare two records of generic characters. */
{
    return _tcsncmp (pKey1, pKey2, KEY_SIZE);
}

static BOOL Scan (LPTNODE pNode)

/* Recursively scan and print the contents of a binary tree. */
{
    if (pNode == NULL) return TRUE;
    Scan (pNode->Left);
    _tprintf (_T ("%s\n"), pNode->pData);
    Scan (pNode->Right);
    return TRUE;
}
```

Run 5–2 shows `sortBT` sorting small and large text files that were generated with `randfile`. `randfile`, introduced in Chapter 1, places 8 random digits in the first 8 bytes of each record to form a sort key. The "x" at the right end of each line is a visual cue and has no other meaning.

Run 5–2   `sortBT`: Sorting Small and Large Text Files

The `timep` utility shows the execution time; see Chapter 6 for the `timep` implementation.

Note: This search tree implementation is clearly not efficient because the tree may become unbalanced. Implementing a balanced search tree would be worthwhile but would not change the program's memory management.

Memory-Mapped Files

Dynamic memory in heaps must be physically allocated in a paging file. The OS's memory management controls page movement between physical memory and the paging file and also maps the process's virtual address space to the paging file. When the process terminates, the physical space in the file is deallocated.

Windows memory-mapped file functionality can also map virtual memory space directly to normal files. This has several advantages.

- There is no need to perform direct file I/O (reads and writes).

- The data structures created in memory will be saved in the file for later use by the same or other programs. Be careful about pointer usage, as Program 5–5 illustrates.

- Convenient and efficient in-memory algorithms (sorts, search trees, string processing, and so on) can process file data even though the file may be much larger than available physical memory. The performance will still be influenced by paging behavior if the file is large.

- File processing performance is frequently much faster than using the `ReadFile()` and `WriteFile()` file access functions.

- There is no need to manage buffers and the file data they contain. The OS does this hard work and does it efficiently with a high degree of reliability.

- Multiple processes (Chapter 6) can share memory by mapping their virtual address spaces to the same file or to the paging file (interprocess memory sharing is the principal reason for mapping to the paging file).

- There is no need to consume paging file space.

The OS itself uses memory mapping to implement DLLs and to load and execute executable (`.EXE`) files. DLLs are described at the end of this chapter.

Caution: When reading or writing a mapped file, it's a good idea to use SEH to catch any `EXCEPTION_IN_PAGE_ERROR` exceptions. The *Examples* file programs all do this, but the SEH is omitted from the program listings for brevity.

File Mapping Objects

The first step is to create a Windows kernel *file mapping object*, which has a handle, on an open file and then map all or part of the file to the process's address space. File mapping objects can be given names so that they are accessible to other processes for shared memory. Also, the mapping object has protection and security attributes and a size.

```
HANDLE CreateFileMapping (
    HANDLE hFile,
    LPSECURITY_ATTRIBUTES lpsa,
    DWORD dwProtect,
    DWORD dwMaximumSizeHigh,
    DWORD dwMaximumSizeLow,
    LPCTSTR lpMapName)
```

Return: A file mapping handle, or NULL on failure.

Parameters

hFile is the handle of an open file with protection flags compatible with dwProtect. The value INVALID_HANDLE_VALUE refers to the paging file, and you can use this value for interprocess memory sharing without creating a separate file.

LPSECURITY_ATTRIBUTES allows the mapping object to be secured.

dwProtect specifies the mapped file access with the following flags. Additional flags are allowed for specialized purposes. For example, the SEC_IMAGE flag specifies an executable image; see the MSDN documentation for more information.

- PAGE_READONLY means that the program can only read the pages in the mapped region; it can neither write nor execute them. hFile must have GENERIC_READ access.

- PAGE_READWRITE gives full access to the object if hFile has both GENERIC_READ and GENERIC_WRITE access.

- PAGE_WRITECOPY means that when mapped memory is changed, a private (to the process) copy is written to the paging file and not to the original file. A debugger might use this flag when setting breakpoints in shared code.

`dwMaximumSizeHigh` and `dwMaximumSizeLow` specify the size of the mapping object. If they are both 0, the current file size is used; be sure to specify these two size values when using the paging file.

- If the file is expected to grow, use a size equal to the expected file size, and, if necessary, the file size will be set to that size immediately.

- Do not map to a file region beyond this specified size; the mapping object cannot grow.

- An attempt to create a mapping on a zero-length file will fail.

- Unfortunately, you need to specify the mapping size with two 32-bit integers. There is no way to use a single 64-bit integer.

`lpMapName` names the mapping object, allowing other processes to share the object; the name is case-sensitive. Use `NULL` if you are not sharing memory.

An error is indicated by a return value of `NULL` (not `INVALID_HANDLE_VALUE`).

Opening an Existing File Mapping

You can obtain a file mapping handle for an existing, named mapping by specifying the existing mapping object's name. The name comes from a previous call to `CreateFileMapping`. Two processes can share memory by sharing a file mapping. The first process creates the named mapping, and subsequent processes open this mapping with the name. The open will fail if the named object does not exist.

```
HANDLE OpenFileMapping (
    DWORD dwDesiredAccess,
    BOOL bInheritHandle,
    LPCTSTR lpMapName)

Return: A file mapping handle, or NULL on failure.
```

`dwDesiredAccess` is checked against the access to the named object created with `CreateFileMapping`; see the upcoming `MapViewOfFile` description for the possible values. `lpMapName` is the name created by a `CreateFileMapping` call. Handle inheritance (`bInheritHandle`) is a subject for Chapter 6.

The `CloseHandle` function, as expected, destroys mapping handles.

Mapping Objects to Process Address Space

The next step is to map a file into the process's virtual address space. From the programmer's perspective, this allocation is similar to `HeapAlloc`, although it is much coarser, with larger allocation units. A pointer to the allocated block (or file *view*) is returned; the difference lies in the fact that the allocated block is backed by a user-specified file rather than the paging file. The file mapping object plays the same role played by the heap when `HeapAlloc` is used.

```
LPVOID MapViewOfFile (
    HANDLE hMapObject,
    DWORD dwAccess,
    DWORD dwOffsetHigh,
    DWORD dwOffsetLow,
    SIZE_T cbMap)
```

Return: The starting address of the block (file view), or NULL on failure.

Parameters

`hMapObject` identifies a file mapping object obtained from either `CreateFile-Mapping` or `OpenFileMapping`.

   `dwAccess` must be compatible with the mapping object's access. The three flag values we'll use are `FILE_MAP_WRITE`, `FILE_MAP_READ`, and `FILE_MAP-_ALL_ACCESS`. (This is the bit-wise "or" of the previous two flags.) See MSDN for the other two flag values, `FILE_MAP_COPY` and `FILE_MAP_EXECUTE`.

   `dwOffsetHigh` and `dwOffsetLow` specify the starting location of the mapped file region. The start address must be a multiple of the allocation granularity (normally 64K; use `GetSystemInfo()` to get the actual value). Use a zero offset to map from the beginning of the file.

   `cbMap` is the size, in bytes, of the mapped region. Zero indicates the entire file at the time of the `MapViewOfFile` call.

   `MapViewOfFileEx` is similar except that you can specify the starting memory address in an additional parameter. Windows fails if the process has already mapped the requested space. See MSDN for more explanation.

Closing the Mapping Handle

You can elect to close the mapping handle returned by `CreateFileMapping` as soon as `MapViewOfFile` succeeds if you do not need to use the mapping handle again to create other views on the file mapping. Many programmers prefer to do this so as to free resources as soon as possible, and there is the benefit that you do not need to maintain the mapping handle value. However, the example programs and Figure 5–2 do not close the mapping handle until all views are unmapped.

Just as it is necessary to release memory allocated in a heap with `HeapFree`, it is necessary to release file views.

```
BOOL UnmapViewOfFile (LPVOID lpBaseAddress)
```

Figure 5–3 shows the relationship between process address space and a mapped file.

`FlushViewOfFile` forces the system to write "dirty" (changed) pages to disk. Normally, a process accessing a file through mapping and another process accessing it through conventional file I/O will not have coherent views of the file. Performing the file I/O without buffering will not help because the mapped memory will not be written to the file immediately.

Therefore, it is not a good idea to access a mapped file with `ReadFile` and `WriteFile`; coherency is not ensured. On the other hand, processes that share a file through shared memory will have a coherent view of the file. If one process changes a mapped memory location, the other process will obtain that new value when it accesses the corresponding area of the file in its mapped memory. This mechanism is il-

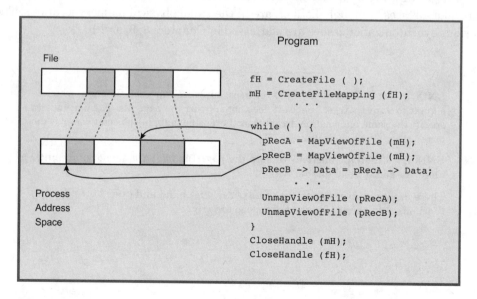

Figure 5–3 A File Mapped into Process Address Space

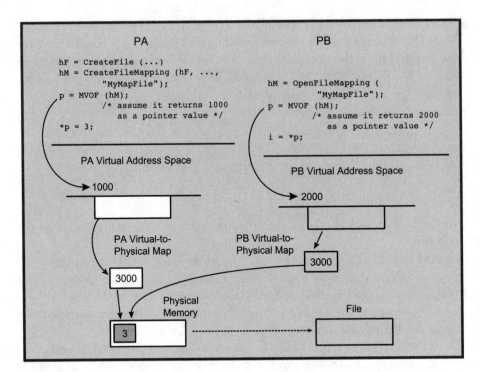

Figure 5–4   Shared Memory

lustrated in Figure 5–4, and the two views are coherent because both processes' virtual addresses, although distinct, are in the same physical memory locations. The obvious synchronization issues are addressed in Chapters 8, 9, and 10.[5]

UNIX, at the SVR4 and 4.3+BSD releases, supports the mmap function, which is similar to MapViewOfFile, but it does not support the page file. The parameters specify the same information except that there is no mapping object. munmap is the UnmapViewOfFile equivalent.

UNIX has different functions to map the page file to share memory: shmget, shmctl, shmat, and shmdt.

There are no equivalents to the CreateFileMapping and OpenFileMapping functions. Any normal file can be mapped directly.

---

[5] Statements regarding coherency of mapped views do not apply to network files. The files must be local.

File Mapping Limitations

File mapping, as mentioned previously, is a powerful and useful feature. The disparity between Win32's 64-bit file system and Win32's 32-bit addressing limits these benefits; Win64 does not have these limitations.

The principal Win32 problem is that if the file is large (greater than 2–3GB in this case), it is not possible to map the entire file into virtual memory space. Furthermore, the entire 3GB will not be available because virtual address space will be allocated for other purposes and available contiguous blocks will be much smaller than the theoretical maximum. Win64 removes this limitation.

When you're dealing with large files that cannot be mapped to one view in Win32, create code that carefully maps and unmaps file regions as they are needed. This technique can be as complex as managing memory buffers, although it is not necessary to perform the explicit reads and writes.

File mapping has two other notable limitations in both Win32 and Win64.

- An existing file mapping cannot be expanded. You need to know the maximum size when creating the file mapping, and it may be difficult or impossible to determine this size.

- There is no way to allocate memory within a mapped memory region without creating your own memory management functions. It would be convenient if there were a way to specify a file mapping and a pointer returned by `MapViewOfFile` and obtain a heap handle.

Summary: File Mapping

Here is the standard sequence required by file mapping.

1. Open the file. Be certain that it has at least `GENERIC_READ` access.

2. If the file is new, set its length either with `CreateFileMapping` (step 3) or by using `SetFilePointerEx` followed by `SetEndOfFile`.

3. Map the file with `CreateFileMapping` or `OpenFileMapping`.

4. Create one or more views with `MapViewOfFile`.

5. Access the file through memory references. If necessary, change the mapped regions with `UnmapViewOfFile` and `MapViewOfFile`. Use SEH to protect against `EXCEPTION_IN_PAGE_ERROR` exceptions.

6. On completion, perform, in order, `UnmapViewOfFile`, `CloseHandle` for the mapping handle, and `CloseHandle` for the file handle.

Example: Sequential File Processing with Mapped Files

`cci` (Program 2–3) illustrates sequential file processing by encrypting files. This is an ideal application for memory-mapped files because the most natural way to convert the data is to process it one character at a time without being concerned with file I/O. Program 5–3 simply maps the input file and the output file and converts the characters one at a time.

This example clearly illustrates the trade-off between the file mapping complexity required to initialize the program and the resulting processing simplicity. This complexity may not seem worthwhile given the simplicity of a simple file I/O implementation, but there is a significant performance advantage. Appendix C and the *Examples* file contain additional performance comparisons and examples; the highlights are summarized here.

- Compared with the best sequential file processing techniques, the performance improvements can be 3:1 or greater.

- You can gain similar advantages with random access; the *Examples* file contains a memory-mapped version (`RecordAccessMM`) of Chapter 3's `RecordAccess` (Program 3–1) example so that you can compare the performance of two solutions to the same problem. A batch file, `RecordAccessTIME.bat`, exercises the two programs with large data sets; Appendix C has results on several computers.[6]

- The performance advantage can disappear for larger files. In this example, on Win32 systems, as the input file size approaches about one half of the physical memory size, normal sequential scanning is preferable. The mapping performance degrades at this point because the input file fills one half of the memory, and the output file, which is twice as long, fills the other half, forcing parts of the output files to be flushed to disk. Thus, on a 1.5GB RAM computer, mapping performance degenerates for input files longer than about 700MB. Many file processing applications deal with smaller files and can take advantage of file mapping.

- Memory mapping performs well with multithreaded programs (Chapter 7). An additional *Examples* file project, `wcMT`, implements a multithreaded "word count" program using memory mapping, and you can compare its performance to the file access version, `wc`.

- `cci_fMM` (Program 5–3) will work with files larger than 4GB but only on a Win64 system.

---

[6] Memory management is a good strategy for record access in *many,* but not all, situations. For example, if records are as large as or larger than the page size, you may not get any benefit and may even decrease performance compared to normal file access.

Program 5–3 shows only the function, cci_fMM, without SEH (see the *Examples* file). The main program is the same as for Program 2–3. Run 5–3 shows the results, comparing the output and timing with cci, which uses normal file access.

Program 5–3 cci_fMM: File Conversion with Memory Mapping

```
/* Chapter 5. cci_fMM.c: Memory-mapped implementation. */

#include "Everything.h"
BOOL cci_f (LPCTSTR fIn, LPCTSTR fOut, DWORD shift)
/* Caesar cipher function.
 * fIn:   Source file pathname.
 * fOut:  Destination file pathname.
 * shift: Numberic shift value. */
{
    BOOL complete = FALSE;
    __try {
        HANDLE hIn, hOut;
        HANDLE hInMap, hOutMap;
        LPTSTR pIn, pInFile, pOut, pOutFile;
        LARGE_INTEGER fileSize;

        /* Open the input file. */
        hIn = CreateFile (fIn, GENERIC_READ, 0, NULL,
            OPEN_EXISTING, FILE_ATTRIBUTE_NORMAL, NULL);

        /* Get the input file size. */
        GetFileSizeEx (hIn, &fileSize);
        if (fileSize.HighPart > 0 && sizeof(SIZE_T) == 4)
            ReportException (_T ("File is too large for Win32."), 4);

        /* Create a file mapping object on the entire input file. */
        hInMap = CreateFileMapping (hIn, NULL, PAGE_READONLY,
                0, 0, NULL);
        /* Map the input file */
        pInFile = MapViewOfFile (hInMap, FILE_MAP_READ, 0, 0, 0);

        /*  Create/Open the output file. */
        /* The output file MUST have Read/Write access. */
        hOut = CreateFile (fOut, GENERIC_READ | GENERIC_WRITE,
            0, NULL, CREATE_ALWAYS, FILE_ATTRIBUTE_NORMAL, NULL);

        /* Map the output file. CreateFileMapping will expand
           the file if it is smaller than the mapping. */

        hOutMap = CreateFileMapping (hOut, NULL, PAGE_READWRITE,
                fileSize.HighPart, fileSize.LowPart, NULL);
        pOutFile = MapViewOfFile (hOutMap, FILE_MAP_WRITE, 0, 0,
                (SIZE_T)fileSize.QuadPart);
```

```
/* Move input file to output file, doing the work in memory. */
__try
{
    pIn = pInFile;
    pOut = pOutFile;
    while (pIn < pInFile + fileSize.QuadPart) {
        *pOut = (*pIn + shift) % 256;
        pIn++; pOut++;
    }
    complete = TRUE;
}
__except(GetExceptionCode() == EXCEPTION_IN_PAGE_ERROR ?
        EXCEPTION_EXECUTE_HANDLER : EXCEPTION_CONTINUE_SEARCH)
{
    complete = FALSE;
    ReportError(_T("Fatal Error accessing mapped file."),
        9, TRUE);
}

/* Close all views and handles. */
UnmapViewOfFile (pOutFile); UnmapViewOfFile (pInFile);
CloseHandle (hOutMap); CloseHandle (hInMap);
CloseHandle (hIn); CloseHandle (hOut);
return complete;
}

__except (EXCEPTION_EXECUTE_HANDLER) {
    /* Delete output file if the operation not successful. */
    if (!complete)
        DeleteFile (fOut);
    return FALSE;
}
}
```

Example: Sorting a Memory-Mapped File

Another advantage of memory mapping is the ability to use convenient memory-based algorithms to process files. Sorting data in memory, for instance, is much easier than sorting records in a file.

Program 5–4 sorts a file with fixed-length records. This program, called sortFL, is similar to Program 5–1 in that it assumes an 8-byte sort key at the start of the record, but it is restricted to fixed records.

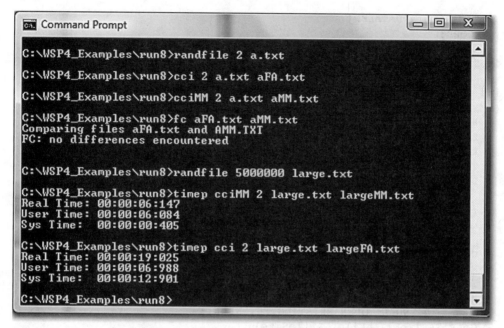

Run 5–3 cciMM: File Conversion with Memory-Mapped Files

The sorting is performed by the <stdlib.h> C library function qsort. Notice that qsort requires a programmer-defined record comparison function, which is the same as the KeyCompare function in Program 5–2.

This program structure is straightforward. Simply create the file mapping on a temporary copy of the input file, create a single view of the file, and invoke qsort. There is no file I/O. Then the sorted file is sent to standard output using _tprintf, although a null character is appended to the file map.

Exception and error handling are omitted in the listing but are in the *Examples* solution on the book's Web site.

Run 5–4 shows the same operations as Run 5–2 for sortBT. sortFL is much faster, requiring about 3 seconds to sort a 1,000,000 record file, rather than over 2 minutes.

Program 5–4 sortFL: Sorting a File with Memory Mapping

```
/* Chapter 5. sortFL. File sorting. Fixed-length records. */
/* Usage: sortFL file */

#include "Everything.h"
typedef struct _RECORD {
   TCHAR key[KEY_SIZE];
```

```
    TCHAR data[DATALEN];
} RECORD;

#define RECSIZE sizeof (RECORD)

int _tmain (int argc, LPTSTR argv[])
{
    HANDLE hFile = INVALID_HANDLE_VALUE, hMap = NULL;
    LPVOID pFile = NULL;
    LARGE_INTEGER fileSize;
    TCHAR tempFile[MAX_PATH];
    LPTSTR pTFile;

    /* Create the name for a temporary file to hold a copy of
       the file to be sorted. Sorting is done in the temp file. */
    _stprintf (tempFile, _T ("%s.tmp"), argv[1]);
    CopyFile (argv[1], tempFile, TRUE);

    /* Map the temporary file and sort it in memory. */
    hFile = CreateFile (tempFile, GENERIC_READ | GENERIC_WRITE,
            0, NULL, OPEN_EXISTING, 0, NULL);
    GetFileSizeEx (hFile, &fileSize);
    fileSize.QuadPart += 2;
    hMap = CreateFileMapping (hFile, NULL, PAGE_READWRITE,
            fileSize.HighPart, fileSize.LowPart, NULL);
    pFile = MapViewOfFile (hMap, FILE_MAP_ALL_ACCESS, 0, 0, 0);

    qsort (pFile, FsLow / RECSIZE, RECSIZE, KeyCompare);
                            /* KeyCompare is as in Program 5-2. */

    /* Print the sorted file. */
    pTFile = (LPTSTR) pFile;
    pTFile[fileSize.QuadPart/TSIZE] = '\0';
    _tprintf (_T ("%s"), pFile);
    UnmapViewOfFile (pFile);
    CloseHandle (hMap);
    CloseHandle (hFile);
    DeleteFile (tempFile);
    return 0;
}
```

This implementation is straightforward, but there is an alternative that does not require mapping. Just allocate memory, read the complete file, sort it in memory, and write it. Such a solution, included in the *Examples* file, would be as effective as Program 5–4 and is often faster, as shown in Appendix C.

```
C:\WSP4_Examples\run8>randfile 4 small.txt

C:\WSP4_Examples\run8>cat small.txt
FileName small.txt
2a35c1e9. Record Number: 00000000.abcdefghijklmnopqrstuvwxyz x
7d2ebe6e. Record Number: 00000001.abcdefghijklmnopqrstuvwxyz x
c200c90f. Record Number: 00000002.abcdefghijklmnopqrstuvwxyz x
28325d9c. Record Number: 00000003.abcdefghijklmnopqrstuvwxyz x

C:\WSP4_Examples\run8>sortFL small.txt
28325d9c. Record Number: 00000003.abcdefghijklmnopqrstuvwxyz x
2a35c1e9. Record Number: 00000000.abcdefghijklmnopqrstuvwxyz x
7d2ebe6e. Record Number: 00000001.abcdefghijklmnopqrstuvwxyz x
c200c90f. Record Number: 00000002.abcdefghijklmnopqrstuvwxyz x

C:\WSP4_Examples\run8>randfile 1000000 large.txt

C:\WSP4_Examples\run8>timep sortFL -n large.txt
Real Time: 00:00:03:123
User Time: 00:00:02:776
Sys Time:  00:00:00:265

C:\WSP4_Examples\run8>_
```

Run 5–4   `sortFL`: Sorting in Memory with File Mapping

Based Pointers

File maps are convenient, as the preceding examples demonstrate. Suppose, however, that the program creates a data structure with pointers in a mapped file and expects to access that file in the future. Pointers will all be relative to the virtual address returned from `MapViewOfFile`, and they will be meaningless when mapping the file the next time. The solution is to use based pointers, which are actually offsets relative to another pointer. The Microsoft C syntax, available in Visual C++ and some other systems, is:

```
type __based (base) declarator
```

Here are two examples.

```
LPTSTR pInFile = NULL;
DWORD __based (pInFile) *pSize;
TCHAR __based (pInFile) *pIn;
```

Notice that the syntax forces use of the *, a practice that is contrary to Windows convention but which the programmer could easily fix with a *typedef*.

Example: Using Based Pointers

Previous programs have shown how to sort files in various situations. The object, of course, is to illustrate different ways to manage memory, not to discuss sorting algorithms. Program 5–1 uses a binary search tree that is destroyed after each sort, and Program 5–4 sorts an array of fixed-size records in mapped memory.

Suppose you need to maintain a permanent index file representing the sorted keys of the original file. The apparent solution is to map a file that contains the permanent index in a search tree or sorted key form to memory. Unfortunately, there is a major difficulty with this solution. All pointers in the tree, as stored in the file, are relative to the address returned by `MapViewOfFile`. The next time the program runs and maps the file, the pointers will be useless.

Program 5–5, together with Program 5–6, solves this problem, which is characteristic of any mapped data structure that uses pointers. The solution uses the __based keyword available with Microsoft C. An alternative is to map the file to an array and use indexing to access records in the mapped files.

The program is written as yet another version of the `sort` command, this time called `sortMM`. There are enough new features, however, to make it interesting.

- The records are of varying lengths.

- The program uses the first field of each record as a key of 8 characters.

- There are two file mappings. One mapping is for the original file, and the other is for the file containing the sorted keys. The second file is the *index file*, and each of its records contains a key and a pointer (base address) in the original file. `qsort` sorts the key file, much as in Program 5–4.

- The index file is saved and can be used later, and there is an option (`-I`) that bypasses the sort and uses an existing index file. The index file can also be used to perform a fast key file search with a binary search (using, perhaps, the C library `bsearch` function) on the index file.

- The input file itself is not changed; the index file is the result. `sortMM` does, however, display the sorted result, or you can use the `-n` option to suppress printing and then use the `-I` option with an index file created on a previous run.

Figure 5–5 shows the relationship of the index file to the file to be sorted. Program 5–5, `sortMM`, is the main program that sets up the file mapping, sorts the index file, and displays the results. It calls a function, `CreateIndexFile`, shown in Program 5–6.

Run 5–6, after the program listings, shows `sortMM` operation, and the timing can be compared to Run 5–4 for `sortFL`; `sortFL` is much faster, as creating the sorted index file requires numerous references to scattered locations in the

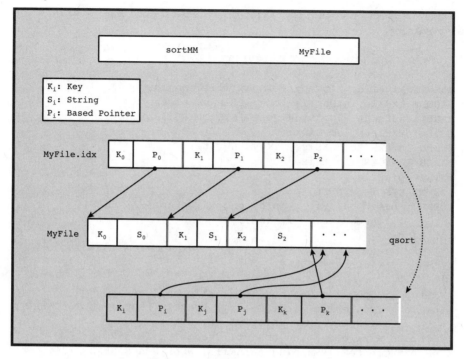

Figure 5–5 Sorting with a Memory-Mapped Index File

mapped data file. However, once the index file is created, the -I option allows you to access the sorted data very quickly.

Caution: These two programs make some implicit assumptions, which we'll review after the program listings and the run screenshot.

Program 5–5 sortMM: Based Pointers in an Index File

```
/* Chapter 5, sortMM command. Memory-Mapped version */

/*   sortMM [options] [file]
     Options:
     -r Sort in reverse order - tested in KeyCompare (not shown here)
     -I Use an existing index file to produce the sorted file.

     This limited implementation sorts on the first field only.
     The key field is 8 characters, starting at record position 0. */

#include "Everything.h"

int KeyCompare (LPCTSTR, LPCTSTR);
VOID CreateIndexFile (LARGE_INSTEGER, LPCTSTR, LPTSTR);
```

```
DWORD_PTR kStart = 0, kSize = 8; /* Key start position & size */
BOOL reverse;

int _tmain (int argc, LPTSTR argv[])
{
    HANDLE hInFile, hInMap;/* Input file handles. */
    HANDLE hXFile, hXMap;/* Index file handles. */
    HANDLE hStdOut = GetStdHandle (STD_OUTPUT_HANDLE);
    BOOL idxExists, noPrint;
    DWORD indexSize, rXSize, iKey, nWrite;
    LARGE_INTEGER inputSize;
    LPTSTR pInFile = NULL;
    LPBYTE pXFile = NULL, pX;
    TCHAR __based (pInFile) *pIn, indexFileName[MAX_PATH],
            ChNewLine = _T('\n');
    int FlIdx =
        Options (argc, argv, _T ("rIn"), &reverse, &idxExists,
            &noPrint, NULL);

    /* Step 1: Open and Map the Input File. */
    hInFile = CreateFile (argv[FlIdx], GENERIC_READ | GENERIC_WRITE,
            0, NULL, OPEN_EXISTING, 0, NULL);
    /* Create a file mapping object. Use the file size. */
    hInMap = CreateFileMapping (hInFile, NULL, PAGE_READWRITE,
            0, 0, NULL);
    pInFile = MapViewOfFile (hInMap, FILE_MAP_ALL_ACCESS, 0, 0, 0);
    if (!GetFileSizeEx (hInFile, &inputSize))
        ReportError (_T("Failed to get input file size."), 5, TRUE);

    /* Steps 2 and 3. Create the index file if necessary. */
    _stprintf (indexFileName, _T ("%s.idx"), argv[FlIdx]);
    if (!idxExists)
        CreateIndexFile (inputSize, indexFileName, pInFile);

    /* Step 4. Map the index file. */
    hXFile = CreateFile (indexFileName, GENERIC_READ | GENERIC_WRITE,
            0, NULL, OPEN_EXISTING, 0, NULL);
    /* Create a file mapping object. Use the index file size. */
    hXMap = CreateFileMapping (hXFile, NULL, PAGE_READWRITE,
            0, 0, NULL);
    pXFile = MapViewOfFile (hXMap, FILE_MAP_ALL_ACCESS, 0, 0, 0);
    indexSize = GetFileSize (hXFile, NULL); /* idx file isn't huge */
    /* Individual index record size - Key plus a pointer. */
    rXSize = kSize * TSIZE + sizeof (LPTSTR);

    /* Step 5. Sort the index file using qsort. */
    if (!idxExists)
        /* KeyCompare uses the global variables kSize and kStart. */
        qsort (pXFile, indexSize / rXSize, rXSize, KeyCompare);
```

```
/* Step 6. Output the sorted input file. */
/* Point to the first pointer in the index file. */
pX = pXFile + rXSize - sizeof (LPTSTR);
if (!noPrint) {
    for (iKey = 0; iKey < indexSize / rXSize; iKey++) {
        WriteFile (hStdOut, &ChNewLine, TSIZE, &nWrite, NULL);
        /* The cast on pX is important, as it is a pointer to a
           character and we need the 4 or 8-byte based pointer. */
        pIn = (TCHAR __based (pInFile)*) *(DWORD *)pX;
        while ((SIZE_T) pIn < inputSize.QuadPart &&
               (*pIn != CR || *(pIn + 1) != LF)) {
            WriteFile (hStdOut, pIn, TSIZE, &nWrite, NULL);
            pIn++;
        }
        pX += rXSize; /* Advance to the next index file pointer */
    }

    /* Done. Free all the handles and maps. */
    UnmapViewOfFile (pInFile);
    CloseHandle (hInMap); CloseHandle (hInFile);
    UnmapViewOfFile (pXFile);
    CloseHandle (hXMap); CloseHandle (hXFile);
    return 0;
    }
}
```

Program 5–6 is the `CreateIndexFile` function, which creates the index file. It scans the input file to find the bound of each varying-length record to set up the structure shown in Figure 5–5.

Program 5–6 sortMM: Creating the Index File

```
VOID CreateIndexFile (LARGE_INTEGER inputSize, LPCTSTR indexFileName,
                LPTSTR pInFile)
{
    HANDLE hXFile;
    TCHAR __based (pInFile) *pInScan = 0;
    DWORD nWrite;

    /* Step 2: Create an index file.
       Do not map it yet as its length is unknown. */
    hXFile = CreateFile (indexFileName, GENERIC_READ | GENERIC_WRITE,
        FILE_SHARE_READ, NULL, CREATE_ALWAYS, 0, NULL);

    /* Step 3. Scan the complete file, writing keys
       and record pointers to the key file. */
    while ((DWORD_PTR) pInScan < inputSize.QuadPart) {
```

```
        WriteFile (hXFile, pInScan + kStart, kSize * TSIZE,
            &nWrite, NULL);
        WriteFile (hXFile, &pInScan, sizeof (LPTSTR), &nWrite, NULL);
        while ((DWORD) (DWORD_PTR)pInScan <
                inputSize.QuadPart - sizeof(TCHAR) &&
                ((*pInScan != CR)|| (*(pInScan + 1) != LF))) {
            pInScan++; /* Skip to end of line. */
        }
        pInScan += 2; /* Skip past CR, LF. */
    }
    CloseHandle (hXFile);
    return;
}
```

Run 5–6   sortMM: Sorting Using Based Pointers and Mapping

A Comment about Alignment

`sortMM` illustrates based pointers in mapped files. The program also allows for different key length and key start positions, which Program 5–5 sets to 8 and 0, respectively. However, the index file has the pointer directly after the key, so these values should be a multiple of the pointer size (4 or 8) to avoid possible alignment exceptions. An exercise asks you to overcome this limitation.

We're also assuming implicitly that page sizes and `MapViewOfFile` return values are multiples of pointer, `DWORD`, and other object sizes.

Dynamic Link Libraries

We have now seen that memory management and file mapping are important and useful techniques in a wide class of programs. The OS itself also uses memory management, and DLLs are the most visible and important use because Windows applications use DLLs extensively. DLLs are also essential to higher-level technologies, such as COM, and many software components are provided as DLLs.

The first step is to consider the different methods of constructing libraries of commonly used functions.

Static and Dynamic Libraries

The most direct way to construct a program is to gather the source code of all the functions, compile them, and link everything into a single executable image. Common functions, such as `ReportError`, can be put into a library to simplify the build process. This technique was used with all the sample programs presented so far, although there were only a few functions, most of them for error reporting.

This monolithic, single-image model is simple, but it has several disadvantages.

- The executable image may be large, consuming disk space and physical memory at run time and requiring extra effort to manage and deliver to users.

- Each program update requires a rebuild of the complete program even if the changes are small or localized.

- Every program in the computer that uses the functions will have a copy of the functions, possibly different versions, in its executable image. This arrangement increases disk space usage and, perhaps more important, physical memory usage when several such programs are running concurrently.

- Distinct versions of the program, using different techniques, might be required to get the best performance in different environments. For example, the `cci_f` function is implemented differently in Program 2–3 (`cci`) and Program 5–3 (`cci_fMM`). The only method of executing different implementations is to decide which of the two versions to run based on environmental factors.

DLLs solve these and other problems quite neatly.

- Library functions are not linked at build time. Rather, they are linked at program load time *(implicit linking)* or at run time *(explicit linking)*. As a result, the program image can be much smaller because it does not include the library functions.

- DLLs can be used to create *shared libraries*. Multiple programs share a single library in the form of a DLL, and only a single copy is loaded into memory. All programs map the DLL code to their process address space, although each process has a distinct copy of the DLL's global variables. For example, the `Re-portError` function was used by nearly every example program; a single DLL implementation could be shared by all the programs.

- New versions or alternative implementations can be supported simply by supplying a new version of the DLL, and all programs that use the library can use the new version without modification.

- The library will run in the same processes as the calling program.

DLLs, sometimes in limited form, are used in nearly every OS. For example, UNIX uses the term "shared libraries" for the same concept. Windows uses DLLs to implement the OS interfaces, among other things. The entire Windows API is supported by a DLL that invokes the Windows kernel for additional services.

Multiple Windows processes can share DLL code, but the code, when called, runs as part of the calling process and thread. Therefore, the library will be able to use the resources of the calling process, such as file handles, and will use the calling thread's stack. DLLs should therefore be written to be thread-safe. (See Chapters 8, 9, and 10 for more information on thread safety and DLLs. Programs 12–5 and 12–6 illustrate techniques for creating thread-safe DLLs.) A DLL can also export variables as well as function entry points.

Implicit Linking

Implicit or *load-time* linking is the easier of the two techniques. The required steps, using Microsoft Visual C++, are as follows.

1. The functions in a new DLL are collected and built as a DLL rather than, for example, a console application.

2. The build process constructs a .LIB library file, which is a *stub* for the actual code and is linked into the calling program at build time, satisfying the function references. The .LIB file contains code that loads the DLL at program load time. It also contains a stub for each function, where the stub calls the DLL. This file should be placed in a common user library directory specified to the project.

3. The build process also constructs a .DLL file that contains the executable image. This file is typically placed in the same directory as the application that will use it, and the application loads the DLL during its initialization. The alternative search locations are described in the next section.

4. Take care to export the function interfaces in the DLL source, as described next.

Exporting and Importing Interfaces

The most significant change required to put a function into a DLL is to declare it to be exportable (UNIX and some other systems do not require this explicit step). This is achieved either by using a .DEF file or, more simply, with Microsoft C/C++, by using the __declspec (dllexport) storage modifier as follows:

```
__declspec (dllexport) DWORD MyFunction (...);
```

The build process will then create a .DLL file and a .LIB file. The .LIB file is the stub library that should be linked with the calling program to satisfy the external references and to create the actual links to the .DLL file at load time.

The calling or *client* program should declare that the function is to be imported by using the __declspec (dllimport) storage modifier. A standard technique is to write the include file by using a preprocessor variable created by appending the Microsoft Visual C++ project name, in uppercase letters, with _EXPORTS.

One further definition is necessary. If the calling (importing) client program is written in C++, __cplusplus is defined, and it is necessary to specify the C calling convention, using:

```
extern "C"
```

For example, if MyFunction is defined as part of a DLL build in project MyLibrary, the header file would contain:

```
#if defined(MYLIBRARY_EXPORTS)
#define LIBSPEC __declspec (dllexport)
#elif defined(__cplusplus)
#define LIBSPEC extern "C" __declspec (dllimport)
```

```
#else
#define LIBSPEC __declspec (dllimport)
#endif
LIBSPEC DWORD MyFunction (...);
```

Visual C/C++ automatically defines `MYLIBRARY_EXPORTS` when invoking the compiler within the `MyLibrary` DLL project. A client project that uses the DLL does not define `MYLIBRARY_EXPORTS`, so the function name is imported from the library.

When building the calling program, specify the `.LIB` file. When executing the calling program, ensure that the `.DLL` file is available to the calling program; this is frequently done by placing the `.DLL` file in the same directory as the executable. As mentioned previously, there is a set of DLL search rules that specify the order in which Windows searches for the specified `.DLL` file *as well as* for all other DLLs or executables that the specified file requires, stopping with the first instance located. The following default *safe DLL search mode* order is used for both explicit and implicit linking:

- The directory containing the loaded application.

- The system directory. You can determine this path with `GetSystem-Directory`; normally its value is `C:\WINDOWS\SYSTEM32`.

- The 16-bit Windows system directory. There is no function to obtain this path, and it is obsolete for our purposes.

- The Windows directory (`GetWindowsDirectory`).

- The current directory.

- Directories specified by the `PATH` environment variable, in the order in which they occur.

Note that the standard order can be modified, as explained in the "Explicit Linking" section. For some additional detailed information on the search strategy, see MSDN and the `SetDllDirectory` function. `LoadLibraryEx`, described in the next section, also alters the search strategy.

You can also export and import variables as well as function entry points, although the examples do not illustrate this capability.

Explicit Linking

Explicit or *run-time* linking requires the program to request specifically that a DLL be loaded or freed. Next, the program obtains the address of the required entry point and uses that address as the pointer in the function call. The function is not declared in the calling program; rather, you declare a variable as a pointer to a function. Therefore, there is no need for a library at link time. The three required functions are LoadLibrary (or LoadLibraryEx), GetProcAddress, and FreeLibrary. *Note:* The function definitions show their 16-bit legacy through far pointers and different handle types.

The two functions to load a library are LoadLibrary and LoadLibraryEx.

```
HMODULE LoadLibrary (LPCTSTR lpLibFileName)
```

```
HMODULE LoadLibraryEx (
    LPCTSTR lpLibFileName,
    HANDLE hFile,
    DWORD dwFlags)
```

In both cases, the returned handle (HMODULE rather than HANDLE; you may see the equivalent macro, HINSTANCE) will be NULL on failure. The .DLL suffix is not required on the file name. .EXE files can also be loaded with the Load-Library functions. Pathnames must use backslashes (\); forward slashes (/) will not work. The name is the one in the .DEF module definition file (see MSDN for details).

Note: If you are using C++ and __dllexport, the decorated name is exported, and the decorated name is required for GetProcAddress. Our examples avoid this difficult problem by using C.

Since DLLs are shared, the system maintains a reference count to each DLL (incremented by the two load functions) so that the actual file does not need to be remapped. Even if the DLL file is found, LoadLibrary will fail if the DLL is implicitly linked to other DLLs that cannot be located.

LoadLibraryEx is similar to LoadLibrary but has several flags that are useful for specifying alternative search paths and loading the library as a data file. The hFile parameter is reserved for future use. dwFlags can specify alternate behavior with one of three values.

1. LOAD_WITH_ALTERED_SEARCH_PATH overrides the previously described standard search order, changing just the first step of the search strategy. The pathname specified as part of lpLibFileName is used rather than the directory from which the application was loaded.

2. LOAD_LIBRARY_AS_DATAFILE allows the file to be data only, and there is no preparation for execution, such as calling DllMain (see the "DLL Entry Point" section later in the chapter).

3. DONT_RESOLVE_DLL_REFERENCE means that DllMain is not called for process and thread initialization, and additional modules referenced within the DLL are not loaded.

When you're finished with a DLL instance, possibly to load a different version of the DLL, free the library handle, thereby freeing the resources, including virtual address space, allocated to the library. The DLL will, however, remain loaded if the reference count indicates that other processes are still using it.

```
BOOL FreeLibrary (HMODULE hLibModule)
```

After loading a library and before freeing it, you can obtain the address of any entry point using GetProcAddress.

```
FARPROC GetProcAddress (
    HMODULE hModule,
    LPCSTR lpProcName)
```

hModule is an instance produced by LoadLibrary or GetModuleHandle (see the next paragraph). lpProcName, which cannot be Unicode, is the entry point name. The return result is NULL in case of failure. FARPROC, like "long pointer," is an anachronism.

You can obtain the file name associated with an hModule handle using Get-ModuleFileName. Conversely, given a file name (either a .DLL or .EXE file), GetModuleHandle will return the handle, if any, associated with this file if the current process has loaded it.

The next example shows how to use the entry point address to invoke a function.

Example: Explicitly Linking a File Conversion Function

Program 2–3 is an encryption conversion program that calls the function cci_f (Program 2–5) to process the file using file I/O. Program 5–3 (cciMM) is an alternative function that uses memory mapping to perform exactly the same operation. The circumstances under which cciMM is faster were described earlier. Furthermore, if you are running on a 32-bit computer, you will not be able to map files larger than about 1.5GB.

Program 5–7 reimplements the calling program so that it can decide which implementation to load at run time. It then loads the DLL and obtains the address of the cci_f entry point and calls the function. There is only one entry point in this case, but it would be equally easy to locate multiple entry points. The main program is as before, except that the DLL to use is a command line parameter. Exercise 5–10 suggests that the DLL should be determined on the basis of system and file characteristics. Also notice how the **FARPROC** address is cast to the appropriate function type using the required, but complex, C syntax. The cast even includes __cdecl, the linkage type, which is also used by the DLL function. Therefore, there are no assumptions about the build settings for the calling program ("client") and called function ("server").

Program 5–7 cciEL: File Conversion with Explicit Linking

```
/* Chapter 5. cci Explicit Link version. */

#include "Everything.h"

int _tmain (int argc, LPTSTR argv[])
{
    BOOL (__cdecl *cci_f) (LPCTSTR, LPCTSTR, DWORD);
    HMODULE hDLL;
    FARPROC pcci;

    /* Load the cipher function. */
    hDLL = LoadLibrary (argv[4]);

    /*  Get the entry point address. */
    pcci = GetProcAddress (hDLL, "cci_f");
    cci_f = (BOOL (__cdecl *)(LPCTSTR, LPCTSTR, DWORD)) pcci;

    /*  Call the function. */
    if (!cci_f (argv[2], argv[3], atoi(argv[1]) ) ) {
        FreeLibrary (hDLL);
        ReportError (_T ("cci failed."), 6, TRUE);
    }
    FreeLibrary (hDLL);
    return 0;
}
```

Building the `cci_f` DLLs

This program was tested with the two file conversion functions, which must be built as DLLs with different names but identical entry points. There is only one entry point in this case. The only significant change in the source code is the addition of a storage modifier, `__declspec (dllexport)`, to export the function.

Run 5–7 shows the results, which are comparable to Run 5–3.

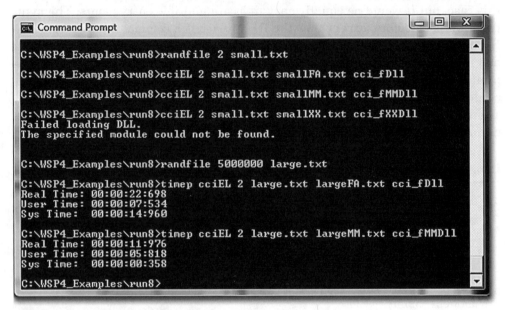

```
Command Prompt                                                    _ □ X

C:\WSP4_Examples\run8>randfile 2 small.txt

C:\WSP4_Examples\run8>cciEL 2 small.txt smallFA.txt cci_fDll

C:\WSP4_Examples\run8>cciEL 2 small.txt smallMM.txt cci_fMMDll

C:\WSP4_Examples\run8>cciEL 2 small.txt smallXX.txt cci_fXXDll
Failed loading DLL.
The specified module could not be found.

C:\WSP4_Examples\run8>randfile 5000000 large.txt

C:\WSP4_Examples\run8>timep cciEL 2 large.txt largeFA.txt cci_fDll
Real Time: 00:00:22:698
User Time: 00:00:07:534
Sys Time:  00:00:14:960

C:\WSP4_Examples\run8>timep cciEL 2 large.txt largeMM.txt cci_fMMDll
Real Time: 00:00:11:976
User Time: 00:00:05:818
Sys Time:  00:00:00:358

C:\WSP4_Examples\run8>
```

Run 5–7   `cciEL`: Explicit Linking to a DLL

The DLL Entry Point

Optionally, you can specify an entry point for every DLL you create, and this entry point is normally invoked automatically every time a process attaches or detaches the DLL. `LoadLibraryEx`, however, allows you to prevent entry point execution. For implicitly linked (load-time) DLLs, process attachment and detachment occur when the process starts and terminates. In the case of explicitly linked DLLs, `LoadLibrary`, `LoadLibraryEx`, and `FreeLibrary` cause the attachment and detachment calls.

The entry point is also invoked when new threads (Chapter 7) are created or terminated by the process.

The DLL entry point, `DllMain`, is introduced here but will not be fully exploited until Chapter 12 (Program 12–5), where it provides a convenient way for threads to manage resources and so-called Thread Local Storage (TLS) in a thread-safe DLL.

```
BOOL DllMain (
    HINSTANCE hDll,
    DWORD Reason,
    LPVOID lpReserved)
```

The `hDll` value corresponds to the instance obtained from `LoadLibrary`. `lpReserved`, if `NULL`, indicates that the process attachment was caused by `LoadLibrary`; otherwise, it was caused by implicit load-time linking. Likewise, `FreeLibrary` gives a `NULL` value for process detachment.

Reason will have one of four values: `DLL_PROCESS_ATTACH`, `DLL_THREAD-_ATTACH`, `DLL_THREAD_DETACH`, and `DLL_PROCESS_DETACH`. DLL entry point functions are normally written as `switch` statements and return `TRUE` to indicate correct operation.

The system serializes calls to `DllMain` so that only one thread at a time can execute it (Chapter 7 introduces threads). This serialization is essential because `DllMain` must perform initializations that must complete without interruption. As a consequence, however, there should not be any blocking calls, such as I/O or wait functions (see Chapter 8), within the entry point, because they would prevent other threads from entering. Furthermore, you cannot call other DLLs from `Dll-Main` (there are a few exceptions, such as `InitializeCriticalSection`).

`LoadLibrary` and `LoadLibraryEx`, in particular, should never be called from a DLL entry point, as that would create additional DLL entry point calls.

An advanced function, `DisableThreadLibraryCalls`, will disable thread attach/detach calls for a specified DLL instance. As a result, Windows does not need to load the DLL's initialization or termination code every time a thread is created or terminates. This can be useful if the DLL is only used by some of the threads.

DLL Version Management

A common problem with DLLs concerns difficulties that occur as a library is upgraded with new symbols and features are added. A major DLL advantage is that multiple applications can share a single implementation. This power, however, leads to compatibility complications, such as the following.

- A new version may change behavior or interfaces, causing problems to existing applications that have not been updated.

- Applications that depend on new DLL functionality sometimes link with older DLL versions.

DLL version compatibility problems, popularly referred to as "DLL hell," can be irreconcilable if only one version of the DLL is to be maintained in a single directory. However, it is not necessarily simple to provide distinct version-specific directories for different versions. There are several solutions.

- Use the DLL version number as part of the .DLL and .LIB file names, usually as a suffix. For example, Utility_4_0.DLL and Utility_4_0.LIB are used in the *Examples* projects to correspond with the book edition number. By using either explicit or implicit linking, applications can then determine their version requirements and access files with distinct names. This solution is commonly used with UNIX applications.

- Microsoft introduced the concept of side-by-side DLLs or assemblies and components. This solution requires adding a manifest, written in XML, to the application so as to define the DLL requirements. This topic is beyond the book's scope, but additional information can be found on the MSDN Web site.

- The .NET Framework provides additional support for side-by-side execution.

The first approach, including the version number as part of the file name, is used in the *Examples* file, as mentioned in the first bullet.

To provide additional support so that applications can determine additional DLL information beyond just the version number, DllGetVersion is a user-provided callback function; many Microsoft DLLs support this callback function as a standard method to obtain version information dynamically. The function operates as follows:

```
HRESULT CALLBACK DllGetVersion(
        DLLVERSIONINFO *pdvi

)
```

- Information about the DLL is returned in the `DLLVERSIONINFO` structure, which contains `DWORD` fields for `cbSize` (the structure size), `dwMajorVersion`, `dwMinorVersion`, `dwBuildNumber`, and `dwPlatformID`.

- The last field, `dwPlatformID`, can be set to `DLLVER_PLATFORM_NT` if the DLL cannot run on Windows 9x (this should no longer be an issue!) or to `DLLVER_PLATFORM_WINDOWS` if there are no restrictions.

- The `cbSize` field should be set to `sizeof(DLLVERSIONINFO)`. The normal return value is `NOERROR`.

- `Utility_4_0` implements `DllGetVersion`.

Summary

Windows memory management includes the following features.

- Logic can be simplified by allowing the Windows heap management and exception handlers to detect and process allocation errors.

- Multiple independent heaps provide several advantages over allocation from a single heap, but there is a cost of extra complexity to assure that blocks are freed, or resized, from the correct heap.

- Memory-mapped files, also available with UNIX but not with the C library, allow files to be processed in memory, as illustrated by several examples. File mapping is independent of heap management, and it can simplify many programming tasks. Appendix C shows the performance advantage of using memory-mapped files.

- DLLs are an essential special case of mapped files, and DLLs can be loaded either explicitly or implicitly. DLLs used by numerous applications should provide version information.

Looking Ahead

This completes coverage of what can be achieved within a single process. The next step is to learn how to manage concurrent processing, first with processes (Chapter 6) and then with threads (Chapter 7). Subsequent chapters show how to synchronize and communicate between concurrent processing activities.

Additional Reading

Memory Mapping, Virtual Memory, and Page Faults

Russinovich, Solomon, and Ionescu (*Windows Internals: Including Windows Server 2008 and Windows Vista, Fifth Edition*) describe the important concepts, and most OS texts provide good in-depth discussion.

Data Structures and Algorithms

Search trees and sort algorithms are explained in numerous texts, including Cormen, Leiserson, Rivest, and Stein's *Introduction to Algorithms*.

Using Explicit Linking

DLLs and explicit linking are fundamental to the operation of COM, which is widely used in Windows software development. Chapter 1 of Don Box's *Essential COM* shows the importance of `LoadLibrary` and `GetProcAddress`.

Exercises

5–1. Design and carry out experiments to evaluate the performance gains from the `HEAP_NO_SERIALIZE` flag with `HeapCreate` and `HeapAlloc`. How are the gains affected by the heap size and by the block size? Are there differences under different Windows versions? The *Examples* file contains a program, `HeapNoSr.c`, to help you get started on this exercise and the next one.

5–2. Modify the test in the preceding exercise to determine whether `malloc` generates exceptions or returns a null pointer when there is no memory. Is this the correct behavior? Also compare `malloc` performance with the results from the preceding exercise.

5–3. Windows versions differ significantly in terms of the overhead memory in a heap. Design and carry out an experiment to measure how many fixed-size blocks each system will give in a single heap. Using SEH to detect when all blocks have been allocated makes the program easier. A test program, `clear.c`, in the *Examples* file will show this behavior.

5–4. Modify `sortFL` (Program 5–4) to create `sortHP`, which allocates a memory buffer large enough to hold the file, and read the file into that buffer. There is no memory mapping. Compare the performance of the two programs.

5–5. Compare random file access performance using conventional file access (Chapter 3's RecordAccess) and memory mapping (RecordAccessMM).

5–6. Program 5–5 exploits the __based pointers that are specific to Microsoft C. If you have a compiler that does not support this feature (or simply for the exercise), reimplement Program 5–5 with a macro, arrays, or some other mechanism to generate the based pointer values.

5–7. Write a search program that will find a record with a specified key in a file that has been indexed by Program 5–5. The C library bsearch function would be convenient here.

5–8. Enhance sortMM (Programs 5–5 and 5–6) to remove all implicit alignment assumptions in the index file. See the comments after the program listings.

5–9. Implement the tail program from Chapter 3 with memory mapping.

5–10. Modify Program 5–7 so that the decision as to which DLL to use is based on the file size and system configuration. The .LIB file is not necessary, so figure out how to suppress .LIB file generation. Use GetVolumeInformation to determine the file system type. Create additional DLLs for the conversion function, each version using a different file processing technique, and extend the calling program to decide when to use each version.

5–11. Put the ReportError, PrintStrings, PrintMsg, and ConsolePrompt utility functions into a DLL and rebuild some of the earlier programs. Do the same with Options and GetArgs, the command line option and argument processing functions. It is important that both the utility DLL and the calling program also use the C library in DLL form. Within Visual Studio, for instance, you can select "Use Run-Time Library (Multithreaded DLL)" in the project settings. Note that DLLs must, in general, be multithreaded because they will be used by threads from several processes. See the Utilities_4_0 project in the *Examples* file for a solution.

5–12. Build project Version (in the *Examples* file), which uses version.c. Run the program on as many different Windows versions as you can access. What are the major and minor version numbers for those systems, and what other information is available? The following screenshot, Exercise Run 5–12, shows the result on a Vista computer with four processors. The "Max appl addr" value is wrong, as this is a 64-bit system. Can you fix this defect?

```
Command Prompt

C:\WSP4_Examples\run8>version
Major Version:        6
Minor Version:        0
Build Number:         6001
Platform ID:          2
Platorm is NT?(0/1)   1
Service Pack:         Service Pack 1

OEM Id:               0
Processor Arch:       0
Page Size:            1000
Min appl addr:        00010000
Max appl addr:        7FFEFFFF
ActiveProcMask:       f
Number processors:    4
Processor type:       586
Alloc grnrty:         10000
Processor level:      16
Processor rev:        515
OEM Id:               0

Sys  Affinity Mask  f
Proc Affinity Mask  f

C:\WSP4_Examples\run8>_
```

Exercise Run 5–12   version: System Version and Other Information

CHAPTER

6 | Process Management

A process contains its own independent virtual address space with both code and data, protected from other processes. Each process, in turn, contains one or more independently executing *threads*. A thread running within a process can execute application code, create new threads, create new independent processes, and manage communication and synchronization among the threads.

By creating and managing processes, applications can have multiple, concurrent tasks processing files, performing computations, or communicating with other networked systems. It is even possible to improve application performance by exploiting multiple CPU processors.

This chapter explains the basics of process management and also introduces the basic synchronization operations and wait functions that will be important throughout the rest of the book.

Windows Processes and Threads

Every process contains one or more threads, and the Windows thread is the basic executable unit; see the next chapter for a threads introduction. Threads are scheduled on the basis of the usual factors: availability of resources such as CPUs and physical memory, priority, fairness, and so on. Windows has long supported multiprocessor systems, so threads can be allocated to separate processors within a computer.

From the programmer's perspective, each Windows process includes resources such as the following components:

- One or more threads.

- A virtual address space that is distinct from other processes' address spaces. Note that shared memory-mapped files share physical memory, but the sharing processes will probably use different virtual addresses to access the mapped file.

- One or more code segments, including code in DLLs.

- One or more data segments containing global variables.

- Environment strings with environment variable information, such as the current search path.

- The process heap.

- Resources such as open handles and other heaps.

Each thread in a process shares code, global variables, environment strings, and resources. Each thread is independently scheduled, and a thread has the following elements:

- A stack for procedure calls, interrupts, exception handlers, and automatic storage.

- Thread Local Storage (TLS)—An arraylike collection of pointers giving each thread the ability to allocate storage to create its own unique data environment.

- An argument on the stack, from the creating thread, which is usually unique for each thread.

- A context structure, maintained by the kernel, with machine register values.

Figure 6–1 shows a process with several threads. This figure is schematic and does not indicate actual memory addresses, nor is it drawn to scale.

This chapter shows how to work with processes consisting of a single thread. Chapter 7 shows how to use multiple threads.

Note: Figure 6–1 is a high-level overview from the programmer's perspective. There are numerous technical and implementation details, and interested readers can find out more in Russinovich, Solomon, and Ionescu, *Windows Internals: Including Windows Server 2008 and Windows Vista.*

A UNIX process is comparable to a Windows process.

Threads, in the form of POSIX Pthreads, are now nearly universally available and used in UNIX and Linux. Pthreads provides features similar to Windows threads, although Windows provides a broader collection of functions.

Vendors and others have provided various thread implementations for many years; they are not a new concept. Pthreads is, however, the most widely used standard, and proprietary implementations are long obsolete. There is an open source Pthreads library for Windows.

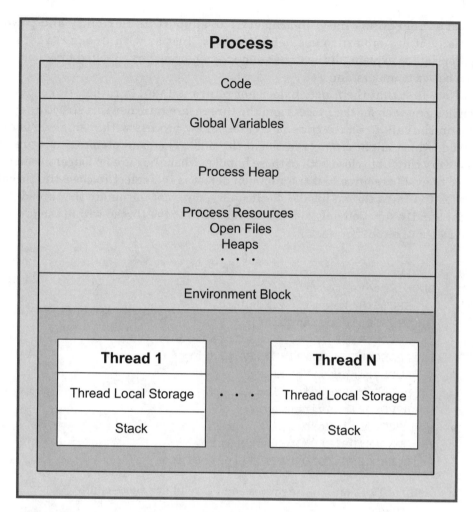

Figure 6–1   A Process and Its Threads

Process Creation

The fundamental Windows process management function is CreateProcess, which creates a process with a single thread. Specify the name of an executable program file as part of the CreateProcess call.

It is common to speak of *parent* and *child* processes, but Windows does not actually maintain these relationships. It is simply convenient to refer to the process that creates a child process as the parent.

CreateProcess has 10 parameters to support its flexibility and power. Initially, it is simplest to use default values. Just as with CreateFile, it is appropriate to explain all the CreateProcess parameters. Related functions are then easier to understand.

Note first that the function does not return a HANDLE; rather, two separate handles, one each for the process and the thread, are returned in a structure specified in the call. CreateProcess creates a new process with a single *primary* thread (which might create additional threads). The example programs are always very careful to close both of these handles when they are no longer needed in order to avoid resource leaks; a common defect is to neglect to close the thread handle. Closing a thread handle, for instance, does not terminate the thread; the CloseHandle function only deletes the reference to the thread within the process that called CreateProcess.

```
BOOL CreateProcess (
    LPCTSTR lpApplicationName,
    LPTSTR lpCommandLine,
    LPSECURITY_ATTRIBUTES lpsaProcess,
    LPSECURITY_ATTRIBUTES lpsaThread,
    BOOL bInheritHandles,
    DWORD dwCreationFlags,
    LPVOID lpEnvironment,
    LPCTSTR lpCurDir,
    LPSTARTUPINFO lpStartupInfo,
    LPPROCESS_INFORMATION lpProcInfo)

Return: TRUE only if the process and thread are successfully
    created.
```

Parameters

Some parameters require extensive explanations in the following sections, and many are illustrated in the program examples.

lpApplicationName and lpCommandLine (this is an LPTSTR and not an LPCTSTR) together specify the executable program and the command line arguments, as explained in the next section.

lpsaProcess and lpsaThread point to the process and thread security attribute structures. NULL values imply default security and will be used until Chapter 15, which covers Windows security.

bInheritHandles indicates whether the new process inherits copies of the calling process's inheritable open handles (files, mappings, and so on). Inherited handles have the same attributes as the originals and are discussed in detail in a later section.

dwCreationFlags combines several flags, including the following.

- CREATE_SUSPENDED indicates that the primary thread is in a suspended state and will run only when the program calls ResumeThread.

- DETACHED_PROCESS and CREATE_NEW_CONSOLE are mutually exclusive; don't set both. The first flag creates a process without a console, and the second flag gives the new process a console of its own. If neither flag is set, the process inherits the parent's console.

- CREATE_UNICODE_ENVIRONMENT should be set if UNICODE is defined.

- CREATE_NEW_PROCESS_GROUP specifies that the new process is the root of a new process group. All processes in a group receive a console control signal (Ctrl-c or Ctrl-break) if they all share the same console. Console control handlers were described in Chapter 4 and illustrated in Program 4–5. These process groups have limited similarities to UNIX process groups and are described later in the "Generating Console Control Events" section.

Several of the flags control the priority of the new process's threads. The possible values are explained in more detail at the end of Chapter 7. For now, just use the parent's priority (specify nothing) or NORMAL_PRIORITY_CLASS.

lpEnvironment points to an environment block for the new process. If NULL, the process uses the parent's environment. The environment block contains name and value strings, such as the search path.

lpCurDir specifies the drive and directory for the new process. If NULL, the parent's working directory is used.

lpStartupInfo is complex and specifies the main window appearance and standard device handles for the new process. We'll use two principal techniques to set the start up information. Programs 6–1, 6–2, 6–3, and others show the proper sequence of operations, which can be confusing.

- Use the parent's information, which is obtained from GetStartupInfo.

- First, clear the associated STARTUPINFO structure before calling CreateProcess, and then specify the standard input, output, and error handles by setting the STARTUPINFO standard handler fields (hStdInput, hStdOutput, and hStdError). For this to be effective, also set another STARTUPINFO member, dwFlags, to STARTF_USESTDHANDLES, and set all the handles that the child process will require. Be certain that the handles are inheritable and that the CreateProcess bInheritHandles flag is set. The "Inheritable Handles" subsection gives more information.

lpProcInfo specifies the structure for containing the returned process, thread handles, and identification. The PROCESS_INFORMATION structure is as follows:

```
typedef struct _PROCESS_INFORMATION {
    HANDLE hProcess;
    HANDLE hThread;
    DWORD dwProcessId;
    DWORD dwThreadId;
} PROCESS_INFORMATION;
```

Why do processes and threads need handles in addition to IDs? The ID is unique to the object for its entire lifetime and in all processes, although the ID is invalid when the process or thread is destroyed and the ID may be reused. On the other hand, a given process may have several handles, each having distinct attributes, such as security access. For this reason, some process management functions require IDs, and others require handles. Furthermore, process handles are required for the general-purpose, handle-based functions. Examples include the wait functions discussed later in this chapter, which allow waiting on handles for several different object types, including processes. Just as with file handles, process and thread handles should be closed when no longer required.

Note: The new process obtains environment, working directory, and other information from the CreateProcess call. Once this call is complete, any changes in the parent will not be reflected in the child process. For example, the parent might change its working directory after the CreateProcess call, but the child process working directory will not be affected unless the child changes its own working directory. The two processes are entirely independent.

The UNIX/Linux and Windows process models are considerably different. First, Windows has no equivalent to the UNIX fork function, which makes a copy of the parent, including the parent's data space, heap, and stack. fork is difficult to emulate exactly in Windows, and while this may seem to be a limitation, fork is also difficult to use in a multithreaded UNIX program because there are numerous problems with creating an exact replica of a multithreaded program with exact copies of all threads and synchronization objects, especially on a multiprocessor computer. Therefore, fork, by itself, is not really appropriate in any multithreaded application.

CreateProcess is, however, similar to the common UNIX sequence of successive calls to fork and execl (or one of five other exec functions). In contrast to Windows, the search directories in UNIX are determined entirely by the PATH environment variable.

As previously mentioned, Windows does not maintain parent-child relationships among processes. Thus, a child process will continue to run after the creating parent process terminates. Furthermore, there are no UNIX-style process groups in Windows. There is, however, a limited form of process group that specifies all the processes to receive a console control event.

Windows processes are identified both by handles and by process IDs, whereas UNIX has no process handles.

Specifying the Executable Image and the Command Line

Either lpApplicationName or lpCommandLine specifies the executable image name. Usually, only lpCommandLine is specified, with lpApplicationName being NULL. Nonetheless, there are detailed rules for lpApplicationName.

- If lpApplicationName is not NULL, it specifies the executable module. Specify the full path and file name, or use a partial name and the current drive and directory will be used; there is no additional searching. Include the file extension, such as .EXE or .BAT, in the name. This is not a command line, and it should not be enclosed with quotation marks.

- If the lpApplicationName string is NULL, the first white-space-delimited token in lpCommandLine is the program name. If the name does not contain a full directory path, the search sequence is as follows:

  1. The directory of the current process's image

  2. The current directory

  3. The Windows system directory, which can be retrieved with GetSystem-Directory

  4. The Windows directory, which is retrievable with GetWindowsDirectory

  5. The directories as specified in the environment variable PATH

The new process can obtain the command line using the usual argv mechanism, or it can invoke GetCommandLine to obtain the command line as a single string.

Notice that the command line is not a constant string. A program could modify its arguments, although it is advisable to make any changes in a copy of the argument string.

It is not necessary to build the new process with the same UNICODE definition as that of the parent process. All combinations are possible. Using _tmain as described in Chapter 2 is helpful in developing code for either Unicode or ASCII operation.

Inheritable Handles

Frequently, a child process requires access to an object referenced by a handle in the parent; if this handle is inheritable, the child can receive a copy of the parent's open handle. The standard input and output handles are frequently shared with the child in this way, and Program 6-1 is the first of several examples. To make a handle inheritable so that a child receives and can use a copy requires several steps.

- The `bInheritHandles` flag on the `CreateProcess` call determines whether the child process will inherit copies of the inheritable handles of open files, processes, and so on. The flag can be regarded as a master switch applying to all handles.

- It is also necessary to make an individual handle inheritable, which is not the default. To create an inheritable handle, use a `SECURITY_ATTRIBUTES` structure at creation time or duplicate an existing handle.

- The `SECURITY_ATTRIBUTES` structure has a flag, `bInheritHandle`, that should be set to `TRUE`. Also, set `nLength` to `sizeof (SECURITY_ATTRIBUTES)`.

The following code segment shows how to create an inheritable file or other handle. In this example, the security descriptor within the security attributes structure is `NULL`; Chapter 15 shows how to include a security descriptor.

```
HANDLE h1, h2, h3;
SECURITY_ATTRIBUTES sa =
    {sizeof(SECURITY_ATTRIBUTES), NULL, TRUE };
...
h1 = CreateFile (..., &sa, ... ); /* Inheritable. */
h2 = CreateFile (..., NULL, ... ); /* Not inheritable. */
h3 = CreateFile (..., &sa, ...);
    /* Inheritable. You can reuse sa. */
```

A child process still needs to know the value of an inheritable handle, so the parent needs to communicate handle values to the child using an interprocess communication (IPC) mechanism or by assigning the handle to standard I/O in the `STARTUPINFO` structure, as in the next example (Program 6–1) and in several additional examples throughout the book. This is generally the preferred

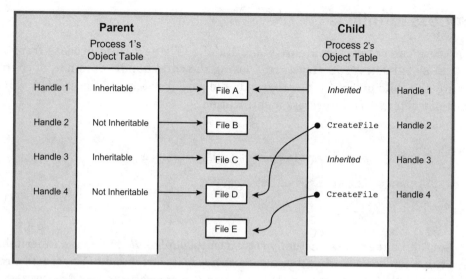

Figure 6–2   Process Handle Tables

technique because it allows I/O redirection in a standard way and no changes are needed in the child program.

Alternatively, nonfile handles and handles that are not used to redirect standard I/O can be converted to text and placed in a command line or in an environment variable. This approach is valid if the handle is inheritable because both parent and child processes identify the handle with the same handle value. Exercise 6–2 suggests how to demonstrate this, and a solution is presented in the *Examples* file.

The inherited handles are distinct copies. Therefore, a parent and child might be accessing the same file using different file pointers. Furthermore, each of the two processes can and should close its own handle.

Figure 6–2 shows how two processes can have distinct handle tables with two distinct handles associated with the same file or other object. Process 1 is the parent, and Process 2 is the child. The handles will have identical values in both processes if the child's handle has been inherited, as is the case with Handles 1 and 3.

On the other hand, the handle values may be distinct. For example, there are two handles for File D, where Process 2 obtained a handle by calling `CreateFile` rather than by inheritance. Also, as is the case with Files B and E, one process may have a handle to an object while the other does not. This would be the case when the child process creates the handle. Finally, while not shown in the figure, a process can have multiple handles to refer to the same object.

Process Identities

A process can obtain the identity and handle of a new child process from the
PROCESS_INFORMATION structure. Closing the child handle does not, of course,
destroy the child process; it destroys only the parent's access to the child. A pair of
functions obtain current process identification.

```
HANDLE GetCurrentProcess (VOID)

DWORD GetCurrentProcessId (VOID)
```

GetCurrentProcess actually returns a *pseudohandle* and is not inheritable.
This value can be used whenever a process needs its own handle. You create a real
process handle from a process ID, including the one returned by GetCurrent-
ProcessId, by using the OpenProcess function. As is the case with all sharable
objects, the open call will fail if you do not have sufficient security rights.

```
HANDLE OpenProcess (
    DWORD dwDesiredAccess,
    BOOL bInheritHandle,
    DWORD dwProcessId)

Return: A process handle, or NULL on failure.
```

Parameters

dwDesiredAccess determines the handle's access to the process. Some of the
values are as follows.

- SYNCHRONIZE—This flag enables processes to wait for the process to
  terminate using the wait functions described later in this chapter.

- PROCESS_ALL_ACCESS—All the access flags are set.

- PROCESS_TERMINATE—It is possible to terminate the process with the
  TerminateProcess function.

- PROCESS_QUERY_INFORMATION—The handle can be used by GetExit-
  CodeProcess and GetPriorityClass to obtain process information.

`bInheritHandle` specifies whether the new process handle is inheritable. `dwProcessId` is the identifier of the process to be opened, and the returned process handle will reference this process.

Finally, a running process can determine the full pathname of the executable used to run it with `GetModuleFileName` or `GetModuleFileNameEx`, using a `NULL` value for the `hModule` parameter. A call with a non-null `hModule` value will return the DLL's file name, not that of the `.EXE` file that uses the DLL.

Duplicating Handles

The parent and child processes may require different access to an object identified by a handle that the child inherits. A process may also need a real, inheritable process handle—rather than the pseudohandle produced by `GetCurrent-Process`—for use by a child process. To address this issue, the parent process can create a duplicate handle with the desired access and inheritability. Here is the function to duplicate handles:

```
BOOL DuplicateHandle (
    HANDLE hSourceProcessHandle,
    HANDLE hSourceHandle,
    HANDLE hTargetProcessHandle,
    LPHANDLE lphTargetHandle,
    DWORD dwDesiredAccess,
    BOOL bInheritHandle,
    DWORD dwOptions)
```

Upon completion, `lphTargetHandle` receives a copy of the original handle, `hSourceHandle`. `hSourceHandle` is a handle in the process indicated by `hSourceProcessHandle` and must have `PROCESS_DUP_HANDLE` access; `DuplicateHandle` will fail if the source handle does not exist in the source process. The new handle, which is pointed to by `lphTargetHandle`, is valid in the target process, `hTargetProcessHandle`. Note that three processes are involved, including the calling process. Frequently, these target and source processes are the calling process, and the handle is obtained from `GetCurrentProcess`. Also notice that it is possible, but generally not advisable, to create a handle in another process; if you do this, you then need a mechanism for informing the other process of the new handle's identity.

`DuplicateHandle` can be used for any handle type.

If dwDesiredAccess is not overridden by DUPLICATE_SAME_ACCESS in dwOptions, it has many possible values (see MSDN).

dwOptions is any combination of two flags.

- DUPLICATE_CLOSE_SOURCE causes the source handle to be closed and can be specified if the source handle is no longer useful. This option also assures that the reference count to the underlying file (or other object) remains constant.

- DUPLICATE_SAME_ACCESS uses the access rights of the duplicated handle, and dwDesiredAccess is ignored.

Reminder: The Windows kernel maintains a reference count for all objects; this count represents the number of distinct handles referring to the object. This count is not available to the application program. An object cannot be destroyed (e.g., deleting a file) until the last handle is closed and the reference count becomes zero. Inherited and duplicate handles are both distinct from the original handles and are represented in the reference count. Program 6–1, later in the chapter, uses inheritable handles.

Next, we learn how to determine whether a process has terminated.

Exiting and Terminating a Process

After a process has finished its work, the process (actually, a thread running in the process) can call ExitProcess with an exit code.

```
VOID ExitProcess (UINT uExitCode)
```

This function does not return. Rather, the calling process and all its threads terminate. Termination handlers are ignored, but there will be detach calls to DllMain (see Chapter 5). The exit code is associated with the process. A return from the main program, with a return value, will have the same effect as calling ExitProcess with the return value as the exit code.

Another process can use GetExitCodeProcess to determine the exit code.

```
BOOL GetExitCodeProcess (
    HANDLE hProcess,
    LPDWORD lpExitCode)
```

The process identified by `hProcess` must have `PROCESS_QUERY_INFOR-MATION` access (see `OpenProcess`, discussed earlier). `lpExitCode` points to the `DWORD` that receives the value. One possible value is `STILL_ACTIVE`, meaning that the process has not terminated.

Finally, one process can terminate another process if the handle has `PROCESS_TERMINATE` access. The terminating function also specifies the exit code.

```
BOOL TerminateProcess (
    HANDLE hProcess,
    UINT uExitCode)
```

Caution: Before exiting from a process, be certain to free all resources that might be shared with other processes. In particular, the synchronization resources of Chapter 8 (mutexes, semaphores, and events) must be treated carefully. SEH (Chapter 4) can be helpful in this regard, and the `ExitProcess` call can be in the handler. However, `__finally` and `__except` handlers are *not* executed when `ExitProcess` is called, so it is not a good idea to exit from inside a program. `TerminateProcess` is especially risky because the terminated process will not have an opportunity to execute its SEH or DLL `DllMain` functions. Console control handlers (Chapter 4 and later in this chapter) are a limited alternative, allowing one process to send a signal to another process, which can then shut itself down cleanly.

Program 6–3 shows a technique whereby processes cooperate. One process sends a shutdown request to a second process, which proceeds to perform an orderly shutdown.

UNIX processes have a process ID, or pid, comparable to the Windows process ID. `getpid` is similar to `GetCurrentProcessId`, but there are no Windows equivalents to `getppid` and `getgpid` because Windows has no process parents or UNIX-like groups.

Conversely, UNIX does not have process handles, so it has no functions comparable to `GetCurrentProcess` or `OpenProcess`.

UNIX allows open file descriptors to be used after an exec if the file descriptor does not have the close-on-exec flag set. This applies only to file descriptors, which are then comparable to inheritable file handles.

UNIX exit, actually in the C library, is similar to ExitProcess; to terminate another process, signal it with SIGKILL.

Waiting for a Process to Terminate

The simplest, and most limited, method to synchronize with another process is to wait for that process to complete. The general-purpose Windows wait functions introduced here have several interesting features.

- The functions can wait for many different types of objects; process handles are just the first use of the wait functions.

- The functions can wait for a single process, the first of several specified processes, or all processes in a collection to complete.

- There is an optional time-out period.

The two general-purpose wait functions wait for synchronization objects to become *signaled*. The system sets a process handle, for example, to the signaled state when the process terminates or is terminated. The wait functions, which will get lots of future use, are as follows:

```
DWORD WaitForSingleObject (
   HANDLE hObject,
   DWORD dwMilliseconds)
```

```
DWORD WaitForMultipleObjects (
   DWORD nCount,
   CONST HANDLE *lpHandles,
   BOOL fWaitAll,
   DWORD dwMilliseconds)

Return: The cause of the wait completion, or 0XFFFFFFFF for an
   error (use GetLastError for more information).
```

Specify either a single process handle (hObject) or an array of distinct object handles in the array referenced by lpHandles. nCount, the size of the array, should not exceed MAXIMUM_WAIT_OBJECTS (defined as 64 in winnt.h).

dwMilliseconds is the time-out period in milliseconds. A value of 0 means that the function returns immediately after testing the state of the specified objects, thus allowing a program to poll for process termination. Use INFINITE for no time-out to wait until a process terminates.

fWaitAll, a parameter of the second function, specifies (if TRUE) that it is necessary to wait for all processes, rather than only one, to terminate.

The possible successful return values for this function are as follows.

- WAIT_OBJECT_0 means that the handle is signaled in the case of WaitFor-SingleObject or all nCount objects are simultaneously signaled in the special case of WaitForMultipleObjects with fWaitAll set to TRUE.

- WAIT_OBJECT_0+n, where $0 \leq n <$ nCount. Subtract WAIT_OBJECT_0 from the return value to determine which process terminated when waiting for any of a collection of processes to terminate. If several handles are signaled, the returned value is the minimum of the signaled handle indices. WAIT_ABANDONED_0 is a possible base value when using mutex handles; see Chapter 8.

- WAIT_TIMEOUT indicates that the time-out period elapsed before the wait could be satisfied by signaled handle(s).

- WAIT_FAILED indicates that the call failed; for example, the handle may not have SYNCHRONIZE access.

- WAIT_ABANDONED_0 is not possible with processes. This value is discussed in Chapter 8 along with mutex handles.

Determine the exit code of a process using GetExitCodeProcess, as described in the preceding section.

Environment Blocks and Strings

Figure 6–1 includes the process environment block. The environment block contains a sequence of strings of the form

```
Name = Value
```

```
DWORD GetEnvironmentVariable (
    LPCTSTR lpName,
    LPTSTR lpValue,
    DWORD cchValue)

BOOL SetEnvironmentVariable (
    LPCTSTR lpName,
    LPCTSTR lpValue)
```

Each environment string, being a string, is NULL-terminated, and the entire block of strings is itself NULL-terminated. PATH is one example of a commonly used environment variable.

To pass the parent's environment to a child process, set lpEnvironment to NULL in the CreateProcess call. Any process, in turn, can interrogate or modify its environment variables or add new environment variables to the block.

The two functions used to get and set variables are as follows:

lpName is the variable name. On setting a value, the variable is added to the block if it does not exist and if the value is not NULL. If, on the other hand, the value is NULL, the variable is removed from the block. The "=" character cannot appear in an environment variable name, since it's used as a separator.

There are additional requirements. Most importantly, the environment block strings must be sorted alphabetically by name (case-insensitive, Unicode order). See MSDN for more details.

GetEnvironmentVariable returns the length of the value string, or 0 on failure. If the lpValue buffer is not long enough, as indicated by cchValue, then the return value is the number of characters actually required to hold the complete string. Recall that GetCurrentDirectory (Chapter 2) uses a similar mechanism.

Process Security

Normally, CreateProcess gives PROCESS_ALL_ACCESS rights. There are, however, several specific rights, including PROCESS_QUERY_INFORMATION, CREATE_PROCESS, PROCESS_TERMINATE, PROCESS_SET_INFORMATION, DUPLICATE_HANDLE, and CREATE_THREAD. In particular, it can be useful to limit PROCESS_TERMINATE rights to the parent process given the frequently mentioned dangers of terminating a running process. Chapter 15 describes security attributes for processes and other objects.

UNIX waits for process termination using wait and waitpid, but there are no time-outs even though waitpid can poll (there is a nonblocking option). These functions wait only for child processes, and there is no equivalent to the multiple wait on a collection of processes, although it is possible to wait for all processes in a process group. One slight difference is that the exit code is returned with `wait` and `waitpid`, so there is no need for a separate function equivalent to `GetExit-CodeProcess`.

UNIX also supports environment strings similar to those in Windows. `getenv` (in the C library) has the same functionality as `GetEnvironmentVariable` except that the programmer must be sure to have a sufficiently large buffer. `putenv`, `setenv`, and `unsetenv` (not in the C library) are different ways to add, change, and remove variables and their values, with functionality equivalent to `SetEnvironmentVariable`.

Example: Parallel Pattern Searching

Now is the time to put Windows processes to the test. This example, `grepMP`, creates processes to search for patterns in files, one process per search file. The simple pattern search program is modeled after the UNIX `grep` utility, although the technique would apply to any program that uses standard output. The search program should be regarded as a black box and is simply an executable program to be controlled by a parent process; however, the project and executable (`grep.exe`) are in the *Examples* file.

The command line to the program is of the form

```
grepMP pattern F1 F2 ... FN
```

The program, Program 6–1, performs the following processing:

- Each input file, `F1` to `FN`, is searched using a separate process running the same executable. The program creates a command line of the form `grep pattern FK`.

- The temporary file handle, specified to be inheritable, is assigned to the hStdOutput field in the new process's start-up information structure.

- Using `WaitForMultipleObjects`, the program waits for all search processes to complete.

- As soon as all searches are complete, the results (temporary files) are displayed in order, one at a time. A process to execute the `cat` utility (Program 2–3) outputs the temporary file.

- `WaitForMultipleObjects` is limited to `MAXIMUM_WAIT_OBJECTS` (64) handles, so the program calls it multiple times.

- The program uses the `grep` process exit code to determine whether a specific process detected the pattern.

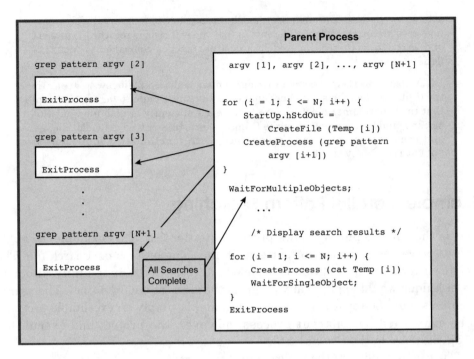

Figure 6-3 File Searching Using Multiple Processes

Figure 6–3 shows the processing performed by Program 6–1, and Run 6–1 shows program execution and timing results.

Program 6-1 grepMP: Parallel Searching

```
/* Chapter 6. grepMP. */
/* Multiple process version of grep command. */

#include "Everything.h"
int _tmain (DWORD argc, LPTSTR argv[])
/* Create a separate process to search each file on the
   command line. Each process is given a temporary file,
   in the current directory, to receive the results. */
{
    HANDLE hTempFile;
    SECURITY_ATTRIBUTES stdOutSA = /* SA for inheritable handle. */
        {sizeof (SECURITY_ATTRIBUTES), NULL, TRUE};
    TCHAR commandLine[MAX_PATH + 100];
    STARTUPINFO startUpSearch, startUp;
    PROCESS_INFORMATION processInfo;
```

```
DWORD iProc, exitCode, dwCreationFlags = 0;
HANDLE *hProc; /* Pointer to an array of proc handles. */
typedef struct {TCHAR tempFile[MAX_PATH];} PROCFILE;
PROCFILE *procFile; /* Pointer to array of temp file names. */

GetStartupInfo (&startUpSearch);
GetStartupInfo (&startUp);
procFile = malloc ((argc - 2) * sizeof (PROCFILE));
hProc = malloc ((argc - 2) * sizeof (HANDLE));

/* Create a separate "grep" process for each file. */
for (iProc = 0; iProc < argc - 2; iProc++) {
    _stprintf (commandLine, _T ("grep \"%s\" \"%s\""),
            argv[1], argv[iProc + 2]);
    GetTempFileName (_T ("."), _T ("gtm"), 0,
            procFile[iProc].tempFile); /* For search results. */
    hTempFile = /* This handle is inheritable */
        CreateFile (procFile[iProc].tempFile,
            GENERIC_WRITE,
            FILE_SHARE_READ | FILE_SHARE_WRITE, &stdOutSA,
            CREATE_ALWAYS, FILE_ATTRIBUTE_NORMAL, NULL);
    startUpSearch.dwFlags = STARTF_USESTDHANDLES;
    startUpSearch.hStdOutput = hTempFile;
    startUpSearch.hStdError = hTempFile;
    startUpSearch.hStdInput = GetStdHandle (STD_INPUT_HANDLE);

    /* Create a process to execute the command line. */
    CreateProcess (NULL, commandLine, NULL, NULL, TRUE,
        dwCreationFlags, NULL, NULL, &startUpSearch, &processInfo);
    /* Close unwanted handles. */
    CloseHandle (hTempFile); CloseHandle (processInfo.hThread);
    hProc[iProc] = processInfo.hProcess;
}

/* Processes are all running. Wait for them to complete. */
for (iProc = 0; iProc < argc - 2; iProc += MAXIMUM_WAIT_OBJECTS)
    WaitForMultipleObjects ( /* Allows a large # of processes */
            min (MAXIMUM_WAIT_OBJECTS, argc - 2 - iProc),
            &hProc[iProc], TRUE, INFINITE);
/* Result files sent to std output using "cat." */
for (iProc = 0; iProc < argc - 2; iProc++) {
    if (GetExitCodeProcess(hProc[iProc], &exitCode) && exitCode==0)
    {
        /* Pattern was detected -- List results. */
        if (argc > 3) _tprintf (_T ("%s:\n"), argv[iProc + 2]);
        _stprintf (commandLine, _T ("cat \"%s\""),
                procFile[iProc].tempFile);
        CreateProcess (NULL, commandLine, NULL, NULL, TRUE,
            dwCreationFlags, NULL, NULL, &startUp, &processInfo);
        WaitForSingleObject (processInfo.hProcess, INFINITE);
```

```
            CloseHandle (processInfo.hProcess);
            CloseHandle (processInfo.hThread);
        }

        CloseHandle (hProc[iProc]);
        DeleteFile (procFile[iProc].tempFile);
    }
    free (procFile);
    free (hProc);
    return 0;
}
```

Run 6-1   grepMP: Parallel Searching

Run 6–1 shows `grepMP` execution for large and small files, and the run contrasts sequential `grep` execution with parallel `grepMP` execution to perform the same task. The test computer has four processors; a single or dual processor computer will give different timing results. Notes after the run explain the test operation and results.

Run 6–1 uses files and obtains results as follows:

- The small file test searches two *Examples* files, `Presidents.txt` and `Monarchs.txt`, which contain names of U.S. presidents and English monarchs, along with their dates of birth, death, and term in office. The "i" at the right end of each line is a visual cue and has no other meaning. The same is true of the "x" at the end of the `randfile`-generated files.

- The large file test searches four `randfile`-generated files, each with 10 million 64-byte records. The search is for a specific record number (`1234562`), and each file has a different random key (the first 8 bytes).

- `grepMP` is more than four times faster than four sequential `grep` executions (Real Time is 15 seconds compared to 77 seconds), so the multiple processes gain even more performance than expected, despite the process creation overhead.

- `timep` is Program 6–2, the next example. Notice, however, that the `grepMP` system time is zero, as the time applies to `grepMP` itself, not the grep processes that it creates.

Processes in a Multiprocessor Environment

In Program 6–1, the processes and their primary (and only) threads run almost totally independently of one another. The only dependence is created at the end of the parent process as it waits for all the processes to complete so that the output files can be processed sequentially. Therefore, the Windows scheduler can and will run the process threads concurrently on the separate processors of a multiprocessor computer. As Run 6–1 shows, this can result in substantial performance improvement when performance is measured as elapsed time to execute the program, and no explicit program actions are required to get the performance improvement.

The performance improvement is not linear in terms of the number of processors due to overhead costs and the need to output the results sequentially. Nonetheless, the improvements are worthwhile and result automatically as a consequence of the program design, which delegates independent computational tasks to independent processes.

It is possible, however, to constrain the processes to specific processors if you wish to be sure that other processors are free to be allocated to other critical tasks.

This can be accomplished using the processor affinity mask (see Chapter 9) for a process or thread.

Finally, it is possible to create independent threads within a process, and these threads will also be scheduled on separate processors. Chapter 7 describes threads and related performance issues.

Process Execution Times

You can determine the amount of time that a process has consumed (elapsed, kernel, and user times) using the `GetProcessTimes` function.

```
BOOL GetProcessTimes (
    HANDLE hProcess,
    LPFILETIME lpCreationTime,
    LPFILETIME lpExitTime,
    LPFILETIME lpKernelTime,
    LPFILETIME lpUserTime)
```

The process handle can refer to a process that is still running or to one that has terminated. Elapsed time can be computed by subtracting the creation time from the exit time, as shown in the next example. The `FILETIME` type is a 64-bit item; create a union with a `LARGE_INTEGER` to perform the subtraction.

Chapter 3's `lsW` example showed how to convert and display file times, although the kernel and user times are elapsed times rather than calendar times.

`GetThreadTimes` is similar and requires a thread handle for a parameter.

Example: Process Execution Times

The next example (Program 6–2) implements the familiar `timep` (time print) utility that is similar to the UNIX `time` command (`time` is supported by the Windows command prompt, so a different name is appropriate). `timep` prints elapsed (or real), user, and system times.

This program uses `GetCommandLine`, a Windows function that returns the complete command line as a single string rather than individual `argv` strings.

The program also uses a utility function, `SkipArg`, to scan the command line and skip past the executable name. `SkipArg` is in the *Examples* file.

Program 6–2 timep: Process Times

```
/* Chapter 6. timep. */

#include "Everything.h"
int _tmain (int argc, LPTSTR argv[])
{
    STARTUPINFO startUp;
    PROCESS_INFORMATION procInfo;
    union { /* Structure required for file time arithmetic. */
        LONGLONG li;
        FILETIME ft;
    } createTime, exitTime, elapsedTime;
    FILETIME kernelTime, userTime;
    SYSTEMTIME elTiSys, keTiSys, usTiSys, startTimeSys;
    LPTSTR targv = SkipArg (GetCommandLine ());
    HANDLE hProc;

    GetStartupInfo (&startUp);
    GetSystemTime (&startTimeSys);

    /* Execute the command line; wait for process to complete. */
    CreateProcess (NULL, targv, NULL, NULL, TRUE,
            NORMAL_PRIORITY_CLASS, NULL, NULL, &startUp, &procInfo);
    hProc = procInfo.hProcess;
    WaitForSingleObject (hProc, INFINITE);

    GetProcessTimes (hProc, &createTime.ft,
            &exitTime.ft, &kernelTime, &userTime);
    elapsedTime.li = exitTime.li - createTime.li;
    FileTimeToSystemTime (&elapsedTime.ft, &elTiSys);
    FileTimeToSystemTime (&kernelTime, &keTiSys);
    FileTimeToSystemTime (&userTime, &usTiSys);
    _tprintf (_T ("Real Time: %02d:%02d:%02d:%03d\n"),
            elTiSys.wHour, elTiSys.wMinute, elTiSys.wSecond,
            elTiSys.wMilliseconds);
    _tprintf (_T ("User Time: %02d:%02d:%02d:%03d\n"),
            usTiSys.wHour, usTiSys.wMinute, usTiSys.wSecond,
            usTiSys.wMilliseconds);
    _tprintf (_T ("Sys Time: %02d:%02d:%02d:%03d\n"),
            keTiSys.wHour, keTiSys.wMinute, keTiSys.wSecond,
            keTiSys.wMilliseconds);

    CloseHandle (procInfo.hThread); CloseHandle (procInfo.hProcess);
    CloseHandle (hProc);
    return 0;
}
```

Using the `timep` Command

`timep` was useful to compare different programming solutions, such as the various Caesar cipher (`cci`) and sorting utilities, including `cci` (Program 2–3) and `sortMM` (Program 5–5). Appendix C summarizes and briefly analyzes some additional results, and there are other examples throughout the book.

Notice that measuring a program such as `grepMP` (Program 6–1) gives kernel and user times only for the parent process. Job objects, described near the end of this chapter, allow you to collect information on a collection of processes. Run 6–1 and Appendix C show that, on a multiprocessor computer, performance can improve as the separate processes, or more accurately, threads, run on different processors. There can also be performance gains if the files are on different physical drives. On the other hand, you cannot always count on such performance gains; for example, there might be resource contention or disk thrashing that could impact performance negatively.

Generating Console Control Events

Terminating a process can cause problems because the terminated process cannot clean up. SEH does not help because there is no general method for one process to cause an exception in another.[1] Console control events, however, allow one process to send a console control signal, or event, to another process in certain limited circumstances. Program 4–5 illustrated how a process can set up a handler to catch such a signal, and the handler could generate an exception. In that example, the user generated a signal from the user interface.

It is possible, then, for a process to generate a signal event in another specified process or set of processes. Recall the `CreateProcess` creation flag value, `CREATE_NEW_PROCESS_GROUP`. If this flag is set, the new process ID identifies a group of processes, and the new process is the *root* of the group. All new processes created by the parent are in this new group until another `CreateProcess` call uses the `CREATE_NEW_PROCESS_GROUP` flag.

One process can generate a `CTRL_C_EVENT` or `CTRL_BREAK_EVENT` in a specified process group, identifying the group with the root process ID. The target processes must have the same console as that of the process generating the event. In particular, the calling process cannot be created with its own console (using the `CREATE_NEW_CONSOLE` or `DETACHED_PROCESS` flag).

---

[1] Chapter 10 shows an indirect way for one thread to cause an exception in another thread, and the same technique is applicable between threads in different processes.

```
BOOL GenerateConsoleCtrlEvent (
    DWORD dwCtrlEvent,
    DWORD dwProcessGroup)
```

The first parameter, then, must be one of either CTRL_C_EVENT or CTRL-_BREAK_EVENT. The second parameter identifies the process group.

Example: Simple Job Management

UNIX shells provide commands to execute processes in the background and to obtain their current status. This section develops a simple "job shell"[2] with a similar set of commands. The commands are as follows.

- jobbg uses the remaining part of the command line as the command for a new process, or *job,* but the jobbg command returns immediately rather than waiting for the new process to complete. The new process is optionally given its own console, or is *detached,* so that it has no console at all. Using a new console avoids console contention with jobbg and other jobs. This approach is similar to running a UNIX command with the & option at the end.

- jobs lists the current active jobs, giving the job numbers and process IDs. This is similar to the UNIX command of the same name.

- kill terminates a job. This implementation uses the TerminateProcess function, which, as previously stated, does not provide a clean shutdown. There is also an option to send a console control signal.

It is straightforward to create additional commands for operations such as suspending and resuming existing jobs.

Because the shell, which maintains the job list, may terminate, the shell employs a user-specific shared file to contain the process IDs, the command, and related information. In this way, the shell can restart and the job list will still be intact. Furthermore, several shells can run concurrently. You could place this information in the registry rather than in a temporary file (see Exercise 6–9).

Concurrency issues will arise. Several processes, running from separate command prompts, might perform job control simultaneously. The job management functions use file locking (Chapter 3) on the job list file so that a user can invoke

---

[2] Do not confuse these "jobs" with the Windows job objects described later. The jobs here are managed entirely from the programs developed in this section.

job management from separate shells or processes. Also, Exercise 6–8 identifies a defect caused by job id reuse and suggests a fix.

The full program in the *Examples* file has a number of additional features, not shown in the listings, such as the ability to take command input from a file. Job-Shell will be the basis for a more general "service shell" in Chapter 13 (Program 13–3). Windows services are background processes, usually servers, that can be controlled with start, stop, pause, and other commands.

Creating a Background Job

Program 6–3 is the job shell that prompts the user for one of three commands and then carries out the command. This program uses a collection of job management functions, which are shown in Programs 6–4, 6–5, and 6–6. Run 6–6 then demonstrates how to use the JobShell system.

Program 6-3 JobShell: Create, List, and Kill Background Jobs

```
/* Chapter 6. */
/* JobShell.c -- job management commands:
   jobbg -- Run a job in the background.
   jobs -- List all background jobs.
   kill -- Terminate a specified job of job family.
        There is an option to generate a console control signal. */

#include "Everything.h"
#include "JobMgt.h"

int _tmain (int argc, LPTSTR argv[])
{
   BOOL exitFlag = FALSE;
   TCHAR command[MAX_COMMAND_LINE], *pc;
   DWORD i, localArgc; /* Local argc. */
   TCHAR argstr[MAX_ARG][MAX_COMMAND_LINE];
   LPTSTR pArgs[MAX_ARG];

   for (i = 0; i < MAX_ARG; i++) pArgs[i] = argstr[i];
   /* Prompt user, read command, and execute it. */
   _tprintf (_T ("Windows Job Management\n"));
   while (!exitFlag) {
      _tprintf (_T ("%s"), _T ("JM$"));
      _fgetts (command, MAX_COMMAND_LINE, stdin);
      pc = strchr (command, '\n');
      *pc = '\0';
      /* Parse the input to obtain command line for new job. */
      GetArgs (command, &localArgc, pArgs); /* See Appendix A. */
      CharLower (argstr[0]);
```

```
    if (_tcscmp (argstr[0], _T ("jobbg")) == 0) {
        Jobbg (localArgc, pArgs, command);
    }
    else if (_tcscmp (argstr[0], _T ("jobs")) == 0) {
        Jobs (localArgc, pArgs, command);
    }
    else if (_tcscmp (argstr[0], _T ("kill")) == 0) {
        Kill (localArgc, pArgs, command);
    }
    else if (_tcscmp (argstr[0], _T ("quit")) == 0) {
        exitFlag = TRUE;
    }
    else _tprintf (_T ("Illegal command. Try again\n"));
    }
    return 0;
}


/* jobbg [options] command-line [Options are mutually exclusive]
        -c: Give the new process a console.
        -d: The new process is detached, with no console.
        If neither is set, the process shares console with jobbg. */
int Jobbg (int argc, LPTSTR argv[], LPTSTR command)
{
    DWORD fCreate;
    LONG jobNumber;
    BOOL flags[2];
    STARTUPINFO startUp;
    PROCESS_INFORMATION processInfo;
    LPTSTR targv = SkipArg (command);

    GetStartupInfo (&startUp);
    Options (argc, argv, _T ("cd"), &flags[0], &flags[1], NULL);
        /* Skip over the option field as well, if it exists. */
    if (argv[1][0] == '-') targv = SkipArg (targv);

    fCreate = flags[0] ? CREATE_NEW_CONSOLE :
            flags[1] ? DETACHED_PROCESS : 0;

        /* Create job/thread suspended. Resume once job entered. */
    CreateProcess (NULL, targv, NULL, NULL, TRUE,
            fCreate | CREATE_SUSPENDED | CREATE_NEW_PROCESS_GROUP,
            NULL, NULL, &startUp, &processInfo);
        /* Create a job number and enter the process ID and handle
            into the job "data base." */

    jobNumber = GetJobNumber (&processInfo, targv); /* See JobMgt.h */
    if (jobNumber >= 0)
        ResumeThread (processInfo.hThread);
    else {
        TerminateProcess (processInfo.hProcess, 3);
```

```
        CloseHandle (processInfo.hProcess);
        ReportError (_T ("Error: No room in job list."), 0, FALSE);
        return 5;
    }
    CloseHandle (processInfo.hThread);
    CloseHandle (processInfo.hProcess);
    _tprintf (_T (" [%d] %d\n"), jobNumber, processInfo.dwProcessId);
    return 0;
}


/* jobs: List all running or stopped jobs. */
int Jobs (int argc, LPTSTR argv[], LPTSTR command)
{
    if (!DisplayJobs ()) return 1; /* See job mgmt functions. */
    return 0;
}


/* kill [options] jobNumber
    -b Generate a Ctrl-Break
    -c Generate a Ctrl-C
        Otherwise, terminate the process. */
int Kill (int argc, LPTSTR argv[], LPTSTR command)
{
    DWORD ProcessId, jobNumber, iJobNo;
    HANDLE hProcess;
    BOOL cntrlC, cntrlB;

    iJobNo =
        Options (argc, argv, _T ("bc"), &cntrlB, &cntrlC, NULL);

    /* Find the process ID associated with this job. */
    jobNumber = _ttoi (argv[iJobNo]);
    ProcessId = FindProcessId (jobNumber); /* See job mgmt. */
    hProcess = OpenProcess (PROCESS_TERMINATE, FALSE, ProcessId);
    if (hProcess == NULL) { /* Process ID may not be in use. */
        ReportError (_T ("Process already terminated.\n"), 0, FALSE);
        return 2;
    }
    if (cntrlB)
        GenerateConsoleCtrlEvent (CTRL_BREAK_EVENT, ProcessId);
    else if (cntrlC)
        GenerateConsoleCtrlEvent (CTRL_C_EVENT, ProcessId);
    else
        TerminateProcess (hProcess, JM_EXIT_CODE);
    WaitForSingleObject (hProcess, 5000);
    CloseHandle (hProcess);
    _tprintf (_T ("Job [%d] terminated or timed out\n"), jobNumber);
    return 0;
}
```

Notice how the `jobbg` command creates the process in the suspended state and then calls the job management function, `GetJobNumber` (Program 6–4), to get a new job number and to register the job and its associated process. If the job cannot be registered for any reason, the job's process is terminated immediately. Normally, the job number is generated correctly, and the primary thread is resumed and allowed to run.

Getting a Job Number

The next three programs show three individual job management functions. These functions are all included in a single source file, `JobMgt.c`.

The first, Program 6–4, shows the `GetJobNumber` function. Notice the use of file locking with a completion handler to unlock the file. This technique protects against exceptions and inadvertent transfers around the unlock call. Such a transfer might be inserted accidentally during code maintenance even if the original program is correct. Also notice how the record past the end of the file is locked in the event that the file needs to be expanded with a new record.

There's also a subtle defect in this function; a code comment identifies it, and Exercise 6–8 suggests a fix.

Program 6–4 `JobMgt`: Creating New Job Information

```
/* Job management utility function. */

#include "Everything.h"
#include "JobMgt.h" /* Listed in Appendix A. */
void GetJobMgtFileName (LPTSTR);
LONG GetJobNumber (PROCESS_INFORMATION *pProcessInfo,
      LPCTSTR command)

/* Create a job number for the new process, and enter
   the new process information into the job database. */
{
    HANDLE hJobData, hProcess;
    JM_JOB jobRecord;
    DWORD jobNumber = 0, nXfer, exitCode, fileSizeLow, fileSizeHigh;
    TCHAR jobMgtFileName[MAX_PATH];
    OVERLAPPED regionStart;

    if (!GetJobMgtFileName (jobMgtFileName)) return -1;
                /* Produces "\tmp\UserName.JobMgt" */
    hJobData = CreateFile (jobMgtFileName,
        GENERIC_READ | GENERIC_WRITE,
        FILE_SHARE_READ | FILE_SHARE_WRITE,
        NULL, OPEN_ALWAYS, FILE_ATTRIBUTE_NORMAL, NULL);
```

```
   if (hJobData == INVALID_HANDLE_VALUE) return -1;

   /* Lock the entire file plus one possible new
      record for exclusive access. */
   regionStart.Offset = 0;
   regionStart.OffsetHigh = 0;
   regionStart.hEvent = (HANDLE)0;

   /* Find file size: GetFileSizeEx is an alternative */
   fileSizeLow = GetFileSize (hJobData, &fileSizeHigh);
   LockFileEx (hJobData, LOCKFILE_EXCLUSIVE_LOCK,
         0, fileSizeLow + SJM_JOB, 0, &regionStart);

   __try {
      /* Read records to find empty slot. */
      /* See text comments and Exercise 6-8 regarding a potential
         defect (and fix) caused by process ID reuse. */
      while (ReadFile (hJobData, &jobRecord, SJM_JOB, &nXfer, NULL)
            && (nXfer > 0)) {
         if (jobRecord.ProcessId == 0) break;
         hProcess = OpenProcess(PROCESS_ALL_ACCESS,
               FALSE, jobRecord.ProcessId);
         if (hProcess == NULL) break;
         if (GetExitCodeProcess (hProcess, &exitCode)
               && (exitCode != STILL_ACTIVE)) break;
         jobNumber++;
      }

      /* Either an empty slot has been found, or we are at end
         of file and need to create a new one. */
      if (nXfer != 0) /* Not at end of file. Back up. */
         SetFilePointer (hJobData, -(LONG)SJM_JOB,
               NULL, FILE_CURRENT);
      jobRecord.ProcessId = pProcessInfo->dwProcessId;
      _tcsnccpy (jobRecord.commandLine, command, MAX_PATH);
      WriteFile (hJobData, &jobRecord, SJM_JOB, &nXfer, NULL);
   } /* End try. */

   __finally {
      UnlockFileEx (hJobData, 0, fileSizeLow + SJM_JOB, 0,
            &regionStart);
      CloseHandle (hJobData);
   }
   return jobNumber + 1;
}
```

Listing Background Jobs

Program 6–5 shows the `DisplayJobs` job management function.

Program 6–5 JobMgt: Displaying Active Jobs

```
BOOL DisplayJobs (void)

/* Scan the job database file, reporting job status. */
{
    HANDLE hJobData, hProcess;
    JM_JOB jobRecord;
    DWORD jobNumber = 0, nXfer, exitCode, fileSizeLow, fileSizeHigh;
    TCHAR jobMgtFileName[MAX_PATH];
    OVERLAPPED regionStart;

    GetJobMgtFileName (jobMgtFileName);
    hJobData = CreateFile (jobMgtFileName,
            GENERIC_READ | GENERIC_WRITE,
            FILE_SHARE_READ | FILE_SHARE_WRITE,
            NULL, OPEN_EXISTING, FILE_ATTRIBUTE_NORMAL, NULL);

    regionStart.Offset = 0;
    regionStart.OffsetHigh = 0;
    regionStart.hEvent = (HANDLE)0;

    /* Demonstration: GetFileSize instead of GetFileSizeEx */
    fileSizeLow = GetFileSize (hJobData, &fileSizeHigh);
    LockFileEx (hJobData, LOCKFILE_EXCLUSIVE_LOCK,
            0, fileSizeLow, fileSizeHigh, &regionStart);

    __try {
    while (ReadFile (hJobData, &jobRecord, SJM_JOB, &nXfer, NULL)
            && (nXfer > 0)){
        jobNumber++;
        if (jobRecord.ProcessId == 0)
            continue;
        hProcess = OpenProcess (PROCESS_ALL_ACCESS, FALSE,
                jobRecord.ProcessId);
        if (hProcess != NULL)
            GetExitCodeProcess (hProcess, &exitCode);
        _tprintf (_T (" [%d] "), jobNumber);
        if (hProcess == NULL)
            _tprintf (_T (" Done"));
        else if (exitCode != STILL_ACTIVE)
            _tprintf (_T ("+ Done"));
        else _tprintf (_T (" "));
        _tprintf (_T (" %s\n"), jobRecord.commandLine);
```

```
        /* Remove processes that are no longer in system. */
        if (hProcess == NULL) { /* Back up one record. */
            SetFilePointer (hJobData, -(LONG)nXfer,
                    NULL, FILE_CURRENT);
            jobRecord.ProcessId = 0;
            WriteFile (hJobData, &jobRecord, SJM_JOB, &nXfer, NULL);
        }
    } /* End of while. */
    } /* End of __try. */

    __finally {
        UnlockFileEx (hJobData, 0, fileSizeLow, fileSizeHigh,
                    &regionStart);
        CloseHandle (hJobData);
    }

    return TRUE;
}
```

Finding a Job in the Job List File

Program 6–6 shows the final job management function, `FindProcessId`, which obtains the process ID of a specified job number. The process ID, in turn, can be used by the calling program to obtain a handle and other process status information.

Program 6–6   `JobMgt`: Getting the Process ID from a Job Number

```
DWORD FindProcessId (DWORD jobNumber)

/* Obtain the process ID of the specified job number. */
{
    HANDLE hJobData;
    JM_JOB jobRecord;
    DWORD nXfer;
    TCHAR jobMgtFileName[MAX_PATH];
    OVERLAPPED regionStart;

    /* Open the job management file. */
    GetJobMgtFileName (jobMgtFileName);

    hJobData = CreateFile (jobMgtFileName, GENERIC_READ,
            FILE_SHARE_READ | FILE_SHARE_WRITE,
            NULL, OPEN_EXISTING, FILE_ATTRIBUTE_NORMAL, NULL);
    if (hJobData == INVALID_HANDLE_VALUE) return 0;
```

```
/* Position to the entry for the specified job number.
 * The full program assures that jobNumber is in range. */
SetFilePointer (hJobData, SJM_JOB * (jobNumber - 1),
     NULL, FILE_BEGIN);

/* Lock and read the record. */
regionStart.Offset = SJM_JOB * (jobNumber - 1);
regionStart.OffsetHigh = 0; /* Assume a "short" file. */
regionStart.hEvent = (HANDLE)0;
LockFileEx (hJobData, 0, 0, SJM_JOB, 0, &regionStart);
ReadFile (hJobData, &jobRecord, SJM_JOB, &nXfer, NULL);
UnlockFileEx (hJobData, 0, SJM_JOB, 0, &regionStart);
CloseHandle (hJobData);
return jobRecord.ProcessId;
}
```

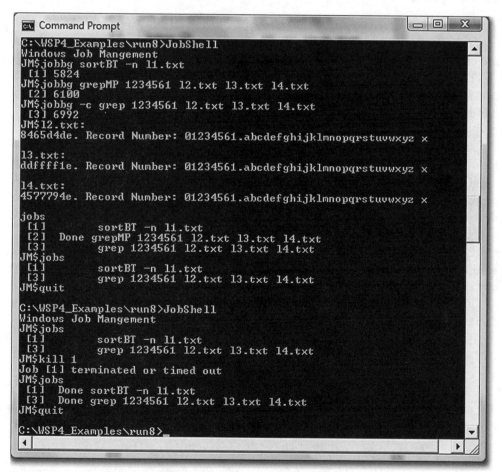

Run 6–6 JobShell: Managing Multiple Processes

Run 6–6 shows the job shell managing several jobs using `grep`, `grepMP`, and `sortBT` (Chapter 5). Notes on Run 6–6 include:

- This run uses the same four 640MB files (`ll.txt`, etc.) as Run 6–1.

- You can quit and reenter `JobShell` and see the same jobs.

- A "Done" job is listed only once.

- The `grep` job uses the `-c` option, so the results appear in a separate console (not shown in the screenshot).

- `JobShell` and the `grepMP` job contend for the main console, so some output can overlap, although the problem does not occur in this example.

Job Objects

You can collect processes together into *job objects* where the processes can be controlled together, and you can specify resource limits for all the job object member processes and maintain accounting information.

The first step is to create an empty job object with `CreateJobObject`, which takes two arguments, a name and security attributes, and returns a job object handle. There is also an `OpenJobObject` function to use with a named object. `CloseHandle` destroys the job object.

`AssignProcessToJobObject` simply adds a process specified by a process handle to a job object; there are just two parameters. A process cannot be a member of more than one job, so `AssignProcessToJobObject` fails if the process associated with the handle is already a member of some job. A process that is added to a job inherits all the limits associated with the job and adds its accounting information to the job, such as the processor time used.

By default, a new child process created by a process in the job will also belong to the job unless the `CREATE_BREAKAWAY_FROM_JOB` flag is specified in the `dwCreationFlags` argument to `CreateProcess`.

Finally, you can specify control limits on the processes in a job using `SetInformationJobObject`.

```
BOOL SetInformationJobObject (
    HANDLE hJob,
    JOBOBJECTINFOCLASS JobObjectInformationClass,
    LPVOID lpJobObjectInformation,
    DWORD cbJobObjectInformationLength)
```

- `hJob` is a handle for an existing job object.

- `JobObjectInformationClass` specifies the information class for the limits you wish to set. There are five values; `JobObjectBasicLimitInformation` is one value and is used to specify information such as the total and per-process time limits, working set size limits,[3] limits on the number of active processes, priority, and processor affinity (the processors of a multiprocessor computer that can be used by threads in the job processes).

- `lpJobObjectInformation` points to the actual information required by the preceding parameter. There is a different structure for each class.

- `JOBOBJECT_BASIC_ACCOUNTING_INFORMATION` allows you to get the total time (user, kernel, and elapsed) of the processes in a job.

- `JOB_OBJECT_LIMIT_KILL_ON_JOB_CLOSE` will terminate all processes in the job object when you close the last handle referring to the object.

- The last parameter is the length of the preceding structure.

`QueryJobInformationObject` obtains the current limits. Other information classes impose limits on the user interface, I/O completion ports (see Chapter 14), security, and job termination.

Example: Using Job Objects

Program 6–7, `JobObjectShell`, illustrates using job objects to limit process execution time and to obtain user time statistics. `JobObjectShell` is a simple extension of `JobShell` that adds a command line time limit argument, in seconds. This limit applies to every process that `JobObjectShell` manages.

When you list the running processes, you will also see the total number of processes and the total user time on a four-processor computer.

Caution: The term "job" is used two ways here, which is confusing. First, the program uses Windows job objects to monitor all the individual processes. Then, borrowing some UNIX terminology, the program also regards each managed process to be a "job."

First, we'll modify the usual order and show Run 6–7, which runs the command:

```
JobObjectShell 60
```

---

[3] The working set is the set of virtual address space pages that the OS determines must be loaded in memory before any thread in the process is ready to run. This subject is covered in most OS texts.

to limit each process to a minute. The example then runs to shell commands:

```
timep grep 1234561 12.txt 13.txt 14.txt
timep grepMP 1234561 12.txt 13.txt 14.txt
```

as in Run 6–6. Note how the jobs command counts the processes that timep creates as well as those that grepMP creates to search the files, resulting in seven processes total. There is also a lot of contention for the console, mixing output from several processes, so you might want to run this example with the -c option.

There are also a few unexpected results, which are described for further investigation in Exercise 6–12.

Program 6–7 gives the JobObjectShell listing; it's an extension of Job-Shell (Program 6–3), so the listing is shortened to show the new code. There are

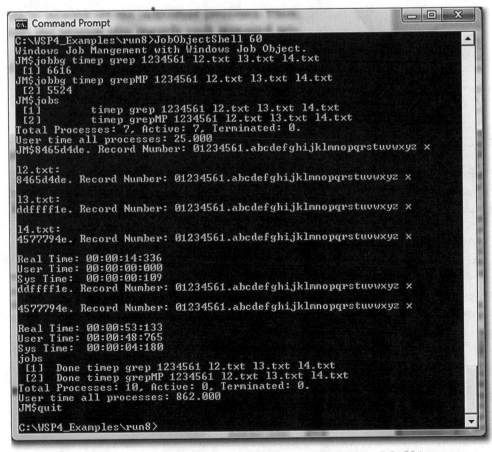

Run 6–7   JobObjectShell: Monitoring Processes with a Job Object

some deviations from the MSDN documentation, which are described in Exercise 6–12 for investigation.

Program 6–7 `JobObjectShell`: Monitoring Processes with a Job Object

```
/* Chapter 6 */
/* JobObjectShell.c JobShell extension
   Enhances JobShell with a time limit on each process.
   The process time limit (seconds) is argv[1] (if present)
      0 or omitted means no process time limit
*/

#include "Everything.h"
#include "JobManagement.h"

#define MILLION 1000000
HANDLE hJobObject = NULL;

JOBOBJECT_BASIC_LIMIT_INFORMATION basicLimits =
          {0, 0, JOB_OBJECT_LIMIT_PROCESS_TIME};

int _tmain (int argc, LPTSTR argv[])
{
    LARGE_INTEGER processTimeLimit;
    . . .
    hJobObject = NULL;
    processTimeLimit.QuadPart = 0;
    if (argc >= 2) processTimeLimit.QuadPart = atoi(argv[1]);
    basicLimits.PerProcessUserTimeLimit.QuadPart =
        processTimeLimit.QuadPart * 10 * MILLION;

    hJobObject = CreateJobObject(NULL, NULL);
    SetInformationJobObject(hJobObject,
        JobObjectBasicLimitInformation, &basicLimits,
        sizeof(JOBOBJECT_BASIC_LIMIT_INFORMATION));
    . . .
    /* Process commands. Call Jobbg, Jobs, etc. - listed below */
    CloseHandle (hJobObject);

    return 0;
}

/* Jobbg: Execute a command line in the background, put
   the job identity in the user's job file, and exit.
*/
int Jobbg (int argc, LPTSTR argv[], LPTSTR command)
{
    /* Execute the command line (targv) and store the job id,
       the process id, and the handle in the jobs file. */
```

```
    DWORD fCreate;
    LONG jobNumber;
    BOOL flags[2];

    STARTUPINFO startUp;
    PROCESS_INFORMATION processInfo;
    LPTSTR targv = SkipArg (command);

    GetStartupInfo (&startUp);

        /* Determine the options. */
    Options (argc, argv, _T ("cd"), &flags[0], &flags[1], NULL);

        /* Skip over the option field as well, if it exists. */
    if (argv[1][0] == '-')
        targv = SkipArg (targv);

    fCreate = flags[0] ? CREATE_NEW_CONSOLE : flags[1] ?
            DETACHED_PROCESS : 0;

    /* Create the job/thread suspended.
        Resume it once the job is entered properly. */
    CreateProcess (NULL, targv, NULL, NULL, TRUE,
            fCreate | CREATE_SUSPENDED | CREATE_NEW_PROCESS_GROUP,
            NULL, NULL, &startUp, &processInfo);

    AssignProcessToJobObject(hJobObject, processInfo.hProcess);

    jobNumber = GetJobNumber (&processInfo, targv);
    if (jobNumber >= 0)
        ResumeThread (processInfo.hThread);
    else {
        TerminateProcess (processInfo.hProcess, 3);
        CloseHandle (processInfo.hThread);
        CloseHandle (processInfo.hProcess);
        return 5;
    }

    CloseHandle (processInfo.hThread);
    CloseHandle (processInfo.hProcess);
    _tprintf (_T (" [%d] %d\n"), jobNumber, processInfo.dwProcessId);
    return 0;
}

/* Jobs: List all running or stopped jobs that have
    been created by this user under job management;
    that is, have been started with the jobbg command.
    List summary process count and user time information.
*/
```

```
int Jobs (int argc, LPTSTR argv[], LPTSTR command)
{
    JOBOBJECT_BASIC_ACCOUNTING_INFORMATION BasicInfo;

    DisplayJobs (); /* Not job objects, but jobbg created processes */

    /* Dispaly the job object information */
    QueryInformationJobObject(hJobObject,
        JobObjectBasicAccountingInformation, &BasicInfo,
        sizeof(JOBOBJECT_BASIC_ACCOUNTING_INFORMATION), NULL);
    _tprintf (_T("Total Processes: %d, Active: %d, Terminated: %d.\n"),
        BasicInfo.TotalProcesses, BasicInfo.ActiveProcesses,
        BasicInfo.TotalTerminatedProcesses);
    _tprintf (_T("User time all processes: %d.%03d\n"),
        BasicInfo.TotalUserTime.QuadPart / MILLION,
        (BasicInfo.TotalUserTime.QuadPart % MILLION) / 10000);

    return 0;
}
```

Summary

Windows provides a straightforward mechanism for managing processes and synchronizing their execution. Examples have shown how to manage the parallel execution of multiple processes and how to obtain information about execution times. Windows does not maintain a parent-child relationship among processes, so the programmer must manage this information if it is required, although job objects provide a convenient way to group processes.

Looking Ahead

Threads, which are independent units of execution within a process, are described in the next chapter. Thread management is similar in some ways to process management, and there are exit codes, termination, and waiting on thread handles. To illustrate this similarity, grepMP (Program 6–1) is reimplemented with threads in Chapter 7's first example program.

Chapter 8 then introduces synchronization, which coordinates operation between threads in the same or different processes.

Exercises

6–1. Extend Program 6–1 (`grepMP`) so that it accepts command line options and not just the pattern.

6–2. Rather than pass the temporary file name to the child process in Program 6–1, convert the inheritable file handle to a `DWORD` (a `HANDLE` requires 4 bytes in Win32; investigate the Win64 `HANDLE` size) and then to a character string. Pass this string to the child process on the command line. The child process, in turn, must convert the character string back to a handle value to use for output. The `catHA.c` and `grepHA.c` programs in the *Examples* file illustrate this technique. Is this technique advisable, or is it poor practice, in your opinion?

6–3. Program 6–1 waits for all processes to complete before listing the results. It is impossible to determine the order in which the processes actually complete within the current program. Modify the program so that it can also determine the termination order. *Hint:* Modify the call to `WaitForMultipleObjects` so that it returns after each individual process terminates. An alternative would be to sort by the process termination times.

6–4. The temporary files in Program 6–1 must be deleted explicitly. Can you use `FILE_FLAG_DELETE_ON_CLOSE` when creating the temporary files so that deletion is not required?

6–5. Determine any `grepMP` performance advantages (compared with sequential execution) on different multiprocessor systems or when the files are on separate or network drives. Appendix C presents some partial results, as does Run 6–1.

6–6. Can you find a way to collect the user and kernel time required by `grepMP`? It may be necessary to modify `grepMP` to use job objects.

6–7. Enhance the `DisplayJobs` function (Program 6–5) so that it reports the exit code of any completed job. Also, give the times (elapsed, kernel, and user) used so far by all jobs.

6–8. The job management functions have a defect that is difficult to fix. Suppose that a job is killed and the executive reuses its process ID before the process ID is removed from the job management file. There could be an `OpenProcess` on the process ID that now refers to a totally different process. The fix requires creating a helper process that holds duplicated handles for every created process so that the ID will not be reused. Another technique would be to include the process start time in the job management file. This time should be the same as the process start time of the process obtained from the process ID. *Note:* Process IDs will be reused quickly. UNIX, however, increments a counter to get a new process ID, and IDs will repeat only after the 32-bit counter wraps around. Therefore, Windows programs cannot assume that IDs will not, for all practical purposes, be reused.

6–9. Modify `JobShell` so that job information is maintained in the registry rather than in a temporary file.

6–10. Enhance `JobShell` so that the `jobs` command will include a count of the number of handles that each job is using. *Hint:* Use `GetProcessHandle-Count` (see MSDN).

6–11. `Jobbg` (in the `JobShell` listing) currently terminates a process if there is no room in the table for a new entry. Enhance the program to reserve a table location before creating the process, so as to avoid `TerminateProcess`.

6–12. `JobObjectShell` exhibits several anomalies and defects. Investigate and fix or explain them, if possible.

- Run 6–7 shows seven total processes, all active, after the first two jobs are started. This value is correct (do you agree?). After the jobs terminate, there are now 10 processes, none of which are active. Is this a bug (if so, is the bug in the program or in Windows?), or is the number correct?

- Program 6–7 shows plausible user time results in seconds (do you agree?). It obtains these results by dividing the total user time by 1,000,000, implying that the time is returned in microseconds. MSDN, however, says that the time is in 100 ns units, so the division should be by 10,000,000. Investigate. Is MSDN wrong?

- Does the limit on process time actually work, and is the program implemented correctly? `sortBT` (Program 5–1) is a time-consuming program for experimentation.

7 | Threads and Scheduling

The thread is the basic unit of execution in Windows, and a process can contain multiple, independent threads sharing the process's address space and other resources. Chapter 6 limited processes to a single thread, but there are many situations in which multiple threads are desirable. This chapter describes and illustrates Windows thread management and introduces program parallelism. The example programs use threads to simplify program design and to enhance performance. Chapter 8 continues with a description of synchronization objects and the performance impact, positive and negative. Chapter 9 examines performance tuning and trade-off issues and describes new NT6 locking and thread pool features. Chapter 10 describes advanced synchronization programming methods and models that greatly simplify the design and development of reliable multithreaded programs. The remaining chapters and example programs use threads and synchronization as a basic tool.

This chapter ends with a very brief discussion of fibers, which allow you to create separate tasks within a thread, followed by an introduction to parallelism. *Fibers are rarely used, and many readers might wish to skip the topic.*

Thread Overview

A *thread* is an independent unit of execution within a process. The multithreaded programming challenge requires organization and coordination of thread execution to simplify programs and to take advantage of the inherent parallelism of the program and the host computer.

Traditionally, programs execute as a single thread of execution. While several processes can execute concurrently, as in the Chapter 6 examples, and even interact through mechanisms such as shared memory or pipes (Chapter 11), concurrent single-threaded processes have several disadvantages.

- It is expensive and time consuming for the OS to switch running processes, and, in cases such as the multiprocess search (grepMP, Program 6–1), the processes are all executing the same program. Threads allow concurrent file or other processing within a single process, reducing overall system overhead.

- Except in the case of shared memory, processes are not tightly coupled, and it is difficult to share resources, such as open files.

- It is difficult and inefficient for single-threaded processes to manage several concurrent and interacting tasks, such as waiting for and processing user input, waiting for file or network input, and performing computation.

- I/O-bound programs, such as the Caesar cipher conversion program in Chapter 2 (cci, Program 2–3) are confined to a simple read-modify-write model. When you're processing sequential files, it can be more efficient to initiate as many read and write operations as possible. Windows also allows asynchronous overlapped I/O (Chapter 14), but threads can frequently achieve the same effect with less programming effort.

- The Windows executive will schedule independent threads on separate processors of a multiprocessor[1] computer, frequently improving performance by exploiting the multiple processors to execute application components concurrently.

This chapter discusses Windows threads and how to manage them. The examples illustrate thread usage with parallel file searching and a multithreaded sort. These two examples contrast I/O- and compute-intensive concurrent activities performed with threads. The chapter also presents an overview of Windows process and thread scheduling and concludes with a brief introduction to parallelism.

Perspectives and Issues

This chapter and those that follow take the point of view that not only do threads make certain programs simpler to design and implement but, with attention to a few basic rules and programming models, threaded programs also can improve performance and be reliable, easy to understand, and maintainable. Thread management functions are very similar to the process management functions so that, as just one example, there is a GetThreadExitCode function that is comparable to GetProcessExitCode.

---

[1] Multiple CPUs are common, even on laptops. Several processors may be on a single "multicore" chip, and, in turn, a computer may have several multicore chips. In Edition 3, we used the term "symmetric multiprocessing" (SMP), but this does not accurately describe multiple multicore chips in a single computer. We use both "multiprocessor" and "multicore" from now on to describe multiple processors accessing common, shared memory.

This point of view is not universally accepted. Many writers and software developers mention thread risks and issues and prefer to use multiple processes when concurrency is required. Common issues and concerns include the following.

- Threads share storage and other resources within a process, so one thread can accidentally modify another thread's data, leading to defects such as race conditions and deadlocks.

- In certain circumstances, concurrency can drastically degrade, rather than improve, performance.

- Converting legacy single-threaded programs to exploit threads can be challenging, partly for the reasons above as well as lack of program understanding.

These concerns are real but are generally avoidable with careful design and programming, and many of the issues are inherent to concurrency, whether using threads within a process, multiple processes, or special-purpose techniques, such as Windows asynchronous I/O (Chapter 14).

Thread Basics

Figure 6–1 in the previous chapter shows how threads exist in a process environment. Figure 7–1 illustrates threads by showing a multithreaded server that can process simultaneous requests from multiple networked clients; a distinct thread is dedicated to each client. A Chapter 11 example implements this model.

Threads within a process share data and code, but individual threads also have their own unique storage in addition to the shared data. Windows provides data for individual threads in several ways. Be aware, however, that the data is not totally protected from other threads within the process; the programmer must assure that threads do not access data assigned to other threads.

- Each thread has its own stack for function calls and other processing.

- The calling process can pass an argument (`Arg` in Figure 7–1), usually a pointer, to a thread at creation time. This argument is actually on the thread's stack.

- Each thread can allocate its own Thread Local Storage (TLS) indexes and can read and set TLS values. TLS, described later, provides small pointer arrays to threads, and a thread can access only its own TLS array. Among other advantages, TLS assures that threads will not modify one another's data.

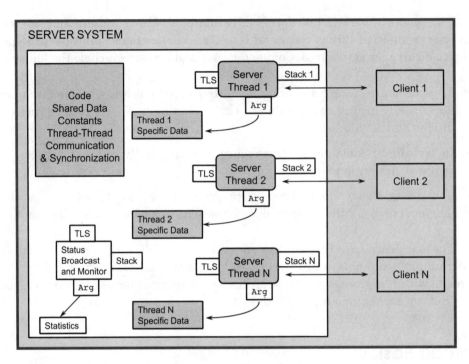

Figure 7-1   Threads in a Server Environment

The thread argument can point to an arbitrary data structure. In Figure 7–1's server example, this structure might contain the current request and the thread's response to that request as well as other working storage.

Windows programs can exploit multiprocessor systems by allowing different threads, even from the same process, to run concurrently on separate processors. This capability, if used properly, can enhance performance, but without sufficient care and a good strategy to exploit multiple processors, execution can actually be slower than on a single-processor computer, as we'll see in Chapter 9.

Thread Management

It should come as no surprise that threads, like any other Windows object, have handles and that there is a `CreateThread` system call to create an executable thread in the calling process's address space. As with processes, we will sometimes speak of "parent" and "child" threads, although the OS does not make any such distinction. `CreateThread` has several unique requirements.

CreateThread

The `CreateThread` function allows you to:

- Specify the thread's start address within the process's code.

- Specify the stack size, and the stack space is allocated from the process's virtual address space. The default stack size is the parent's virtual memory stack size (normally 1MB). One page is initially committed to the stack. New stack pages are committed as required until the stack reaches its maximum size and cannot grow anymore.

- Specify a pointer to a thread argument. The argument can be nearly anything and is interpreted by the thread and its parent.

- `CreateThread` returns a thread's ID value and its handle. A `NULL` handle value indicates a failure.

```
HANDLE CreateThread (
    LPSECURITY_ATTRIBUTES lpsa,
    DWORD dwStackSize,
    LPTHREAD_START_ROUTINE lpStartAddr,
    LPVOID lpThreadParm,
    DWORD dwCreationFlags,
    LPDWORD lpThreadId)
```

Parameters

`lpsa` is the familiar security attributes structure.

`dwStackSize` is the byte size of the new thread's stack. Use 0 to default to the primary thread's stack size.

`lpStartAddr` points to the thread function (within the calling process) to be executed. This function accepts a single pointer argument and returns a 32-bit `DWORD` exit code. The thread can interpret the argument as a `DWORD` or a pointer. The thread function signature, then, is as follows:

```
DWORD WINAPI ThreadFunc (LPVOID)
```

lpThreadParm is the pointer passed as the thread argument and is interpreted by the thread and its parent, normally as a pointer to an argument structure.

dwCreationFlags, if 0, means that the thread is ready to run immediately. If dwCreationFlags is CREATE_SUSPENDED, the new thread will be in the suspended state, requiring a ResumeThread function call to move the thread to the ready state.

lpThreadId points to a DWORD that receives the new thread's identifier. The pointer can also be NULL, indicating that no thread ID will be returned.

The CreateRemoteThread function allows a thread to be created in another process. Compared with CreateThread, there is an additional parameter for the process handle, and the function addresses must be in the target process's address space. CreateRemoteThread is one of several interesting, and potentially dangerous, ways for one process to affect another directly, and it might be useful in writing, for example, a debugger. There is no way to call this function usefully and safely in normal applications. Avoid it!

ExitThread

All threads in a process can exit using the ExitThread function. A common alternative, however, is for a thread to return from the thread function using the exit code as the return value. The thread's stack is deallocated and all handles referring to the thread are signaled. If the thread is linked to one or more DLLs (either implicitly or explicitly), then the DllMain functions (Chapter 4) of each DLL will be called with DLL_THREAD_DETACH as the "reason."

```
VOID ExitThread (DWORD dwExitCode)
```

When the last thread in a process exits, the process itself terminates.

One thread can terminate another thread with the TerminateThread function, but the thread's resources will not be deallocated, completion handlers do not execute, and there is no notification to attached DLLs. It is best if the thread terminates itself with a return statement; TerminateThread usage is strongly discouraged, and it has the same disadvantages as TerminateProcess.

GetExitCodeThread

A terminated thread (again, a thread normally should terminate itself) will continue to exist until the last handle to it is closed using CloseHandle. Any other thread, perhaps one waiting for some other thread to terminate, can retrieve the exit code.

```
BOOL GetExitCodeThread (
    HANDLE hThread,
    LPDWORD lpExitCode)
```

`lpExitCode` will contain the thread's exit code. If the thread is still running, the value is `STILL_ACTIVE`.

Thread Identity

You can obtain thread IDs and handles using functions that are similar to those used with processes.

- `GetCurrentThread` returns a noninheritable pseudohandle to the calling thread.

- `GetCurrentThreadId` obtains the thread ID rather than the handle.

- `GetThreadId` obtains a thread's ID from its handle.

- `OpenThread` creates a thread handle from a thread ID. `OpenProcess` was very useful in `JobShell` (Program 6–3), and you can use `OpenThread` in a similar fashion.

Additional Thread Management Functions

While the thread management functions just discussed are sufficient in most cases, including the examples in this book, two additional functions were introduced in XP and Windows 2003 (that is, NT5). Brief descriptions follow.

1. `GetProcessIdOfThread`, which requires Windows 2003 or later (XP does not support it), finds the process ID of a thread from the thread's handle. You could use this function in a program that manages or interacts with threads in other processes. If necessary, use `OpenProcess` to obtain a process handle.

2. `GetThreadIOPendingFlag` determines whether the thread, identified by its handle, has any outstanding I/O requests. For example, the thread might be blocked on a `ReadFile` operation. The result is the status at the time that the function is executed; the actual status could change at any time if the target thread completes or initiates an operation.

Suspending and Resuming Threads

Every thread has a *suspend count*, and a thread can execute only if this count is 0. One thread can increment or decrement the suspend count of another thread using SuspendThread and ResumeThread. Recall that a thread can be created in the suspended state with a count of 1.

```
DWORD ResumeThread (HANDLE hThread)

DWORD SuspendThread (HANDLE hThread)
```

Both functions, if successful, return the previous suspend count. 0xFFFFFFFF indicates failure.

Waiting for Threads to Terminate

One thread can wait for another thread to terminate in the same way that threads wait for process termination (Chapter 6). Use a wait function (WaitForSingle-Object or WaitForMultipleObjects) using thread handles instead of process handles. Note that the handles in the array passed to WaitForMultipleObjects do not all need to be of the same type; for example, thread, process, and other handle types can be mixed in a single call.

WaitForMultipleObjects can wait for only MAXIMUM_WAIT_OBJECTS (64) handles at one time, but you can perform a series of waits if you have a large number of threads. Program 6–1 already illustrated this technique; most programs in this book will perform single waits.

The wait function waits for the object, indicated by the handle, to become *signaled*. In the case of threads, ExitThread and TerminateThread set the object to the signaled state, releasing all other threads waiting on the object, including threads that might wait in the future after the thread terminates. Once a thread handle is signaled, it never becomes nonsignaled. The same is true of process handles but not of handles to some other objects, such as mutexes and events (see the next chapter).

Note that multiple threads can wait on the same object. Similarly, the ExitProcess function sets the process state and the states of all its threads to signaled.

Threads are a well-established concept in many OSs, and historically, many UNIX vendors and users have provided their own proprietary implementations. Some thread libraries have been implemented outside the kernel. POSIX Pthreads are now the standard. Pthreads are part of all commercial UNIX and Linux implementations. The system calls are distinguished from normal UNIX system calls by the pthread_ prefix name. Pthreads are also supported on some proprietary non-UNIX systems.

pthread_create is the equivalent of CreateThread, and pthread_exit is the equivalent of ExitThread. One thread waits for another to exit with pthread-_join. Pthreads provide the very useful pthread_cancel function, which, unlike TerminateThread, ensures that completion handlers and cancellation handlers are executed. Thread cancellation would be a welcome addition to Windows, but Chapter 10 will show a method to achieve the same effect.

Using the C Library in Threads

Most code requires the C library, even if it is just to manipulate strings. Historically, the C library was written to operate in single-threaded processes, so some functions use global storage to store intermediate results. Such libraries are not *thread-safe* because two separate threads might, for example, be simultaneously accessing the library and modifying the library's global storage. Proper design of threaded code is discussed again in Chapter 8, which describes Windows synchronization.

The strtok function is an example of a C library function that is not thread-safe. strtok, which scans a string to find the next occurrence of a token, maintains *persistent state* between successive function calls, and this state is in static storage, shared by all the threads calling the function.

Microsoft C solves such problems by supplying a thread-safe C library implementation named LIBCMT.LIB. There is more. Do not use CreateThread; if you do, there is a risk of different threads accessing and modifying the same data that the library requires for correct operation. Instead, use a special C function, _beginthreadex, to start a thread and create thread-specific working storage for LIBCMT.LIB. Use _endthreadex in place of ExitThread to terminate a thread.

Note: There is a _beginthread function, intended to be simpler to use, *but you should never use it*. First, _beginthread does not have security attributes or flags and does not return a thread ID. More importantly, it actually closes the thread handle it creates, and the returned thread handle may be invalid by the time the parent thread stores it. Also avoid _endthread; it does not allow for a return value.

The _beginthreadex arguments are exactly the same as for the Windows functions but without the Windows type definitions; therefore, be sure to cast the _beginthreadex return value to a HANDLE to avoid warning messages. Be certain to define _MT before any include files; this definition is in Environment.h for the sample programs. That is all there is to it. When you're using the Visual Studio development environment, be sure to do the following:

- Open the `Project Properties` pages.

- Under `Configuration Properties`, expand `C/C++`.

- Select `Code Generation`.

- For the `Runtime Library`, specify `Multi-threaded DLL (/MD)`.

- Terminate threads with `_endthreadex` or simply use a `return` statement at the end of the thread routine.

All examples will operate this way, and the programs will never use `CreateThread` directly, even if the thread functions do not use the C library.

Thread-Safe Libraries

User-developed libraries must be carefully designed to avoid thread safety issues, especially when persistent state is involved. A Chapter 12 example (Program 12–5), where a DLL maintains state in a parameter, shows one strategy.

Another Chapter 12 example (Program 12–6) demonstrates an alternative approach that exploits the `DllMain` function and TLS, which is described later in this chapter.

Example: Multithreaded Pattern Searching

Program 6–1, `grepMP`, used processes to search multiple files simultaneously. Program 7–1, `grepMT`, includes the `grep` pattern searching source code so that threads can perform the searching within a single process. The pattern searching code relies on the C library for file I/O. The main control program is similar to the process implementation.

This example also shows that a form of asynchronous I/O is possible with threads without using the explicit methods of Chapter 14. In this example, the program is managing concurrent I/O to multiple files, and the main thread, or any other thread, can perform additional processing before waiting for I/O completion. In the author's opinion, threads are a much simpler method of achieving asynchronous I/O, and Chapter 14 compares the methods, allowing readers to form their own opinions. We will see, however, that asynchronous I/O, combined with I/O completion ports, is useful and often necessary when the number of threads is large. Furthermore, as of NT6, extended asynchronous I/O often performs very well.

`grepMT`, for the purposes of illustration, differs in another way from `grepMP`. Here, `WaitForMultipleObjects` waits for a *single* thread to terminate rather than waiting for all the threads. The appropriate output is displayed before waiting for another thread to complete. The completion order will, in most cases, vary from one run to the next. It is easy to modify the program to display the results in the order of the command line arguments; just imitate grepMP.

Finally, notice that there is a limit of 64 threads due to the value of MAXIMUM_WAIT_OBJECTS, which limits the number of handles in the WaitForMultipleObjects call. If more threads are required, create the appropriate logic to loop on either WaitForSingleObject or WaitForMultipleObjects.

Caution: grepMT performs asynchronous I/O in the sense that separate threads are concurrently, and synchronously, reading different files with read operations that block until the read is complete. You can also concurrently read from the same file if you have distinct handles on the file (typically, one per thread). These handles should be generated by CreateFile rather than DuplicateHandle. Chapter 14 describes asynchronous I/O, with and without user threads, and an example in the *Examples* file (cciMT; see Chapter 14) has several threads performing I/O to the same file.

Note: You can perform all sorts of parallel file processing using this design. All that is required is to change the "ThGrep" function at the end of Program 7–1. An exercise suggests that you implement a parallel word count (wc) program this way, but you could also edit files or compile source code files in parallel.

Program 7–1 grepMT: Multithreaded Pattern Searching

```
/* Chapter 7. grepMT. */
/* Parallel grep -- multiple thread version. */

#include "Everything.h"
typedef struct { /* grep thread's data structure. */
    int argc;
    TCHAR targv[4][MAX_PATH];
} GREP_THREAD_ARG;
typedef GREP_THREAD_ARG *PGR_ARGS;
static DWORD WINAPI ThGrep (PGR_ARGS pArgs);

int _tmain (int argc, LPSTR argv[])
{
    GREP_THREAD_ARG * gArg;
    HANDLE * tHandle;
    DWORD threadIndex, exitCode;
    TCHAR commandLine[MAX_COMMAND_LINE];
    int iThrd, threadCount;
    STARTUPINFO startUp;
    PROCESS_INFORMATION processInfo;

    GetStartupInfo (&startUp);
    /* Boss thread: create separate "grep" thread for each file. */
    tHandle = malloc ((argc - 2) * sizeof (HANDLE));
    gArg = malloc ((argc - 2) * sizeof (GREP_THREAD_ARG));
```

```
    for (iThrd = 0; iThrd < argc - 2; iThrd++) {
        _tcscpy (gArg[iThrd].targv[1], argv[1]); /* Pattern. */
        _tcscpy (gArg[iThrd].targv[2], argv[iThrd + 2]);
        GetTempFileName /* Temp file name. */
                (".", "Gre", 0, gArg[iThrd].targv[3]);
        gArg[iThrd].argc = 4;

        /* Create a worker thread to execute the command line. */
        tHandle[iThrd] = (HANDLE)_beginthreadex (
                NULL, 0, ThGrep, &gArg[iThrd], 0, NULL);
    }
    /* Redirect std output for file listing process. */
    startUp.dwFlags = STARTF_USESTDHANDLES;
    startUp.hStdOutput = GetStdHandle (STD_OUTPUT_HANDLE);

    /* Worker threads are all running. Wait for them to complete. */
    threadCount = argc - 2;
    while (threadCount > 0) {
        threadIndex = WaitForMultipleObjects (
                threadCount, tHandle, FALSE, INFINITE);
        iThrd = (int) threadIndex - (int) WAIT_OBJECT_0;
        GetExitCodeThread (tHandle[iThrd], &exitCode);
        CloseHandle (tHandle[iThrd]);
        if (exitCode == 0) { /* Pattern found. */
            if (argc > 3) {
            /* Print file name if more than one. */
                _tprintf (_T ("\n**Search results - file: %s\n"),
                        gArg[iThrd].targv[2]);
                fflush (stdout);
            }
            /* Use the "cat" program to list the result files. */
            _stprintf (commandLine, _T ("%s%s"), _T ("cat "),
                    gArg[iThrd].targv[3]);
            CreateProcess (NULL, commandLine, NULL, NULL,
                    TRUE, 0, NULL, NULL, &startUp, &processInfo);
            WaitForSingleObject (processInfo.hProcess, INFINITE);
            CloseHandle (processInfo.hProcess);
            CloseHandle (processInfo.hThread);
        }
        DeleteFile (gArg[iThrd].targv[3]);

        /* Adjust thread and file name arrays. */
        tHandle[iThrd] = tHandle[threadCount - 1];
        _tcscpy (gArg[iThrd].targv[3], gArg[threadCount - 1].targv[3]);
        _tcscpy (gArg[iThrd].targv[2], gArg[threadCount - 1].targv[2]);
        threadCount--;
    }
}
```

```
/* The form of the grep thread function code is:
static DWORD WINAPI ThGrep (PGR_ARGS pArgs)
{
    . . .
} */
```

Run 7–1 shows grepMT operation and compares the performance with grepMP, using the same four 640MB files.

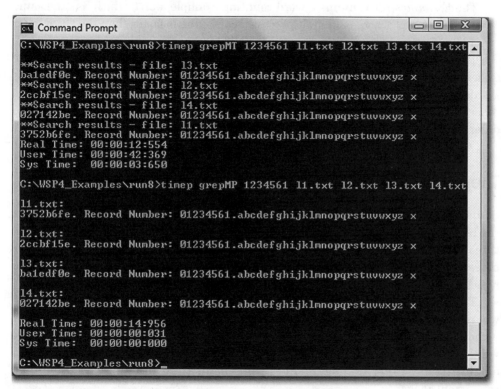

Run 7–1   grepMT: Multithreaded Pattern Searching

Performance Impact

grepMP and grepMT are comparable in terms of program structure and complexity, but grepMT has the expected advantage of better performance; it is more efficient for the kernel to switch between threads than between processes. Run 7–1 shows that the theoretical advantage is real, but not large (12.554 versus 14.956 seconds). Specifically, if you are processing multiple large files of about the same size, with one thread per file, performance improves nearly linearly with the number of files up to the number of processors on the computer. You may not see this improvement with smaller files, however, because of the thread creation and management overhead. Chapter 9 shows how to improve performance slightly more with NT6 thread pools.

Both implementations exploit multiprocessor systems, giving a considerable improvement in the elapsed time; threads, whether in the same process or in different processes, run in parallel on the different processors. The measured user time actually exceeds the elapsed time because the user time is the total for all the processors.

The *Examples* file contains a word counting example, wcMT, which has the same structure as grepMT and, on a multiprocessor computer, is faster than the Cygwin wc command (Cygwin, an open source set of UNIX/Linux commands, implements wc).

There is a common misconception, however, that this sort of parallelism using either grepMP or grepMT yields performance improvements only on multiprocessor systems. You can also gain performance when there are multiple disk drives or some other parallelism in the storage system. In such cases, multiple I/O operations to different files can run concurrently.

The Boss/Worker and Other Threading Models

grepMT illustrates the "boss/worker" threading model, and Figure 6–3 illustrates the relationship if "thread" is substituted for "process." The boss thread (the main thread in this case) assigns tasks for the worker threads to perform. Each worker thread is given a file to search, and the worker threads pass their results to the boss thread in a temporary file.

There are numerous variations, such as the *work crew model* in which the workers cooperate on a single task, each performing a small piece. The next example uses a work crew (see Figure 7–2). The workers might even divide up the work themselves without direction from the boss. Multithreaded programs can employ nearly every management arrangement that humans use to manage concurrent tasks.

The two other major models are the *client/server model* (illustrated in Figure 7–1 and developed in Chapter 11) and the *pipeline model*, where work moves from one thread to the next (see Chapter 10 and Figure 10–1 for an example of a multistage pipeline).

There are many advantages to using these models when designing a multithreaded program, including the following.

- Most multithreaded programming problems can be solved using one of the standard models, expediting design, development, and debugging.

- Not only does using a well-understood and tested model avoid many of the mistakes that are so easy to make in a multithreaded program, but the model also helps you obtain the best performance.

- The models correspond naturally to the structures of most programming problems.

- Programmers who maintain the program will be able to understand it much more easily if documentation describes the program in terms that everyone understands.

- Troubleshooting an unfamiliar program is much easier if you analyze it in terms of models. Frequently, an underlying problem is found when the program is seen to violate the basic principles of one of the models.

- Many common defects, such as race conditions and deadlocks, are also described by simple models, as are effective methods of using the synchronization objects described in Chapters 9 and 10.

These classical thread models are used in many OSs. The Component Object Model (COM), widely used in Windows systems, uses different terminology.

Example: Merge-Sort—Exploiting Multiple Processors

This example, diagrammed in Figure 7–2, shows how to use threads to get significant performance gains, especially on a multiprocessor computer. The basic idea is to divide the problem into component tasks, give each task to a separate thread, and then combine the results to get the complete solution. The Windows executive will automatically assign the threads to separate processors, so the threads will execute in parallel, reducing elapsed time.

This strategy, often called the *divide and conquer strategy* or the *work crew model,* is useful both for performance and as an algorithm design method. grepMT, Program 7–1, could be considered one example; it creates a thread for each file or pattern matching task.

Next, consider another example in which a single task, sorting a file, is divided into subtasks delegated to separate threads.

Merge-sort, in which the array to be sorted is divided into smaller arrays, is a classic divide and conquer algorithm. Each small array is sorted individually, and the individual sorted arrays are merged in pairs to yield larger sorted arrays. The pairwise merging continues until completion. Generally, merge-sort starts with small arrays, which can be sorted efficiently with a simple algorithm. This example starts with larger arrays so that there can be one array for each processor. Figure 7–2 is a sketch of the algorithm.

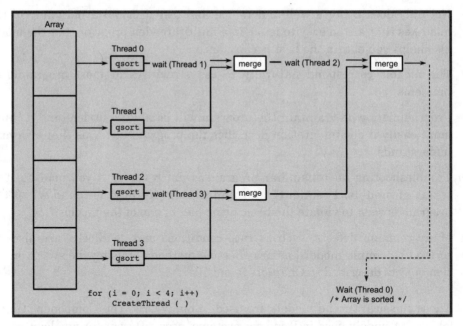

Figure 7–2   Merge-Sort with Multiple Threads

Program 7–2 shows the implementation details. The user specifies the number of tasks on the command line. Exercise 7–9 suggests that `sortMT` use `Get-SystemInfo` to find the number of processors and then create one thread per processor.

Notice that the program runs efficiently on single-processor systems with sufficient memory and gains a significant performance improvement on multiprocessor systems. *Caution:* The algorithm as shown will work only if the number of records in the sort file is divisible by the number of threads and if the number of threads is a power of 2. Exercise 7–8 removes these limitations.

Note: In understanding this program, concentrate on the thread management logic separately from the logic that determines which portion of the array a thread should sort. Notice too that the C library `qsort` function is used, so there is no need to be concerned with developing an efficient basic sort function.

Additional Point to Notice: The thread creation loop (look for the comment "Create the sorting threads" on the second page of the listing) creates the worker threads in the suspended state. The threads are resumed only after all the worker threads are created. The reason for this can be seen from Figure 7–2; consider what would happen if Thread 0 waits for Thread 1 before Thread 1 is created. There would then be no handle to wait for. This is an example of a "race" condition where two or more threads make unsafe assumptions about the progress of the other threads. Exercises 7–10 and 7–13 investigate this further.

Program 7–2 sortMT: Merge-Sort with Multiple Threads

```
/* Chapter 7. SortMT.
   File sorting with multiple threads (a work crew).
   sortMT [options] nt file */

#include "Everything.h"
#define DATALEN 56 /* Key: 8 bytes; Data: 56 bytes. */
#define KEYLEN 8
typedef struct _RECORD {
      CHAR key[KEYLEN];
      TCHAR data[DATALEN];
} RECORD;
#define RECSIZE sizeof (RECORD)
typedef RECORD * LPRECORD;

typedef struct _THREADARG {        /* Thread argument */
   DWORD iTh;                      /* Thread number: 0, 1, 2, ... */
   LPRECORD lowRecord;             /* Low record */
   LPRECORD highRecord;            /* High record */
} THREADARG, *PTHREADARG;

static int KeyCompare (LPCTSTR, LPCTSTR);
static DWORD WINAPI SortThread (PTHREADARG pThArg);
static DWORD nRec; /* Total number of records to be sorted. */
static HANDLE *pThreadHandle;

int _tmain (int argc, LPTSTR argv[])
{
   HANDLE hFile, mHandle;
   LPRECORD pRecords = NULL;
   DWORD lowRecordNum, nRecTh, numFiles, iTh;
   LARGE_INTEGER fileSize;
   BOOL noPrint;
   int iFF, iNP;
   PTHREADARG threadArg;
   LPTSTR stringEnd;

   iNP = Options (argc, argv, _T ("n"), &noPrint, NULL);
   iFF = iNP + 1;
   numFiles = _ttoi (argv[iNP]);

   /* Open the file and map it */
   hFile = CreateFile (argv[iFF], GENERIC_READ | GENERIC_WRITE,
          0, NULL, OPEN_EXISTING, 0, NULL);
   /* For technical reasons, we need to add bytes to the end. */
   SetFilePointer(hFile, 2, 0, FILE_END);
   SetEndOfFile(hFile);
```

```
    mHandle = CreateFileMapping(hFile, NULL, PAGE_READWRITE,
                            0, 0, NULL);

    /* Get the file size. */
    GetFileSizeEx (hFile, &fileSize);
    nRec = fileSize.QuadPart / RECSIZE;/* Total number of records. */
    nRecTh = nRec / numFiles;/* Records per thread. */
    threadArg = malloc (numFiles*sizeof (THREADARG)); /* thread args */
    pThreadHandle = malloc (numFiles * sizeof (HANDLE));

    /* Map the entire file */
    pRecords = MapViewOfFile(mHandle, FILE_MAP_ALL_ACCESS, 0, 0, 0);
    CloseHandle (mHandle);

    /* Create the sorting threads. */
    lowRecordNum = 0;
    for (iTh = 0; iTh < numFiles; iTh++) {
        threadArg[iTh].iTh = iTh;
        threadArg[iTh].lowRecord = pRecords + lowRecordNum;
        threadArg[iTh].highRecord = pRecords + (lowRecordNum + nRecTh);
        lowRecordNum += nRecTh;
        pThreadHandle[iTh] = (HANDLE)_beginthreadex (NULL,
            0, SortThread, &threadArg[iTh], CREATE_SUSPENDED, NULL);
    }

    /* Resume all the initially suspened threads. */
    for (iTh = 0; iTh < numFiles; iTh++)
        ResumeThread (pThreadHandle[iTh]);

    /* Wait for the sort-merge threads to complete. */
    WaitForSingleObject (pThreadHandle[0], INFINITE);
    for (iTh = 0; iTh < numFiles; iTh++)
        CloseHandle (pThreadHandle[iTh]);

    /*  Print out the entire sorted file as one single string. */
    stringEnd = (LPTSTR) pRecords + nRec*RECSIZE;
    *stringEnd =_T('\0');
    if (!noPrint) {
        _tprintf (_T("%s"), (LPCTSTR) pRecords);
    }
    UnmapViewOfFile(pRecords);
    /* Restore the file length */
    SetFilePointer(hFile, -2, 0, FILE_END);
    SetEndOfFile(hFile);

    CloseHandle(hFile);
    free (threadArg); free (pThreadHandle);
    return 0;
} /* End of _tmain. */
```

```
static VOID MergeArrays (LPRECORD, DWORD);

DWORD WINAPI SortThread (PTHREADARG pThArg)
{
    DWORD groupSize = 2, myNumber, twoToI = 1;
          /* twoToI = 2^i, where i is the merge step number. */
    DWORD_PTR numbersInGroup;
    LPRECORD first;

    myNumber = pThArg->iTh;
    first = pThArg->lowRecord;
    numbersInGroup = pThArg->highRecord - first;

    /* Sort this portion of the array. */
    qsort (first, numbersInGroup, RECSIZE, KeyCompare);

    /* Either exit the thread or wait for the adjoining thread. */
    while ((myNumber % groupSize) == 0 && numbersInGroup < nRec) {
             /* Merge with the adjacent sorted array. */
        WaitForSingleObject (pThreadHandle[myNumber + twoToI],
                             INFINITE);
        MergeArrays (first, numbersInGroup);
        numbersInGroup *= 2;
        groupSize *= 2;
        twoToI *=2;
    }
    return 0;
}


static VOID MergeArrays (LPRECORD p1, DWORD nRecs)
{
    /* Merge adjacent arrays, with nRecs records. p1 is the first */
    DWORD iRec = 0, i1 = 0, i2 = 0;
    LPRECORD pDest, p1Hold, pDestHold, p2 = p1 + nRecs;

    pDest = pDestHold = malloc (2 * nRecs * RECSIZE);
    p1Hold = p1;

    while (i1 < nRecs && i2 < nRecs) {
        if (KeyCompare ((LPCTSTR)p1, (LPCTSTR)p2) <= 0) {
            memcpy (pDest, p1, RECSIZE);
            i1++; p1++; pDest++;
        }
        else {
            memcpy (pDest, p2, RECSIZE);
            i2++; p2++; pDest++;
        }
    }
    if (i1 >= nRecs)
        memcpy (pDest, p2, RECSIZE * (nRecs - i2));
```

```
        else
            memcpy (pDest, p1, RECSIZE * (nRecs - i1));

        memcpy (p1Hold, pDestHold, 2 * nRecs * RECSIZE);
        free (pDestHold);
        return;
}
```

Run 7–2a `sortMT`: Sorting with Multiple Threads

Run 7–2a shows sorting of large and small files, with 1, 2, 4, and 8 threads for the large file. The test computer has four processors, and four threads give the best results. Also note that the first single-thread run is slower than the second; this may be explained by the fact that the file is cached in memory during the second run. `sortFL` (Program 5–4) was the best previous result, 3.123 seconds.

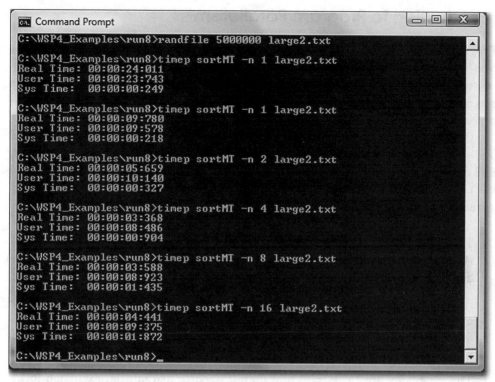

```
Command Prompt                                                    _  □  X

C:\WSP4_Examples\run8>randfile 5000000 large2.txt

C:\WSP4_Examples\run8>timep sortMT -n 1 large2.txt
Real Time: 00:00:24:011
User Time: 00:00:23:743
Sys Time:  00:00:00:249

C:\WSP4_Examples\run8>timep sortMT -n 1 large2.txt
Real Time: 00:00:09:780
User Time: 00:00:09:578
Sys Time:  00:00:00:218

C:\WSP4_Examples\run8>timep sortMT -n 2 large2.txt
Real Time: 00:00:05:659
User Time: 00:00:10:140
Sys Time:  00:00:00:327

C:\WSP4_Examples\run8>timep sortMT -n 4 large2.txt
Real Time: 00:00:03:368
User Time: 00:00:08:486
Sys Time:  00:00:00:904

C:\WSP4_Examples\run8>timep sortMT -n 8 large2.txt
Real Time: 00:00:03:588
User Time: 00:00:08:923
Sys Time:  00:00:01:435

C:\WSP4_Examples\run8>timep sortMT -n 16 large2.txt
Real Time: 00:00:04:441
User Time: 00:00:09:375
Sys Time:  00:00:01:872

C:\WSP4_Examples\run8>_
```

Run 7–2b `sortMT`: Sorting with Multiple Threads and a Larger File

An additional screenshot, Run 7–2b, uses a 5,000,000 record (320MB) file so that the time improvements are more significant.

Performance

Multiprocessor systems give good results when the number of threads is the same as the number of processors. Performance improves with more threads but not linearly because of the merging. Additional threads beyond the processor count slow the program.

Divide and conquer is more than just a strategy for algorithm design; it can also be the key to exploiting multiprocessors. The single-processor results can vary. On a computer with limited memory (that is, insufficient physical memory to hold the entire file), using multiple threads might increase the sort time because the threads contend for available physical memory. On the other hand, multiple threads can improve performance with a single processor when there is sufficient memory. The results are also heavily dependent on the initial data arrangement.

Introduction to Program Parallelism

Programs 7–1 and 7–2 share some common properties that permit "paralleliza-tion" so that subtasks can execute concurrently, or "in parallel" on separate pro-cessors. Parallelization is the key to future performance improvement, since we can no longer depend on increased CPU clock rates and since multicore and multi-processor systems are increasingly common.

Chapter 10 discusses these technology trends and parallelism in more detail and relates these trends to the thread pools available in NT6 (Windows 7, Vista, and Server 2008). However, sortMT, wcMT, and grepMT have already illustrated the potential performance benefits from parallelism. The properties that enabled parallelism include the following:

- There are separate worker subtasks that can run independently, without any interaction between them. For example, grepMT can process each file indepen-dently, and sortMT can sort subsets of the entire array.

- As subtasks complete, a master program can combine, or "reduce," the results of several subtasks into a single result. Thus, sortMT merges sorted arrays to form larger sorted arrays. grepMT and wcMT simply display the results from the individual files, in order.

- The programs are "lock-free" and do not need to use mutual exclusion locks, such as the mutexes described next in Chapter 8. The only synchronization re-quired is for the boss thread to wait for the worker threads to complete.

- The worker subtasks run as individual threads, potentially running on sepa-rate processors.

- Program performance scales automatically, up to some limit, as you run on systems with more processors; the programs themselves do not, in general, de-termine the processor count on the host computer. Instead, the Windows ker-nel assigns worker subtasks to available processors.

- If you "serialize" the program by replacing the thread creation calls with di-rect function calls and remove the wait calls, you should get precisely the same results as the parallel program.[2] The serialized program is, moreover, much easier to debug.

---

[2] This statement fails, or is only approximately true, if operation order and associativity are important. For example, if you sum floating-point numbers, the order is important. In these cases, the multi-threaded results will also vary from run to run, and the serial execution is one of many possible multi-threaded execution sequences.

- The maximum performance improvement is limited by the program's "parallelism," thread management overhead, and computations that cannot be parallelized. The maximum parallelism for sortMT is determined by the command line parameter specifying the number of threads, although the merging steps do not use all the threads. grepMT parallelism cannot be larger than the number of files on the command line. Computations that cannot be parallelized include initialization and reducing worker results.

Be aware, however, that these two examples are relatively simple and "coarse grained." The subtasks are easy to identify and run for a relatively long time period, although the subtasks will require different amounts of time, depending primarily on the file sizes. In general, correct program parallelization that improves performance significantly can be challenging.

Thread Local Storage

Threads may need to allocate and manage their own storage independently of and protected from other threads in the same process. One technique is to have the creating thread call CreateThread (or _beginthreadex) with lpvThreadParm pointing to a data structure that is unique for each thread. The thread can then allocate additional data structures and access them through lpvThreadParm. Program 7–1 used this technique.

Windows also provides TLS, which gives each thread its own array of pointers. Figure 7–3 shows this TLS arrangement.

Initially, no TLS indexes (rows) are allocated, but new rows can be allocated and deallocated at any time, with at least TLS_MINIMUM_AVAILABLE (64) indexes

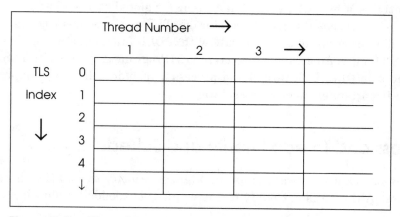

Figure 7–3   Thread Local Storage within a Process

for any process. The number of columns can change as new threads are created and old ones terminate.

The first issue is TLS index management. The primary thread is a logical place to do this, but any thread can manage thread indexes.

`TlsAlloc` returns the allocated index (≥ 0), with −1 (`0xFFFFFFFF`) if no index is available.

```
DWORD TlsAlloc (VOID)

BOOL TlsFree (DWORD dwIndex)
```

An individual thread can get and set its values (void pointers) from its slot using a TLS index.

The programmer must ensure that the TLS index parameter is valid—that is, that it has been allocated with `TlsAlloc` and has not been freed.

```
LPVOID TlsGetValue (DWORD dwTlsIndex)

BOOL TlsSetValue (DWORD dwTlsIndex,
    LPVOID lpTlsValue)
```

TLS provides a convenient mechanism for storage that is global within a thread but unavailable to other threads. Normal global storage is shared by all threads. Although no thread can access another thread's TLS, any thread can call `TlsFree` and destroy an index for all threads, so use `TlsFree` carefully. TLS is frequently used by DLLs as a replacement for global storage in a library; each thread, in effect, has its own global storage. TLS also provides a convenient way for a calling program to communicate with a DLL function, and this is the most common TLS use. An example in Chapter 12 (Program 12–5) exploits TLS to build a thread-safe DLL; DLL thread and process attach/detach calls (Chapter 5) are another important element in the solution.

Process and Thread Priority and Scheduling

The Windows kernel always runs the highest-priority thread that is ready for execution. A thread is not ready if it is waiting, suspended, or blocked for some reason.

Threads receive priority relative to their process priority classes. Process priority classes are set initially by `CreateProcess` (Chapter 6), and each has a *base priority,* with values including:

- `IDLE_PRIORITY_CLASS`, for threads that will run only when the system is idle.

- `NORMAL_PRIORITY_CLASS`, indicating no special scheduling requirements.

- `HIGH_PRIORITY_CLASS`, indicating time-critical tasks that should be executed immediately.

- `REALTIME_PRIORITY_CLASS`, the highest possible priority.

The two extreme classes are rarely used, and the normal class can be used normally, as the name suggests. Windows is not a real-time OS, and using `REALTIME_PRIORITY_CLASS` can prevent other essential threads from running. Set and get the priority class with:

```
BOOL SetPriorityClass (HANDLE hProcess,
    DWORD dwPriority)

DWORD GetPriorityClass (HANDLE hProcess)
```

You can use the values listed above as well as:

- Two additional priority classes, `ABOVE_NORMAL_PRIORITY_CLASS` (which is below `HIGH_PRIORITY_CLASS`) and `BELOW_NORMAL_PRIORITY_CLASS` (which is above `IDLE_PRIORITY_CLASS`).

- `PROCESS_MODE_BACKGROUND_BEGIN`, which lowers the priority of the process and its threads for background work without affecting the responsiveness of foreground[3] processes and threads. The handle must represent the calling process; a process cannot put another into background mode. You need NT6 (Windows Vista or later) to use this mode.

- `PROCESS_MODE_BACKGROUND_END`, which restores the process priority to the value before it was set with `PROCESS_MODE_BACKGROUND_BEGIN`.

---

[3] Foreground threads and processes ("tasks") are generally those that need to respond quickly, such as a thread that interacts directly with the user. Background tasks do not need to respond quickly; examples include file processing or time-consuming computations.

A process can change or determine its own priority or that of another process, security permitting.

Thread priorities are either absolute or are set relative to the process base priority. At thread creation time, the priority is set to that of the process. The relative thread priorities are in a range of ±2 "points" from the process's base. The symbolic names of the resulting common thread priorities, starting with the five relative priorities, are:

- `THREAD_PRIORITY_LOWEST`

- `THREAD_PRIORITY_BELOW_NORMAL`

- `THREAD_PRIORITY_NORMAL`

- `THREAD_PRIORITY_ABOVE_NORMAL`

- `THREAD_PRIORITY_HIGHEST`

- `THREAD_PRIORITY_TIME_CRITICAL` is 15, or 31 if the process class is `REALTIME_PRIORITY_CLASS`.

- `THREAD_PRIORITY_IDLE` is 1, or 16 for `REALTIME_PRIORITY_CLASS` processes.

- `THREAD_MODE_BACKGROUND_BEGIN` and `THREAD_MODE_BACKGROUND_END` are similar to `PROCESS_MODE_BACKGROUND_BEGIN` and `PROCESS_MODE-_BACKGROUND_END`. You need Windows Vista, or later, to use these modes.

Use these values to set and read a thread's relative priority. Note the signed integer priority argument.

```
BOOL SetThreadPriority (HANDLE hThread,
    int nPriority)

int GetThreadPriority (HANDLE hThread)
```

There are actually two additional thread priority values. They are absolute rather than relative and are used only in special cases.

- `THREAD_PRIORITY_IDLE` is a value of 1 (or 16 for real-time processes).

- `THREAD_PRIORITY_TIME_CRITICAL` is 15 (or 31 for real-time processes).

Thread priorities change automatically with process priority. In addition, Windows may adjust thread priorities dynamically on the basis of thread behavior. You can enable and disable this feature with the `SetThreadPriorityBoost` function.

Thread and Process Priority Cautions

Use high thread priorities and process priority classes with caution or, better yet, not at all, unless there is a proven requirement. Definitely avoid real-time priorities for normal user processes; our examples never use real-time priorities, and real-time applications are out of scope. Among other dangers, user threads may preempt threads in the executive.

Furthermore, everything that we say in the following chapters about the correctness of threaded programs assumes, without comment, that thread scheduling is *fair*. Fairness ensures that all threads will, eventually, run. Without fairness, a low-priority thread could hold resources required by a high-priority thread. *Thread starvation* and *priority inversion* are terms used to describe the defects that occur when scheduling is not fair.

Thread States

Figure 7–4, which is taken from Custer's *Inside Windows NT,* page 210 (also see Russinovich, Solomon, and Ionescu), shows how the executive manages threads and shows the possible thread states. This figure also shows the effect of program actions. Such state diagrams are common to all multitasking OSs and help clarify how a thread is scheduled for execution and how a thread moves from one state to another.

Here is a quick summary of the fundamentals; see the references for more information.

- A thread is in the *running* state when it is actually running on a processor. More than one thread can be in the running state on a multiprocessor computer.

- The executive places a running thread in the *wait* state when the thread performs a wait on a nonsignaled handle, such as a thread or process handle, or on a synchronization object handle (Chapter 8). I/O operations will also wait for completion of a disk or other data transfer, and numerous other functions can cause waiting. It is common to say that a thread is *blocked,* or *sleeping,* when in the wait state.

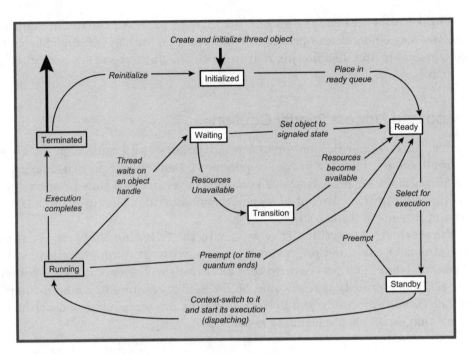

Figure 7–4 Thread States and Transitions
(From *Inside Windows NT*, by Helen Custer. Copyright ©
1993, Microsoft Press. Reproduced by permission of Microsoft Press. All rights reserved.)

- A thread is *ready* if it could be running. The executive's scheduler could put it
  in the running state at any time. The scheduler will run the highest-priority
  ready thread when a processor becomes available, and it will run the one that
  has been in the ready state for the longest time if several threads have the
  same high priority. The thread moves through the *standby* state before entering the ready state.

- Normally, the scheduler will place a ready thread on any available processor.
  The programmer can specify a thread's *processor affinity* (see Chapter 9),
  which will limit the processors that can run that specific thread. In this way,
  the programmer can allocate processors to threads and prevent other threads
  from using these processors, helping to assure responsiveness for some
  threads. The appropriate functions are `SetProcessAffinityMask` and `Get-
  ProcessAffinityMask`. `SetThreadIdealProcessor` can specify a pre-
  ferred processor that the scheduler will use whenever possible; this is less
  restrictive than assigning a thread to a single processor with the affinity
  mask.

- The executive will move a running thread to the ready state if the thread's time slice expires without the thread waiting. Executing `Sleep(0)` will also move a thread from the running state to the ready state.

- The executive will place a waiting thread in the ready state as soon as the appropriate handles are signaled, although the thread actually goes through an intermediate *transition* state. It is common to say that the thread *wakes up*.

- There is no way for a program to determine the state of another thread (of course, a thread, if it is running, must be in the running state, so it would be meaningless for a thread to find its own state). Even if there were, the state might change before the inquiring thread would be able to act on the information.

- A thread, regardless of its state, can be *suspended*, and a ready thread will not be run if it is suspended. If a running thread is suspended, either by itself or by a thread on a different processor, it is placed in the ready state.

- A thread is in the *terminated* state after it terminates and remains there as long as there are any open handles on the thread. This arrangement allows other threads to interrogate the thread's state and exit code.

Pitfalls and Common Mistakes

There are several factors to keep in mind as you develop threaded programs; lack of attention to a few basic principles can result in serious defects, and it is best to avoid the problems in the first place than try to find them during testing or debugging.

The essential factor is that the threads execute asynchronously. There is no sequencing unless you create it explicitly. This asynchronous behavior is what makes threads so useful, but without proper care, serious difficulties can occur.

Here are a few guidelines; there are more in later chapters. The example programs attempt to adhere to all these guidelines. There may be a few inadvertent violations, however, which illustrates the multithreaded programming challenges.

- Make no assumptions about the order in which the parent and child threads execute. It is possible for a child thread to run to completion before the parent returns from `CreateThread`, or, conversely, the child thread may not run at all for a considerable period of time. On a multiprocessor computer, the parent and one or more children may even run concurrently.

- Ensure that all initialization required by the child is complete before the `CreateThread` call, or else use thread suspension or some other technique. Failure by the parent to initialize data required by the child is a common cause of "race conditions" wherein the parent "races" the child to initialize data before the child needs it. `sortMT` illustrates this principle.

- Be certain that each distinct child has its own data structure passed through the thread function's parameter. Do not assume that one child thread will complete before another (this is another form of race condition).

- Any thread, at any time, can be preempted, and any thread, at any time, may resume execution.

- Do not use thread priority as a substitute for explicit synchronization.

- Do not use reasoning such as "that will hardly ever happen" as an argument that a program is correct. If it can happen, it will, possibly at a very embarrassing moment.

- Even more so than with single-threaded programs, testing is necessary, but not sufficient, to ensure program correctness. It is common for a multithreaded program to pass extensive tests despite code defects. There is no substitute for careful design, implementation, and code inspection.

- Threaded program behavior varies widely with processor speed, number of processors, OS version, and more. Testing on a variety of systems can isolate numerous defects, but the preceding precaution still applies.

- Be certain that threads have a sufficiently large stack, although the default 1MB is usually sufficient.

- Threads should be used only as appropriate. Thus, if there are activities that are naturally concurrent, each such activity can be represented by a thread. If, on the other hand, the activities are naturally sequential, threads only add complexity and performance overhead.

- If you use a large number of threads, be careful, as the numerous stacks will consume virtual memory space and thread context switching may become expensive. "Large" is a relative term and could mean hundreds or thousands. In other cases, it could mean more threads than the number of processors.

- Fortunately, correct programs are frequently the simplest and have the most elegant designs. Avoid complexity wherever possible.

Timed Waits

The final function, `Sleep`, allows a thread to give up the processor and move from the running to the wait state for a specified period of time. A thread can, for example, perform a task periodically by sleeping after carrying out the task. Once the time period is over, the scheduler moves the thread back to the ready state. A program in Chapter 11 (Program 11–4) uses this technique.

```
VOID Sleep (DWORD dwMilliseconds)
```

The time period is in milliseconds and can even be `INFINITE`, in which case the thread will never resume. A 0 value will cause the thread to relinquish the remainder of the time slice; the kernel moves the thread from the running state to the ready state (Figure 7–4).

The function `SwitchToThread` provides another way for a thread to yield its processor to another ready thread if there is one that is ready to run.

The UNIX `sleep` function is similar to `Sleep`, but time periods are measured in seconds. To obtain millisecond resolution, use the `select` or `poll` functions with no file descriptors.

Fibers

Note: Fibers are of specialized interest. See the comment after the first bulleted item below to determine if you want to skip this section.

A *fiber*, as the name implies, is a piece of a thread. More precisely, a fiber is a unit of execution that can be scheduled by the application rather than by the kernel. An application can create numerous fibers, and the fibers themselves determine which fiber will execute next. The fibers have independent stacks but otherwise run entirely in the context of the thread on which they are scheduled, having access, for example, to the thread's TLS and any mutexes[4] owned by the thread. Furthermore, fiber management occurs entirely in user space outside the kernel. Fibers can be thought of as lightweight threads, although there are numerous differences.

A fiber can execute on any thread, but never on two at one time. Therefore, a fiber should not access thread-specific data, such as TLS, as the data will have no meaning if the fiber is later rescheduled to run on another thread.

Fibers can be used for several purposes.

- Most importantly, many applications, especially some written for UNIX using proprietary thread implementations, now generally obsolete, are written to schedule their own threads. Fibers make it easier to port such applications to Windows but otherwise do not provide advantages over properly used threads. *Most readers will not have such requirements and may want to skip this section.*

---

[4] A mutex, as explained in Chapter 8, is a synchronization object that threads can own.

- A fiber does not need to block waiting for a file lock, mutex, named pipe input, or other resource. Rather, one fiber can poll the resource and, if the resource is not available, switch control to another specific fiber.

- Fibers operate as part of a *converted* thread (see the first numbered item below) and have access to thread and process resources. A fiber is not, however, bound to a specific thread and can run on any thread (but not on more than one at a time).

- Unlike threads, fibers are not preemptively scheduled. The Windows executive, in fact, is not aware of fibers; fibers are managed within the fiber DLL entirely within user space.

- Fibers allow you to implement *co-routines*, whereby an application switches among several interrelated tasks. Threads do not allow this. The programmer has no direct control over which thread will be executed next.

- Major software vendors have used fibers and claim performance advantages. For example, Oracle Database 10g has an optional "fiber mode" (see http://download.oracle.com/owsf_2003/40171_colello.ppt; this presentation also describes the threading model).

Seven functions make up the fiber API. They are used in the following sequence and as shown in Figure 7–5.

1. A thread must first enable fiber operation by calling `ConvertThreadTo-Fiber` or `ConvertThreadToFiberEx`. The thread then consists of a single fiber. This call provides a pointer to fiber data, which can be used in much the same way that the thread argument was used to create unique data for a thread.

2. The application can create additional fibers using `CreateFiber`. Each fiber has a start address, a stack size, and a parameter. Each new fiber is identified by an address rather than by a handle.

3. An individual fiber can obtain its data, as received from `CreateFiber`, by calling `GetFiberData`.

4. Similarly, a fiber can obtain its identity with `GetCurrentFiber`.

5. A running fiber yields control to another fiber by calling `SwitchToFiber`, indicating the address of the other fiber. Fibers must explicitly indicate the next fiber that is to run within the thread.

6. The `DeleteFiber` function deletes an existing fiber and all its associated data.

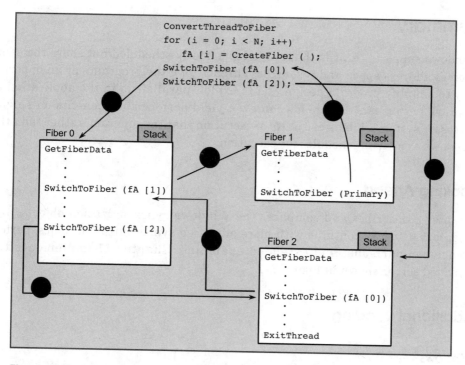

Figure 7–5   Control Flow among Fibers in a Thread

7. New functions, such as `ConvertFiberToThread` (which releases resources created by `ConvertThreadToFiber`), have been added to XP (NT 5.1), along with fiber local storage.

Figure 7–5 shows fibers in a thread. This example shows two ways in which fibers schedule each other.

- *Master-slave* **scheduling**. One fiber decides which fiber to run, and that fiber always yields control to the master fiber. Fiber 1 in Figure 7–5 behaves in this way. The *Examples* file contains `grepMF`, a `grepMT` variation, that uses master-slave scheduling.

- *Peer-to-peer* **scheduling**. A fiber determines the next fiber to run. The determination can be based on policies such as round-robin scheduling, priority scheduling based on a priority scheme, and so on. Co-routines would be implemented with peer-to-peer scheduling. In Figure 7–5, Fibers 0 and 2 switch control in this way.

Summary

Windows supports threads that are independently scheduled but share the same process address space and resources. Threads give the programmer an opportunity to simplify program design and to exploit parallelism in the application to improve performance. Threads can even yield performance benefits on single-processor systems. Fibers are units of execution that the program, rather than the Windows executive, schedules for execution.

Looking Ahead

Chapter 8 describes and compares the Windows synchronization objects, and Chapters 9 and 10 continue with more advanced synchronization topics, performance comparisons, and extended examples. Chapter 11 implements the threaded server shown in Figure 7–1.

Additional Reading

Windows

Multithreading Applications in Win32, by Jim Beveridge and Robert Wiener, is an entire book devoted to Win32 threads.

UNIX and Pthreads

Both *Advanced Programming in the UNIX Environment,* by W. Richard Stevens and Stephen A. Rago, and *Programming with POSIX Threads,* by David Butenhof, are recommended. The second book provides numerous guidelines for threaded program design and implementation. The information applies to Windows as well as to Pthreads, and many of the examples can be easily ported to Windows. There is also good coverage of the boss/worker, client/server, and pipeline threading models, and Butenhof's presentation is the basis for the model descriptions in this chapter.

Exercises

7–1. Implement a set of functions that will suspend and resume threads but also allow you to obtain a thread's suspend count.

7–2. Compare the performance of the parallel word count programs, one using threads (wcMT) and the other using processes (similar to Program 6–1, grepMP). Compare the results with those in Appendix C.

7–3. Perform additional performance studies with grepMT where the files are on different disk drives or are networked files. Also determine the performance gain on as many multiprocessor systems as are available.

7–4. Modify grepMT, Program 7–1, so that it puts out the results in the same order as that of the files on the command line. Does this affect the performance measurements in any way?

7–5. Further enhance grepMT, Program 7–1, so that it prints the time required by each worker thread. GetThreadTimes will be useful, and this function is similar to GetProcessTimes (Chapter 6).

7–6. The *Examples* file includes a multithreaded word count program, wcMT.c, that has a structure similar to that of grepMT.c. A defective version, wcMTx.c, is also included. Without referring to the correct solution, analyze and fix the defects in wcMTx.c, including any syntax errors. Also, create test cases that illustrate these defects and carry out performance experiments similar to those suggested for grepMT. If you use Cygwin (open source UNIX/Linux commands and shells), compare the performance of Cygwin's wc with that of wcMT, especially on multiprocessor systems.

7–7. The *Examples* file includes grepMTx.c, which is defective because it violates basic rules for thread safety. Describe the failure symptoms, identify the errors, and fix them.

7–8. sortMT requires that the number of records in the array to be sorted be divisible by the number of threads and that the number of threads be a power of 2. Remove these restrictions.

7–9. Enhance sortMT so that if the number of threads specified on the command line is zero, the program will determine the number of processors on the host computer using GetSystemInfo. Set the number of threads to different multiples (1, 2, 4, and so on) of the number of processors and determine the effect on performance.

7–10. Modify sortMT so that the worker threads are not suspended when they are created. What failure symptoms, if any, does the program demonstrate as a result of the race condition defect?

7–11. sortMT reads the entire file in the primary thread before creating the sorting threads. Modify the program so that each thread reads the portion of the file that it requires. Next, modify the program to use mapped files.

7–12. Is there any performance benefit if you give some of the threads in sortMT higher priority than others? For example, it might be beneficial to give the threads that only sort and do not merge, such as Thread 3 in Figure 7–2, a higher priority. Explain the results.

7–13. sortMT creates all the threads in a suspended state so as to avoid a race condition. Modify the program so that it creates the threads in reverse order and in a running state. Are there any remaining race conditions? Compare performance with the original version.

7–14. Quicksort, the algorithm generally used by the C library qsort function, is usually fast, but it can be slow in certain cases. Most texts on algorithms show a version that is fastest when the array is reverse sorted and slowest when it is already sorted. The Microsoft C library implementation is different. Determine from the library code which sequences will produce the best and worst behavior, and study sortMT's performance in these extreme cases. What is the effect of increasing or decreasing the number of threads? *Note:* The C library source code can be installed in the CRT directory under your Visual Studio installation. Look for qsort.c.

7–15. The *Examples* file contains a defective sortMTx.c program. Demonstrate the defects with test cases and then explain and fix the defects without reference to the correct solutions. *Caution:* The defective version may have syntax errors as well as errors in the thread logic.

7–16. One of the technical reviewers suggested an interesting sortMT enhancement that may provide improved performance. The idea is to modify the MergeArrays function so that it does not need to allocate the destination record storage. Instead, preallocate a second array as large as the array being sorted. Each worker thread can then use the appropriate portion of the preallocated array. Finally, eliminate the memcpy at the end. *Hint:* Alternate the merge direction on even and odd passes. Compare the resulting performance to Runs 7–2a and 7–2b.

CHAPTER

8 | Thread Synchronization

Threads can simplify program design and implementation and also improve performance, but thread usage requires care to ensure that shared resources are protected against simultaneous modification and that threads run only when appropriate. This chapter shows how to use Windows synchronization objects— CRITICAL_SECTIONs, mutexes, semaphores, and events[1]—to solve these problems and describes some of the problems, such as deadlocks and race conditions, that can occur with improper synchronization object use. Some synchronization objects can be used to synchronize threads in the same process or in separate processes.

The examples illustrate the synchronization objects and discuss the performance impacts, both positive and negative, of different synchronization methods. The following chapters then show how to use synchronization to solve additional programming problems, improve performance, avoid pitfalls, and use more advanced NT6 features, such as "slim reader/writer" (SRW) locks and Windows condition variables.

Thread synchronization is a fundamental and interesting topic, and it is essential in nearly all threaded applications. *Nonetheless, readers who are primarily interested in interprocess communication, network programming, and building threaded servers might want to skip to Chapter 11.*

The Need for Thread Synchronization

Chapter 7 showed how to create and manage worker threads, where each worker thread accesses its own resources and runs to completion without interacting with other threads. Each thread in the Chapter 7 examples processes a separate file or a separate storage area, yet simple synchronization during thread creation and termination is still necessary. For example, the grepMT worker threads all run

---

[1] The last three are Windows *kernel* objects referenced with HANDLEs. The first is not a kernel object.

independently of one another, but the boss thread must wait for the workers to complete before reporting the results the worker threads generated. Notice that the boss shares memory with the workers, but the program design assures that the boss will not access the memory until the worker terminates. This design enables the parallelism described in Chapter 7.

sortMT is slightly more complicated because the workers need to synchronize by waiting for adjacent workers to complete, and the worker threads are not allowed to start until the boss thread has created all the workers. As with grepMT, synchronization consists of waiting for one or more threads to terminate.

In many cases, however, it is necessary for two or more threads to coordinate execution throughout each thread's lifetime. For instance, several threads may share data, and this raises the issue of mutual exclusion. In other cases, a thread cannot proceed until another thread reaches a designated point. How can the programmer assume that two or more threads do not, for example, simultaneously modify the same global storage, such as the performance statistics? Furthermore, how can the programmer ensure that a thread does not attempt to remove an element from a queue before there are any elements in the queue or that two threads do not attempt to remove the same element?

Several examples illustrate situations that can prevent code from being thread-safe. (Code is thread-safe if several threads can execute the code simultaneously without any undesirable results.) Thread safety is discussed later in this and the following chapters.

Figure 8–1 shows what can happen when two unsynchronized threads share a resource such as a memory location. Both threads increment variable N, but, because of the particular sequence in which the threads *might* execute, the final value of N is 5, whereas the correct value is 6. Notice that the particular result shown here is not predictable; a different thread execution sequence could yield the correct results. Execution on a multiprocessor computer can aggravate this problem.

Critical Code Regions

Incrementing N with a single statement such as N++ is no better because the compiler will generate a sequence of one or more machine-level instructions that are not necessarily executed *atomically* as a single unit.

The core problem is that there is a *critical code region*[2] (the code that increments N in this example) such that, once a thread starts to execute the critical region, no other thread can be allowed to enter until the first thread exits

---

[2] The term "critical code section" is common but can cause confusion with Windows CRITICAL_SECTION objects, which, while related to critical code regions (or sections), are not the same thing.

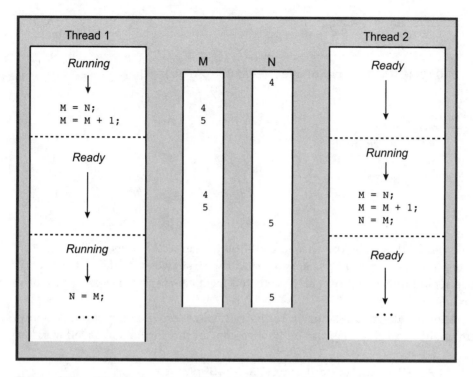

Figure 8–1   Unsynchronized Threads Sharing Memory

from the code region. This critical code region problem can be considered a type of race condition because the first thread "races" to complete the critical region before any other thread starts to execute the same critical code region. Thus, we need to synchronize thread execution in order to ensure that only one thread at a time executes the critical region.

There can be more than one critical code region for a variable, such as N in Figure 8–1. Typically, there might be a critical code region that decrements N. Generalizing, we need to synchronize thread execution in order to ensure that only one thread at a time executes *any* of the critical regions for a data item. We need to avoid problems such as having one thread increment N while another is decrementing it.

Defective Solutions to the Critical Code Region Problem

Similarly unpredictable results will occur with a code sequence that attempts to protect the increment with a global polled flag (in this case, the variable `Flag`).

```
BOOL Flag = FALSE;
DWORD N;
. . .
DWORD WINAPI ThreadFunc(TH_ARGS pArgs)
{
    . . .
    while (Flag) Sleep (1000);
    Flag = TRUE;
    N++;
    Flag = FALSE;
    . . .
}
```

Even in this case, the thread could be preempted between the time `Flag` is tested and the time `Flag` is set to TRUE; the first two statements form a critical code region that is not properly protected from concurrent access by two or more threads.

Another attempted solution to the critical code region synchronization problem might be to give each thread its own copy of the variable N, as follows:

```
DWORD WINAPI ThreadFunc (TH_ARGS pArgs)
{   DWORD N;
    ... N++; ...
}
```

This approach is no better, however, because each thread has its own copy of the variable on its stack, where it may have been required to have N represent, for example, the total number of threads in operation. Such a solution is necessary, however, in the common case in which each thread needs its own distinct copy of the variable and the increment is not a critical code region.

Notice that such problems are not limited to threads within a single process. They can also occur if two processes share mapped memory or modify the same file.

volatile Storage

Yet another latent defect exists even after we solve the synchronization problem. An optimizing compiler might leave the value of N in a register rather than storing it back in N. An attempt to solve this problem by resetting compiler optimization switches would impact performance throughout the code. The correct solution is to use the ANSI C `volatile` storage qualifier, which ensures that the variable will be stored in memory after modification and will always be fetched from memory before use. The `volatile` qualifier informs the compiler that the variable can change value at any time. Be aware, however, that the `volatile` qualifier can negatively affect performance, so use it only as required.

As a simple guideline, use `volatile` for any variable that is accessed by concurrent threads and is:

- Modified by at least one thread, and

- Accessed, even if read-only, by two or more threads, and correct program operation depends on the new value being visible to all threads immediately

This guideline is overly cautious; Program 8–1 shows a situation where the variable meeting these guidelines does not necessarily need to be `volatile`. If a modifying thread returns from or calls another function after modifying the variable, the variable will not be held in a register.

There is another situation where you need to use `volatile`; the parameters to the "interlocked functions," described soon, require `volatile` variables.

Memory Architecture and Memory Barriers

Even the `volatile` modifier does not assure that changes are visible to other processors in a specific order, because a processor might hold the value in cache before committing it to main memory and alter the order in which different processes see the changed values. To assure that changes are visible to other processors in the desired order, use *memory barriers* (or "fences"); the interlocked functions (next section) provide a memory barrier, as do all the synchronization functions in this chapter.

To help clarify this complex issue, Figure 8–2 shows the memory subsystem architecture of a typical multiprocessor computer. In this case, the computer has four processors on two dual-core chips and is similar to the computer used with many of the "run" screenshots in this chapter and Chapter 7.

The components are listed here, along with *representative* values[3] for total size, line size (that is, the number of bytes in a single chunk), and latency (access) times in processor cycles:

- The four processor cores, which include the registers that hold computed values as well as values loaded from memory.

- Level 1 (L1) cache. The instruction and data caches are usually separate, and each processor core has a distinct cache. When you modify a `volatile` vari-

---

[3] See the chip manufacturer's specifications for actual values and architectural details. The information here is similar to that of the Intel Core 2 Quad processor.

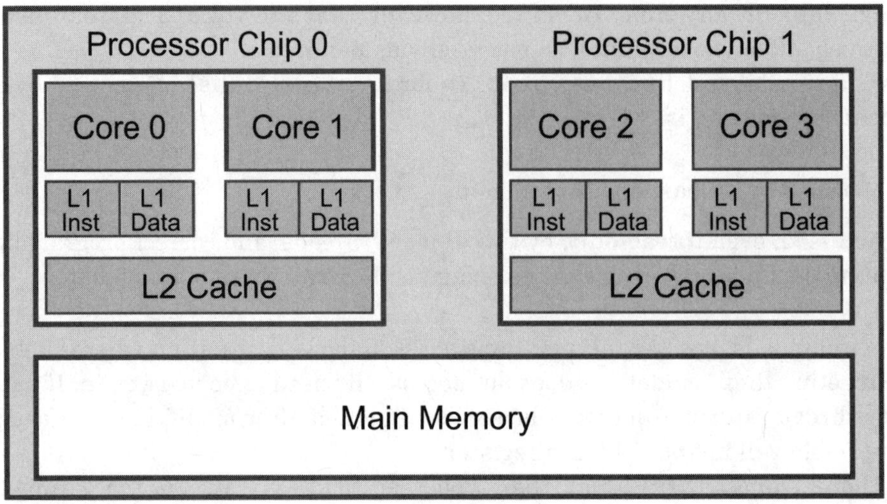

Figure 8–2   Memory System Architecture

able, the new value will be stored in the core's L1 data cache but won't necessarily be stored in the L2 cache or main memory. *Size:* 32KB, *Line Size:* 64 bytes, *Latency:* 3 cycles.

- Level 2 (L2) cache. Each processor chip has its own L2 cache, shared by the two cores. *Size:* 6MB, *Line Size:* 64 bytes, *Latency:* 14 cycles.

- Main Memory, which is shared by all processor cores and is not part of the processor chips. *Size:* Multiple GB, *Line Size:* N/A, *Latency:* 100+ cycles.

Figure 8–2 represents the most common "symmetric multiprocessing" (SMP) shared memory architecture, although the processors are not entirely symmetric because of the L2 cache. Nonuniform memory access (NUMA) is more complex because the main memory is partitioned among the processors; NUMA is not coverd here.

Figure 8–2 shows that `volatile` only assures that the new data value will be in the L1 cache; there is no assurance that the new value will be visible to threads running on other cores. A memory barrier, however, assures that the value is moved to main memory. Furthermore, the barrier assures cache coherence. Thus, if Core 0 updates variable N at a memory barrier, and Core 3's L1 cache has a value representing N, the N value in Core 3's L1 (and L2) cache is either updated or removed so that the new value is visible to Core 3 and all other cores concurrently.

There is a performance cost, however, as moving data between main memory, processor cores, and caches can require hundreds of cycles, whereas a pipelined processor can access register values in less than a cycle.

Figure 8–2 also shows that it's important to assure that shared variables are aligned on their natural boundaries. If, for example, a `LARGE_INTEGER` were aligned on a 4-byte (but not 8-byte) boundary, it might also cross a cache line boundary. It would then be possible that only part of the new value would become visible to other processors, resulting in a "word tear" bug. By default, most compilers align data items on their natural boundaries.

Interlocked Functions: Introduction

If all we need is to increment, decrement, or exchange variables, as in this simple initial example, then the *interlocked* functions will suffice, and the variables need to be `volatile`. The interlocked functions are simpler and faster than any of the alternatives, although they do generate a memory barrier with the performance impact described previously.

The first two members of the interlocked function family are `Interlocked-Increment` and `InterlockedDecrement`; other interlocked functions are described in a later section. These two instructions apply to 32-bit signed integers (the "Addend," which must be aligned on a 4-byte boundary to assure correct operation) and return the resulting `Addend` value.

These functions have limited utility, but they should be used wherever possible to simplify code and improve performance.

```
LONG InterlockedIncrement (
    LONG volatile *Addend)
```

```
LONG InterlockedDecrement (
    LONG volatile *Addend)
```

Use `InterlockedIncrement64` and `InterlockedDecrement64` to increment and decrement 64-bit values, but be sure that the `Addend` is aligned on a 64-bit (8-byte) boundary.

If your code will run on processors that support "acquire" and "release" semantics, such as the Itanium (but not Intel x86 and x64), you could use `Interlocked-IncrementAcquire` and `InterlockedIncrementRelease` to gain performance. See MSDN for more information.

The task of incrementing N in Figure 8–1 can be implemented with a single line:

```
InterlockedIncrement (&N);
```

N is a signed `volatile` `LONG` integer, and the function returns its new value, although another thread could modify N's value before the thread that called `InterlockedIncrement` can use the returned value.

Be careful, however, not to call this function twice in succession if, for example, you need to increment the variable by 2 and correct program operation depends on the variable being even. The thread might be preempted between the two calls. Instead, use the `InterlockedExchangeAdd` function described near the end of the chapter.

Local and Global Storage

Another requirement for correct thread code is that global storage not be used for local purposes. For example, the earlier `ThreadFunc` example would be necessary and appropriate if each thread required its own separate copy of N. N might hold temporary results or retain the argument. If, however, N represents thread-specific data and were placed in global storage, all threads would share a single copy of N, resulting in incorrect behavior no matter how well your program synchronized access.

Here is an example of such incorrect usage, which often occurs when converting a legacy single-threaded program to multithreaded operation and using a function (`ThreadFunc`, in this case) as a thread function. N should be a local variable, allocated on the thread function's stack as its value is used within the function.

```
DWORD N;
. . .
DWORD WINAPI ThreadFunc (TH_ARGS pArgs)
{
    ...
    N = 2 * pArgs->Count; ...
    /* Use N; value is specific to this call to ThreadFunc */
}
```

Comment: Finding and removing global variables, such as N in this fragment, is a major challenge when converting legacy, single-threaded programs to use threads. In the code fragment above, the function was called sequentially, and, in the multithreaded version, several threads can be executing the function concurrently. The problem is also challenging when we have a situation such as the following legacy code fragment, where results are accumulated in the global variable:

```
DWORD N = 0;
. . .
for (int i = 0; i < MAX; ++i) {
    ... Allocate and initialize pArgs data ...
    N += ThreadFunc(pArgs);
}
. . .
DWORD WINAPI ThreadFunc (ARGS pArgs)
{
    DWORD result;
    ...
    result = ...;
    return result;
}
```

The challenge occurs when converting `ThreadFunc` to a thread function executed by two or more threads running in parallel. This and the following chapters deal with many similar situations.

Summary: Thread-Safe Code

Before proceeding to the synchronization objects, here are five initial guidelines to help ensure that the code will run correctly in a threaded environment.

1. Variables that are local to the thread should not be global and should be on the thread's stack or in a data structure or TLS that only the individual thread can access directly.

2. If a function is called by several threads and a thread-specific state value, such as a counter, is to persist from one function call to the next, do not store it in a global variable or structure. Instead, store the state value in TLS or in a data structure dedicated to that thread, such as the data structure passed to the thread when it is created. Programs 12–5 and 12–6 show the required techniques when building thread-safe DLLs.

3. Avoid race conditions such as the uninitialized variables that would occur in Program 7–2 (`sortMT`) if the threads were not created in a suspended state. If some condition is assumed to hold at a specific point in the program, wait on a synchronization object to ensure that the condition does hold.

4. Threads should not, in general, change the process environment because that would affect all threads. Thus, a thread should not set the standard input or output handles or change environment variables. An exception would be the primary thread, which might make such changes before creating any other threads. In this case, all threads would share the same environment, since the primary thread can assure that there are no other threads in the process at the time the environment is changed.

5. Variables shared by all threads should be static or in global storage and protected with the synchronization or interlocked mechanisms that create a memory barrier.

The next section discusses the synchronization objects. With that discussion, there will be enough to develop a simple producer/consumer example.

Thread Synchronization Objects

Two mechanisms discussed so far allow processes and threads to synchronize with one another.

1. A thread can wait for another process to terminate by waiting on the process handle with `WaitForSingleObject` or `WaitForMultipleObjects`. A thread can wait for another thread to terminate, regardless of how the thread terminates, in the same way.

2. File locks are specifically for synchronizing file access.

Windows NT5 and NT6 provide four other objects designed for thread and process synchronization. Three of these objects—*mutexes*, *semaphores*, and *events*—are kernel objects that have handles. Events are also used for other purposes, such as asynchronous I/O (Chapter 14).

The fourth object, the `CRITICAL_SECTION`, is discussed first. Because of their simplicity and performance advantages, `CRITICAL_SECTION`s are the preferred mechanism when they are adequate for a program's requirements.

Caution: There are risks inherent to the use of synchronization objects if they are not used properly. These risks, such as deadlocks, are described in this and subsequent chapters, along with techniques for developing reliable code. First, however, we'll show some synchronization examples in realistic situations.

New in Windows Vista and Windows Server 2008: Windows kernel 6 (NT 6) introduced SRW locks (see Chapter 9) and condition variables (see Chapter 10), which are welcome additions. However, at the time of writing, most applications will need to support Windows XP. This situation may change in the future.

Two other synchronization objects, waitable timers and I/O completion ports, are deferred until we've described the prerequisite asynchronous I/O techniques in Chapter 14.

CRITICAL_SECTION Objects

A critical code region, as described earlier, is a code region that only one thread can execute at a time; more than one thread executing the critical code region concurrently can result in unpredictable and incorrect results.

Windows provides the CRITICAL_SECTION object as a simple "lock" mechanism for implementing and enforcing the critical code region concept.

CRITICAL_SECTION (CS) objects are initialized and deleted but do not have handles and are not shared with other processes. Declare a CS variable as a CRITICAL_SECTION. Threads enter and leave a CS, and only one thread at a time can be in a specific CS. A thread can, however, enter and leave a specific CS at multiple points in the program.

To initialize and delete a CRITICAL_SECTION variable and its resources, use InitializeCriticalSection and DeleteCriticalSection, respectively. You cannot perform any operations on a CS before initializing it or after deleting it, although you can reinitialize a CS.

```
VOID InitializeCriticalSection (
    LPCRITICAL_SECTION lpCriticalSection)
```

```
VOID DeleteCriticalSection (
    LPCRITICAL_SECTION lpCriticalSection)
```

EnterCriticalSection blocks a thread if another thread is in the section, and multiple threads can wait simultaneously on the same CS. One waiting thread unblocks when another thread executes LeaveCriticalSection; you cannot predict which waiting thread will unblock.

We say that a thread *owns* the CS once it returns from EnterCriticalSection, and LeaveCriticalSection relinquishes ownership. *Always be certain to leave a CS; failure to do so will cause other threads to wait forever, even if the owning thread terminates.* The examples use __finally blocks to leave CSs.

We will often say that a CS is *locked* or *unlocked,* and entering a CS is the same as locking the CS.

```
VOID EnterCriticalSection (
   LPCRITICAL_SECTION lpCriticalSection)

VOID LeaveCriticalSection (
   LPCRITICAL_SECTION lpCriticalSection)
```

If a thread already owns the CS, it can enter again without blocking; that is, CRITICAL_SECTIONs are *recursive*. Windows maintains a count so that the thread must leave as many times as it enters in order to unlock the CS for other threads. This capability can be useful in implementing recursive functions and making shared library functions thread-safe.

Leaving a CS that a thread does not own can produce unpredictable results, including thread blockage.

There is no time-out from EnterCriticalSection; a thread will block forever if the owning thread never leaves the CS. You can, however, test or poll to see whether another thread owns a CS using TryEnterCriticalSection.

```
BOOL TryEnterCriticalSection (
   LPCRITICAL_SECTION lpCriticalSection)
```

A TRUE return value from TryEnterCriticalSection indicates that the calling thread now owns the CS. A FALSE return indicates that some other thread already owns the CS, and it is not safe to execute the critical code region.

CRITICAL_SECTIONs have the advantage of not being kernel objects and are maintained in user space. This almost always provides performance improvements compared to using a Windows mutex kernel object with similar functionality, especially in NT5 and later (and this book assumes you are using NT5 or NT6). We will discuss the performance benefit after introducing kernel synchronization objects.

Adjusting the Spin Count

Normally, if a thread finds that a CS is already owned when executing `Enter-CriticalSection`, it enters the kernel and blocks until the `CRITICAL_SECTION` is released, which is time consuming. On multiprocessor systems, however, you can require that the thread try again (that is, spin) before blocking, as the owning thread may be running on a separate processor and could release the CS at any time. This can be useful for performance when there is high contention among threads for a single `CRITICAL_SECTION` that is never held for more than a few instructions. Performance implications are discussed later in this chapter and the next.

The two functions to adjust spin count are `SetCriticalSectionSpinCount`, which allows you to adjust the count dynamically, and `InitializeCritical-SectionAndSpinCount`, which is a substitute for `InitializeCritical-Section`. Spin count tuning is a topic in Chapter 9.

A `CRITICAL_SECTION` for Protecting Shared Variables

Using `CRITICAL_SECTION`s is simple, and one common use is to allow threads to access global shared variables. For example, consider a threaded server (as in Figure 7–1) in which there might be a need to maintain usage statistics such as:

- The total number of requests received
- The total number of responses sent
- The number of requests currently being processed by server threads

Because the count variables are global to the process, two threads must not modify the counts simultaneously. `CRITICAL_SECTION` objects provide one means of ensuring this, as shown by the code sequence below and in Figure 8–3. Program 8–1, much simpler than the server system, illustrates this `CRITICAL_SECTION` usage.

CSs can be used to solve problems such as the one shown in Figure 8–1, in which two threads increment the same variable. The following code segment will do more than increment the variable because simple incrementing is possible with the interlocked functions. This example also uses an intermediate variable; this unnecessary inefficiency more clearly illustrates the solution to the problem in Figure 8–1.

```
CRITICAL_SECTION cs1;
volatile DWORD N = 0;
```

```
/* N is a global variable, shared by all threads. */
InitializeCriticalSection (&cs1);
    . . .
/* Create one or more threads using ThreadFunc */
    . . .
DWORD WINAPI ThreadFunc (TH_ARGS pArgs);
{
    DWORD M;
    __try {
        EnterCriticalSection (&cs1);
        if (N < N_MAX) { M = N; M += 1; N = M; }
    } __finally {
        LeaveCriticalSection (&cs1)
    }
}
    ...
DeleteCriticalSection (&cs1);
```

Figure 8–3 shows one possible execution sequence for the Figure 8–1 example and illustrates how CSs solve the critical code region synchronization problem.

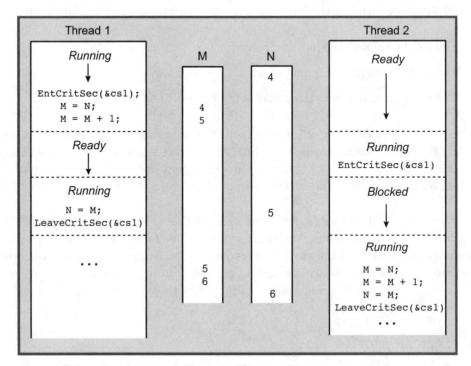

Figure 8–3   Synchronized Threads Sharing Memory

Protect a Variable with a Single Synchronization Object

Each variable, or collection of variables, that is accessed in a critical code section should be guarded by the *same* CS (or other synchronization object) everywhere. Otherwise, two threads could still modify the variable concurrently. For example, the following thread function, which uses two CS and interlocked functions, is defective (N is, as before, a global `volatile DWORD`, and `cs1` and `cs2` are global CSs).

```
DWORD WINAPI ThreadFunc (ARGS pArgs)
{
    . . .
    EnterCriticalSection(&cs1);
    N += 5;
    LeaveCriticalSection(&cs1);
    . . .
    InterlockedDecrement(&N);
    . . .
    EnterCriticalSection(&cs2);
    N -= 5;
    LeaveCriticalSection(&cs2);
    . . .
}
```

Example: A Simple Producer/Consumer System

Program 8–1 shows how CS lock objects can be useful. The program also shows how to build protected data structures for storing object state and introduces the concept of an *invariant*, which is a property of an object's state that is guaranteed (by the proper program implementation) to be true outside a critical code region. Here is a description of the problem.

- There are two threads in addition to the primary thread, a *producer* and a *consumer*, that act entirely asynchronously.

- The producer periodically creates messages containing a table of numbers, such as current stock prices, periodically updating the table.

- The consumer, on request from the user, displays the current data. The requirement is that the displayed data must be the *most recent complete set of data, but no data should be displayed twice.*

- Do not display data while the producer is updating it, and do not display old data. Note that, by design, many produced messages are never used and are "lost." This example is a special case of the pipeline model in which data moves from one thread to the next.

- As an integrity check, the producer also computes a simple checksum[4] of the data in the table, and the consumer validates the checksum to ensure that the data has not been corrupted in transmission from one thread to the next. If the consumer accesses the table while it is still being updated, the table will be invalid; the CS ensures that this does not happen. The message block invariant is that the checksum is correct for the current message contents.

- The two threads also maintain statistics on the total number of messages produced, consumed, and lost.

The final output (see Run 8–1 after Program 8–1) shows the actual number computed at stop time, since the number computed after a consume command is probably stale. Additional comments follow the program listing and the run screenshot.

Program 8–1 `simplePC`: A Simple Producer and Consumer

```
/* Chapter 8. simplePC.c */
/* Maintain two threads, a producer and a consumer. */
/* The producer periodically creates checksummed data buffers, */
/* or "message blocks," that the consumer displays when prompted. */

#include "Everything.h"
#include <time.h>
#define DATA_SIZE 256

typedef struct MSG_BLOCK_TAG { /* Message block */
   CRITICAL_SECTION mGuard;/* Guard the message block structure*/
   DWORD fReady, fStop;
      /* ready state flag, stop flag*/
   volatile DWORD nCons, mSequence; /* Msg block sequence number*/
   DWORD nLost;
   time_t mTimestamp;
   DWORD mChecksum; /* Message contents mChecksum*/
   DWORD mData[DATA_SIZE]; /* Message Contents*/
} MSG_BLOCK;

/* Single message block, ready to fill with a new message. */
MSG_BLOCK mBlock = { 0, 0, 0, 0, 0 };
```

---

[4] This checksum, an "exclusive or" of the message bits, is for illustration only. Much more sophisticated message digest techniques are available for use in production applications.

```
DWORD WINAPI Produce (void *);
DWORD WINAPI Consume (void *);
void MessageFill (MSG_BLOCK *);
void MessageDisplay (MSG_BLOCK *);

DWORD _tmain (DWORD argc, LPTSTR argv [])
{
    DWORD status;
    HANDLE hProduce, hConsume;

    /* Initialize the message block CRITICAL SECTION */
    InitializeCriticalSection (&mBlock.mGuard);

    /* Create the two threads */
    hProduce = (HANDLE)_beginthreadex (NULL, 0, Produce,
            NULL, 0, NULL);
    hConsume = (HANDLE)_beginthreadex (NULL, 0, Consume,
            NULL, 0, NULL);

    /* Wait for the producer and consumer to complete */

    status = WaitForSingleObject (hConsume, INFINITE);
    status = WaitForSingleObject (hProduce, INFINITE);

    DeleteCriticalSection (&mBlock.mGuard);

    _tprintf (_T("Producer and consumer threads have terminated\n"));
    _tprintf (_T("Messages produced: %d, Consumed: %d, Lost: %d.\n"),
        mBlock.mSequence, mBlock.nCons,
        mBlock.mSequence - mBlock.nCons);
    return 0;
}

DWORD WINAPI Produce (void *arg)
/* Producer thread -- create new messages at random intervals. */
{
    srand ((DWORD)time(NULL)); /* Seed the random # generator */

    while (!mBlock.fStop) {
        /* Random Delay */
        Sleep(rand()/100);

        /* Get the buffer, fill it */
        EnterCriticalSection (&mBlock.mGuard);
        __try {
            if (!mBlock.fStop) {
                mBlock.fReady = 0;
                MessageFill (&mBlock);
                mBlock.fReady = 1;
                InterlockedIncrement (&mBlock.mSequence);
```

```
            }
        }
        __finally { LeaveCriticalSection (&mBlock.mGuard); }
    }
    return 0;
}


DWORD WINAPI Consume (void *arg)
{
    CHAR command, extra;
    /* Consume the NEXT message when prompted by the user */
    while (!mBlock.fStop) { /* Only thread accessing stdin, stdout */
        _tprintf (_T("\n**Enter 'c' for Consume; 's' to stop: "));
        _tscanf ("%c%c", &command, &extra);
        if (command == 's') {
            /* ES not needed here. This is not a read/modify/write.
             * The producer sees the new value after consumer returns */
            mBlock.fStop = 1;
        } else if (command == 'c') { /* Get a new buffer to consume */
            EnterCriticalSection (&mBlock.mGuard);
            __try {
                if (mBlock.fReady == 0)
                    _tprintf (_T("No new messages. Try again later\n"));
                else {
                    MessageDisplay (&mBlock);
                    mBlock.nLost = mBlock.mSequence - mBlock.nCons + 1;
                    mBlock.fReady = 0; /* No new messages are ready */
                    InterlockedIncrement(&mBlock.nCons);
                }
            }
            __finally { LeaveCriticalSection (&mBlock.mGuard); }
        } else {
            _tprintf (_T("Illegal command. Try again.\n"));
        }
    }
    return 0;
}


void MessageFill (MSG_BLOCK *msgBlock)
{
    /* Fill the message buffer, including checksum and timestamp. */
    DWORD i;
    msgBlock->mChecksum = 0;
    for (i = 0; i < DATA_SIZE; i++) {
        msgBlock->mData[i] = rand();
        msgBlock->mChecksum ^= msgBlock->mData[i];
    }
    msgBlock->mTimestamp = time(NULL);
    return;
}
```

```
void MessageDisplay (MSG_BLOCK *msgBlock)
{
    /* Display message buffer, timestamp, and validate checksum. */
    DWORD i, tcheck = 0;

    for (i = 0; i < DATA_SIZE; i++)
        tcheck ^= msgBlock->mData[i];
    _tprintf (_T("\nMessage number %d generated at: %s"),
        msgBlock->mSequence, _tctime (&(msgBlock->mTimestamp)));
    _tprintf (_T("First and last entries: %x %x\n"),
        msgBlock->mData[0], msgBlock->mData[DATA_SIZE-1]);
    if (tcheck == msgBlock->mChecksum)
        _tprintf (_T("GOOD ->mChecksum was validated.\n"));
    else
        _tprintf (_T("BAD  ->mChecksum failed. message corrupted\n"));

    return;
}
```

Run 8–1 shows four consumed messages. You can estimate the time between consume commands from the message time stamp and the message number.

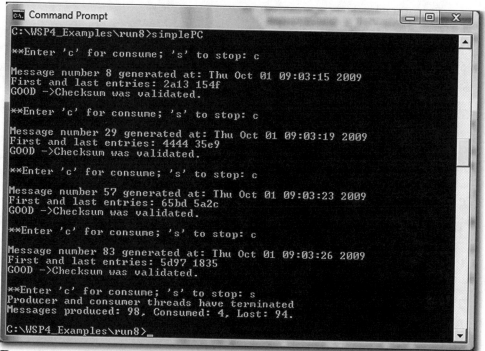

Run 8–1   `simplePC`: Periodic Messages, Consumed on Demand

Comments on the Simple Producer/Consumer Example

This example illustrates several points and programming conventions that are important throughout this and the following chapters.

- The CRITICAL_SECTION object is a part of the object (the message block) that it protects.

- Every access to the message block is performed in a critical code region, with one exception described next.

- When the Consume thread receives a stop command, it sets the message block's stop flag. There is no need to use the message's CS, because the new value does not depend on the old flag value (there is no "read/modify/write"), and the compiler will store the value when Consume returns. Furthermore, only one thread modifies the stop flag, which is not volatile.

- The producer thread only knows that it should stop by examining a flag in the message block, where the flag is set by the consumer. Because one thread cannot send any sort of signal to another and TerminateThread has undesirable side effects, this technique is the simplest way to stop another thread. The threads must cooperate for this method to be effective. This solution requires, however, that the thread must not be blocked so that it can test the flag; Chapter 10 shows how to cancel a blocked thread.

- Any variable that is accessed and modified with interlocked instructions is volatile. mChecksum and mData are not volatile because the CS enter and leave statements create memory barriers assuring that the consumer's changes are visible to the producer.

- Termination handlers ensure that the CS is released. This technique helps to ensure that later code modifications do not inadvertently skip the Leave-CriticalSection call. It is important, however, that the __try statement is *immediately after* the EnterCriticalSection so that there is no possibility of an exception or other transfer of control between the call to Enter-CriticalSection and the __try block.

- The MessageFill and MessageDisplay functions are called only within critical code regions, and both functions use local rather than global storage for their computations. Incidentally, these two functions are useful in subsequent examples; there is no need to list them again.

- The producer does not have a useful way to tell the consumer that there is a new message, so the consumer simply has to wait until the ready flag, indicating a new message, is set. Event kernel objects will give us a way to eliminate this inefficiency.

- One of the invariant properties that this program ensures is that the message block checksum is always correct, *outside* the critical code regions. Another invariant property is:

```
0 <= nLost + nCons <= sequence
```

The `CRITICAL_SECTION` object is a powerful synchronization mechanism, yet it does not provide all the functionality needed. The inability to signal another thread was noted earlier, and there is also no time-out capability. The Windows kernel synchronization objects address these limitations and more.

Mutexes

A *mutex* ("mutual exclusion") object provides locking functionality beyond that of `CRITICAL_SECTIONs`. Because mutexes can be named and have handles, they can also be used for interprocess synchronization between threads in separate processes. For example, two processes that share memory by means of memory-mapped files can use mutexes to synchronize access to the shared memory.

Mutex objects are similar to CSs, but in addition to being process-sharable, mutexes allow time-out values and become signaled when *abandoned* by a terminating thread.[5] A thread gains mutex ownership (or *locks* the mutex) by successfully waiting on the mutex handle (`WaitForSingleObject` or `WaitForMultipleObjects`), and it releases ownership with `ReleaseMutex`.

As always, threads should be careful to release resources they own as soon as possible. A thread can acquire a specific mutex several times; the thread will not block if it already has ownership. Ultimately, it must release the mutex the same number of times. This recursive ownership feature, also available with CSs, can be useful for restricting access to a recursive function or in an application that implements nested transactions.

Windows functions are `CreateMutex`, `ReleaseMutex`, and `OpenMutex`.

```
HANDLE CreateMutex (
    LPSECURITY_ATTRIBUTES lpsa,
    BOOL bInitialOwner,
    LPCTSTR lpMutexName)
```

---

[5] As a rule of thumb, use a `CRITICAL_SECTION` if the limitations are acceptable, and use mutexes when you have more than one process or need some other mutex capability. Also, CSs are nearly always much faster. This topic is discussed in detail in Chapter 9, which also describes the more efficient NT6 SRW locks.

Parameters

- The `bInitialOwner` flag, if `TRUE`, gives the calling thread immediate owner-ship of the new mutex. This flag is ignored if the mutex already exists, as de-termined by the name.

- `lpMutexName` indicates the mutex name; unlike files, mutex names are case-sensitive. The mutexes are unnamed if the parameter is `NULL`. Events, mu-texes, semaphores, file mapping, and other kernel objects used in this book all share the same name space, which is distinct from the file system name space. Therefore, all named synchronization objects should have distinct names. These names are limited to 260 characters.

- A `NULL` return `HANDLE` value indicates failure.

Windows Vista and Server 2008 (NT 6) also provide `CreateMutexEx`, which has an extra `DWORD dwDesiredAccess` parameter that specifies the same secu-rity and access rights values, with the same meanings, as used in the optional se-curity attributes structure (the parameter values do not need to be identical). One possible value is `MUTEX_ALL_ACCESS`, which would normally be used only by an administrator. `CreateMutexEx` changes the parameter order and replaces `BOOL bInitialOwner` with `DWORD dwFlags` with only one possible non-zero value. See MSDN for additional information.

`OpenMutex` is for opening an existing named mutex. This function is not discussed further but is used in some examples. It allows threads in different processes to synchronize just as if the threads were in the same process. The `Create` in one process must precede the `Open` in another. Semaphores and events also have `Create` and `Open` functions, as do file mappings (Chapter 5). The assumption always is that one process, such as a server, first performs a `Create` call, failing if the named object has already been created. Alternatively, all processes can use the `Create` call with the same name if the order is not important.

`ReleaseMutex` relinquishes mutex ownership. It fails if the thread does not own the mutex.

```
BOOL ReleaseMutex (HANDLE hMutex)
```

The POSIX Pthreads specification supports mutexes. The four basic functions are as follows:

- `pthread_mutex_init`

- `pthread_mutex_destroy`

- `pthread_mutex_lock`

- `pthread_mutex_unlock`

`pthread_mutex_lock` will block and is therefore nearly equivalent (there are some small differences) to `WaitForSingleObject` when used with a mutex handle. `pthread_mutex_trylock` is a nonblocking, polling version that corresponds to `WaitForSingleObject` with a zero time-out value. Pthreads do not provide for a time-out.

The Pthreads `pthread_spinlock_t` is similar to the Windows `CRITICAL-_SECTION`.

These functions operate on `pthread_mutex_t` type variables, which, by default, are not recursive. However, there is an option to set the recursive attribute.

Abandoned Mutexes

If a thread terminates without releasing a mutex that it owns, the mutex becomes "abandoned" and the handle is in the signaled state. `WaitForSingleObject` will return `WAIT_ABANDONED_0`, and `WaitForMultipleObjects` will use `WAIT-_ABANDONED_0` as the base value to indicate that the signaled handle(s) represents abandoned mutex(es).

The fact that abandoned mutex handles are signaled is a useful feature not available with CSs. If an abandoned mutex is detected, there is a strong possibility of a defect in the thread code or program failure because threads should be programmed to release their resources before terminating. It is also possible that the thread was terminated by some other thread.

Mutexes, `CRITICAL_SECTIONS`, and Deadlocks

Although CSs and mutexes can solve problems such as the one in Figure 8–1, you must use them carefully to avoid *deadlocks,* in which two threads become blocked while each is waiting for a resource owned by the other thread. Incidentally, the same caution applies to file locking (Chapter 3).

Deadlocks are one of the most common and insidious defects in synchronization, and they frequently occur when two or more mutexes must be locked at the same time. Consider the following problem.

- There are two linked lists, Lists A and B, each containing identical structures and maintained by worker threads.

- For one class of list element, correct operation depends on a given element, X, being either in both lists or in neither; it is an error if an element of this class is in just one list. This is an informal statement of the invariant.

- In other situations, an element is allowed to be in one list but not in the other. *Motivation:* The lists might be employees in Departments A and B, where some employees are allowed to be in both departments.

- Therefore, distinct mutexes (or CRITICAL_SECTIONs) are required for both lists, but both mutexes must be locked when adding or deleting a shared element. Using a single mutex would degrade performance, prohibiting concurrent independent updates to the two lists, because the mutex would be "too large."

Here is a *defective* implementation of the worker thread functions for adding and deleting shared list elements.

```
static struct {
    /* Invariant: List is a valid list. */
    HANDLE guard; /* Mutex handle. */
    struct ListStuff;
} ListA, ListB;
...
DWORD WINAPI AddSharedElement (void *arg)
/* Add a shared element to lists A and B. */
{ /* Invariant: New element is in both or neither list. */
    WaitForSingleObject (ListA.guard, INFINITE);
    WaitForSingleObject (ListB.guard, INFINITE);
    /* Add the element to both lists ... */
    ReleaseMutex (ListB.guard);
    ReleaseMutex (ListA.guard);
    return 0;
}
DWORD WINAPI DeleteSharedElement (void *arg)
/* Delete a shared element to lists A and B. */
{
    WaitForSingleObject (ListB.guard, INFINITE);
    WaitForSingleObject (ListA.guard, INFINITE);
    /* Delete the element from both lists ... */
    ReleaseMutex (ListB.guard);
    ReleaseMutex (ListA.guard);
    return 0;
}
```

The code may appear to be correct by all the previous guidelines. However, a preemption of the `AddSharedElement` thread immediately after it locks List A and immediately before it tries to lock List B will deadlock if the `Delete-SharedElement` thread starts before the add thread resumes. Each thread owns a mutex the other requires, and neither thread can proceed to the `ReleaseMutex` call that would unblock the other thread.

Notice that deadlocks are really another form of race condition, as one thread races to acquire all its mutexes before the other thread starts to do so.

One way to avoid deadlock is the "try and back off" strategy, whereby a thread calls `WaitForSingleObject` with a finite time-out value and, when detecting an owned mutex, "backs off" by yielding the processor or sleeping for a brief time before trying again. Designing for deadlock-free systems is even better and more efficient, as described next.

A far simpler and superior method, covered in nearly all OS texts, is to specify a "mutex hierarchy" such that all threads are programmed to assure that they acquire the mutexes in exactly the same order and release them in the opposite order. This hierarchical sequence might be arbitrary or could be natural from the structure of the problem, but, whatever the hierarchy, all threads must observe it. In this example, all that is needed is for the delete function to wait for Lists A and B in order, and the threads will never deadlock as long as this hierarchical sequence is observed everywhere by all threads.

Another technique to reduce deadlock potential is to put the two mutex handles in an array and use `WaitForMultipleObjects` with the `fWaitAll` flag set to `TRUE` so that a thread acquires either both or neither of the mutexes in an atomic operation. This technique assumes that you do not need to acquire the mutexes sequentially and that acquisition is centralized, so it can be difficult to use successfully. This technique is not possible with `CRITICAL_SECTION`s.

Finally, notice that you could create deadlocks with three or more mutexes; all that is required is a cyclic dependency among the mutexes.

Review: Mutexes versus `CRITICAL_SECTIONS`

As stated several times, the two lock objects, mutexes and `CRITICAL_SECTION`s, are very similar and solve the same basic problems. In particular, both objects can be owned by a single thread, and other threads attempting to gain ownership will block until the object is released. Mutexes do provide greater flexibility, but with a performance penalty. In summary, these are the differences:

- Mutexes, when abandoned by a terminated thread, are signaled so that other threads are not blocked forever. This allows the application to continue execution, but an abandoned mutex almost certainly indicates a serious program bug or failure.

- Mutex waits can time out, whereas you can only poll a CS.

- Mutexes can be named and are sharable by threads in different processes.

- The thread that creates a mutex can specify immediate ownership. This is only a slight convenience, as the thread could immediately acquire the mutex with the next statement.

- CSs are almost always considerably faster than mutexes. There is more on this in Chapter 9, and Chapter 9's SRW locks provide an additional, faster option.

Heap Locking

A pair of functions—HeapLock and HeapUnlock—is available to synchronize heap access (Chapter 5). The heap handle is the only argument. No other thread can allocate or free memory from the heap while a thread owns the heap lock. These functions cannot be used if the heap was created with the HEAP_NO-_SERIALIZE flag.

Although rarely used, heap locking can assure that no other thread modifies the heap if, for example, the locking thread is using HeapWalk to examine the heap for diagnostic purposes.

Semaphores

Semaphores, the second of the three kernel synchronization objects, maintain a count, and the semaphore object is in the signaled state when the count is greater than 0. The semaphore is unsignaled when the count is 0.

Threads wait in the normal way, using one of the wait functions. When a waiting thread is released, the semaphore's count is decremented by 1.

The semaphore functions are CreateSemaphore, CreateSemaphoreEx, OpenSemaphore, and ReleaseSemaphore. The last function can increment the count by 1 or more. These functions are comparable to their mutex counterparts.

```
HANDLE CreateSemaphore (
   LPSECURITY_ATTRIBUTES lpsa,
   LONG lSemInitial,
   LONG lSemMax,
   LPCTSTR lpSemName)
```

lSemMax, which must be 1 or greater, is the maximum value for the semaphore. lSemInitial, with $0 \leq$ lSemInitial $\leq$ lSemMax, is the initial value, and the semaphore value is never allowed to go outside of this range. A NULL return value indicates failure.

You can decrease the count only by 1 with any given wait operation, but a semaphore release can increment its count by any value up to the maximum.

```
BOOL ReleaseSemaphore (
    HANDLE hSemaphore,
    LONG cReleaseCount,
    LPLONG lpPreviousCount)
```

Notice that you can find the count preceding the release, but the pointer can be NULL if there is no need for this value.

The release count must be greater than 0, but if it would cause the semaphore count to exceed the maximum, the call will fail, returning FALSE, and the count will remain unchanged. Use the previous count value with caution, as other threads can change the semaphore count. Also, you cannot determine whether the count is at its maximum because there is no legal release count in that state. An example in the *Examples* file code demonstrates using the previous count.

While it is tempting to think of a mutex as a special case of a semaphore with a maximum value of 1, this would be misleading because there is no semaphore ownership. Any thread can release a semaphore, not just the one that performed the wait. Likewise, since there is no ownership, there is no concept of an abandoned semaphore.

Using Semaphores

The classic semaphore application regards the semaphore count as representing the number of available resources, such as the number of messages waiting in a queue. The semaphore maximum then represents the maximum queue size. Thus, a producer would place a message in the buffer and call ReleaseSemaphore, usually with a release count of 1. Consumer threads would wait on the semaphore, consuming a message and decrementing the semaphore count.

The potential race condition in sortMT (Program 7–2) illustrates another use of a semaphore to control the exact number of threads to wake up. All the threads could be created without being suspended. All of them would immediately wait on a semaphore initialized to 0. The boss thread, rather than resuming the threads, would simply call ReleaseSemaphore with a count of 4 (or whatever the number of threads is), and the four threads could then proceed.

While semaphores can be convenient, they are redundant in the sense that mutexes and events (described in the next major section), used together, are more powerful than semaphores. See Chapter 10 for more information.

A Semaphore Limitation

There is still an important limitation with the Windows semaphore implementation. How can a thread request that the count be decremented by two or more? The thread can wait twice in succession, as shown below, but this would not be an atomic operation because the thread could be preempted between waits. A deadlock could occur, as described next.

```
/* hSem is a semaphore handle.
The maximum semaphore count is 2. */
    . . .
/* Decrement the semaphore by 2. */
WaitForSingleObject (hSem, INFINITE);
WaitForSingleObject (hSem, INFINITE);
    . . .
/* Release two semaphore counts. */
ReleaseSemaphore (hSem, 2, &PrevCount);
```

To see how a deadlock is possible in this situation, suppose that the maximum and original semaphore counts are set to 2 and that the first of two threads completes the first wait and is then preempted. A second thread could then complete the first wait, reducing the count to 0. Both threads will block forever because neither will be able to get past the second wait.

A possible correct solution, shown in the following code fragment, is to protect the waits with a mutex or CRITICAL_SECTION.

```
/* Decrement the semaphore by 2. */
EnterCriticalSection (&csSem);
WaitForSingleObject (hSem, INFINITE);
WaitForSingleObject (hSem, INFINITE);
LeaveCriticalSection (&csSem);
    . . .
ReleaseSemaphore (hSem, 2, &PrevCount);
```

Even this implementation, in general form, is limited. Suppose, for example, that the semaphore has two remaining units, and that Thread A needs three units and Thread B needs just two. If Thread A arrives first, it will complete two waits and block on the third while owning the mutex. Thread B, which only needs the two remaining units, will still be blocked.

Another proposed solution would be to use `WaitForMultipleObjects` with the same semaphore handle used several times in the handle array. This suggestion fails for two reasons. First, `WaitForMultipleObjects` will return an error if it detects two handles for the same object. What is more, the handles would all be signaled, even if the semaphore count were only 1, which would defeat the purpose.

Exercise 10–10 provides a complete solution to this multiple-wait problem.

The Windows semaphore design would be more convenient if we could perform an atomic multiple-wait operation.

Events

Events are the final kernel synchronization object. Events can signal other threads to indicate that some condition, such as a message being available, now holds.

The important additional capability offered by events is that multiple threads can be released from a wait simultaneously when a single event is signaled. Events are classified as manual-reset and auto-reset, and this event property is set by the `CreateEvent` call.

- A manual-reset event can signal several threads waiting on the event simultaneously and can be reset.

- An auto-reset event signals a single thread waiting on the event, and the event is reset automatically.

Events use six new functions: `CreateEvent`, `CreateEventEx`, `OpenEvent`, `SetEvent`, `ResetEvent`, and `PulseEvent`. Here is the `CreateEvent` definition.

```
HANDLE CreateEvent (
    LPSECURITY_ATTRIBUTES lpsa,
    BOOL bManualReset,
    BOOL bInitialState,
    LPTCSTR lpEventName)
```

Specify a manual-reset event by setting `bManualReset` to TRUE. Similarly, the event is initially set to the signaled state if `bInitialState` is TRUE. You open a named event, possibly from another process, with `OpenEvent`.

The following three functions control events:

```
BOOL SetEvent (HANDLE hEvent)

BOOL ResetEvent (HANDLE hEvent)

BOOL PulseEvent (HANDLE hEvent)
```

A thread can signal an event using `SetEvent`. If the event is auto-reset, a single waiting thread, possibly one of many, is released, and the event automatically returns to the nonsignaled state. If no threads are waiting on the event, the event remains in the signaled state until a thread waits on it, and the thread is immediately released. Notice that a semaphore with a maximum count of 1 would have the same effect.

If, on the other hand, the event is manual-reset, it remains signaled until a thread calls `ResetEvent` for that event. During this time, all waiting threads are released, and it is possible that other threads will wait, and be released, before the reset.

`PulseEvent` releases all threads currently waiting on a manual-reset event, but the event is then automatically reset. In the case of an auto-reset event, `PulseEvent` releases a single waiting thread, if any.

Note: While many writers and even some Microsoft documentation (see the remarks in the MSDN `PulseEvent` entry) advise readers to avoid `PulseEvent`, I find it not only useful but essential, as discussed extensively, with examples, in Chapter 10. However, as we'll see, even that use has its risks, which are only resolved through the NT6 condition variables described in Chapter 10. For now, do not use `PulseEvent`.

Notice that `ResetEvent` is useful only after a manual-reset event is signaled with `SetEvent`. Be careful when using `WaitForMultipleObjects` to wait for *all* events to become signaled. A waiting thread will be released only when all events are simultaneously in the signaled state, and some signaled events might be reset before the thread is released.

Exercise 8–5 suggests how to modify `sortMT`, Program 7–2, to exploit events.

Pthreads' *condition variables* are somewhat comparable to events, but they are used in conjunction with a mutex. This is actually very useful and is described in Chapter 10, and Windows condition variables are available with NT6. `pthread_cond_init` and `pthread_cond_destroy` create and destroy condition variables. `pthread_cond_wait` and `pthread_cond_timedwait` are the waiting functions. `pthread_cond_signal` signals one waiting thread, as when pulsing a Windows auto-reset event. `pthread_cond_broadcast` signals all waiting threads and is therefore similar to `PulseEvent` applied to a manual-reset event. There is no exact equivalent of `Pulse-Event` or of `ResetEvent` used with manual-reset events.

Review: The Four Event Usage Models

The combination of auto- and manual-reset events with `SetEvent` and `Pulse-Event` gives four distinct ways to use events. Each combination is unique and each is useful, or even necessary, in some situations, and each model combination will be used in an example or exercise, either in this chapter or Chapter 10.

Warning: Events, if not used properly, can cause race conditions, deadlocks, and other subtle and difficult-to-diagnose errors. Chapter 10 describes techniques that are almost always required if you are using events in any but the simplest situations.

Table 8–1 describes the four situations.

Table 8–1 Summary of Event Behavior

	Auto-Reset Event	Manual-Reset Event
`SetEvent`	Exactly one thread is released. If none is currently waiting on the event, the first thread to wait on it in the future will be released immediately. The event is automatically reset.	All currently waiting threads are released. The event remains signaled until reset by some thread.
`PulseEvent`	Exactly one thread is released, but only if a thread is currently waiting on the event. The event is then reset to nonsignaled.	All currently waiting threads, if any, are released, and the event is then reset to nonsignaled.

An auto-reset event can be thought of as a door with a spring that slams the door shut, whereas a manual-reset event does not have a spring and will remain open. Using this metaphor, `PulseEvent` opens the door and immediately shuts it after one (auto-reset) or all (manual-reset) waiting threads, if any, go through the door. It is difficult, however, to know if anyone is waiting at the door. `SetEvent` opens the door and releases it.

Example: A Producer/Consumer System

This example extends Program 8–1 so that the consumer can wait until there is an available message. This eliminates the problem that requires the consumer to try again if a new message is not available. The resulting program, Program 8–2, is called `eventPC`.

Notice that the solution uses a mutex rather than a `CRITICAL_SECTION`; there is no reason for this other than to illustrate mutex usage. The use of an auto-reset event and `SetEvent` in the producer are, however, essential for correct operation to ensure that just one thread is released.

Also notice how the mutex and event are both associated with the message block data structure. The mutex enforces the critical code region for accessing the data structure object, and the event signals that there is a new message. Generalizing, the mutex ensures the message block's invariants, and the event signals that the object is in a specified state. Later chapters use this basic technique extensively.

Program 8–2   `eventPC`: A Signaling Producer and Consumer

```
/* Chapter 8. eventPC.c */
/* Maintain two threads, a producer and a consumer. */
/* The producer periodically creates checksummed data buffers, */
/* or "message blocks," signaling the consumer that a message */
/* is ready. The consumer displays when prompted. */

#include "Everything.h"
#include <time.h>
#define DATA_SIZE 256

typedef struct MSG_BLOCK_TAG { /* Message block */
    HANDLE mGuard;/* Mutex to uard the message block structure*/
    HANDLE mReady; /* "Message ready" auto-reset event */
    DWORDfReady, fStop;
        /* ready state flag, stop flag*/
    volatile DWORD nCons, mSequence; /* Msg block mSequence number*/
    DWORD nLost;
    time_t mTimestamp;
    DWORDmChecksum; /* Message contents mChecksum*/
    DWORDmData[DATA_SIZE]; /* Message Contents*/
} MSG_BLOCK;
/* ... */

DWORD _tmain (DWORD argc, LPTSTR argv[])
{
    HANDLE hProduce, hConsume;

    /* Initialize the message block mutex and event (auto-reset) */
    mBlock.mGuard = CreateMutex (NULL, FALSE, NULL);
    mBlock.mReady = CreateEvent (NULL, FALSE, FALSE, NULL);

    /* Create the two threads */
    hProduce = (HANDLE)_beginthreadex (NULL, 0, Produce,
                                    NULL, 0, NULL);
    hConsume = (HANDLE)_beginthreadex (NULL, 0, Consume,
                                    NULL, 0, NULL);
```

```
    /* Wait for the producer and consumer to complete */
    WaitForSingleObject (hConsume, INFINITE);
    WaitForSingleObject (hProduce, INFINITE);

    CloseHandle (mBlock.mGuard);
    CloseHandle (mBlock.mReady);

    _tprintf (_T("Producer and consumer threads have terminated\n"));
    _tprintf
       (_T("Messages produced: %d, Consumed: %d, Known Lost: %d\n"),
       mBlock.mSequence, mBlock.nCons,
       mBlock.mSequence - mBlock.nCons);
    return 0;
}

DWORD WINAPI Produce (void *arg)
/* Producer thread -- create new messages at random intervals. */
{
    srand ((DWORD)time(NULL)); /* Seed the random # generator */

    while (!mBlock.fStop) {
        /* Random Delay */
        Sleep(rand()/5); /* wait a long period for the next message */
            /* Adjust the divisor to change message generation rate */

        /* Get the buffer, fill it */
        WaitForSingleObject (mBlock.mGuard, INFINITE);
        __try {
            if (!mBlock.fStop) {
                mBlock.fReady = 0;
                MessageFill (&mBlock);
                mBlock.fReady = 1;
                InterlockedIncrement(&mBlock.mSequence);
                SetEvent(mBlock.mReady); /* Signal message ready. */
            }
        }
        __finally { ReleaseMutex (mBlock.mGuard); }
    }
    return 0;
}

DWORD WINAPI Consume (void *arg)
{
    DWORD ShutDown = 0;
    CHAR command[10];
    /* Consume the NEXT message when prompted by the user */
    while (!ShutDown) { /* Only thread accessing stdin, stdout */
        _tprintf (_T ("\n**Enter 'c' for Consume; 's' to stop: "));
        _tscanf (_T("%s"), command);
        if (command[0] == 's') {
```

```
                  WaitForSingleObject (mBlock.mGuard, INFINITE);
                  ShutDown = mBlock.fStop = 1;
                  ReleaseMutex (mBlock.mGuard);
          } else if (command[0] == 'c') { /* New buffer to consume */
                  WaitForSingleObject (mBlock.mReady, INFINITE);
                  WaitForSingleObject (mBlock.mGuard, INFINITE);
                  __try {
                          if (!mBlock.fReady) _leave; /* Don't process twice */
                          /* Wait for the event indicating a message is ready */
                          MessageDisplay (&mBlock);
                          InterlockedIncrement(&mBlock.nCons);
                          mBlock.nLost = mBlock.mSequence - mBlock.nCons;
                          mBlock.fReady = 0; /* No new messages are ready */
                  }
                  __finally { ReleaseMutex (mBlock.mGuard); }
          } else {
                  _tprintf (_T("Illegal command. Try again.\n"));
          }
      }
      return 0;
}
```

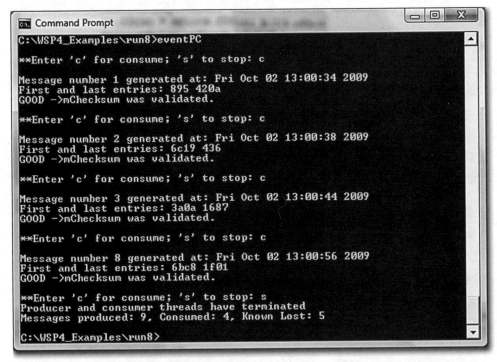

Run 8–2 eventPC: Producing and Consuming Messages

Note: It is possible that the consumer, having received the message ready event, will not actually process the current message if the producer generates yet another message before the consumer acquires the mutex. This behavior could cause a consumer to process a single message twice if it were not for the test at the start of the consumer's __try block. Chapter 10 addresses this and similar issues.

Run 8–2 shows eventPC execution, along with the summary of messages produced (12), consumed (4), and known to be lost (7). *Question:* Is it a defect that the number sum of consumed and known lost messages is less than the number produced? If so, how would you fix the defect?

Review: Windows Synchronization Objects

Table 8–2 reviews and compares the essential features of the Windows synchronization objects.

Table 8–2   Comparison of Windows Synchronization Objects

	CRITICAL_SECTION	Mutex	Semaphore	Event
Named, Securable Synchronization Object	No	Yes	Yes	Yes
Accessible from Multiple Processes	No	Yes	Yes	Yes
Synchronization	Enter	Wait	Wait	Wait
Release/Signal	Leave	Release or abandoned	Any thread can release	Set, pulse
Ownership	One thread at a time. The owning thread can enter multiple times without blocking.	One thread at a time. The owning thread can wait multiple times without blocking.	N/A. Many threads at a time, up to the maximum count.	N/A. Any thread can set or pulse an event.
Effect of Release	One waiting thread can enter.	One waiting thread can gain ownership after last release.	Multiple threads can proceed, depending on release count.	One or several waiting threads will proceed after a set or pulse.

Message and Object Waiting

The function `MsgWaitForMultipleObjects` is similar to `WaitForMultiple-Objects`. Use this function to allow a thread to process user interface events, such as mouse clicks, while waiting on synchronization objects.

More Mutex and `CRITICAL_SECTION` Guidelines

We are now familiar with all the Windows synchronization objects and have explored their utility in the examples. Mutexes and CSs, the two lock objects, were the first objects described and, because events will be used extensively in the next chapter, it is worthwhile to conclude this chapter with some guidelines for using mutexes and CSs to help ensure program correctness, maintainability, and performance.

Nearly everything is stated in terms of mutexes; the statements also apply to CSs unless noted otherwise.

Note: Many of these guidelines are paraphrased from *Programming with POSIX Threads* by David Butenhof.

- If there is no time-out associated with `WaitForSingleObject` on a mutex handle (CSs do not have a time-out), the calling thread could block forever. It is the programmer's responsibility to ensure that an owned (or locked) mutex is eventually unlocked.

- If a thread terminates or is terminated before it leaves (unlocks) a CS, the CS is left in an unstable state and subsequent behavior, such as attempts to enter the CS, is undefined. Mutexes have the useful abandonment property, and an abandoned mutex indicates a program bug or failure.

- If `WaitForSingleObject` times out waiting for a mutex, do not access the resources that the mutex is designed to protect.

- There may be multiple threads waiting on a given locked mutex. When the mutex is unlocked, *exactly one* of the waiting threads is given mutex ownership and moved to the ready state by the OS scheduler based on priority and scheduling policy. Do not assume that any particular thread will have priority; as always, program so that your application will operate correctly regardless of which waiting thread gains mutex ownership and resumes execution. The same comment applies to threads waiting on an event; do not assume that a specific thread will be the one released when the event is signaled or that threads will be unblocked in any specific order.

- A critical code region is everything between the points where the thread gains and relinquishes mutex ownership. A single mutex can be used to define several critical regions. If properly implemented, at most one thread can execute a mutex's critical code region at any time.

- *Mutex granularity* affects performance and is an important consideration. *Each critical code region should be just as long as necessary, and no longer, and a mutex should be owned just as long as necessary, and no longer.* Large critical code regions, locked for a long period of time, defeat concurrency and can impact performance.

- Minimize lock usage; locks decrease performance, so use them only when absolutely required. Chapter 9 describes a situation not requiring any locks, although locking might, at first, appear to be necessary. Be aware, however, not to introduce subtle race conditions while minimizing lock usage and critical code region size.

- Associate the mutex directly with the resource it is designed to protect, possibly in a data structure. (Programs 8–1 and 8–2 use this technique.).

- Document the invariant as precisely as possible, in words or even as a logical, or Boolean, expression. The invariant is a property of the protected resource that you guarantee holds outside the critical code region. An invariant might be of the form "the element is in both or neither list," "the checksum on the data buffer is valid," or "the linked list is valid." A precisely stated invariant can be used with the ASSERT macro at the end of a critical code region (the *Examples* eventPC source file is one of several that uses ASSERT). An example of a well-stated invariant is:

```
0 <= nLost + nCons && nLost + nCons <= sequence
```

- Ensure that each critical code region has exactly one entrance, where the thread locks the mutex, and exactly one exit, where the thread unlocks the mutex. Avoid complex conditional code and avoid premature exits, such as break, return, and goto statements, from within the critical code region. Termination handlers are useful for protecting against such problems.

- If the critical code region becomes too lengthy (longer than one page, perhaps), but all the logic is required, consider putting the code in a function so that the synchronization logic will be easy to comprehend. For example, the code to delete a node from a balanced search tree while the tree is locked might best be put in a function.

More Interlocked Functions

InterlockedIncrement and InterlockedDecrement have already been shown to be useful when all you need to do is perform very simple operations on thread-shared variables. Several other functions allow you to perform atomic operations to compare and exchange variable pairs.

Interlocked functions are as useful as they are efficient; they are implemented in user space using atomic machine instructions (for this reason, they are sometimes called "compiler intrinsic statements").

InterlockedExchange (also see InterlockedExchange64) stores one variable into another, as follows:

```
LONG InterlockedExchange (
    LONG volatile *Target,
    LONG Value)
```

The function returns the original value of *Target and sets *Target to Value.

InterlockedExchangePointer is similar and uses pointer-sized variables; that is, 32-bit pointers when the program is built for 32-bit operation or 64-bit pointers when built for 64-bit operation.

All the interlocked functions described here support 64-bit versions, so there is no need to mention this for the individual functions.

Note: An additional function, InterlockedExchangeAcquire, is supported only on the Itanium processor.

InterlockedExchangeAdd adds the second value to the first.

```
LONG InterlockedExchangeAdd (
    LONG volatile *Addend,
    LONG Increment)
```

Increment is added to *Addend, and the original value of *Addend is returned. This function allows you to increment a variable by 2 (or more) atomically, which is not possible with successive calls to InterlockedIncrement.

An additional *Examples* program, wcInterlocked, shows a variation of the familiar wc example using InterlockedExchangeAdd in the thread functions.

The next function, InterlockedCompareExchange, is similar to InterlockedExchange except that the exchange is done only if a comparison is satisfied.

```
PVOID InterlockedCompareExchange (
    LONG volatile *Destination,
    LONG Exchange,
    LONG Comparand)
```

InterlockedCompareExchange atomically performs the following, where Temp is a LONG:

```
Temp = *Destination;
if (*Destination == Comparand) *Destination = Exchange;
return Temp;
```

One use of the InterlockedCompareExchange functions is to implement a code "lock," similar to a CRITICAL_SECTION. *Destination is the *lock variable*, with 0 indicating unlocked and 1 indicating locked. Exchange is 1, Comparand is 0, and *Destination is initialized to 0 (unlocked). A calling thread knows that it owns the lock if the function returns 0. Otherwise, it should sleep or "spin"—that is, execute a meaningless loop that consumes time for a short period and then try again. This spinning is essentially what EnterCriticalSection does when waiting for a CRITICAL_SECTION with a nonzero spin count; see Chapter 9 for more information.

Finally, there is a family of interlocked logical functions for logical and, or, and exclusive or, and there are 8-bit, 16-bit, and 64-bit versions as well as the default for 32 bits. Hence, we have InterlockedAnd, InterlockedAnd64, Interlocked-And16, InterlockedAnd8, InterlockedXor, and so on.

Memory Management Performance Considerations

Program 9–1, in the next chapter, illustrates the potential performance impact when multiple threads contend for a shared resource. A similar effect is seen if threads perform memory management using malloc and free from the multithreaded Standard C library because these functions synchronize access to a heap data structure. Here are two possible methods to improve memory management performance.

- Each thread that performs memory management can create a HANDLE to its own heap using HeapCreate (Chapter 5). Memory allocation is then performed using HeapAlloc and HeapFree rather than using malloc and free.

- Consider an open source alternative such as the Hoard Memory Manager (use your favorite search engine).

Summary

Windows supports a complete set of synchronization operations that allows threads and processes to be implemented safely. Synchronization introduces a host of program design and development issues that you need to consider carefully to ensure both program correctness and good performance.

Looking Ahead

Chapter 9 concentrates on multithreaded and synchronization performance issues. The first topic is the performance impact of multiprocessor systems; in some cases, resource contention can dramatically reduce performance, and several strategies are provided to assure robust or even improved performance on multiprocessor systems. Trade-offs between mutexes and CRITICAL_SECTIONs, followed by CRITICAL_SECTION tuning with spin counts, are treated next, followed by the NT6 SRW locks. The chapter concludes with guidelines summarizing the performance-enhancing techniques, as well as performance pitfalls.

Additional Reading

Windows

Synchronization issues are independent of the OS, and many OS texts discuss the issue at length and within a more general framework.

Other books on Windows synchronization have already been mentioned. When dealing with more general Windows books, however, exercise caution many have not been updated to reflect the NT5 and NT6 features.

David Butenhof's *Programming with POSIX Threads* is recommended for in-depth thread and synchronization understanding, even for Windows programmers. The discussions and descriptions generally apply equally well to Windows, and porting the example programs can be a good exercise.

Exercises

8–1. The *Examples* file contains a defective version of simplePC.c (Program 8–1) called simplePCx.c. Test this program and describe the defect symptoms, if any. Fix the program without reference to the correct solution.

8–2. Modify simplePC.c so that the time period between new messages is increased. (*Suggestion:* Eliminate the division in the sleep call.) Ensure that the logic that determines whether there is a new message is correct. Also experiment with the defective version, `simplePCx.c`.

8–3. Reimplement `simplePC.c` with a mutex.

8–4. Reimplement `sortMT.c` (Program 7–2) using a semaphore rather than thread suspension to synchronize worker thread start-up.

8–5. Reimplement `sortMT.c` (Program 7–2) using an event rather than thread suspension to synchronize worker thread start-up. The recommended solution uses `SetEvent` and a manual-reset event. Other combinations would not be assured of correct operation. Explain.

8–6. Experiment with Program 8–2 by using different combinations of auto- and manual-reset events and `SetEvent` and `PulseEvent` (the current solution uses `SetEvent` and an auto-reset event). Are the alternate implementations and the original implementation correct, given the definition of the program's intended functionality? (See the note after Program 8–2.) Explain the results and explain how the alternate functionality might be useful. Can you make any of the alternate implementations work by changing the program logic?

8–7. Create a worker thread pool but control the rate of worker thread operation so that only one thread is allowed to run in any 1-second interval. Modify the program so that two threads can run in the interval but the overall rate of thread operation is limited to one per second. *Hint:* The worker threads should wait on an event (what type of event?), and a controlling thread should signal the event (`SetEvent` or `PulseEvent`?) every second.

8–8. *Advanced exercise:* `CRITICAL_SECTION`s are intended to be used by threads within the same process. What happens if you create a CS in shared, memory-mapped storage? Can both processes use the CS? You can perform this experiment by modifying Program 8–1 so that the producer and consumer run in different processes.

9 | Locking, Performance, and NT6 Enhancements

Chapter 8 introduced synchronization operations and demonstrated their use in some relatively simple examples. Chapter 10 provides more complex but realistic and useful message passing and compound object examples and describes a general model that solves many practical problems and enhances program reliability. This chapter is concerned first with locking performance implications and techniques to minimize the impact. The chapter then describes Windows NT6 (Vista, Server 2008, ...) SRW locks and NT6 thread pools, which provide additional performance improvements and programming conveniences. The chapter ends with a continuation of the parallelism discussion started in Chapter 7.

While thread synchronization is essential, there are some significant performance pitfalls, and we describe some of the major issues, both on single-processor and multiprocessor systems. There are also trade-offs among alternative solutions. For example, CRITICAL_SECTIONs (CSs) and mutexes are nearly identical functionally and solve the same fundamental problem. CSs are generally the most efficient locking mechanism, and SRW locks are even better. In other cases, interlocked operations are sufficient, and it may even be possible to avoid locking synchronization altogether with careful design and implementation.

CS–mutex trade-offs form the first topic, along with multiprocessor implications. CS spin counts, semaphore throttles, and processor affinity are other topics.

Note: Microsoft has implemented substantial performance improvements in NT5 and again in NT6; these improvements are particularly significant when using multiple processors. Consequently, some programming guidelines in this book's third edition, while appropriate for NT4 and older systems, are now obsolete and often counter productive.

Synchronization Performance Impact

Synchronization can and will impact your program's performance. There are several reasons for this:

- Locking operations, waiting, and even interlocked operations are inherently time consuming.

- Locking that requires kernel operation and waiting is expensive.

- Only one thread at a time can execute a critical code region, reducing concurrency and having the effect of serializing execution of critical code regions.

- Processor contention for memory and cache access on multiprocessor systems can produce unexpected effects, such as false sharing (described later).

CRITICAL_SECTION–Mutex Trade-offs

The first step is to assess the locking performance impact and compare CRITICAL_SECTIONs to mutexes. Program 9–1 shows statsMX.c, which uses a mutex to lock access to a thread-specific data structure. statsCS.c, not shown but in the *Examples* file, does exactly the same thing using a CRITICAL-_SECTION, and statsIN.c uses interlocked functions. Finally, statsNS.c, also not shown, uses no locking at all; by design, locking is not necessary in this example because each worker accesses its own unique storage. However, see the cautionary note after the bulleted list following the program. The actual programs allow any number of worker threads.

This set of examples not only illustrates the relative performance impact of three types of locking but also shows the following concepts.

- Locking is sometimes avoidable or can be minimized with careful program design. For example, the total amount of work performed is accumulated in the boss after the threads complete, so the example has no locking requirement for this computation. However, if each thread updated the global work completed variable, then the update operation would require a lock.

- The interlocked functions work well in some simple situations, such as incrementing a shared variable, as in Program 9–1.

- CSs are significantly faster than mutexes in most situations.

- A common technique is to specify the thread argument data structure so that it contains state data to be maintained by the thread along with a reference to a mutex or other locking object.

- Program 9–1 carefully aligns the thread argument data structure on cache line boundaries (defined to be 64 bytes in the listing). The alignment implementation uses the __declspec(align) modifier on the structure definition and the _aligned_malloc and _aligned_free memory management calls (all are Microsoft extensions). The cache alignment is to avoid a "false-sharing" performance bug, as described after the program listing.

Program 9–1 statsMX: Maintaining Thread Statistics

```
/* Chapter 9. statsMX.c                                   */
/* Simple boss/worker system, where each worker reports   */
/* its work output back to the boss for display.          */
/* MUTEX VERSION                                           */

#include "Everything.h"
#define DELAY_COUNT 20
#define CACHE_LINE_SIZE 64

/* Usage: statsMX nthread ntasks */
/* start up nthread worker threads, each assigned to perform   */
/* "ntasks" work units. Each thread reports its progress        */
/* in its own unshared slot in a work performed array           */

DWORD WINAPI Worker (void *);

__declspec(align(CACHE_LINE_SIZE))
typedef struct _THARG {
    HANDLE hMutex;
    int threadNumber;
    unsigned int tasksToComplete;
    unsigned int tasksComplete;
} THARG;

int _tmain (DWORD argc, LPTSTR argv[])
{
    INT nThread, iThread;
    HANDLE *hWorkers, hMutex;
    unsigned int tasksPerThread, totalTasksComplete;
    THARG **pThreadArgsArray, *pThreadArg;

    nThread = _ttoi(argv[1]);
    tasksPerThread = _ttoi(argv[2]);

    /* Create the mutex */
    hMutex = CreateMutex (NULL, FALSE, NULL);
    hWorkers = malloc (nThread * sizeof(HANDLE));
    pThreadArgsArray = malloc (nThread * sizeof(THARG *));
```

```
    for (iThread = 0; iThread < nThread; iThread++) {
        /* Fill in the thread arg */
        pThreadArg = (pThreadArgsArray[iThread] =
            _aligned_malloc (sizeof(THARG), CACHE_LINE_SIZE));
        pThreadArg->threadNumber = iThread;
        pThreadArg->tasksToComplete = tasksPerThread;
        pThreadArg->tasksComplete = 0;
        pThreadArg->hMutex = hMutex;
        hWorkers[iThread] = (HANDLE)_beginthreadex (NULL, 0, Worker,
                pThreadArg, 0, NULL);
    }

    /* Wait for the threads to complete */
    for (iThread = 0; iThread < nThread; iThread++)
        WaitForSingleObject (hWorkers[iThread], INFINITE);
    CloseHandle (hMutex);
    free (hWorkers);
    _tprintf (_T("Worker threads have terminated\n"));

    totalTasksComplete = 0;
    for (iThread = 0; iThread < nThread; iThread++) {
        pThreadArg = pThreadArgsArray[iThread];
        _tprintf (_T("Tasks completed by thread %5d: %6d\n"), iThread,
                pThreadArg->tasksComplete);
        totalTasksComplete += pThreadArg->tasksComplete;
        _aligned_free (pThreadArg);
    }
    _tprintf (_T("Total work performed: %d.\n"), totalTasksComplete);
    free (pThreadArgArray);

    return 0;
}

DWORD WINAPI Worker (void *arg)
{
    THARG * threadArgs;
    int iThread;

    threadArgs = (THARG *)arg;
    iThread = threadArgs->threadNumber;

    while (threadArgs->tasksComplete < threadArgs->tasksToComplete) {
        delay_cpu (DELAY_COUNT);
        WaitForSingleObject (threadArgs->hMutex, INFINITE);
        (threadArgs->tasksComplete)++;
        ReleaseMutex (threadArgs->hMutex);
    }
    return 0;
}
```

You can use the `timep` program from Chapter 6 (Program 6–2) to examine the behavior of the different implementations. Run 9–1a shows the results with 32 threads and 256,000 work units for `statsNS` (no synchronization), `statsIN` (interlocked), `statsCS` (`CRITICAL_SECTION`), and `statsMX` (mutex). The test system has four processors.

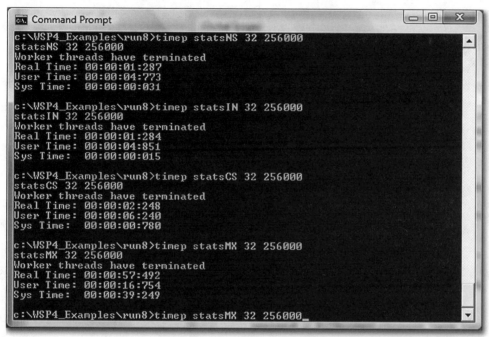

Run 9–1a `statsXX`: Performance with Different Locking Techniques

Additional tests performed on otherwise idle systems with 256,000 work units and 1, 2, 4, 8, 16, 32, 64, and 128 worker threads show similar results, as follows:

- The NS (no synchronization) and IN (interlocked functions) versions are always fastest, as is to be expected, and they really cannot be distinguished in this example. The CS version is noticeably slower, by a factor of 2 or more compared to IN, showing a typical synchronization slowdown. The MX (mutex) version, however, can take 2 to 30 times longer to execute than CS.

- Prior to NT5, CS performance did not always scale with the number of threads when the thread count exceeded 4. CS scalability is a significant NT5 improvement.

- NT6 SRW locks (later in this chapter) generally have performance between the interlocked functions and CSs.

- NT6 thread pools (later in this chapter) provide slight additional performance gains.

- Any type of locking, even interlocked locking, is expensive compared to no locking at all, but, of course, you frequently need locking. This example was deliberately designed so that locking is not required so as to illustrate locking costs.

- Mutexes are very slow, and unlike the behavior with CSs, performance degrades rapidly as the processor count increases. For instance, Table 9–1 shows the elapsed `statsMX` and `statsCS` times (seconds) for 64 threads and 256,000 work units on 1-, 2-, 4-, and 8-processor systems. Table C-5 (Appendix C) contains additional data. CS performance, however, improves with processor count and clock rate.

Table 9–1   Mutex and CS Performance with Multiple Processors

#Processors, Clock rate	statsMX	statsCS
1, 1.4GHz	55.03	14.15
2, 2.0GHz	93.11	5.30
4, 2.4GHz	118.3	4.34
8, 1.7GHz	262.2	2.02

False Sharing

The `pThreadArgsArray` array deliberately uses integers in cache-line aligned `THARG` structures to avoid the potential performance degradation caused by "false-sharing" cache contention (see Figure 8–2) on multiprocessor systems. The false-sharing problem can occur when:

- Two or more threads on different processors concurrently modify adjacent (that is, on the same cache line) task counts or other variables, making the modification in their respective cache lines.

- At the next memory barrier, the system would need to make the cache lines consistent, slowing the program.

False-sharing prevention requires that each thread's working storage be properly separated and aligned according to cache line size, as was done in Program 9–1, at some cost in program complexity and memory.

A Model Program for Performance Experimentation

The *Examples* file includes a project, TimedMutualExclusion, that generalizes Program 9–1 and enables experimentation with different boss/worker models, application program characteristics, and Windows locking and threading mechanisms (not all of which have been described yet). Program features, controlled from the command line, include the following:

- The lock type (CS, mutex, or SRW lock).

- The lock holding time, or *delay,* which models the amount of work performed in the critical code section.

- The number of worker threads, limited only by system resources.

- Thread pool usage, if any.

- The number of *sleep points* where a worker yields the processor, using Sleep(0), while owning the lock. Sleep points model a worker thread that waits for I/O or an event, while the delay models CPU activity.

The delay and sleep point parameters significantly affect performance because they affect the amount of time that a worker holds a lock, preventing other workers from running.

The program listing contains extensive comments explaining how to run the program and set the parameters. Exercise 9–1 suggests some experiments to perform on as wide a variety of systems as you can access. A variation, Timed-MutualExclusionSC, supports spin counts, as explained in the next section.

Note: TimedMutualExclusion is a *simple* model that captures many worker thread features. It can often be tuned or modified to represent a real application, and if the model shows performance problems, the application is at risk for similar problems. On the other hand, good performance in the model does not necessarily indicate good performance in the real application, even though the model may assist you in application performance tuning.

Tuning Multiprocessor Performance with CS Spin Counts

CRITICAL_SECTION locking (enter) and unlocking (leave) are efficient because CS testing is performed in user space without making the kernel system call that a mutex makes. Unlocking is performed entirely in user space, whereas ReleaseMutex requires a system call. CS operation is as follows.

- A thread executing `EnterCriticalSection` tests the CS's lock bit. If the bit is off (unlocked), then `EnterCriticalSection` sets it atomically as part of the test and proceeds without ever waiting. Thus, locking an unlocked CS is extremely efficient, normally taking just one or two machine instructions. The owning thread identity is maintained in the CS data structure, as is a recursion count.

- If the CS is locked, `EnterCriticalSection` enters a tight loop on a multiprocessor system, repetitively testing the lock bit without yielding the processor (of course, the thread could be preempted). The CS spin count determines the number of times `EnterCriticalSection` repeats the loop before giving up and calling `WaitForSingleObject`. A single-processor system gives up immediately; spin counts are useful only on a multiprocessor system where a different processor could change the lock bit.

- Once `EnterCriticalSection` gives up testing the lock bit (immediately on a single-processor system), `EnterCriticalSection` enters the kernel and the thread goes into a wait state, using a semaphore wait. Hence, CS locking is efficient when contention is low or when the spin count gives another processor time to unlock the CS.

- `LeaveCriticalSection` is implemented by turning off the lock bit, after checking that the thread actually owns the CS. `LeaveCriticalSection` also notifies the kernel, using `ReleaseSemaphore`, in case there are any waiting threads.

Consequently, CSs are efficient on single-processor systems if the CS is likely to be unlocked, as shown by the CS version of Program 9–1. The multiprocessor advantage is that the CS can be unlocked by a thread running on a different processor while the waiting thread spins.

The next steps show how to set spin counts and how to tune an application by determining the best spin count value. Again, spin counts are useful only on multiprocessor systems; they are ignored on single-processor systems.

Setting the Spin Count

You can set CS spin counts at CS initialization or dynamically. In the first case, replace `InitializeCriticalSection` with `InitializeCriticalSection-AndSpinCount`, where there is an additional count parameter. There is no way to read a CS's spin count.

```
VOID InitializeCriticalSectionAndSpinCount (
    LPCRITICAL_SECTION lpCriticalSection,
    DWORD dwCount)
```

You can change a spin count at any time.

```
VOID SetCriticalSectionSpinCount (
    LPCRITICAL_SECTION lpCriticalSection,
    DWORD dwCount)
```

MSDN mentions that 4,000 is a good spin count for heap management and that you can improve performance with a small spin count when a critical code section has short duration. The best value is, however, application specific, so spin counts should be adjusted with the application running in a realistic multiprocessor environment. The best values will vary according to the number of processors, the nature of the application, and so on.

`TimedMutualExclusionSC` is in the *Examples* file. It is a variation of the `TimedMutualExclusion` program, and it includes a spin count argument on the command line. You can run it on your host processor to find a good value for this particular test program on your multiprocessor systems, as suggested in Exercise 9–2.

NT6 Slim Reader/Writer Locks

NT6 supports SRW locks.[1] As the name implies, SRWs add an important feature: they can be locked in *exclusive mode* ("write") and *shared mode* ("read"), and they are light weight ("slim"). Exclusive mode is comparable to `CRITICAL_SECTION` and mutex locking, and shared mode grants read-only access. The locking logic is similar to file locking (Chapter 3), as are the benefits.

SRWs have several features that are different from `CRITICAL_SECTION`s.

- An SRW lock can be acquired in either mode, but you cannot upgrade or downgrade the mode between shared and exclusive.

---

[1] Some writers use the term "Vista SRW locks" because Vista was the first Windows release to support this feature.

- SRW locks are light weight and small, the size of a pointer (either 32 or 64 bits). Also, there is no associated kernel object for waiting, thus SRW locks require minimal resources.

- SRW locks do not support recursion because there is insufficient state information in the lock.

- You cannot configure or adjust the spin count; Microsoft implemented a spin count value that they determined to provide good results in a wide variety of situations.

- While you do need to initialize an SRW lock, there is no need to delete it.

- There is no nonblocking call equivalent to `TryEnterCriticalSection`.

- Both CSs and SRW locks can be used with Windows condition variables (Chapter 10).

With this `CRITICAL_SECTION` comparison, the API is self-explanatory, using the `SRWLOCK` and `PSRWLOCK` types. The initialization function (there is no delete function) is:

```
VOID InitializeSRWLock (
    PSRWLOCK pSRWLock)
```

There are two SRW acquisition and release functions, corresponding to the two modes. SRWs use the terms "acquire" and "release," as opposed to "enter" and "leave." You need to release a lock with the function corresponding to the acquisition. The functions for shared, or read, mode are:

```
VOID AcquireSRWLockShared (
    PSRWLOCK pSRWLock)

VOID ReleaseSRWLockShared (
    PSRWLOCK pSRWLock)
```

The two corresponding functions for exclusive, or write, mode are:

```
VOID AcquireSRWLockExclusive (
    PSRWLOCK pSRWLock)

VOID ReleaseSRWLockExclusive (
    PSRWLOCK pSRWLock)
```

There is one additional SRW function, `SleepConditionVariableSRW`, which Chapter 10 describes along with condition variables.

You can now use SRW locks in exclusive mode the same way that you use CSs, and you can also use shared mode if the critical code region does not change the guarded state variables. The advantage of shared mode is that multiple threads can concurrently own an SRW in shared mode, which can improve concurrency in many applications.

In summary, SRWs provide improved locking performance compared to mutexes and CSs for three principal reasons:

- SRWs are light weight, both in implementation and in resource requirements.

- SRWs allow shared mode access.

- SRWs do not support recursion, simplifying the implementation.

To test SRW locks, there is an SRW version of `statsMX` called `statsSRW`. `TimedMutualExclusion` also has an option to use SRWs, and there is also an exclusive/shared parameter that specifies the percentage of shared acquisitions. See the code comments. Program 9–2 uses both an SRW lock and a thread pool (see the next section).

Run 9–1b compares `statsSRW` and `statsCS` performance for several thread count values, running on the same four-processor system used in Run 9–1a.

The experimental results confirm that SRW locks, used in exclusive mode (the worst case), are faster than CSs (by a factor of 2 in this case). Appendix C shows timing results on several machines under a variety of circumstances. An exercise suggests testing a situation in which CSs can be more competitive.

The POSIX Pthreads specification supports reader/writer locks. The type is `pthread_rwlock_t`, and there are the expected functions for locking and unlocking, with a try option.

```
Command Prompt                                                          _  □  X

c:\WSP4_Examples\run8>timep statsSRW 32 256000
statsSRW 32 256000
Worker threads have terminated
Real Time: 00:00:01:244
User Time: 00:00:04:446
Sys Time:  00:00:00:015

c:\WSP4_Examples\run8>timep statsCS 32 256000
statsCS 32 256000
Worker threads have terminated
Real Time: 00:00:02:191
User Time: 00:00:06:115
Sys Time:  00:00:00:780

c:\WSP4_Examples\run8>timep statsSRW 64 256000
statsSRW 64 256000
Worker threads have terminated
Real Time: 00:00:02:321
User Time: 00:00:08:923
Sys Time:  00:00:00:015

c:\WSP4_Examples\run8>timep statsCS 64 256000
statsCS 64 256000
Worker threads have terminated
Real Time: 00:00:04:511
User Time: 00:00:12:495
Sys Time:  00:00:02:184

c:\WSP4_Examples\run8>timep statsSRW 256 256000
statsSRW 256 256000
Worker threads have terminated
Real Time: 00:00:08:948
User Time: 00:00:34:788
Sys Time:  00:00:00:031

c:\WSP4_Examples\run8>timep statsCS 256 256000
statsCS 256 256000
Worker threads have terminated
Real Time: 00:00:18:287
User Time: 00:00:50:294
Sys Time:  00:00:08:486

c:\WSP4_Examples\run8>
```

Run 9–1b `statsXX`: Comparing SRW and CS Performance

Thread Pools to Reduce Thread Contention

Programs with numerous threads can cause performance problems beyond locking issues. These problems include:

- Each thread has a distinct stack, with 1MB as the default stack size. For instance, 1,000 threads consume 1GB of virtual address space.

- Thread context switching is time consuming.

- Thread context switches can cause page faults during stack access.

Nonetheless, it is very natural to use multiple threads, where each thread represents a distinct activity, such as a worker processing its own work unit. It is difficult, and often self-defeating, to attempt to multiplex user-created worker threads. For example, an application cannot effectively determine how to load-balance tasks among the worker threads; this is a problem for the kernel's scheduler to solve. Furthermore, reducing the number of threads has the effect of serializing activities that are inherently parallel.

Several useful techniques and Windows features can help address this problem:

- Semaphore throttles, a simple programming technique that is still useful on NT4 and, to a lesser extent, on NT5 and NT6. The next section has a brief description.

- I/O completion ports, which are described and illustrated in Chapter 14, with a very brief description in a following section.

- Asynchronous I/O (overlapped and extended), also covered in Chapter 14. Generally, asynchronous I/O is difficult to program and does not provide performance advantages until NT6. Extended I/O, but not overlapped I/O, gives excellent performance on NT6 (Vista, Server 2008, ...) and can be worth the programming effort.

- NT6 thread pools, where the application submits callback functions to a thread pool. The kernel executes the callback functions from worker threads. Typically, the number of worker threads is the same as the number of processors, although the kernel may make adjustments. We describe thread pools after the semaphore throttle section.

- Asynchronous procedure calls (APC), which are important in the next chapter.

- A parallelization framework, such as OpenMP, Intel Thread Building Blocks, or Cilk++. These frameworks are language extensions that express program parallelism; as language extensions, they are out of scope for this book. Nonetheless, there's a (very) brief overview at the end of this chapter.

Before proceeding to NT6 thread pools, there are short descriptions of semaphore throttles and I/O completion ports. These descriptions help to motivate NT6 thread pools.

Semaphore "Throttles" to Reduce Thread Contention

Semaphores give a natural way to retain a simple threading model while still minimizing the number of active, contending threads. The solution is simple conceptually and can be added to an existing application program, such as the `statsMX` and `TimedMutualExclusion` examples, very quickly. The solution, called a *semaphore throttle,* uses the following techniques. We'll assume that you are using a mutex, some other kernel object, or file locks and have a good reason for doing so.

- The boss thread creates a semaphore with a small maximum value, such as 4, which represents the maximum number of active threads, possibly the number of processors, compatible with good performance. Set the initial count to the maximum value as well. This number can be a parameter and tuned to the best value after experimentation, just as spin lock counts can be tuned.

- Each worker thread waits on the semaphore before entering its critical code section. The semaphore wait can immediately precede the mutex or other wait.

- The worker thread should then release the semaphore (release count of 1) immediately after leaving the critical code section.

- If the semaphore maximum is 1, the mutex is redundant.

- Overall CS or mutex contention decreases as the thread execution is serialized with only a few threads waiting on the mutex or CS.

The semaphore count simply represents the number of threads that can be active at any one time, limiting the number of threads contending for the mutex, CS, processors, or other resource. The boss thread can even throttle the workers and dynamically tune the application by waiting on the semaphore to reduce the count if the boss determines that the workers are running too slowly (for example, the boss could monitor exit flags maintained by each worker, as in Program 8–1), and it can release semaphore units to allow more workers to run. Note, however, that the maximum semaphore count is set at create time and cannot be changed.

The following code fragment illustrates a modified worker loop with two semaphore operations.

```
WaitForSingleObject (hThrottleSem, INFINITE);
while (TRUE) { /* Worker loop */
    WaitForSingleObject (hMutex, INFINITE);
        ... Critical code section ...
    ReleaseMutex (hMutex);
} /* End of worker loop */
ReleaseSemaphore (hThrottleSem, 1, NULL);
```

There is one more variation. If a particular worker is considered to be "expensive" in some sense, it can be made to wait for several semaphore units. As noted in the previous chapter, however, two successive waits can create a deadlock. An exercise in the next chapter shows how to build an atomic multiple-wait compound semaphore object.

`TimedMutualExclusion`, the familiar example, adds a sixth parameter that is the initial throttle semaphore count for the number of active threads. You can experiment with this count as suggested in one of the exercises.

Comment: As mentioned previously, this technique is useful mostly on older Windows releases with multiple processors, before NT5. NT5 and NT6 have improved synchronization performance, so you should experiment carefully before deploying a semaphore throttle solution. Nonetheless:

- Throttles are still useful in some NT5 and NT6 systems when using mutexes and multiple processors (see Run 9–1c and Table 9–1, later in this chapter).

- I've also found semaphore throttles useful to limit concurrent access to other resources, such as files and memory. Thus, if multiple threads all have large, thread-specific memory requirements, limiting the number of active threads can reduce page faults and thrashing.

- You can add a semaphore throttle very easily to an existing program, and you do not need to depend on the Windows version or new functionality, such as thread pools.

Run 9–1c compares `statsMX` and `statsMX_ST` (the semaphore throttle version) for a large number of threads (256). `statsMX_ST` is slightly but consistently faster (about 24 seconds faster over nearly 8 minutes).

Run 9–1c `statsMX`: Using a Semaphore Throttle

I/O Completion Ports

Chapter 14 describes I/O completion ports, which provide another mechanism to avoid thread contention by limiting the number of threads. I/O completion ports allow a small number of threads to manage a large number of concurrent I/O operations. Individual I/O operations are started asynchronously so that the operation is, in general, not complete when the read or write call returns. However, as outstanding operations complete, data processing is handed off to one of a small number of worker threads. Chapter 14 has an example using a server communicating with remote clients (Program 14–4).

NT6 Thread Pools

NT6 thread pools are easy to use, and it's also simple to upgrade an existing program to use a thread pool rather than threads. The major thread pool features are as follows:

- The application program creates "work objects" rather than threads and submits the work objects to the thread pool. Each work object is a callback function and a parameter value and is identified by handle-like (but not a HANDLE) structure that identifies the work object.

- The thread pool manages a small number of "worker threads" (not to be confused with the application worker threads in preceding examples). Windows then assigns work objects to worker threads, and a worker thread executes a work object by calling the callback function with the work object's parameter.

- When a work object completes, it returns to the Windows worker thread, which can then execute another work object. Notice that a callback function should never call ExitThread or _endthreadex, as that would terminate the Windows worker thread. A work object can, however, submit another work object, which could be itself, requesting that the same work object be executed again.

- Windows can adjust the number of worker threads based on application behavior. The application can, however, set upper and lower bounds on the number of worker threads.

- There is a default thread pool, but applications can create additional pools. However, the pools will all contend for the same processor resources, so the examples use the default pool.

Thread pools allow the Windows kernel to exploit sophisticated techniques to determine how many worker threads to create and when to call the work objects. Furthermore, invoking a callback function avoids the overhead of thread context switching, and this is most effective when the work item callback functions are short.

NT5 supports thread pools, and we use them in later chapters. NT6 introduced a new and more powerful thread pool API, which we use in this chapter. MSDN compares the API functions (search for "thread pool API").

We convert `statsSRW` to `statsSRW_VTP` (for "Vista Thread Pool") to illustrate the changes. The *Examples* file also contains `wcMT_VTP`, a conversion of Chapter 7's multithreaded `wc` (word count) utility.

The conversion steps are as follows; function descriptions follow:

- Add an initialization call to `InitializeThreadpoolEnvironment` and, optionally, modify the environment.

- Create a work object (callback function and argument), which is similar to creating a thread in the suspended state. This creates a work object handle to use with the other functions; note that this is not a `HANDLE` but a `PTP_WORK` object.

- Submit the work object using `SubmitThreadPoolWork`, which is analogous to `ResumeThread`.

- Replace the thread wait call with calls to `WaitForThreadpoolWorkCallbacks`. The calling, or boss, thread will block until all calls to the work object complete.

- Replace the thread handle `CloseHandle` calls with calls to `CloseThreadpoolWork`.

We describe each function in turn and then show the `statsSRW_VTP` listing and performance results.

Caution: Be careful using the C library in the callback functions because the Windows executive does not use `_beginthreadex`. Many functions, such as `printf` statements, will usually work if you use the multithreaded C library (see Chapter 7). However, some C library functions, such as `strtok`, could fail in a callback function.

CreateThreadpoolWork

This is the thread pool work object creation function.

```
PTP_WORK CreateThreadpoolWork (
   PTP_WORK_CALLBACK pfnwk,
   PVOID pv,
   PTP_CALLBACK_ENVIRON pcbe)
```

Parameters

- pfnwk is the callback function; the function signature is described later.

- pv is optional. The value will be passed as a parameter to every call to the callback function. Notice that every call to the callback function for this work object receives the same value.

- pcbe is an optional TP_CALLBACK_ENVIRON structure. The default is usually sufficient, but see the InitializeThreadpoolEnviroment function to understand the advanced options, and Chapter 14 has more on the thread pool environment.

- The return value is the thread pool work object and is NULL in case of failure.

SubmitThreadpoolWork

Each call to this function posts a work object (that is, a callback function call and parameter) to the thread pool. The Windows executive's thread pool implementation decides when to call the individual instances. The callbacks can execute in parallel on separate processors.

```
VOID SubmitThreadpoolWork (
   PTP_WORK pwk)
```

pwk is the value that CreateThreadpoolWork returned. Assuming that this value is valid, SubmitThreadpoolWork never fails, since all the required resources were allocated previously.

The callback function associated with pwd will be called once for every Submit-ThreadpoolWork call. The Windows kernel scheduler determines which of several threads will run a specific call. The programmer does not need to manage threads but still must manage synchronization. Furthermore, a specific callback instance might run on different threads at different points.

WaitForThreadpoolWorkCallbacks

This wait function does not have a time-out and returns when all submitted work objects (callbacks) complete. Optionally, you can cancel callbacks for the work objects that have not started, using the second parameter, but callbacks that have started will run to completion. The first parameter is the thread pool work object.

```
VOID WaitForThreadpoolWorkCallbacks (
    PTP_WORK pwk,
    BOOL fCancelPendingCallbacks)
```

CloseThreadpoolWork

All that is required is a valid work object.

```
VOID CloseThreadpoolWork (
    PTP_WORK pwk)
```

The Callback Function

This is our first use of callback functions, although we'll see them again with extended I/O and timers (Chapter 14) and APCs (Chapter 10). The thread pool will invoke this function once for every SubmitThreadpoolWork invocation.

The callback function replaces the thread function.

```
VOID CALLBACK WorkCallback (
    PTP_CALLBACK_INSTANCE Instance,
    PVOID Context,
    PTP_WORK Work)
```

Work is the work object, and Context is the pv value from the work object creating CreateThreadpoolWork call. The Instance value identifies this specific callback instance (not the work object, which may have multiple instances), allowing the callback function to provide the Windows executive with information that may help scheduling. Specifically, `CallbackMayRunLong` informs the executive that the callback instance may execute for a long time so that the executive can attempt to assign an existing or new worker thread to this instance. Normally, callback instances are expected to execute quickly.

Using Thread Pools

Program 9–2 modifies Program 9–1 to use an SRW lock and a thread pool.

Program 9–2 `statsSRW_VTP`: Thread Performance with a Thread Pool

```
/* Chapter 9. statsSRW_VTP.c                              */
/* Simple boss/worker system, where each worker reports   */
/* its work output back to the boss for display.          */
/* SLIM READER/WRITER VERSION, with a VISTA (NT6) THREAD POOL */

#include "Everything.h"
#define DELAY_COUNT 20
#define CACHE_LINE_SIZE 64

/* Usage: statsSRW_VTP nthread ntasks */

VOID CALLBACK Worker (PTP_CALLBACK_INSTANCE, PVOID, PTP_WORK);
int workerDelay = DELAY_COUNT;

__declspec(align(CACHE_LINE_SIZE))
typedef struct _THARG {
    SRWLOCK SRWL;
    int threadNumber;
    unsigned int tasksToComplete;
    unsigned int tasksComplete;
} THARG;

int _tmain (DWORD argc, LPTSTR argv[])
{
    INT nThread, iThread;
    HANDLE *pWorkObjects;
    SRWLOCK srwl;
    unsigned int tasksPerThread, totalTasksComplete;
    THARG ** pThreadArgsArray, *pThreadArg;
    TP_CALLBACK_ENVIRON cbe;  /* Callback environment */
    BOOL traceFlag = FALSE;

    nThread = _ttoi(argv[1]);
    tasksPerThread = _ttoi(argv[2]);
```

```
    /* Initialize the SRW lock */
    InitializeSRWLock (&srwl);

    pWorkObjects = malloc (nThread * sizeof(PTP_WORK));
    pThreadArgsArray = malloc (nThread * sizeof(THARG *));

    InitializeThreadpoolEnvironment (&cbe);

    for (iThread = 0; iThread < nThread; iThread++) {
        /* Fill in the thread arg */
        pThreadArg = (pThreadArgsArray[iThread] =
                _aligned_malloc (sizeof(THARG), CACHE_LINE_SIZE));
        pThreadArg->threadNumber = iThread;
        pThreadArg->tasksToComplete = tasksPerThread;
        pThreadArg->tasksComplete = 0;
        pThreadArg->SRWL = srwl;
        pWorkObjects[iThread] =
                CreateThreadpoolWork (Worker, pThreadArg, &cbe);
        SubmitThreadpoolWork (pWorkObjects[iThread]);
    }

    /* Wait for the threads to complete */
    for (iThread = 0; iThread < nThread; iThread++) {
        /* Wait for the thread pool work item to complete */
        WaitForThreadpoolWorkCallbacks (pWorkObjects[iThread], FALSE);
        CloseThreadpoolWork(pWorkObjects[iThread]);
    }

    free (pWorkObjects);
    _tprintf (_T("Worker threads have terminated\n"));
    totalTasksComplete = 0;
    for (iThread = 0; iThread < nThread; iThread++) {
        pThreadArg = pThreadArgsArray[iThread];
        _tprintf (_T("Tasks completed by thread %5d: %6d\n"), iThread,
                pThreadArg->tasksComplete);
        totalTasksComplete += pThreadArg->tasksComplete;
        _aligned_free (pThreadArg);
    }
    free (pThreadArgsArray);

    _tprintf (_T("Total work performed: %d.\n"), totalTasksComplete);

    return 0;
}

VOID CALLBACK Worker (PTP_CALLBACK_INSTANCE Instance, PVOID Context,
                        PTP_WORK Work)
{
    THARG *pTa;
    threadArgs = (THARG *)Context;
```

```
while (threadArgs->tasksComplete < threadArgs->tasksToComplete) {
    delay_cpu (workerDelay);
    AcquireSRWLockExclusive (&(threadArgs->SRWL));
    (threadArgs->tasksComplete)++;
    ReleaseSRWLockExclusive (&(threadArgs->SRWL));
}
return;
}
```

Run 9–2 compares performance for `statsSRW`, which uses worker threads, and `statsSRW_VTP`, which uses work objects, on a four-processor system, with the expectation that the second program will be faster.

- First, the two programs are run with large "tasks to complete" values (the second command line argument) for the worker threads (or work objects); this means that the workers are long running. It turns out that the VTP is a bit slower (3.954 seconds instead of 3.481 seconds).

- However, when there is a large number of workers (the first command line argument), each with a small amount of work, the thread pool solution is faster. See the second pair of test runs, where the thread pool version requires 2.596 seconds, and the threads version requires 3.368 seconds.

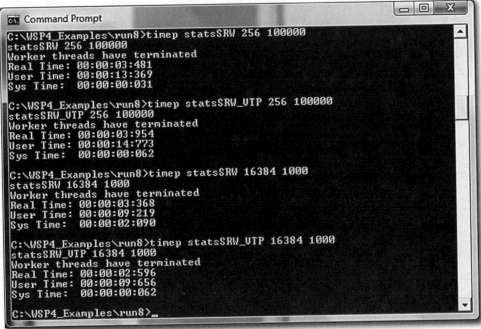

Run 9–2   `statsSRW`: Using a Thread Pool, Fast and Slow Workers

If you test `statsSRW_VTP`, it is interesting to add a call to `GetCurrentThreadId` from within the `worker` callback function. You can either print the value or add a field to the thread argument to display within the boss function. You will find that Windows will use a small number of threads, typically one per processor.

Submitting Callbacks to the Thread Pool

`TrySubmitThreadpoolCallback` is an alternative to the `CreateThreadpool-Work`, `SubmitThreadpoolWork`, `CloseThreadpoolWork` sequence.

```
BOOL TrySubmitThreadpoolCallback (
    PTP_SIMPLE_CALLBACK pfnwk,
    PVOID pv,
    PTP_CALLBACK_ENVIRON pcbe)
```

The callback function is a different type: `PTP_SIMPLE_CALLBACK` instead of `PTP_WORK_CALLBACK`. The work item is omitted because it's not required.

```
VOID CALLBACK SimpleCallback (
    PTP_CALLBACK_INSTANCE Instance,
    PVOID Context)
```

The Thread Pool Environment

Both `CreateThreadpoolWork` and `TrySubmitThreadpoolCallback` have optional callback environment parameters, which are frequently `NULL` for the default value. However, the callback environment can be useful, and Chapter 14 describes some advanced thread pool techniques that use the environment.

The `wcMT_VTP` example in the *Examples* file illustrates a simple environment use in which the environment is set to indicate that the callback functions are long running. However, in this example, there was no measurable effect on performance, just as with Run 9–2.

The Process Thread Pool

Each process has a dedicated thread pool. When you use `CreateThreadpool-Work`, `SubmitThreadpoolWork`, and `TrySubmitThreadpoolCallback`, the callback functions are all executed using the process thread pool. Therefore, several distinct callback functions could contend for this pool, and this is normally the desired behavior because it allows the executive to schedule work objects with the available resources.

Our examples (`statsSRW_VTP` and `wcMT_VTP`) both share the property that there is only one callback function, and the callback functions dominate execution time.

You can, however, create additional thread pools with `CreateThreadPool`; however, test carefully to see if this provides any benefit or if it degrades performance.

Other Threadpool Callback Types

`CreateThreadpoolWork` associates a work callback function with a `TP_WORK` structure. In the examples here, the work function performs computation and possibly I/O (see the `wcMT_VTP` example in the *Examples* file). There are, however, other callback types that can be associated with the process thread pool.

- `CreateThreadpoolTimer` specifies a callback function to execute after a time interval and possibly periodically after that. The callback will execute on a thread in the pool. Chapter 14 has an example, `TimeBeep_TPT`.

- `CreateThreadpoolIo` specifies a callback function to execute when an overlapped I/O operation completes on a `HANDLE`. Again, see Chapter 14.

- `CreateThreadpoolWait` specifies a callback function to execute when an object, specified by `SetThreadpoolWait`, is signaled.

Summary: Locking Performance

We now have four locking mechanisms as well as thread pools and the possibility of no locking. The seven `stats` program variations (including `statsMX_ST`) illustrate the relative performance, although, as with any statement about performance, results may vary depending on a wide variety of software and hardware factors. Nonetheless, as a generalization, the mechanisms, from fastest to slowest, are:

- No synchronization, which is possible in some situations.

- Interlocked functions.

- SRW locks with a worker thread pool (NT6 only). The locks are exclusive mode. A mix of shared and exclusive locking could improve performance.

- SRW locks with conventional thread management (NT6 only).

- Critical sections, which can be optimized with spin count tuning.

- Mutexes, which can be dramatically slower than the alternatives, especially with multiple processors. A semaphore throttle can be marginally useful in some cases with a large number of threads.

Appendix C gives additional results, using other systems and different parameter values.

Parallelism Revisited

Chapter 7 discussed some basic program characteristics that allow application threads to run in parallel, potentially improving program performance, especially on multiprocessor systems.

Parallelism has become an important topic because it is the key to improving application performance, since processor clock rates no longer increase regularly as they have in the past. Most systems today and in the foreseeable future, whether laptops or servers, will have clock rates in the 2–3GHz range. Instead, chip makers are marketing multicore chips with 2, 4, or more processors on a single chip. In turn, system vendors are installing multiple multicore chips in their systems so that systems with 4, 8, 16, or more total processors are common.[2]

Therefore, if you want to increase your application's performance, you will need to exploit its inherent parallelism using threads, NT6 thread pools, and, possibly, parallelism frameworks (which this section surveys). We've seen several simple examples, but these examples give only a partial view of what can be achieved:

- In most cases, such as wcMT and grepMT, the parallel operations are straightforward. There is one thread per file.

- sortMT is more complex, as it divides a single data structure, an array, into multiple parts, sorts them, and merges the results. This is a simplistic use of the divide and conquer strategy.

- cciMT (Chapter 14) divides the file into multiple segments and works on them independently.

In each case, the maximum potential speedup, compared to a single-threaded implementation or running on a single processor, is easy to determine. For example,

---

[2] Nearly all desktop systems, most laptops, and many notebooks sold today have multiple processors and cost less than single-processor systems sold a few years ago. The "Additional Reading" section suggests references for parallelism and the appropriate technology trends.

the speedup for `wcMT` and `grepMT` is limited by the minimum of the number of processors and the number of files.

A Better Foundation and Extending Parallel Program Techniques

The previous parallelism discussion was very informal and intuitive, and the implementation, such as `wcMT`, are all boss/worker models where the workers are long-lived, executing for essentially the entire duration of the application execution.

While a formal discussion is out of scope for this book, it's important to be aware that parallelism has been studied extensively, and there is a solid theoretical foundation along with definitions for important concepts. There are also analytical methods to determine algorithmic complexity and parallelism. Interested readers will find several good treatments; for example, see Chapter 27 of Cormen, Leiserson, Rivest, and Stein, *Introduction to Algorithms,* Third Edition.

Furthermore, parallel programming techniques are far more extensive than the boss/worker examples used here. For example:

- Parallel sort-merge can be made far more effective than `sortMT`'s rudimentary divide and conquer design.

- Recursion and divide and conquer techniques are important for exploiting finer-grained program parallelism where parallel tasks can be short-lived relative to total program duration.

- Computational tasks that are amenable to parallel programming include, but are hardly limited to, matrix multiplication, fast Fourier transformations, and searching. Usually, a new thread is created for every recursive function call.

- Games and simulations are other application types that can often be decomposed into parallel components.

In short, parallelism is increasingly important to program performance. Our examples have suggested the possibilities, but there are many more that are beyond this book's scope.

Parallel Programming Alternatives

Once you have identified the parallel components in your program, the next issue is to determine how to implement the parallelism. There are several alternatives; we've been using the first two, which Windows supports well.

- The most direct approach is to "do it yourself" (DIY), as in some of the examples. This requires direct thread management and synchronization. DIY is manageable and effective for smaller programs or programs with a simple parallel structure. However, DIY can become complex and error prone, but not impossible, when implementing recursion.

- Thread pools, both legacy and NT6 thread pools, enable advanced kernel scheduling and resource allocation methods that can enhance performance. Be aware, however, that the NT6 thread pool API is limited to that kernel; this should become less of an issue in coming years.

- Use a parallelism framework, which extends the programming language to help you express program parallelism. See the next section.

Parallelism Frameworks

Several popular "parallelism frameworks" offer alternatives to DIY or thread pools. Framework properties include:

- Programming language extensions that express program parallelism. The two most common extensions are to express *loop parallelism* (that is, every loop iteration can execute concurrently) and *fork-join parallelism* (that is, a function call can run independently from the calling program, which eventually must wait for the called function to complete). The language extensions may take the form of compiler directives or actual extensions that require compiler front ends.

- The supported languages almost always include C and C++, often C# and Java, and Fortran for scientific and engineering applications.

- There is run-time support for efficient scheduling, locking, and other tasks.

- There is support for result "reduction" where the results from parallel tasks are combined (for instance, word counts from individual files are summed), and there is care to minimize locking.

- Parallel code can be serialized for debugging and produces the same results as the parallel code.

- The frameworks frequently contain tools for race detection and identifying and measuring parallelism during program execution.

- The frameworks are sometimes open source and portable to UNIX and Linux.

Popular parallelism frameworks include:[3]

- OpenMP is open source, portable, and scalable. Numerous compilers and development environments, including Visual C++, support OpenMP.

- Intel Thread Building Blocks (TBB) is a C++ template library. The commercial release is available on Windows as well as many Linux and UNIX systems.

- Intel's Cilk++ supports C and C++. Cilk++ is available on Windows and Linux and provides a simple language extension with three key words along with a run-time library for "work stealing" scheduling. Cilk++ also provides flexible reduction templates.

- .NET Framework 4's Task Parallel Library (TPL), not yet available, will simplify creating applications with parallelism and concurrency.

Do Not Forget the Challenges

As stated previously, this book takes the point of view that multithreaded programming is straightforward, beneficial, and even enjoyable. Nonetheless, there are numerous pitfalls, and we've provided numerous guidelines to help produce reliable multithreaded programs; there are even more guidelines in the next chapter. Nonetheless, do not overlook the challenges when developing multithreaded applications or converting legacy systems. These challenges are daunting even when using a parallelism framework. Here are some of the notable challenges that you can expect and that have been barriers to successful implementations:

- Identifying the independent subtasks is not always straightforward. This is especially true for legacy applications that may have been developed with no thought toward parallelism and threading.

- Too many subtasks can degrade performance; you may need to combine smaller subtasks.

- Too much locking can degrade performance, and too little can cause race conditions.

- Global variables, which are common in large, single-threaded applications, can cause races if independent subtasks modify global variables. For example, a global variable might contain the sum or other combination of results from separate loop iterations; if the iterations run in parallel, you will need to find

---

[3] Wikipedia covers all of these, and a Web search will yield extensive additional information. This list is not complete, and it will take time for one or more frameworks to become dominant.

a way to combine ("reduce") the independent results to produce a single result without causing a data race.

- There can be subtle performance issues due to the memory cache architecture and the combination of multiple multicore chips.

Processor Affinity

The preceding discussion has assumed that all processors of a multiprocessor system are available to all threads, with the kernel making scheduling decisions and allocating processors to threads. This approach is simple, natural, consistent with multiprocessors, and almost always the best approach. It is possible, however, to assign threads to specific processors by setting processor affinity. Processor affinity can be used in several situations.

- You can dedicate a processor to a small set of one or more threads and exclude other threads from that processor. This assumes, however, that you control all the running applications, and even then, Windows can schedule its own threads on the processor.

- You can assign a collection of threads to a processor pair sharing L2 cache (see Figure 8–2) to minimize the delay caused by memory barriers.

- You may wish to test a processor. Such diagnostic testing, however, is out of scope for this book.

- Worker threads that contend for a single resource can be allocated to a single processor.

You may wish to skip this section, considering the specialized nature of the topic.

System, Process, and Thread Affinity Masks

Each process has its own process affinity mask, which is a bit vector. There is also a system affinity mask.

- The system mask indicates the processors configured on this system.

- The process mask indicates the processors that can be used by the process's threads. By default, its value is the same as the system mask.

- Each individual thread has a thread affinity mask, which must be a subset of the process affinity mask. Initially, a thread's affinity mask is the same as the process mask.

- Affinity masks are pointers (either 32 or 64 bits). Win32 supports up to 32 processors. Consult MSDN if you need to deal with more than 64 processors on Win64.

There are functions to get and set the masks, although you can only read (get) the system mask and can only set thread masks. The set functions use thread and process handles, so one process or thread can set the affinity mask for another, assuming access rights, or for itself. Setting a mask has no effect on a thread that might already be running on a processor that is masked out; only future scheduling is affected.

A single function, `GetProcessAffinityMask`, reads both the system and process affinity masks. On a single-processor system, the two mask values will be 1.

```
BOOL GetProcessAffinityMask (
   HANDLE hProcess,
   LPDWORD lpProcessAffinityMask,
   LPDWORD lpSystemAffinityMask)
```

The process affinity mask, which will be inherited by any child process, is set with `SetProcessAffinityMask`.

```
BOOL SetProcessAffinityMask (
   HANDLE hProcess,
   DWORD_PTR dwProcessAffinityMask)
```

The new mask must be a *subset* of the values obtained from `GetProcessAffinityMask`. It does not, however, need to be a proper subset. Such a limitation would not make sense because you would not be able to restore a system mask to a previous value. The new value affects all the threads belonging to this process.

Thread masks are set with a similar function.

```
DWORD_PTR SetThreadAffinityMask (
   HANDLE hThread,
   DWORD dwThreadAffinityMask)
```

These functions are not designed consistently. `SetThreadAffinityMask` returns a `DWORD` with the previous affinity mask; 0 indicates an error. `SetThread-AffinityMask`, however, returns a `BOOL` and does not return the previous value.

`SetThreadIdealProcessor` is a variation of `SetThreadAffinityMask`. You specify the preferred ("ideal") processor number (not a mask), and the scheduler will assign that processor to the thread if possible, but it will use a different processor if the preferred processor is not available. The return value gives the previous preferred processor number, if any.

Finding the Number of Processors

The system affinity mask does indicate the number of processors on the system; all that is necessary is to count the number of bits that are set. It is easier, however, to call `GetSystemInfo`, which returns a `SYSTEM_INFO` structure whose fields include the number of processors and the active processor mask, which is the same as the system mask. A simple program and project, `version`, in the *Examples* file, displays this information along with the Windows version. See Exercise 6–12 for `version` output on the system used for the run screenshots in this chapter.

Performance Guidelines and Pitfalls

Multiple threads can provide significant programming advantages, including simpler programming models and performance improvement. However, there are several performance pitfalls that can have drastic and unexpected negative performance impact, and the impact is not always consistent on different computers, even when they are running the same Windows version. Some simple guidelines, summarizing the experience in this chapter, will help you to avoid these pitfalls. Some of these guidelines are adapted from Butenhof's *Programming with POSIX Pthreads,* as are many of the designing, debugging, and testing hints in the next chapter.

In all cases, of course, it's essential to maintain program correctness. For example, while the `statsXX` programs, as written, can run without locking, that is not the case in general. Likewise, when you make a critical code section as small as possible, be sure not to move critical code out of the code section. Thus, if the critical code section adds an element to a search tree, all the code required for the insertion operation must be in the critical code section.

- Beware of conjecture and theoretical arguments about performance, which often sound convincing but can be wrong in practice. Test the conjecture with a simple prototype, such as `TimedMutualExclusion`, or with alternative implementations of your application.

- Test application performance on as wide a variety of systems as are available to you. It is helpful to run with different memory configurations, processor types, Windows versions, and number of processors. *An application may perform very well on one system and then have extremely poor performance on a similar one;* see the discussion after Program 9–1.

- Locking is expensive; use it only as required. Hold (own) a lock, regardless of the type, only as long as required and no longer (see earlier comment). As an additional example, consider the message structures used in `simplePC` (Program 8–1). The critical code section incudes everything that modifies the message structure, and nothing else, and the invariant holds everywhere outside the critical code section.

- Use distinct locks for distinct resources so that locking is as granular as possible. In particular, avoid global locks.

- High lock contention hinders good performance. The greater the frequency of thread locking and unlocking, and the larger the number of threads, the greater the performance impact. Performance degradation can be drastic and is not just linear in the number of threads. Note, however, that this guideline involves a trade-off with fine-grained locking, which can increase locking frequency.

- CSs provide an efficient, lightweight locking mechanism. When using CSs in a performance-critical multiprocessor application, tune performance with the CS spin counts. SRW locks are even more efficient but do not have adjustable spin counts.

- Semaphores can reduce the number of active contending threads without forcing you to change your programming model.

- Multiprocessors can cause severe, often unexpected, performance impacts in cases where you might expect improved performance. This is especially true when using mutexes. Reducing contention and using thread affinity are techniques to maintain good performance.

- Investigate using commercially available profiling and performance analysis tools, which can help clarify the behavior of the threads in your program and locate time-consuming code segments.

Summary

Synchronization can impact program performance on both single-processor and multiprocessor systems; in some cases, the impact can be severe. Careful program design and selection of the appropriate synchronization objects can help assure good performance. This chapter discussed a number of useful techniques and guidelines and illustrated performance issues with a simple test program that captures the essential characteristics of many real programming situations.

Looking Ahead

Chapter 10 shows how to use Windows synchronization in more general ways, particularly for message passing and correct event usage. It also discusses several programming models, or patterns, that help ensure correctness and maintainability, as well as good performance. Chapter 10 creates several compound synchronization objects that are useful for solving a number of important problems. Subsequent chapters use threads and synchronization as required for applications, such as servers. There are also a few more basic threading topics; for example, Chapter 12 illustrates and discusses thread safety and reentrancy in DLLs.

Additional Reading

Chapter 10 provides information sources that apply to this chapter as well. Duffy's *Concurrent Programming on Windows*, in addition to covering the synchronization API, also gives insight into the internal implementation and performance implications and compares the Windows features with features available in .NET. In particular, see Chapter 6 for synchronization and Chapter 7 for thread pools.

Chapter 27 of Cormen, Leiserson, Rivest, and Stein, *Introduction to Algorithms, Third Edition,* is invaluable for understanding parallelism and effective parallel algorithm design.

The Wikipedia "Multi-core" entry gives a good introduction to the commercial and technical incentives as well as long-term trends for multicore systems.

Exercises

9–1. Experiment with the `statsXX` variations on your own system and on as many different systems (both hardware and Windows versions) as are available to you. Do you obtain similar results as those reported in this chapter and in Appendix C?

9–2. Use `TimedMutualExclusionSC`, included in the *Examples* file, to experiment with `CRITICAL_SECTION` spin counts to see whether adjusting the count can improve and tune multiprocessor performance when you have a large number of threads. Results will vary from system to system, and I have found approximately optimal points ranging from 2,000 to 10,000. How do the best results compare with exclusive-mode SRW locks?

9–3. Experiment with the statsXX variations by modifying the delay time in the worker function. For example, increasing the delay should increase the total elapsed time for all variations, but the relative impact of the locking model could be less.

9–4. Use TimedMutualExclusion to experiment with delay and sleep point counts.

9–5. TimedMutualExclusion also uses a semaphore throttle to limit the number of running threads. Experiment with the count on both single-processor and multiprocessor systems. If an NT4 system is available, compare the results with NT5 and NT6.

9–6. Do the seven statsXX variations all operate correctly, ignoring performance, on multiprocessor systems? Experiment with a large number of worker threads. Run on a multiprocessor Windows 2003 or 2008 server. Can you reproduce the "false-sharing" performance problem described earlier?

9–7. Enhance Program 9–2 (statsSRW_VTP) to display the thread number as suggested after the program listing.

9–8. What is the effect of using an NT6 thread pool with a CS or mutex? Suggestion: Modify statsSRW_VTP. What is the effect of using a semaphore throttle with a CS (modify statsMX_ST)?

9–9. Rewrite statsSRW_VTP to use TrySubmitThreadpoolCallback. Compare the results and ease of programming with statsSRW_VTP.

9–10. Use processor affinity as a possible performance-enhancement technique by modifying this chapter's programs.

9–11. Run 9–1b compared SRWs with CSs, and SRWs were always considerably faster. Modify the statsXX programs so that they each use a pair of locks (be careful to avoid deadlocks!), each guarding a separate variable. Are CSs more competitive in this situation?

9–12. The statsXX programs have an additional command line parameter, not shown in the listings, that controls the delay time in the worker threads. Repeat the comparisons in Runs 9–1a and 9–1b with larger and smaller delays (changing the amount of contention). What is the effect?

10 Advanced Thread Synchronization

The preceding chapter described Windows performance issues and how to deal with them in realistic situations. Chapter 8 described several simple problems that require synchronization. This chapter solves additional practical but more complex synchronization problems, relying on the ideas introduced in Chapters 8 and 9.

The first step is to combine two or more synchronization objects and data to create compound objects. The most useful combination is the "condition variable model" involving a mutex and one or more events. The condition variable model is essential in numerous practical situations and prevents many serious program race condition defects that occur when programmers do not use Windows synchronization objects, especially events, properly. Events are complex, and their behavior varies depending on the choices illustrated in Table 8–1, so they should be used according to well-understood models. In fact, even the condition variable model described here has limitations that we'll describe.

NT6 (Windows Vista, Windows Server 2008, and Windows 7) added condition variables to the Windows API, which is a significant advance that will be easy to understand after we cover the condition variable model. Programmers, however, will not be able to use condition variables if they need to support NT5 (Windows XP and Server 2003), which will probably be a requirement for many years after publication. NT6 condition variables are essential for a totally correct implementation that overcomes all the event limitations.

Subsequent sections show how to use asynchronous procedure calls (APCs) so that individual, cooperating threads can be controlled and canceled in an orderly manner.

Additional performance issues are discussed as appropriate.

The Condition Variable Model and Safety Properties

Threaded programs are much easier to develop, understand, and maintain if we use well-understood and familiar techniques and models. Chapter 7 discussed this and introduced the boss/worker and work crew models to establish a useful framework for understanding many threaded programs. The critical code region concept is essential when using mutexes, and it's also useful to describe the invariants of your data structure. Finally, even defects have models, as we saw with the deadlock example. *Note:* Microsoft has its own distinct set of models, such as the apartment model and free threading. These terms are most often used with COM.

Using Events and Mutexes Together

The next step is to describe how to use mutexes and events together, generalizing Program 8–2, where we had the following situation, which will occur over and over again. *Note:* This discussion applies to CRITICAL_SECTIONs and SRW locks as well as to mutexes.

- The mutex and event are both associated with the message block or other data structure.

- The mutex defines the critical code section for accessing the data structure.

- The event signals that there is a new message or some other significant change to the data structure.

- Generalizing, the mutex ensures the object's invariants (or safety properties), and the event signals that the object has changed state (e.g., a message has been added or removed from a message buffer), possibly being put into a known state (e.g., there is at least one message in the message buffer).

- One thread (the producer in Program 8–2) locks the data structure, changes the object's state by creating a new message, and signals the event associated with the fact that there is a new message.

- At least one other thread (the consumer in this example) waits on the event for the object to reach the desired state. The wait must occur outside the critical code region so that the producer can access the object.

- A consumer thread can also lock the mutex, test the object's state (e.g., is there a new message in the buffer?), and avoid the event wait if the object is already in the desired state.

This general situation, where one thread changes a state variable and other threads wait for the change, occurs in numerous situations. The example here involves producers, consumers, and message passing; Programs 10–1 and 10–2 provide a different example.

The Condition Variable Model

Now let's combine all of this into a single code fragment that represents what we will call the *condition variable model* (CV model) with two variations, the *signal* and *broadcast* CV models. The first examples use the broadcast variation. The result is a program model that will occur frequently and can solve a wide variety of synchronization problems. For convenience, the example is stated in terms of a producer and a consumer.

The discussion may seem a bit abstract, but once the techniques are understood, we will be able to solve synchronization problems that would be very difficult without a good model.

The code fragment has several key elements.

- A data structure of type STATE_TYPE that contains all the data or *state variables* such as the messages, checksums, and counters used in Program 8–2.

- A mutex (alternatively, an SRW or CRITICAL_SECTION) and one or more events associated with, and usually a part of, the data structure.

- One or more Boolean functions to evaluate the *condition variable predicates*, which are the conditions (states) on which a thread might wait. Examples include "a new message is ready," "there is available space in the buffer," and "the queue is not empty." A distinct event may be associated with each condition variable predicate, or one event may be used to represent simply a change of state or a combination (logical "or") of several predicates. In the latter case, test individual predicate functions with the mutex locked to determine the actual state. If the predicate (logical expression) is simple, there is no need for a separate function.

The following code segment shows a producer and consumer using these principles, with a single event and condition variable predicate (implemented with a function, cvp, that is assumed but not shown). When the producer signals that a desired state has been reached, the signal should be broadcast to all waiting consumers. For instance, the producer may have created several messages, and the state is changed by increasing the message count. In many situations, you want to release only a single thread, as discussed after the code fragment.

This code segment is designed to operate under all NT kernel versions and even Windows 9x. SignalObjectAndWait will then simplify the solution. We show this full solution, appropriate for obsolete Windows versions, because:

- The usage pattern is still common in existing programs.

- Understanding the segment will make it easier to see the usefulness of SignalObjectAndWait and NT6 condition variables.

- The usage pattern is still useful when using a CRITICAL_SECTION in place of a mutex.

NT6 condition variables will further simplify and improve the solution.

Note and caution: This example deliberately uses PulseEvent, even though many writers and some of the Microsoft documentation warn against its use (see the remarks section in the MSDN entry). The ensuing discussion and examples will justify this choice, but with an additional cautionary note in the SignalObjectAndWait section. Also, there is a WaitForSingleObject call with a finite time-out, making the loop a form of polling loop; we show later how to eliminate the time-out.

```
typedef struct STATE_TYPE_T {
    HANDLE sGuard; /* Mutex to protect the object. */
    HANDLE cvpSet; /* Manual-reset event -- cvp () holds. */
    ... other events ...
    /* State structure with counts, checksums, etc. */
    struct STATE_VAR_TYPE stateVar;
} STATE_TYPE state;
...
/* Initialize state, creating the mutex and event. */
...
/* PRODUCER thread that modifies state. */
WaitForSingleObject (state.sGuard, INFINITE);
/* Change state so that the CV predicate holds. */
/* Example: one or more messages are now ready. */
state.stateVar.msgCount += N;
PulseEvent (state.cvpSet);
ReleaseMutex (state.sGuard);
/* End of the interesting part of the producer. */
...
/* CONSUMER thread function waits for a particular state. */
WaitForSingleObject (state.sGuard, INFINITE);
while (!cvp (&state)) {
    ReleaseMutex (state.sGuard);
    /* The timeout is required, making this loop poll */
    WaitForSingleObject (state.cvpSet, TimeOut);
    WaitForSingleObject (state.sGuard, INFINITE);
}
```

```
/* This thread now owns the mutex and cvp (&state) holds. */
/* Take appropriate action, perhaps modifying state. */
...
    ReleaseMutex (state.sGuard);
/* End of the interesting part of the consumer. */
```

Comments on the Condition Variable Model

The essential feature in the code segment is the loop in the consumer code. The loop body consists of three steps: (1) unlock the mutex that was locked prior to entering the loop; (2) wait, with a finite time-out, on the event; and (3) lock the mutex again. *The event wait time-out is significant,* as explained later.

Pthreads, as implemented in many UNIX and other systems, combine these three steps into a single function, pthread_cond_wait, combining a mutex and a condition variable (which is similar but not identical to the Windows event). Windows NT6 condition variables do the same thing. This is the reason for the term "condition variable model." There is also a timed version, which allows a time-out on the event wait.

Importantly, the single Pthreads function implements the first two steps (the mutex release and event wait) as an atomic operation so that no other thread can run before the calling thread waits on the event (or condition variable).

The Pthreads designers and the NT6 designers made a wise choice; the two functions (with and without a time-out) are the only ways to wait on a condition variable in Pthreads, so a condition variable must always be used with a mutex. Windows (before NT6) forces you to use two or three separate function calls, and you need to do it in just the right way to avoid problems.

Another motivation for learning the CV model, besides simplifying programs, is that it is essential if you ever need to use Pthreads or convert a Pthreads program to Windows.

Note: Windows NT Version 4.0 introduced a new function, SignalObject-AndWait (SOAW), that performs the first two steps atomically. The later examples assume that this function is available, in keeping with the policy established in Chapter 1. Nonetheless, the CV model introduction does not use SOAW in order to motivate its later usage, and a few examples have alternative implementations on the book's *Examples* file that use a CS in place of a mutex. (SOAW cannot be used with a CS.) Appendix C (Table C–6) shows that SignalObjectAndWait provides significant performance advantages.

Using the Condition Variable Model

The CV model, when implemented properly, works as follows in the producer/consumer context.

- The producer locks the mutex, changes state, pulses the event when appropriate, and unlocks the mutex. For example, the producer pulses the event when one or more messages are ready.

- The `PulseEvent` call should be with the mutex locked so that no other thread can modify the object, perhaps invalidating the condition variable predicate.

- The consumer tests the condition variable predicate *with the mutex locked.* If the predicate holds, there is no need to wait.

- If the predicate does not hold, the consumer must unlock the mutex before waiting on the event. Otherwise, no thread could ever modify the state and set the event.

- The event wait must have a time-out just in case the producer pulses the event in the interval between the mutex release (step 1) and the event wait (step 2). That is, without the *finite* time-out, there could be a "lost signal," which is another example of a race condition. APCs, described later in this chapter, can also cause lost signals. The time-out value used in the producer/consumer segment is a tunable parameter. (See Appendix C for comments on optimal values.)

- The consumer always retests the predicate after the event wait. Among other things, this is necessary in case the event wait has timed out. Also, the state may have changed. For example, the producer may have produced two messages and then released three waiting consumers, so one of the consumers will test the state, find no more messages, and wait again. Finally, the retest protects against spurious wakeups that might result from a thread setting or pulsing the event without the mutex locked. There is no way to avoid this time-out and polling loop until we get to `SignalObjectAndWait` and the Windows NT6 condition variables.

- The consumer always owns the mutex when it leaves the loop, regardless of whether the loop body was executed.

Condition Variable Model Variations

Notice, first, that the preceding code fragment uses a manual-reset event and calls `PulseEvent` rather than `SetEvent`. Is this the correct choice, and could the event be used differently? The answer is yes to both questions.

Referring back to Table 8–1, we see that the example has the property that *multiple threads* will be released. This is correct in this example, where several messages are produced and there are multiple consuming threads, and we need to broadcast the change. However, if the producer creates just one message and there are multiple consuming threads, the event should be auto-reset and the producer should call `SetEvent` to ensure that exactly one thread is released. This variation is the "signal CV" model rather than the "broadcast CV" model. It is still essential for the released consumer thread, which will then own the mutex and can remove a message.

Of the four combinations in Table 8–1, two are useful in the CV model. Considering the other two combinations, auto-reset/`PulseEvent` would have the same effect as auto-reset/`SetEvent` (the signal CV model) because of the time-out, but the dependence on the time-out would reduce responsiveness. The manual-reset/`SetEvent` combination causes spurious signals (the condition variable predicate test offers protection, however), because some thread must reset the event, and there will be a race among the threads before the event is reset.

In summary:

- Auto-reset/`SetEvent` is the signal CV model, which releases a single waiting thread.

- Manual-reset/`PulseEvent` is the broadcast CV model, which releases all waiting threads.

- Pthreads and NT6 condition variables make the same distinction but do not require the finite time-out in the event wait for the broadcast model, whereas the time-out is essential in Windows because the mutex release and event wait are not performed atomically.

- This will change, however, when we introduce `SignalObjectAndWait`.

An Example Condition Variable Predicate

Consider the condition variable predicate:

```
state.stateVar.count >= K;
```

In this case, a consumer thread will wait until the count is sufficiently large. This shows, for example, how to implement a multiple-wait semaphore; recall that normal semaphores do not have an atomic wait for multiple units. The consumer thread would then decrement the count by K after leaving the loop but before releasing the mutex.

Notice that the broadcast CV model is appropriate in this case because a single producer may increase the count so as to satisfy several but not all of the waiting consumers.

Semaphores and the Condition Variable Model

In some cases, a semaphore would be appropriate rather than an event, and semaphores have the advantage of specifying the exact number of threads to be released. For example, if each consumer were known to consume exactly one message, the producer could call `ReleaseSemaphore` with the exact number of messages produced. In the more general case, however, the producer does not know how the individual consumers will modify the state variable structure, so the CV model can solve a wider class of problems.

The CV model is powerful enough to implement semaphores. As described earlier, the basic technique is to define a predicate stating that "the semaphore count is nonzero" and create a state structure containing the count and maximum value. Exercise 10–10 shows a complete solution that allows for an atomic wait for multiple units.

Using `SignalObjectAndWait`

The consumer loop in the preceding code segment is critical to the CV model because it waits for a state change and then tests to see if the desired state holds. The state may not hold if the event is too *coarse,* indicating, for example, that there was simply some state change, not necessarily the required change. Furthermore, a different consumer thread might have made some other state change, such as emptying the message buffer. The loop required two waits and a mutex release, as follows:

```
while (!cvp (&state)) {
    ReleaseMutex (state.sGuard);
    WaitForSingleObject (state.cvpSet, TimeOut);
    WaitForSingleObject (state.sGuard, INFINITE);
}
```

The time-out on the first wait (the event wait) is necessary in order to avoid missed signals and other potential problems. This code will work if you replace the mutexes with CSs.

SOAW is an important enhancement that eliminates the need for the time-out and combines the first two loop statements; that is, the mutex release and the event wait. In addition to the program simplicity benefit, performance generally improves because a system call is eliminated and there is no need to tune the wait time-out period.

```
DWORD SignalObjectAndWait (
    HANDLE hObjectToSignal,
    HANDLE hObjectToWaitOn,
    DWORD dwMilliseconds,
    BOOL bAlertable)
```

This function simplifies the consumer loop, where the two handles are the mutex and event handles, respectively. There is no event wait time-out because the calling thread waits on the second handle *immediately* after the first handle is signaled (which, in this case, means that the mutex is released). The signal and wait are atomic so that no other thread can possibly signal the event between the time that the calling thread releases the mutex and the thread waits on the second handle. The simplified consumer loop, then, is as follows.

```
while (!cvp (&state)) {
    SignalObjectAndWait (state.sGuard, state.cvpSet,
        INFINITE, FALSE);
    WaitForSingleObject (state.sGuard, INFINITE);
}
```

The final argument, `bAlertable`, is `FALSE` here but will be set to `TRUE` in the later sections on APCs.

In general, the two handles can be for any appropriate synchronization objects. You cannot, however, use a `CRITICAL_SECTION` as the signaled object; kernel objects are necessary.

Many program examples, both in the book and in the *Examples* file, use `SignalObjectAndWait`, although some alternative solutions are also included and are mentioned in the text. If you want to use a `CRITICAL_SECTION` instead of a mutex, use the signal/wait pair in the original code segment and be certain to have a finite time-out period on the event wait.

The section on APCs shows a different technique to signal waiting threads with the additional advantage of signaling a specific waiting thread, whereas, when using events, there is no easy way to control which thread is signaled.

`PulseEvent`: One More Caution

`SignalObjectAndWait`, used with `PulseEvent`, appears to implement the broadcast CV model properly, and it nearly does. The remaining problem is that the Windows executive can, under some circumstances, preempt a waiting thread (such as one waiting on `SignalObjectAndWait`) just as another thread calls `PulseEvent`, resulting in a missed signal and possibly a permanently blocked thread. This is `PulseEvent`'s fatal flaw and the principal reason that MSDN warns against it.

Unfortunately, it's frequently necessary to use the CV model (e.g., you need to port a Pthreads program or you need the underlying functionality). Fortunately, there are several defenses against this flaw:

- Use a finite time-out with SOAW, treating a time-out as a spurious signal detected when the loop retests the predicate. You could also gain performance using a CS or an SRW lock rather than a mutex and then wait on the event with a finite time-out.

- Use the much faster Windows condition variables if you do not need to support NT5 (Windows XP, etc.).

- Assure that your program never uses the functions that would cause the executive to preempt a waiting thread. `GetThreadContext` is one such function and is very rare. However, if you are writing a library, there is no direct way to assure that the calling program respects such limitations.

- Pulse the event multiple times so that the waiting thread will eventually receive the signal. This is the approach used in Programs 10–3 and 10–4 where new messages are generated continuously.

- Avoid the broadcast model, which we can do in Programs 10–4 and 10–5. The signal model is sufficient if you need to signal only a single thread.

- Program 10–4 uses `PulseEvent`, but comments after the program describe variations that do not require it.

Example: A Threshold Barrier Object

Suppose that you wish to have the worker threads wait until there are enough workers to form a work crew to work in parallel on a task, as in Program 7–1 (sortMT). Or, you may want to wait until all threads have finished the first phase of a parallel computation before proceeding to the next phase. Once the threshold is reached, all the workers start operation, and if any other workers arrive later, they do not wait. This problem is solvable with a threshold barrier compound object.

Programs 10–1 and 10–2 show the implementation of the three functions that support the threshold barrier compound object. Two of the functions, `Create-ThresholdBarrier` and `CloseThresholdBarrier`, manage a `THB_OBJECT`. The threshold number of threads is a parameter to `CreateThresholdBarrier`.

Program 10–1 shows the appropriate part of the header file, `SynchObj.h`, while Program 10–2 shows the implementation of the three functions. Notice that the barrier object has a mutex, an event, a counter, and a threshold. The condition variable predicate is documented in the header file—that is, the event is to be set exactly when the count is greater than or equal to the threshold.

Program 10–1   `SynchObj.h`: Part 1—Threshold Barrier Definitions

```
/* THRESHOLD BARRIER - TYPE DEFINITION AND FUNCTIONS */
typedef struct THRESHOLD_BARRIER_TAG { /* Threshold Barrier */
    HANDLE bGuard;/* mutex for the object */
    HANDLE bEvent;/* auto-reset event: bCount >= bThreshold */
    DWORD bCount; /* number of threads that have reached the Barrier */
    DWORD bThreshold;/* Barrier threshold */
} THRESHOLD_BARRIER, *THB_OBJECT;

DWORD CreateThresholdBarrier (THB_OBJECT *, DWORD /* threshold */);
DWORD WaitThresholdBarrier (THB_OBJECT);
DWORD CloseThresholdBarrier (THB_OBJECT);

/* Error Values */
#define SYNCH_OBJ_NOMEM 1  /* Unable to allocate resources */
#define SYNCH_OBJ_CREATE_FAILURE 2
#define SYNCH_OBJ_BUSY 3  /* Object is in use and cannot be closed */
```

Program 10–2 now shows the implementation of the three functions. A test program, `testTHB.c`, is in the *Examples* file. Notice how the `WaitThreshold-Barrier` function contains the familiar condition variable loop. Also notice that the wait function not only waits on the event but also signals the event. The previous producer/consumer example waited and signaled in separate functions.

Finally, the condition variable predicate is, in this case, persistent. Once it becomes true, it will never change, unlike the situation in other examples. This allows a further simplification in `WaitThresholdBarrier`. `SetEvent` is okay because there is no need to reset the event, although `PulseEvent` would also work and would adhere to the CV model. Later examples do use the CV model.

Program 10–2   `ThbObject`: Implementing the Threshold Barrier

```
/* ThbObject. Program 10-2        */
/* threshold Barrier compound synch objects library*/

#include "Everything.h"
#include "synchobj.h"
```

```
/*********************/
/*  THRESHOLD barrier OBJECTS */
/*********************/

DWORD CreateThresholdBarrier (THB_OBJECT *pThb, DWORD bValue)
{
    THB_OBJECT objThb;
    /* Initialize a barrier object */
    objThb = malloc (sizeof(THRESHOLD_BARRIER));
    if (objThb == NULL) return SYNCH_OBJ_NOMEM;

    objThb->bGuard = CreateMutex (NULL, FALSE, NULL);
    if (objThb->bGuard == NULL) return SYNCH_OBJ_CREATE_FAILURE;

    /* Manual reset event */
    objThb->bEvent = CreateEvent (NULL, TRUE, FALSE, NULL);
    if (objThb->bEvent == NULL) return SYNCH_OBJ_CREATE_FAILURE;

    objThb->bThreshold = bValue;
    objThb->bCount = 0;

    *pThb = objThb;

    return 0;
}

DWORD WaitThresholdBarrier (THB_OBJECT thb)
{
    /* Wait for the specified number of threads to reach */
    /* the barrier, then broadcast on the CV */

    WaitForSingleObject (thb->bGuard, INFINITE);
    thb->bCount++;  /* A new thread has arrived */
    while (thb->bCount < thb->bThreshold) {
        SignalObjectAndWait(thb->bGuard, thb->bEvent, INFINITE, FALSE);
        WaitForSingleObject(thb->bGuard, INFINITE);
    }
    SetEvent (thb->bEvent); /* Broadcast to all waiting threads */
    /* NOTE: We are broadcasting to all waiting threads.
     * HOWEVER, SetEvent is OK because the condition is persistent
     * and there is no need to reset the event. */
    ReleaseMutex (thb->bGuard);
    return 0;
}

DWORD CloseThresholdBarrier (THB_OBJECT thb)
{
    /* Destroy component mutex and event once it is safe to do so */
    WaitForSingleObject (thb->bGuard, INFINITE);
```

```
    /* Be certain that no thread is waiting on the object. */
    if (thb->bCount < thb->bThreshold) {
        ReleaseMutex (thb->bGuard);
        return SYNCH_OBJ_BUSY;
    }

    /* Now release the mutex and close the handle */
    ReleaseMutex (thb->bGuard);
    CloseHandle (thb->bEvent);
    CloseHandle (thb->bGuard);
    free (thb);
    return 0;
}
```

Run 10–2 shows the test program, testTHB, with command line parameters to start 10 short-lived threads and a barrier of 5. Each thread prints its start and stop time, and testTHB starts new threads at random intervals averaging one thread every 1.5 seconds (approximately). The first five threads end at about the same time immediately after the fifth thread arrives. Later threads end shortly after they start.

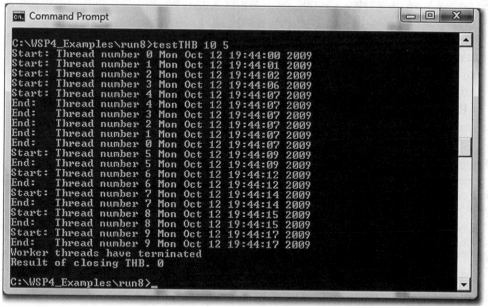

Run 10–2 testTHB: Testing the Threshold Barrier Functions

Comments on the Threshold Barrier Implementation

The threshold barrier object implemented here is limited for simplicity. In general, we would want to emulate Windows objects more closely by:

- Allowing the object to have security attributes (Chapter 15)

- Allowing the object to be named

- Permitting multiple objects on the object and not destroying it until the reference count is 0

- Allowing the object to be shared between processes

The *Examples* file contains a full implementation of one such object, a multiple wait semaphore, and the techniques used there can then be used for any of the objects in this chapter.

A Queue Object

So far, we have associated a single event with each mutex, but in general there might be more than one condition variable predicate. For example, in implementing a first in, first out (FIFO) queue, a thread that removes an element from the queue needs to wait on an event signifying that the queue is not empty, while a thread placing an element in the queue must wait until the queue is not full. The solution is to provide two events, one for each condition. Notice, however, that there is a single mutex.

Program 10–3 shows the definitions of a queue object and its functions. Programs 10–4 and 10–5 show the queue functions and a program that uses them.

Program 10–3 `SynchObj.h`: Part 2—Queue Definitions

```
/* Definitions of synchronized, general bounded queue structure. */
/* Queues are implemented as arrays with indices to youngest */
/* and oldest messages, with wrap around. */
/* Each queue also contains a guard mutex and */
/* "not empty" and "not full" condition variables. */
/* Finally, there is a pointer to an array of character messages. */

typedef struct QUEUE_OBJECT_TAG { /* General-purpose queue */
    HANDLE qGuard;/* Guard the message block*/
    HANDLE qNe;/* Event: Queue is not empty*/
    HANDLE qNf;/* Event: Queue is not full*/
        /* These two events are manual-reset for the broadcast model
         * and auto-reset for the signal model */
    DWORD qSize;/* Queue max size size*/
```

```
    DWORD qFirst;/* Index of oldest message*/
    DWORD qLast;/* Index of youngest msg*/
    char*msgArray;/* array of qSize messages*/
} QUEUE_OBJECT;

/* Queue management functions */
DWORD QueueInitialize (QUEUE_OBJECT *, DWORD, DWORD);
DWORD QueueDestroy (QUEUE_OBJECT *);
DWORD QueueDestroyed (QUEUE_OBJECT *);
DWORD QueueEmpty (QUEUE_OBJECT *);
DWORD QueueFull (QUEUE_OBJECT *);
DWORD QueueGet (QUEUE_OBJECT *, PVOID, DWORD, DWORD);
DWORD QueuePut (QUEUE_OBJECT *, PVOID, DWORD, DWORD);
DWORD QueueRemove (QUEUE_OBJECT *, PVOID, DWORD);
DWORD QueueInsert (QUEUE_OBJECT *, PVOID, DWORD);
```

Program 10–4 shows the functions, such as QueueInitialize and Queue-Get, that are defined at the end of Program 10–3. Notice that QueueGet and QueuePut provide synchronized access, while QueueRemove and QueueInsert, which the first two functions call, are not themselves synchronized and could be used in a single-threaded program. The first two functions provide for a time-out, so the normal condition variable model is extended slightly. The time-out parameter is used when the mutex guard is replaced with a CRITICAL_SECTION.

QueueEmpty and QueueFull are two other essential functions used to implement condition variable predicates.

This implementation uses PulseEvent and manual-reset events (the broadcast model) so that multiple threads are notified when the queue is not empty or not full.

A nice feature of the implementation is the symmetry of the QueueGet and QueuePut functions. Note, for instance, how they use the empty and full predicates and how they use the events. This simplicity is not only pleasing in its own right, but it also has the very practical benefit of making the code easier to write, understand, and maintain. The condition variable model enables this simplicity and its benefits.

Finally, C++ programmers will notice that a synchronized queue class could be constructed from this code; Exercise 10–7 suggests doing this.

Program 10–4   QueueObj: The Queue Management Functions

```
/* Chapter 10. QueueObj. */
/* Queue function */
```

```
#include "Everything.h"
#include "SynchObj.h"

/* Finite bounded queue management functions. */
DWORD QueueGet (QUEUE_OBJECT *q, PVOID msg, DWORD mSize,
                DWORD maxWait)
{
    DWORD TotalWaitTime = 0;
    BOOL TimedOut = FALSE;

    WaitForSingleObject (q->qGuard, INFINITE);
    if (q->msgArray == NULL) return 1;  /* Queue has been destroyed */

    while (QueueEmpty (q) && !TimedOut) {
        ReleaseMutex (q->qGuard);
        WaitForSingleObject (q->qNe, CV_TIMEOUT);
        if (maxWait != INFINITE) {
            TotalWaitTime += CV_TIMEOUT;
            TimedOut = (TotalWaitTime > maxWait);
        }
        WaitForSingleObject (q->qGuard, INFINITE);
    }

    /* remove the message from the queue */
    if (!TimedOut) QueueRemove (q, msg, mSize);
    /* Signal that the queue is not full as we've removed a message */
    PulseEvent (q->qNf);
    ReleaseMutex (q->qGuard);

    return TimedOut ? WAIT_TIMEOUT : 0;
}

DWORD QueuePut (QUEUE_OBJECT *q, PVOID msg, DWORD mSize,
                DWORD maxWait)
{
    DWORD TotalWaitTime = 0;
    BOOL TimedOut = FALSE;

    WaitForSingleObject (q->qGuard, INFINITE);
    if (q->msgArray == NULL) return 1;  /* Queue has been destroyed */

    while (QueueFull (q) && !TimedOut) {
        ReleaseMutex (q->qGuard);
        WaitForSingleObject (q->qNf, CV_TIMEOUT);
        if (maxWait != INFINITE) {
            TotalWaitTime += CV_TIMEOUT;
            TimedOut = (TotalWaitTime > maxWait);
        }
        WaitForSingleObject (q->qGuard, INFINITE);
    }
```

```
        /* Put the message in the queue */
        if (!TimedOut) QueueInsert (q, msg, mSize);
        /* Signal queue not empty as we've inserted a message */
        PulseEvent (q->qNe);
        ReleaseMutex (q->qGuard);

        return TimedOut ? WAIT_TIMEOUT : 0;
}

DWORD QueueInitialize (QUEUE_OBJECT *q, DWORD mSize, DWORD nMsgs)
{
        /* Initialize queue, including its mutex and events */
        /* Allocate storage for all messages. */

        if ((q->msgArray = calloc (nMsgs, mSize)) == NULL) return 1;
        q->qFirst = q->qLast = 0;
        q->qSize = nMsgs;

        q->qGuard = CreateMutex (NULL, FALSE, NULL);
        /* Manual reset events. */
        q->qNe = CreateEvent (NULL, TRUE, FALSE, NULL);
        q->qNf = CreateEvent (NULL, TRUE, FALSE, NULL);
        return 0;
}

DWORD QueueDestroy (QUEUE_OBJECT *q)
{
        /* Free all the resources created by QueueInitialize */
        WaitForSingleObject (q->qGuard, INFINITE);
        free (q->msgArray);
        q->msgArray = NULL;
        CloseHandle (q->qNe);
        CloseHandle (q->qNf);
        ReleaseMutex (q->qGuard);
        CloseHandle (q->qGuard);

        return 0;
}

DWORD QueueEmpty (QUEUE_OBJECT *q)
{
        return (q->qFirst == q->qLast);
}

DWORD QueueFull (QUEUE_OBJECT *q)
{
        return ((q->qFirst - q->qLast) == 1 ||
                (q->qLast == q->qSize-1 && q->qFirst == 0));
}
```

```
DWORD QueueRemove (QUEUE_OBJECT *q, PVOID msg, DWORD mSize)
{
    char *pm;

    if (QueueEmpty(q)) return 1; /* Error - Q is empty */
    pm = q->msgArray;

    /* Remove oldest ("first") message */
    memcpy (msg, pm + (q->qFirst * mSize), mSize);
    q->qFirst = ((q->qFirst + 1) % q->qSize);
    return 0; /* no error */
}

DWORD QueueInsert (QUEUE_OBJECT *q, PVOID msg, DWORD mSize)
{
    char *pm;

    if (QueueFull(q)) return 1; /* Error - Q is full */
    pm = q->msgArray;

    /* Add a new youngest ("last") message */
    memcpy (pm + (q->qLast * mSize), msg, mSize);
    q->qLast = ((q->qLast + 1) % q->qSize);
    return 0;
}
```

Example: Using Queues in a Multistage Pipeline

The boss/worker model, along with its variations, is one popular multithreaded programming model, and Program 8–2 is a simple producer/consumer model, a special case of the more general pipeline model.

Another important special case consists of a single boss thread that produces work items for a limited number of worker threads, placing the work items in a queue. This message-passing technique can be helpful when creating a scalable server that has a large number (perhaps thousands) of clients and it is not feasible to have a worker thread for each client. Chapter 14 discusses the scalable server problem in the context of I/O completion ports.

In the pipeline model, each thread, or group of threads, does some work on work items, such as messages, and passes the work items on to other threads for additional processing. A manufacturing assembly line is analogous to a thread pipeline. Queues are an ideal mechanism for pipeline implementations.

Program 10–5, ThreeStage, creates multiple production and consumption stages, and each stage maintains a queue of work to perform. Each queue has a bounded, finite length. There are three pipeline stages in total connecting the four work stages. The program structure is as follows.

- Producers create checksummed unit messages periodically, using the same message creation function as in Program 8–2, except that each message has a destination field indicating which consumer thread is to receive the message; each producer communicates with a single consumer. The number of producer/consumer pairs is a command line parameter. The producer then sends the unit message to the transmitter thread by placing the message in the transmission queue. If the queue is full, the producer waits until the queue state changes.

- The transmitter thread gathers all the available unit messages (but, arbitrarily, no more than five at a time) and creates a transmission message that contains a header block with the number of unit messages. The transmitter then puts each transmission message in the receiver queue, blocking if the queue is full. The transmitter and receiver might, in general, communicate over a network connection. The 5:1 blocking factor is easy to adjust.

- The receiver thread processes the unit messages in each transmission message, putting each unit message in the appropriate consumer queue if the queue is not full.

- Each consumer thread receives unit messages as they are available and puts the message in a log file.

Figure 10–1 shows the system. Notice how it models networking communication where messages between several sender/receiver pairs are combined and transmitted over a shared facility.

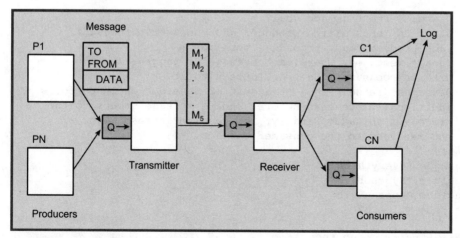

Figure 10–1 Multistage Pipeline

Program 10–5 shows the implementation, which uses the queue functions in Program 10–4. The message generation and display functions are not shown; they were first seen in Program 8–1. The message blocks are augmented, however, to contain source and destination fields along with the checksum and data.

One of the complexities in Program 10–5 is forcing all the threads to shut down in an orderly way without resorting to the very undesirable Terminate-Thread function, as was done in Edition 3. The solution is:

- Producer threads have an argument with the work goal, and the threads terminate after producing the required number of messages followed by a final "end message" with a negative sequence number.

- The consumer threads also have work goals, and they also look for messages with a negative sequence number in case the consumer goal does not match the producer goal.

- The transmitter and receiver threads know the number of consumers and can decrement the number of active consumers upon processing a message with a negative sequence. The threads terminate when the count reaches 0.

- The transmitter and receiver also test a global ShutDown flag. However, it is impossible to test this flag while waiting for a message. A later solution, ThreeStageCancel, will use the flag.

Program 10–5   ThreeStage: A Multistage Pipeline

```
/* Chapter 10. ThreeStage */
/* Three-stage producer/consumer system. */

/* Usage: ThreeStage npc goal. */
/* Start up "npc" paired producer and consumer threads. */
/* Each producer must produce a total of */
/* "goal" messages, where each message is tagged */
/* with the consumer that should receive it. */
/* Messages are sent to a "transmitter thread," which performs */
/* additional processing before sending message groups to the */
/* "receiver thread." Finally, the receiver thread sends */
/* the messages to the consumer threads. */

#include "Everything.h"
#include "SynchObj.h"
#include "messages.h"
#include <time.h>

#define DELAY_COUNT 1000
```

```c
#define MAX_THREADS 1024

/* Q lengths and blocking factors. These are arbitrary and */
/* can be adjusted for performance tuning. The current values are */
/* not well balanced. */

#define TBLOCK_SIZE 5 /* Trsmttr combines 5 messages at a time. */
#define TBLOCK_TIMEOUT 50 /* Trsmttr time-out waiting for messages. */
#define P2T_QLEN 10 /* Producer to transmitter queue length. */
#define T2R_QLEN 4 /* Transmitter to receiver queue length. */
#define R2C_QLEN 4 /* Receiver to consumer queue length --
                       there is one such queue for each consumer. */

DWORD WINAPI Producer (PVOID);
DWORD WINAPI Consumer (PVOID);
DWORD WINAPI Transmitter (PVOID);
DWORD WINAPI Receiver (PVOID);

typedef struct THARG_TAG {
    DWORD threadNumber;
    DWORD workGoal;      /* used by producers */
    DWORD workDone;      /* Used by producers and consumers */
} THARG;

/* Grouped messages sent by the transmitter to receiver*/
typedef struct T2R_MSG_OBJ_TAG {
    DWORD numMessages; /* Number of messages contained*/
    MSG_BLOCK messages [TBLOCK_SIZE];
} T2R_MSG_OBJ;

/* Argument for transmitter and receiver threads */
typedef struct TR_ARG_TAG {
    DWORD nProducers;  /* Number of active producers */
} TR_ARG;

QUEUE_OBJECT p2tq, t2rq, *r2cqArray;

static volatile DWORD ShutDown = 0;
static DWORD EventTimeout = 50;
DWORD trace = 0;

DWORD main (DWORD argc, char * argv[])
{
    DWORD tStatus, nThread, iThread, goal;
    HANDLE *producerThreadArray, *consumerThreadArray,
           transmitterThread, receiverThread;
    THARG *producerArg, *consumerArg;
    TR_ARG transmitterArg, receiverArg;

    srand ((int)time(NULL));/* Seed the RN generator */
```

```
nThread = atoi(argv[1]);
receiverArg.nProducers = transmitterArg.nProducers = nThread;

goal = atoi(argv[2]);
if (argc >= 4) trace = atoi(argv[3]);

producerThreadArray = malloc (nThread * sizeof(HANDLE));
producerArg = calloc (nThread, sizeof (THARG));
consumerThreadArray = malloc (nThread * sizeof(HANDLE));
consumerArg = calloc (nThread, sizeof (THARG));

QueueInitialize (&p2tq, sizeof(MSG_BLOCK), P2T_QLEN);
QueueInitialize (&t2rq, sizeof(T2R_MSG_OBJ), T2R_QLEN);

/* Allocate, initialize Receiver to Consumer queues */
r2cqArray = calloc (nThread, sizeof(QUEUE_OBJECT));

for (iThread = 0; iThread < nThread; iThread++) {
    /* Initialize r2c queue for this consumer thread */
    QueueInitialize (&r2cqArray[iThread],
                    sizeof(MSG_BLOCK), R2C_QLEN);
    /* Fill in the thread arg */
    consumerArg[iThread].threadNumber = iThread;
    consumerArg[iThread].workGoal = goal;
    consumerArg[iThread].workDone = 0;
    consumerThreadArray[iThread] = (HANDLE)_beginthreadex (NULL, 0,
            Consumer, &consumerArg[iThread], 0, NULL);

    producerArg[iThread].threadNumber = iThread;
    producerArg[iThread].workGoal = goal;
    producerArg[iThread].workDone = 0;
    producerThreadArray[iThread] = (HANDLE)_beginthreadex (NULL, 0,
            Producer, &producerArg[iThread], 0, NULL);
}

transmitterThread = (HANDLE)_beginthreadex (NULL, 0, Transmitter,
                    &transmitterArg, 0, NULL);
receiverThread = (HANDLE)_beginthreadex (NULL, 0, Receiver,
                    &receiverArg, 0, NULL);

_tprintf (_T("BOSS: All threads are running\n"));

/* Wait for the producers to complete */
for (iThread = 0; iThread < nThread; iThread++) {
    WaitForSingleObject (producerThreadArray[iThread], INFINITE);
    _tprintf (_T("BOSS: Producer %d produced %d work units\n"),
        iThread, producerArg[iThread].workDone);
}
```

```
    /* Producers have completed their work. */
    _tprintf (_T("BOSS: All producers have completed their work.\n"));

    /* Wait for the consumers to complete */
    for (iThread = 0; iThread < nThread; iThread++) {
        WaitForSingleObject (consumerThreadArray[iThread], INFINITE);
        _tprintf (_T("BOSS: consumer %d consumed %d work units\n"),
            iThread, consumerArg[iThread].workDone);
    }
    _tprintf (_T("BOSS: All consumers have completed their work.\n"));

    ShutDown = 1; /* Set a shutdown flag. */
    WaitForSingleObject (transmitterThread, INFINITE);
    WaitForSingleObject (receiverThread, INFINITE);

    QueueDestroy (&p2tq);
    QueueDestroy (&t2rq);
    for (iThread = 0; iThread < nThread; iThread++) {
        QueueDestroy (&r2cqArray[iThread]);
        CloseHandle(consumerThreadArray[iThread]);
        CloseHandle(producerThreadArray[iThread]);
    }
    free (r2cqArray);
    free (producerThreadArray); free (consumerThreadArray);
    free (producerArg); free(consumerArg);
    CloseHandle(transmitterThread); CloseHandle(receiverThread);
    _tprintf (_T("System has finished. Shutting down\n"));
    return 0;
}

DWORD WINAPI Producer (PVOID arg)
{
    THARG * parg;
    DWORD iThread;
    MSG_BLOCK msg;

    parg = (THARG *)arg;
    iThread = parg->threadNumber;
    while (parg->workDone < parg->workGoal) {
        /* Periodically produce work units until goal is satisfied */
        /* messages receive source and destination address which are */
        /* the same in this case but could, in general, be different. */
        delay_cpu (DELAY_COUNT * rand() / RAND_MAX);
        MessageFill (&msg, iThread, iThread, parg->workDone);

        /* put the message in the queue */
        QueuePut (&p2tq, &msg, sizeof(msg), INFINITE);

        parg->workDone++;
    }
```

```
    /*Send a final "done" message (negative sequence number) */
    MessageFill (&msg, iThread, iThread, -1);
    QueuePut (&p2tq, &msg, sizeof(msg), INFINITE);
    return 0;
}

DWORD WINAPI Transmitter (PVOID arg)
{
    /* Obtain multiple producer messages, combining into a single */
    /* compound message for the receiver */

    DWORD tStatus, im;
    T2R_MSG_OBJ t2r_msg = {0};
    TR_ARG * tArg = (TR_ARG *)arg;

    while (!ShutDown) {
        t2r_msg.numMessages = 0;
        /* pack the messages for transmission to the receiver */
        for (im = 0; im < TBLOCK_SIZE; im++) {
            tStatus = QueueGet (&p2tq, &t2r_msg.messages[im],
                        sizeof(MSG_BLOCK), INFINITE);
            if (tStatus != 0) break;
            t2r_msg.numMessages++;
            /* Decrement number of active consumers if negative seq # */
            if (t2r_msg.messages[im].sequence < 0) {
                tArg->nProducers--;
                if (tArg->nProducers <= 0) break;
            }
        }

        /* Transmit the block of messages */
        tStatus = QueuePut (&t2rq, &t2r_msg,
                        sizeof(t2r_msg), INFINITE);
        if (tStatus != 0) return tStatus;
        /* Terminate the transmitter if there are no active consumers */
        if (tArg->nProducers <=0) return 0;
    }
    return 0;
}

DWORD WINAPI Receiver (PVOID arg)
{
    /* Obtain compound messages from transmitter and unblock them */
    /* and transmit to the designated consumer. */

    DWORD tStatus, im, ic;
    T2R_MSG_OBJ t2r_msg;
    TR_ARG * tArg = (TR_ARG *)arg;
```

```
    while (!ShutDown) {
        tStatus = QueueGet (&t2rq, &t2r_msg,
                            sizeof(t2r_msg), INFINITE);
        if (tStatus != 0) return tStatus;
        /* Distribute the messages to the proper consumer */
        for (im = 0; im < t2r_msg.numMessages; im++) {
            ic = t2r_msg.messages[im].destination;
            tStatus = QueuePut (&r2cqArray[ic], &t2r_msg.messages[im],
                                sizeof(MSG_BLOCK), INFINITE);
            if (tStatus != 0) return tStatus;
            if (t2r_msg.messages[im].sequence < 0) {
                tArg->nProducers--;
                if (tArg->nProducers <= 0) break;
            }
        }
        /* Terminate the transmitter if there are no active consumers */
        if (tArg->nProducers <= 0) return 0;
    }
    return 0;
}

DWORD WINAPI Consumer (PVOID arg)
{
    THARG * carg;
    DWORD tStatus, iThread;
    MSG_BLOCK msg;
    QUEUE_OBJECT *pr2cq;

    carg = (THARG *) arg;
    iThread = carg->threadNumber;

    carg = (THARG *)arg;
    pr2cq = &r2cqArray[iThread];

    while (carg->workDone < carg->workGoal) {
        /* Receive and display messages */
        tStatus = QueueGet (pr2cq, &msg, sizeof(msg), INFINITE);
        if (tStatus != 0) return tStatus;
        if (msg.sequence < 0) return 0;  /* Last Message */
        carg->workDone++;
    }

    return 0;
}
```

Queue Management Function Comments and Performance

Program 10–5 and the queue management functions can be implemented in several different ways, and the version shown here is actually the slowest and scales poorly as the thread count increases. The following comments that refer to performance are based on that data. The *Examples* file contains several variations, and subsequent run screen shots will show the operation and performance.

- `ThreeStage`, Program 10–5, uses the broadcast model (manual-reset/ `PulseEvent`) to allow for the general case in which multiple messages may be requested or created by a single thread. This is the only version subject to the risk of a missed `PulseEvent` signal.

- `ThreeStageCS` uses a `CRITICAL_SECTION`, rather than a mutex, to protect the queue object. However, you must use an `EnterCriticalSection` followed by an event wait rather than `SignalObjectAndWait` with a finite time-out. Two files provided with the *Examples*, `QueueObjCS.c` and `QueueObjCS_Sig.c`, implement the queue management functions.

```
Command Prompt                                              _ □ X

C:\WSP4_Examples\run8>timep ThreeStage 32 4000
BOSS: All threads are running
BOSS: All producers have completed their work.
BOSS: All consumers have completed their work.
System has finished. Shutting down
Real Time: 00:00:21:981
User Time: 00:00:08:034
Sys Time:  00:00:24:523

C:\WSP4_Examples\run8>timep ThreeStage 64 4000
BOSS: All threads are running
BOSS: All producers have completed their work.
BOSS: All consumers have completed their work.
System has finished. Shutting down
Real Time: 00:01:22:957
User Time: 00:00:22:963
Sys Time:  00:01:25:582

C:\WSP4_Examples\run8>timep ThreeStage_Sig 32 4000
BOSS: All threads are running
BOSS: All producers have completed their work.
BOSS: All consumers have completed their work.
System has finished. Shutting down
Real Time: 00:00:03:171
User Time: 00:00:03:151
Sys Time:  00:00:03:837

C:\WSP4_Examples\run8>timep ThreeStage_Sig 64 4000
BOSS: All threads are running
BOSS: All producers have completed their work.
BOSS: All consumers have completed their work.
System has finished. Shutting down
Real Time: 00:00:06:319
User Time: 00:00:06:099
Sys Time:  00:00:08:346
```

Run 10–5a   `ThreeStage[_Sig]`: Mutex Broadcast and Signaling

- `ThreeStage_noSOAW` does not use `SignalObjectAndWait`; instead it uses successive mutex and event waits with a time-out. This corresponds to the code fragment at the beginning of the chapter.

- `ThreeStage_Sig` uses the signal model (auto-reset/`SetEvent`) with `SignalObjectAndWait` and will work if only one message is produced at a time, as is the case in this example. There are significant performance advantages because only a single thread is released to test the predicate.

- `ThreeStageCS_Sig` is like `ThreeStage_Sig`, except that it uses a CS in place of a mutex. It combines the features of `ThreeStageCS` and `ThreeStage_Sig`.

- `ThreeStageSig_noSOAW` combines the `ThreeStage_noSOAW` and `ThreeStage_Sig` features.

- `ThreeStageCV` uses Windows NT6 condition variables, which are described later in the chapter.

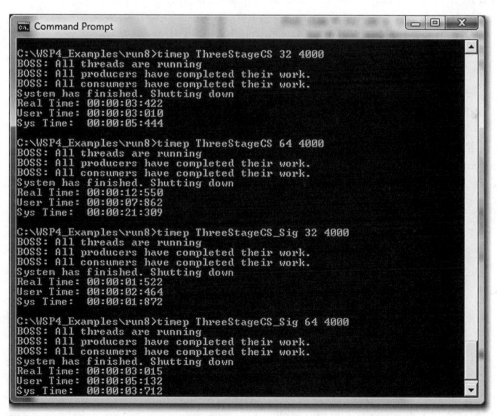

Run 10-5b `ThreeStageCS[_Sig]`: CS Broadcast and Signaling

Appendix C also shows the comparative performance of these implementations; the run screen shots here show some initial results.

Run 10–5a compares `ThreeStage` and `ThreeStage_Sig` with 32 and 64 producer/consumer pairs. Both use a mutex, but `ThreeStage`, which broadcasts, performs poorly and does not scale as we go from 32 to 64 threads.

Run 10–5b makes the same comparison, but with a `CRITICAL_SECTION` and a time-out in the consumer loop. CS performance is much better, as expected, but, again, the broadcast model does not scale well with the number of producer/consumer pairs.

Windows NT6 Condition Variables

Windows Vista and 2008 Server support condition variable objects whose behavior is similar to Pthreads condition variables and the CV model we've used in this chapter. Furthermore, Windows condition variables (WCV, a nonstandard but convenient abbreviation) use `CRITICAL_SECTION` and SRW lock objects (Chapter 8) rather than mutexes, and the WCV objects are also user, not kernel, objects, providing additional performance benefits. The only significant limitations are:

- Condition variables cannot be shared between processes the way you can share named mutexes and events.

- There is nothing comparable to `SignalObjectAndWait`'s alertable state (see the upcoming "Asynchronous Procedure Calls" section), so you cannot cancel threads waiting on condition variables.

First, the type for a WCV object is `CONDITION_VARIABLE`. Initialize WCVs just as you would a `CRITICAL_SECTION` with the `InitializeConditionVariable` function. There is no `DeleteConditionVariable` function analogous to `Delete-CriticalSection` for the same reason that there is no delete function for SRW locks.

```
VOID InitializeConditionVariable (
    PCCONDITION_VARIABLE pConditionVariable)
```

Use `SleepConditionVariableCS` with a `CRITICAL_SECTION` to wait for a signal to a WCV. Be sure to initialize both the CS and the WCV before their first use. There is a time-out, and the function looks similar to `SignalObjectAndWait`, except there is no alertable flag.

```
BOOL WINAPI SleepConditionVariableCS (
   PCONDITION_VARIABLE pConditionVariable,
   PCRITICAL_SECTION pCriticalSection,
   DWORD dwMilliseconds)
```

SleepConditionVariableSRW is an alternative, using SRW locks. The parameters are the same as for SleepConditionVariableCS, except there is an additional parameter to indicate whether the SRW lock is in shared or exclusive mode.

Signal, or "wake up," a condition variable with WakeConditionVariable (corresponding to the "signal" model) and WakeAllConditionVariable (corresponding to the "broadcast" model).

Revising QueueObject (Program 10–4) is simple. First, modify SynchObj.h (Program 10–3) by replacing the three HANDLE items with CRITICAL_SECTION (for qGuard) and CONDITION_VARIABLE (for qNf and qNe). Then, QueueObjectCV is simpler, as there is no need for the additional wait after the SOAW call, as Program 10–6 shows. Note that there is no need to modify utility functions such as QueueEmpty and QueueRemove.

Program 10–6 implements the signal, rather than the broadcast, version. It also uses a CS, but the *Examples* file version uses an SRW lock, so there are illustrations of both techniques. MSDN's example code (search for "Using Condition Variables") is very similar, also using queues with "not empty" and "not full" predicates.

Program 10–6   QueueObjCV: The Queue Management Functions

```
/* Chapter 10. QueueObjCV. */
/* Queue functions - Using Windows NT6 Condition Variables*/

#include "Everything.h"
#include "SynchObj.h"


/* Finite bounded queue management functions. */

DWORD QueueGet (QUEUE_OBJECT *q, PVOID msg, DWORD mSize,
               DWORD maxWait)
{
   EnterCriticalSection (&q->qGuard);
   while (QueueEmpty (q)) {
      SleepConditionVariableCS (&q->qNe, &q->qGuard, INFINITE);
   }
```

```
    /* remove the message from the queue */
    QueueRemove (q, msg, mSize);

    /* Signal that the queue is not full as we've removed a message */
    WakeConditionVariable (&q->qNf);
    LeaveCriticalSection (&q->qGuard);
    return 0;
}


DWORD QueuePut (QUEUE_OBJECT *q, PVOID msg, DWORD mSize,
                DWORD maxWait)
{
    EnterCriticalSection (&q->qGuard);
    while (QueueFull (q)) {
        SleepConditionVariableCS(&q->qNf, &q->qGuard, INFINITE)
    }
    /* Put the message in the queue */
    QueueInsert (q, msg, mSize);

    /* Signal that the queue is not empty; we've inserted a message */
    WakeConditionVariable (&q->qNe);
    LeaveCriticalSection (&q->qGuard);
    return 0;
}

DWORD QueueInitialize (QUEUE_OBJECT *q, DWORD mSize, DWORD nMsgs)
{
    /* Initialize queue, including its mutex and events */
    /* Allocate storage for all messages. */

    q->qFirst = q->qLast = 0;
    q->qSize = nMsgs;

    InitializeCriticalSection(&q->qGuard);
    InitializeConditionVariable(&q->qNe);
    InitializeConditionVariable(&q->qNf);

    if ((q->msgArray = calloc (nMsgs, mSize)) == NULL) return 1;
    return 0; /* No error */
}

DWORD QueueDestroy (QUEUE_OBJECT *q)
{
    /* Free all the resources created by QueueInitialize */
    EnterCriticalSection (&q->qGuard);
    free (q->msgArray);
    LeaveCriticalSection (&(q->qGuard));
    DeleteCriticalSection (&(q->qGuard));
    return 0;
}
```

```
DWORD QueueEmpty (QUEUE_OBJECT *q)
{
    return (q->qFirst == q->qLast);
}

DWORD QueueFull (QUEUE_OBJECT *q)
{
    return ((q->qFirst - q->qLast) == 1 ||
           (q->qLast == q->qSize-1 && q->qFirst == 0));
}

DWORD QueueRemove (QUEUE_OBJECT *q, PVOID msg, DWORD mSize)
{
    char *pm;

    if (QueueEmpty(q)) return 1; /* Error - Q is empty */
    pm = q->msgArray;
    /* Remove oldest ("first") message */
    memcpy (msg, pm + (q->qFirst * mSize), mSize);
    q->qFirst = ((q->qFirst + 1) % q->qSize);
    return 0; /* no error */
}

DWORD QueueInsert (QUEUE_OBJECT *q, PVOID msg, DWORD mSize)
{
    char *pm;

    if (QueueFull(q)) return 1; /* Error - Q is full */
    pm = q->msgArray;
    /* Add a new youngest ("last") message */
    memcpy (pm + (q->qLast * mSize), msg, mSize);
    q->qLast = ((q->qLast + 1) % q->qSize);
    return 0;
}
```

The modified solution, in the *Examples* file, is ThreeStageCV, and it does provide the anticipated performance improvements relative to ThreeStageCS (the CRITICAL_SECTION solution), as shown in Run 10–6.

```
Command Prompt                                                    _ □ X

C:\WSP4_Examples\run8>timep ThreeStageCS 64 4000
BOSS: All threads are running
BOSS: All producers have completed their work.
BOSS: All consumers have completed their work.
System has finished. Shutting down
Real Time: 00:00:13:018
User Time: 00:00:07:222
Sys Time:  00:00:23:509

C:\WSP4_Examples\run8>timep ThreeStageCS 128 4000
BOSS: All threads are running
BOSS: All producers have completed their work.
BOSS: All consumers have completed their work.
System has finished. Shutting down
Real Time: 00:00:50:947
User Time: 00:00:23:602
Sys Time:  00:01:25:457

C:\WSP4_Examples\run8>timep ThreeStageCV 64 4000
BOSS: All threads are running
BOSS: All producers have completed their work.
BOSS: All consumers have completed their work.
System has finished. Shutting down
Real Time: 00:00:02:507
User Time: 00:00:06:021
Sys Time:  00:00:02:776

C:\WSP4_Examples\run8>timep ThreeStageCV 128 4000
BOSS: All threads are running
BOSS: All producers have completed their work.
BOSS: All consumers have completed their work.
System has finished. Shutting down
Real Time: 00:00:05:740
User Time: 00:00:12:636
Sys Time:  00:00:07:659
```

Run 10–6 ThreeStageCV: Condition Variable and CS Performance

Asynchronous Procedure Calls

A complexity in ThreeStage (Program 10–5), as it is currently written, is the way that the transmitter and receiver threads test the message sequence numbers and track the number of active consumers. This solution assumes that the transmitter and receiver threads know the number of consumers and understand the message structure, which may not always be the case. In general, it would be convenient if the boss thread were able to cancel the transmitter and receiver threads directly.

Another open problem is that there is no general method (other than TerminateThread) to signal, or cause an action in, a specific thread. Events signal one thread waiting on an auto-reset event or all the threads waiting on a manual-reset event, but there is no way to assure that the signal goes to a particular thread. The solution used so far is simply to wake up all the waiting threads so they can individually determine whether it is time to proceed. An alternative solution, occasionally used, is to assign events to specific threads so that the signaling thread can determine which event to pulse or set.

APCs provide a solution to both of these problems. The sequence of actions is as follows, where the boss thread needs to control a cooperating worker or target thread.

- The boss thread specifies an APC callback routine to be executed by the target thread by queuing the APC to the target. More than one APC can be queued to a specific thread.

- The target thread enters an *alertable* wait state indicating that the thread can safely execute the APC. The order of these first two steps is irrelevant, so there is no concern here with race conditions.

- A thread in an alertable wait state will execute all queued APCs, one at a time.

- An APC can carry out any appropriate action, such as freeing resources or raising an exception. In this way, the boss thread can cause an exception to occur in the target, although the exception will not occur until the target has entered an alertable state.

APC execution is asynchronous in the sense that a boss thread can queue an APC to a target at any time, but the execution is synchronous in the sense that it can occur only when the target thread allows it to occur by entering an alertable wait state. Also notice that APCs give a limited sort of thread pool (see Chapter 9); the target thread is the "pool," and the queued functions are the callback functions.

Alertable wait states appear once more in Chapter 14, which covers asynchronous I/O.

The following sections describe the required functions and illustrate their use with another variation of the `ThreeStage` program. In the *Examples* file, the source file is `ThreeStageCancel.c`, and the project to build this version is `ThreeStageCancel`.

Queuing Asynchronous Procedure Calls

One thread (the boss) queues an APC to a target thread using `QueueUserAPC`.

```
DWORD QueueUserAPC (
    PAPCFUNC pfnAPC,
    HANDLE hThread,
    ULONG_PTR dwData)
```

`pfnAPC` is a pointer to the actual function that the target thread will execute. `hThread` is the handle of the target thread. `dwData` is a pointer-sized argument value that will be passed to the APC function when it is executed.

`ThreeStageCancel.c`, in the main function (compare to Program 10–5), uses `QueueUserAPC` calls to cancel the transmitter and receiver threads after the consumer and producer threads terminate, as follows:

```
tstatus = QueueUserAPC
    (QueueShutDown, transmitterThread, 1);
if (tstatus == 0) ReportError (
    "Failed queuing APC for transmitter", 8, FALSE);
tstatus = QueueUserAPC
    (QueueShutDown, receiverThread, 2);
if (tstatus == 0) ReportError (...);
```

The `QueueUserAPC` return value is nonzero for success or zero for failure. `GetLastError()`, however, does not return a useful value, so the `ReportError` call does not request an error message (the last argument is `FALSE`).

`QueueShutDown` is an additional queue function, where the argument specifies shutting down the get queue (value 1) or the put queue (value 2). The function also sets flags that `QueueGet` and `QueuePut` test, so an APC queued by some other thread will not inadvertently shut down the queue.

Program 10–7 shows `QueueShutDown` working with modified versions of `QueueGet` and `QueuePut` (Program 10–4). As a result, the queue functions return nonzero values, causing the transmitter and receiver threads to unblock and exit.

Alertable Wait States

The last `SignalObjectAndWait` parameter, `bAlertable`, has been `FALSE` in previous examples. By using `TRUE` instead, we indicate that the wait is a so-called alertable wait, and the thread enters an alertable wait state. The behavior is as follows.

- If one or more APCs are queued to the thread (as a QueueUserAPC target thread) *before* either hObjectToWaitOn (normally an event) is signaled or the time-out expires, then the APCs are executed (there is no guaranteed order) and Signal-ObjectAndWait returns with a return value of WAIT_IO_COMPLETION.

- If an APC is never queued, then SignalObjectAndWait behaves in the normal way; that is, it waits for the object to be signaled or the time-out period to expire.

Alterable wait states will be used again with asynchronous I/O (Chapter 14); the name WAIT_IO_COMPLETION comes from this usage. A thread can also enter an alertable wait state with other alertable wait functions such as WaitFor-SingleObjectEx, WaitForMultipleObjectsEx, and SleepEx, and these functions will also be useful when performing asynchronous I/O.

We can now modify QueueGet and QueuePut (see Program 10–4) to perform an orderly shutdown after an APC is performed, even though the APC function, QueueShutDown, does not do anything other than print a message and return. All that is required is to enter an alertable wait state and to test the Signal-ObjectAndWait return value, as shown by the following modified queue functions (see QueueObjCancel.c in the *Examples* file).

This version uses the signal CV model with an auto-reset event and SetEvent; there is no need to be concerned with the PulseEvent missed signal issues.

Program 10–7   QueueObjCancel:
Queue Functions Modified for Cancellation

```
/* Chapter 10. QueueObjCancel. Prepare to be cancelled */
/* Queue functions. Signal model       */

#include "Everything.h"
#include "SynchObj.h"

static BOOL shutDownGet = FALSE;
static BOOL shutDownPut = FALSE;

void WINAPI QueueShutDown (DWORD n)
{
    _tprintf (_T("In ShutDownQueue callback. %d\n"), n);
    if (n%2 != 0) shutDownGet = TRUE;
    if ( (n/2) % 2 != 0) shutDownPut = TRUE;
    /* Free any resource (none in this example). */
    return;
}
```

```
DWORD QueueGet (QUEUE_OBJECT *q, PVOID msg, DWORD mSize, DWORD maxWait)

{
    if (q->msgArray == NULL) return 1;   /* Queue has been destroyed */

    WaitForSingleObject (q->qGuard, INFINITE);
    while (!shutDownGet && QueueEmpty (q)) {
        if (SignalObjectAndWait (q->qGuard, q->qNe, INFINITE, TRUE) ==
                    WAIT_IO_COMPLETION && shutDownGet) {
            continue;
        }
        WaitForSingleObject (q->qGuard, INFINITE);
    }
    /* remove the message from the queue */
    if (!shutDownGet) {
        QueueRemove (q, msg, mSize);
        /* Signal queue not full as we've removed a message */
        SetEvent (q->qNf);
        ReleaseMutex (q->qGuard);
    }
    return shutDownGet ? WAIT_TIMEOUT : 0;
}

DWORD QueuePut (QUEUE_OBJECT *q, PVOID msg, DWORD mSize, DWORD maxWait)
{
    if (q->msgArray == NULL) return 1;   /* Queue has been destroyed */

    WaitForSingleObject (q->qGuard, INFINITE);
    while (!shutDownPut && QueueFull (q)) {
        if (SignalObjectAndWait(q->qGuard, q->qNf, INFINITE, TRUE) ==
                    WAIT_IO_COMPLETION && shutDownPut) {
            continue;
        }
        WaitForSingleObject (q->qGuard, INFINITE);
    }
    /* Put the message in the queue */
    if (!shutDownPut) {
        QueueInsert (q, msg, mSize);
        /* Signal queue not empty as we've inserted a message */
        SetEvent (q->qNe);
        ReleaseMutex (q->qGuard);
    }
    return shutDownPut ? WAIT_TIMEOUT : 0;
}
```

The APC routine could be either `ShutDownReceiver` or `ShutDownTrans-`
`mitter`, as the receiver and transmitter threads use both `QueueGet` and
`QueuePut`. If it were necessary for the shutdown functions to know which thread

they are executed from, use different APC argument values for the third `QueueUserAPC` arguments in the code segment preceding Program 10–7.

The thread exit code will be `WAIT_TIMEOUT` to maintain consistency with previous versions. A `DllMain` function can perform additional cleanup in a `DllMain` function if appropriate.

An alternative to testing the return value for `WAIT_IO_COMPLETION` would be for the shutdown functions to raise an exception, place the `QueuePut` body in a try block, and add an exception handler.

APCs and Missed Signals

A kernel mode APC (used in asynchronous I/O) can momentarily move a waiting thread out of its wait state, potentially causing a missed `PulseEvent` signal. Some documentation warns against `PulseEvent` for this reason, as discussed earlier in the "PulseEvent: Another Caution" section. Should there be a situation where a missed signal could occur, include a finite time-out period on the appropriate wait calls, or use Windows NT6 condition variables. Better yet, avoid `PulseEvent`.

Safe Thread Cancellation

The preceding example and discussion show how we can safely cancel a target thread that uses alertable wait states. Such cancellation is sometimes called *synchronous cancellation,* despite the use of APCs, because the cancellation, which is caused by the boss's `QueueUserAPC` call, can only take effect when the target thread permits cancellation by entering a safe alertable wait state.

Synchronous cancellation requires the target thread to cooperate and allow itself to be canceled from time to time. Event waits are a natural place to enter an alertable wait state because, as a system shuts down, the event may never be signaled again. Mutex waits could also be alertable to allow thread waiting on a resource that may not become available again. For example, a boss thread could break deadlocks with this technique.

Asynchronous thread cancellation might appear useful to signal a compute-bound thread that seldom, if ever, waits for I/O or events. Windows does not allow asynchronous cancellation, and it would be a risky operation. You do not know the state of the thread to be canceled and whether it owns locks or other resources. There are techniques, using processor-specific code, to interrupt a specified thread, but the techniques not only are risky but are nonportable.

Pthreads for Application Portability

Pthreads have been mentioned several times as the alternative threading and synchronization model available with UNIX, Linux, and other non-Windows systems. There is an open source Windows Pthreads library, and with this library, you can write portable threaded applications that can run on a wide variety of systems. The *Examples* file discusses this subject in more detail. The `ThreeStagePthreads` project uses the open source library and points to the download site.

Thread Stacks and the Number of Threads

Two more cautions, which are related, are in order. First, give some thought to the thread stack size, where 1MB is the default. This should be sufficient in most cases, but if there is any doubt, determine the maximum amount of stack space each thread will require, including the requirements of any library functions or recursive functions that the thread calls. A stack overflow will corrupt other memory or cause an exception.

Second, a large number of threads with large stacks will require large amounts of virtual memory for the process and could affect paging behavior and the paging file. For example, using 1,000 threads would not be unreasonable in some of the examples in this and later chapters. Allowing 1MB per thread stack results in 1GB of virtual address space. Preventive measures include careful stack sizing, thread pools, and multiplexing operations within a single thread. Furthermore, parallelism frameworks (previous chapter) generally assure that there are bounds on the total stack size and task-switching times.

Hints for Designing, Debugging, and Testing

At the risk of presenting advice that is contrary to that given in many other books and technical articles, which stress testing and little else, my personal advice is to balance your efforts so that you pay attention to design, implementation, and use of familiar programming models. The best debugging technique is not to create the bugs in the first place; this advice, of course, is easier to give than to follow. Nonetheless, when defects do occur, as they will, code inspection, balanced with debugging, often is most effective in finding and fixing the defects' root causes.

Overdependence on testing is not advisable because many serious defects will elude the most extensive and expensive testing. Testing can only reveal defects; it cannot prove that they do not exist, and testing shows only defect symptoms, not root causes. As a personal example, I ran a version of a multiple semaphore wait function that used the CV model without the finite time-out on the event variable wait. The defect, which could cause a thread to block indefinitely, did not show up in over a year of use; eventually, however, something would have failed. Simple code inspection and knowledge of the condition variable model revealed the error.

Debugging is also problematic because debuggers change timing behavior, masking the very race conditions that you wish to expose. For example, debugging is unlikely to find a problem with an incorrect choice of event type (auto-reset or manual-reset) and `SetEvent`/`PulseEvent`. You have to think carefully about what you wish to achieve.

Having said all that, testing on a wide variety of platforms, which must include multiprocessor systems, is an essential part of any multithreaded software development project.

Avoiding Incorrect Code

Every bug you don't put in your code in the first place is one more bug you won't find in testing or production. Here are some hints, most of which are taken, although rephrased, from Butenhof's *Programming with POSIX Threads (PWPT)*.

- **Avoid relying on thread inertia.** Threads are asynchronous, but we often assume, for example, that a parent thread will continue running after creating one or more child threads. The assumption is that the parent's "inertia" will keep it running before the children run. This assumption is especially dangerous on a multiprocessor system, but it can also lead to problems on single-processor systems.

- **Never bet on a thread race.** Nearly anything can happen in terms of thread scheduling. Your program has to assume that any ready thread can start running at any time and that any running thread can be preempted at any time. "No ordering exists between threads unless you cause ordering" (*PWPT*, p. 294).

- **Scheduling is not the same as synchronization.** Scheduling policy and priorities cannot ensure proper synchronization. Use synchronization objects instead.

- **Sequence races can occur even when you use locks to protect shared data.** Just because data is protected, there is no assurance as to the order in which different threads will access the shared data. For example, if one thread adds money to a bank account and another makes a withdrawal, there is no assurance, using a lock alone, that the deposit will be made before the withdrawal. Exercise 10–14 shows how to control thread execution order.

- **Cooperate to avoid deadlocks.** You need a well-understood lock hierarchy, used by all threads, to ensure that deadlocks will not occur.

- **Never share events between predicates.** Each event used in a condition variable implementation should be associated with a distinct predicate. Furthermore, an event should always be used with the same mutex.

- **Beware of sharing stacks and related memory corrupters.** Always remember that when you return from a function or when a thread terminates, memory that is local to the function or thread is no longer valid. Memory on a thread's stack can be used by other threads, but you have to be sure that the first thread continues to exist. This behavior is not unique to thread functions, of course.

- **Be sure to use the `volatile` storage modifier.** Whenever a shared variable can be changed in one thread and accessed in another, the variable should be `volatile` to ensure that each thread stores and fetches the variable to and from memory, rather than assuming that the variable is held in a register that is specific to the thread. However, do not overuse `volatile`; any function call or return will assure that registers are stored; furthermore, every synchronization call will erect a memory barrier.

- **Use memory barriers so that processors have coherent memory views** (see Chapter 8 and Figure 8–2). `volatile` is not sufficient. Memory barriers assure that memory accesses issued by the processors are visible in a particular order.

Here are some additional guidelines and rules of thumb that can be helpful.

- **Use the condition variable model properly,** being certain not to use two distinct locks with the same event. Understand the condition variable model on which you depend. Be certain that the invariant holds before waiting on a condition variable.

- **Understand your invariants and condition variable predicates,** even if they are stated only informally. Be certain that the invariant always holds outside the critical code section.

- **Keep it simple.** Multithreaded programming is complex enough without the burden of additional complex, poorly understood thread models and logic. If a program becomes overly complex, assess whether the complexity is really necessary or is the result of poor design. Careful use of standard threading models can simplify your program and make it easier to understand, and lack of a good model may be a symptom of a poorly designed program.

- **Test on both single-processor and multiprocessor systems and on systems with different clock rates, cache architectures, and other characteristics.** Some defects will never, or rarely, show up on a single-processor system but will occur immediately on a multiprocessor system, and conversely. Likewise, a variety of system characteristics helps ensure that a defective program has more opportunity to fail.

- **Testing is necessary but not sufficient to ensure correct behavior.** There have been a number of examples of programs, known to be defective, that seldom fail in routine or even extensive tests.

- **Be humble.** After all these precautions, bugs will still occur. This is true even with single-threaded programs; threads simply give us more, different, and very interesting ways to cause problems. This adage has been proved many times in preparing this book, where several reviewers and I found bugs (not always subtle bugs, either) in the example programs.

Beyond the Windows API

We have intentionally limited coverage to the Windows API. Microsoft does, however, provide additional access to kernel objects, such as threads. For example, the .NET `ThreadPool` class, accessible through C++, C#, and other languages, allows you to create a pool of threads and to queue work items to the threads (the `ThreadPool` method is `QueueUserWorkItem`).

Microsoft also implements the Microsoft Message Queuing (MSMQ) service, which provides messaging services between networked systems. The examples in this chapter should help show the value of a general-purpose message queuing system. MSMQ is documented in MSDN.

Summary

Multithreaded program development is much simpler if you use well-understood and familiar programming models and techniques. This chapter has shown the utility of the condition variable model and has solved several relatively complex but important programming problems. APCs allow one thread to signal and cause actions in another thread, which allows thread cancellation so that all threads in a system can shut down properly.

Synchronization and thread management are complex because there are multiple ways to solve a given problem, and the different techniques involve complexity and performance trade-offs. The three-stage pipeline example was implemented several different ways in order to illustrate the options.

Use of careful program design and implementation is the best way to improve program quality. Overdependence on testing and debugging, without attention to detail, can lead to serious problems that may be very difficult to detect and fix.

Looking Ahead

Chapter 11 introduces interprocess communication using Windows proprietary anonymous and named pipes. The named pipe example programs show a multithreaded server that can process requests from multiple networked clients. Chapter 12 then converts the example to sockets, which are an industry standard and allow interoperability with Linux, UNIX, and other systems.

Additional Reading

David Butenhof's *Programming with POSIX Threads* was the source of much of the information and programming guidelines at the end of the chapter. The threshold barrier solution, Programs 10–1 and 10–2, was adapted from Butenhof as well.

"Strategies for Implementing POSIX Condition Variables in Win32," by Douglas Schmidt and Irfan Pyarali (posted at http://www.cs.wustl.edu/~schmidt/win32-cv-1.html), discusses Windows event limitations along with condition variables emulation, thoroughly analyzing and evaluating several approaches. Reading this paper will increase your appreciation of the new functions. Another paper by the same authors (http://www.cs.wustl.edu/~schmidt/win32-cv-2.html) builds object-oriented wrappers around Windows synchronization objects to achieve a platform-independent synchronization interface. The open source Pthreads implementation, which is based on the Schmidt and Pyarali work, is available at http://sources.redhat.com/pthreads-win32/.

Exercises

10–1. Revise Program 10–1 so that it does not use the `SignalObjectAndWait` function.

10–2. Modify `eventPC` (Program 8–2) so that there can be multiple consumers and so that it uses the condition variable model. Which event type is appropriate?

10–3. Change the logic in Program 10–2 so that the event is signaled only once.

10–4. Replace the mutex in the queue object used in Program 10–2 with a CS. What are the effects on performance and throughput? The solution is in the *Examples* file, and Appendix C contains experimental data.

10–5. Program 10–4 uses the broadcast CV model to indicate when the queue is either not empty or not full. Would the signal CV model work? Would the signal model even be preferable in any way? Appendix C contains experimental data.

10–6. Experiment with the queue lengths and the transmitter-receiver blocking factor in Program 10–5 to determine the effects on performance, throughput, and CPU load.

10–7. *For C++ programmers*: The code in Programs 10–3 and 10–4 could be used to create a synchronized queue class in C++; create this class and modify Program 10–5 to test it. Which of the functions should be public and which should be private?

10–8. Study the performance behavior of Program 10–5 if CRITICAL_SECTIONs are used instead of mutexes.

10–9. Improve Program 10–5 so that it is not necessary to terminate the transmitter and receiver threads. The threads should shut themselves down.

10–10. The *Examples* file contains MultiSem.c, which implements a multiple-wait semaphore modeled after the Windows objects (they can be named, secured, and process shared, and there are two wait models), and TestMultiSem.c is a test program. Build and test this program. How does it use the CV model? Is performance improved by using a CRITICAL_SECTION or Windows condition variable? What are the invariants and condition variable predicates?

10–11. Illustrate the various guidelines at the end of this chapter in terms of bugs you have encountered or in the defective versions of the programs provided in the *Examples* file.

10–12. Read "Strategies for Implementing POSIX Condition Variables in Win32" by Schmidt and Pyarali (see the Additional Reading section). Apply their fairness, correctness, serialization, and other analyses to the CV models (called "idioms" in their paper) in this chapter. Notice that this chapter does not directly emulate condition variables; rather, it tackles the easier problem of emulating normal condition variable usage, whereas Schmidt and Pyarali emulate condition variables used in an arbitrary context.

10–13. Convert one of Chapter 9's statsXX programs to create a thread pool using APCs.

10–14. Two projects in the *Examples* file, batons and batonsMultipleEvents, show alternative solutions to the problem of serializing thread execution. The code comments give background and acknowledgments. The second solution associates a unique event with each thread so that specific threads can be signaled. The implementation uses C++ in order to take advantage of the C++ Standard Template Library (STL). Compare and contrast these two solutions, and use the second as a means to become familiar with the STL.

10–15. Perform tests to compare NT6 condition variable performance with the other `ThreeStage` implementations.

10–16. Modify `QueueObjectCV.c` (which implements the message queue management functions with condition variables) so that it uses SRW (slim reader/writer) locks. Test with `ThreeStage.c` and compare performance with the original implementation. Further modify the implementation to use thread pooling.

CHAPTER

11 | Interprocess Communication

Chapter 6 showed how to create and manage processes, and Chapters 7 to 10 showed how to manage and synchronize threads within processes. So far, however, we have not been able to perform direct process-to-process communication other than through shared memory (Chapter 5).

The next step is to provide sequential interprocess communication (IPC) between processes[1] using filelike objects. Two primary Windows mechanisms for IPC are the anonymous pipe and the named pipe, both of which are accessed with the familiar `ReadFile` and `WriteFile` functions. Simple anonymous pipes are character-based and half-duplex. As such, they are well suited for redirecting the output of one program to the input of another, as is common with communicating Linux and UNIX programs. The first example shows how to do this with Windows anonymous pipes.

Named pipes are much more powerful than anonymous pipes. They are full-duplex and message-oriented, and they allow networked communication. Furthermore, there can be multiple open handles on the same pipe. These capabilities, coupled with convenient transaction-oriented named pipe functions, make named pipes appropriate for creating client/server systems. This capability is shown in this chapter's second example, a multithreaded client/server command processor, modeled after Figure 7–1, which was used to introduce threads. Each server thread manages communication with a different client, and each thread/client pair uses a distinct handle, or named pipe instance. Mailslots, which allow for one-to-many message broadcasting and are also filelike, are used to help clients locate servers.

---

[1] The Windows system services also allow processes to communicate through mapped files, as demonstrated in the semaphore exercise in Chapter 10 (Exercise 10–10). Additional mechanisms for IPC include files, sockets, remote procedure calls, COM, and message posting. Chapter 12 describes sockets.

Anonymous Pipes

Windows anonymous pipes allow one-way (half-duplex), byte-based IPC. Each pipe has two handles: a read handle and a write handle. The `CreatePipe` function is:

```
BOOL CreatePipe (
    PHANDLE phRead,
    PHANDLE phWrite,
    LPSECURITY_ATTRIBUTES lpsa,
    DWORD cbPipe)
```

The pipe handles are often inheritable; the next example shows the reasons. `cbPipe`, the pipe byte size, is only a suggestion, and 0 specifies the default value.

In order to use the pipe for IPC, there must be another process, and that process requires one of the pipe handles. Assume that the parent process, which calls `CreatePipe`, wishes to write data for a child to use. The problem, then, is to communicate the read handle (`phRead`) to the child. The parent achieves this by setting the child procedure's input handle in the start-up structure to `*phRead` (see Chapter 6 for process management and the start-up structure).

Reading a pipe read handle will block if the pipe is empty. Otherwise, the read will accept as many bytes as are in the pipe, up to the number specified in the `ReadFile` call. A write operation to a full pipe, which is implemented in a memory buffer, will also block.

Finally, anonymous pipes are one-way. Two pipes are required for bidirectional communication.

Example: I/O Redirection Using an Anonymous Pipe

Program 11–1 shows a parent process, `Redirect`, that creates two processes from the command line and pipes them together. The parent process sets up the pipe and redirects standard input and output. Notice how the anonymous pipe handles are inheritable and how standard I/O is redirected to the two child processes; these techniques were described in Chapter 6.

The location of `WriteFile` in `Program2` on the right side of Figure 11–1 assumes that the program reads a large amount of data, processes it, and then writes out results. Alternatively, the write could be inside the loop, putting out results after each read.

Close the pipe and thread handles at the earliest possible point. Figure 11–1 does not show the handle closings, but Program 11–1 does. The parent should

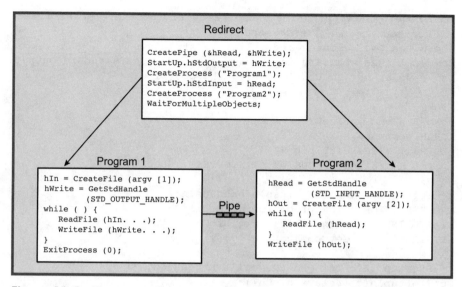

Figure 11-1   Process-to-Process Communication Using an Anonymous Pipe

close the standard output handle immediately after creating the first child process so that the second process will be able to recognize an end of file when the first process terminates. If there were still an open handle, the second process might not terminate because the application would not indicate an end of file.

Program 11–1 uses an unusual syntax; the = sign is the pipe symbol separating the two commands. The vertical bar (|) would conflict with the command processor. Figure 11–1 schematically shows the execution of the command:

```
$ Redirect Program1 arguments = Program2 arguments
```

In UNIX or at the Windows command prompt, the corresponding command would be:

```
$ Program1 arguments | Program2 arguments
```

Program 11–1   Redirect: Interprocess Communication

```
/* Chapter 11. Redirect: Anonymous Pipe IPC example. */

#include "Everything.h"

int _tmain (int argc, LPTSTR argv[])
```

```
/* Pipe together two programs whose names are on the command line:
       Redirect command1 = command2
   where the two commands are arbitrary strings.
   command1 uses standard input, and command2 uses standard output.
   Use = so as not to conflict with the DOS pipe. */
{
   DWORD i;
   HANDLE hReadPipe, hWritePipe;
   TCHAR command1[MAX_PATH];
   SECURITY_ATTRIBUTES pipeSA =
              {sizeof(SECURITY_ATTRIBUTES), NULL, TRUE};

   /* Initialize for inheritable handles. */
   PROCESS_INFORMATION procInfo1, procInfo2;
   STARTUPINFO startInfoCh1, startInfoCh2;
   LPTSTR targv = GetCommandLine ();

   /* Startup info for the two child processes. */
   GetStartupInfo (&startInfoCh1);
   GetStartupInfo (&startInfoCh2);

   targv = SkipArg (targv);
   i = 0;     /* Get the two commands. */
   while (*targv != _T ('=') && *targv != _T ('\0')) {
      command1[i] = *targv;
      targv++; i++;
   }
   command1[i] = '\0';
   if (*targv == '\0')
      ReportError (_T ("No command separator found."), 2, FALSE);
   targv = SkipArg (targv);

   /* Create anonymous pipe - default size & inheritable handles. */
   CreatePipe (&hReadPipe, &hWritePipe, &pipeSA, 0);

   /* Set the output handle to the inheritable pipe handle,
      and create the first processes. */
   startInfoCh1.hStdInput  = GetStdHandle (STD_INPUT_HANDLE);
   startInfoCh1.hStdError  = GetStdHandle (STD_ERROR_HANDLE);
   startInfoCh1.hStdOutput = hWritePipe;
   startInfoCh1.dwFlags = STARTF_USESTDHANDLES;

   CreateProcess (NULL, command1, NULL, NULL,
         TRUE,     /* Inherit handles. */
         0, NULL, NULL, &startInfoCh1, &procInfo1);

   CloseHandle (procInfo1.hThread); CloseHandle (hWritePipe);

   /* Repeat (symmetrically) for the second process. */
   startInfoCh2.hStdInput  = hReadPipe;
```

```
startInfoCh2.hStdError  = GetStdHandle (STD_ERROR_HANDLE);
startInfoCh2.hStdOutput = GetStdHandle (STD_OUTPUT_HANDLE);
startInfoCh2.dwFlags = STARTF_USESTDHANDLES;

CreateProcess (NULL, targv, NULL, NULL,
      TRUE,    /* Inherit handles. */
      0, NULL, NULL, &startInfoCh2, &procInfo2);
CloseHandle (procInfo2.hThread);
CloseHandle (hReadPipe);

/* Wait for both processes to complete.
   The first one should finish first, but it doesn't matter. */
WaitForSingleObject (procInfo1.hProcess, INFINITE);
WaitForSingleObject (procInfo2.hProcess, INFINITE);
CloseHandle (procInfo1.hProcess);
CloseHandle (procInfo2.hProcess);
return 0;
}
```

Run 11–1 shows output from grepMT, Chapter 7's multithreaded pattern search program piped to FIND, which is a similar Windows command. While this may seem a bit artificial, cat is the book's only sample program that accepts standard input, and it also shows that Redirect works with third-party programs that accept standard input.

These examples search the presidents and monarchs files, first used in Chapter 6, for individuals named "James" and "George" who lived in any part of the eighteenth century (the search is not entirely accurate) or "William" who lived in any part of the nineteenth century. The file names were shortened to decrease the horizontal space.

```
C:\WSP4_Examples\run8>Redirect grepMT James mnch.txt pres.txt = FIND "17"
16331014 16850423 16890906 17010906 JamesII                          i
17510316 18090300 18170300 18390628 Madison,James                    i
17580428 18170300 18250209 18310704 Monroe,James                     i
17951102 18450304 18490300 18490300 Polk,JamesK                      i
17910423 18570304 18610304 18680601 Buchanan,James                   i

C:\WSP4_Examples\run8>Redirect grepMT George mnch.txt pres.txt = FIND "17"
17620812 18210719 18300626 18300626 GeorgeIV                         i
17380604 17610922 18200129 18200129 GeorgeIII                        i
16600328 17141020 17270611 17270611 GeorgeI                          i
16831110 17271011 17601025 17601025 GeorgeII                         i
17320222 17890204 17970303 17991214 Washington,George                i

C:\WSP4_Examples\run8>Redirect grepMT William mnch.txt pres.txt = FIND "18"
17650821 18310908 18370620 18370620 WilliamIV                        i
18570915 19090300 19130304 19300308 Taft,WilliamHoward               i
18430129 18970300 19010914 19010914 McKinley,William                 i
17730209 18410304 18410404 18410404 Harrison,WilliamHenry            i

C:\WSP4_Examples\run8>
```

Run 11–1 Redirect: Using an Anonymous Pipe

Named Pipes

Named pipes have several features that make them an appropriate general-purpose mechanism for implementing IPC-based applications, including networked file access and client/server systems,[2] although anonymous pipes remain a good choice for simple byte-stream IPC, such as the preceding example, where communication is within a single computer. Named pipe features (some are optional) include the following.

- Named pipes are message-oriented, so the reading process can read varying-length messages precisely as sent by the writing process.

- Named pipes are bidirectional, so two processes can exchange messages over the same pipe.

- There can be multiple, independent instances of pipes with the same name. For example, several clients can communicate concurrently with a single server using distinct instances of a named pipe. Each client can have its own named pipe instance, and the server can respond to a client using the same instance.

- Networked clients can access the pipe by name. Named pipe communication is the same whether the two processes are on the same machine or on different machines.

- Several convenience and connection functions simplify named pipe request/response interaction and client/server connection.

Named pipes are generally preferable to anonymous pipes, although Program 11–1 and Figure 11–1 did illustrate a situation in which anonymous pipes are useful. Use named pipes any time your communication channel needs to be bidirectional, message-oriented, networked, or available to multiple client processes. The upcoming examples could not be implemented using anonymous pipes.

Using Named Pipes

`CreateNamedPipe` creates the first instance of a named pipe and returns a handle. The function also specifies the pipe's maximum number of instances and, hence, the number of clients that can be supported simultaneously.

---

[2] This statement requires a major qualification. Windows Sockets (Chapter 12) is the preferred API for most networking applications and higher-level protocols (http, ftp, and so on), especially where TCP/IP-based interoperability with non-Windows systems is required. Many developers prefer to limit named pipe usage to IPC within a single computer or to communication within Windows networks.

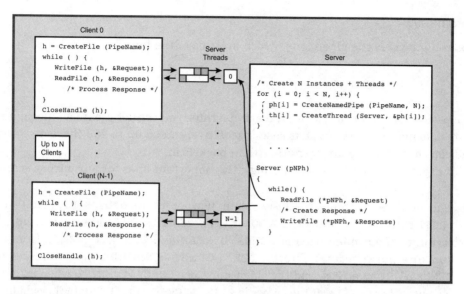

Figure 11–2   Clients and Servers Using Named Pipes

Normally, the creating process is regarded as the *server. Client* processes, possibly on other systems, open the pipe with `CreateFile`.

Figure 11–2 shows an illustrative client/server relationship, and the pseudocode shows one scheme for using named pipes. Notice that the server creates multiple instances of the same pipe, each of which can support a client. The server also creates a thread for each named pipe instance, so that each client has a dedicated thread and named pipe instance. Figure 11–2, then, shows how to implement the multithreaded server model of Figure 7–1.

Creating Named Pipes

Here is the specification of the `CreateNamedPipe` function.

```
HANDLE CreateNamedPipe (
    LPCTSTR lpName,
    DWORD dwOpenMode,
    DWORD dwPipeMode,
    DWORD nMaxInstances,
    DWORD nOutBufferSize,
    DWORD nInBufferSize,
    DWORD nDefaultTimeOut,
    LPSECURITY_ATTRIBUTES lpSecurityAttributes)
```

Parameters

lpName indicates the pipe name, which must be of the form:

    \\.\pipe*pipename*

The period (.) stands for the local machine; thus, you cannot create a pipe on a remote machine. The pipename is case-insensitive, can be up to 256 characters long, and can contain any character other than backslash.

dwOpenMode specifies several flags; the important ones for our purposes are:

- One of three mutually exclusive data flow description flags—PIPE_ACCESS-
  _DUPLEX, PIPE_ACCESS_INBOUND, or PIPE_ACCESS_OUTBOUND. The value determines the combination of GENERIC_READ and GENERIC_WRITE from the server's perspective. Thus, PIPE_ACCESS_INBOUND gives the server GENERIC_READ access, and the client must use GENERIC_WRITE when connecting with CreateFile. If the access is PIPE_ACCESS_DUPLEX, data flows bidirectionally, and the client can specify GENERIC_READ, GENERIC_WRITE, or both.

- FILE_FLAG_OVERLAPPED enables asynchronous I/O (Chapter 14).

The mode can also specify FILE_FLAG_WRITE_THROUGH (not used with message pipes), FILE_FLAG_FIRST_PIPE_INSTANCE, and more (see MSDN).

dwPipeMode has three mutually exclusive flag pairs. They indicate whether writing is message-oriented or byte-oriented, whether reading is by messages or blocks, and whether read operations block.

- PIPE_TYPE_BYTE and PIPE_TYPE_MESSAGE indicate whether data is written to the pipe as a stream of bytes or messages. Use the same type value for all pipe instances with the same name.

- PIPE_READMODE_BYTE and PIPE_READMODE_MESSAGE indicate whether data is read as a stream of bytes or messages. PIPE_READMODE_MESSAGE requires PIPE_TYPE_MESSAGE.

- PIPE_WAIT and PIPE_NOWAIT determine whether ReadFile will block. Use PIPE_WAIT because there are better ways to achieve asynchronous I/O.

nMaxInstances determines the maximum number of pipe instances. As Figure 11–2 shows, use this same value for every CreateNamedPipe call for a given pipe. Use the value PIPE_UNLIMITED_INSTANCES to have Windows base the number on available computer resources.

nOutBufferSize and nInBufferSize give the sizes, in bytes, of the input and output buffers used for the named pipes. Specify 0 to get default values.

nDefaultTimeOut is a default time-out period (in milliseconds) for the Wait-NamedPipe function, which is discussed in an upcoming section. This situation, in which the create function specifies a time-out for a related function, is unique.

The error return value is INVALID_HANDLE_VALUE because pipe handles are similar to file handles.

lpSecurityAttributes operates as in all the other create functions.

The first CreateNamedPipe call actually creates the named pipe and an instance. Closing the last handle to an instance will delete the instance (usually, there is only one handle per instance). Closing the last instance of a named pipe will delete the pipe, making the pipe name available for reuse.

Named Pipe Client Connections

Figure 11–2 shows that a client connects to a named pipe using CreateFile with the pipe name. In many cases, the client and server are on the same machine, and the name would take this form:

```
\\.\pipe\[path]pipename
```

If the server is on a different machine, the name would take this form:

```
\\servername\pipe\pipename
```

Using the name period (.) when the server is local—rather than using the local machine name—delivers significantly better connection-time performance.

Named Pipe Status Functions

There are seven functions to interrogate pipe status information, and an eighth sets state information. They are mentioned briefly, and Program 11–3 demonstrates several of the functions.

- GetNamedPipeHandleState returns information, given an open handle, on whether the pipe is in blocking or nonblocking mode, whether it is message-oriented or byte-oriented, the number of pipe instances, and so on.

- SetNamedPipeHandleState allows the program to set the same state attributes. The mode and other values are passed by address rather than by value, which is necessary so that a NULL value specifies that the mode should not be changed. See the full *Examples* code of Program 11–2 for an example.

- `GetNamedPipeInfo` determines whether the handle is for a client or server instance, the buffer sizes, and so on.

- Five functions get information about the client name and the client and server session ID and process ID. Representative names are `GetNamedPipeClient-SessionId` and `GetNamedPipeServerProcessId`.

Named Pipe Connection Functions

The server, after creating a named pipe instance, can wait for a client connection (`CreateFile` or `CallNamedPipe`, described in a subsequent function) using `ConnectNamedPipe`.

```
BOOL ConnectNamedPipe (
    HANDLE hNamedPipe,
    LPOVERLAPPED lpOverlapped)
```

With `lpOverlapped` set to NULL, `ConnectNamedPipe` will return as soon as there is a client connection. Normally, the return value is TRUE. However, it would be FALSE if the client connected between the server's `CreateNamedPipe` call and the `Connect-NamedPipe` call. In this case, `GetLastError` returns ERROR_PIPE_CONNECTED, and the connection is valid despite the FALSE return value.

Following the return from `ConnectNamedPipe`, the server can read requests using `ReadFile` and write responses using `WriteFile`. Finally, the server should call `DisconnectNamedPipe` to free the handle (pipe instance) for connection with another client.

`WaitNamedPipe`, the final function, is for use by the client to synchronize connections to the server. The call will return successfully as soon as the server has a pending `ConnectNamedPipe` call. By using `WaitNamedPipe`, the client can be certain that the server is ready for a connection and the client can then call `CreateFile`. Nonetheless, the client's `CreateFile` call could fail if some other client opens the named pipe using `CreateFile` or if the server closes the instance handle; that is, there is a race involving the server and the clients. The server's `ConnectNamedPipe` call will not fail. Notice that there is a time-out period for `WaitNamedPipe` that, if specified, will override the time-out period specified with the server's `CreateNamedPipe` call.

Client and Server Named Pipe Connection

The proper connection sequences for the client and server are as follows. First is the server sequence, in which the server makes a client connection, communicates with the client until the client disconnects (causing `ReadFile` to return `FALSE`), disconnects the server-side connection, and then connects to another client.

```
/* Named pipe server connection sequence. */
hNp = CreateNamedPipe ("\\\\.\\pipe\\my_pipe", ...);
while (... /* Continue until server shuts down. */) {
    ConnectNamedPipe (hNp, NULL);
    while (ReadFile (hNp, Request, ...) {
        ...
        WriteFile (hNp, Response, ...);
    }
    DisconnectNamedPipe (hNp);
}
CloseHandle (hNp);
```

The client connection sequence is as follows, where the client terminates after it finishes, allowing another client to connect on the same named pipe instance. As shown, the client can connect to a networked server if it knows the server name.

```
/* Named pipe client connection sequence. */
WaitNamedPipe ("\\\\ServerName\\pipe\\my_pipe",
        NMPWAIT_WAIT_FOREVER);
hNp =
        CreateFile ("\\\\ServerName\\pipe\\my_pipe", ...);
while (... /* Run until there are no more requests. */ {
    WriteFile (hNp, Request, ...);
    ...
    ReadFile (hNp, Response);
}
CloseHandle (hNp); /* Disconnect from the server. */
```

Notice the race conditions between the client and the server. First, the client's `WaitNamedPipe` call will fail if the server has not yet created the named pipe; the failure test is omitted for brevity but is included in the sample programs in the *Examples* file. Next, the client may, in rare circumstances, complete its `Create-File` call before the server calls `ConnectNamedPipe`. In that case, `Connect-NamedPipe` will return `FALSE` to the server, but the named pipe communication will still function properly.

The named pipe instance is a global resource, so once the client disconnects, another client can connect with the server.

Named Pipe Transaction Functions

Figure 11–2 shows a typical client configuration in which the client does the following:

- Opens an instance of the pipe, creating a long-lived connection to the server and consuming a pipe instance
- Repetitively sends requests and waits for responses
- Closes the connection

The common WriteFile, ReadFile sequence could be regarded as a single client transaction, and Windows provides such a function for message pipes.

```
BOOL TransactNamedPipe (
    HANDLE hNamedPipe,
    LPVOID lpWriteBuf,
    DWORD cbWriteBuf,
    LPVOID lpReadBuf,
    DWORD cbReadBuf,
    LPDWORD lpcbRead,
    LPOVERLAPPED lpOverlapped)
```

The parameter usage is clear because this function combines WriteFile and ReadFile on the named pipe handle. Both the output and input buffers are specified, and *lpcbRead receives the message length. Overlapped operations (Chapter 14) are possible. More typically, the function waits for the response.

TransactNamedPipe is convenient, but, as in Figure 11–2, it requires a permanent connection, which limits the number of clients.[3]

CallNamedPipe is the second client convenience function:

---

[3] Note that TransactNamedPipe is more than a mere convenience compared with WriteFile and ReadFile and can provide some performance advantages. One experiment shows throughput enhancements ranging from 57% (small messages) to 24% (large messages).

```
BOOL CallNamedPipe (
    LPCTSTR lpPipeName,
    LPVOID lpWriteBuf,
    DWORD cbWriteBuf,
    LPVOID lpReadBuf,
    DWORD cbReadBuf,
    LPDWORD lpcbRead,
    DWORD dwTimeOut)
```

CallNamedPipe does not require a permanent connection; instead, it makes a temporary connection by combining the following complete sequence:

```
CreateFile
WriteFile
ReadFile
CloseHandle
```

into a single function. The benefit is that clients do not have long-lived connections, and the server can service more clients at the cost of per-request connection overhead.

The parameter usage is similar to that of TransactNamedPipe except that a pipe name, rather than a handle, specifies the pipe. CallNamedPipe is synchronous (there is no overlapped structure). It specifies a time-out period, in milliseconds, for the connection but not for the transaction. There are three special values for dwTimeOut:

- NMPWAIT_NOWAIT

- NMPWAIT_WAIT_FOREVER

- NMPWAIT_USE_DEFAULT_WAIT, which uses the default time-out period specified by CreateNamedPipe

Peeking at Named Pipe Messages

In addition to reading a named pipe using ReadFile, you can also determine whether there is actually a message to read using PeekNamedPipe. This is useful to poll the named pipe (an inefficient operation), determine the message length so as to allocate a buffer before reading, or look at the incoming data so as to prioritize its processing.

```
BOOL PeekNamedPipe (
    HANDLE hPipe,
    LPVOID lpBuffer,
    DWORD cbBuffer,
    LPDWORD lpcbRead,
    LPDWORD lpcbAvail,
    LPDWORD lpcbMessage)
```

PeekNamedPipe nondestructively reads any bytes or messages in the pipe, but it does not block; it returns immediately.

Test *lpcbAvail to determine whether there is data in the pipe; if there is, *lpcbAvail will be greater than 0. lpBuffer and lpcbRead can be NULL, but if you need to look at the data, call PeekNamedPipe a second time with a buffer and count large enough to receive the data (based on the *lpcbAvail value). If a buffer is specified with lpBuffer and cbBuffer, then *lpcbMessage will tell whether there are leftover message bytes that could not fit into the buffer, allowing you to allocate a large buffer before reading from the named pipe. This value is 0 for a byte mode pipe.

Again, PeekNamedPipe reads nondestructively, so a subsequent ReadFile is required to remove messages or bytes from the pipe.

The UNIX FIFO is similar to a named pipe, thus allowing communication between unrelated processes. There are limitations compared with Windows named pipes.

- FIFOs are half-duplex.

- FIFOs are limited to a single machine.

- FIFOs are still byte-oriented, so it is easiest to use fixed-size records in client/server applications. Nonetheless, individual read and write operations are atomic.

A server using FIFOs must use a separate FIFO for each client's response, although all clients can send requests to a single, well-known FIFO. A common practice is for the client to include a FIFO name in a connect request.

The UNIX function mkfifo is a limited version of CreateNamedPipe.

If the clients and server are to be networked, use sockets or a similar transport mechanism. Sockets are full-duplex, but there must still be one separate connection per client.

Example: A Client/Server Command Line Processor

Everything required to build a request/response client/server system is now available. This example is a command line server that executes a command on behalf of the client. Features of the system include:

- Multiple clients can interact with the server.

- The clients can be on different systems on the network, although the clients can also be on the server machine.

- The server is multithreaded, with a thread dedicated to each named pipe instance. That is, there is a *thread pool* of worker threads[4] ready for use by connecting clients. Worker threads are allocated to a client on the basis of the named pipe instance that the system allocates to the client.

- The individual server threads process a single request at a time, simplifying concurrency control. Each thread handles its own requests independently. Nonetheless, exercise the normal precautions if different server threads are accessing the same file or other resource.

Program 11–2 shows the single-threaded client, and its server is Program 11–3. The server corresponds to the model in Figures 7–1 and 11–2. The client request is simply the command line. The server response is the resulting output, which is sent in several messages. The programs also use the include file `ClientServer.h`, which is included in the *Examples* file, and defines the request and response data structures as well as the client and server pipe names.

The client in Program 11–2 also calls a function, `LocateServer`, which finds a server pipe by name. `LocateServer` uses a mailslot, described in a later section and shown in Program 11–5.

The defined records have `DWORD32` length fields; this is done to emphasize the field size.

Program 11–2   `clientNP`: Named Pipe Connection-Oriented Client

```
/* Chapter 11. Client/server system. CLIENT .
   clientNP -- connection-oriented client. */
/* Execute a command line (on the server); display the response. */
/* The client creates a long-lived connection with the server
   (consuming a pipe instance) and prompts user for a command. */

#include "Everything.h"
```

---

[4] This application-managed thread pool is different from the NT6 thread pool (see Chapter 10).

```
#include "ClientServer.h" /* Defines the request, records. */

int _tmain (int argc, LPTSTR argv[])
{
    HANDLE hNamedPipe = INVALID_HANDLE_VALUE;
    TCHAR quitMsg[] = _T ("$Quit");
    TCHAR serverPipeName[MAX_PATH];
    REQUEST request;/* See ClientServer.h */
    RESPONSE response;/* See ClientServer.h */
    DWORD nRead, nWrite, npMode = PIPE_READMODE_MESSAGE | PIPE_WAIT;

    LocateServer (serverPipeName, MAX_PATH);

    /* Obtain a handle to a NP instance */
    while (INVALID_HANDLE_VALUE == hNamedPipe) {
        WaitNamedPipe (serverPipeName, NMPWAIT_WAIT_FOREVER);
        /* An instance has become available. Attempt to open it
         * before another thread, or the server closes the instance */
        hNamedPipe = CreateFile (serverPipeName,
            GENERIC_READ | GENERIC_WRITE, 0, NULL,
            OPEN_EXISTING, FILE_ATTRIBUTE_NORMAL, NULL);
    }

    /*  Read NP handle in waiting, message mode. Note the 2nd argument
     *  is an address. Client and server may be on the same computer, so
     *  do not set the collection mode and timeout (last 2 args) */
    SetNamedPipeHandleState (hNamedPipe, &npMode, NULL, NULL);
    /* Prompt the user for commands. Terminate on "$Quit". */
    request.command = 0;
    request.rqLen = RQ_SIZE;
    while (ConsolePrompt (promptMsg, request.record,
                MAX_RQRS_LEN, TRUE)
            && (_tcscmp (request.record, quitMsg) != 0)) {
        WriteFile (hNamedPipe, &request, RQ_SIZE, &nWrite, NULL);

        /* Read each response and send it to std out */
        while (ReadFile (hNamedPipe, &response, RS_SIZE, &nRead, NULL))
        {
            if (response.rsLen <= 1) { break; /* Server response end */
            _tprintf (_T ("%s"), response.record);
        }
    }

    _tprintf (_T("Quit command received. Disconnect."));
    CloseHandle (hNamedPipe);
    return 0;
}
```

Program 11–3 is the server program, including the server thread function, that processes the requests from Program 11–2. The server also creates a "server broadcast" thread (see Program 11–4) to broadcast its pipe name on a mailslot to clients that want to connect. Program 11–2 calls the `LocateServer` function, shown in Program 11–5, which reads the information sent by this process. Mailslots are described later in this chapter.

While the code is omitted in Program 11–4, the server (in the *Examples* file) optionally secures its named pipe to prevent access by unauthorized clients. Chapter 15 describes object security and how to use this option. Also, see the example for the server process shutdown logic.

Program 11–3   `serverNP`: Multithreaded Named Pipe Server Program

```
/* Chapter 11. ServerNP.
 * Multithreaded command line server. Named pipe version. */

#include "Everything.h"
#include "ClientServer.h" /* Request & response message definitions. */

typedef struct {     /* Argument to a server thread. */
   HANDLE hNamedPipe;  /* Named pipe instance. */
   DWORD threadNumber;
   TCHAR tempFileName[MAX_PATH]; /* Temporary file name. */
} THREAD_ARG;
typedef THREAD_ARG *LPTHREAD_ARG;

volatile static int shutDown = 0;
static DWORD WINAPI Server (LPTHREAD_ARG);
static DWORD WINAPI Connect (LPTHREAD_ARG);
static DWORD WINAPI ServerBroadcast (LPLONG);
static BOOL  WINAPI Handler (DWORD);
static THREAD_ARG threadArgs[MAX_CLIENTS];

_tmain (int argc, LPTSTR argv[])
{
   /* MAX_CLIENTS is defined in ClientServer.h. */
   /* Limited to MAXIMUM_WAIT_OBJECTS WaitForMultipleObjects */
   /* is used by the main thread to wait for the server threads */

   HANDLE hNp, hMonitor, hSrvrThread[MAX_CLIENTS];
   DWORD iNp, monitorId, threadId;
   LPSECURITY_ATTRIBUTES pNPSA = NULL;

   /* Console control handler to permit server shutdown */
   SetConsoleCtrlHandler (Handler, TRUE);

   /* Create a thread broadcast pipe name periodically. */
```

```
    hMonitor = (HANDLE)_beginthreadex (NULL, 0, ServerBroadcast,
                            NULL, 0, &monitorId);

    /* Create a pipe instance for every server thread.
     * Create a temp file name for each thread.
     * Create a thread to service that pipe. */

    for (iNp = 0; iNp < MAX_CLIENTS; iNp++) {
        hNp = CreateNamedPipe ( SERVER_PIPE, PIPE_ACCESS_DUPLEX,
                PIPE_READMODE_MESSAGE | PIPE_TYPE_MESSAGE | PIPE_WAIT,
                MAX_CLIENTS, 0, 0, INFINITE, pNPSA);

        threadArgs[iNp].hNamedPipe = hNp;
        threadArgs[iNp].threadNumber = iNp;
        GetTempFileName (_T ("."), _T ("CLP"), 0,
                        threadArgs[iNp].tempFileName);
        hSrvrThread[iNp] = (HANDLE)_beginthreadex (NULL, 0, Server,
                        &threadArgs[iNp], 0, &threadId);
    }

    /* Wait for all the threads to terminate. */
    WaitForMultipleObjects (MAX_CLIENTS, hSrvrThread, TRUE, INFINITE);
    _tprintf (_T ("All Server worker threads have shut down.\n"));

    WaitForSingleObject (hMonitor, INFINITE);
    _tprintf (_T ("Monitor thread has shut down.\n"));

    CloseHandle (hMonitor);
    for (iNp = 0; iNp < MAX_CLIENTS; iNp++) {
        /* Close pipe handles and delete temp files */
        /* Closing temp files is redundant; the worker threads do it */
        CloseHandle (hSrvrThread[iNp]);
        DeleteFile (threadArgs[iNp].tempFileName);
    }

    _tprintf (_T ("Server process will exit.\n"));
    return 0;
}

static DWORD WINAPI Server (LPTHREAD_ARG pThArg)
/* Server thread function. One thread for every potential client. */
{
    /* Each thread keeps its own request, response,
     * and bookkeeping data structures on the stack.
     * Also, each thread creates an additional "connect thread"
     * so that the main worker thread can test the shutdown flag
     * periodically while waiting for a client connection. */

    HANDLE hNamedPipe, hTmpFile = INVALID_HANDLE_VALUE,
            hConTh = NULL, hClient;
```

```
    DWORD nXfer, conThStatus, clientProcessId;
    STARTUPINFO startInfoCh;
    SECURITY_ATTRIBUTES tempSA =
          {sizeof (SECURITY_ATTRIBUTES), NULL, TRUE};
    PROCESS_INFORMATION procInfo;
    FILE *fp;
    REQUEST request;
    RESPONSE response;

    GetStartupInfo (&startInfoCh);
    hNamedPipe = pThArg->hNamedPipe;

    /* Open temporary results file for connections to this instance. */
    hTmpFile = CreateFile (pThArg->tempFileName,
          GENERIC_READ | GENERIC_WRITE,
          FILE_SHARE_READ | FILE_SHARE_WRITE, &tempSA,
          CREATE_ALWAYS, FILE_ATTRIBUTE_TEMPORARY, NULL);

while (!shutDownFlag) { /* Connection loop */
    /* Create a connection thread, and wait for it to terminate */
    /* Use timeout on wait so that shutdown flag can be tested */
    hConTh = (HANDLE)_beginthreadex (NULL, 0, Connect,
                              pThArg, 0, NULL);

    /* Wait for a client connection. */
    while (!shutDownFlag &&
       WaitForSingleObject (hConTh, CS_TIMEOUT) == WAIT_TIMEOUT)
       { /* Empty loop body */};
    if (shutDownFlag) _tprintf(_T("Thread %d received shutdown\n"),
                     pThArg->threadNumber);
    if (shutDownFlag) continue;/* Could be set by other threads */

    CloseHandle (hConTh); hConTh = NULL;
    /* A connection now exists */
    GetNamedPipeClientProcessId(pThArg->hNamedPipe,
                 &clientProcessId);
    _tprintf(_T("Connect to client process id: %d\n"),
                     clientProcessId);
    while (!shutDownFlag && ReadFile (hNamedPipe, &request,
                     RQ_SIZE, &nXfer, NULL)) {
       _tprintf(_T("Command from client thread: %d. %s\n"),
             clientProcessId, request.record);
       /* Receive new commands until the client disconnects */
       shutDownFlag = shutDownFlag ||
                 (_tcscmp (request.record, shutRequest) == 0);
       if (shutDownFlag)  continue;

       /* Main command loop */
       /* Create a process to carry out the command. */
       startInfoCh.hStdOutput = hTmpFile;
```

```
            startInfoCh.hStdError = hTmpFile;
            startInfoCh.hStdInput = GetStdHandle (STD_INPUT_HANDLE);
            startInfoCh.dwFlags = STARTF_USESTDHANDLES;

            CreateProcess (NULL, request.record, NULL,
                NULL, TRUE, /* Inherit handles. */
                0, NULL, NULL, &startInfoCh, &procInfo);

            CloseHandle (procInfo.hThread);
            WaitForSingleObject (procInfo.hProcess, INFINITE);
            CloseHandle (procInfo.hProcess);

            /* Respond a line at a time. It is convenient to use
               C library line-oriented routines at this point. */
            fp = _tfopen (pThArg->tempFileName, _T ("r"));
            while (_fgetts(response.record, MAX_RQRS_LEN, fp) != NULL) {
                response.rsLen = strlen(response.record) + 1;
                WriteFile (hNamedPipe, &response,
                    response.rsLen+sizeof(response.rsLen), &nXfer, NULL);
            }
            /* Write a terminating record. */
            _tcscpy (response.record, _T(""));
            response.rsLen = 0;
            WriteFile (hNamedPipe, &response, sizeof(response.rsLen),
                    &nXfer, NULL);
            FlushFileBuffers (hNamedPipe);
            fclose (fp);

            /* Erase temp file contents */
            SetFilePointer (hTmpFile, 0, NULL, FILE_BEGIN);
            SetEndOfFile (hTmpFile);
        }   /* End of main command loop. Get next command */

        /* Client has disconnected or there was a shutdown requrest */
        /* Terminate this client connection and then wait for another */
        FlushFileBuffers (hNamedPipe);
        DisconnectNamedPipe (hNamedPipe);
    }

    /*  Force connection thread to shut down if it is still active */
    if (hConTh != NULL) {
        GetExitCodeThread (hConTh, &conThStatus);
        if (conThStatus == STILL_ACTIVE) {
            hClient = CreateFile (SERVER_PIPE,
                GENERIC_READ | GENERIC_WRITE, 0, NULL,
                OPEN_EXISTING, FILE_ATTRIBUTE_NORMAL, NULL);
            if (hClient != INVALID_HANDLE_VALUE) CloseHandle (hClient);
            WaitForSingleObject (hConTh, INFINITE);
        }
    }
```

```
    _tprintf (_T("Thread %d shutting down.\n"), pThArg->threadNumber);
    /* End of command processing loop. Free thread resources; exit. */
    CloseHandle (hTmpFile); hTmpFile = INVALID_HANDLE_VALUE;
    DeleteFile (pThArg->tempFileName);
    _tprintf (_T ("Exiting server thread number %d\n"),
                pThArg->threadNumber);
    return 0;
}

static DWORD WINAPI Connect (LPTHREAD_ARG pThArg)
{
    /* Connection thread allowing server to poll ShutDown flag. */
    ConnectNamedPipe (pThArg->hNamedPipe, NULL);
    return 0;
}

BOOL WINAPI Handler (DWORD CtrlEvent)
{
    /* Shut down the system. */
    shutDownFlag = TRUE;
    return TRUE;
}
```

Comments on the Client/Server Command Line Processor

This solution includes a number of features as well as limitations that will be addressed in later chapters.

- Multiple client processes can connect with the server and perform concurrent requests; each client has a dedicated server (or worker) thread allocated from the thread pool.

- The server and clients can run from separate command prompts or can run under control of JobShell (Program 6–3).

- If all the named pipe instances are in use when a client attempts to connect, the new client will wait until a different client disconnects on receiving a $Quit command, making a pipe instance available for another client. Several new clients may be attempting to connect concurrently and will race to open the available instance; threads that lose this race will need to wait again.

- Each server thread performs synchronous I/O, but some server threads can be processing requests while others are waiting for connections or client requests.

- Extension to networked clients is straightforward, subject to the limitations of named pipes discussed earlier in this chapter. Simply change the pipe names in the header file or add a client command line parameter for the server name.

- Each server worker thread creates a simple connection thread, which calls `ConnectNamedPipe` and terminates as soon as a client connects. This allows a worker thread to wait, with a time-out, on the connection thread handle and test the global shutdown flag periodically. If the worker threads blocked on `ConnectNamedPipe`, they could not test the flag and the server could not shut down. For this reason, the server thread performs a `CreateFile` on the named pipe in order to force the connection thread to resume and shut down. Asynchronous I/O (Chapter 14) is an alternative, so that an event could be associated with the `ConnectNamedPipe` call. The comments in the *Examples* file source provide additional alternatives and information. Without this solution, connection threads might never terminate by themselves, resulting in resource leaks. Chapter 12 discusses this subject.

- There are a number of opportunities to enhance the system. For example, there could be an option to execute an in-process server by using a DLL that implements some of the commands. This enhancement is added in Chapter 12.

- The number of server threads is limited by the `WaitForMultipleObjects` call in the main thread. While this limitation is easily overcome, the system here is not truly scalable; too many threads will impair performance, as we saw in Chapter 10. Chapter 14 uses asynchronous I/O ports to address this issue.

Running the Client and Server

The details of how clients locate servers are explained in the next section ("Mailslots"). However, we can now show the programs in operation. Run 11–3 shows the server, Program 11–3, which was started using `JobShell` from

Run 11–3   `serverNP`: Servicing Several Clients

Chapter 6. The server accepts connections from three client processes, reporting the connections and the commands.

Run 11–4 shows one of the clients in operation; this is the client represented by process ID 15872 in Run 11–3. The commands are familiar from previous chapters.

```
Command Prompt - clientNP                                    [ _ ][ □ ][ X ]
c:\WSP4_Examples\run8>clientNP
Looking for a server.
Server has been located. Pipe Name: \\.\PIPE\SERVER.

Enter Command: timep statsCS 64 10000
statsCS 64 10000
Worker threads have terminated
Real Time:  00:00:00:231
User Time:  00:00:00:624
Sys Time:   00:00:00:093

Enter Command: Redirect grepMT James mnch.txt pres.txt = FIND "17"
16331014 16850423 16890906 17010906 JamesII          i
17510316 18090300 18170300 18390628 Madison,James     i
17580428 18170300 18250209 18310704 Monroe,James      i
17951102 18450304 18490300 18490300 Polk,JamesK       i
17910423 18570304 18610304 18680601 Buchanan,James    i

Enter Command: lsW -l *.txt

    64000000      10/12/2009 00:52:26 m1.txt
    64000000      10/12/2009 00:52:43 m2.txt
    64000000      10/12/2009 00:52:58 m3.txt
    64000000      10/12/2009 00:53:13 m4.txt
    64000000      10/12/2009 00:53:30 m5.txt
    64000000      10/12/2009 00:53:45 m6.txt
    64000000      10/12/2009 00:54:01 m7.txt
    64000000      10/12/2009 00:54:16 m8.txt
        3968      09/20/2009 14:49:29 mnch.txt
        3968      09/20/2009 14:49:29 Monarchs.TXT
        2816      09/20/2009 14:56:27 pres.txt
        2816      09/20/2009 14:56:27 Presidents.TXT
        2048      09/29/2009 21:35:16 small.txt
         384      09/27/2009 19:11:05 small2.txt
Enter Command: timep sortBT -n m2.txt
Real Time:  00:02:36:529
User Time:  00:00:13:962
Sys Time:   00:02:19:262

Enter Command:
```

Run 11–4   `clientNP`: Client Commands and Results

Mailslots

A Windows mailslot, like a named pipe, has a name that unrelated processes can use for communication. Mailslots are a broadcast mechanism, similar to datagrams (see Chapter 12), and behave differently from named pipes, making them useful in some important but limited situations. Here are the significant mailslot characteristics:

- A mailslot is one-directional.

- A mailslot can have multiple writers and multiple readers, but frequently it will be one-to-many of one form or the other.

- A writer (client) does not know for certain that all, some, or any readers (servers) actually received the message.

- Mailslots can be located over a network domain.

- Message lengths are limited.

Using a mailslot requires the following operations.

- Each server creates a mailslot handle with `CreateMailslot`.

- The server then waits to receive a mailslot message with a `ReadFile` call.

- A write-only client should open the mailslot with `CreateFile` and write messages with `WriteFile`. The open will fail (name not found) if there are no waiting readers.

A client's message can be read by *all* servers; all of them receive the same message.

There is one further possibility. The client, in performing the `CreateFile`, can specify a name of this form:

```
\\*\mailslot\mailslotname
```

In this way, the * acts as a wildcard, and the client can locate every server in the *domain*, a networked group of systems assigned a common name by the network administrator. The client can then connect to one of the servers, assuming that they all provide the same basic functionality, although the server responses could contain information (current load, performance, etc.) that would influence the client's choice.

Using Mailslots

The preceding client/server command processor suggests several ways that mailslots might be useful. Here is one scenario that will solve the server location problem in the preceding client/server system (Programs 11–2 and 11–3).

The *application server*, acting as a *mailslot client*, periodically broadcasts its name and a named pipe name. Any *application client* that wants to find a server can receive this name by being a *mailslot server*. In a similar manner, the command line server can periodically broadcast its status, including information such as utilization, to the clients. This situation could be described as a single writer (the mailslot client) and multiple readers (the mailslot servers). If there were multiple mailslot clients (that is, multiple application servers), there would be a many-to-many situation.

Alternatively, a single reader could receive messages from numerous writers, perhaps giving their status—that is, there would be multiple writers and a single reader. This usage, for example, in a bulletin board application, justifies the term *mailslot*. These first two uses—name and status broadcast—can be combined so that a client can select the most appropriate server.

The inversion of the terms *client* and *server* is confusing in this context, but notice that both named pipe and mailslot servers perform the `CreateNamedPipe` (or `CreateMailSlot`) calls, while the client (named pipe or mailslot) connects using `CreateFile`. Also, in both cases, the client performs the first `WriteFile` and the server performs the first `ReadFile`.

```
HANDLE CreateMailslot (LPCTSTR lpName,
    DWORD cbMaxMsg,
    DWORD dwReadTimeout,
    LPSECURITY_ATTRIBUTES lpsa)
```

Figure 11–3 shows the use of mailslots for the first approach.

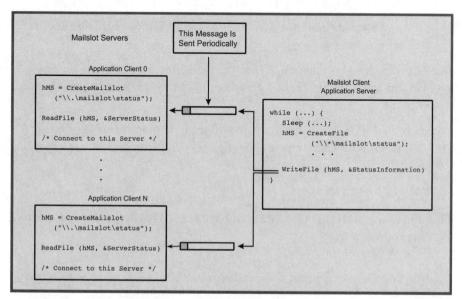

Figure 11–3 Clients Using a Mailslot to Locate a Server

Creating and Opening a Mailslot

The mailslot servers (readers) use `CreateMailslot` to create a mailslot and to get a handle for use with `ReadFile`. There can be only one mailslot of a given name on a specific machine, but several systems in a network can use the same name to take advantage of mailslots in a multireader situation.

Parameters

`lpName` points to a mailslot name of this form:

```
\\.\mailslot\[path]name
```

The name must be unique. The period (.) indicates that the mailslot is created on the current machine. The path, if any, represents a pseudo directory, and path components are separated by backslash characters.

`cbMaxMsg` is the maximum size (in bytes) for messages that a client can write. A value of 0 means no limit.

`dwReadTimeout` is the number of milliseconds that a read operation will wait. A value of 0 causes an immediate return, and `MAILSLOT_WAIT_FOREVER` is an infinite wait (no time-out).

The client (writer), when opening a mailslot with `CreateFile`, can use the following name forms.

\\.\mailslot*[path]name* specifies a local mailslot.

computername\mailslot*[path]name* specifies a mailslot on a specified machine.

domainname\mailslot*[path]name* specifies all mailslots on machines in the domain. In this case, the maximum message length is 424 bytes.

\mailslot[path]name* specifies all mailslots on machines in the domain. In this case, the maximum message length is also 424 bytes.

Finally, the client must specify the `FILE_SHARE_READ` flag.

The functions `GetMailslotInfo` and `SetMailslotInfo` are similar to their named pipe counterparts.

UNIX does not have a facility comparable to mailslots. A broadcast or multicast TCP/IP datagram, however, could be used for this purpose.

Pipe and Mailslot Creation, Connection, and Naming

Table 11–1 summarizes the valid pipe names that can be used by application clients and servers. It also summarizes the functions to create and connect with named pipes.

Table 11–2 gives similar information for mailslots. Recall that the mailslot client (or server) may not be the same process or even on the same computer as the application client (or server).

Table 11–1   Named Pipes: Creating, Connecting, and Naming

	Application Client	Application Server
Named Pipe Handle or Connection	`CreateFile`	`CreateNamedPipe`
	`CallNamedPipe`, `TransactNamedPipe`	
Pipe Name	`\\.\`*pipename* (pipe is local)	`\\.\`*pipename* (pipe is created locally)
	`\\`*sys_name*`\`*pipename* (pipe is local or remote)	

Table 11–2   Mailslots: Creating, Connecting, and Naming

	Mailslot Client	Mailslot Server
Mailslot Handle	`CreateFile`	`CreateMailslot`
Mailslot Name	`\\.\`*msname* (mailslot is local)	`\\.\`*msname* (mailslot is created locally)
	`\\`*sys_name*`\`*mailslot*`\`*msname* (mailslot is on a specific remote system) `\\`*domain_name*`\`*mailslot*`\`*msname* (all domain mailslots with this name)	
	`\\*\`*mailslot*`\`*msname* (all mailslots with this name)	

Example: A Server That Clients Can Locate

Program 11–4 shows the thread function that the command line server (Program 11–3), *acting as a mailslot client*, uses to broadcast its pipe name to waiting clients. There can be multiple servers with different characteristics and pipe names, and the clients obtain their names from the well-known mailslot name. Program 11–3 starts this function as a thread.

Note: In practice, many client/server systems invert the location logic used here. The alternative is to have the application client also act as the mailslot client and broadcast a message requesting a server to respond on a specified named pipe; the client determines the pipe name and includes that name in the message. The application server, acting as a mailslot server, then reads the request and creates a connection on the specified named pipe.

Program 11–4's inverted logic solution has advantages, although it consumes a mailslot name:

- The latency time to discover a server decreases because there is no need to wait for a server to broadcast its name.

- Network bandwidth and CPU cycles are used only as required when a client needs to discover a server.

Program 11–4   SrvrBcst: Mailslot Client Thread Function

```
int _tmain (int argc, LPTSTR argv[])
{
    BOOL exit;
    MS_MESSAGE mailSlotNotify;
    DWORD nXfer;
    HANDLE hMailSlot;

    /* Open the mailslot for the MS "client" writer. */
    while (TRUE) {
        exit = FALSE;
        while (!exit) { /* Wait for a client to create a MS. */
            hMailSlot = CreateFile (MS_CLTNAME,
                GENERIC_WRITE | GENERIC_READ,
                    FILE_SHARE_READ | FILE_SHARE_WRITE,
                    NULL, OPEN_EXISTING, FILE_ATTRIBUTE_NORMAL, NULL);
            if (hMailSlot == INVALID_HANDLE_VALUE) {
                Sleep (5000);
            }
            else exit = TRUE;
        }
```

```
    /* Send out the message to the mailslot. */
    /* Avoid an "information discovery" security exposure. */
    ZeroMemory(&mailSlotNotify, sizeof(mailSlotNotify));
    mailSlotNotify.msStatus = 0;
    mailSlotNotify.msUtilization = 0;

    _tcscpy (mailSlotNotify.msName, SERVER_PIPE);
    WriteFile (hMailSlot, &mailSlotNotify, MSM_SIZE, &nXfer, NULL);
    CloseHandle (hMailSlot);

    /* Wait for another client to open a mailslot. */
  }

  /* Not reachable. */
  return(0);
}
```

Program 11–5 shows the LocSrver function called by the client (see Program 11–2) so that it can locate the server.

Program 11–5   LocSrver: Mailslot Server

```
/* Chapter 11. LocSrver.c */
/* Find a server by reading the mailslot
   used to broadcast server names. */

#include "Everything.h"
#include "ClientServer.h" /* Defines mailslot name. */

BOOL LocateServer (LPTSTR pPipeName, DWORD size)
{
    HANDLE hMailSlot;
    MS_MESSAGE serverMsg;
    BOOL found = FALSE;
    DWORD cbRead;

    hMailSlot = CreateMailslot (MS_SRVNAME, 0, CS_TIMEOUT, NULL);
        if (hMailSlot == INVALID_HANDLE_VALUE)
            ReportError (_T ("MS create error."), 11, TRUE);

    /* Communicate with the server to be certain that it is running.
     * Server must have time to find the mailslot & send pipe name. */

    while (!found) {
        _tprintf (_T ("Looking for a server.\n"));
        found = ReadFile (hMailSlot, &serverMsg,
                sizeof(serverMsg), &cbRead, NULL);
    }
```

```
    _tprintf (_T ("Server has been located.\n"));

    /* Close the mailslot. */
    CloseHandle (hMailSlot);
    if (found) _tcsncpy (pPipeName, serverMsg.msName, size-1);
    return found;
}
```

Summary

Windows pipes and mailslots, which are accessed with file I/O operations, provide stream-oriented interprocess and networked communication. The examples show how to pipe data from one process to another and a simple, multithreaded client/ server system. Pipes also provide another thread synchronization method because a reading thread blocks until another thread writes to the pipe.

Looking Ahead

Chapter 12 shows how to use industry-standard, rather than Windows propri- etary, interprocess and networking communication. The same client/server sys- tem, with some server enhancements, will be rewritten to use the standard methods.

Exercises

11–1. Carry out experiments to determine the accuracy of the performance advantages cited for `TransactNamedPipe`. You will need to make some changes to the server code as given. Also compare the results with the current implementation.

11–2. Use the `JobShell` program from Chapter 6 to start the server and several clients, where each client is created using the "detached" option. Eventually, shut down the server by sending a console control event through the `kill` command. Can you suggest any improvements to the `serverNP` shutdown logic so that a connected server thread can test the shutdown flag while blocked waiting for a client request? *Hint:* Create a read thread similar to the connection thread.

11–3. Enhance the server so that the name of its named pipe is an argument on the command line. Bring up multiple server processes with different pipe names using the job management programs in Chapter 6. Verify that multiple clients simultaneously access this multiprocess server system.

11–4. Run the client and server on different systems to confirm correct network operation. Modify SrvrBcst (Program 11–4) so that it includes the server machine name in the named pipe. Also, modify the mailslot name, currently hard-coded in Program 11–4, so that the name is taken from the mailslot response from the application server.

11–5. Modify the server so that you measure the server's utilization. (In other words, what percentage of elapsed time is spent in the server?) Maintain performance information and report this information to the client on request. Consider using the Request.Command field to hold the information.

11–6. Enhance the server location programs so that the client will find the server with the lowest utilization rate.

11–7. serverNP is designed to run indefinitely as a server, allowing clients to connect, obtain services, and disconnect. When a client disconnects, it is important for the server to free *all* associated resources, such as memory, file handles, and thread handles. Any remaining resource leaks will ultimately exhaust computer resources, causing the server to fail, and before failure there will probably be significant performance degradation. Carefully examine serverNP to ensure that there are no resource leaks, and, if you find any, fix them. (Also, please inform the author using the e-mail address in the preface.) *Note:* Resource leaks are a common and serious defect in many production systems. No "industry-strength" quality assurance effort is complete if it has not addressed this issue.

11–8. *Extended exercise:* Synchronization objects can synchronize threads in different processes on the same machine, but they cannot synchronize threads running in processes on different machines. Use named pipes and mailslots to create emulated mutexes, events, and semaphores to overcome this limitation.

CHAPTER

12 | Network Programming with Windows Sockets

Named pipes and mailslots are suitable for interprocess communication between processes on the same computer or processes on Windows computers connected by a local or wide area network. The client/server application system developed in Chapter 11, starting with Program 11–2, demonstrated these capabilities.

Named pipes and mailslots (both simply referred to here as "named pipes" unless the distinction is important) have the distinct drawback, however, of not being an industry standard. Therefore, programs such as those in Chapter 11 will not port easily to non-Windows machines, nor will they interoperate with non-Windows machines. This is the case even though named pipes are protocol-independent and can run over industry-standard protocols such as TCP/IP.

Windows provides interoperability by supporting Windows Sockets, which are nearly the same as, and interoperable with, Berkeley Sockets, a de facto industry standard. This chapter shows how to use the Windows Sockets (or "Winsock") API by modifying Chapter 11's client/server system. The resulting system can operate over TCP/IP-based wide area networks, and the server, for instance, can accept requests from UNIX, Linux, and other non-Windows clients.

Readers who are familiar with Berkeley Sockets may want to proceed directly to the programming examples, which not only use sockets but also show new server features and additional thread-safe library techniques.

Winsock, by enabling standards-based interoperability, allows programmers to exploit higher-level protocols and applications, such as ftp, http, RPCs, and COM, all of which provide different, and higher-level, models for standard, interoperable, networked interprocess communication.

In this chapter, the client/server system is a vehicle for demonstrating Winsock, and, in the course of modifying the server, interesting new features are added. In particular, *DLL entry points* (Chapter 5) and *in-process DLL servers* are used for the first time. (These new features could have been incorporated in the initial Chapter 11 version, but doing so would have distracted from the development and understanding of the basic system architecture.) Finally, additional examples show how to create reentrant thread-safe libraries.

Winsock, because of conformance to industry standards, has naming conventions and programming characteristics somewhat different from the Windows functions described so far. The Winsock API is not strictly a part of the Windows API. Winsock also provides additional functions that are not part of the standard; these functions are used only as absolutely required. Among other advantages, programs will be more portable to other operating systems.

Windows Sockets

The Winsock API was developed as an extension of the Berkeley Sockets API into the Windows environment, and all Windows versions support Winsock. Winsock's benefits include the following.

- Porting code already written for Berkeley Sockets is straightforward.

- Windows machines easily integrate into TCP/IP networks, both IPv4 and IPv6. IPv6, among other features, allows for longer IP addresses, overcoming the 4-byte address limit of IPv4.

- Sockets can be used with Windows overlapped I/O (Chapter 14), which, among other things, allows servers to scale when there is a large number of active clients.

- Sockets can be treated as file `HANDLE`s for use with `ReadFile`, `WriteFile`, and, with some limitations, other Windows functions, just as UNIX allows sockets to be used as file descriptors. This capability is convenient whenever there is a need to use asynchronous I/O and I/O completion ports (Chapter 14).

- Windows provides nonportable extensions.

- Sockets can support protocols other than TCP/IP, but this chapter assumes TCP/IP. See MSDN if you use some other protocol, particularly Asynchronous Transfer Mode (ATM).

Winsock Initialization

The Winsock API is supported by a DLL (`WS2_32.DLL`) that can be accessed by linking `WS2_32.LIB` with your program (these names do not change on 64-bit machines). The DLL needs to be initialized with a nonstandard, Winsock-specific function, `WSAStartup`, which must be the first Winsock function a program calls. `WSACleanup` should be called when the program no longer needs to use Winsock functionality. *Note:* The prefix `WSA` denotes "Windows Sockets asynchronous. . . ." The asynchronous capabilities will not be used here because we'll use threads for asynchronous operation.

`WSAStartup` and `WSACleanup`, while always required, may be the only nonstandard functions you will use. A common practice is to use `#ifdef` statements to test the `WIN32` macro (normally defined from Visual Studio) so that the `WSA` functions are called only if you are building on Windows. This approach assumes, of course, that the rest of your code is platform-independent.

```
int WSAStartup (
    WORD wVersionRequired,
    LPWSADATA lpWSAData);
```

Parameters

`wVersionRequired` indicates the highest version of the Winsock DLL that you need and can use. Nonetheless, Version 2.x is available on all current Windows versions, and the examples use 2.0.

The return value is nonzero if the DLL cannot support the version you want.

The low byte of `wVersionRequired` specifies the major version, and the high byte specifies the minor version, which is the opposite of what you might expect. The `MAKEWORD` macro is usually used; thus, `MAKEWORD (2, 0)` represents Version 2.0.

`lpWSAData` points to a `WSADATA` structure that returns information on the configuration of the DLL, including the highest version available. The Visual Studio on-line help shows how to interpret the results.

`WSAGetLastError` can be used to get the error; `GetLastError` also works but is not entirely reliable. The *Examples* file socket programs use `WSAReportError`, a `ReportError` variation that uses `WSAGetLastError`.

When a program has completed or no longer needs to use sockets, it should call `WSACleanup` so that `WS2_32.DLL`, the sockets DLL, can free resources allocated for this process.

Creating a Socket

Once the Winsock DLL is initialized, you can use the standard (i.e., Berkeley Sockets) functions to create sockets and connect for client/server or peer-to-peer communication.

A Winsock `SOCKET` data type is analogous to the Windows `HANDLE` and can even be used with `ReadFile` and other Windows functions requiring a `HANDLE`. Call the `socket` function in order to create (or open) a `SOCKET` and return its value.

```
SOCKET socket (int af, int type, int protocol);
```

Parameters

The type `SOCKET` is actually defined as an `int`, so UNIX code will port without the necessity of using the Windows type definitions.

`af` denotes the address family, or protocol; use `PF_INET` (or `AF_INET`, which has the same value but is more properly used with the `bind` call) to designate IP (the Internet protocol component of TCP/IP).

`type` specifies connection-oriented (`SOCK_STREAM`) or datagram communications (`SOCK_DGRAM`), slightly analogous to named pipes and mailslots, respectively.

`protocol` is unnecessary when `af` is `AF_INET`; use 0.

`socket` returns `INVALID_SOCKET` on failure.

You can use Winsock with protocols other than TCP/IP by specifying different protocol values; we will use only TCP/IP.

`socket`, like all the other standard functions, does not use uppercase letters in the function name. This is a departure from the Windows convention and is due to the need to conform to industry standards.

Socket Server Functions

In this discussion, a *server* is a process that accepts connections on a specified port. While sockets, like named pipes, can be used for peer-to-peer communication, this distinction is convenient and reflects the manner in which two machines connect to one another.

Unless specifically mentioned, the socket type will always be `SOCK_STREAM` in the examples. `SOCK_DGRAM` is described later in this chapter.

Binding a Socket

A server should first create a socket (using `socket`) and then "bind" the socket to its address and *endpoint* (the communication path from the application to a service). The `socket` call, followed by the `bind`, is analogous to creating a named pipe. There is, however, no name to distinguish sockets on a given machine. A *port number* is used instead as the service endpoint. A given server can have multiple endpoints. The `bind` function is shown here.

```
int bind (
    SOCKET s,
    const struct sockaddr *saddr,
    int namelen);
```

Parameters

`s` is an unbound `SOCKET` returned by `socket`.

`saddr`, filled in before the call, specifies the protocol and protocol-specific information, as described next. The port number is part of this structure.

`namelen` is `sizeof(sockaddr)`.

The return value is normally 0 or `SOCKET_ERROR` in case of error. The `sockaddr` structure is defined as follows.

```
struct sockaddr {
    u_short sa_family;
    char sa_data [14];
    };
typedef struct sockaddr SOCKADDR, *PSOCKADDR;
```

The first member, `sa_family`, is the protocol. The second member, `sa_data`, is protocol-specific. The Internet version of `sockaddr` is `sockaddr_in`, and we use `sockaddr_in` in the examples.

```
struct sockaddr_in {
    short sin_family; /* AF_INET */
    u_short sin_port;
    struct in_addr sin_addr; /* 4-byte IP addr */
    char sin_zero [8];
    };

typedef struct sockaddr_in SOCKADDR_IN,
    *PSOCKADDR_IN;
```

Note the use of a short integer for the port number. The port number and other information must also be in the proper byte order, big-endian, so as to allow interoperability. The `sin_addr` member has a submember, `s_addr`, which is filled in with the familiar 4-byte IP address, such as `127.0.0.1`, to indicate the machine from which connections will be accepted. Normally, applications accept connections from any machine, so the value `INADDR_ANY` is common, although this symbolic value must be converted to the correct form, as in the next code fragment.

Use the `inet_addr` function to convert a known IP address text string (use `char` characters, not Unicode) into the required form so that you can initialize the `sin_addr.s_addr` member of a `sockaddr_in` variable, as follows:

```
sa.sin_addr.s_addr = inet_addr ("192.13.12.1");
```

A bound socket, with a protocol, port number, and IP address, is sometimes said to be a *named socket*.

Putting a Bound Socket into the Listening State

`listen` makes a server socket available for client connection. There is no analogous named pipe function.

```
int listen (SOCKET s, int nQueueSize);
```

nQueueSize indicates the number of connection requests you are willing to have queued at the socket. There is no upper bound in Winsock Version 2.0.

Accepting a Client Connection

Finally, a server can wait for a client to connect, using the `accept` function, which returns a new connected socket for use in the I/O operations. Notice that the original socket, now in the listening state, is used solely as an `accept` parameter and is not used directly for I/O.

`accept` blocks until a client connection request arrives, and then it returns the new I/O socket. It is possible to make a socket be nonblocking (see MSDN), but the server (Program 12–2) uses a separate accepting thread so that the server does not block. Call `accept` after the socket is placed in the listening state with calls to `bind` and `listen`.

```
SOCKET accept (
    SOCKET s,
    LPSOCKADDR lpAddr,
    LPINT lpAddrLen);
```

Parameters

s, the first argument, is the listening socket.

lpAddr points to a `sockaddr_in` structure that gives the address of the client machine.

lpAddrLen points to a variable that will receive the length of the returned `sockaddr_in` structure. Initialize this variable to `sizeof(struct sockaddr_in)` before the `accept` call.

Disconnecting and Closing Sockets

Disconnect a socket using

```
shutdown (s, how)
```

where s is the value returned by `accept`. The how value indicates if you want to disconnect send operations (`SD_SEND`), receive operations (`SD_RECEIVE`), or both (`SD_BOTH`). The effects of shutting down sending and/or receiving are:

- `SD_SEND` or `SD_BOTH` — Subsequent `send` calls will fail and the sender will send a `FIN` (no more data from the sender). You cannot re-enable sending on the socket.

- `SD_RECEIVE` or `SD_BOTH` — Subsequent `recv` calls will fail and the sender will send a FIN (no more data from the sender). Any queued data or data that arrives later is lost. There is no way to re-enable receiving on the socket.

`shutdown` does not close the socket or free its resources, but it does assure that all data is sent or received before the socket is closed. Nonetheless, an application should not reuse a socket after calling `shutdown`.

If you shut down a socket for sending only, you can still receive, so if there is possibility of more data, call `recv` until it returns 0 bytes. Once there is no more data, shut down receiving. If there is a socket error, then a clean disconnect is impossible.

Likewise, if you shut down a socket for receiving only, you can still send remaining data. For example, a server might stop receiving requests while it still has response or other data to transmit before shutting down sending.

Once you are finished with a socket, you can close it with

```
closesocket (SOCKET s)
```

The server first closes the socket created by `accept`, not the listening `socket`. The server should not close the listening socket until the server shuts down or will no longer accept client connections. Even if you are treating a socket as a `HANDLE` and using `ReadFile` and `WriteFile`, `CloseHandle` alone will not destroy the socket; use `closesocket`.

Example: Preparing for and Accepting a Client Connection

The following code fragment shows how to create a socket and then accept client connections. This example uses two standard functions, `htons` ("host to network short") and `htonl` ("host to network long"), that convert integers to big-endian form, as IP requires.[1]

The server port can be any unassigned short integer. Well-known ports (0–1023) and registered ports (1024–49151, with some exceptions) should not be used for your server. Select a port from the an unassigned range such as 48557–48618, 48620–49150, or 49152 and above. However, check www.iana.org/assignments/port-numbers to be certain that your port number is currently unassigned. You may also find that the port you select is in use by some other process on your computer, so you'll need to make another selection. The examples use `SERVER_PORT`, defined in `ClientServer.h` as `50000`.

---

[1] Windows supports little-endian, and `htons` and `htonl` perform the required conversion. The functions are implemented on non-Windows machines to behave as required by the machine architecture.

```
struct sockaddr_in srvSAddr; /* Server address struct. */
struct sockaddr_in connectAddr;
SOCKET srvSock, sockio;
DWORD addrLen;
...
srvSock = socket (AF_INET, SOCK_STREAM, 0);
srvSAddr.sin_family = AF_INET;
srvSAddr.sin_addr.s_addr = htonl (INADDR_ANY);
srvSAddr.sin_port = htons (SERVER_PORT);
bind (srvSock, (struct sockaddr *) &srvSAddr,
      sizeof srvSAddr);
listen (srvSock, 5);
addrLen = sizeof (connectAddr);
sockio = accept (srvSock,
      (struct sockaddr *) &connectAddr, &addrLen);
... Receive requests and send responses ...
/* Requests and Responses complete. Shutdown socket */
shutdown (sockio, SD_BOTH);
closesocket (sockio);
```

Socket Client Functions

A client station wishing to connect to a server must also create a socket with the socket function. The next step is to connect with a server, specifying a port, host address, and other information. There is just one additional function, connect.

Connecting to a Server

If there is a server with a listening socket, the client can connect with the connect function.

```
int connect (
    SOCKET s,
    LPSOCKADDR lpName,
    int nNameLen);
```

Parameters

s is a socket created with the socket function.

lpName points to a sockaddr_in structure that has been initialized with the port number and IP address of a machine with a socket, bound to the specified port, that is in listening mode.

Initialize nNameLen with sizeof (struct sockaddr_in).

A return value of 0 indicates a successful connection, whereas SOCKET_ERROR indicates failure, possibly because there is no listening socket at the specified address.

Example: Client Connecting to a Server

The following code sequence allows a client to connect to a server. Just two function calls are required, but be certain to initialize the address structure before the connect call. Error testing is omitted here but should be included in actual programs. In the example, assume that the IP address (a text string such as 192.76.33.4) is given in argv [1] on the command line.

```
SOCKET clientSock;
...
clientSock = socket (AF_INET, SOCK_STREAM, 0);
memset (&clientSAddr, 0, sizeof (clientSAddr));
clientSAddr.sin_family = AF_INET;
clientSAddr.sin_addr.s_addr = inet_addr (argv [1]);
clientSAddr.sin_port = htons (SERVER_PORT);
conVal = connect (clientSock,
        (struct sockaddr *) &clientSAddr,
        sizeof (clientSAddr));
```

Sending and Receiving Data

Socket programs exchange data using send and recv, which have nearly identical argument forms (the send buffer has the const modifier). Only send is shown here.

```
int send (
    SOCKET s,
    const char * lpBuffer,
    int nBufferLen,
    int nFlags);
```

The return value is the actual number of bytes transmitted. An error is indicated by the return value SOCKET_ERROR.

nFlags can be used to indicate urgency (such as out-of-band data), and the MSG_PEEK flag can be used to look at incoming data without reading it.

The most important fact to remember is that send and recv *are not atomic,* and there is no assurance that all the requested data has been received or sent. "Short sends" are extremely rare but possible, as are "short receives." There is no concept of a message as with named pipes; therefore, you need to test the return value and resend or transmit until all data has been transmitted.

You can also use ReadFile and WriteFile with sockets by casting the socket to a HANDLE in the function call.

Comparing Named Pipes and Sockets

Named pipes, described in Chapter 11, are very similar to sockets, but there are significant usage differences.

- Named pipes can be message-oriented, which can simplify programs.

- Named pipes require ReadFile and WriteFile, whereas sockets can also use send and recv.

- Sockets, unlike named pipes, are flexible so that a user can select the protocol to use with a socket, such as TCP or UDP. The user can also select protocols based on quality of service and other factors.

- Sockets are based on an industry standard, allowing interoperability with non-Windows machines.

There are also differences in the server and client programming models.

Comparing Named Pipe and Socket Servers

When using sockets, call accept repetitively to connect to multiple clients. Each call will return a different connected socket. Note the following differences relative to named pipes.

- Named pipes require you to create each named pipe instance with Create-NamedPipe. accept creates the socket instances.

- There is no upper bound on the number of socket clients (listen limits only the number of queued clients), but there can be a limit on the number of named pipe instances, depending on the first call to CreateNamedPipe.

- There are no socket convenience functions comparable to TransactNamedPipe.

- Named pipes do not have explicit port numbers and are distinguished by name.

A named pipe server requires two function calls (`CreateNamedPipe` and `ConnectNamedPipe`) to obtain a usable `HANDLE`, whereas socket servers require four function calls (`socket`, `bind`, `listen`, and `accept`).

Comparing Named Pipes and Socket Clients

Named pipes use `WaitNamedPipe` followed by `CreateFile`. The socket sequence is in the opposite order because the `socket` function can be regarded as the creation function, while `connect` is the blocking function.

An additional distinction is that `connect` is a socket client function, while the similarly named `ConnectNamedPipe` is a server function.

Example: A Socket Message Receive Function

It is frequently convenient to send and receive messages as a single unit. Named pipes can do this, as shown in Chapter 11. Sockets, however, require that you provide a mechanism to specify and determine message boundaries. One common method is to create a message header with a length field, followed by the message itself, and we'll use message headers in the following examples. Later examples use a different technique, end-of-string null characters, to mark message boundaries. Fixed-length messages provide yet another solution.

The following function, `ReceiveMessage`, receives message length headers and message bodies. The `SendMessage` function is similar.

Notice that the message is received in two parts: the header and the contents. The user-defined `MESSAGE` type with a 4-byte message length header is:

```
typedef struct {
   LONG32 msgLen;/* Message length, excluding this field */
   BYTE record [MAX_MSG_LEN];
} MESSAGE;
```

Even the 4-byte header requires repetitive `recv` calls to ensure that it is read in its entirety because `recv` is not atomic.

Note: The message length variables are fixed-precision `LONG32` type to remind readers that the length, which is included in messages that may be transferred to and from programs written in other languages (such as Java) or running on other machines, where long integers may be 64 bits, will have a well-defined, unambiguous length.

```
DWORD ReceiveMessage (MESSAGE *pMsg, SOCKET sd)
{
   /* A message has a 4-byte length field, followed
      by the message contents. */
   DWORD disconnect = 0;
   LONG32 nRemainRecv, nXfer;
   LPBYTE pBuffer;
   /* Read message. */
   /* First the length header, then contents. */
   nRemainRecv = 4; /* Header field length. */
   pBuffer = (LPBYTE) pMsg; /* recv may not */
   /* Receive the header. */
   while (nRemainRecv > 0 && !disconnect) {
      nXfer = recv (sd, pBuffer, nRemainRecv, 0);
      disconnect = (nXfer == 0);
      nRemainRecv -=nXfer; pBuffer += nXfer;
   }
   /* Read the message contents. */
   nRemainRecv = pMsg->msgLen;
   /* Exclude buffer overflow */
   nRemainRecv = min(nRemainRecv, MAX_RQRS_LEN);
   while (nRemainRecv > 0 && !disconnect) {
      nXfer = recv (sd, pBuffer, nRemainRecv, 0);
      disconnect = (nXfer == 0);
      nRemainRecv -=nXfer; pBuffer += nXfer;
   }
   return disconnect;
}
```

Example: A Socket-Based Client

Program 12–1 reimplements the client program, which in named pipe form is
Program 11–2, clientNP. The conversion is straightforward, with several small
differences.

- Rather than locating a server using mailslots, the user enters the IP address
  on the command line. If the IP address is not specified, the default address is
  127.0.0.1, which indicates the current machine.

- Functions for sending and receiving messages, such as ReceiveMessage, are
  used but are not shown here.

- The port number, SERVER_PORT, is defined in the header file, Client-Server.h.

While the code is written for Windows, there are no Windows dependencies other than the WSA calls.

Comment: The programs in this chapter do not use generic characters. This is a simplification driven by the fact that inet_addr does not accept Unicode strings.

Program 12–1 clientSK: Socket-Based Client

```
/* Chapter 12. clientSK.c */
/* Single-threaded command line client. */
/* WINDOWS SOCKETS VERSION. */
/* Reads a sequence of commands to send to a server process */
/* over a socket connection. Wait for and display response. */

#include "Everything.h"
#include "ClientServer.h"/* Defines request and response records. */

static BOOL SendRequestMessage (REQUEST *, SOCKET);
static BOOL ReceiveResponseMessage (RESPONSE *, SOCKET);

struct sockaddr_in clientSAddr;/* Client Socket address structure */

int main (int argc, LPSTR argv[])
{
    SOCKET clientSock = INVALID_SOCKET;
    REQUEST request;/* See clntcrvr.h */
    RESPONSE response;/* See clntcrvr.h */
    WSADATA WSStartData;   /* Socket library data structure   */
    BOOL quit = FALSE;
    DWORD conVal;

    /* Initialize the WS library. Ver 2.0 */
    WSAStartup (MAKEWORD (2, 0), &WSStartData);
    /* Connect to the server */
    /* Follow the standard client socket/connect sequence */
    clientSock = socket(AF_INET, SOCK_STREAM, 0);
    memset (&clientSAddr, 0, sizeof(clientSAddr));
    clientSAddr.sin_family = AF_INET;
    if (argc >= 2)
        clientSAddr.sin_addr.s_addr = inet_addr (argv[1]);
    else
        clientSAddr.sin_addr.s_addr = inet_addr ("127.0.0.1");

    clientSAddr.sin_port = htons(SERVER_PORT);
    conVal = connect (clientSock, (struct sockaddr *)&clientSAddr,
                   sizeof(clientSAddr));
```

```
    /*  Main loop to prompt user, send request, receive response */
    while (!quit) {
        _tprintf (_T("%s"), _T("\nEnter Command: "));
        fgets (request.record, MAX_RQRS_LEN, stdin);
        /* Get rid of the new line at the end */
        request.record[strlen(request.record)-1] = '\0';
        if (strcmp (request.record, "$Quit") == 0) quit = TRUE;
        SendRequestMessage (&request, clientSock);
        if (!quit) ReceiveResponseMessage (&response, clientSock);
    }

    shutdown (clientSock, SD_BOTH); /* Disallow sends and receives */
    closesocket (clientSock);
    WSACleanup();
    _tprintf (_T("\n****Leaving client\n"));
    return 0;
}
```

Running the Socket Client

The socket server is complex with long program listings. Therefore, Run 12–1 shows the client in operation, assuming that there is a running server. The commands are familiar, and operation is very similar to Chapter 11's named pipe client.

Run 12–1 clientSK: Socket Client Operation

Example: A Socket-Based Server with New Features

serverSK, Program 12–2, is similar to serverNP, Program 11–3, but there are several changes and improvements.

- Rather than creating a fixed-size thread pool, we now create *server threads on demand*. Every time the server accepts a client connection, it creates a server worker thread, and the thread terminates when the client quits.

- The server creates a separate *accept thread* so that the main thread can poll the global shutdown flag while the accept call is blocked. While it is possible to specify nonblocking sockets, threads provide a convenient and uniform solution. It's worth noting that a lot of the extended Winsock functionality is designed to support asynchronous operation, and Windows threads allow you to use the much simpler and more standard synchronous socket functionality.

- The thread management is improved, at the cost of some complexity, so that the state of each thread is maintained.

- This server also supports *in-process servers* by loading a DLL during initialization. The DLL name is a command line option, and the server thread first tries to locate an entry point in the DLL. If successful, the server thread calls the DLL entry point; otherwise, the server creates a process, as in serverNP. A sample DLL is shown in Program 12–4. The DLL needs to be trusted, however, because any unhandled exception could crash or corrupt the server, as would changes to the environment.

In-process servers could have been included in serverNP if desired. The biggest advantage of in-process servers is that no context switch to a different process is required, potentially improving performance. The disadvantage is that the DLL runs in the server process and could corrupt the server, as described in the last bullet. Therefore, use only trusted DLLs.

The server code is Windows-specific, unlike the client, due to thread management and other Windows dependencies.

The Main Program

Program 12–2 shows the main program and the thread to accept client connections. It also includes some global declarations and definitions, including an enumerated type, SERVER_THREAD_STATE, used by each individual server thread.

Program 12–3 shows the server thread function; there is one instance for each connected client. The server state can change in both the main program and the server thread.

The server state logic involves both the boss and server threads. Exercise 12–6 suggests an alternative approach where the boss is not involved.

Program 12–2 `serverSK`: Socket-Based Server with In-Process Servers

```
/* Chapter 12. Client/server. SERVER PROGRAM. SOCKET VERSION. */
/* Execute the command in the request and return a response. */
/* Commands will be executed in process if a shared library */
/* entry point can be located, and out of process otherwise. */
/* ADDITIONAL FEATURE: argv [1] can be name of a DLL supporting */
/* in-process servers. */

#include "Everything.h"
#include "ClientServer.h"/* Defines the request and response records.
*/

struct sockaddr_in srvSAddr;/* Server's Socket address structure */
struct sockaddr_in connectSAddr;/* Connected socket */
WSADATA WSStartData;        /* Socket library data structure   */

enum SERVER_THREAD_STATE {SERVER_SLOT_FREE, SERVER_THREAD_STOPPED,
                    SERVER_THREAD_RUNNING, SERVER_SLOT_INVALID};

typedef struct SERVER_ARG_TAG { /* Server thread arguments */
    CRITICAL_SECTION threadCs;
    DWORDnumber;
    SOCKET sock;
    enum SERVER_THREAD_STATE thState;
    HANDLE hSrvThread;
    HINSTANCE hDll; /* Shared library handle */
} SERVER_ARG;

static BOOL ReceiveRequestMessage (REQUEST *pRequest, SOCKET);
static BOOL SendResponseMessage (RESPONSE *pResponse, SOCKET);
static DWORD WINAPI Server (PVOID);
static DWORD WINAPI AcceptThread (PVOID);
static BOOL  WINAPI Handler (DWORD);

volatile static int shutFlag = 0;
static SOCKET SrvSock = INVALID_SOCKET, connectSock = INVALID_SOCKET;

int main (int argc, LPCTSTR argv [])
{
    /* Server listening and connected sockets. */
    DWORD iThread, tStatus;
    SERVER_ARG sArgs[MAX_CLIENTS];
    HANDLE hAcceptThread = NULL;
    HINSTANCE hDll = NULL;
```

```c
/* Console control handler to permit server shutdown */
SetConsoleCtrlHandler (Handler, TRUE);

/* Initialize the WS library. Ver 2.0 */
WSAStartup (MAKEWORD (2, 0), &WSStartData);

/* Open command library DLL if it is specified on command line */
if (argc > 1) hDll = LoadLibrary (argv[1]);

/* Initialize thread arg array */
for (iThread = 0; iThread < MAX_CLIENTS; iThread++) {
    InitializeCriticalSection (&sArgs[iThread].threadCs);
    sArgs[iThread].number = iThread;
    sArgs[iThread].thState = SERVER_SLOT_FREE;
    sArgs[iThread].sock = 0;
    sArgs[iThread].hDll = hDll;
    sArgs[iThread].hSrvThread = NULL;
}
/* Follow standard server socket/bind/listen/accept sequence */
SrvSock = socket(PF_INET, SOCK_STREAM, 0);

/* Prepare the socket address structure for binding the
    server socket to port number "reserved" for this service.
    Accept requests from any client machine.  */

srvSAddr.sin_family = AF_INET;
srvSAddr.sin_addr.s_addr = htonl(INADDR_ANY);
srvSAddr.sin_port = htons(SERVER_PORT);
bind (SrvSock, (struct sockaddr *)&srvSAddr, sizeof(srvSAddr));
listen (SrvSock, MAX_CLIENTS);

/* Main thread becomes listening/connecting/monitoring thread */
/* Find an empty slot in the server thread arg array */
while (!shutFlag) {
    iThread = 0;
    while (!shutFlag) {
        /* Continuously poll thread State of all server slots */
        EnterCriticalSection(&sArgs[iThread].threadCs);
        __try {
            if (sArgs[iThread].thState ==
                SERVER_THREAD_STOPPED) {
                /* stopped, either normally or a shutdown request */
                /* Wait for it to stop, and free the slot */
                WaitForSingleObject(sArgs[iThread].hSrvThread,
                            INFINITE);
                CloseHandle (sArgs[iThread].hSrvThread);
                sArgs[iThread].hSrvThread = NULL;
                sArgs[iThread].thState = SERVER_SLOT_FREE;
            }
            /* Free slot or shut down. Use slot for new connection */
```

```
            if (sArgs[iThread].thState == SERVER_SLOT_FREE
                 ||shutFlag) break;
        }
        __finally {
            LeaveCriticalSection(&sArgs[iThread].threadCs);
        }

        iThread = (iThread++) % MAX_CLIENTS;
        if (iThread == 0) Sleep(50); /* Break the polling loop */
        /* An alternative: use an event to signal a free slot */
    }
    if (shutFlag) break;
    /* sArgs[iThread] == SERVER_SLOT_FREE */
    /* Wait for a connection on this socket */
    /* Use a separate accept thread to poll the shutFlag flag */
    hAcceptThread = (HANDLE)_beginthreadex (NULL, 0, AcceptThread,
                    &sArgs[iThread], 0, NULL);
    while (!shutFlag) {
        tStatus = WaitForSingleObject (hAcceptThread, CS_TIMEOUT);
        if (tStatus == WAIT_OBJECT_0) {
            /* sArgs[iThread] == SERVER_THREAD_RUNNING */
            if (!shutFlag) {
                CloseHandle (hAcceptThread);
                hAcceptThread = NULL;
            }
            break;
        }
    }
}   /* OUTER while (!shutFlag) */

/* shutFlag == TRUE */
_tprintf(_T("Shutdown in process. Wait for server threads\n"));
/* Wait for any active server threads to terminate */
/* Try continuously as some threads may be long running. */

while (TRUE) {
    int nRunningThreads = 0;
    for (iThread = 0; iThread < MAX_CLIENTS; iThread++) {
        EnterCriticalSection(&sArgs[iThread].threadCs);
        __try {
            if (
                sArgs[iThread].thState == SERVER_THREAD_RUNNING ||
                sArgs[iThread].thState == SERVER_THREAD_STOPPED) {
                    if (WaitForSingleObject
                        (sArgs[iThread].hSrvThread, 10000) ==
                                WAIT_OBJECT_0) {
                    CloseHandle (sArgs[iThread].hSrvThread);
                    sArgs[iThread].hSrvThread = NULL;
                    sArgs[iThread].thState = SERVER_SLOT_INVALID;
                } else
```

```
                        if (WaitForSingleObject
                            (sArgs[iThread].hSrvThread, 10000) ==
                                    WAIT_TIMEOUT) {
                            nRunningThreads++;
                        } else {
                            _tprintf(_T("Error waiting: slot %d\n"), iThread);
                        }

                    }
                }
                __finally { LeaveCriticalSection(&sArgs[iThread].threadCs);}
            }
        if (nRunningThreads == 0) break;
    }

    if (hDll != NULL) FreeLibrary (hDll);

    /* Redundant shutdown */
    shutdown (SrvSock, SD_BOTH);
    closesocket (SrvSock);
    WSACleanup();
    if (hAcceptThread != NULL)
        WaitForSingleObject(hAcceptThread, INFINITE));
    return 0;
}

static DWORD WINAPI AcceptThread (PVOID pArg)
{
    LONG addrLen;
    SERVER_ARG * pThArg = (SERVER_ARG *)pArg;

    addrLen = sizeof(connectSAddr);
    pThArg->sock =
        accept (SrvSock, (struct sockaddr *)&connectSAddr, &addrLen);

    /* A new connection. Create a server thread */
    EnterCriticalSection(&(pThArg->threadCs));
    __try {
        pThArg->hSrvThread = (HANDLE)_beginthreadex (NULL, 0, Server,
                    pThArg, 0, NULL);
        pThArg->thState = SERVER_THREAD_RUNNING;
    }
    __finally { LeaveCriticalSection(&(pThArg->threadCs)); }
    return 0;
}

BOOL WINAPI Handler (DWORD CtrlEvent)
{
    /* Shutdown the program */
    _tprintf (_T("In console control handler\n"));
```

```
        InterlockedIncrement (&shutFlag);
        return TRUE;
}
```

The Server Thread

Program 12–3 shows the socket server thread function. There are many similarities to the named pipe server function, and some code is elided for simplicity. Also, the code uses some of the global declarations and definitions from Program 12–2.

Program 12–3   serverSK: Server Thread Code

```
static DWORD WINAPI Server (PVOID pArg)

/* Server thread function. One thread for every potential client. */
{
    /* Each thread keeps its own request, response,
        and bookkeeping data structures on the stack. */
    BOOL done = FALSE;
    STARTUPINFO startInfoCh;
    SECURITY_ATTRIBUTES tempSA = {. . .}; /* Inheritable handles */
    PROCESS_INFORMATION procInfo;
    SOCKET connectSock;
    int commandLen;
    REQUEST request;/* Defined in ClientServer.h */
    RESPONSE response;/* Defined in ClientServer.h.*/
    char sysCommand[MAX_RQRS_LEN], tempFile[100];
    HANDLE hTmpFile;
    FILE *fp = NULL;
    int (__cdecl *dl_addr)(char *, char *);
    SERVER_ARG * pThArg = (SERVER_ARG *)pArg;
    enum SERVER_THREAD_STATE threadState;

    GetStartupInfo (&startInfoCh);

    connectSock = pThArg->sock;
    /* Create a temp file name */
    _stprintf (tempFile, _T("ServerTemp%d.tmp"), pThArg->number);

    while (!done && !shutFlag) { /* Main Server Command Loop. */
        done = ReceiveRequestMessage (&request, connectSock);

        request.record[sizeof(request.record)-1] = '\0';
        commandLen = strcspn (request.record, "\n\t");
        memcpy (sysCommand, request.record, commandLen);
        sysCommand[commandLen] = '\0';
        _tprintf (_T("Command received on server slot %d: %s\n"),
```

```
                    pThArg->number, sysCommand);

        /* Retest shutFlag; could be set in console control handler. */
        done = done || (strcmp (request.record, "$Quit") == 0)
                || shutFlag;
        if (done) continue;

        /* Open the temporary results file. */
        hTmpFile = CreateFile (tempFile, GENERIC_READ | GENERIC_WRITE,
            FILE_SHARE_READ | FILE_SHARE_WRITE, &tempSA,
            CREATE_ALWAYS, FILE_ATTRIBUTE_NORMAL, NULL);

        /* Check for shared library command. For simplicity, shared */
        /* library commands take precedence over process commands */
        dl_addr = NULL; /* will be set if GetProcAddress succeeds */
        if (pThArg->hDll != NULL) { /* Try Server "In process" */
            char commandName[256] = "";
            int commandNameLength = strcspn (sysCommand, " ");
            strncpy (commandName, sysCommand,
                min(commandNameLength, sizeof(commandName)));
            dl_addr = (int (*)(char *, char *))GetProcAddress
                (pThArg->hDll, commandName);
            /* Trust this DLL not to corrupt the server */
            if (dl_addr != NULL) { /* Call the DLL */
                (*dl_addr)(request.record, tempFile);
            }
        }

        if (dl_addr == NULL) { /* No inprocess support */
            /* Create a process to carry out the command. */
            /* Same as in serverNP*/
            . . .
        }

        /* Respond a line at a time. It is convenient to use
           C library line-oriented routines at this point. */

        /* Send temp file, one line at a time, to the client. */
        /* Same as in serverNP */
            . . .
    }   /* End of main command loop. Get next command */

/* done || shutFlag */
/* End of command processing loop. Free resources; exit thread. */
_tprintf (_T("Shuting down server thread # %d\n"), pThArg->number);
closesocket (connectSock);
```

```
EnterCriticalSection(&(pThArg->threadCs));
__try {
    threadState = pThArg->thState = SERVER_THREAD_STOPPED;
}
__finally { LeaveCriticalSection(&(pThArg->threadCs)); }

return threadState;
}
```

Running the Socket Server

Run 12–3 shows the server in operation, with several printed information messages that are not in the listings for Programs 12–2 and 12–3. The server has several clients, one of which is the client shown in Run 12–1 (slot 0).

The termination at the end occurs in the accept thread; the shutdown closes the socket, causing the accept call to fail. An exercise suggests ways to make this shutdown cleaner.

```
C:\WSP4_Examples\run8>serverSK
Client accepted on slot: 0, using server thread 4260.
Client accepted on slot: 1, using server thread 6240.
Command received on server slot 1: timep statsCS 64 10000
Client accepted on slot: 2, using server thread 5844.
Command received on server slot 2: lsW -l *.txt
Command received on server slot 0: Redirect grepMT James mnch.txt pres
.txt = FIND "17"
Command received on server slot 1: timep randfile 100000 m2.txt
Command received on server slot 0: timep statsMX 64 10000
Command received on server slot 2: cat m2.txt
Command received on server slot 0: timep sortBT -n m2.txt
Command received on server slot 1: $Quit
Shuting down server thread number 1
Command received on server slot 2: lsW -l *.txt
Command received on server slot 2: $Quit
Shuting down server thread number 2
Command received on server slot 0: $Quit
Shuting down server thread number 0
In console control handler
Server shutdown in process. Wait for all server threads
Server thread on slot 0 stopped.
Server thread on slot 1 stopped.
Server thread on slot 2 stopped.
accept: invalid socket error
A blocking operation was interrupted by a call to WSACancelBlockingCal
l.


C:\WSP4_Examples\run8>
```

Run 12–3 `serverSK`: Requests from Several Clients

A Security Note

This client/server system, as presented, is *not* secure. If you are running the server on your computer and someone else knows the port and your computer name, your computer is at risk. The other user, running the client, can run commands on your computer that could, for example, delete or modify files.

A complete discussion of security solutions is well beyond this book's scope. Nonetheless, Chapter 15 shows how to secure Windows objects, and Exercise 12–15 suggests using Secure Sockets Layer (SSL).

In-Process Servers

As mentioned previously, in-process servers are a major enhancement in `serverSK`. Program 12–4 shows how to write a DLL to provide these services. Two familiar functions are shown, a word counting function and a `toupper` function.

By convention, the first parameter is the command line, while the second is the name of the output file. Beyond that, always remember that the function will execute in the same thread as the server thread, so there are strict requirements for thread safety, including but not limited to the following:

- The functions should not change the process environment in any way. For example, if one of the functions changes the working directory, that change will affect the entire process.

- Similarly, the functions should not redirect standard input or output.

- Programming errors, such as allowing a subscript or pointer to go out of bounds or the stack to overflow, could corrupt another thread or the server process itself. More generally, the function should not generate any unhandled exception because the server will not be able to do anything other than shut down.

- Resource leaks, such as failing to deallocate memory or to close handles, will ultimately affect the server application.

Processes do not have such stringent requirements because a process cannot normally corrupt other processes, and resources are freed when the process terminates. A typical development methodology, then, is to develop and debug a service as a process, and when it is judged to be reliable, convert it to a DLL.

Program 12–4 shows a small DLL library with two simple functions, `wcip` and `toupperip`, which have functionality from programs in previous chapters. The code is in C, avoiding C++ decorated names. These examples do not support Unicode as currently written.

Program 12–4   `commandIP`: Sample In-Process Servers

```c
/* Chapter 12. commands.c              */
/*                                     */
/* "In Process Server" commands to use with serverSK, etc.*/
/*                                     */
/* There are several commands implemented as DLLs*/
/* Each command function must be a thread-safe function */
/* and take two parameters. The first is a string:*/
/* command arg1 arg2 ... argn (i.e.; a RESTRICTED command*/
/* line with no spaces or quotes in the command or args)*/
/* and the second is the file name for the output*/
/* The code is C, without decorated names*/

#include <stdio.h>
#include <stdlib.h>
#include <string.h>
#include <ctype.h>

static void ExtractToken (int, char *, char *);

__declspec (dllexport)
int __cdecl wcip (char * command, char * output_file)
/* word count; in process (ONE FILE ONLY)*/
/* Count the number of characters, works, and lines in*/
/* the file specified as the second token in "command"*/
/* NOTE: Simple version; results may differ from wc utility*/
{
    FILE * fIn, *fOut;
    int ch, c, nl, nw, nc;
    char inputFile[256];

    ExtractToken (1, command, inputFile);

    fIn = fopen (inputFile, "r");
    if (fIn == NULL) return 1;

    ch = nw = nc = nl = 0;
    while ((c = fgetc (fIn)) != EOF) {
        if (c == '\0') break;
        if (isspace(c) && isalpha(ch))
            nw++;
        ch = c;
        nc++;
        if (c == '\n')
            nl++;
    }
    fclose (fIn);
```

```
    /* Write the results */
    fOut = fopen (output_file, "w");
    if (fOut == NULL) return 2;
    fprintf (fOut, " %9d %9d %9d %s\n", nl, nw, nc, inputFile);
    fclose (fOut);
    return 0;
}


__declspec (dllexport)
int __cdecl toupperip (char * command, char * output_file)
/* convert input to upper case; in process*/
/* Input file is the second token ("toupperip" is the first)*/
{
    FILE * fIn, *fOut;
    int c;
    char inputFile[256];

    ExtractToken (1, command, inputFile);

    fIn = fopen (inputFile, "r");
    if (fIn == NULL) return 1;
    fOut = fopen (output_file, "w");
    if (fOut == NULL) return 2;

    while ((c = fgetc (fIn)) != EOF) {
        if (c == '\0') break;
        if (isalpha(c)) c = toupper(c);
        fputc  (c, fOut);
    }
    fclose (fIn); fclose (fOut);
    return 0;
}

static void ExtractToken (int it, char * command, char * token)
{
    /* Extract token number "it" (first token is number 0)*/
    /* from "command". Result goes in "token"*/
    /* tokens are white space delimited*/
    . . . (see the Examples file
    return;
}
```

Line-Oriented Messages, DLL Entry Points, and TLS

serverSK and clientSK communicate using messages, where each message is composed of a 4-byte length header followed by the message content. A common alternative to this approach is to have the messages delimited by null characters.

The difficulty with delimited messages is that there is no way to know the message length in advance, and each incoming character must be examined. Receiving a single character at a time would be inefficient, however, so incoming characters are stored in a buffer, and the buffer contents might include one or more null characters and parts of one or more messages. *Buffer contents and state must be retained between calls to the message receive function.* In a single-threaded environment, static storage can be used, but multiple threads cannot share the same static storage.

In more general terms, we have a *multithreaded persistent state problem.* This problem occurs any time a thread-safe function must maintain information from one call to the next. The Standard C library `strtok` function, which scans a string for successive instances of a token, is a common alternative example of this problem.

Solving the Multithreaded Persistent State Problem

The first of this chapter's two solutions to the persistent state problem uses a combination of the following components.

- A DLL for the message send and receive functions.

- An entry point function in the DLL.

- Thread Local Storage (TLS, Chapter 7). The DLL index is created when the process attaches, and it is destroyed when the process detaches. The index number is stored in static storage to be accessed by all the threads.

- A structure containing a buffer and its current state. A structure is allocated every time a thread attaches, and the address is stored in the TLS entry for that thread. A thread's structure is deallocated when the thread detaches.

- This solution does have a significant limitation; you can only use one socket with this library per thread. The second solution, later in the chapter, overcomes this limitation.

The TLS, then, plays the role of static storage, and each thread has its own unique copy of the static storage.

Example: A Thread-Safe DLL for Socket Messages

Program 12–5 is the DLL containing two character string ("CS" in names in this example) or socket streaming functions: `SendCSMessage` and `ReceiveCSMessage`, along with a `DllMain` entry point (see Chapter 5). These two functions are similar to and essentially replace `ReceiveMessage`, listed earlier in this chapter, and the functions used in Programs 12–1 and 12–2.

The DllMain function is a representative solution of a multithreaded persistent state problem, and it combines TLS and DLLs. The resource deallocation in the DLL_THREAD_DETACH case is especially important in a server environment; without it, the server would eventually exhaust resources, typically resulting in either failure or performance degradation or both. *Note:* This example illustrates concepts that are not directly related to sockets, but it is included here, rather than in earlier chapters, because this is a convenient place to illustrate thread-safe DLL techniques in a realistic example.

If this DLL is to be loaded dynamically, you must load it before starting any threads that use the DLL; otherwise, there will not be a DLL_THREAD_ATTACH call to DllMain.

The *Examples* file contains client and server code, slightly modified from Programs 12–1 and 12–2, that uses this DLL.

Program 12–5   SendReceiveSKST: Thread-Safe DLL

```
/* SendReceiveSKST.c -- Multithreaded streaming socket DLL. */
/* Messages are delimited by null characters ('\0') */
/* so the message length is not known ahead of time. Incoming */
/* data is buffered and preserved from one function call to */
/* the next. Therefore, use Thread Local Storage (TLS) */
/* so that each thread has its own private "static storage." */

#include "Everything.h"
#include "ClientServer.h"/* Defines MESSAGE records. */

typedef struct STATIC_BUF_T {
/* "staticBuf" contains "staticBufLen" characters of residual data */
/* There may or may not be end-of-string (null) characters */
    char staticBuf[MAX_RQRS_LEN];
    LONG32 staticBufLen;
} STATIC_BUF;

static DWORD tlsIndex = TLS_OUT_OF_INDEXES; /* Initialize TLS index */
/* A single threaded library would use the following: */
static char staticBuf[MAX_RQRS_LEN];
static LONG32 staticBufLen;
*/

/* number of attached, detached threads and processes. */
static volatile long nPA = 0, nPD = 0, nTA = 0, nTD = 0;

/* DLL main function. */
BOOL WINAPI DllMain(HINSTANCE hinstDLL, DWORD fdwReason,
                    LPVOID lpvReserved)
```

```
{
    STATIC_BUF * pBuf;

    switch (fdwReason) {
        case DLL_PROCESS_ATTACH:
            tlsIndex = TlsAlloc();
            InterlockedIncrement (&nPA);
            /* There is no thread attach call for other threads created
                BEFORE this DLL was loaded.
                Perform thread attach operations during process attach
                Load this DLL before creating threads that use DLL. */

        case DLL_THREAD_ATTACH:
            /* Indicate that memory has not been allocated  */
            InterlockedIncrement (&nTA);
            /* Slots are initialized to 0 */
            return TRUE; /* This value is ignored */

        case DLL_PROCESS_DETACH:
            /* Free remaining resources this DLL uses. Some thread
                DLLs may not have been called. */
            InterlockedIncrement (&nPD);
            /* Count this as detaching the primary thread as well */
            InterlockedIncrement (&nTD);
            pBuf = TlsGetValue (tlsIndex);
            if (pBuf != NULL) {
                free (pBuf);
                pBuf = NULL;
            }
            TlsFree(tlsIndex);
            return TRUE;

        case DLL_THREAD_DETACH:
            /* May not be called for every thread using the DLL */
            InterlockedIncrement (&nTD);
            pBuf = TlsGetValue (tlsIndex);
            if (pBuf != NULL) {
                free (pBuf);
                pBuf = NULL;
            }
            return TRUE;

        default: return TRUE;
    }
}


__declspec(dllexport)
BOOL ReceiveCSMessage (MESSAGE *pMsg, SOCKET sd)
{
    /* FALSE return indicates an error or disconnect */
```

```
BOOL disconnect = FALSE;
LONG32 nRemainRecv, nXfer, k; /* Must be signed integers */
LPBYTE pBuffer, message;
CHAR tempBuff[MAX_MESSAGE_LEN+1];
STATIC_BUF *pBuff;

if (pMsg == NULL) return FALSE;
pBuff = (STATIC_BUF *) TlsGetValue (tlsIndex);
if (pBuff == NULL) { /* First time initialization. */
   /* Only threads that need this storage will allocate it */
   pBuff = malloc (sizeof (STATIC_BUF));
   if (pBuff == NULL) return FALSE; /* Error */
   TlsSetValue (tlsIndex, pBuff);
   pBuff->staticBufLen = 0; /* Intialize state */
}

message = pMsg->record;
/* Read up to the null character, leaving residual data
 * in the static buffer */

for (k = 0; k < pBuff->staticBufLen && pBuff->staticBuf[k] != '\0';
        k++) {
   message[k] = pBuff->staticBuf[k];
} /* k is the number of characters transferred */
if (k < pBuff->staticBufLen) { /* a null was found in staticBuf */
   message[k] = '\0';
   pBuff->staticBufLen -= (k+1); /* Adjust the buffer state */
   memcpy (pBuff->staticBuf, &(pBuff->staticBuf[k+1]),
        pBuff->staticBufLen);
   return TRUE; /* No socket input required */
}

/* the entire static buffer was transferred. No null found */
nRemainRecv = sizeof(tempBuff) -
        sizeof(CHAR) - pBuff->staticBufLen;
pBuffer = message + pBuff->staticBufLen;
pBuff->staticBufLen = 0;

while (nRemainRecv > 0 && !disconnect) {
   nXfer = recv (sd, tempBuff, nRemainRecv, 0);
   if (nXfer <= 0) {
      disconnect = TRUE;
      continue;
   }

   /* Transfer to target message up to null, if any */
   for (k = 0; k < nXfer && tempBuff[k] != '\0'; k++) {
      *pBuffer = tempBuff[k];
      nRemainRecv -= nXfer; pBuffer++;
   }
```

```
        if (k < nXfer) { /* null has been found */
            *pBuffer = '\0';
            nRemainRecv = 0;
            /* Adjust the static buffer state for the next
             * ReceiveCSMessage call */
            memcpy (pBuff->staticBuf, &tempBuff[k+1], nXfer - k - 1);
            pBuff->staticBufLen = nXfer -k - 1;
        }
    }
    return !disconnect;
}


__declspec(dllexport)
BOOL SendCSMessage (MESSAGE *pMsg, SOCKET sd)
{
    /* Send the the request to the server on socket sd */
    BOOL disconnect = FALSE;
    LONG32 nRemainSend, nXfer;
    LPBYTE pBuffer;

    if (pMsg == NULL) return FALSE;
    pBuffer = pMsg->record;
    if (pBuffer == NULL) return FALSE;
    nRemainSend = min(strlen (pBuffer) + 1, MAX_MESSAGE_LEN);

    while (nRemainSend > 0 && !disconnect)  {
        /* send does not guarantee that the entire message is sent */
        nXfer = send (sd, pBuffer, nRemainSend, 0);
        if (nXfer <= 0) {
            disconnect = TRUE;
        }
        nRemainSend -=nXfer; pBuffer += nXfer;
    }
    return !disconnect;
}
```

Comments on the DLL and Thread Safety

- DllMain, with DLL_THREAD_ATTACH, is called whenever a new thread is created, but there is not a distinct DLL_THREAD_ATTACH call for the primary thread or any other threads that exist when the DLL is loaded. The DLL's DLL_PROCESS_ATTACH case must handle these cases.

- In general, and even in this case (consider the accept thread), some threads may not require the allocated memory, but DllMain cannot distinguish the different thread types. Therefore, the DLL_THREAD_ATTACH case does not actually allocate any memory, and there is no need to call `TlsSetValue` because Windows initializes the value to `NULL`. The `ReceiveCSMessage` entry point allocates the memory the first time it is called. In this way, the thread-specific memory is allocated only by threads that require it, and different thread types can allocate exactly the resources they require.

• While this DLL is thread-safe, a given thread can use these routines with only one socket at a time because the persistent state is associated with the thread, not the socket. The next example addresses this issue.

• The DLL source code on the *Examples* file is instrumented to print the total number of `DllMain` calls by type.

• There is still a resource leak risk, even with this solution. Some threads, such as the accept thread, may never terminate and therefore will never be detached from the DLL. `ExitProcess` will call `DllMain` with `DLL_PROCESS_DETACH` but not with `DLL_THREAD_DETACH` for threads that are still active. This does not cause a problem in this case because the accept thread does not allocate any resources, and even memory is freed when the process terminates. There would, however, be an issue if threads allocated resources such as temporary files; the ultimate solution would be to create a globally accessible list of resources. The `DLL_PROCESS_DETACH` code would then have the task of scanning the list and deallocating the resources; this is left as an exercise.

Example: An Alternative Thread-Safe DLL Strategy

Program 12–5, while typical of the way in which TLS and `DllMain` are combined to create thread-safe libraries, has two major weaknesses noted in the comments in the previous section. First, the state is associated with the thread rather than with the socket, so a given thread can process only one socket at a time. Second, there is the resource leak risk mentioned in the last bullet above.

An effective alternative approach to thread-safe library functions is to create a handle-like structure that is passed to every function call. The state is then maintained in the structure. The application explicitly manages the state, so you can manage multiple sockets in a thread, and you can even use the sockets with fibers (there might be one socket, or more, per fiber). Many UNIX and Linux applications use this technique to create thread-safe C libraries; the main disadvantage is that the functions require an additional parameter for the state structure.

Program 12–6 modifies Program 12–5. Notice that `DllMain` is not necessary, but there are two new functions to initialize and free the state structure. The send and receive functions require only minimal changes. An associated server, `serverSKHA`, is included in the *Examples* file and requires only slight changes in order to create and close the socket handle (`HA` denotes "handle").

Program 12–6   SendReceiveSKHA: Thread-Safe DLL with a State Structure

```
/* SendReceiveSKHA.c -- multithreaded streaming socket. */
/* This is a modification of SendReceiveSKST.c to illustrate a */
/* different thread-safe library technique. */
/* State is preserved in a handle-like state structure rather than */
/* using TLS. This allows a thread to use several sockets at once. */
/* Messages are delimited by null characters ('\0'). */

#include "Everything.h"
#include "ClientServer.h"/* Defines MESSAGEa. */

typedef struct SOCKET_HANDLE_T {
/* Current socket state */
/* Contains "staticBuffLen" characters of residual data */
/* There may or may not be end-of-string (null) characters */
    SOCKET sk;
    char staticBuff[MAX_RQRS_LEN];
    LONG32 staticBuffLen;
} SOCKET_HANDLE, * PSOCKET_HANDLE;

/* Functions to create and close "streaming socket handles" */
__declspec (dllexport)
PVOID CreateCSSocketHandle (SOCKET s)
{
    PVOID p;
    PSOCKET_HANDLE ps;

    p = malloc (sizeof(SOCKET_HANDLE));
    if (p == NULL) return NULL;
    ps = (PSOCKET_HANDLE)p;
    ps->sk = s;
    ps->staticBuffLen = 0; /* Initialize buffer state */
    return p;
}

__declspec (dllexport)
BOOL CloseCSSocketHandle (PSOCKET_HANDLE psh)
{
    if (psh == NULL) return FALSE;
    free (psh);
    return TRUE;
}

__declspec(dllexport)
BOOL ReceiveCSMessage (MESSAGE *pMsg, PSOCKET_HANDLE psh)
/*  Use PVOID so that calling program does not need to include the */
/* SOCKET_HANDLE definition. */
```

```
{
    /* TRUE return indicates an error or disconnect */
    BOOL disconnect = FALSE;
    LONG32 nRemainRecv = 0, nXfer, k; /* Must be signed integers */
    LPSTR pBuffer, message;
    CHAR tempBuff[MAX_RQRS_LEN+1];
    SOCKET sd;

    if (psh == NULL) return FALSE;
    sd = psh->sk;

    /* This is all that's changed from SendReceiveSKST! */
    message = pMsg->record;
    /* Read up to the null character, leaving residual data
     * in the static buffer */

    for (k = 0;
          k < psh->staticBuffLen && psh->staticBuff[k] != '\0'; k++) {
        message[k] = psh->staticBuff[k];
    }  /* k is the number of characters transferred */
    if (k < psh->staticBuffLen) { /* null found in buffer */
        message[k] = '\0';
        psh->staticBuffLen -= (k+1); /* Adjust buffer state */
        memcpy (psh->staticBuff, &(psh->staticBuff[k+1]),
                psh->staticBuffLen);
        return TRUE; /* No socket input required */
    }

    /* The entire static buffer was transferred. No null found */
    nRemainRecv = sizeof(tempBuff) - 1 - psh->staticBuffLen;
    pBuffer = message + psh->staticBuffLen;
    psh->staticBuffLen = 0;

    while (nRemainRecv > 0 && !disconnect) {
        nXfer = recv (sd, tempBuff, nRemainRecv, 0);
        if (nXfer <= 0) {
            disconnect = TRUE;
            continue;
        }

        nRemainRecv -=nXfer;
        /* Transfer to target message up to null, if any */
        for (k = 0; k < nXfer && tempBuff[k] != '\0'; k++) {
            *pBuffer = tempBuff[k];
            pBuffer++;
        }
        if (k >= nXfer) { /* null not found, read more */
            nRemainRecv -= nXfer;
        } else { /* null has been found */
            *pBuffer = '\0';
```

```
            nRemainRecv = 0;
            memcpy (psh->staticBuff, &tempBuff[k+1], nXfer - k - 1);
            psh->staticBuffLen = nXfer -k - 1;
        }
    }
    return !disconnect;
}


__declspec(dllexport)
BOOL SendCSMessage (MESSAGE *pMsg, PSOCKET_HANDLE psh)
{
    /* Send the the request to the server on socket sd */
    BOOL disconnect = FALSE;
    LONG32 nRemainSend, nXfer;
    LPSTR pBuffer;
    SOCKET sd;

    if (psh == NULL || pMsg == NULL) return FALSE;
    sd = psh->sk;

    pBuffer = pMsg->record;
    /* Ignore Win64 conversion warning. strlen is size_t */
    nRemainSend = min(strlen (pBuffer) + 1, MAX_MESSAGE_LEN);

    while (nRemainSend > 0 && !disconnect)  {
        /* send does not guarantee that the entire message is sent */
        nXfer = send (sd, pBuffer, nRemainSend, 0);
        if (nXfer <= 0) {
            disconnect = TRUE;
        }
        nRemainSend -=nXfer; pBuffer += nXfer;
    }

    return !disconnect;
}
```

Datagrams

Datagrams are similar to mailslots and are used in similar circumstances. There is no connection between the sender and receiver, and there can be multiple receivers. Delivery to the receiver is not ensured with either mailslots or datagrams, and successive messages will not necessarily be received in the order they were sent.

The first step in using datagrams is to specify SOCK_DGRAM in the type field when creating the socket with the socket function.

Next, use `sendto` and `recvfrom`, which take the same arguments as `send` and `recv`, but add two arguments to designate the partner station. Thus, the `sendto` function is as follows.

```
int sendto (
    SOCKET s,
    LPSTR lpBuffer,
    int nBufferLen,
    int nFlags,
    LPSOCKADDR lpAddr,
    int nAddrLen);
```

`lpAddr` points to an `sockaddr` address structure where you can specify the name of a specific machine and port, or you can specify that the datagram is to be broadcast to multiple computers; see the next section.

When using `recvfrom`, you specify the computers (perhaps all) from which you are willing to accept datagrams; also see the next section.

As with mailslots, datagram messages should be short; MSDN recommends 512 as the length limit for the data portion, as that limit avoids having the message sent in fragments.

Datagram Broadcasting

Several steps are necessary to broadcast `sendto` messages to multiple computers. Here are the basic steps; see MSDN for complete details:

- Set the `SOCK_DGRAM` socket options by calling `setsockopt`, specifying the `SO_BROADCAST` option. Also, set this option for sockets that are to receive broadcast messages.

- Set the client's `lpAddr sin_addr_in.s_addr` value to `INADDR_BROADCAST`.

- Set the port number as in the preceding examples.

- The broadcasts will be sent to and received by all computer interfaces (that is, all computers with a datagram socket with the `SO_BROADCAST` option) to that port.

Using Datagrams for Remote Procedure Calls

A common datagram usage is to implement RPCs. Essentially, in the most common situation, a client sends a request to a server using a datagram. Because delivery is not ensured, the client will retransmit the request if a response, also using a datagram, is not received from the server after a wait period. The server must be prepared to receive the same request several times.

The important point is that the RPC client and server do not require the overhead of a stream socket connection; instead, they communicate with simple requests and responses. As an option, the RPC implementation ensures reliability through time-outs and retransmissions, simplifying the application program. Alternatively, the client and server are frequently implemented so as to use *stateless protocol* (they do not maintain any state information about previous messages), so each request is independent of other requests. Again, application design and implementation logic are greatly simplified.

Berkeley Sockets versus Windows Sockets

Programs that use standard Berkeley Sockets calls will port to Windows Sockets, with the following important exceptions.

- You must call `WSAStartup` to initialize the Winsock DLL.

- You must use `closesocket` (which is not portable), rather than `close`, to close a socket.

- You must call `WSACleanup` to shut down the DLL.

Optionally, you can use the Windows data types such as `SOCKET` and `LONG` in place of `int`, as was done in this chapter. Programs 12–1 and 12–2 were ported from UNIX, and the effort was minimal. It was necessary, however, to modify the DLL and process management sections. Exercise 12–12 suggests that you port these two programs back to UNIX.

Overlapped I/O with Windows Sockets

Chapter 14 describes asynchronous I/O, which allows a thread to continue running while an I/O operation is in process. Sockets with Windows asynchronous I/O are discussed in that chapter.

Most asynchronous programming can be achieved uniformly and easily using threads. For example, `serverSK` uses an accept thread rather than a nonblocking socket. Nonetheless, I/O completion ports, which are associated with asynchronous I/O, are important for scalability when there is a large number of clients. This topic is also described in Chapter 14, and Chapter 9 discussed the same situation in the context of NT6 thread pools.

Windows Sockets Additional Features

Windows Sockets 2 adds several areas of functionality, including those listed here.

- Standardized support for overlapped I/O (see Chapter 14). This is considered to be the most important enhancement.

- Scatter/gather I/O (sending and receiving from noncontiguous buffers in memory).

- The ability to request quality of service (speed and reliability of transmission).

- The ability to organize sockets into groups. The quality of service of a socket group can be configured, so it does not have to be done on a socket-by-socket basis. Also, the sockets belonging to a group can be prioritized.

- Piggybacking of data onto connection requests.

- Multipoint connections (comparable to conference calls).

Summary

Windows Sockets allows the use of an industry-standard API, so that your programs can be interoperable and nearly portable in source code form. Winsock is capable of supporting nearly any network protocol, but TCP/IP is the most common.

Winsock is comparable to named pipes (and mailslots) in both functionality and performance, but portability and interoperability are important reasons for considering sockets. Keep in mind that socket I/O is not atomic, so it is necessary to ensure that a complete message is transmitted.

This chapter covered the Winsock essentials, which are enough to build a workable client/server application system. There is, however, much more, including asynchronous usage; see the Additional Reading references for more information.

This chapter also provided examples of using DLLs for in-process servers and for creating thread-safe libraries.

Looking Ahead

Chapters 11 and 12 have shown how to develop servers that respond to client requests. Servers, in various forms, are common Windows applications. Chapter 13 describes Windows Services, which provide a standard way to create and manage servers, in the form of services, permitting automated service start-up, shutdown, and monitoring. Chapter 13 shows how to turn a server into a manageable service.

Additional Reading

Windows Sockets

Network Programming for Microsoft Windows by Jim Ohlund is a good Winsock reference.

Berkeley Sockets and TCP/IP

W. R. Stevens's *TCP/IP Illustrated, Volume 3,* covers sockets and much more, while the first two volumes in the series describe the protocols and their implementation. The same author's *UNIX Network Programming* provides comprehensive coverage that is valuable even for non-UNIX machines. Another reference is Michael Donahoo and Kenneth Calvert, *TCP/IP Sockets in C: Practical Guide for Programmers.*

Exercises

12–1. Use WSAStartup to determine the highest and lowest Winsock version numbers supported on the machines accessible to you.

12–2. Use the JobShell program from Chapter 6 to start the server and several clients, where each client is created using the "detached" option. Eventually, shut down the server by sending a console control event through the kill command. Can you suggest any improvements in the serverSK shutdown logic?

12–3. Modify the client and server programs (Programs 12–1 and 12–2) so that they use datagrams to locate a server. The mailslot solution in Chapter 11 could be used as a starting point.

12–4. Modify the named pipe server in Chapter 11 (Program 11–3) so that it creates threads on demand instead of a server thread pool. Rather than predefining a fixed maximum for the number of named pipe instances, allow the application to determine the maximum.

12–5. Perform experiments to determine whether in-process servers are faster than out-of-process servers. For example, you can use the word count example (Program 12–4); there is an executable wc program as well as the DLL function shown in Program 12–4.

12–6. The number of clients that serverSK can support is bounded by the array of server thread arguments. Modify the program so that there is no such bound. You will need to create a data structure that allows you to add and delete thread arguments, and you also need to be able to scan the structure for terminated server threads. An alternative, and arguably simpler, approach would be to have each server thread manage its own state without the boss thread being involved other than to ask the server threads to shut down and wait for them to complete.

12–7. Develop additional in-process servers. For example, convert the grep program (see Chapter 6).

12–8. Enhance the server (Program 12–2) so that you can specify multiple DLLs on the command line.

12–9. Investigate the setsockopt function and the SO_LINGER option. Apply the option to one of the server examples.

12–10. Ensure that serverSK is free of resource leaks. Do the same with serverSKST, which was modified to use the DLL in Program 12–5.

12–11. Extend the exception handler in Program 12–4 so that it reports the exception and exception type at the end of the temporary file used for the server results.

12–12. *Extended exercise (requires extra equipment):* If you have access to a UNIX machine that is networked to your Windows machine, port clientSK to the UNIX machine and have it access serverSK to run Windows programs. You will, of course, need to convert data types such as DWORD and SOCKET to other types (unsigned int and int, respectively, in these two cases). Also, you will need to ensure that the message length is transmitted in big-endian format. Use functions such as htonl to convert the message lengths. Finally, port serverSK to UNIX so that Windows machines can execute UNIX commands on a remote system. Convert the DLL calls to shared library calls.

12–13. serverSK shuts down the accept thread by closing the connection socket (see Run 12–3). Is there a better way to terminate the accept thread? Potential approaches to investigate include queuing an APC as in Chapter 10. Or, can you use the Windows extended function, AcceptEx (Chapter 14 may help)?

12–14. A comment after Program 12–5 (SendReceiveSKST) mentions that you cannot assure that DLL_THREAD_DETACH will be invoked for every thread, and, therefore, there could be resource leaks (memory, temporary files, open file handles, etc.). Implement a solution in SendReceiveSKST that uses DLL_PROCESS_DETACH to free all allocated memory. Because you cannot find the allocated memory with TlsGetValue, maintain a list of all allocated memory.

12–15. Read about the SSL in MSDN and the Additional Reading references. Enhance the programs to use SSL for secure client/server communication.

13 | Windows Services

The server programs in Chapters 11 and 12 are console applications. In principle, the servers could run indefinitely, serving numerous clients as they connect, send requests, receive responses, and disconnect. That is, these servers could provide continuous services, but to be fully effective, the services should be manageable.

Windows Services,[1] previously known as NT Services, provide the management capabilities required to convert the servers into services that can be initiated on command or at boot time, before any user logs in, and can also be paused, resumed, terminated, and monitored. The registry maintains information about services.

Ultimately, any server, such as those developed in Chapters 11 and 12, should be converted to a service, especially if it is to be widely used by customers or within an organization.

Windows provides a number of services; examples include the DNS Client, several SQL Server services, and Terminal Services. The computer management snap-in, accessible from the Control Panel, displays the full set of services.

Chapter 6's JobShell (Program 6–3) provides rudimentary server management by allowing you to bring up a server under job control and send a termination signal. Windows Services, however, are much more comprehensive and robust, and the main example is a conversion of JobShell so that it can control Windows Services.

This chapter also shows how to convert an existing console application into a Windows service and how to install, monitor, and control the service. Logging, which allows a service to log its actions to a file, is also described.

---

[1] This terminology can be confusing because Windows provides numerous services that are not the Windows Services described here. However, the context should make the meaning clear, just as using the term "Windows" throughout the book when talking specifically about the API has not been a problem.

Writing Windows Services—Overview

Windows Services run under the control of a Service Control Manager (SCM). You can interact with the SCM to control services in three ways:

1. Use the management snap-in labeled Services under Systems and Maintenance, Administrative Tools in the Control Panel.

2. Control services with the `sc.exe` command line tool.

3. Control the SCM programmatically, as Program 13-3 demonstrates.

Converting a console application, such as `serverNP` or `serverSK`, to a Windows Service requires three major steps to place the program under the SCM.

1. Create a new `main()` entry point that registers the service with the SCM, supplying the logical service entry points and names.

2. Convert the old `main()` entry point function to *ServiceMain()*, which registers a service control handler and informs the SCM of its status. The remaining code is essentially that of the existing program, although you can add event logging commands. The name *ServiceMain()* is a placeholder for the name of a logical service, and there can be one or more logical services in a single process.

3. Write the service control handler function to respond to commands from the SCM.

As we describe these three steps, there are several references to creating, starting, and controlling services. Later sections describe the specifics, and Figure 13–1, later in the chapter, illustrates the component interactions.

The `main()` Function

The new `main()` function, which the SCM calls, has the task of registering the service with the SCM and starting the service control dispatcher. This requires a call to the `StartServiceCtrlDispatcher` function with the name(s) and entry point(s) of one or more logical services.

```
BOOL StartServiceCtrlDispatcher (
    SERVICE_TABLE_ENTRY *lpServiceStartTable)
```

The single parameter, `lpServiceStartTable`, is the address of an array of `SERVICE_TABLE_ENTRY` items, where each item is a logical service name and entry point. The end of the array is indicated by a pair of `NULL` entries.

The return is `TRUE` if the registration was successful.

The main thread of the service process that calls `StartServiceCtrl-Dispatcher` connects the thread to the SCM. The SCM registers the service(s) with the calling thread as the service control dispatcher thread. The SCM does not return to the calling thread until all services have terminated. Notice, however, that the logical services do not actually start at this time; starting the service requires the `StartService` function, which we describe later.

Program 13–1 shows a typical service main program with a single logical service.

Program 13–1   `main`: The Main Service Entry Point

```
#include "Everything.h"

void WINAPI ServiceMain (DWORD argc, LPTSTR argv[]);
static LPTSTR serviceName = _T("SocketCommandLineService");

/* Main routine that starts the service control dispatcher. */
VOID _tmain (int argc, LPTSTR argv[])
{
    SERVICE_TABLE_ENTRY dispatchTable[] =
    {
        { serviceName, ServiceMain },
        { NULL, NULL }
    };

    if (!StartServiceCtrlDispatcher (dispatchTable))
        ReportError (_T("Failed to start srvc ctrl dis."), 1, TRUE);
    /* ServiceMain () will not run until started by the SCM. */
    /* Return here only when all services have terminated. */
    return;
}
```

ServiceMain() Functions

The dispatch table specifies the functions, as shown in Program 13–1, and each function represents a logical service. The functions are enhanced versions of the base program that is being converted to a service, and the SCM invokes each logical service on its own thread. A logical service may, in turn, start up additional threads, such as the server worker threads that `serverSK` and `serverNP` create. Frequently, there is just one logical service within a Windows Service. In Program 13–2, the logical service is adapted from the main server (Program 12–2). It would be possible, however, to run both socket and named pipe logical services under the same Windows service, in which case you would supply two service main functions.

While the *ServiceMain()* function is an adaptation of a main() function with argument count and argument string parameters, there is one small change. The function should be declared void WINAPI rather than having an int return of a normal main() function.

Registering the Service Control Handler

A service control handler, called by the SCM, must be able to control the associated logical service. The console control handler in serverSK, which sets a global shutdown flag, illustrates, in limited form, what is expected of a handler. First, however, each logical service must immediately register a handler using RegisterServiceCtrlHandlerEx. The function call should be at the beginning of *ServiceMain()* and not called again. The SCM, after receiving a control request for the service, calls the handler.

```
SERVICE_STATUS_HANDLE
    RegisterServiceCtrlHandlerEx (
    LPCTSTR lpServiceName,
    LPHANDLER_FUNCTION_EX lpHandlerProc,
    LPVOID lpContext)
```

Parameters

lpServiceName is the user-supplied service name provided in the service table entry for this logical service; it should match a ServiceMain function name registered with StartServiceCtrlDispatcher.

lpHandlerProc is the address of the extended handler function, described in a later section.

lpContext is user-defined data passed to the control handler. This allows a single control handler to distinguish between multiple services using the same handler.

The return value, which is a SERVICE_STATUS_HANDLE object, is 0 if there is an error, and the usual methods can be used to analyze errors.

Setting the Service Status

Now that the handler is registered, the next immediate task is to set the service status to SERVICE_START_PENDING using SetServiceStatus. SetService-

Status will also be used in several other places to set different values, informing the SCM of the service's current status. A later section and Table 13–3 describe the valid status values in addition to SERVICE_START_PENDING.

The service control handler must set the status every time it is called, even if there is no status change.

Furthermore, any of the service's threads can call SetServiceStatus at any time to report progress, errors, or other information, and services frequently have a thread dedicated to periodic status updates. The time period between status update calls is specified in a member field in a data structure parameter. The SCM can assume an error has occurred if a status update does not occur within this time period.

```
BOOL SetServiceStatus (
    SERVICE_STATUS_HANDLE hServiceStatus,
    LPSERVICE_STATUS lpServiceStatus)
```

Parameters

hServiceStatus is the SERVICE_STATUS_HANDLE returned by Register-ServiceCtrlHandlerEx. The RegisterServiceCtrlHandlerEx call must therefore precede the SetServiceStatus call.

lpServiceStatus, pointing to a SERVICE_STATUS structure, describes service properties, status, and capabilities.

The SERVICE_STATUS Structure

The SERVICE_STATUS structure definition is:

```
typedef struct _SERVICE_STATUS {
    DWORD dwServiceType;
    DWORD dwCurrentState;
    DWORD dwControlsAccepted;
    DWORD dwWin32ExitCode;
    DWORD dwServiceSpecificExitCode;
    DWORD dwCheckPoint;
    DWORD dwWaitHint;
} SERVICE_STATUS, *LPSERVICE_STATUS;
```

Parameters

dwWin32ExitCode is the normal thread exit code for the logical service. The service must set this to NO_ERROR while running and on normal termination. Despite the name, you can use this field on 64-bit applications; there will be "32" references in other nSames.

dwServiceSpecificExitCode can be used to indicate an error while the service is starting or stopping, but this value will be ignored unless dwWin32ExitCode is set to ERROR_SERVICE_SPECIFIC_ERROR.

dwCheckPoint should be incremented periodically by the service to report its progress during all steps, including initialization and shutdown. This value is invalid and should be 0 if the service does not have a start, stop, pause, or continue operation pending.

dwWaitHint, in milliseconds, is the elapsed time between calls to SetService-Status with either an incremented value of dwCheckPoint value or a change in dwCurrentState. As mentioned previously, the SCM can assume that an error has occurred if this time period passes without such a SetServiceStatus call.

The remaining SERVICE_STATUS members are now described in individual sections.

Service Type

dwServiceType must be one of the values described in Table 13–1.

Table 13-1 Service Types

Value	Meaning
SERVICE_WIN32_OWN_PROCESS	Indicates that the Windows service runs in its own process with its own resources. *Program 13–2 uses this value.*
SERVICE_WIN32_SHARE_PROCESS	Indicates a Windows service that shares a process with other services, consolidating several services into a single process, which can reduce overall resource requirements.
SERVICE_KERNEL_DRIVER	Indicates a Windows device driver and is reserved for system use.
SERVICE_FILE_SYSTEM_DRIVER	Specifies a Windows file system driver and is also reserved for system use.
SERVICE_INTERACTIVE_PROCESS	This flag can be combined with only the two SERVICE_WIN32_X values. However, interactive services pose a security risk and should not be used.

Table 13–2 Service State Values

Value	Meaning
SERVICE_STOPPED	The service is not running.
SERVICE_START_PENDING	The service is in the process of starting but is not yet ready to respond to requests. For example, the worker threads have not yet been started.
SERVICE_STOP_PENDING	The service is stopping but has not yet completed shutdown. For example, a global shutdown flag may have been set, but the worker threads have not yet responded.
SERVICE_RUNNING	The service is running.
SERVICE_CONTINUE_PENDING	The service is in the process of resuming from the pause state, but it is not yet running.
SERVICE_PAUSE_PENDING	The service pause is in process, but the service is not yet safely in the pause state.
SERVICE_PAUSED	The service is paused.

Table 13–3 Controls That a Service Accepts (Partial List)

Value	Meaning
SERVICE_ACCEPT_STOP	Enables SERVICE_CONTROL_STOP.
SERVICE_ACCEPT_PAUSE_CONTINUE	Enables SERVICE_CONTROL_PAUSE and SERVICE_CONTROL_CONTINUE.
SERVICE_ACCEPT_SHUTDOWN (The ControlService function cannot send this control code.)	Notifies the service when system shutdown occurs. This enables the system to send a SERVICE_CONTROL_SHUTDOWN value to the service. For Windows system use only.
SERVICE_ACCEPT_PARAMCHANGE	The startup parameters can change without restarting. The notification is SERVICE_CONTROL_PARAMCHANGE.

For our purposes, the type is almost always SERVICE_WIN32_OWN_PROCESS, and SERVICE_WIN32_SHARE_PROCESS is the only other value suitable for user-mode services. Showing the different values, however, does indicate that services play many different roles.

Service State

dwCurrentState indicates the current service state. Table 13–2 shows the different possible values.

Controls Accepted

dwControlsAccepted specifies the control codes that the service will accept and process through its service control handler (see the next section). Table 13–3 enumerates three values used in a later example, and the appropriate values should be combined by bit-wise "or" ($|$). See the MSDN entry for SERVICE_STATUS for the three additional values.

Service-Specific Code

Once the handler has been registered and the service status has been set to SERVICE_START_PENDING, the service can initialize itself and set its status again. In the case of converting serverSK, once the sockets are initialized and the server is ready to accept clients, the status should be set to SERVICE_RUNNING.

The Service Control Handler

The service control handler, the callback function specified in Register-ServiceCtrlHandlerEx, has the following form:

```
DWORD WINAPI HandlerEx (
    DWORD dwControl,
    DWORD dwEventType,
    LPVOID lpEventData,
    LPVOID lpContext)
```

The dwControl parameter indicates the actual control signal sent by the SCM that should be processed.

There are 14 possible values for dwControl, including the controls mentioned in Table 13–3. Five control values of interest in the example are listed here:

SERVICE_CONTROL_STOP

SERVICE_CONTROL_PAUSE

SERVICE_CONTROL_CONTINUE

SERVICE_CONTROL_INTERROGATE

SERVICE_CONTROL_SHUTDOWN

User-defined values in the range 128–255 are also permitted but will not be used here.

dwEventType is usually 0, but nonzero values are used for device management, which is out of scope for this book. lpEventData provides additional data required by some of these events.

Finally, lpContext is user-defined data passed to RegisterServiceCtrl-HandlerEx when the handler was registered.

The handler is invoked by the SCM in the same thread as the main program, and the function is usually written as a switch statement. This is shown in the examples.

Event Logging

Services run "headless" without user interaction, so it is not generally appropriate for a service to display status messages directly. Prior to Vista and NT6, some services would create a console, message box, or window for user interaction; those techniques are no longer available.

The solution is to log events to a log file or use Windows event logging functionality. Such events are maintained within Windows and can be viewed from the event viewer provided in the control panel's Administrative Tools.

The upcoming SimpleService example (Program 13–2) logs significant service events and errors to a log file; an exercise asks you to modify the program to use Windows events.

Example: A Service "Wrapper"

Program 13–2 performs the conversion of an arbitrary _tmain to a service. The conversion to a service depends on carrying out the tasks we've described. The existing server code (that is, the old _tmain function) is invoked as a thread or process from the function ServiceSpecific. Therefore, the code here is essentially a wrapper around an existing server program.

The command line option –c specifies that the program is to run as a standalone program, perhaps for debugging. Without the option, there is a call to StartServiceCtrlDispatcher.

Another addition is a log file; the name is hard-coded for simplicity. The service logs significant events to that file. Simple functions to initialize and close the log and to log messages are at the end.

Several other simplifications and limitations are noted in the comments.

Program 13–2 SimpleService: A Service Wrapper

```
/*Chapter 13. SimpleService.c
   Simplest example of a Windows Service
   All it does is update the checkpoint counter
   and accept basic controls.
   You can also run it as a stand-alone application. */

#include "Everything.h"
#include <time.h>
#define UPDATE_TIME 1000/* One second between updates */

VOID LogEvent (LPCTSTR, WORD), LogClose();
BOOL LogInit(LPTSTR);
void WINAPI ServiceMain (DWORD argc, LPTSTR argv[]);
VOID WINAPI ServerCtrlHandler(DWORD);
void UpdateStatus (int, int);
int  ServiceSpecific (int, LPTSTR *);

static BOOL shutDown = FALSE, pauseFlag = FALSE;
static SERVICE_STATUS hServStatus;
static SERVICE_STATUS_HANDLE hSStat; /* handle for setting status */

static LPTSTR serviceName = _T("SimpleService");
static LPTSTR logFileName = _T(".\\LogFiles\\SimpleServiceLog.txt");
static BOOL consoleApp = FALSE, isService;

/*  Main routine that starts the service control dispatcher */
/*  Optionally, run as a stand-alone console program*/
/*  Usage: simpleService [-c]              */
/*          -c says to run as a console app, not a service*/

VOID _tmain (int argc, LPTSTR argv[])
{
    SERVICE_TABLE_ENTRY DispatchTable[] =
    {
        { serviceName,       ServiceMain},
        { NULL,              NULL }
    };

    Options (argc, argv, _T("c"), &consoleApp, NULL);
    isService = !consoleApp;
    /* Initialize log file */
    if (!LogInit (logFileName)) return;

    if (isService) {
       LogEvent(_T("Starting Dispatcher"), EVENTLOG_SUCCESS);
       StartServiceCtrlDispatcher (DispatchTable);
    } else {
```

```c
        LogEvent(_T("Starting application"), EVENTLOG_SUCCESS);
        ServiceSpecific (argc, argv);
    }
    LogClose();
    return;
}

/* ServiceMain entry point, called by main program.  */
void WINAPI ServiceMain (DWORD argc, LPTSTR argv[])
{
    LogEvent (_T("Entering ServiceMain."), EVENTLOG_SUCCESS);

    hServStatus.dwServiceType = SERVICE_WIN32_OWN_PROCESS;
    hServStatus.dwCurrentState = SERVICE_START_PENDING;
    hServStatus.dwControlsAccepted = SERVICE_ACCEPT_STOP |
        SERVICE_ACCEPT_SHUTDOWN | SERVICE_ACCEPT_PAUSE_CONTINUE;
    hServStatus.dwWin32ExitCode = NO_ERROR;
    hServStatus.dwServiceSpecificExitCode = 0;
    hServStatus.dwCheckPoint = 0;
    hServStatus.dwWaitHint = 2 * UPDATE_TIME;

    hSStat =
        RegisterServiceCtrlHandler( serviceName, ServerCtrlHandler);

    if (hSStat == 0) {
        LogEvent (_T("Cannot register handler"), EVENTLOG_ERROR_TYPE);
        hServStatus.dwCurrentState = SERVICE_STOPPED;
        hServStatus.dwWin32ExitCode = ERROR_SERVICE_SPECIFIC_ERROR;
        hServStatus.dwServiceSpecificExitCode = 1;
        UpdateStatus (SERVICE_STOPPED, -1);
        return;
    }

    LogEvent (_T("Control handler registered"), EVENTLOG_SUCCESS);
    SetServiceStatus (hSStat, &hServStatus);
    LogEvent (_T("Status SERVICE_START_PENDING"), EVENTLOG_SUCCESS);

    /*  Start service-specific work; the generic work is complete */
    ServiceSpecific (argc, argv);

    /*  only return here when the ServiceSpecific function
        completes, indicating system shutdown. */
    LogEvent (_T("Service threads shut down"), EVENTLOG_SUCCESS);
    LogEvent (_T("Set SERVICE_STOPPED status"), EVENTLOG_SUCCESS);
    UpdateStatus (SERVICE_STOPPED, 0);
    LogEvent (_T("Status set to SERVICE_STOPPED"), EVENTLOG_SUCCESS);
    return;
}
```

```
/* service-specific function, or "main"; called from ServiceMain */
int ServiceSpecific (int argc, LPTSTR argv[])
{
    UpdateStatus (-1, -1); /* change to status; increment checkpoint */
    /* Start the server as a thread or process */
    /* Assume the service starts in 2 seconds. */
    UpdateStatus (SERVICE_RUNNING, -1);
    LogEvent (_T("Status update. Service running"), EVENTLOG_SUCCESS);

    /* Update the status periodically. */
    /*** The update loop could be on a separate thread ***/
    /* Also, check the pauseFlag - See Exercise 13-1 */
    LogEvent (_T("Starting main service loop"), EVENTLOG_SUCCESS);
    while (!shutDown) { /* shutDown is set on a shutDown control */
        Sleep (UPDATE_TIME);
        UpdateStatus (-1, -1);   /* Assume no change */
        LogEvent (_T("Status update. No change"), EVENTLOG_SUCCESS);
    }
    LogEvent (_T ("Server process has shut down."), EVENTLOG_SUCCESS);
    return 0;
}

/* Control Handler Function */
VOID WINAPI ServerCtrlHandler( DWORD dwControl)
{
    switch (dwControl) {
    case SERVICE_CONTROL_SHUTDOWN:
    case SERVICE_CONTROL_STOP:
        shutDown = TRUE;/* Set the global shutDown flag */
        UpdateStatus (SERVICE_STOP_PENDING, -1);
        break;
    case SERVICE_CONTROL_PAUSE:
        pauseFlag = TRUE;
        /* Pause implementation is Exercise 13-1 */
        break;
    case SERVICE_CONTROL_CONTINUE:
        pauseFlag = FALSE;
        /* Continue is also an exercise */
        break;
    case SERVICE_CONTROL_INTERROGATE:
        break;
    default:
        if (dwControl > 127 && dwControl < 256) /* User Defined */
        break;
    }
    UpdateStatus (-1, -1);
    return;
}
```

```c
void UpdateStatus (int NewStatus, int Check)
/*  Set service status and checkpoint (specific value or increment) */
{
    if (Check < 0 ) hServStatus.dwCheckPoint++;
    else        hServStatus.dwCheckPoint = Check;

    if (NewStatus >= 0) hServStatus.dwCurrentState = NewStatus;
    if (isService) {
        if (!SetServiceStatus (hSStat, &hServStatus)) {
            LogEvent (_T("Cannot set status"), EVENTLOG_ERROR_TYPE);
            hServStatus.dwCurrentState = SERVICE_STOPPED;
            hServStatus.dwWin32ExitCode = ERROR_SERVICE_SPECIFIC_ERROR;
            hServStatus.dwServiceSpecificExitCode = 2;
            UpdateStatus (SERVICE_STOPPED, -1);
            return;
        } else {
            LogEvent (_T("Service Status updated."), EVENTLOG_SUCCESS);
        }
    } else {
        LogEvent (_T("Stand-alone status updated."), EVENTLOG_SUCCESS);
    }
    return;
}


/* Simple file based event logging */
static FILE * logFp = NULL;
/* Very primitive logging service, using a file */
VOID LogEvent (LPCTSTR UserMessage, WORD type)
{
    TCHAR cTimeString[30] = _T("");
    time_t currentTime = time(NULL);
    _tcsncat (cTimeString, _tctime(&currentTime), 30);
    /* Remove the new line at the end of the time string */
    cTimeString[_tcslen(cTimeString)-2] = _T('\0');
    _ftprintf(logFp, _T("%s. "), cTimeString);
    if (type == EVENTLOG_SUCCESS || type == EVENTLOG_INFORMATION_TYPE)
        _ftprintf(logFp, _T("%s"), _T("Information. "));
    else if (type == EVENTLOG_ERROR_TYPE)
        _ftprintf(logFp, _T("%s"), _T("Error.      "));
    else if (type == EVENTLOG_WARNING_TYPE)
        _ftprintf(logFp, _T("%s"), _T("Warning.    "));
    else
        _ftprintf(logFp, _T("%s"), _T("Unknown.    "));

    _ftprintf(logFp, _T("%s\n"), UserMessage);
    fflush(logFp);
    return;
}
```

```
BOOL LogInit(LPTSTR name)
{
    logFp = _tfopen (name, _T("a+"));
    if (logFp != NULL) LogEvent (_T("Initialized Logging"),
            EVENTLOG_SUCCESS);
    return (logFp != NULL);
}

VOID LogClose()
{
    LogEvent (_T("Closing Log"), EVENTLOG_SUCCESS);
    return;
}
```

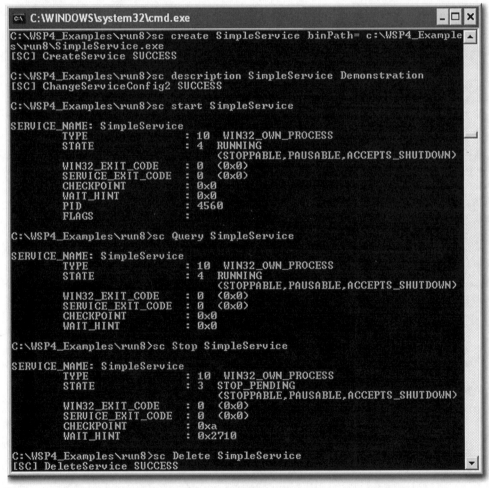

Run 13–2a   SimpleService: Controlled by sc

Running the Simple Service

Run 13–2a shows the sc command tool creating, starting, querying, stopping, and deleting SimpleService. Only an administrator can perform these steps.

Run 13–2b shows the log file.

```
/cygdrive/c/WSP4_Examples/LogFiles                                    _ □ ×
Tue Oct 20 12:59:49 200. Information. Initialized Logging
Tue Oct 20 12:59:49 200. Information. Starting Service Control Dispatcher
Tue Oct 20 12:59:50 200. Information. Entering ServiceMain.
Tue Oct 20 12:59:50 200. Information. Control handler registered successfully
Tue Oct 20 12:59:50 200. Information. Service status set to SERVICE_START_PENDING
Tue Oct 20 12:59:50 200. Information. Service Status updated.
Tue Oct 20 12:59:50 200. Information. Service Status updated.
Tue Oct 20 12:59:50 200. Information. Status update. Service is now running
Tue Oct 20 12:59:50 200. Information. Starting main service server loop
Tue Oct 20 12:59:51 200. Information. Service Status updated.
Tue Oct 20 12:59:51 200. Information. Status update. No change
. . .
Tue Oct 20 12:59:56 200. Information. Service Status updated.
Tue Oct 20 12:59:56 200. Information. Status update. No change
Tue Oct 20 12:59:56 200. Information. Server process has shut down.
Tue Oct 20 12:59:56 200. Information. Service threads shut down
Tue Oct 20 12:59:56 200. Information. Set SERVICE_STOPPED status
Tue Oct 20 12:59:56 200. Information. Closing Log
```

Run 13–2b   SimpleServiceLog.txt: The Log File

Managing Windows Services

Once a service has been written, the next task is to put the service under the control of the SCM so that the SCM can start, stop, and otherwise control the service. While sc.exe and the Services administrative tool can do this, you can also manage services programmatically, as we'll do next.

There are several steps to open the SCM, create a service under SCM control, and then start the service. These steps do not directly control the service; they are directives to the SCM, which in turn controls the specified service.

Opening the SCM

A separate process, running as "Administrator," is necessary to create the service, much as JobShell (Chapter 6) starts jobs. The first step is to open the SCM, obtaining a handle that then allows the service creation.

```
SC_HANDLE OpenSCManager (
    LPCTSTR lpMachineName,
    LPCTSTR lpDatabaseName,
    DWORD dwDesiredAccess)
```

Parameters

lpMachineName is NULL if the SCM is on the local computer, but you can also access the SCM on networked machines.

lpDatabaseName is also normally NULL.

dwDesiredAccess is normally SC_MANAGER_ALL_ACCESS, but you can specify more limited access rights, as described in the on-line documentation.

Creating and Deleting a Service

Call CreateService to register a service.

```
SC_HANDLE CreateService (
    SC_HANDLE hSCManager,
    LPCTSTR lpServiceName,
    LPCTSTR lpDisplayName,
    DWORD dwDesiredAccess,
    DWORD dwServiceType,
    DWORD dwStartType,
    DWORD dwErrorControl,
    LPCTSTR lpBinaryPathName,
    LPCTSTR lpLoadOrderGroup,
    LPDWORD lpdwTagId,
    LPCTSTR lpDependencies,
    LPCTSTR lpServiceStartName,
    LPCTSTR lpPassword);
```

As part of CreateService operation, new services are entered into the registry under:

```
HKEY_LOCAL_MACHINE\SYSTEM\CurrentControlSet\Services
```

Do not, however, attempt to bypass CreateService by manipulating the registry directly; we just point this out to indicate how Windows keeps service information.

Parameters

hSCManager is the SC_HANDLE obtained from OpenSCManager.

`lpServiceName` is the name used for future references to the service and is one of the logical service names specified in the dispatch table in the `StartServiceCtrlDispatcher` call. Notice that there is a separate `CreateService` call for each logical service.

`lpDisplayName` is the name displayed to the user to represent the service in the Services administrative tool (accessed from the Control Panel under Administrative Tools) and elsewhere. You will see this name entered immediately after a successful `CreateService` call.

`dwDesiredAccess` can be `SERVICE_ALL_ACCESS` or combinations of `GENERIC_READ`, `GENERIC_WRITE`, and `GENERIC_EXECUTE`. See the MSDN documentation for additional details.

`dwServiceType` has values as in Table 13–1.

`dwStartType` specifies how the service is started. `SERVICE_DEMAND_START` is used in our examples, but other values (`SERVICE_BOOT_START` and `SERVICE_SYSTEM_START`) allow device driver services to be started at boot time or at system start time, and `SERVICE_AUTO_START` specifies that a service is to be started at machine start-up.

`lpBinaryPathName` gives the service's executable as a full path; the `.exe` extension is necessary. Use quotes if the path contains spaces.

Other parameters specify account name and password, groups for combining services, and dependencies when there are several interdependent services.

Service configuration parameters of an existing service can be changed with `ChangeServiceConfig` and `ChangeServiceConfig2`, which is simpler and is not, perhaps for that reason, called `ChangeServiceConfigEx`. Identify the service by its handle, and you can specify new values for most of the parameters. For example, you can provide a new `dwServiceType` or `dwStartType` value but not a new value for `dwAccess`.

There is also an `OpenService` function to obtain a handle to a named service. Use `DeleteService` to unregister a service from the SCM and `CloseServiceHandle` to close `SC_HANDLE`s.

Starting a Service

A service, once created, is not running. Start the *ServiceMain()* function by specifying the handle obtained from `CreateService` along with the `argc`, `argv` command line parameters expected by the service's main function (that is, the function specified in the dispatch table).

```
BOOL StartService (
   SC_HANDLE hService,
   DWORD argc,
   LPTSTR argv[])
```

Controlling a Service

Control a service by telling the SCM to invoke the service's control handler with the specified control.

```
BOOL ControlService (
   SC_HANDLE hService,
   DWORD dwControlCode,
   LPSERVICE_STATUS lpServStat)
```

The interesting dwControlCode values for our examples are:

SERVICE_CONTROL_STOP

SERVICE_CONTROL_PAUSE

SERVICE_CONTROL_CONTINUE

SERVICE_CONTROL_INTERROGATE

SERVICE_CONTROL_SHUTDOWN

or a user-specified value in the range 128–255. Additional named values notify a service that start-up values have changed or there are changes related to binding.

SERVICE_CONTROL_INTERROGATE tells the service to report its status with SetServiceStatus, but it's of limited use, as the SCM receives periodic updates.

lpServStat points to a SERVICE_STATUS structure that receives the current status. This is the same structure as that used by the SetServiceStatus function.

Querying Service Status

Obtain a service's current status in a SERVICE_STATUS structure with the following:

```
BOOL QueryServiceStatus (
    SC_HANDLE hService,
    LPSERVICE_STATUS lpServiceStatus)
```

There's a distinction between calling QueryServiceStatus, which gets the current status information from the SCM, and ControlService with a SERVICE_CONTROL_INTERROGATE control code. The former tells the service to update the SCM rather than the application program.

Summary: Service Operation and Management

Figure 13–1 shows the SCM and its relation to the services and to a service control program, such as the one in Program 13–3 in the next section. In particular, a service must register with the SCM, and all commands to the service pass through the SCM.

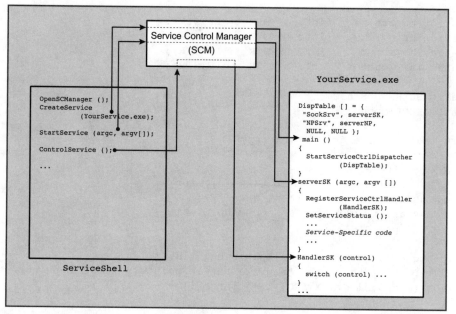

Figure 13–1 Controlling Windows Services through the SCM

Example: A Service Control Shell

You can control Windows Services from the Administrative Tools, where there is a Services icon. Alternatively, you can control services from the Windows command `sc.exe`. Finally, you can control a service from within an application, as illustrated in the next example, `ServiceShell` (Program 13–3), which is a modification of Chapter 6's `JobShell` (Program 6–3).

This example is intended to show how to control services from a program; it does not supplant `sc.exe` or the Services Administrative tool.

Program 13-3   `ServiceShell`: A Service Control Program

```
/* Chapter 13 */
/* ServiceShell.c  Windows Service Management shell program.
   This program modifies Chapter 6's Job Management program,
   managing services rather than jobs. */
/* Illustrates service control from a program
   In general, use the sc.exe command or the "Services"
   Administrative tools */
/* commandList supported are:
      create    Create a service
      delete    Delete a service
      start  Start a service
      control    Control a service */
#include "Everything.h"

static int Create    (int, LPTSTR *, LPTSTR);
static int Delete    (int, LPTSTR *, LPTSTR);
static int Start     (int, LPTSTR *, LPTSTR);
static int Control   (int, LPTSTR *, LPTSTR);

static SC_HANDLE hScm;
static BOOL debug;

int _tmain (int argc, LPTSTR argv[])
{
    BOOL exitFlag = FALSE;
    TCHAR command[MAX_COMMAND_LINE+10], *pc;
    DWORD i, locArgc; /* Local argc */
    TCHAR argstr[MAX_ARG][MAX_COMMAND_LINE];
    LPTSTR pArgs[MAX_ARG];

    debug = (argc > 1); /* simple debug flag */
    /* Prepare the local "argv" array as pointers to strings */
    for (i = 0; i < MAX_ARG; i++) pArgs[i] = argstr[i];
```

```
    /*  Open the SC Control Manager on the local machine,
        with the default database, and all access. */
    hScm = OpenSCManager (NULL, SERVICES_ACTIVE_DATABASE,
        SC_MANAGER_ALL_ACCESS);

    /*  Main command processing loop  */
    _tprintf (_T("\nWindows Service Management"));
    while (!exitFlag) {
        _tprintf (_T("\nSM$"));
        _fgetts (command, MAX_COMMAND_LINE, stdin);
        /*  Replace the new line character with a string end. */
        pc = _tcschr (command, _T('\n')); *pc = _T('\0');

        if (debug) _tprintf (_T("%s\n"), command);
        /*  Convert the command to "argc, argv" form. */
        GetArgs (command, &locArgc, pArgs);
        CharLower (argstr[0]);  /* The command is case-insensitive */

        if (debug) _tprintf (_T("\n%s %s %s %s"), argstr[0], argstr[1],
            argstr[2], argstr[3]);

        if (_tcscmp (argstr[0], _T("create")) == 0) {
            Create (locArgc, pArgs, command);
        }
        else if (_tcscmp (argstr[0], _T("delete")) == 0) {
            Delete (locArgc, pArgs, command);
        }
        else if (_tcscmp (argstr[0], _T("start")) == 0) {
            Start (locArgc, pArgs, command);
        }
        else if (_tcscmp (argstr[0], _T("control")) == 0) {
            Control (locArgc, pArgs, command);
        }
        else if (_tcscmp (argstr[0], _T("quit")) == 0) {
            exitFlag = TRUE;
        }
        else _tprintf (_T("\nCommand not recognized"));
    }

    CloseServiceHandle (hScm);
    return 0;
}

int Create (int argc, LPTSTR argv[], LPTSTR command)
{
    /*  Create a new service as a "demand start" service:
        argv[1]: Service Name
        argv[2]: Display Name
        argv[3]: binary executable */
```

```
    SC_HANDLE hSc;
    TCHAR executable[MAX_PATH+1],
        quotedExecutable[MAX_PATH+3] = _T("\"");

    /* You need full path name, add quotes if there are spaces */
    GetFullPathName (argv[3], MAX_PATH+1, executable, NULL);
    _tcscat(quotedExecutable, executable);
    _tcscat(quotedExecutable, _T("\""));
    if (debug) _tprintf (_T("\nService Full Path Name: %s"),
            executable);

    hSc = CreateService (hScm, argv[1], argv[2],
        SERVICE_ALL_ACCESS, SERVICE_WIN32_OWN_PROCESS,
        SERVICE_DEMAND_START, SERVICE_ERROR_NORMAL,
        quotedExecutable, NULL, NULL, NULL, NULL, NULL);
        CloseServiceHandle (hSc); /* No need to retain the handle as
                            OpenService will query the service DB */
    return 0;
}

/*  Delete a service
        argv[1]: ServiceName to delete  */
int Delete (int argc, LPTSTR argv[], LPTSTR command)
{
    SC_HANDLE hSc;

    if (debug) _tprintf (_T("\nAbout to delete service: %s"), argv[1]);
    hSc = OpenService(hScm,  argv[1], DELETE);
    DeleteService (hSc);
    CloseServiceHandle (hSc);
    return 0;
}

/*  Start a named service.
        argv[1]: Service name to start */
int Start (int argc, LPTSTR argv[], LPTSTR command)
{
    SC_HANDLE hSc;
    TCHAR workingDir[MAX_PATH+1];
    LPTSTR argvStart[] = {argv[1], workingDir};

    GetCurrentDirectory (MAX_PATH+1, workingDir);

    /* Get a handle to service named on the command line (argv[1]) */
    hSc = OpenService(hScm,  argv[1], SERVICE_ALL_ACCESS);

    /*  Start the service with one arg, the working directory */
    /*  The service name is from the program command line (argv[1]) */
     */
    StartService (hSc, 2, argvStart);
```

```
        CloseServiceHandle (hSc);

        return 0;
}


/*  Control a named service.
        argv[1]:  Service name to control
        argv[2]:  Control command (case insenstive):
                  stop
                  pause
                  resume
                  interrogate
                  user   user defined
                  */
static LPCTSTR commandList[] =
    {  _T("stop"), _T("pause"), _T("resume"),
       _T("interrogate"), _T("user") };
static DWORD controlsAccepted[] = {
    SERVICE_CONTROL_STOP, SERVICE_CONTROL_PAUSE,
    SERVICE_CONTROL_CONTINUE, SERVICE_CONTROL_INTERROGATE, 128 };

int Control (int argc, LPTSTR argv[], LPTSTR command)
{
    SC_HANDLE hSc;
    SERVICE_STATUS sStatus;
    DWORD dwControl, i;
    BOOL found = FALSE;

    if (debug) _tprintf (_T("\nAControl service: %s"), argv[1]);

    for (i= 0;
           i < sizeof(controlsAccepted)/sizeof(DWORD) && !found; i++)
        found = (_tcscmp (commandList[i], argv[2]) == 0);
    if (!found) {
        _tprintf (_T("\nIllegal Control command %s"), argv[1]);
        return 1;
    }
    dwControl = controlsAccepted[i-1];
    if (dwControl == 128) dwControl = _ttoi (argv[3]);
    if (debug) _tprintf (_T("\ndwControl = %d"), dwControl);

    hSc = OpenService(hScm,  argv[1],
        SERVICE_INTERROGATE | SERVICE_PAUSE_CONTINUE |
        SERVICE_STOP | SERVICE_USER_DEFINED_CONTROL |
        SERVICE_QUERY_STATUS );

    ControlService (hSc, dwControl, &sStatus);

    if (dwControl == SERVICE_CONTROL_INTERROGATE) {
        QueryServiceStatus (hSc, &sStatus);
```

```
        _tprintf (_T("\nStatus from QueryServiceStatus"));
        _tprintf (_T("\nSerice Status"));
        _tprintf (_T("\ServiceType: %d"), sStatus.dwServiceType);
        _tprintf (_T("\CurrentState: %d"), sStatus.dwCurrentState);
        _tprintf (_T("\ControlsAccd: %d"), sStatus.dwControlsAccepted);
        _tprintf (_T("\Win32ExitCode: %d"), sStatus.dwWin32ExitCode);
        _tprintf (_T("\ServiceSpecificExitCode: %d"),
                sStatus.dwServiceSpecificExitCode);
        _tprintf (_T("\CheckPoint: %d"), sStatus.dwCheckPoint);
        _tprintf (_T("\ndwWaitHint: %d"), sStatus.dwWaitHint);

    }
    if (hSc != NULL) CloseServiceHandle (hSc);
    return 0;
}
```

Run 13–3 shows `SimpleService` operation.

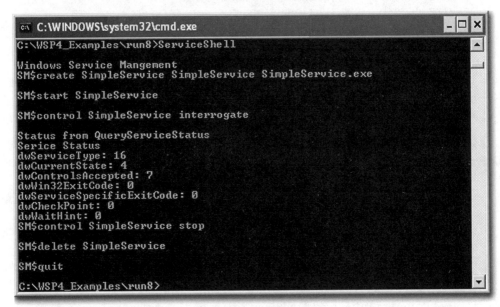

Run 13–3   `ServiceShell`: Managing Services

Sharing Kernel Objects with a Service

There can be situations in which a service and applications share a kernel object.
For example, the service might use a named mutex to protect a shared memory

region used to communicate with applications. Furthermore, in this example, the file mapping would also be a shared kernel object.

There is a difficulty caused by the fact that applications run in a security context separate from that of services, which can run under the system account. Even if no protection is required, it is not adequate to create and/or open the shared kernel objects with a NULL security attribute pointer (see Chapter 15). Instead, a non-NULL discretionary access control list is required at the very least—that is, the applications and the service need to use a non-NULL security attribute structure. In general, you may want to secure the objects, and, again, this is the subject of Chapter 15.

Also notice that if a service runs under the system account, there can be difficulties in accessing resources on other machines, such as shared files, from within a service.

Notes on Debugging a Service

A service is expected to run continuously, so it must be reliable and as defect-free as possible. While a service can be attached to the debugger and event logs can be used to trace service operation, these techniques are most appropriate after a service has been deployed.

During initial development and debugging, however, it is often easier to take advantage of the service wrapper presented in Program 13–2, which allows operation as either a service or a stand-alone application based on the command line -c option.

- Develop the "preservice" version as a stand-alone program. serverSK, for example, was developed in this way.

- Instrument the program with event logging or a log file.

- Once the program is judged to be ready for deployment as a service, run it without the -c command line option so that it runs as a service.

- Additional testing on a service is essential to detect both additional logic errors and security issues. Services can run under the system account and do not, for instance, necessarily have access to user objects, and the stand-alone version may not detect such problems.

- Normal events and minor maintenance debugging can be performed using information in the log file or event log. Even the status information can help determine server health and defect symptoms.

- If extensive maintenance is necessary, you can debug as a normal application using the -c option.

Summary

Windows services provide standardized capabilities to add user-developed services to Windows computers. An existing stand-alone program can be converted to a service using the methods in this chapter.

A service can be created, controlled, and monitored using the Administrative Tools or the ServiceShell program presented in this chapter. The SCM controls and monitors deployed services, and there are registry entries for all services.

Looking Ahead

Chapter 14 describes asynchronous I/O, which provides two techniques that allow multiple read and write operations to take place concurrently with other processing. It is not necessary to use threads; only one user thread is required.

In most cases, multiple threads are easier to program than asynchronous I/O, and thread performance is generally superior. However, asynchronous I/O is essential to the use of I/O completion ports, which are extremely useful when building scalable servers that can handle large numbers of clients.

Chapter 14 also describes waitable timers.

Additional Reading

Kevin Miller's *Professional NT Services* thoroughly covers the subject. Device drivers and their interaction with services were not covered in this chapter; a book such as Walter Oney's *Programming the Microsoft Windows Driver Model, Second Edition*, can provide that information.

Exercises

13–1. Modify Program 13–2 (SimpleService) to use Windows events instead of a log file. The principal functions to use are RegisterEventSource, ReportEvent, and DeregisterEventSource, all described in MSDN. Also consider using Vista event logging. Alternatively, use an open source logging system such as NLog (http://nlog-project.org/home).

13–2. Extend serviceSK to accept pause controls in a meaningful way. As suggested behavior for a paused service, it should maintain existing connections but not accept new connections. Furthermore, it should complete and respond to requests that are currently being processed, but it should not accept any more client requests.

13–3. `ServiceShell`, when interrogating service status, simply prints out the numbers. Extend it so that status is presented in a more readable form.

13–4. Convert `serverNP` (Program 12–3) into a service.

13–5. Test `serviceSK` in the *Exercises* file. Modify `serviceSK` so that it uses event logging.

14 Asynchronous Input/Output and Completion Ports

Input and output are inherently slow compared with other processing due to factors such as the following:

- Delays caused by track and sector seek time on random access devices, such as disks

- Delays caused by the relatively slow data transfer rate between a physical device and system memory

- Delays in network data transfer using file servers, storage area networks, and so on

All I/O in previous examples has been *thread-synchronous*, so that the entire thread waits until the I/O operation completes.

This chapter shows how a thread can continue without waiting for an operation to complete—that is, threads can perform *asynchronous* I/O. Examples illustrate the different techniques available in Windows.

Waitable timers, which require some of the same techniques, are also described here.

Finally, and more important, once standard asynchronous I/O is understood, we are in a position to use *I/O completion ports,* which are extremely useful when building scalable servers that must be able to support large numbers of clients without creating a thread for each client. Program 14–4 modifies an earlier server to exploit I/O completion ports.

Overview of Windows Asynchronous I/O

There are three techniques for achieving asynchronous I/O in Windows; they differ in both the methods used to start I/O operations and those used to determine when operations are complete.

- **Multithreaded I/O**. Each thread within a process or set of processes performs normal synchronous I/O, but other threads can continue execution.

- **Overlapped I/O (with waiting)**. A thread continues execution after issuing a read, write, or other I/O operation. When the thread requires the I/O results before continuing, it waits on either the file handle or an event specified in the `ReadFile` or `WriteFile` overlapped structure.

- **Overlapped I/O with completion routines (or "extended I/O" or "alertable I/O")**. The system invokes a specified *completion routine* callback function within the thread when the I/O operation completes. The term "extended I/O" is easy to remember because it requires extended functions such as `WriteFileEx` and `ReadFileEx`.

The terms "overlapped I/O" and "extended I/O" are used for the last two techniques; they are, however, two forms of overlapped I/O that differ in the way Windows indicates completed operations.

The threaded server in Chapter 11 uses multithreaded I/O on named pipes. `grepMT` (Program 7–1) manages concurrent I/O to several files. Thus, we have existing programs that perform multithreaded I/O to achieve a form of asynchronous I/O.

Overlapped I/O is the subject of the next section, and the examples implement file conversion (simplified Caesar cipher, first used in Chapter 2) with this technique in order to illustrate sequential file processing. The example is a modification of Program 2–3. Following overlapped I/O, we explain extended I/O with completion routines.

Note: Overlapped and extended I/O can be complex and seldom yield large performance benefits on Windows XP. Threads frequently overcome these problems, *so some readers might wish to skip ahead to the sections on waitable timers and I/O completion ports (but see the next note),* referring back as necessary. Before doing so, however, you will find asynchronous I/O concepts in both old and very new technology, so it can be worthwhile to learn the techniques. Also, the asynchronous procedure call (APC) operation (Chapter 10) is very similar to extended I/O. There's a final significant advantage to the two overlapped I/O techniques: you can cancel outstanding I/O operations, allowing cleanup.

NT6 Note: NT6 (including Windows 7) provides an exception to the comment about performance. NT6 extended and overlapped I/O provide good performance compared to simple sequential I/O; we'll show the results here.

Finally, since I/O performance and scalability are almost always the principal objectives (in addition to correctness), remember that memory-mapped I/O can be very effective when processing files (Chapter 5), although it is not trivial to recover from memory-mapped I/O errors.

Overlapped I/O

The first requirement for asynchronous I/O, whether overlapped or extended, is to set the overlapped attribute of the file or other handle. Do this by specifying the `FILE_FLAG_OVERLAPPED` flag on the `CreateFile` or other call that creates the file, named pipe, or other handle. Sockets (Chapter 13), whether created by `socket` or `accept`, have the attribute set by default. An overlapped socket can be used asynchronously in all Windows versions.

Until now, overlapped structures have only been used with `LockFileEx` and as an alternative to `SetFilePointerEx` (Chapter 3), but they are essential for overlapped I/O. These structures are optional parameters on four I/O functions that can potentially block while the operation completes:

ReadFile

WriteFile

TransactNamedPipe

ConnectNamedPipe

Recall that when you're specifying `FILE_FLAG_OVERLAPPED` as part of dw-AttrsAndFlags (for `CreateFile`) or as part of dwOpenMode (for `CreateNamedPipe`), the pipe or file is to be used only in overlapped mode. Overlapped I/O does not work with anonymous pipes.

Consequences of Overlapped I/O

Overlapped I/O is asynchronous. There are several consequences when starting an overlapped I/O operation.

- I/O operations do not block. The system returns immediately from a call to `ReadFile`, `WriteFile`, `TransactNamedPipe`, or `ConnectNamedPipe`.

- A returned `FALSE` value does not necessarily indicate failure because the I/O operation is most likely not yet complete. In this normal case, `GetLast-Error()` will return `ERROR_IO_PENDING`, indicating no error. Windows provides a different mechanism to indicate status.

- The returned number of bytes transferred is also not useful if the transfer is not complete. Windows must provide another means of obtaining this information.

- The program may issue multiple reads or writes on a single overlapped file handle. Therefore, the handle's file pointer is meaningless. There must be another method to specify file position with each read or write. This is not a problem with named pipes, which are inherently sequential.

- The program must be able to wait (synchronize) on I/O completion. In case of multiple outstanding operations on a single handle, it must be able to determine which operation has completed. I/O operations do not necessarily complete in the same order in which they were issued.

The last two issues—file position and synchronization—are addressed by the overlapped structures.

Overlapped Structures

The OVERLAPPED structure (specified, for example, by the lpOverlapped parameter of ReadFile) indicates the following:

- The file position (64 bits) where the read or write is to start, as discussed in Chapter 3

- The event (manual-reset) that will be signaled when the operation completes

Here is the OVERLAPPED structure.

```
typedef struct _OVERLAPPED {
    DWORD Internal;
    DWORD InternalHigh;
    DWORD Offset;
    DWORD OffsetHigh;
    HANDLE hEvent;
} OVERLAPPED
```

The file position (pointer) must be set in both Offset and OffsetHigh. Do not set Internal and InternalHigh, which are reserved for the system. Currently, Windows sets Internal to the I/O request error code and InternalHigh to the number of bytes transferred. However, MSDN warns that this behavior may change in the future, and there are other ways to get the information.

hEvent is an event handle (created with `CreateEvent`). The event can be named or unnamed, but it *must* be a manual-reset event (see Chapter 8) when used for overlapped I/O; the reasons are explained soon. The event is signaled when the I/O operation completes.

Alternatively, hEvent can be `NULL`; in this case, the program can wait on the file handle, which is also a synchronization object (see the upcoming list of cautions). *Note:* For convenience, the term "file handle" is used to describe the handle with `ReadFile`, `WriteFile`, and so on, even though this handle could refer to a pipe or device rather than to a file.

This event is immediately reset (set to the nonsignaled state) by the system when the program makes an I/O call. When the I/O operation completes, the event is signaled and remains signaled until it is used with another I/O operation. The event needs to be manual-reset because multiple threads might wait on it (although our example uses only one thread).

Even if the file handle is synchronous (it was created without `FILE_FLAG_OVERLAPPED`), the overlapped structure is an alternative to `SetFile-Pointer` and `SetFilePointerEx` for specifying file position. In this case, the `ReadFile` or other call does not return until the operation is complete. This feature was useful in Chapter 3.

Notice also that an outstanding I/O operation is uniquely identified by the combination of file handle and overlapped structure.

Here are a few cautions to keep in mind.

- Do not reuse an `OVERLAPPED` structure while its associated I/O operation, if any, is outstanding.

- Similarly, do not reuse an event while it is part of an `OVERLAPPED` structure.

- If there is more than one outstanding request on an overlapped handle, use events, rather than the file handle, for synchronization. We provide examples of both forms.

- As with any automatic variable, if the `OVERLAPPED` structure or event is an automatic variable in a block, be certain not to exit the block before synchronizing with the I/O operation. Also, close the event handle before leaving the block to avoid a resource leak.

Overlapped I/O States

An overlapped `ReadFile` or `WriteFile` operation—or, for that matter, one of the two named pipe operations—returns immediately. In most cases, the I/O will not be complete, and the read or write returns FALSE. GetLastError returns ERROR_IO_PENDING. However, test the read or write return; if it's TRUE, you can get the transfer count immediately and proceed without waiting.

After waiting on a synchronization object (an event or, perhaps, the file handle) for the operation to complete, you need to determine how many bytes were transferred. This is the primary purpose of GetOverlappedResult.

```
BOOL GetOverlappedResult (
    HANDLE hFile,
    LPOVERLAPPED lpOverlapped,
    LPWORD lpcbTransfer,
    BOOL bWait)
```

The handle and overlapped structure combine to indicate the specific I/O operation. bWait, if TRUE, specifies that GetOverlappedResult will wait until the specified operation is complete; otherwise, it returns immediately. In either case, the function returns TRUE only if the operation has completed successfully. GetLastError returns ERROR_IO_INCOMPLETE in case of a FALSE return from GetOverlappedResult, so it is possible to poll for I/O completion with this function.

The number of bytes transferred is in *lpcbTransfer. Be certain that the overlapped structure is unchanged from when it was used with the overlapped I/O operation.

Canceling Overlapped I/O Operations

The Boolean NT6 function CancelIoEx cancels outstanding overlapped I/O operations on the specified handle in the current process. The arguments are the handle and the overlapped structure. All pending operations issued by the calling thread using the handle and overlapped structure are canceled. Use NULL for the overlapped structure to cancel all operations using the handle.

CancelIoEx cancels I/O requests in the calling thread only.

The canceled operations will usually complete with error code ERROR_OPERATION_ABORTED and status STATUS_CANCELLED, although the status would be STATUS_SUCCESS if the operation completed before the cancellation call.

CancelIoEx does not, however, wait for the cancellation to complete, so it's still essential to wait in the normal way before reusing the OVERLAPPED structure for another I/O operation.

Program 14-4 (serverCP) exploits CancelIoEx.

Example: Synchronizing on a File Handle

Overlapped I/O can be useful and relatively simple when there is only one outstanding operation. The program can synchronize on the file handle rather than on an event.

The following code fragment shows how a program can initiate a read operation to read a portion of a file, continue to perform other processing, and then wait on the handle.

```
OVERLAPPED ov = { 0, 0, 0, 0, NULL /* No event. */ };
HANDLE hF;
DWORD nRead;
BYTE buffer [BUF_SIZE];
...
hF = CreateFile ( ..., FILE_FLAG_OVERLAPPED, ... );
ReadFile (hF, buffer, sizeof (buffer), &nRead, &ov);
/* Perform other processing. nRead probably not valid. */
/* Wait for the read to complete. */
WaitForSingleObject (hF, INFINITE);
GetOverlappedResult (hF, &ov, &nRead, FALSE);
```

Example: File Conversion with Overlapped I/O and Multiple Buffers

Program 2–3 (cci) encrypted a file to illustrate sequential file conversion, and Program 5-3 (cciMM) showed how to perform the same sequential file processing with memory-mapped files. Program 14–1 (cciOV) performs the same task using overlapped I/O and multiple buffers holding fixed-size records.

Figure 14–1 shows the program organization and an operational scenario with four fixed-size buffers. The program is implemented so that the number of buffers is defined in a preprocessor variable, but the following discussion assumes four buffers.

First, the program initializes all the overlapped structures with events and file positions. There is a separate overlapped structure for each input and each output buffer. Next, an overlapped read is issued for each of the four input buffers. The program then uses WaitForMultipleObjects to wait for a single event, indicating either a read or a write completed. When a read completes, the buffer is copied and converted into the corresponding output buffer and the write is initiated. When a write completes, the next read is initiated. Notice that the events associated with the input and output buffers are arranged in a single array to be used as an argument to WaitForMultipleObjects.

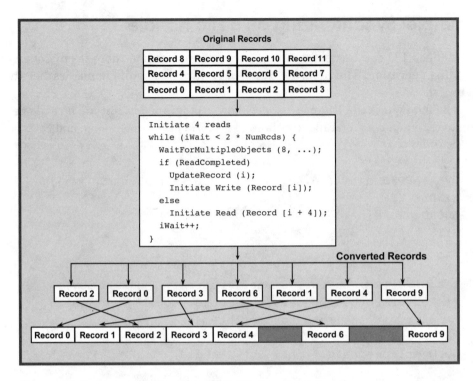

Figure 14–1 An Asynchronous File Update Model

Program 14–1 cciOV: File Conversion with Overlapped I/O

```
/* Chapter 14. cciOV.
   OVERLAPPED simplified Caesar cipher file conversion. */
/* cciOV shift file1 file2 */
/* This program illustrates overlapped asynch I/O. */

#include "Everything.h"

#define MAX_OVRLP 4/* Must be <= 32 due to WaitForMultipleObjects */
#define REC_SIZE 0x4000 /* Selected experimentally for performance */

int _tmain (int argc, LPTSTR argv[])
{
    HANDLE hInputFile, hOutputFile;
    DWORD shift, nIn[MAX_OVRLP], nOut[MAX_OVRLP], ic, i;
    /* There is a copy of each of the following structures */
    /* for each outstanding overlapped I/O operation */
    OVERLAPPED overLapIn[MAX_OVRLP], overLapOut[MAX_OVRLP];
    /* The first event index is 0 for read, 1 for write */
    /* WaitForMultipleObjects requires a contiguous array */
```

```
HANDLE hEvents[2][MAX_OVRLP];
/* The first index on these two buffers is the I/O operation */
CHAR rawRec[MAX_OVRLP][REC_SIZE], ccRec[MAX_OVRLP][REC_SIZE];
LARGE_INTEGER curPosIn, curPosOut, fileSize;
LONGLONG nRecords, iWaits;

shift = _ttoi(argv[1]);

hInputFile = CreateFile (argv[2], GENERIC_READ,
        0, NULL, OPEN_EXISTING, FILE_FLAG_OVERLAPPED, NULL);
hOutputFile = CreateFile (argv[3], GENERIC_WRITE,
        0, NULL, CREATE_ALWAYS, FILE_FLAG_OVERLAPPED, NULL);

/* Compute total number of records - There may be a
   partial record at the end. */
GetFileSizeEx (hInputFile, &fileSize);
nRecords = (fileSize.QuadPart + REC_SIZE - 1) / REC_SIZE;

/*  Create the manual-reset, unsignaled events for
    the overlapped structures. Initiate a read on
    each buffer, corresponding to the overlapped structure. */
curPosIn.QuadPart = 0;
for (ic = 0; ic < MAX_OVRLP; ic++) {
    /* Input and output complete events. */
    hEvents[0][ic] = overLapIn[ic].hEvent =
            CreateEvent (NULL, TRUE, FALSE, NULL);
    hEvents[1][ic] = overLapOut[ic].hEvent =
            CreateEvent (NULL, TRUE, FALSE, NULL);
    /* Set file position. */
    overLapIn[ic].Offset = curPosIn.LowPart;
    overLapIn[ic].OffsetHigh = curPosIn.HighPart;
    if (curPosIn.QuadPart < fileSize.QuadPart)
        ReadFile (hInputFile, rawRec[ic], REC_SIZE,
                &nIn[ic], &overLapIn[ic]);
    curPosIn.QuadPart += (LONGLONG)REC_SIZE;
}

/*  All read operations running. Wait for read & write events.
    Continue until all records have been processed. */

iWaits = 0;
while (iWaits < 2 * nRecords) {
    ic = WaitForMultipleObjects (2 * MAX_OVRLP, hEvents[0],
                    FALSE, INFINITE) - WAIT_OBJECT_0;
    iWaits++;

    if (ic < MAX_OVRLP) { /* A read completed. */
        GetOverlappedResult (hInputFile, &overLapIn[ic],
                        &nIn[ic], FALSE);
```

```
                  /* Reset event before the next WFMO call. Otherwise,
                   * event won't be reset until next Read for this ic value */
                  ResetEvent (hEvents[0][ic]);
                  /* Process record and start write at same position. */
                  curPosIn.LowPart = overLapIn[ic].Offset;
                  curPosIn.HighPart = overLapIn[ic].OffsetHigh;
                  curPosOut.QuadPart = curPosIn.QuadPart;
                  overLapOut[ic].Offset = curPosOut.LowPart;
                  overLapOut[ic].OffsetHigh = curPosOut.HighPart;

                  /* Encrypt the record. */
                  for (i = 0; i < nIn[ic]; i++)
                      ccRec[ic][i] = (rawRec[ic][i] + shift) % 256;
                  WriteFile (hOutputFile, ccRec[ic], nIn[ic],
                          &nOut[ic], &overLapOut[ic]);

                  /* Prepare input overlapped structure for next read, which
                     is initiated after the write completes. */

                  curPosIn.QuadPart += REC_SIZE * (LONGLONG) (MAX_OVRLP);
                  overLapIn[ic].Offset = curPosIn.LowPart;
                  overLapIn[ic].OffsetHigh = curPosIn.HighPart;

              } else if (ic < 2 * MAX_OVRLP) {/* A write completed. */
                  /* Start the read. Check first to not read past file end */
                  ic -= MAX_OVRLP;/* Set the output buffer index. */
                  GetOverlappedResult (hOutputFile, &overLapOut[ic],
                                    &nOut[ic], FALSE);
                  ResetEvent (hEvents[1][ic]);
                  curPosIn.LowPart = overLapIn[ic].Offset;
                  curPosIn.HighPart = overLapIn[ic].OffsetHigh;
                  /* Start a new read. */
                  if (curPosIn.QuadPart < fileSize.QuadPart) {
                      ReadFile (hInputFile, rawRec[ic], REC_SIZE,
                              &nIn[ic], &overLapIn[ic]);
                  }
              }
              else/* Impossible unless wait failed error. */
                  ReportError (_T ("Multiple wait error."), 0, TRUE);
          }

          /*  Close all events. */
          for (ic = 0; ic < MAX_OVRLP; ic++) {
              CloseHandle (hEvents[0][ic]);
              CloseHandle (hEvents[1][ic]);
          }
          CloseHandle (hInputFile);
          CloseHandle (hOutputFile);
          return 0;

      }
```

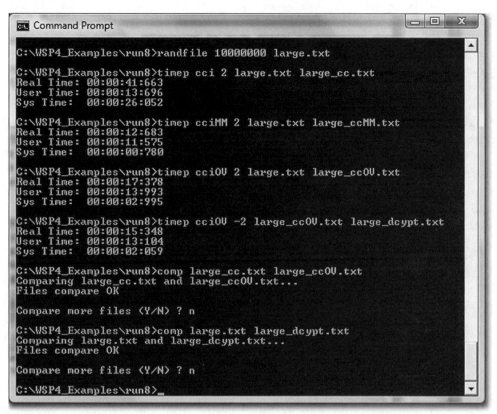

Run 14–1 cciOV: Comparing Performance and Testing Results

Run 14–1 shows cci timings converting the same 640MB file with cci, cciMM, and cciOV on a four-processor Windows Vista machine.

Memory mapping and overlapped I/O provide the best performance, with memory-mapped I/O showing a consistent advantage (12.7 seconds compared to about 16 seconds in this test). Run 14–1 also compares the converted files and the decrypted file as an initial correctness test.

The cciOV timing results in Run 14–1 depend on the record size (the REC_SIZE macro in the listing). The 0x4000 (16K) value worked well, as did 8K. However, 32K required twice the time. An exercise suggests experimenting with the record size on different systems and file sizes. Appendix C shows additional timing results on several systems for the different cci implementations.

Caution: The elapsed time in these tests can occasionally increase significantly, sometimes by factors of 2 or more. However, Run 14–1 contains typical results that I've been able to reproduce consistently. Nonetheless, be aware that you might see much longer times, depending on numerous factors such as other machine activity.

Extended I/O with Completion Routines

There is an alternative to using synchronization objects. Rather than requiring a thread to wait for a completion signal on an event or handle, the system can invoke a user-specified completion, or callback, routine when an I/O operation completes. The completion routine can then start the next I/O operation and perform any other bookkeeping. The completion or callback routine is similar to Chapter 10's asynchronous procedure call and requires alertable wait states.

How can the program specify the completion routine? There are no remaining `ReadFile` or `WriteFile` parameters or data structures to hold the routine's address. There is, however, a family of extended I/O functions, identified by the `Ex` suffix and containing an extra parameter for the completion routine address. The read and write functions are `ReadFileEx` and `WriteFileEx`, respectively. It is also necessary to use one of five alertable wait functions:

- `WaitForSingleObjectEx`
- `WaitForMultipleObjectsEx`
- `SleepEx`
- `SignalObjectAndWait`
- `MsgWaitForMultipleObjectsEx`

Extended I/O is sometimes called *alertable I/O,* and Chapter 10 used alertable wait states for thread cancellation. The following sections show how to use the extended functions.

`ReadFileEx`, `WriteFileEx`, and Completion Routines

The extended read and write functions work with open file, named pipe, and mailslot handles if `FILE_FLAG_OVERLAPPED` was used at open (create) time. Notice that the flag sets a handle attribute, and while overlapped I/O and extended I/O are distinguished, a single overlapped flag enables both types of asynchronous I/O on a handle.

Overlapped sockets (Chapter 12) operate with `ReadFileEx` and `WriteFileEx`.

```
BOOL ReadFileEx (
    HANDLE hFile,
    LPVOID lpBuffer,
    DWORD nNumberOfBytesToRead,
    LPOVERLAPPED lpOverlapped,
    LPOVERLAPPED_COMPLETION_ROUTINE lpcr)

BOOL WriteFileEx (
    HANDLE hFile,
    LPVOID lpBuffer,
    DWORD nNumberOfBytesToWrite,
    LPOVERLAPPED lpOverlapped,
    LPOVERLAPPED_COMPLETION_ROUTINE lpcr)
```

The two functions are familiar but have an extra parameter to specify the completion routine. The completion routine could be NULL; there's no easy way to get the results.

The overlapped structures must be supplied, but there is no need to specify the hEvent member; the system ignores it. It turns out, however, that this member is useful for carrying information, such as a sequence number, to identify the I/O operation, as shown in Program 14–2.

In comparison to ReadFile and WriteFile, notice that the extended functions do not require the parameters for the number of bytes transferred. That information is conveyed as an argument to the completion routine.

The completion routine has parameters for the byte count, an error code, and the overlapped structure. The last parameter is necessary so that the completion routine can determine which of several outstanding operations has completed. Notice that the same cautions regarding reuse or destruction of overlapped structures apply here as they did for overlapped I/O.

```
VOID WINAPI FileIOCompletionRoutine (
    DWORD dwError,
    DWORD cbTransferred,
    LPOVERLAPPED lpo)
```

As was the case with CreateThread, which also specified a function name, *FileIOCompletionRoutine* is a placeholder and not an actual function name.

Common dwError values are 0 (success) and ERROR_HANDLE_EOF (when a read tries to go past the end of the file). The overlapped structure is the one used by the completed ReadFileEx or WriteFileEx call.

Two things must happen before the completion routine is invoked by the system.

1. The I/O operation must complete.

2. The calling thread must be in an alertable wait state, notifying the system that it should execute any queued completion routines.

How does a thread get into an alertable wait state? It must make an explicit call to one of the alertable wait functions described in the next section. In this way, the thread can ensure that the completion routine does not execute prematurely. A thread can be in an alertable wait state only while it is calling an alertable wait function; on return, the thread is no longer in this state.

Once these two conditions have been met, completion routines that have been queued as the result of I/O completion are executed. *Completion routines are executed in the same thread that made the original I/O call and is in the alertable wait state.* Therefore, the thread should enter an alertable wait state only when it is safe for completion routines to execute.

Alertable Wait Functions

There are five alertable wait functions, and the three that relate directly to our current needs are described here.

```
DWORD WaitForSingleObjectEx (
    HANDLE hObject,
    DWORD dwMilliseconds,
    BOOL bAlertable)

DWORD WaitForMultipleObjectsEx (
    DWORD cObjects,
    LPHANDLE lphObjects,
    BOOL fWaitAll,
    DWORD dwMilliseconds,
    BOOL bAlertable)

DWORD SleepEx (
    DWORD dwMilliseconds,
    BOOL bAlertable)
```

Each alertable wait function has a bAlertable flag that must be set to TRUE when used for asynchronous I/O. The functions are extensions of the familiar Wait and Sleep functions.

Time-outs, as always, are in milliseconds. These three functions will return as soon as *any one* of the following situations occurs.

- Handle(s) are signaled so as to satisfy one of the two wait functions in the normal way.

- The time-out period expires.

- At least one completion routine or user APC (see Chapter 10) is queued to the thread and `bAlertable` is set. Completion routines are queued when their associated I/O operation is complete (see Figure 14–2) or `QueueUserAPC` queues a user APC. Windows executes all queued user APCs and completion routines before returning from an alertable wait function. Note how this allows I/O operation cancellation with a user APC, as was done in Chapter 10.

Also notice that no events are associated with the `ReadFileEx` and `Write-FileEx` overlapped structures, so any handles in the wait call will have no direct relation to the I/O operations. `SleepEx`, on the other hand, is not associated with a synchronization object and is the easiest of the three functions to use. `SleepEx` is usually used with an `INFINITE` time-out so that the function will return only after one or more of the currently queued completion routines have finished.

Execution of Completion Routines and the Alertable Wait Return

As soon as an extended I/O operation is complete, its associated completion routine, with the overlapped structure, byte count, and error status arguments, is queued for execution.

All of a thread's queued completion routines are executed when the thread enters an alertable wait state. They are executed sequentially but not necessarily in the same order as I/O completion. The alertable wait function returns only after the completion routines return. This property is essential to the proper operation of most programs because it assumes that the completion routines can prepare for the next use of the overlapped structure and perform related operations to get the program to a known state before the alertable wait returns.

`SleepEx` and the wait functions will return `WAIT_IO_COMPLETION` if one or more queued completion routines were executed.

Here are two final points.

1. Use an `INFINITE` time-out value with any alertable wait function. Without the possibility of a time-out, the wait function will return only after all queued completion routines have been executed or the handles have been signaled.

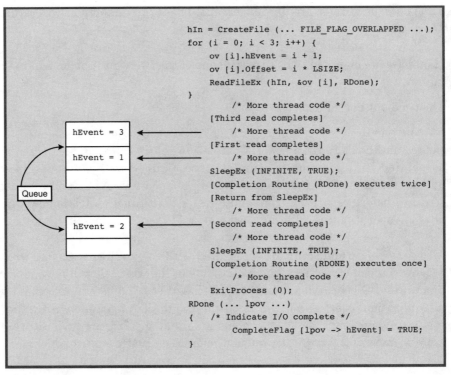

```
hIn = CreateFile (... FILE_FLAG_OVERLAPPED ...);
for (i = 0; i < 3; i++) {
    ov [i].hEvent = i + 1;
    ov [i].Offset = i * LSIZE;
    ReadFileEx (hIn, &ov [i], RDone);
}
        /* More thread code */
[Third read completes]
        /* More thread code */
[First read completes]
        /* More thread code */
SleepEx (INFINITE, TRUE);
[Completion Routine (RDone) executes twice]
[Return from SleepEx]
        /* More thread code */
[Second read completes]
        /* More thread code */
SleepEx (INFINITE, TRUE);
[Completion Routine (RDONE) executes once]
        /* More thread code */
ExitProcess (0);
RDone (... lpov ...)
{   /* Indicate I/O complete */
        CompleteFlag [lpov -> hEvent] = TRUE;
}
```

hEvent = 3

hEvent = 1

Queue

hEvent = 2

Figure 14–2 Asynchronous I/O with Completion Routines

2. It is common practice to use the hEvent data member of the overlapped structure to convey information to the completion routine because Windows ignores this field.

Figure 14–2 illustrates the interaction among the main thread, the completion routines, and the alertable waits. In this example, three concurrent read operations are started, and two are completed by the time the alertable wait is performed.

Example: File Conversion with Extended I/O

Program 14–2, cciEX, reimplements Program 14–1, cciOV. These programs show the programming differences between the two asynchronous I/O techniques. cciEX is similar to Program 14–1 but moves most of the bookkeeping code to the completion routines, and many variables are global so as to be accessible from the completion routines.

Program 14–2   cciEX: File Conversion with Extended I/O

```
/* Chapter 14. cciEX.
      EXTENDED simplified Caesar cipher conversion. */
/* cciEX file1 file2  */
/* This program illustrates Extended (a.k.a.
   alterable or completion routine asynch) I/O.
   It was developed by restructuring cciOV. */

#include "Everything.h"

#define MAX_OVRLP 4
#define REC_SIZE 0x8000 /* Size is not as important as with cciOV */

static VOID WINAPI ReadDone (DWORD, DWORD, LPOVERLAPPED);
static VOID WINAPI WriteDone (DWORD, DWORD, LPOVERLAPPED);

/* The first overlapped structure is for reading,
   and the second is for writing. Structures and buffers are
   provided for each outstanding operation */
OVERLAPPED overLapIn[MAX_OVRLP], overLapOut[MAX_OVRLP];
CHAR rawRec[MAX_OVRLP][REC_SIZE], cciRec[MAX_OVRLP][REC_SIZE];
HANDLE hInputFile, hOutputFile;
LONGLONG nRecords, nDone;
LARGE_INTEGER fileSize;
DWORD shift;

int _tmain (int argc, LPTSTR argv[])
{
    DWORD ic;
    LARGE_INTEGER curPosIn;

    shift = _ttoi(argv[1]);
    hInputFile = CreateFile (argv[2], GENERIC_READ,
          0, NULL, OPEN_EXISTING, FILE_FLAG_OVERLAPPED, NULL);
    hOutputFile = CreateFile (argv[3], GENERIC_WRITE,
          0, NULL, CREATE_ALWAYS, FILE_FLAG_OVERLAPPED, NULL);

    /* Compute total number of records to process.
       There may not be a partial record at the end. */
    GetFileSizeEx (hInputFile, &fileSize);
    nRecords = (fileSize.QuadPart + REC_SIZE - 1) / REC_SIZE;

    /* Initiate read on buffer paired with an overlapped structure*/
    curPosIn.QuadPart = 0;
    for (ic = 0; ic < MAX_OVRLP; ic++) {
        overLapIn[ic].hEvent = (HANDLE)ic;/* Overload event field to */
        overLapOut[ic].hEvent = (HANDLE)ic;/* hold the event number. */
        /* Set file position. */
```

```
        overLapIn[ic].Offset = curPosIn.LowPart;
        overLapIn[ic].OffsetHigh = curPosIn.HighPart;
        if (curPosIn.QuadPart < fileSize.QuadPart)
            ReadFileEx (hInputFile, rawRec[ic], REC_SIZE,
                    &overLapIn[ic], ReadDone);
        curPosIn.QuadPart += (LONGLONG) REC_SIZE;
    }

    /*  All read operations are running. Enter an alterable
        wait state; continue until all records have been processed. */
    nDone = 0;
    while (nDone < 2* nRecords) {
        SleepEx (0, TRUE);
    }

    CloseHandle (hInputFile); CloseHandle (hOutputFile);
    return 0;
}

static VOID WINAPI ReadDone (DWORD Code, DWORD nBytes,
                        LPOVERLAPPED pOv)
{
    LARGE_INTEGER curPosIn, curPosOut;
    DWORD i, ic; /* Represents value from event field */

    nDone++;
    /* Process the record and initiate the write. */
    /* Get the overlapped structure ID from the event field. */
    ic = PtrToInt(pOv->hEvent);
    curPosIn.LowPart = overLapIn[ic].Offset;
    curPosIn.HighPart = overLapIn[ic].OffsetHigh;
    curPosOut.QuadPart = (curPosIn.QuadPart / REC_SIZE) * REC_SIZE;
    overLapOut[ic].Offset = curPosOut.LowPart;
    overLapOut[ic].OffsetHigh = curPosOut.HighPart;

    /* Encrypt the characters */
    for (i = 0; i < nBytes; i++)
        cciRec[ic][i] = (rawRec[ic][i] + shift) % 256;
    WriteFileEx (hOutputFile, cciRec[ic], nBytes,
        &overLapOut[ic], WriteDone);

    /* Prepare the input overlapped structure
        for the next read, which will be initiated
        after the write, issued above, completes. */
    curPosIn.QuadPart += REC_SIZE * (LONGLONG) (MAX_OVRLP);
    overLapIn[ic].Offset = curPosIn.LowPart;
    overLapIn[ic].OffsetHigh = curPosIn.HighPart;

    return;
}
```

```
static VOID WINAPI WriteDone (DWORD Code, DWORD nBytes,
                              LPOVERLAPPED pOv)
{
    LARGE_INTEGER curPosIn;
    DWORD ic;
    nDone++;
    /* Get the overlapped structure ID from the event field. */
    ic = PtrToInt(pOv->hEvent);

    /* Start the read. The file position was already set in the input
       overlapped structure. Check first, however, to assure not to
       read past the end of file. */
    curPosIn.LowPart = overLapIn[ic].Offset;
    curPosIn.HighPart = overLapIn[ic].OffsetHigh;
    if (curPosIn.QuadPart < fileSize.QuadPart) {
        /* Start a new read. */
        ReadFileEx (hInputFile, rawRec[ic], REC_SIZE,
                &overLapIn[ic], ReadDone);
    }
    return;
}
```

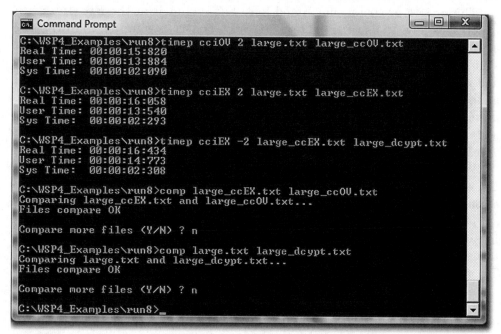

Run 14–2 `cciEX`: Overlapped I/O with Completion Routines

Run 14–2 and Appendix C show that `cciEX` performs competitively with `cciOV`, which was slower than the memory-mapped version on the tested four-processor Windows Vista computer. Based on these results, asynchronous overlapped I/O is a good choice for sequential and possibly other file I/O but does not compete with memory-mapped I/O. The choice between the overlapped and extended overlapped I/O is somewhat a matter of taste (I found `cciEX` slightly easier to write and debug).

Asynchronous I/O with Threads

Overlapped and extended I/O achieve asynchronous I/O within a single user thread. These techniques are common, in one form or another, in many older OSs for supporting limited forms of asynchronous operation in single-threaded systems.

Windows, however, supports threads, so the same functional effect is possible by performing synchronous I/O operations in multiple, separate threads, at the possible performance cost due to thread management overhead. Threads also provide a uniform and, arguably, much simpler way to perform asynchronous I/O. An alternative to Programs 14–1 and 14–2 is to give each thread its own handle to the file and each thread could synchronously process every fourth record.

The `cciMT` program, not listed here but included in the *Examples* file, illustrates how to use threads in this way. `cciMT` is simpler than the two asynchronous I/O programs because the bookkeeping is less complex. Each thread simply maintains its own buffers on its own stack and performs the read, convert, and write sequence synchronously in a loop. The performance is superior to the results in Run 14–2, so the possible performance impact is not realized. In particular, the 640MB file conversions, which require about 16 seconds for `cciOV` and `cciEX`, require about 10 seconds for `cciMT`, running on the same machine. This is better than the memory-mapped performance (about 12 seconds).

What would happen if we combined memory mapping and multiple threads? `cciMTMM`, also in the *Examples* file, shows even better results, namely about 4 seconds for this case. Appendix C has results for several different machines.

My personal preference is to use threads rather than asynchronous I/O for file processing, and they provide the best performance in most cases. Memory mapping can improve things even more, although it's difficult to recover from I/O errors, as noted in Chapter 5. The programming logic is simpler, but there are the usual thread risks.

There are some important exceptions to this generalization.

- The situation shown earlier in the chapter in which there is only a single outstanding operation and the file handle can be used for synchronization.

- Asynchronous I/O can be canceled. However, with small modifications, `cciMT` can be modified to use overlapped I/O, with the reading or writing thread waiting on the event immediately after the I/O operation is started. Exercise 14–10 suggests this modification.

- Multithreaded programs have many risks and can be a challenge to get right, as Chapters 7 through 10 describe. A source file, cciMT_dh.c, that's in the unzipped *Examples,* documents several pitfalls I encountered while developing cciMT; don't try to use this program because it is not correct!

- Asynchronous I/O completion ports, described at the end of this chapter, are useful with servers.

- NT6 executes asynchronous I/O programs very efficiently compared to normal file I/O (see Run 14–1 and Appendix C).

Waitable Timers

Windows supports waitable timers, a type of waitable kernel object.

You can always create your own timing signal using a timing thread that sets an event after waking from a Sleep call. serverNP (Program 11–3) also uses a timing thread to broadcast its pipe name periodically. Therefore, waitable timers are a redundant but useful way to perform tasks periodically or at specified absolute or relative times.

As the name suggests, you can wait for a waitable timer to be signaled, but you can also use a callback routine similar to the extended I/O completion routines. A waitable timer can be either a *synchronization timer* or a *manual-reset (or notification) timer.* Synchronization and manual-reset timers are comparable to auto-reset and manual-reset events; a synchronization timer becomes unsignaled after a wait completes on it, and a manual-reset timer must be reset explicitly. In summary:

- There are two ways to be notified that a timer is signaled: either wait on the timer or have a callback routine.

- There are two waitable timer types, which differ in whether or not the timer is reset automatically after a wait.

The first step is to create a timer handle with CreateWaitableTimer.

```
HANDLE CreateWaitableTimer (
    LPSECURITY_ATTRIBUTES lpTimerAttributes,
    BOOL bManualReset,
    LPCTSTR lpTimerName);
```

The second parameter, bManualReset, determines whether the timer is a synchronization timer or a manual-reset notification timer. Program 14–3 uses a synchronization timer, but you can change the comment and the parameter setting to obtain a notification timer. Notice that there is also an OpenWaitable-Timer function that can use the optional name supplied in the third argument.

The timer is initially inactive, but SetWaitableTimer activates it, sets the timer to unsignaled, and specifies the initial signal time and the time between periodic signals.

```
BOOL SetWaitableTimer (
    HANDLE hTimer,
    const LARGE_INTEGER *pDueTime,
    LONG lPeriod,
    PTIMERAPCROUTINE pfnCompletionRoutine,
    LPVOID lpArgToCompletionRoutine,
    BOOL fResume);
```

hTimer is a valid timer handle created using CreateWaitableTimer.

The second parameter, pointed to by pDueTime, is either a positive absolute time or a negative relative time and is actually expressed as a FILETIME with a resolution of 100 nanoseconds. FILETIME variables were introduced in Chapter 3 and were used in Chapter 6's timep (Program 6–2).

The third parameter specifies the interval between signals, using millisecond units. If this value is 0, the timer is signaled only once. A positive value indicates that the timer is a periodic timer and continues signaling periodically until you call CancelWaitableTimer. Negative interval values are not allowed.

pfnCompletionRoutine, the fourth parameter, specifies the time-out call-back function (completion routine) to be called when the timer is signaled *and* the thread enters an alertable wait state. The routine is called with the pointer specified in the fifth parameter, lpArgToCompletionRoutine, as an argument.

Having set a synchronization timer, you can now call SleepEx or other alertable wait function to enter an alertable wait state, allowing the completion routine to be called. Alternatively, wait on the timer handle. As mentioned previously, a manual-reset waitable timer handle will remain signaled until the next call to SetWaitableTimer, whereas Windows resets a synchronization timer immediately after the first wait after the set.

The complete version of Program 14–3 in the *Examples* file allows you to experiment with using the four combinations of the two timer types and with choosing between using a completion routine or waiting on the timer handle.

The final parameter, fResume, is concerned with power conservation. See the MSDN documentation for more information.

Use CancelWaitableTimer to cancel the last effect of a previous SetWaitableTimer, although it will not change the timer's signaled state; use another SetWaitableTimer call to do that.

Example: Using a Waitable Timer

Program 14–3 shows how to use a waitable timer to signal the user periodically.

Program 14–3   TimeBeep: A Periodic Signal

```
/* Chapter 14 -  TimeBeep. Periodic alarm. */
/* Usage: TimeBeep period (in ms). */
/* This implementation uses kernel object "waitable timers".
   This program uses a console control handler to catch
   control C signals; see the end of Chapter 7.  */

#include "Everything.h"

static BOOL WINAPI Handler (DWORD CntrlEvent);
static VOID APIENTRY Beeper (LPVOID, DWORD, DWORD);
volatile static LONG exitFlag = 0;

HANDLE hTimer;

int _tmain (int argc, LPTSTR argv [])
{
    DWORD count = 0, period;
    LARGE_INTEGER dueTime;

    if (argc >= 2) period = _ttoi (argv [1]) * 1000;

    SetConsoleCtrlHandler (Handler, TRUE);

    dueTime.QuadPart = -(LONGLONG)period * 10000;
            /*  Due time is negative for first time-out relative to
                current time. Period is in ms (10**-3 sec) whereas
                the due time is in 100 ns (10**-7 sec) units to be
                consistent with a FILETIME. */

    hTimer = CreateWaitableTimer (NULL,
        FALSE /*TRUE*/,/* Not manual reset ("notification") timer, but
                        a "synchronization timer." */
        NULL);
```

```
    SetWaitableTimer (hTimer,
          &dueTime /* relative time of first signal. Positive value
                would indicate an absolute time. */,
          period  /* Time period in ms */,
          Beeper  /* Timer function */,
          &count  /* Parameter passed to timer function */,
          FALSE);

    /* Enter the main loop */
    while (!exitFlag) {
        _tprintf (_T("count = %d\n"), count);
        /* count is increased in the timer routine */
        /*  Enter an alertable wait state, enabling the timer routine.
            The timer handle is a synchronization object, so you can
            also wait on it. */
        SleepEx (INFINITE, TRUE);
        /* or WaitForSingleObjectEx (hTimer, INFINITE); Beeper(...); */
    }

    _tprintf (_T("Shut down. count = %d"), count);
    CancelWaitableTimer (hTimer);
    CloseHandle (hTimer);
    return 0;
}

/* Waitable timer callback function */
static VOID APIENTRY Beeper (LPVOID lpCount,
    DWORD dwTimerLowValue, DWORD dwTimerHighValue)
{

    *(LPDWORD)lpCount = *(LPDWORD)lpCount + 1;

    _tprintf (_T("About to perform beep number: %d\n"),
            *(LPDWORD)lpCount);
    Beep (1000 /* Frequency */, 250 /* Duration (ms) */);
    return;
}

BOOL WINAPI Handler (DWORD CntrlEvent)
{
    InterlockedIncrement(&exitFlag);
    _tprintf (_T("Shutting Down\n"));

    return TRUE;
}
```

Comments on the Waitable Timer Example

There are four combinations based on timer type and whether you wait on the handle or use a completion routine. Program 14–3 illustrates using a completion routine and a synchronization timer. The four combinations can be tested using the version of `TimeBeep.c` in the *Examples* file by changing some comments.

Caution: The beep sound may be annoying, so you might want to test this program without anyone else nearby or adjust the frequency and duration.

Threadpool Timers

Alternatively, you can use a different type of timer, specifying that the timer callback function is to be executed within a thread pool (see Chapter 9). `TimeBeep-_TPT` is a simple modification to `TimeBeep`, and it shows how to use `CreateThreadpoolTimer` and `SetThreadpoolTimer`. The new program requires a `FILETIME` structure for the timer due time, whereas the waitable timer used a `LARGE_INTEGER`.

I/O Completion Ports

I/O completion ports combine features of both overlapped I/O and independent threads and are most useful in server programs. To see the requirement for this, consider the servers that we built in Chapters 11 and 12 (and converted to Windows Services in Chapter 13), where each client is supported by a distinct worker thread associated with a socket or named pipe instance. This solution works well when the number of clients is not large.

Consider what would happen, however, if there were 1,000 clients. The current model would then require 1,000 threads, each with a substantial amount of virtual memory space. For example, by default, each thread will consume 1MB of stack space, so 1,000 threads would require 1GB of virtual address space, and thread context switches could increase page fault delays.[1] Furthermore, the threads would contend for shared resources both in the executive and in the process, and the timing data in Chapter 9 showed the performance degradation that can result. Therefore, there is a requirement to allow a small pool of worker threads to serve a large number of clients. Chapter 9 used an NT6 thread pool to address this same problem.

I/O completion ports provide a solution on all Windows versions by allowing you to create a limited number of server threads in a thread pool while having a very large number of named pipe handles (or sockets), each associated with a dif-

---

[1]This problem is less severe, but should not be ignored, on systems with large amounts of memory.

ferent client. Handles are not paired with individual worker server threads; rather, a server thread can process data on any handle that has available data.

An I/O completion port, then, is a set of overlapped handles, and threads wait on the port. When a read or write on one of the handles is complete, one thread is awakened and given the data and the results of the I/O operation. The thread can then process the data and wait on the port again.

The first task is to create an I/O completion port and add overlapped handles to the port.

Managing I/O Completion Ports

A single function, `CreateIoCompletionPort`, both creates the port and adds handles. Since this one function must perform two tasks, the parameter usage is correspondingly complex.

```
HANDLE CreateIoCompletionPort (
    HANDLE FileHandle,
    HANDLE ExistingCompletionPort,
    ULONG_PTR CompletionKey,
    DWORD NumberOfConcurrentThreads);
```

An I/O completion port is a collection of file handles opened in OVERLAPPED mode. `FileHandle` is an overlapped handle to add to the port. If the value is `INVALID_HANDLE_VALUE`, a new I/O completion port is created and returned by the function. The next parameter, `ExistingCompletionPort`, must be NULL in this case.

`ExistingCompletionPort` is the port created on the first call, and it indicates the port to which the handle in the first parameter is to be added. The function also returns the port handle when the function is successful; NULL indicates failure.

`CompletionKey` specifies the key that will be included in the completion packet for `FileHandle`. The key could be a pointer to a structure containing information such as an operation type, a handle, and a pointer to the data buffer. Alternatively, the key could be an index to a table of structures, although this is less flexible.

`NumberOfConcurrentThreads` indicates the maximum number of threads allowed to execute concurrently. Any threads in excess of this number that are waiting on the port will remain blocked even if there is a handle with available data. If this parameter is 0, the number of processors in the system is the limit. The value is ignored except when `ExistingCompletionPort` is NULL (that is, the port is created, not when handles are added).

An unlimited number of overlapped handles can be associated with an I/O completion port. Call `CreateIoCompletionPort` initially to create the port and to specify the maximum number of threads. Call the function again for every overlapped handle that is to be associated with the port. There is no way to remove a handle from a completion port; the handle and completion port are associated permanently.

The handles associated with a port should not be used with `ReadFileEx` or `WriteFileEx` functions. The Microsoft documentation suggests that the files or other objects not be shared using other open handles.

Waiting on an I/O Completion Port

Use `ReadFile` and `WriteFile`, along with overlapped structures (no event handle is necessary), to perform I/O on the handles associated with a port. The I/O operation is then queued on the completion port.

A thread waits for a queued overlapped completion not by waiting on an event but by calling `GetQueuedCompletionStatus`, specifying the completion port. Upon completion, the function returns a key that was specified when the handle (the one whose operation has completed) was initially added to the port with `CreateIoCompletionPort`. This key can specify the identity of the actual handle for the completed operation and other information associated with the I/O operation.

Notice that the Windows thread that initiated the read or write is not necessarily the thread that will receive the completion notification; any waiting thread can receive completion notification. Therefore, the receiving thread can identify the handle of the completed operation from the completion key.

Never hold a lock (mutex, `CRITICAL_SECTION`, etc.) when you call `GetQueuedCompletionStatus`, because the thread that releases the lock is probably not the some thread that acquired it. Owning the lock would not be a good idea in any case as there is an indefinite wait before the completion notification.

There is also a time-out associated with the wait.

```
BOOL GetQueuedCompletionStatus (
    HANDLE CompletionPort,
    LPDWORD lpNumberOfBytesTransferred,
    PULONG_PTR lpCompletionKey,
    LPOVERLAPPED *lpOverlapped,
    DWORD dwMilliseconds);
```

It is sometimes convenient (as in an additional example, `cciMTCP`, in the *Examples* file) to have the operation not be queued on the I/O completion port, making the operation synchronous. In such a case, a thread can wait on the overlapped event. In order to specify that an overlapped operation should *not* be queued on the completion port, you must set the low-order bit in the overlapped structure's event handle; then you can wait on the event for that specific operation. This is an interesting design, but MSDN does document it, although not prominently.

Posting to an I/O Completion Port

A thread can post a completion event, with a key, to a port to satisfy an outstanding call to GetQueuedCompletionStatus. The PostQueuedCompletionStatus function supplies all the required information.

```
BOOL PostQueuedCompletionStatus (
    HANDLE CompletionPort,
    DWORD dwNumberOfBytesTransferred,
    ULONG_PTR dwCompletionKey,
    LPOVERLAPPED lpOverlapped);
```

One common technique is to provide a bogus key value, such as -1, to wake up waiting threads, even though no operation has completed. Waiting threads should test for bogus key values, and this technique can be used, for example, to signal a thread to shut down.

Alternatives to I/O Completion Ports

Chapter 9 showed how a semaphore can be used to limit the number of ready threads, and this technique is effective in maintaining throughput when many threads compete for limited resources.

We could use the same technique with server SK (Program 12–2) and serverNP (Program 11–3). All that is required is to wait on the semaphore after the read request completes, perform the request, create the response, and release the semaphore before writing the response. This solution is much simpler than the I/O completion port example in the next section. One problem with this solution is that there may be a large number of threads, each with its own stack space, which will consume virtual memory. The problem can be partly alleviated by carefully measuring the amount of stack space required. Exercise 14–7 involves experimentation with this alternative solution, and there is an example implementation in the *Examples* file. I/O completion ports also have the advantage that the scheduler posts the completion to the thread most recently executed, as that thread's memory is most likely still in the cache or at least does not need to be paged in.

There is yet another possibility when creating scalable servers. A limited number of worker threads can take work item packets from a queue (see Chapter 10). The incoming work items can be placed in the queue by one or more boss threads, as in Program 10–5.

Example: A Server Using I/O Completion Ports

serverCP (Program 14–4) modifies serverNP (Program 11–3) to use I/O completion ports. This server creates a small server thread pool and a larger pool of overlapped pipe handles along with a completion key for each handle. The overlapped handles are added to the completion port and a ConnectNamedPipe call is issued. The server threads wait for completions associated with both client connections and read operations. After a read is detected, the associated client request is processed and returned to the client (clientNP from Chapter 11).

serverCP's design prevents server threads from blocking during I/O operations or request processing (through an external process). Each client pipe goes through a set of states (see the enum CP_CLIENT_PIPE_STATE type in the listing), and different server threads may process the pipe through stages of the state cycle. The states, which are maintained in a per-pipe CP_KEY structure, proceed as follows:

- connected — The pipe is connected with a server thread.

- requestRead — The server thread reads a request from the client and starts the process from a separate "compute" thread, which calls PostQueued-CompletionStatus when the process completes. The server thread does not block, since the process management is in the compute thread.

- computed — The server thread reads the first temporary file record with the response's first record, and the server thread then writes the record to the client.

- responding — The server thread sends additional response records, one at a time, returning to the responding state until the last response record is sent to the client.

- respondLast — The server thread sends a terminating empty record to the client.

The program listing does not show familiar functions such as the server mailslot broadcast thread function.

Program 14–4   `serverCP`: A Server Using a Completion Port

```
/*  Chapter 14. ServerCP.
 *  Command line server. Named pipe version, COMPLETION PORT example
 *  Assume MAX_SERVER_TH <= 64 (because of WaitForMultipleObject) */

#include "Everything.h"
#include "ClientServer.h" /* Request, response message definitions */

typedef struct {      /* Argument to a server thread. */
   HANDLE hCompPort;/* Completion port handle. */
   DWORD threadNum;
} SERVER_THREAD_ARG;
typedef SERVER_THREAD_ARG *LPSERVER_THREAD_ARG;

enum CP_CLIENT_PIPE_STATE { connected, requestRead, computed,
                            responding, respondLast };
/* Argument structure for each named pipe instance */
typedef struct {/* Completion port keys refer to these structures */
     HANDLE hCompPort;
     HANDLE hNp;/* which represent outstanding ReadFile  */
     HANDLE hTempFile;
     FILE *tFp;/* Used by server process to hold result */
     TCHAR tmpFileName[MAX_PATH]; /* Temp file name for respnse. */
     REQUESTrequest;/* and ConnectNamedPipe operations */
     DWORD nBytes;
     enum CP_CLIENT_PIPE_STATE npState;
     LPOVERLAPPED pOverLap;
} CP_KEY;

OVERLAPPED overLap;
volatile static int shutDown = 0;
static DWORD WINAPI Server (LPSERVER_THREAD_ARG);
static DWORD WINAPI ServerBroadcast (LPLONG);
static BOOL  WINAPI Handler (DWORD);
static DWORD WINAPI ComputeThread (PVOID);

static CP_KEY Key[MAX_CLIENTS_CP];

_tmain (int argc, LPTSTR argv[])
{
   HANDLE hCompPort, hMonitor, hSrvrThread[MAX_CLIENTS];
   DWORD iNp, iTh;
   SECURITY_ATTRIBUTES tempFileSA = {sizeof (SECURITY_ATTRIBUTES),
                                     NULL,  TRUE};
   SERVER_THREAD_ARG ThArgs[MAX_SERVER_TH]; /* MAX_SERVER_TH <= 64 */
   OVERLAPPED ov = {0};

   /* Console control handler to permit server shutDown */
```

```
SetConsoleCtrlHandler (Handler, TRUE);

/* Create a thread broadcast pipe name periodically. */
hMonitor = (HANDLE) _beginthreadex (NULL, 0, ServerBroadcast, NULL,
                0, NULL);

hCompPort = CreateIoCompletionPort (INVALID_HANDLE_VALUE, NULL, 0,
                MAX_SERVER_TH);

/* Create an overlapped named pipe for every potential client, */
/* add to the completion port */
/* Assume that the maximum number of clients far exceeds */
/* the number of server threads*/
for (iNp = 0; iNp < MAX_CLIENTS_CP; iNp++) {
    memset (&Key[iNp], 0, sizeof(CP_KEY));
    Key[iNp].hCompPort = hCompPort;
    Key[iNp].hNp =  CreateNamedPipe ( SERVER_PIPE,
        PIPE_ACCESS_DUPLEX | FILE_FLAG_OVERLAPPED,
        PIPE_READMODE_MESSAGE | PIPE_TYPE_MESSAGE,
        MAX_CLIENTS_CP, 0, 0, INFINITE, &tempFileSA);
    GetTempFileName (_T("."), _T "CLP"), 0, Key[iNp].tmpFileName);
    Key[iNp].pOverLap = &overLap;
    /* Add the named pipe instance to the completion port */
    CreateIoCompletionPort (Key[iNp].hNp, hCompPort,
            (ULONG_PTR)&Key[iNp], 0);
    ConnectNamedPipe (Key[iNp].hNp, &ov);
    Key[iNp].npState = connected;
}

/* Create server worker threads and a temp file name for each.*/
for (iTh = 0; iTh < MAX_SERVER_TH; iTh++) {
    ThArgs[iTh].hCompPort = hCompPort;
    ThArgs[iTh].threadNum = iTh;
    hSrvrThread[iTh] = (HANDLE)_beginthreadex (NULL, 0, Server,
                    &ThArgs[iTh], 0, NULL);
}
_tprintf (_T("All server threads running.\n"));

/* Wait for all server threads (<= 64) to terminate. */
WaitForMultipleObjects (MAX_SERVER_TH, hSrvrThread,
            TRUE, INFINITE);
WaitForSingleObject (hMonitor, INFINITE);
_tprintf (_T ("Monitor and server threads have shut down.\n"));

CloseHandle (hMonitor);
for (iTh = 0; iTh < MAX_SERVER_TH; iTh++) {
    /* Close pipe handles */
    CloseHandle (hSrvrThread[iTh]);
}
```

```
        CloseHandle (hCompPort);

        return 0;
}

static DWORD WINAPI Server (LPSERVER_THREAD_ARG pThArg)
/* Server thread function. . */
{
    DWORD nXfer;
    BOOL disconnect = FALSE;
    CP_KEY *pKey;
    RESPONSE response;
    OVERLAPPED serverOv = {0}, * pOv = NULL;

    /* Main server thread loop to process completions */
    while (!disconnect && !shutDown) {
        if (!GetQueuedCompletionStatus (pThArg->hCompPort, &nXfer,
                (PULONG_PTR)&pKey, &pOv, INFINITE))
        {
            DWORD errCode = GetLastError();
            if (errCode == ERROR_OPERATION_ABORTED) continue;
            if (errCode != ERROR_MORE_DATA)
                ReportError (_T("GetQueuedCompletionStatus error."),
                    0, TRUE);
        }
        if (shutDown) continue;

        /* npState: connected, requestRead, ... */
        switch (pKey->npState) {
            case connected:
                {   /* A connection has completed, read a request */
                    /* Open temp results file for this connection. */

                    _tcscpy (pKey->request.record, _T(""));
                    pKey->request.rqLen = 0;
                    pKey->npState = requestRead;
                    disconnect = !ReadFile (pKey->hNp, &(pKey->request),
                        RQ_SIZE, &(pKey->nBytes), &serverOv)
                      && GetLastError() != ERROR_IO_PENDING;
                    continue;
                }
            case requestRead:
                { /* A read has completed. process the request */
                    /* Thread to process request asynchronously. */
                    /* This server is free to process other requests. */
                    HANDLE hComputeThread;
                    DWORD computeExitCode;
                    hComputeThread = (HANDLE)_beginthreadex (NULL, 0,
                            ComputeThread, pKey, 0, NULL);
                    if (NULL == hComputeThread) continue;
```

```
                WaitForSingleObject(hComputeThread, INFINITE);
                GetExitCodeThread (hComputeThread, &computeExitCode);
                CloseHandle (hComputeThread);

                pKey->npState = computed;
                if (computeExitCode != 0)
                {
                    pKey->npState = respondLast;
                }

                PostQueuedCompletionStatus (pKey->hCompPort, 0,
                    (ULONG_PTR)pKey, pKey->pOverLap);
                continue;
        }
    case computed:
        {
            /* Results are in the temp file */
            /* Respond a line at a time. It is convenient to use
                C library line-oriented routines at this point. */
            pKey->tFp = _tfopen (pKey->tmpFileName, _T ("r"));
            pKey->npState = responding;
            if (_fgetts (response.record, MAX_RQRS_LEN,
                    pKey->tFp) != NULL) {
                response.rsLen = strlen(response.record) + 1;
                disconnect = !WriteFile (pKey->hNp, &response,
                    response.rsLen + sizeof(response.rsLen),
                    &nXfer, &serverOv)
                    && GetLastError() != ERROR_IO_PENDING;
            } else {
                /* Bad read; post completion; go to next state */
                pKey->npState = respondLast;
                PostQueuedCompletionStatus (pKey->hCompPort, 0,
                    (ULONG_PTR)pKey, pKey->pOverLap);
            }
            continue;
        }
    case responding:
        {
            /* In the process of responding a record at a time */
            /* Continue in this state until no more records */
            if (_fgetts (response.record, MAX_RQRS_LEN,
                    pKey->tFp) != NULL) {
                response.rsLen = strlen(response.record) + 1;
                disconnect = !WriteFile (pKey->hNp, &response,
                    response.rsLen + sizeof(response.rsLen),
                    &nXfer, &serverOv)
                    && GetLastError() != ERROR_IO_PENDING;
            }
```

```
                    else {
                        pKey->npState = respondLast;
                        PostQueuedCompletionStatus (pKey->hCompPort, 0,
                            (ULONG_PTR)pKey, pKey->pOverLap);
                    }
                    continue;
                }
            case respondLast:
                {
                    /* Send end of response indicator. */
                    /* Stay connected. */
                    pKey->npState = connected;
                    _tcscpy (response.record, _T(""));
                    response.rsLen = 0;
                    disconnect = !WriteFile (pKey->hNp, &response,
                            sizeof(response.rsLen), &nXfer, &serverOv)
                        && GetLastError() != ERROR_IO_PENDING;
                    continue;
                }
            default:
                {
                    /* No recovery attempted (a good exercise!) */
                    return 1;
                }
        }

        FlushFileBuffers (pKey->hNp);
        DisconnectNamedPipe (pKey->hNp);
        if (disconnect) {
            ConnectNamedPipe (pKey->hNp, &serverOv);
            pKey->npState = connected;
        } else {
            _tprintf (_T("Thread %d shutting down\n"),
                    pThArg->threadNum);
            /* End of command processing. Free resources; thread exit */
            DeleteFile (pKey->tmpFileName);
            return 0;
        }
    }
    return 0;
}

static DWORD WINAPI ComputeThread (PVOID pArg)
{
    PROCESS_INFORMATION procInfo;
    STARTUPINFO startInfo;
    CP_KEY *pKey = (CP_KEY *)pArg;
    SECURITY_ATTRIBUTES tempSA =
            {sizeof(SECURITY_ATTRIBUTES), NULL, TRUE};
    GetStartupInfo (&startInfo);
```

```
    /* Open temp file, erasing previous contents */
    pKey->hTempFile =
        CreateFile (pKey->tmpFileName, GENERIC_READ | GENERIC_WRITE,
        FILE_SHARE_READ | FILE_SHARE_WRITE, &tempSA,
        CREATE_ALWAYS, FILE_ATTRIBUTE_TEMPORARY, NULL);

    if (pKey->hTempFile != INVALID_HANDLE_VALUE) {
        startInfo.hStdOutput = pKey->hTempFile;
        startInfo.hStdError = pKey->hTempFile;
        startInfo.hStdInput = GetStdHandle (STD_INPUT_HANDLE);
        startInfo.dwFlags = STARTF_USESTDHANDLES;
        CreateProcess (NULL, pKey->request.record, NULL, NULL,
                TRUE, /* Inherit handles. */
                0, NULL, NULL, &startInfo, &procInfo);

        /* Server process is running */
        CloseHandle (procInfo.hThread);
        WaitForSingleObject (procInfo.hProcess, INFINITE);
        CloseHandle (procInfo.hProcess);
        CloseHandle(pKey->hTempFile);
    } else { /* To do: Come here if CreateProcess fails. */
        ReportError (_T("Compute thread failed."));
        return 1;
    }

    return 0;
}

static DWORD WINAPI ServerBroadcast (LPLONG pNull)
{
    MS_MESSAGE MsNotify;
    DWORD nXfer, iNp;
    HANDLE hMsFile;

    /* Open the mailslot for the MS "client" writer. */
    while (!shutDown) { /* Run as long as there are server threads */
        /* Wait for another client to open a mailslot. */
        Sleep (CS_TIMEOUT);
        hMsFile = CreateFile (MS_CLTNAME, GENERIC_WRITE | GENERIC_READ,
                FILE_SHARE_READ | FILE_SHARE_WRITE,
                NULL, OPEN_EXISTING, FILE_ATTRIBUTE_NORMAL, NULL);
        if (hMsFile == INVALID_HANDLE_VALUE) continue;

        /* Send out the message to the mailslot. */

        MsNotify.msStatus = 0;
        MsNotify.msUtilization = 0;
        _tcscpy (MsNotify.msName, SERVER_PIPE);
        if (!WriteFile (hMsFile, &MsNotify, MSM_SIZE, &nXfer, NULL))
            ReportError (_T ("Server MS Write error."), 13, TRUE);
```

```
        CloseHandle (hMsFile);
    }

    _tprintf (_T("Cancel all outstanding I/O operations.\n"));
    for (iNp = 0; iNp < MAX_CLIENTS_CP; iNp++) {
        CancelIoEx (Key[iNp].hNp, NULL);
    }
    _tprintf (_T ("Shuting down monitor thread.\n"));

    _endthreadex (0);
    return 0;
}

BOOL WINAPI Handler (DWORD CtrlEvent)
{
    /* Same as in serverNP, but it posts a completion */
}
```

Summary

Windows has three methods for performing asynchronous I/O; there are examples of all three, along with performance results, throughout the book to help you decide which to use on the basis of programming simplicity and performance.

Threads provide the most general and simplest technique. Each thread is responsible for a sequence of one or more sequential, blocking I/O operations. Furthermore, each thread should have its own file or pipe handle.

Overlapped I/O allows a single thread to perform asynchronous operations on a single file handle, but there must be an event handle, rather than a thread and file handle pair, for each operation. Wait specifically for each I/O operation to complete and then perform any required cleanup or sequencing operations.

Extended I/O, on the other hand, automatically invokes the completion code, and it does not require additional events.

The one indispensable advantage provided by overlapped I/O is the ability to create I/O completion ports as mentioned previously and illustrated by a program, cciMTCP.c, in the *Examples* file. A single server thread can serve multiple clients, which is important if there are thousands of clients; there would not be enough memory for the equivalent number of servers.

UNIX supports threads through Pthreads, as discussed previously.

System V UNIX limits asynchronous I/O to streams and cannot be used for file or pipe operations.

BSD Version 4.3 uses a combination of signals (SIGIO) to indicate an event on a file descriptor and select a function to determine the ready state of file descriptors. The file descriptors must be set in the O_ASYNC mode. This approach works only with terminals and network communication.

Looking Ahead

Chapter 15 completes the book by showing how to secure Windows objects.

Exercises

14–1. Use asynchronous I/O to merge several sorted files into a larger sorted file.

14–2. Does the FILE_FLAG_NO_BUFFERING flag improve cciOV or cciEX performance? Are there any restrictions on file size? Read the MSDN CreateFile documentation carefully.

14–3. Experiment with the cciOV and cciEX record sizes to determine the performance impact. Is the optimal record size machine-independent? What results to you get on Window XP and Windows 7?

14–4. Modify TimeBeep (Program 14–3) so that it uses a manual-reset notification timer.

14–5. Modify the named pipe client in Program 11–2, clientNP, to use overlapped I/O so that the client can continue operation after sending the request. In this way, it can have several outstanding requests.

14–6. Rewrite the socket server, serverSK in Program 12–2, so that it uses I/O completion ports.

14–7. Rewrite either serverSK or serverNP so that the number of ready worker threads is limited by a semaphore. Experiment with a large thread pool to determine the effectiveness of this alternative.

14–8. Use JobShell (Program 6–3, the job management program) to bring up a large number of clients and compare the responsiveness of serverNP and serverCP. Networked clients can provide additional load. Determine an optimal range for the number of active threads.

14–9. Modify cciMT to use an NT6 thread pool rather than thread management. What is the performance impact? Compare your results with those in Appendix C.

14–10. Modify `cciMT` to use overlapped read/write calls with the event wait immediately following the read/write. This should allow you to cancel I/O operations with a user APC; try to do so. Also, does this change affect performance?

14–11. Modify `serverCP` so that there is no limit on the number of clients. Use `PIPE-_UNLIMITED_INSTANCES` for the `CreateNamedPipe    nMaxInstances` value. You will need to replace the array of `CP_KEY` structures with dynamically allocated structures.

14–12. Review `serverCP`'s error and disconnect processing to be sure all situations are covered. Fix any deficiencies.

15 | Securing Windows Objects

Windows supports a comprehensive security model that prevents unauthorized access to objects such as files, processes, and file mappings. Nearly all sharable objects can be protected, and the programmer has a fine granularity of control over access rights. Windows has Common Criteria Certification at Evaluation Assurance Level 4 (EAL-4), an internationally recognized criteria.

Security is a large subject that cannot be covered completely in a single chapter. Therefore, this chapter concentrates on the immediate problem of showing how to use the Windows security API to protect objects from unauthorized access. While access control is only a subset of Windows security functionality, it is of direct concern to those who need to add security features to their programs. The initial example, Program 15–1, shows how to emulate UNIX file permissions with NT file system (NTFS) files, and a second example applies security to named pipes. The same principles can then be used to secure other objects. The bibliography lists several resources you can consult for additional security information.

Security Attributes

This chapter explores Windows access control by proceeding from the top down to show how to construct an object's security. Following an overview, the Windows functions are described in detail before proceeding to the examples. In the case of files, it is also possible to use Windows Explorer to examine and manage some file security attributes.

Nearly any object created with a `Create` system call has a security attributes parameter. Therefore, programs can secure files, processes, threads, events, semaphores, named pipes, and so on. The first step is to include a `SECURITY_ATTRIBUTES` structure in the `Create` call. Until now, our programs have always used a `NULL` pointer in `Create` calls or have used `SECURITY_ATTRIBUTES` simply to create inheritable handles (Chapter 6). In order to implement security, the important element in the `SECURITY_ATTRIBUTES` structure is `lpSecurityDescriptor`, the pointer to a *security descriptor,* which describes the object's owner and determines which users are allowed or denied various rights.

An individual process is identified by its *access token,* which specifies the owning user and group membership. When a process attempts to access an object, the Windows kernel can determine the process's identity using the token and can then decide from the information in the security descriptor whether or not the process has the required rights to access the object.

Chapter 6 introduced the `SECURITY_ATTRIBUTES` structure; for review, here is the complete structure definition:

```
typedef struct _SECURITY_ATTRIBUTES {
    DWORD nLength;
    LPVOID lpSecurityDescriptor;
    BOOL bInheritHandle;
} SECURITY_ATTRIBUTES, *PSECURITY_ATTRIBUTES;
```

Set `nLength` to `sizeof(SECURITY_ATTRIBUTES)`. `bInheritHandle` indicates whether or not the handle is inheritable by other processes.

Security Overview: The Security Descriptor

Analyzing the security descriptor gives a good overview of essential Windows security elements. This section mentions the various elements and the names of the functions that manage them, starting with security descriptor structure.

A security descriptor is initialized with the function `InitializeSecurity-Descriptor`, and it contains the following:

- The owner security identifier (SID) (described in the next section, which deals with the object's owner)

- The group SID

- A discretionary access control list (DACL)—a list of entries explicitly granting and denying access rights. The term "ACL" without the "D" prefix will refer to DACLs in our discussion.

- A system ACL (SACL), sometimes called an "audit access ACL," controls audit message generation when programs access securable objects; you need to have system administrator rights to set the SACL.

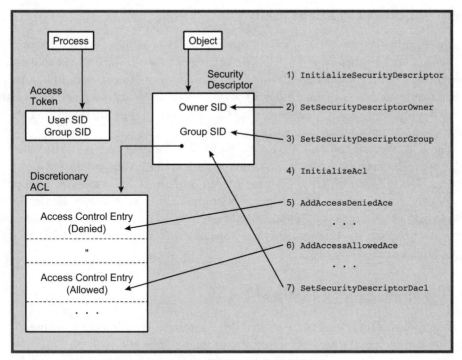

Figure 15–1   Constructing a Security Descriptor

`SetSecurityDescriptorOwner` and `SetSecurityDescriptorGroup` associate SIDs with security descriptors, as described in the upcoming "Security Identifiers" section.

ACLs are initialized using the `InitializeAcl` function and are then associated with a security descriptor using `SetSecurityDescriptorDacl` or `SetSecurityDescriptorSacl`.

Figure 15–1 shows the security descriptor and its components.

Access Control Lists

Each ACL is a set (list) of access control entries (ACEs). There are two types of ACEs: one for access allowed and one for access denied.

You first initialize an ACL with `InitializeAcl` and then add ACEs. Each ACE contains a SID and an *access mask,* which specifies rights to be granted or denied to the user or group specified by the SID. `FILE_GENERIC_READ` and `DELETE` are typical file access rights.

The two functions used to add ACEs to discretionary ACLs are `AddAccessAllowedAce` and `AddAccessDeniedAce`. `AddAuditAccessAce` is for adding to an SACL. Finally, remove ACEs with `DeleteAce` and retrieve them with `GetAce`.

Using Windows Object Security

There are numerous details to fill in, but Figure 15–1 shows the basic structure. Notice that each process also has SIDs (in an access token), which the kernel uses to determine whether access is allowed. The user's access token may also give the owner certain *privileges* (the ability to perform system operations such as system shutdown and to access system resources). These user and group privileges are set when the administrator creates the account.

The kernel scans the ACL for access rights for the user, based on the user's ID and group. The first entry that specifically grants or denies the requested service is decisive. The order in which ACEs are entered into an ACL is therefore important. Frequently, access-denied ACEs come first so that a user who is specifically denied access will not gain access by virtue of membership in a group that does have such access. In Program 15–1, however, it is essential to mix allowed and denied ACEs to obtain the desired semantics.

Object Rights and Object Access

An object, such as a file, gets its security descriptor at creation time, although the program can change the security descriptor at a later time.

A process requests access to the object when it asks for a handle using, for example, a call to `CreateFile`. The handle request contains the desired access, such as `FILE_GENERIC_READ`, in one of the parameters. If the security descriptor grants access to the process, the request succeeds. Different handles to the same object may have different access rights. The access flag values are the same for both allowing and denying rights when creating ACLs.

Standard UNIX provides a simpler security model. It is limited to files and based on file permissions. The example programs in this chapter emulate the UNIX permissions.

Security Descriptor Initialization

The first step is to initialize the security descriptor using the `Initialize-SecurityDescriptor` function. Set the `pSecurityDescriptor` parameter to the address of a valid `SECURITY_DESCRIPTOR` structure. These structures are opaque and are managed with specific functions.

Security descriptors are classified as either *absolute* or *self-relative*. This distinction is ignored for now but is explained near the end of the chapter.

```
BOOL InitializeSecurityDescriptor (
    PSECURITY_DESCRIPTOR pSecurityDescriptor,
    DWORD dwRevision)
```

dwRevision is set to the constant SECURITY_DESCRIPTOR_REVISION.

Security Descriptor Control Flags

Flags within the Control structure of the security descriptor, the SECURITY-_DESCRIPTOR_CONTROL flags, control the meaning assigned to the security descriptor. Several of these flags are set or reset by the upcoming functions and will be mentioned as needed. GetSecurityDescriptorControl and SetSecurityDescriptorControl access these flags, but the examples do not use the flags directly.

Security Identifiers

Windows uses SIDs to identify users and groups. The program can look up a SID from the account name, which can be a user, group, domain, and so on. The account can be on a remote system. The first step is to determine the SID from an account name.

```
BOOL LookupAccountName (
    LPCTSTR lpSystemName,
    LPCTSTR lpAccountName,
    PSID Sid,
    LPDWORD cbSid,
    LPTSTR ReferencedDomainName,
    LPDWORD cbReferencedDomainName,
    PSID_NAME_USE peUse)
```

Parameters

lpSystemName and lpAccountName point to the system and account names. Frequently, lpSystemName is NULL to indicate the local system.

Sid is the returned information, which is of size *cbSid. The function will fail, returning the required size, if the buffer is not large enough.

ReferencedDomainName is a string of length *cbReferencedDomainName characters. The length parameter should be initialized to the buffer size (use the usual techniques to process failures). The return value shows the domain where the name is found. The account name Administrators will return BUILTIN, whereas a user account name will return that same user name.

peUse points to a SID_NAME_USE (enumerated type) variable and can be tested for values such as SidTypeWellKnownGroup, SidTypeUser, SidTypeGroup, and so on.

Getting the Account and User Names

Given a SID, you reverse the process and obtain the account name using LookupAccountSid. Specify the SID and get the name in return. The account name can be any name available to the process. Some names, such as Everyone, are well known.

```
BOOL LookupAccountSid (
    LPCTSTR lpSystemName,
    PSID lpSid,
    LPTSTR lpAccountName,
    LPDWORD cchName,
    LPTSTR lpReferencedDomainName,
    LPDWORD cchReferencedDomainName,
    PSID_NAME_USE peUse)
```

Obtain the process's user account name (the logged-in user) with the GetUserName function.

```
BOOL GetUserName (
    LPTSTR lpBuffer,
    LPDWORD lpnSize)
```

The user name and length are returned in the conventional manner.

Create and manage SIDs using functions such as InitializeSid and AllocateAndInitializeSid. The examples confine themselves, however, to SIDs obtained from account names.

Once SIDs are known, they can be entered into an initialized security descriptor.

```
BOOL SetSecurityDescriptorOwner (
    PSECURITY_DESCRIPTOR pSecurityDescriptor,
    PSID pOwner,
    BOOL bOwnerDefaulted)
```

```
BOOL SetSecurityDescriptorGroup (
    PSECURITY_DESCRIPTOR pSecurityDescriptor,
    PSID pGroup,
    BOOL bGroupDefaulted)
```

`pSecurityDescriptor` points to the appropriate security descriptor, and `pOwner` (or `pGroup`) is the address of the owner's (group's) SID. As always in such situations, assure that these SIDs were not prematurely freed.

`bOwnerDefaulted` (or `bGroupDefaulted`) indicates, if `TRUE`, that a default mechanism is used to derive the owner (or primary group) information. The `SE_OWNER_DEFAULTED` and `SE_GROUP_DEFAULTED` flags within the `SECURITY-_DESCRIPTOR_CONTROL` structure are set according to these two parameters.

The similar functions `GetSecurityDescriptorOwner` and `GetSecurity-DescriptorGroup` return the SID (either owner or group) from a security descriptor.

Managing ACLs

This section shows how to manage ACLs, how to associate an ACL with a security descriptor, and how to add ACEs. Figure 15–1 shows the relationships between these objects and functions.

The first step is to initialize an ACL structure. The ACL should not be accessed directly, so its internal structure is not relevant. The program must, however, provide a buffer to serve as the ACL; the functions manage the contents.

```
BOOL InitializeAcl (
    PACL pAcl,
    DWORD cbAcl,
    DWORD dwAclRevision)
```

pAcl is the address of a programmer-supplied buffer of cbAcl bytes. Subsequent discussion and Program 15–4 will show how to determine the ACL size, but 1KB is more than adequate for most purposes. dwAclRevision should be ACL_REVISION.

Next, add the ACEs in the order desired with the AddAccessAllowedAce and AddAccessDeniedAce functions.

```
BOOL AddAccessAllowedAce (
    PACL pAcl,
    DWORD dwAclRevision
    DWORD dwAccessMask,
    PSID pSid)

BOOL AddAccessDeniedAce (
    PACL pAcl,
    DWORD dwAclRevision,
    DWORD dwAccessMask,
    PSID pSid)
```

pAcl points to the same ACL structure initialized with InitializeAcl, and dwAclRevision is ACL_REVISION. pSid points to a SID, such as one that would be obtained from LookupAccountName.

The access mask (dwAccessMask) determines the rights to be granted or denied to the user or group specified by the SID. The predefined mask values will vary by the object type.

The final step is to associate an ACL with the security descriptor. In the case of the discretionary ACL, use the SetSecurityDescriptorDacl function.

```
BOOL SetSecurityDescriptorDacl (
    PSECURITY_DESCRIPTOR pSecurityDescriptor,
    BOOL bDaclPresent,
    PACL pAcl,
    BOOL fDaclDefaulted)
```

bDaclPresent, if TRUE, indicates that there is an ACL in the pAcl structure. If FALSE, pAcl and fDaclDefaulted, the next two parameters, are ignored. The SECURITY_DESCRIPTOR_CONTROL's SE_DACL_PRESENT flag is also set to this parameter's value.

The final flag is fDaclDefaulted. FALSE indicates an ACL generated by the programmer. TRUE indicates that the ACL was obtained by a default mechanism, such as inheritance. The SE_DACL_DEFAULTED flag in the SECURITY_DESCRIPTOR-_CONTROL is set to this parameter value.

Other functions delete ACEs and read ACEs from an ACL; we discuss them later in this chapter. It is now time for an example.

Example: UNIX-Style Permission for NTFS Files

UNIX file permissions provide a convenient way to illustrate Windows security, even though Windows security is much more general than standard UNIX security.

First, however, here is a very quick review of UNIX file permissions (directories are treated slightly differently).

- Every file has an owning user and group.

- Every file has 9 permission bits, which are specified as 3 octal (base 8) digits.

- The 3 bits in each octal digit grant, or deny, read (high-order bit), write, and execute (low-order bit) permission. Read, write, and execute permissions are displayed as r, w, and x respectively. Execute rights are meaningful for .exe and .bat files but not for .txt files.

- The 3 octal digits, from left to right, represent rights given to the owner, the group, and to everyone else.

- Thus, if you set the permissions to 640, the permissions will be displayed as rw_r_____. The file owner can read and write the file, group members can read it, and everyone else has no access.

The implementation creates nine ACEs to grant or deny read, write, and execute permissions to the owner, group, and everyone. There are two commands.

1. chmodW sets the permissions and is modeled after the UNIX chmod command. The implementation has been enhanced to create the specified file if it does not already exist and to allow the user to specify the group name.

2. lsFP displays the permissions along with other file information and is an extension of the lsW command (Program 3–2). When the long listing is requested, the command displays the owning user and an interpretation of the existing ACLs, which may have been set by chmodW.

Programs 15–1 and 15–2 show the implementation for these two commands. Programs 15–3, 15–4, and 15–5 show three supporting functions:

1. InitializeUnixSA, which creates a valid security attributes structure corresponding to a set of UNIX permissions. This function is general enough that it can be used with objects other than files, such as processes (Chapter 6), named pipes (Chapter 11), and synchronization objects (Chapter 8).

2. ReadFilePermissions.

3. ChangeFilePermissions.

Note: The separate DeniedAceMasks array assures that SYNCHRONIZE rights are never denied because the SYNCHRONIZE flag is set in all three of the macros, FILE_GENERIC_READ, FILE_GENERIC_WRITE, and FILE_GENERIC_EXECUTE, which are combinations of several flags (see the include file, winnt.h). The full program in the *Examples* file provides additional explanation.

The programs that follow are simplifications of the programs from the *Examples* file. For example, the full program checks to see if there is a group name on the command line; here, the name is assumed. Also, there are command line flags to create a file that does not exist and to suppress the warning message if the change fails.

Program 15–1   chmodW: Change File Permissions

```
/* Chapter 15-1. Windows chmodW command */
/* chmodW [options] mode file [groupName]
   Update access rights of the named file. */
/* This program illustrates:
   1.  Setting the file security attributes.
   2.  Changing a security descriptor. */
```

```
#include "Everything.h"

int _tmain (int argc, LPTSTR argv[])
{
    HANDLE hFile, heap = NULL;
    BOOL force, createNew, change, exists;
    DWORD mode, userCount = ACCT_NAME_SIZE;
    TCHAR userName[ACCT_NAME_SIZE];
    int fileIndex, groupIndex, modeIndex;
        /* Array of rights settings in "UNIX order". */
    DWORD allowedAceMasks[] =
        {FILE_GENERIC_READ, FILE_GENERIC_WRITE, FILE_GENERIC_EXECUTE};
    DWORD deniedAceMasks[] =
        {  FILE_GENERIC_READ & ~SYNCHRONIZE,
           FILE_GENERIC_WRITE & ~SYNCHRONIZE,
           FILE_GENERIC_EXECUTE & ~SYNCHRONIZE};
    LPSECURITY_ATTRIBUTES pSa;
    LPCTSTR groupName = NULL;

    modeIndex = Options (argc, argv, _T ("fc"),
                         &force, &createNew, NULL);
    groupIndex = modeIndex + 2;
    fileIndex = modeIndex + 1;
    /* Mode is base 8, convert to decimal */
    mode = _tcstoul(argv[modeIndex], NULL, 8);
    exists = (_taccess (argv[fileIndex], 0) == 0);
    if (!exists && createNew) {
        GetUserName (userName, &userCount);
        pSa = InitializeUnixSA (mode, userName, groupName,
                allowedAceMasks, deniedAceMasks, &heap);
        hFile = CreateFile (argv[fileIndex], 0,
                0, pSa, CREATE_ALWAYS, FILE_ATTRIBUTE_NORMAL, NULL);
        CloseHandle (hFile);
    }
    else if (exists) {
                /* File exists; change permissions. */
        change = ChangeFilePermissions (mode, argv[fileIndex],
                allowedAceMasks,deniedAceMasks);
    }

    DestroyUnixSA (pSa, heap);
    return 0;
}
```

Program 15–2 shows the relevant part of lsFP—namely, the ProcessItem function. Other parts of the program are similar to Chapter 3's lsW Program 3–2.

Program 15–2   lsFP: List File Permissions

```
static BOOL ProcessItem (LPWIN32_FIND_DATA pFileData,
      DWORD numberFlags, LPBOOL flags)

/* List attributes, with file permissions and owner. */
{
   DWORD fileType = FileType(pFileData), Mode, i;
   BOOL dashL = flags[1];
   TCHAR groupName[ACCT_NAME_SIZE], userName[ACCT_NAME_SIZE];
   SYSTEMTIME timeLastWrite;
   TCHAR  permissionString[] = _T("---------");
   const TCHAR RWX[] = {'r','w','x'}, FileTypeChar[] = {' ','d'};

   if (fileType != TYPE_FILE && fileType != TYPE_DIR)
      return FALSE;
   _tprintf (_T ("\n"));

   if (dashL) {
      Mode = ReadFilePermissions (pFileData->cFileName,
            userName, groupName);
      if (Mode == 0xFFFFFFFF)
         Mode = 0;
      for (i = 0; i < 9; i++) {
         if ( (Mode / (1 << (8 - i)) & 0x1) )
            permissionString[i] = RWX[i % 3];
      }
      _tprintf (_T ("%c%s %8.7s %8.7s%10d"),
         FileTypeChar[fileType-1], permissionString, userName,
            groupName,pFileData->nFileSizeLow);
      FileTimeToSystemTime (&(pFileData->ftLastWriteTime),
                      &timeLastWrite);
      _tprintf (_T (" %02d/%02d/%04d %02d:%02d:%02d"),
            timeLastWrite.wMonth, timeLastWrite.wDay,
            timeLastWrite.wYear, timeLastWrite.wHour,
            timeLastWrite.wMinute, timeLastWrite.wSecond);
   }
   _tprintf (_T (" %s"), pFileData->cFileName);
   return TRUE;
}
```

The next step is to show the supporting function implementations. However, Run 15–2 first shows the two new commands in operation. First, a new file is created, and its permissions are seen to be 700 (the owner can read, write, and execute the file; others have no rights). Next, the owner's write permission is removed, and an attempt to write to the file is denied. Once the write permissions are restored, the file write succeeds, and the file listing (`cat` command) shows that the new text is at the end of the file. Finally, others are given read permission.

```
Command Prompt                                          _  □  X

C:\WSP4_Examples\run8>randfile 2 small.txt

C:\WSP4_Examples\run8>lsFP -l small.txt

rwxr-----      jhart      None       128 10/23/2009 22:54:31 small.txt
C:\WSP4_Examples\run8>chmodW 500 small.txt

C:\WSP4_Examples\run8>lsFP -l small.txt

r-x------      jhart      None       128 10/23/2009 22:54:31 small.txt
C:\WSP4_Examples\run8>echo xyz >> small.txt
Access is denied.

C:\WSP4_Examples\run8>chmodW 700 small.txt

C:\WSP4_Examples\run8>echo xyz >> small.txt

C:\WSP4_Examples\run8>cat small.txt
e2b3f479. Record Number: 00000000.abcdefghijklmnopqrstuvwxyz x
29b225be. Record Number: 00000001.abcdefghijklmnopqrstuvwxyz x
xyz

C:\WSP4_Examples\run8>chmodW 744 small.txt

C:\WSP4_Examples\run8>lsFP -l small.txt

rwxr--r--      jhart      None       134 10/23/2009 22:54:56 small.txt
C:\WSP4_Examples\run8>_
```

Run 15–2   `chmodW`, `lsFP`: UNIX-like File Permissions

Example: Initializing Security Attributes

Program 15–3 shows the utility function `InitializeUnixSA`, which creates a security attributes structure containing an ACL with ACEs that emulate UNIX file permissions. There are nine ACEs granting or denying read, write, and execute permissions for the owner, the group, and everyone else. The actual array of three rights (read, write, and execute for files) can vary according to the object type being secured. This structure is not a local variable in the function but must be allocated and initialized and then returned to the calling program; notice the ACE mask arrays in Program 15–1.

Two aspects of this program are interesting and could be modified (see the exercises).

- The function creates a heap and allocates memory from the heap. This greatly simplifies destroying the SA (`DestroyUnixSA` is at the end). The heap is returned from the function; alternatively, you could create an opaque structure containing the heap and the SA.

- The SDs in the SA are "absolute" rather than self-relative; a later section talks about this some more.

Program 15–3 InitUnSA: Initializing Security Attributes

```
/* Set UNIX-style permissions as ACEs in a
   SECURITY_ATTRIBUTES structure. */

#include "Everything.h"

#define ACL_SIZE 1024
#define SID_SIZE SECURITY_MAX_SID_SIZE
#define DOM_SIZE LUSIZE

static VOID FindGroup (DWORD, LPTSTR, DWORD);

LPSECURITY_ATTRIBUTES InitializeUnixSA (DWORD unixPerms,
      LPTSTR usrName, LPTSTR grpName, LPDWORD allowedAceMasks,
      LPDWORD deniedAceMasks, LPHANDLE pSaHeap)

/* Allocate a structure and set the UNIX style permissions
   as specified in unixPerms, which is 9-bits
   (low-order end) giving the required [r,w,x] settings
   for [User,Group,Other] in the familiar UNIX form.
   Return a pointer to a security attributes structure */

{
    HANDLE saHeap = HeapCreate (HEAP_GENERATE_EXCEPTIONS, 0, 0);
    /*  Several memory allocations are necessary to build the SA
        and they are all constructed in this heap.
        This memory MUST be available to the calling program and must
        not be allocated on the stack of this function.*/

    LPSECURITY_ATTRIBUTES pSA = NULL;
    PSECURITY_DESCRIPTOR pSD = NULL;
    PACL pAcl = NULL;
    BOOL success, ok = TRUE;
    DWORD iBit, iSid;

    /* Various tables of User, Group, and Everyone Names, SIDs,
         etc. for use first in LookupAccountName and SID creation. */

    LPTSTR groupNames[3] = {EMPTY, EMPTY, _T ("Everyone")};
    PSID pSidTable[3] = {NULL, NULL, NULL};
    SID_NAME_USE sNamUse[] =
        {SidTypeUser, SidTypeGroup, SidTypeWellKnownGroup};
    TCHAR refDomain[3][DOM_SIZE];
    DWORD refDomainCount[3] = {DOM_SIZE, DOM_SIZE, DOM_SIZE};
    DWORD sidCount[3] = {SID_SIZE, SID_SIZE, SID_SIZE};
```

```
__try {
   /* This is in a try-except block so as to
      free resources in case of any subsequent failure. */

   pSA = HeapAlloc (saHeap, 0, sizeof (SECURITY_ATTRIBUTES));
   pSA->nLength = sizeof (SECURITY_ATTRIBUTES);
   pSA->bInheritHandle = FALSE; /* Programmer can set this later. */

   pSD = HeapAlloc (saHeap, 0, sizeof (SECURITY_DESCRIPTOR));
   pSA->lpSecurityDescriptor = pSD;
   /* Other function calls are tested, but just this test is shown */
   if (!InitializeSecurityDescriptor (pSD,
                   SECURITY_DESCRIPTOR_REVISION))
      ReportException (_T ("I.S.D. Error"), 21);

   /* Set up the table names for the user and group.
      Then get a SID for User, Group, and Everyone. */

   groupNames[0] = usrName;
   if (grpName == NULL || _tcslen(grpName) == 0) {
      /*  No group name specified. Get the user's primary group. */
      /*  Allocate a buffer for the group name */
      groupNames[1] = HeapAlloc (saHeap, 0, ACCT_NAME_SIZE);
      FindGroup (2, groupNames[1], ACCT_NAME_SIZE);
   } else groupNames[1] = grpName;

   /* Look up the three names, creating the SIDs. */
   for (iSid = 0; iSid < 3; iSid++) {
      pSidTable[iSid] = HeapAlloc (saHeap, 0, SID_SIZE);
      LookupAccountName (NULL, groupNames[iSid],
            pSidTable[iSid], &sidCount[iSid],
            refDomain[iSid], &refDomainCount[iSid], &sNamUse[iSid]);
   }

   /* Set the security descriptor owner & group SIDs. */
   SetSecurityDescriptorOwner (pSD, pSidTable[0], FALSE);
   SetSecurityDescriptorGroup (pSD, pSidTable[1], FALSE);

   /* Allocate a structure for the ACL. */
   pAcl = HeapAlloc (saHeap, 0, ACL_SIZE);

   /* Initialize an ACL. */
   InitializeAcl (pAcl, ACL_SIZE, ACL_REVISION);

   /* Add the ACEs. Scan permission bits, adding allowed ACE when
      the bit is set and a denied ACE when the bit is reset. */
   for (iBit = 0; iBit < 9; iBit++) {
      if ((unixPerms >> (8 - iBit) & 0x1) != 0
            && allowedAceMasks[iBit % 3] != 0)
```

```
               AddAccessAllowedAce (pAcl, ACL_REVISION,
                   allowedAceMasks[iBit % 3], pSidTable[iBit / 3]);
           else if (deniedAceMasks[iBit % 3] != 0)
               AddAccessDeniedAce (pAcl, ACL_REVISION,
                   deniedAceMasks[iBit % 3], pSidTable[iBit / 3]);
       }

       /* ACL is now complete. Associate it with security descriptor. */
       SetSecurityDescriptorDacl (pSD, TRUE, pAcl, FALSE);
       IsValidSecurityDescriptor (pSD);
   } /* End of __try-except block. */

__except ((GetExceptionCode() != STATUS_NO_MEMORY) ?
         EXCEPTION_EXECUTE_HANDLER : EXCEPTION_CONTINUE_SEARCH) {
   /* An exception occurred and was reported. All memory allocated to
      create the security descriptor and attributes is freed with a
      single HeapDestroy so that the individual elements do not need
      to be deallocated. */
   if (pSaHeap != NULL)
      HeapDestroy (pSaHeap);
   pSA = NULL;
}
   return pSA;
}
```

Comments on Program 15–3

Program 15–3 may have a straightforward structure, but its operation is hardly simple. Furthermore, it illustrates several points about Windows security that need review.

- Several memory allocations are required to hold information such as the SIDs. They are created in a dedicated heap, which the calling program eventually destroys. The advantage is that it's simple to free the allocated memory (there are seven allocations) with a single HeapDestroy call.

- The security attribute structure in this example is for files, but it is also used with other objects such as named pipes (Chapter 11). Program 15–4 shows how to integrate the security attributes with a file.

- To emulate UNIX behavior, the ACE entry order is critical. Notice that access-denied and access-allowed ACEs are added to the ACL as the permission bits are processed from left (Owner/Read) to right (Everyone/Execute). In this way, permission bits of, say, 460 (in octal) will deny write access to the user even though the user may be in the group.

- The ACEs' rights are access values, such as `FILE_GENERIC_READ` and `FILE_GENERIC_WRITE`, which are similar to the flags used with `Create-File`. The calling program (Program 15–1 in this case) specifies the rights that are appropriate for the object.

- The defined constant `ACL_SIZE` is large enough to contain the nine ACEs. After Program 15–5, it will be apparent how to determine the required size.

- The function uses three SIDs, one each for `User`, `Group`, and `Everyone`. Three different techniques are employed to get the name to use as an argument to `LookupAccountName`. The user name comes from `GetUserName`, or get the user SID from the current token without getting the user name (also avoiding the problem of getting an impersonating name; this is Exercise 15–5). The name for everyone is `Everyone` in a `SidTypeWellKnownGroup`. The group name is a command line argument and is looked up as a `SidType-Group`. Finding the groups that the current user belongs to requires some knowledge of process token, and solving this problem is Exercise 15–12. Incidentally, finding the groups of an arbitrary user is fairly complex.

- The version of the program in the *Examples* file, but not the one shown here, is fastidious about error checking. It even goes to the effort to validate the generated structures using the self-explanatory `IsValidSecurityDescriptor`, `IsValidSid`, and `IsValidAcl` functions. This error testing proved to be helpful during debugging.

Reading and Changing Security Descriptors

Now that a security descriptor is associated with a file, the next step is to determine the security of an existing file and, in turn, change it. The following functions get and set file security in terms of security descriptors.

```
BOOL GetFileSecurity (
   LPCTSTR lpFileName,
   SECURITY_INFORMATION secInfo,
   PSECURITY_DESCRIPTOR pSecurityDescriptor,
   DWORD cbSd,
   LPDWORD lpcbLengthNeeded)

BOOL SetFileSecurity (
   LPCTSTR lpFileName,
   SECURITY_INFORMATION secInfo,
   PSECURITY_DESCRIPTOR pSecurityDescriptor)
```

secInfo is an enumerated type that takes on values such as OWNER-
_SECURITY_INFORMATION, GROUP_SECURITY_INFORMATION, DACL_SECURITY-
_INFORMATION, and SACL_SECURITY_INFORMATION to indicate what part of the
security descriptor to get or set. Combine these values with the bit-wise "or" operator.

To figure out the size of the return buffer for GetFileSecurity, the best
strategy is to call the function twice. The first call simply uses 0 as the cbSd
value. After allocating a buffer, call the function a second time. Program 15–4
operates this way.

Needless to say, the correct file permissions are required in order to carry out
these operations. For example, it is necessary to have WRITE_DAC permission or to
be the object's owner to succeed with SetFileSecurity.

The functions GetSecurityDescriptorOwner and GetSecurity-
DescriptorGroup can extract the SIDs from the security descriptor obtained
with GetFileSecurity. Obtain the ACL with the GetSecurityDescriptor-
Dacl function.

```
BOOL GetSecurityDescriptorDacl (
    PSECURITY_DESCRIPTOR pSecurityDescriptor,
    LPBOOL lpbDaclPresent,
    PACL *pAcl,
    LPBOOL lpbDaclDefaulted)
```

The parameters are nearly identical to those of SetSecurityDescriptor-
Dacl except that the flags are returned to indicate whether a discretionary ACL is
actually present and was set as a default or by a user.

To interpret an ACL, first find out how many ACEs it contains.

```
BOOL GetAclInformation (
    PACL pAcl,
    LPVOID pAclInformation,
    DWORD cbAclInfo,
    ACL_INFORMATION_CLASS dwAclInfoClass)
```

In most cases, the ACL information class, dwAclInfoClass, is AclSize-
Information, and the pAclInformation parameter is a structure of type
ACL_SIZE_INFORMATION. AclRevisionInformation is the other value for the class.

An `ACL_SIZE_INFORMATION` structure has three members: the most important one is `AceCount`, which shows how many entries are in the list. To determine whether the ACL is large enough, look at the `AclBytesInUse` and `AclBytes-Free` members of the `ACL_SIZE_INFORMATION` structure.

The `GetAce` function retrieves ACEs by index.

```
BOOL GetAce (
    PACL pAcl,
    DWORD dwAceIndex,
    LPVOID *pAce)
```

Obtain the ACEs (the total number is now known) by using an index. `pAce` points to an `ACE` structure, which has a member called `Header`, which, in turn, has an `AceType` member. Test the ACE type for `ACCESS_ALLOWED_ACE` and `ACCESS_DENIED_ACE`.

Example: Reading File Permissions

Program 15–4 is the function `ReadFilePermissions`, which Programs 15–1 and 15–2 use. This program methodically uses the preceding functions to extract the information. Its correct operation depends on the fact that the ACL was created by Program 15–3. The function is in the same source module as Program 15–3, so the definitions are not repeated.

Program 15–4   `ReadFilePermissions`: Reading Security Attributes

```
DWORD ReadFilePermissions (LPTSTR lpFileName, LPTSTR userName,
        LPTSTR groupName)
/* Return the UNIX style permissions for a file. */
{
    PSECURITY_DESCRIPTOR pSD = NULL;
    DWORD lenNeeded, permissionBits, iAce;
    BOOL fileDacl, aclDefaulted, ownerDaclDefaulted,
        groupDaclDefaulted;
    DWORD dacl[ACL_SIZE/sizeof(DWORD)];/* ACLS need DWORD alignment */
    PACL pAcl = (PACL) &dacl;
    ACL_SIZE_INFORMATION aclSizeInfo;
    PACCESS_ALLOWED_ACE pAce;
    BYTE aclType;
    PSID pOwnerSid, pGroupSid;
    TCHAR refDomain[2][DOM_SIZE];
    DWORD refDomainCount[2] = {DOM_SIZE, DOM_SIZE};
```

```
    DWORD accountNameSize[2] = {ACCT_NAME_SIZE, ACCT_NAME_SIZE};
    SID_NAME_USE sNamUse[] = {SidTypeUser, SidTypeGroup};

    /* Get the required size for the security descriptor. */
    GetFileSecurity (lpFileName, OWNER_SECURITY_INFORMATION |
            GROUP_SECURITY_INFORMATION | DACL_SECURITY_INFORMATION,
            NULL, 0, &lenNeeded);

    /* Create a security descriptor. */
    pSD = malloc (lenNeeded);
    GetFileSecurity (lpFileName, OWNER_SECURITY_INFORMATION |
            GROUP_SECURITY_INFORMATION | DACL_SECURITY_INFORMATION,
            pSD, lenNeeded, &lenNeeded);
    GetSecurityDescriptorDacl (pSD, &fileDacl, &pAcl, &aclDefaulted);
    /* Get the number of ACEs in the ACL. */
    GetAclInformation (pAcl, &aclSizeInfo,
            sizeof (ACL_SIZE_INFORMATION), AclSizeInformation);

    /* Get Each Ace. We know that this ACL was created by
        our InitializeUnixSA function, so the ACES are in the
        same order as the UNIX permission bits. */
    permissionBits = 0;
    for (iAce = 0; iAce < aclSizeInfo.AceCount; iAce++) {
        GetAce (pAcl, iAce, &pAce);
        aclType = pAce->Header.AceType;
        if (aclType == ACCESS_ALLOWED_ACE_TYPE)
            permissionBits |= (0x1 << (8-iAce));
    }

    /* Find the name of the owner and owning group. */
    /* Find the SIDs first. */

    GetSecurityDescriptorOwner (pSD, &pOwnerSid, &ownerDaclDefaulted);
    GetSecurityDescriptorGroup (pSD, &pGroupSid, &groupDaclDefaulted);
    LookupAccountSid (NULL, pOwnerSid, userName, &accountNameSize[0],
            refDomain[0],&refDomainCount[0], &sNamUse[0]);
    LookupAccountSid (NULL, pGroupSid, groupName, &accountNameSize[1],
            refDomain[1],&refDomainCount[1], &sNamUse[1]);
    free (pSD);
    return permissionBits;
}
```

Example: Changing File Permissions

Program 15–5 completes the collection of file security functions. This function, ChangeFilePermissions, replaces the existing security descriptor with a new one, preserving the user and group SIDs but creating a new discretionary ACL.

Program 15–5   ChangeFilePermissions: Changing Security Attributes

```
BOOL ChangeFilePermissions (DWORD fPerm, LPTSTR fileName,
                   LPDWORD allowedAceMasks, LPDWORD deniedAceMasks)
/* Change permissions in an existing file. The group is unchanged. */
/* Strategy:
    1. Obtain the existing security descriptor using
       the internal function ReadFilePermissions.
    2. Create a security attribute for the owner and permission bits.
    3. Extract the security descriptor.
    4. Set the file security with the new descriptor. */
{
    TCHAR userName[ACCT_NAME_SIZE], groupName[ACCT_NAME_SIZE];
    LPSECURITY_ATTRIBUTES pSA;
    PSECURITY_DESCRIPTOR pSD = NULL;

    ReadFilePermissions (fileName, userName, groupName);
    pSA = InitializeUnixSA (fPerm, userName, groupName,
            allowedAceMasks, deniedAceMasks);
    pSD = pSA->lpSecurityDescriptor;
    SetFileSecurity (fileName, DACL_SECURITY_INFORMATION, pSD);
    return TRUE;
}
```

Securing Kernel and Communication Objects

The preceding sections were concerned mostly with file security, and the same techniques apply to other filelike objects, such as named pipes (Chapter 11), and to kernel objects. Program 15–6, the next example, deals with named pipes, which can be treated in much the same way as files.

Securing Named Pipes

While the code is omitted in the Program 11–3 listing, the server (whose full code appears in the *Examples* file) optionally secures its named pipe to prevent access by unauthorized clients. Optional command line parameters specify the user and group name.

```
Server [UserName GroupName]
```

If the user and group names are omitted, default security is used. Note that the full version of Program 11–3 (in the *Examples* file) and Program 15–6 use techniques from Program 15–3 to create the optional security attributes. However, rather than calling `InitUnixSA`, we now use a simpler function, `Initialize-AccessOnlySA`, which only creates access-allowed ACEs. Program 15–6 shows the relevant code sections that were not shown in Program 11–3. The important security rights for named pipes are follows:

- `FILE_GENERIC_READ`
- `FILE_GENERIC_WRITE`

These two values provide `SYCHRONIZE` rights. The server in Program 15–6 optionally secures its named pipe instances using these rights. Only clients executed by the owner have access, although it would be straightforward to allow group members to access the pipe as well.

Program 15–6 `ServerNP`: Securing a Named Pipe

```
/* Chapter 15. ServerNP. With named pipe security.
 * Multithreaded command line server. Named pipe version.
 * Usage: Server [UserName GroupName]. */
. . .
_tmain (int argc, LPTSTR argv[])
{
    . . .
    HANDLE hNp, hMonitor, hSrvrThread[MAX_CLIENTS];
    DWORD iNp;
    DWORD aceMasks[] =  /* Named pipe access rights */
            {FILE_GENERIC_READ | FILE_GENERIC_WRITE, 0, 0 };

    LPSECURITY_ATTRIBUTES pNPSA = NULL;
    . . .
    if (argc == 4)      /* Optional pipe security. */
       pNPSA = InitializeAccessOnlySA (0440, argv[1], argv[2],
          aceMasks, &hSecHeap);
    . . .
    for (iNp = 0; iNp < MAX_CLIENTS; iNp++) {
       hNp = CreateNamedPipe (SERVER_PIPE, PIPE_ACCESS_DUPLEX,
             PIPE_READMODE_MESSAGE | PIPE_TYPE_MESSAGE | PIPE_WAIT,
             MAX_CLIENTS, 0, 0, INFINITE, pNPSA);

       if (hNp == INVALID_HANDLE_VALUE)
          ReportError (_T ("Failure to open named pipe."), 1, TRUE);
    . . .
}
```

Kernel and Private Object Security

Many objects, such as processes, threads, and mutexes, are *kernel objects*. To get and set kernel security descriptors, use `GetKernelObjectSecurity` and `SetKernelObjectSecurity`, which are similar to the file security functions described in this chapter. However, you need to know the access rights appropriate to an object; the next subsection shows how to find the rights.

It is also possible to associate security descriptors with private, programmer-generated objects, such as a proprietary database. The appropriate functions are `GetPrivateObjectSecurity` and `SetPrivateObjectSecurity`. The programmer must take responsibility for enforcing access and must provide security descriptors with calls to `CreatePrivateObjectSecurity` and `DestroyPrivateObjectSecurity`.

ACE Mask Values

The "user, group, everyone" model that `InitUnixSA` implements will be adequate in many cases, although different models are possible using the same basic techniques.

It is necessary, however, to determine the actual ACE mask values appropriate for a particular kernel object. The values are not always well documented, but there are several ways to determine the values for different kernel objects.

- Read the documentation for the open call for the object in question. The access flags are the same as the flags in the ACE mask. For example, `OpenMutex` uses `MUTEX_ALL_ACCESS` and `SYNCHRONIZE` (the second flag is required for any object that can be used with `WaitForSingleObject` or `WaitForMultipleObjects`). Other objects, such as processes, have many additional access flags.

- The "create" documentation may also supply useful information.

- Inspect the header files `winnt.h` and `winbase.h` for flags that apply to the object.

Example: Securing a Process and Its Threads

The `OpenProcess` documentation shows a fine-grained collection of access rights, which is appropriate considering the various functions that can be performed on a process handle. For example, `PROCESS_TERMINATE` access is required on a process handle in order for a process (actually, a thread within that process) to terminate the process that the handle represents. `PROCESS_QUERY_INFORMATION` access is required in order to perform `GetExitCodeProcess` or `GetPriority-`

`Class` on a process handle. `PROCESS_ALL_ACCESS` permits all access, and `SYNCHRONIZE` access is required to perform a wait function.

To illustrate these concepts, `JobShellSecure.c` upgrades Chapter 6's `JobShell` job management program so that only the owner (or administrator) can access the managed processes. The program is in the *Examples* file.

Overview of Additional Security Features

There is much more to Windows security, but this chapter is an introduction, showing how to secure Windows objects using the security API. The following sections give a brief overview of additional security subjects that some readers will want to explore.

Removing ACEs

The `DeleteAce` function deletes an ACE specified by an index, in a manner similar to that used with `GetAce`.

Absolute and Self-Relative Security Descriptors

Program 15–5, which changed ACLs, had the benefit of simply replacing one security descriptor (SD) with another. To change an existing SD, however, some care is required because of the distinction between absolute (ASD) and self-relative SDs (SRSD). The internal details of these data structures are not important for our purposes, but it is important to understand why there are two distinct SD types and how to convert between them.

- During construction, an SD is absolute, with pointers to various structures in memory. `InitializeSecurityDescriptor` creates an absolute SD. An absolute SD cannot be associated with a permanent object, such as a file, because the structure refers to memory addresses. However, an absolute SD is easy to modify and is fine for a process, thread, event, or other object that is not persistent and is represented by in-memory data structures.

- When the SD is associated with a permanent object, Windows consolidates the SD into a compact "self-relative" structure (SRSD) that can be associated with the object in the file system.

- An SRSD is more compact and more appropriate to pass as a function argument, but it is difficult to change.

- It is possible to convert between the two forms using Windows functions for that purpose. Use `MakeAbsoluteSD` to convert an SRSD, such as the one returned by `GetFileSecurity`. Modify the ASD and then use `MakeSelfRelativeSD` to convert it back. `MakeAbsoluteSD` is one of the more formidable Windows functions, having 11 parameters: two for each of the four SD components, one each for the input and output SDs, and one for the length of the resulting absolute SD.

`InitializeUnixSA` constructs a SA containing multiple ASDs. Exercise 15–16 suggests using only SRSDs.

System ACLs

There is a complete set of functions for managing system ACLs; only system administrators can use it. System ACLs specify which object accesses should be logged. The principal function is `AddAuditAccessAce`, which is similar to `AddAccessAllowedAce`. There is no concept of access denied with system ACLs.

Two other system ACL functions are `GetSecurityDescriptorSacl` and `SetSecurityDescriptorSacl`. These functions are comparable to their discretionary ACL counterparts, `GetSecurityDescriptorDacl` and `SetSecurityDescriptorDacl`.

Access Token Information

Program 15–1 did not solve the problem of obtaining the groups associated with a process in its access token. Program 15–1 simply required the user to specify the group name. You use the `GetTokenInformation` function for this, providing a process handle (Chapter 6). Exercise 15–12 addresses this issue, providing a hint toward the solution. The solution code is also included in the *Examples* file.

SID Management

The examples obtained SIDs from user and group names, but you can also create new SIDs with the `AllocateAndInitializeSid` function. Other functions obtain SID information, and you can even copy (`CopySid`) and compare (`CompareSid`) SIDs.

Summary

Windows implements an extensive security model that goes beyond the one offered by standard UNIX. Programs can secure all objects, not just files. The example programs have shown how to emulate the UNIX permissions and ownership that are set with the umask, chmod, and chown functions. Programs can also set the owner (group and user). The emulation is not easy, but the functionality is much more powerful. The complexity reflects the complexity of the requirements.

Looking Ahead

This chapter completes our presentation of the Windows API.

Additional Reading

Windows

Microsoft Windows Security Resource Kit, Second Edition, by Smith, Komar, and the Microsoft Security Team, and *Microsoft Windows Server 2003 PKI and Certificate Security,* by Brian Komar, provide in depth coverage.

Windows Design and Architecture

Windows Internals: Including Windows Server 2008 and Windows Vista, Fifth Edition, by Solomon, Russinovich, and Ionescu, describes details of Windows security internal implementation.

Common Criteria

See www.commoncriteriaportal.org/thecc.html for information about the Common Criteria levels and the Common Criteria Recognition Agreement.

Exercises

15–1. Extend Program 15–1 so that multiple groups have their own unique permissions. The group name and permission pairs can be separate arguments to the function.

15–2. Extend Program 15–4 so that it can report on all the groups that have ACEs in the object's security descriptor.

15–3. Confirm that chmodW has the desired effect of limiting file access.

15–4. Investigate the default security attributes you get with a file.

15–5. What are some of the other access masks you can use with an ACE? The Microsoft documentation supplies some information.

15–6. Enhance both `chmodW` and `lsFP` so that they produce an error message if asked to deal with a file on a non-NTFS file system. `GetVolume-Information` is required.

15–7. Enhance the `chmodW` command so that there is an `-o` option to set the owning user to be the user of the `chmodW` program.

15–8. Determine the actual size of the ACL buffer that Program 15–3 needs to store the ACEs. Program 15–3 uses 1,024 bytes. Can you determine a formula for estimating the required ACL size?

15–9. The Cygwin Web site (www.cygwin.com) provides an excellent open source Linux-like environment on Windows with a shell and implementations of commands including `chmod` and `ls`. Install this environment and compare the implementations of these two commands with the ones developed here. For example, if you set file permissions using the Cygwin command, does `lsFP` properly show the permissions, and conversely? Compare the Cygwin source code with this chapter's examples to contrast the two approaches to using Windows security.

15–10. The compatibility library contains functions `_open` and `_unmask`, which manage file permissions. Investigate their emulation of UNIX file permissions and compare it with the solutions in this chapter.

15–11. Write a command, `whoami`, that will display your logged-in user name.

15–12. Program 15–3, which created a security descriptor, required the programmer to supply the group name. Modify the program so that it creates permissions for all the user's groups. *Hint:* Use the `OpenProcessToken` function, which returns an array with the group names, although you will need to experiment to find out how the array stores group names. The source program in the *Examples* file contains a partial solution.

15–13. Note in the client/server system that the clients can access exactly the same files and other objects that are available to the server on the server's machine with the server's access rights. Remove this limitation by implementing *security delegation* using the functions `Impersonate-NamedPipeClient` and `RevertToSelf`. Clients that are not in the group used to secure the pipe cannot connect to the server.

15–14. There are several additional Windows functions that you may find useful and that could be applied to simplify or improve this chapter's examples. Look up the following functions: `AreAllAccessesGranted`, `AreAny-AccessesGranted`, `AccessCheck`, and `MapGenericMask`. Can you use these functions to simplify or improve the examples?

15–15. `chmodW` (Program 15–1) calls `GetUserName`, and a code comment suggests an alternative, getting the SID from the current token, to avoid an impersonation problem. Implement and test that change.

15–16. `InitializeUnixSA` uses a heap to simplify destroying the SA structure. An alternative, and arguably superior, method would be to convert all the SDs to be self-relative, use normal (`malloc`) allocations, and use `free`. However, if `InitializeUnixSA` fails before completing, be sure to free the memory that has been allocated.

A | Using the Sample Programs

The book's support Web site (www.jmhartsoftware.com) contains a zip file (the *Examples* file) with the source code for all the sample programs as well as the include files, utility functions, projects, and executables. A number of programs illustrate additional features and solve specific exercises, although the *Examples* file does not include solutions for all exercises or show every alternative implementation.

- All programs have been tested on Windows 7, Vista, XP, Server 2008, and Server 2003 on a wide variety of systems, ranging from laptops to servers. Where appropriate, they have also been tested at one time or another under Windows 9x, although many programs, especially those from later chapters, will not run on Windows 9x or even on NT 4.0, which is also obsolete.

- With a few minor exceptions, nearly all programs compile without warning messages under Microsoft Visual Studio 2005 and 2008 using warning level 3. Visual Studio 2010 (a beta version) easily converted several programs.

- Distinct project directories are provided for Microsoft Visual Studio 2005 and 2008 (32- and 64-bit). The three project directories are `Projects2005`, `Projects2008`, and `Projects2008_64`. The projects build the executable programs in the `run2005`, `run2008`, and `run2008_64` directories, respectively. VS 2010 project and run directories will appear in an updated *Examples* file after VS 2010 is released.

- There is a separate zip file with Visual Studio C++ 6.0 and 7.0 projects; some readers may find these projects convenient, but they are not up to date.

- The generic C library functions are used extensively, as are compiler-specific keywords such as `__try`, `__except`, and `__leave`. The multithreaded C run-time library, `_beginthreadex`, and `_endthreadex` are essential starting with Chapter 7.

- The projects are in release, not debug, form. The projects are all very simple, with minimal dependencies, and can also be created quickly with the desired configuration and as either debug or release versions.

- The projects are defined to build all programs, with the exception of static or dynamic libraries, as *console* applications.

You can also build the programs using open source development tools, such as gcc and g++ in the Gnu Compiler Collection (http://gcc.gnu.org/). Readers interested in these tools should look at the MinGW open source project (www.mingw.org), which describes MinGW as "a port of the GNU Compiler Collection (GCC), and GNU Binutils, for use in the development of native Microsoft Windows applications." I have tested only a few of the programs using these tools, but I have had considerable success using MinGW and have even been able to cross-build, constructing Windows executable programs and DLLs on a Linux system. Furthermore, I've found that gcc and g++ provide very useful 64-bit warning and error messages.

Examples File Organization

The primary directory is named WSP4_Examples ("Windows System Programming, Edition 4 Examples"), and this directory can be copied directly to your hard disk. There is a source file subdirectory for each chapter. All include files are in the Include directory, and the Utility directory contains the common functions such as ReportError. Complete projects are in the project directories. Executables and DLLs for all projects are in the run directories.

Download WindowsSmpEd3 ("Windows Sample Programs, Edition 3") if you want to use Visual Studio 6 or Visual Studio 7.

ReadMe.txt

Everything else you need to know is in the ReadMe.txt file, where you will find information about:

- The directories and their contents
- The source code, chapter by chapter
- The include files
- Utility functions

APPENDIX

B | Source Code Portability: Windows, UNIX, and Linux

A common, but not universal, application requirement, especially for server applications, is that the application must run on some combination of Windows, Linux, and UNIX.[1] This requirement leads to the need for "source code portability" whereby:

- There is a single set of source code for all target platforms.

- Macros and build parameters define the target platform, which could be any of the three operating systems, along with choices of processor architecture, 32-bit or 64-bit, and operating system vendor.

- Conditional compilation statements, while unavoidable, should be minimal, and the bulk of the source code should be the same for all target platforms.

- The source code is compatible with a wide variety of compilers.

- Performance, resource requirements, and other application characteristics should be similar for all targets.

With sufficient care and some exceptions, you can meet these requirements and build nontrivial source code portable applications. This discussion assumes, however, that there is no GUI interface. This appendix starts by describing some

---

[1] More precisely, "UNIX" means the POSIX functions specified in *The Single UNIX Specification* (www.opengroup.org/onlinepubs/007908799/). UNIX and Linux implement this specification. In turn, the specification has its historical origins in UNIX.

techniques that have been successful and have met all the requirements. There are, of course, other ways to achieve source code portability beyond what is described here.

The discussion is limited to the POSIX API that is comparable to the topics in this book, and the discussion is not concerned with the complete POSIX environment. However, it's worth pointing out that Cygwin (www.cygwin.com) provides an excellent open source set of POSIX commands and utilities for Windows.

After the discussion are tables that list the Windows functions and their POSIX equivalents, if any. The tables are organized by chapter.

Source Code Portability Strategies

There are several ways to tackle this problem, although there is no single strategy suitable for all functionality areas. Viable strategies, not always mutually exclusive, include:

- Use libraries, possibly open source or Microsoft-provided, that emulate POSIX functions on Windows. This strategy is common and successful, with some examples in this appendix.

- Use libraries, possibly open source, that emulate Windows functions on UNIX/ Linux. This strategy is rare, and there are no examples here.

- Use industry-standard functions that Microsoft supports directly. This is also a common and successful strategy for some functionality.

- Use macros instead of libraries to emulate one OS under the other. This strategy is also rare, but there is one example in this appendix.

Windows Services for UNIX

Windows Services for UNIX (SFU) is a Microsoft product that provides a UNIX subsystem, also called Interix, for Windows. The subsystem is implemented in user space on the NT kernel. The current version is 3.5, and you can download it from the Microsoft Web site.

In principle, SFU should satisfy all the requirements. Unfortunately, at publication time, Microsoft plans to discontinue support (the plans were announced in 2005). For example, the Web site states that the supported operating systems are "Windows 2000; Windows 2000 Service Pack 3; Windows 2000 Service Pack 4; Windows Server 2003; Windows XP." Furthermore, "the product will not install on Windows 9x or Windows XP Home Edition or Windows Vista. The product should not be installed on Windows Server 2003 R2. This is an unsupported configuration."

The Wikipedia entry (http://en.wikipedia.org/wiki/Microsoft_Windows_Services_for_UNIX) says, "SFU will be available for download until 2009; general support will continue until 2011; extended support until 2014," and citations to the trade press support this statement.

Source Code Portability for Windows Functionality

The following sections describe some techniques, arranged by chapter order. Some areas are easier than others, and in some cases, there are no straightforward solutions.

File and Directory Management

The Standard C library (CLIB) will support normal file I/O without significant performance impact. However, CLIB does not provide directory management, among other limitations.

Another possible solution is to use the normal POSIX functions, such as `open()` and `read()` and the corresponding Windows functions (see Chapter 1 and the `cpUC` project), such as `_open()` and `_read()`. A simple header file, in the *Examples* file, allows you to use the POSIX function names in the source code. The header file also includes definitions to support time, file attributes, and file locking.

There is no POSIX equivalent to the registry.

Exception and Signal Handling

POSIX signal handling is difficult to emulate in Windows except for a few special cases described in Chapter 4. However, you can write in C++ rather than C and use C++ exception handling rather than Structured Exception Handling (SEH) to achieve some of the requirements.

Memory Management and Memory-Mapped File I/O

There are several aspects to portable memory management code.

- The CLIB functions `malloc`, `calloc`, `realloc`, and `free` are sufficient in most cases for application memory management.

- POSIX does not have functions equivalent to the Windows heap management functions, and Chapter 5 describes some heap management advantages. There are, however, open source solutions, available on Windows and UNIX/Linux, that provide the heap management benefits. One such solution is

"Hoard: A Scalable Memory Allocator for Multithreaded Applications" (www.cs.umass.edu/~emery/hoard/asplos2000.pdf).

- Memory-mapped file I/O provides similar performance and programming simplicity advantages on all operating systems. The Web site's `wcMT` (multithreaded word count) example includes portable file memory-mapping code that has been tested on multiple target systems.

Process Management

Windows `CreateProcess` allows you to emulate the POSIX `fork-exec` sequence, as described in Chapter 6. The principal difficulties arise in:

- Emulating the various `exec` options to specify the command line and environment variables
- Passing handles to the child process
- Managing the parent-child relationships, which Windows does not support

I am not aware of a good open source solution to the process management problem. However, it's worth mentioning that I've successfully developed a library, usable from all OSs, that provides a significant subset of the POSIX process management functionality. This subset was sufficient for the project needs. However, the code was developed under nondisclosure, so it's not in the *Examples* file. Suffice it to say, however, that the task was not difficult and required about two days of work.

Thread Management and Synchronization

Thread management and synchronization portability, at first sight, may seem to be intractable, considering the need for correct operation on a wide variety of platforms. Fortunately, it is not difficult at all. Here is one successful approach.

- Develop your source code using the Pthreads API (www.unix.org/version3/ieee_std.html)
- Use the open source Pthreads library for Windows (http://sources.redhat.com/pthreads-win32/)

This open source library provides good performance, compatible with native Windows code. However, at publication time, it does not yet support slim reader/

writer locks (Chapter 9) or thread pools. However, the library is open source, and upgrading this library would be a worthwhile contribution.

I've also had success with a simple set of macros that nicely emulate nearly all Pthreads functionality in Windows. In this case, the client did not want to use open source code. The macros are on the book's Web site.

Interprocess Communication and Network Programming

This problem also has multiple aspects.

- One-directional pipes (Chapter 12) are fairly close in Windows and POSIX, and they are usually associated with process management (mentioned in a previous section).

- Windows supports the sockets API and provides the simplest portability and interoperability strategy for network programming and interprocess communication, even on a single system.

- Named pipes and mailslots are Windows-specific and are best avoided in portable source code.

Services

Windows Services correspond very roughly to POSIX "daemons." Service and daemon management are administrative functions, and there is no direct way to provide portable source code that uses the Windows Services functions.

Asynchronous I/O

The Windows and POSIX models for asynchronous I/O are considerably different. I've found that it's simplest to use threads and avoid asynchronous I/O altogether, although this is a matter of personal taste.

Windows, POSIX, and C Library Comparison Tables

The following tables show the Windows functions described in the main text along with the corresponding UNIX/Linux and ANSI Standard C library functions, if any.

The tables are arranged by chapter (some chapters are combined). Within each chapter, they are sorted first by functionality area (file system, directory management, and so on) and then by the Windows function name.

Each table row gives the following information:

- The functionality area (subject)

- The Windows function name

- The corresponding UNIX function name, in some cases, more than one

- The corresponding C library function name, if any

- Comments as appropriate

The notation used in the tables requires some explanation.

- The Microsoft Visual Studio library contains some UNIX compatibility functions. For example, _open is the compatibility library function for UNIX open. If the UNIX function is in italics, there is a compatibility function. An asterisk next to the name indicates that there is also a wide character Unicode version. For example, there is a _wopen function.

- A program that uses just the Standard C library, and no Windows or UNIX system functions, should compile, build, and run on both systems if normal precautions are taken. Such a program will, however, be limited to file and I/O operations.

- Commas separating functions indicate alternatives, often using different characteristics or emulating one aspect of the Windows function.

- Semicolons separating functions indicate that you use the functions in sequence to emulate the Windows function. Thus, fork; exec corresponds roughly to CreateProcess.

- An underlined entry indicates a global variable, such as errno.

- In a few cases, the UNIX equivalent may be stated imprecisely in terms such as "terminal I/O" for Windows functions such as AllocConsole. Often, "Use C library" is the appropriate comment, as in the case of GetTempFileName. In other cases, the situation is reversed. Thus, under the UNIX signal management functions (sigaddset and so on), the Windows entry is "Use SEH, VEH" to indicate that the programmer should set up structured or vectored exception handlers and filter functions to get the desired behavior. Unlike UNIX, Windows does not support process groups, so the Windows entries are "N/A," although job management, as done by the programs in Chapter 6, could emulate process relationships.

- There are numerous N/A entries, especially for the C library, if there is no comparable function or set of functions. This is the case, for example, with directory management.

- The POSIX threads (Pthreads) functions are the UNIX equivalents shown in the tables for Chapters 7 through 10, even though they are not properly a part of UNIX.

Generally, the correspondence is more precise in the earlier chapters, particularly for file management. The systems tend to diverge with the more advanced functionality, and in many cases, there is no C library equivalent. For example, the UNIX and Windows security models differ significantly, so the relationships shown are, at best, approximations.

These functional correspondences are not exact. There are many differences, small and large, among the three systems. Therefore, these tables are only for guidance. The individual chapters discuss many of the differences.

Chapters 2 and 3: File and Directory Management

Table B-1   Chapters 2 and 3: File and Directory Management

Subject	Windows	UNIX	C Library	Comments
Console I/O	AllocConsole	terminal I/O	N/A	
Console I/O	FreeConsole	terminal I/O	N/A	
Console I/O	ReadConsole	*read*	getc, scanf, gets	
Console I/O	SetConsoleMode	ioctl	N/A	
Console I/O	WriteConsole	*write*	putc, printf, puts	
Directory Mgt	CreateDirectory	*mkdir**	N/A	Make a new directory
Directory Mgt	FindClose	*closedir**	N/A	Close a directory search handle
Directory Mgt	FindFirstFile	*opendir**, *readdir**	N/A	Find first file matching a pattern
Directory Mgt	FindNextFile	*readdir**	N/A	Find subsequent files
Directory Mgt	GetCurrentDirectory	*getcwd**	N/A	
Directory Mgt	GetFullPathName	N/A	N/A	
Directory Mgt	GetSystemDirectory	Well-known pathnames	N/A	
Directory Mgt	RemoveDirectory	*rmdir, unlink**	remove	
Directory Mgt	SearchPath	Use opendir, readdir	N/A	Search for a file on a specified path

Table B-1   Chapters 2 and 3: File and Directory Management (cont.)

Subject	Windows	UNIX	C Library	Comments
Directory Mgt	`SetCurrentDirectory`	*chdir**, `fchdir`	N/A	Change the working directory
Error Handling	`FormatMessage`	`strerror`	`perror`	
Error Handling	`GetLastError`	<u>`errno`</u>	<u>`errno`</u>	Global variable
Error Handling	`SetLastError`	<u>`errno`</u>	<u>`errno`</u>	Global variable
File Locking	`LockFile`	`fcntl (cmd=F_ GETLK, ...)`	N/A	
File Locking	`LockFileEx`	`fcntl (cmd=F_ GETLK, ...)`	N/A	
File Locking	`UnlockFile`	`fcntl (cmd=F_ GETLK, ...)`	N/A	
File Locking	`UnlockFileEx`	`fcntl (cmd=F_ GETLK, ...)`	N/A	
File System	`CloseHandle` (file handle)	*close**	`fclose`	`CloseHandle` is not limited to files
File System	`CopyFile`	`open; read; write; close`	`fopen; fread; fwrite; fclose`	Duplicate a file
File System	`CreateFile`	*open**, *creat**	`fopen`	Open/create a file
File System	`DeleteFile`	*unlink**	`remove`	Delete a file
File System	`FlushFileBuffers`	`fsynch`	`fflush`	Write file buffers
File System	`GetFileAttributes`	*stat**, *fstat**, `lstat`	N/A	

Table B-1   Chapters 2 and 3: File and Directory Management (cont.)

Subject	Windows	UNIX	C Library	Comments
File System	`GetFileInformation-ByHandle`	*stat**, *fstat**, `lstat`	N/A	Fill structure with file info
File System	`GetFileSize`	*stat**, *fstat**, `lstat`	`ftell, fseek`	Get length of file in bytes
File System	`GetFileTime`	*stat**, *fstat**, `lstat`	N/A	
File System	`GetFileType`	*stat**, *fstat**, `lstat`	N/A	Check for character stream device or file
File System	`GetStdHandle`	Use file desc 0, 1, or 2	Use stdin, stdout, stderr	
File System	`GetTempFileName`	Use C library	`tmpnam`	Create a unique file name
File System	`GetTempFileName, CreateFile`	Use C library	`tmpfile`	Create a temporary file
File System	`GetTempPath`	`/temp` path	N/A	Directory for temp files
File System	`MoveFile, MoveFileEx`	Use C library	`rename`	Rename a file or directory
File System	`CreateHardLink`	`link`, *unlink**	N/A	Windows does not support links
File System	N/A	`symlink`	N/A	Create a symbolic link
File System	N/A	`readlink`	N/A	Read name in a symbolic link
File System	N/A, `ReadFile` returns 0 bytes	N/A, `read` returns 0 bytes	`feof`	Rest for end of file
File System	N/A, use multiple `ReadFiles`	`readv`	N/A, use multiple `freads`	Scatter read

Table B–1 Chapters 2 and 3: File and Directory Management (cont.)

Subject	Windows	UNIX	C Library	Comments
File System	N/A, use multiple WriteFiles	writev	N/A, use multiple fwrites	Gather write
File System	ReadFile	*read*	fread	Read data from a file
File System	SetEndOfFile	*chsize**	N/A	
File System	SetFileAttributes	fcntl	N/A	
File System	SetFilePointer	*lseek*	fseek	Set file pointer
FileSystem	SetFilePointer (to 0)	lseek (0)	rewind	
File System	SetFileTime	*utime**	N/A	
File System	SetStdHandle	close, *dup**, *dup2**, or fcntl	freopen	dup2 or fcntl
File System	WriteFile	write	fwrite	Write data to a file
System Info	GetDiskFreeSpace	N/A	N/A	
System Info	GetSystemInfo	getrusage	N/A	
System Info	GetVersion	uname	N/A	
System Info	GetVolume-Information	N/A	N/A	
System Info	GlobalMemoryStatus	getrlimit	N/A	
System Info	Various defined constants	sysconf, pathconf, fpathconf	N/A	
Time	GetSystemTime	Use C library	time, gmtime	

Table B–1   Chapters 2 and 3: File and Directory Management (cont.)

Subject	Windows	UNIX	C Library	Comments
Time	See `ls` program, Program 3–2	Use C library	`asctime`	
Time	`CompareFileTime`	Use C library	`difftime`	Compare "calendar" times
Time	`FileTimeToLocal-FileTime, File-TimeToSystemTime`	Use C library	`localtime`	
Time	`FileTimeToSystem-Time`	Use C library	`gmtime`	
Time	`GetLocalTime`	Use C library	`time, localtime`	
Time	See `touch` program, Program 3–3	Use C library	`strftime`	
Time	`SetLocalTime`	N/A	N/A	
Time	`SetSystemTime`	N/A	N/A	
Time	Subtract file times	Use C library	`difftime`	
Time	`SystemTimeToFile-Time`	Use C library	`mktime`	

Chapter 4: Exception Handling

Table B–2   Chapter 4: Exception Handling

Subject	Windows	UNIX	C Library
SEH	`_try − _except`	Use C library signals	Use C library signals
SEH	`_try − _finally`	Use C library signals	Use C library signals
SEH	`AbnormalTermination`	Use C library signals	Use C library signals
SEH	`GetExceptionCode`	Use C library signals	Use C library signals
SEH	`RaiseException`	Use C library signals	`signal, raise`
Signals	Use `_finally` block	Use C library	`atexit`
Signals	Use C library or terminate process	`kill`	`raise`
Signals	Use C library	Use C library	`signal`
Signals	Use SEH, VEH	`sigemptyset`	N/A
Signals	Use SEH, VEH	`sigfillset`	N/A
Signals	Use SEH, VEH	`sigaddset`	N/A
Signals	Use SEH, VEH	`sigdelset`	N/A
Signals	Use SEH, VEH	`sigismember`	N/A
Signals	Use SEH, VEH	`sigprocmask`	N/A
Signals	Use SEH, VEH	`sigpending`	N/A
Signals	Use SEH, VEH	`sigaction`	N/A
Signals	Use SEH, VEH	`sigsetjmp`	N/A
Signals	Use SEH, VEH	`siglongjmp`	N/A
Signals	Use SEH, VEH	`sigsuspendf`	N/A
Signals	Use SEH, VEH	`psignal`	N/A
Signals	Use SEH, VEH, or C library	Use C library	`abort`

Chapter 5: Memory Management, Memory-Mapped Files, and DLLs

Table B–3   Chapter 5: Memory Management, Memory-Mapped Files, and DLLs

Subject	Windows	UNIX	C Library
Mapped Files	`CreateFileMapping`	`shmget`	N/A
Mapped Files	`MapViewOfFile`	`mmap, shmat`	N/A
Mapped Files	`MapViewOfFileEx`	`mmap, shmat`	N/A
Mapped Files	`OpenFileMapping`	`shmget`	N/A
Mapped Files	`UnmapViewOfFile`	`munmap, shmdt, shmctl`	N/A
Memory Mgt	`GetProcessHeap`	N/A	N/A
Memory Mgt	`GetSystemInfo`	N/A	N/A
Memory Mgt	`HeapAlloc`	sbrk, brk, or C library	`malloc, calloc`
Memory Mgt	`HeapCreate`	N/A	N/A
Memory Mgt	`HeapDestroy`	N/A	N/A
Memory Mgt	`HeapFree`	Use C library	`free`
Memory Mgt	`HeapReAlloc`	Use C library	`realloc`
Memory Mgt	`HeapSize`	N/A	N/A
Shared Memory	`CloseHandle` (map handle)	`shmctl`	N/A
Shared Memory	`CreateFileMapping, OpenFileMapping`	`shmget`	N/A
Shared Memory	`MapViewOfFile`	`shmat`	N/A
Shared Memory	`UnmapViewOfFile`	`shmdt`	N/A
DLLs	`LoadLibrary`	`dlopen`	N/A
DLLs	`FreeLibrary`	`dlclose`	N/A
DLLs	`GetProcAddress`	`dlsyn`	N/A
DLLs	`DllMain`	`pthread_once`	N/A

Chapter 6: Process Management

Table B–4   Chapter 6: Process Management

Subject	Windows	UNIX	C Library	Comments
Process Mgt	CreateProcess	fork (); execl ()*, system()	N/A	There are 6 execxx functions
Process Mgt	ExitProcess	_exit	exit	
Process Mgt	GetCommandLine	argv []	argv []	
Process Mgt	GetCurrentProcess	getpid*	N/A	
Process Mgt	GetCurrentProcessId	getpid*	N/A	
Process Mgt	GetEnvironmentStrings	N/A	getenv	
Process Mgt	GetEnvironmentVariable	N/A	getenv	
Process Mgt	GetExitCodeProcess	wait, waitpid	N/A	
Process Mgt	GetProcessTimes	times, wait3, wait4	N/A	
Process Mgt	GetProcessWorkingSetSize	wait3, wait4	N/A	
Process Mgt	N/A	execl*, execv*, execle*, execve*, execlp*, execvp*	N/A	Windows does not have a direct equivalent
Process Mgt	N/A	fork, vfork	N/A	Windows does not have a direct equivalent
Process Mgt	N/A	getppid	N/A	No parent-child relationships in Windows

Table B–4   Chapter 6: Process Management (cont.)

Subject	Windows	UNIX	C Library	Comments
Process Mgt	N/A	getgid, getegid	N/A	No process groups in Windows
Process Mgt	N/A	getpgrp	N/A	
Process Mgt	N/A	setpgid	N/A	
Process Mgt	N/A	setsid	N/A	
Process Mgt	N/A	tcgetpgrp	N/A	
Process Mgt	N/A	tcsetpgrp	N/A	
Process Mgt	OpenProcess	N/A	N/A	
Process Mgt	SetEnvironmentVariable	putenv	N/A	putenv is not part of the Standard C library
Process Mgt	TerminateProcess	kill	N/A	
Synch: Process	WaitForMultipleObjects (process handles)	waitpid	N/A	
Synch: Process	WaitForSingleObject (process handle)	wait, waitpid	N/A	
Timers	KillTimer	alarm (0)	N/A	
Timers	SetTimer	alarm	N/A	
Timers	Sleep	sleep	N/A	
Timers	Sleep	poll or select, no file descriptor	N/A	

Note: Many UNIX vendors provide proprietary exception handling capabilities.

Chapter 7: Threads and Scheduling

Table B–5   Chapter 7: Threads and Scheduling

Subject	Windows	UNIX/Pthreads	Comments
Thread Mgt	CreateRemoteThread	N/A	
TLS	TlsAlloc	pthread_key_alloc	
TLS	TlsFree	pthread_key_delete	
TLS	TlsGetValue	pthread_getspecific	
TLS	TlsSetValue	pthread_setspecific	
Thread Mgt	CreateThread, _beginthreadex	pthread_create	
Thread Mgt	ExitThread, _endthreadex	pthread_exit	
Thread Mgt	GetCurrentThread	pthread_self	
Thread Mgt	GetCurrentThreadId	N/A	
Thread Mgt	GetExitCodeThread	pthread_yield	
Thread Mgt	ResumeThread	N/A	
Thread Mgt	SuspendThread	N/A	
Thread Mgt	TerminateThread	pthread_cancel	pthread_cancel is safer
Thread Mgt	WaitForSingleObject(thread handle)	pthread_join	
Thread Priority	GetPriorityClass	pthread_attr_getschedpolicy, getpriority	

Table B–5 Chapter 7: Threads and Scheduling (cont.)

Subject	Windows	UNIX/Pthreads	Comments
Thread Priority	`GetThreadPriority`	`pthread_attr_ getschedparam`	
Thread Priority	`SetPriorityClass`	`pthread_attr_ setschedpolicy, setpriority, nice`	
Thread Priority	`SetThreadPriority`	`pthread_attr_ setschedparam`	

Note: Pthreads, while a part of all modern UNIX offerings, are available on non-UNIX systems as well.

Chapters 8–10: Thread Synchronization

Table B–6   Chapters 8–10: Thread Synchronization

Subject	Windows	UNIX/Pthreads	Comments
Synch: CritSec	DeleteCriticalSection		C library is not applicable
Synch: CritSec	EnterCriticalSection	Use mutexes to emulate critical sections. Some systems provide proprietary equivalents.	C library is not applicable
Synch: CritSec	InitializeCriticalSection		
Synch: CritSec	LeaveCriticalSection		
Synch: Event	CloseHandle (event handle)	pthread_cond_destroy	
Synch: Event	CreateEvent	pthread_cond_init	
Synch: Event	PulseEvent	pthread_cond_signal	Manual-reset event
Synch: Event	ResetEvent	N/A	
Synch: Event	SetEvent	pthread_cond_broad-cast	Auto-reset event
Synch: Event	WaitForSingleObject (event handle)	pthread_cond_wait	
Synch: Event	WaitForSingleObject (event handle)	pthread_timed_wait	
Synch: Mutex	CloseHandle (mutex handle)	pthread_mutex_destroy	
Synch: Mutex	CreateMutex	pthread_mutex_init	
Synch: Mutex	ReleaseMutex	pthread_mutex_unlock	
Synch: Mutex	WaitForSingleObject (mutex handle)	pthread_mutex_lock	

Table B–6   Chapters 8–10: Thread Synchronization (cont.)

Subject	Windows	UNIX/Pthreads	Comments
Synch: Sem	`CreateSemaphore`	`semget`	
Synch: Sem	N/A	`semctl`	Windows does not directly support all these options
Synch: Sem	`OpenSemaphore`	`semget`	
Synch: Sem	`ReleaseSemaphore`	`semop (+)`	
Synch: Sem	`WaitForSingleObject` (semaphore handle)	`semop (-)`	Windows can wait for only one count
Synch: SRW	`InitializeSRWLock`	`pthread_rwlock_init`	
Synch: SRW	`AcquireSRWLockShared`	`pthread_rwlock_rdlock`	
Synch: SRW	`AcquireSRWLockExclusive`	`pthread_rwlock_wrlock`	
Synch: SRW	`ReleaseSRWLockShared` `ReleaseSRWLockExclusive`	`pthread_rwlock_unlock`	
Thread Pools	`CreateThreadpoolWork, etc.`	N/A	
Synch: SOAW	`SignalObjectAndWait;` `WaitForSingleObject`	`pthread_cond_wait,` `pthread_cond_timedwait`	Event and mutex handles only
Condition Variable	`InitializeConditionVariable`	`pthread_cond_init`	
Condition Variable	`SleepConditionVariableCS,` `SleepConditionVariableSRW`	`pthread_cond_wait,` `pthread_cond_timedwait`	
User APCs	`QueueUserAPC`	N/A	

Chapter 11: Interprocess Communication

Table B–7   Chapter 11: Interprocess Communication

Subject	Windows	UNIX	C Library	Comments
IPC	CallNamedPipe	N/A	N/A	CreateFile, WriteFile, ReadFile, CloseHandle
IPC	CloseHandle (pipe handle)	close, msgctl	pclose	Not part of the Standard C library—see Stevens and Rago
IPC	ConnectNamedPipe	N/A	N/A	
IPC	CreateMailslot	N/A	N/A	
IPC	CreateNamedPipe	mkfifo, msgget	N/A	
IPC	CreatePipe	*pipe*	popen	Not part of the Standard C library—see Stevens and Rago
IPC	DuplicateHandle	*dup*, *dup2*, or fcntl	N/A	Or use file names CONIN$, CONOUT$
IPC	GetNamedPipeHandle-State	*stat*, *fstat*, lstat64	N/A	
IPC	GetNamedPipeInfo	*stat*, *fstat*, lstat	N/A	
IPC	ImpersonateNamedPipe-Client	N/A	N/A	
IPC	PeekNamedPipe	N/A	N/A	
IPC	ReadFile (named pipe handle)	read (FIFO), msgsnd	N/A	
IPC	RevertToSelf	N/A	N/A	

Table B–7   Chapter 11: Interprocess Communication (cont.)

Subject	Windows	UNIX	C Library	Comments
IPC	SetNamedPipeHandle-State	N/A	N/A	
IPC	TransactNamedPipe	N/A	N/A	WriteFile; ReadFile
IPC	WriteFile (named pipe handle)	write (FIFO), msgrcv	N/A	
Misc.	GetComputerName	uname	N/A	
Misc.	SetComputerName	N/A	N/A	
Security	SetNamedPipeIdentity	Use directory sticky bit	N/A	

Chapter 14: Asynchronous I/O

Table B–8   Chapter 14: Asynchronous I/O

Subject	Windows	UNIX	C Library	Comments
Asynch I/O	GetOverlappedResult	N/A	N/A	
Asynch I/O	ReadFileEx	N/A	N/A	Extended I/O with completion routine
Asynch I/O	SleepEx	N/A	N/A	Alertable wait
Asynch I/O	WaitForMultipleObjects (file handles)	poll, select	N/A	
Asynch I/O	WaitForMultipleObjectsEx	N/A	N/A	Alertable wait
Asynch I/O	WriteFileEx	N/A	N/A	Extended I/O with completion routine
Asynch I/O	WaitForSingleObjectEx	waitpid	N/A	Alertable wait

Chapter 15: Securing Windows Objects

Table B–9   Chapter 15: Securing Windows Objects

Subject	Windows	UNIX	Comments
Security	AddAccessAllowedAce	chmod, fchmod	C library does not support security
Security	AddAccessDeniedAce	chmod, fchmod	
Security	AddAuditAce	N/A	
Security	CreatePrivateObjectSecurity	N/A	
Security	DeleteAce	chmod, fchmod	
Security	DestroyPrivateObjectSecurity	N/A	
Security	GetAce	*stat**, *fstat**, lstat	
Security	GetAclInformation	*stat**, *fstat**, lstat	
Security	GetFileSecurity	*stat**, *fstat**, lstat	
Security	GetPrivateObjectSecurity	N/A	
Security	GetSecurityDescriptorDacl	*stat**, *fstat**, lstat	
Security	GetUserName	getlogin	
Security	InitializeAcl	N/A	
Security	InitializeSecurityDescriptor	*umask*	
Security	LookupAccountName	getpwnam, getgrnam	

Table B–9   Chapter 15: Securing Windows Objects (cont.)

Subject	Windows	UNIX	Comments
Security	LookupAccountSid	getpwuid, getuid, geteuid	C library does not support security
Security	N/A	getpwend, setpwent, endpwent	
Security	N/A	getgrent, setgrent, endgrent	
Security	N/A	setuid, seteuid, setreuid	
Security	N/A	setgid, setegid, setregid	
Security	OpenProcessToken	getgroups, setgroups, initgroups	
Security	SetFileSecurity	*chmod**, fchmod	
Security	SetPrivateObjectSecurity	N/A	
Security	SetSecurityDescriptorDacl	*umask*	
Security	SetSecurityDescriptorGroup	chown, fchown, lchown	
Security	SetSecurityDescriptorOwner	chown, fchown, lchown	
Security	SetSecurityDescriptorSacl	N/A	

APPENDIX

C | Performance Results

The example programs have shown a variety of alternative techniques to implement the same tasks, such as file copying, random record access, and locking, and it is natural to speculate about the performance advantages of these techniques. Application design requires knowledge of, rather than speculation about, the performance impacts of alternative implementations and the potential performance advantages of various Windows versions, hardware configurations, and Windows features, such as threads, memory mapping, and asynchronous I/O.

This appendix contains tables that compare performance directly on several platforms. There are numerous variations for some tasks; consider, for example, the multiple locking and condition variable combinations. The tables show that performance can often vary significantly among different implementations, but, in other cases, the difference is not significant. The tables also show the effect of multiple processors. The tables here are far more comprehensive than the run screenshots throughout the book, as those tests are usually confined to a single machine.

You can run these tests on your own computer, and the Web site contains all the required executables, DLLs, and shell scripts, as well as a "read me" file.

Test Configurations

Testing was performed with a representative variety of applications, based on examples in the book and a range of host computers.

Applications

The tables in this appendix show the times measured with `timep` (Chapter 6) for the test programs running on several different machines. The six functionality areas are as follows.

1. *File copying.* Several different techniques, such as using the C library and the Windows CopyFile function, are measured to determine the performance impact. File copying stresses sequential file I/O without any data processing.

2. *Simple Caesar cipher file conversion.* This shows the effect of memory mapping, larger buffers, the Windows sequential scan flags, and asynchronous I/O. Conversion stresses file I/O with a small amount of data processing as the data is moved, and converted, from one buffer to another.

3. *Word counting.* This test set uses the wc program in its single and multithreaded forms. Simple sequential processing is also tested and turns out to be competitive with the two parallel search methods on a single processor. Word counting increases the amount of data processing and minimizes the output.

4. *Record Access.* This shows the performance differences between direct file I/O (read and write statements) and memory mapping to perform record access in large files.

5. *Locking.* Chapter 9 discussed several locking models and showed some results, and the table here extends those results.

6. *Multithreaded producer/consumer application.* This shows the effects of different synchronization techniques for implementing a multithreaded queuing application in order to evaluate the trade-offs discussed in Chapters 8, 9, and 10 among CRITICAL_SECTIONs, condition variables, mutexes, and the signal and broadcast condition variable models.

All application programs were built with Microsoft Visual Studio 2005 and 2008 as release versions rather than debug versions. Running in debug mode can add significant performance overhead. Nearly 80% overhead was observed in one CPU-intensive test, and the debug executable images can be two or three times larger than the release versions.

The VS 2005 builds are all 32-bit, but there are 32- and 64-bit versions of the VS 2008 builds. In most cases, the results are similar when run on a 64-bit computer, but the 64-bit builds allow much larger files and data structures.

Test Machines

Performance was measured on six computers with a wide variety of CPU, memory, and OS configurations. I've used a broad range of current and relatively inexpensive machines; nonetheless, anyone reading this list in a few years may be tempted to smile indulgently as technical progress obsolesces these computers.

1. A 1.4GHz Intel Celeron M 1-processor laptop with 1.5GB RAM, running Windows XP SP3 (32-bit). This computer is about 5 years old (as of October 2009), but it is still useful; I'm using it to create this document and expect to use it for years to come.

2. A 2GHz Intel Core2 (2-CPU) laptop acquired in June 2008 with 2GB RAM, running Windows Vista SP2 (32-bit).

3. A new (May 2009) 2.83GHz Intel Core2 Quad (4-CPU) desktop with 4MB RAM, running Windows Vista SP2 (32-bit).

4. A new (June 2009) 2.4GHz AMD Phenom 9750 Quad-Core (4-CPU) desktop[1] with 16GB RAM, running Windows Vista SP2 (64-bit). All applications are 64-bit builds. The 64-bit executables are sometimes slower and rarely faster than the 32-bit executables, but they do have the advantage of being able to process large data sets and to map huge files. For a comparison, see test machine 6.

5. A 1.7GHz AMD Quad-Core AMD Opteron Processor 2344 HE server with two cores (8 processors total) and 4GB RAM, running Windows Server 2008 SP1 (32-bit).

6. Windows 7 installed on machine 4 to validate operation on Windows 7 and to see if there are any notable performance differences from Vista. All applications are 32-bit builds, whereas the machine 4 builds are 64-bit.

All file systems were less than 50% full and were not significantly fragmented. In addition, the test machines were all idle except for running the test programs. The CPU-intensive applications give a good indication of relative processing speeds.

The timing programs are all in the *Examples* file so that you can perform these tests on your own test machine.

Performance Measurements

Each application was run five times on the host machine. The batch files clear physical memory before each run of the file access programs so that performance figures would not be improved as the files became cached in memory or the swap file. The tables show the average times in seconds.

Comments are after the tables. Needless to say, generalizations about performance can be perilous because numerous factors, including test program characteristics, contribute to a program's performance. These tests do, however, show

---

[1] Actually, it's on the floor, but we'll use the marketing term, and anyhow, the laptops are on the desktop.

some of the possibilities and show the potential impacts of various operating system versions and different programming techniques. Also bear in mind that the tests measure the time from program start to end but do not measure the time that the computer might take to flush buffers to the disk. Finally, there was no attempt to exploit specific computer features or parameters, such as stripped disks, disk block sizes, multiple disk partitions, and so on.

The Windows performance monitor, available under the control panel's Administrative Tools, displays CPU, kernel, user, and other activities graphically. This tool is invaluable in gaining insight into program behavior beyond the measurements given here.

The host machine variety also shows the impact of features such as cache size and organization, disk speed, and more. For example, machine 4 (Vista, 4-CPU, 64-bit, 2.4GHz desktop) sometimes outperforms machine 2 (Vista, 2-CPU, 32-bit, 2.0GHz laptop) by factors far beyond what can be explained by CPU count and clock speed alone; see the locking results (Table C–5). In some other cases, the results are nearly the same, as with file copying (Table C–1), which is purely serial. The impact of these features can be difficult, if not impossible, to predict accurately. Ultimately, you need to test your application.

One more example will reinforce this point. I recently experimented with a parallelism framework (see Chapter 9) on the 2-CPU Vista laptop (machine 2) and for many programs found consistent performance improvement factors such as 1.5 to 1.9 compared to the serial, single-threaded program. Running on more processors, such as machine 4, gave even better results. However, one test program run on the laptop, a matrix transpose, was consistently slower than the serial version run on the same machine, although the results on other machines were good. The explanation, while not certain, seemed to involve the laptop's cache architecture.

Finally, here is even more advice. First, do not put too much weight on small performance differences, especially when the total times are small (less than a second, for example). In many cases, such as file copying, results can vary widely from one run to the next. Also, beware of the temptation to gain performance at the cost of correctness; multithreaded applications, for instance, can be challenging to get right.

File Copying

Five file copy implementations copy a 320MB file (5,000,000 64-byte records, generated with Chapter 5's RandFile program).

1. cpC (Program 1–1) uses the C library. This test measures the effect of an implementation layered on top of Windows, although the library has the opportunity to perform efficient buffering and other techniques.

2. `cpW` (Program 1–2) is the straightforward Windows implementation with a small buffer (256 bytes).

3. `cpwFA` is a "fast" implementation, using a larger buffer (8,192 bytes, a multiple of the sector size on all host machines) and the sequential scan flags on both the input and output files.

4. `cpCF` (Program 1–3) uses the Windows `CopyFile` function to determine whether the implementation within a single system call is more efficient than what can be achieved with other techniques.

5. `cpUC` is a UNIX implementation using a small buffer (similar to `cpW`). It is modified slightly to use the Visual C++ UNIX compatibility library.

While the results are averages of five test runs, the elapsed time can vary widely. For example, cp (first row), with an average of 2.48 seconds in the second column (2-CPU Vista laptop), had a minimum elapsed time of less than a second and a maximum of more than 10 seconds. This wide variation was typical of nearly all cases on all the machines.

Comments

1. The C library gives competitive performance that is superior to the simplest Windows implementation in many cases, but the UNIX compatibility library is slower.

2. Multiple processors do not make a difference, as the implementations do not exploit parallelism.

3. There is no significant difference between the 32-bit and 64-bit build performance (machines 3, 4, and 6).

4. There are elapsed time performance advantages on Vista and Windows 7 machines obtained by using large buffers, sequential scan flags, or a function such as `CopyFile`.

5. Vista is significantly faster than XP, although the XP laptop may suffer from older disk technology.

6. The Windows 7 times look good compared to Vista on the same hardware platform (machines 4 and 6).

7. Elapsed time results are highly variable, with as much as a 10:1 difference between identical tests run under identical circumstances.

Table C-1   File Copy Performance

	CPU	1.4GHz 1-CPU	2.0GHz 2-CPU	2.83GHz 4-CPU	2.4GHz 4-CPU	1.7GHz 8-CPU	2.4GHz 4-CPU
	OS	XP	Vista	Vista	Vista	Server 2008	Windows 7
	Build CPU	32-bit 32-bit	32-bit 32-bit	32-bit 32-bit	64-bit 64-bit	32-bit 32-bit	32-bit 64-bit
cpC	Real	36.10	2.48	3.33	2.66	2.50	1.87
	User	0.98	0.90	0.55	0.51	0.92	0.56
	System	3.31	1.53	1.37	1.75	1.47	0.92
cpW	Real	33.48	8.58	9.47	9.85	9.83	6.71
	User	0.45	0.53	1.59	0.11	0.58	0.41
	System	10.88	8.24	7.86	8.80	8.56	6.15
cpwFA	Real	40.23	0.92	0.89	1.13	1.22	0.87
	User	0.03	0.03	0.09	0.00	0.03	0.12
	System	2.03	1.03	0.80	1.23	1.17	0.83
cpCF	Real	18.08	0.70	0.79	0.79	1.95	1.19
	User	0.03	0.02	0.02	0.00	0.00	0.00
	System	0.77	0.64	0.62	0.67	1.31	0.58
cpUC	Real	37.61	6.65	4.12	4.34	6.05	3.67
	User	3.63	3.17	1.93	2.32	2.98	1.98
	System	3.92	3.28	2.01	1.68	3.00	1.65

Caesar Cipher File Conversion

Seven programs tested converting the same 320MB file. Table C–2 shows the results.

1. cci is Program 2–3 and is comparable to cpW using a small buffer.

2. cciLBSS uses both a large buffer and sequential scan flags, and it also presizes the output file to the length required.

3. cciOV, Run 14–1, uses overlapped I/O.

4. cciEX, Program 14–2, uses extended I/O.

5. cciMM uses memory mapping for file I/O and calls the functions in Program 5–3.

6. cciMT is a multithreaded implementation of Chapter 14's multiple buffer scheme without asynchronous I/O.

7. cciMTMM is a modification of cciMT and uses memory-mapped files rather than ReadFile and WriteFile.

Comments

1. These results show no consistent benefit to using large buffers and the sequential scan flags, possibly in conjunction.

2. The very large cciOV and cciMT times for test machine 1 (Windows XP) are not misprints; these times are repeatable and are only partially explained by clock rate, disk speed, or similar factors.

3. Extended and overlapped I/O performance are excellent on Windows Vista and Windows 7. Notice that the time is predominantly user time and not system time.

4. Multiple threads do not provide any significant benefit unless the threads are combined with memory-mapped files.

5. Memory-mapped I/O can give good performance, except that test machine 2 (Windows XP, 2 processors) showed poor performance consistently. I don't have a good explanation for this behavior.

Table C–2   File Conversion Performance

		1.4GHz 1-CPU	2.0GHz 2-CPU	2.83GHz 4-CPU	2.4GHz 4-CPU	2.4GHz 4-CPU
	CPU					
	OS	XP	Vista	Vista	Vista	Windows 7
	Build CPU	32-bit 32-bit	32-bit 32-bit	32-bit 32-bit	64-bit 64-bit	32-bit 64-bit
cci	Real	53.80	15.21	18.62	17.83	13.45
	User	4.27	2.03	7.00	6.24	5.41
	System	11.64	11.70	12.34	11.40	7.94
cciLBSS	Real	40.14	13.74	16.67	18.91	13.77
	User	3.13	1.31	5.93	7.16	4.85
	System	1.97	1.25	1.06	1.53	1.31
cciOV	Real	371.2	5.27	7.55	9.37	6.47
	User	3.16	1.62	6.10	8.11	5.37
	System	2.11	1.26	1.42	1.08	1.06
cciEX	Real	62.56	3.21	7.96	10.57	6.29
	User	8.36	1.68	6.58	9.19	5.21
	System	6.02	0.95	0.89	1.28	0.99
cciMM	Real	4.08	37.59	5.82	6.67	5.13
	User	3.16	1.83	5.40	6.61	4.65
	System	0.66	1.86	0.41	0.42	0.48
cciMT	Real	485.6	8.11	5.81	6.20	4.80
	User	2.72	1.47	1.42	5.77	5.09
	System	2.69	2.22	2.48	1.83	1.47
cciMTMM	Real	23.66	2.70	2.44	2.50	2.29
	User	3.11	1.62	5.07	5.20	4.88
	System	0.33	0.21	0.17	0.11	0.16

Word Counting

Four word counting methods compared the efficiencies of multiple threads and sequential processing (see Table C–3).

1. wc, the Cygwin implementation (a free download from www.cygwin.com), is single threaded but well-implemented.

2. wcMT, a variation of Program 7–1, uses a thread for each file and direct (read/write) file I/O.

3. wcMTMM replaces wcMT's direct I/O with file memory mapping.

4. wcMT_VTP is the Vista thread pool variation of wcMTMM.

The eight target files used in the test are each 64MB. Using files with significantly different lengths would reduce the parallelism and multithreaded speedup, as some threads would complete sooner than others. However, wcMT_VTP should adjust to this situation and give better results (this would be a good experiment).

Comments

1. wcMT is slow not because of the threads but because of the direct file reading. A single-threaded version showed similar bad results.

2. The Cygwin wc implementation is competitive on a single processor.

3. Memory-mapped files provide a clear advantage, and the threading is also effective.

4. Multiprocessor machines show the performance gains that are possible using threads. Notice that the total user and system times exceed the real time because the user and system times represent all processors. We'll also see this in other tests.

Table C–3   Word Counting Performance

		1.4GHz 1-CPU	2.0GHz 2-CPU	2.83GHz 4-CPU	2.4GHz 4-CPU	1.7GHz 8-CPU	2.4GHz 4-CPU
	CPU						
	OS	XP	Vista	Vista	Vista	Server 2008	Windows 7
	Build CPU	32-bit 32-bit	32-bit 32-bit	32-bit 32-bit	64-bit 64-bit	32-bit 32-bit	32-bit 64-bit
wc	Real	6.84	22.12	2.45	3.59	7.08	3.57
	User	4.69	3.15	1.81	2.56	5.52	2.31
	System	0.91	1.33	0.64	1.14	1.52	1.23
wcMT	Real	97.78	40.05	41.78	20.71	68.33	28.11
	User	97.12	73.06	153.8	77.89	424.3	96.55
	System	0.64	0.09	0.62	0.70	1.09	0.84
wcMTMM	Real	4.67	1.58	0.56	1.44	0.52	1.45
	User	4.25	2.45	1.83	5.01	3.19	5.09
	System	0.38	0.09	0.09	0.12	0.17	0.11
wcMT_VTP	Real	N/A	3.88	0.58	1.76	0.52	1.84
	User	N/A	7.02	1.64	5.93	3,19	6.10
	System	N/A	0.16	0.20	0.08	0.19	0.14

Random File Record Access

This test set compares `RecordAccess` (Chapter 3) and `RecordAccessMM` (Chapter 5). These programs read and write fixed-length records in large, initially empty files. The programs both interact with the user who specifies read, write, delete, or other operations and specifies a record number and data (for write operations). There is no hashing; this record number is an index into the file, as if it were an array.

An additional program, `RecordAccessTestDataGenerate`, creates text command files to drive the tests. The test set then:

1. Creates empty files with space for 100,000 fixed-length records. The record length is, arbitrarily, 308 bytes.

2. Generates a command file to write 50,000 data records into random locations in the file.

3. Generates a command file to read 100,000 records from the file. Some will not be located, as there are only 50,000 nonempty records.

4. The command files are used as redirected input to both `RecordAccess` and `RecordAccessMM`.

Comments

1. Memory-mapped file I/O is always fastest. However, be aware that these tests use small records; you can get different results if your records are larger than the page size.

2. Vista's random access is much better than XP's. Windows 7 shows poor random access write performance. This result is repeatable, and there is no apparent explanation.

3. The two programs are single threaded, so multiple processors do not provide an advantage.

Table C–4 Random File Record Access

	CPU	1.4GHz 1-CPU	2.0GHz 2-CPU	2.83GHz 4-CPU	2.4GHz 4-CPU	1.7GHz 8-CPU	2.4GHz 4-CPU
	OS	XP	Vista	Vista	Vista	Server 2008	Windows 7
	Build CPU	32-bit 32-bit	32-bit 32-bit	32-bit 32-bit	64-bit 64-bit	32-bit 32-bit	32-bit 64-bit
Write 50K Records Random Access	Real	163.84	18.12	10.88	6.32	8.36	17.64
	User	0.23	0.31	0.28	0.45	0.41	0.44
	System	1.13	1.22	0.72	1.19	0.86	0.95
Read 50K Records Random Access	Real	11.89	0.87	0.61	0.84	0.84	0.42
	User	0.19	0.14	0.11	0.16	0.16	0.17
	System	0.45	0.73	0.50	0.64	0.63	0.25
Write 50K Records Memory Mapped	Real	0.63	0.29	0.24	0.50	0.67	0.33
	User	0.41	0.22	0.17	0.41	0.58	0.27
	System	0.62	0.08	0.08	0.06	0.09	0.06
Read 100K Records Memory Mapped	Real	0.22	0.13	0.14	0.14	0.27	0.11
	User	0.22	0.12	0.11	0.14	0.23	0.08
	System	0.02	0.0	0.03	0.03	0.03	0.03

Locking

The locking tests ran seven of the Chapter 9 `stats` variations to compare the efficiencies of locking by multiple worker threads (see Table C–5). Chapter 9 lists some partial results. The seven programs, listed in order of expected performance from best to worst, are:

1. `statsNS` has no locking synchronization, which is valid in this simple program, as there are no shared variables. The NS results show the actual time that the worker tasks require; the remaining tests show the locking overhead.

2. `statsIN` uses interlocked increment and decrement operations so that locking occurs at the lowest level with atomic processor instructions.

3. `statsSRW_VTP` uses a slim reader/writer (SRW) lock and a Vista thread pool.

4. `statsSRW` uses an SRW lock but conventional thread management.

5. `statsCS` uses a `CRITICAL_SECTION`, but there is no spin lock adjustment. Spin lock experimentation would be interesting but is not included.

6. `statsMX_ST` uses a Windows mutex and a semaphore throttle set to the number of processors, or to the number of threads on a single-processor machine. The performance improvement, if any, is marginal with 64 threads but is better with 128 threads (see Table 9–1).

7. `statsMX` uses a Windows mutex.

In each case, there were 64 worker threads, with each thread performing 256,000 work units. The results are similar when using more threads or fewer threads, although the differences are harder to distinguish for 16 or fewer threads. The mutex cases (`statsMX`, `statsMX_ST`) show the negative impact of more processors contending for the mutex (compare the 4- and 8-processor cases).

See Chapter 9 for more information about these programs and their relative speeds.

Table C–5 Locking Performance

stats		1.4GHz 1-CPU	2.0GHz 2-CPU	2.83GHz 4-CPU	2.4GHz 4-CPU	1.7GHz 8-CPU	2.4GHz 4-CPU
	CPU						
	OS	XP	Vista	Vista	Vista	Server 2008	Windows 7
	Build CPU	32-bit 32-bit	32-bit 32-bit	32-bit 32-bit	64-bit 64-bit	32-bit 32-bit	32-bit 64-bit
NS	Real	0.13	4.42	0.08	1.82	0.11	2.28
	User	0.13	8.64	0.14	7.19	0.75	8.95
	System	0.02	0.03	0.03	0.02	0.00	0.02
IN	Real	0.50	4.46	0.53	1.80	0.48	2.28
	User	0.48	8.83	1.89	7.11	0.47	9.02
	System	0.00	0.02	0.00	0.00	0.00	0.00
SRW_VTP	Real	N/A	5.41	0.64	2.30	0.77	2.75
	User	N/A	10.36	2.26	9.00	5.78	10.89
	System	N/A	0.02	0.02	0.03	0.00	0.00
SRW	Real	N/A	5.24	0.63	2.32	0.84	2.79
	User	N/A	10.16	2.31	9.11	6.21	11.00
	System	N/A	0.05	0.02	0.02	0.00	0.00
CS	Real	1.17	5.30	1.28	5.02	2.02	4.73
	User	1.17	10.08	0.98	11.14	3.72	13.18
	System	0.00	0.14	1.23	3.57	0.20	3.53
MX_ST	Real	59.69	157.9	132.0	110.0	242.5	90.68
	User	17.75	36.26	35.32	37.32	355.8	40.28
	System	41.16	49.44	209.3	194.3	157.9	72.40
MX	Real	31.52	167.6	178.8	115.2	226.2	94.07
	User	9.13	24.66	16.49	26.30	157.7	42.09
	System	21.00	64.16	132.9	84.74	61.67	72.34

Message Passing and Contending for a Single Resource

This test sequence compares different strategies for implementing the queue management functions of Program 10–4, using Program 10–5 (the three-stage pipeline) as a test application. The tests were run on machine 4 (4-CPU, Vista, 32-bit builds) using 1, 2, 4, 8, 16, 32, and 64 threads along with 4,000 work units per thread. Ideally, we would then expect real time to increase linearly with the number of threads, but contention for a single mutex (or CRITICAL_SECTION (CS)) can cause nonlinear degradation as the number of threads increases. Note that these tests do not exercise the file system.

There are six different implementation strategies, and the results are shown in separate columns in Table C–6. The comments following Program 10–4 discuss the results and explain the merits of the different implementations, but notice that the signal model does scale with the number of threads, while the broadcast model does not scale, especially with 32 and 64 threads. Also notice how the broadcast model results in large amounts of system CPU time as multiple threads run, test the predicate, and immediately return to the wait state.

Also notice how CSs compare well with condition variables (the last two columns) in the signal model, even though the CS implementation requires a time-out.

1. ThreeStage. Broadcast model, mutex, event, separate release and wait calls. There is no time-out.

2. ThreeStageCS. Broadcast model, CRITICAL_SECTION, event, separate release and wait calls. The tunable time-out was set to 25 milliseconds, which optimized the 16-thread case.

3. ThreeStage_noSOAW. Broadcast model, mutex, event, with 25-ms time-out.

4. ThreeStage_SIG. Signal model, mutex, event, separate release and wait calls.

5. ThreeStageCS_SIG. Signal model, CRITICAL_SECTION, event, separate release and wait calls.

6. ThreeStageCV. Vista condition variable using WakeConditionVariable (the signal model).

Table C-6 Multithreaded Pipeline Performance on a Four-Processor Desktop

Number of Threads		Broadcast Model	Broadcast Model	Broadcast Model	Signal Model	Signal Model	Signal Model
		Mtx, Evt	CS, Evt	Mtx, Evt	SOAW	CS, Evt	Vista CV
		no T/O	25-ms T/O	25-ms T/O	no T/O	25 ms T/O	WakeCV
1	Real	0.12	0.03	0.10	0.07	0.10	0.05
	User	0.16	0.06	0.06	0.05	0.14	0.09
	System	0.05	0.02	0.11	0.08	0.08	0.02
2	Real	0.17	0.14	0.16	0.17	0.09	0.07
	User	0.17	0.14	0.14	0.09	0.14	0.14
	System	0.17	0.16	0.23	0.14	0.11	0.05
4	Real	0.47	0.27	0.48	0.40	0.15	0.14
	User	0.37	0.31	0.34	0.28	0.16	0.30
	System	0.80	0.19	0.67	0.50	0.30	0.08
8	Real	1.60	0.50	1.43	0.79	0.34	0.32
	User	0.98	0.64	0.84	0.67	0.48	0.52
	System	2.15	0.47	1.87	0.89	0.51	0.17
16	Real	5.71	1.44	5.06	1.56	0.71	0.72
	User	2.37	1.44	2.29	1.20	1.17	1.36
	System	6.49	1.99	6.29	1.58	0.94	0.30
32	Real	21.21	4.33	20.42	3.14	1.42	1.54
	User	6.26	3.03	6.30	2.78	2.18	2.96
	System	23.50	7.27	25.12	3.78	2.04	0.67
64	Real	82.99	16.21	76.51	6.37	2.82	2.47
	User	21.00	7.86	20.09	5.60	4.04	6.27
	System	89.06	28.22	95.08	7.99	4.17	2.50

Running the Tests

The `TimeTest` directory on the book's Web site includes the following batch files:

- `cpTIME.bat`

- `cciTIME.bat` — The word count tests are also in this file

- `RecordAccessTIME.bat`

- `SynchStatsTIME.bat`

- `ThreeStageTime.bat`

The program `RandFile` creates a large ASCII file used in the first two batch files.

Bibliography

Beveridge, Jim, and Wiener, Robert. *Multithreading Applications in Win32: The Complete Guide to Threads,* Addison-Wesley, Reading, MA, 1997. ISBN-13: 9780201442342.

Bott, Ed, and Siechert, Carl. *Microsoft® Windows® XP Networking and Security Inside Out,* Microsoft Press, Redmond, WA, 2005. ISBN-13: 9780735620421.

Box, Don. *Essential COM,* Addison-Wesley, Reading, MA, 1998. ISBN-13: 9780201634464.

Butenhof, David. *Programming with POSIX® Threads,* Addison-Wesley, Reading, MA, 1997. ISBN-13: 9780201633924.

Chen, Raymond. *The Old New Thing: Practical Development Throughout the Evolution of Windows,* Addison-Wesley, Boston, MA, 2007. ISBN-13: 9780321440303.

CCRA. *Common Criteria.* This defines the security assurance levels. www.commoncriteriaportal.org/thecc.html.

Cormen, Thomas H, Leiserson, Charles E., Rivest, Ronald L, and Stein, Clifford. *Introduction to Algorithms, Third Edition,* MIT Press, Cambridge, MA, 2009. ISBN-13: 9780262033848.

Custer, Helen. *Inside Windows NT®,* Microsoft Press, Redmond, WA, 1993. ISBN-13: 9781556154812.

———. *Inside the Windows NT File System,* Microsoft Press, Redmond, WA, 1994. ISBN-13: 9781556156601.

Donahoo, Michael, and Calvert, Kenneth. *TCP/IP Sockets in C: Practical Guide for Programmers,* Morgan Kaufmann, San Francisco, CA, 2001. ISBN-13: 9781558608269.

Dr. International. *Developing International Software, Second Edition,* Microsoft Press, 2002. ISBN-13: 9780735615830.

Duffy, Joe. *Concurrent Programming on Windows,* Addison-Wesley, Boston, MA, 2009. ISBN-13: 9780321434821.

Hennessy, John L., and Patterson, David A. *Computer Architecture: A Quantitative Approach, Third Edition,* Morgan Kaufmann, San Francisco, CA, 2002. ISBN-13: 9781558605961.

Honeycutt, Jerry. *Microsoft® Windows® Registry Guide, Second Edition,* Microsoft Press, Redmond, WA, 2005. ISBN-13: 9780735622180.

Josuttis, Nicolai M. *The C++ Standard Library: A Tutorial and Reference,* Addison-Wesley, Boston, MA, 1999. ISBN-13: 9780201379266.

Kano, Nadine. *Developing International Software for Windows® 95 and Windows NT™,* Microsoft Press, Redmond, WA, 1995. ISBN-13: 9781556158407.

Kernighan, Brian W., and Ritchie, Dennis M. *C Programming Language: ANSI C Version, Second Edition,* Prentice-Hall, Englewood Cliffs, NJ, 1988. ISBN-13: 9780131103627.

Komar, Brian. *Microsoft Windows Server™ 2003 PKI and Certificate Security,* Microsoft Press, Redmond, WA, 2004. ISBN-13: 9780735620216.

Miller, Kevin. *Professional NT Services,* Wrox Press, Indianapolis, IN, 1998. ISBN-13: 9781861001306.

Nagar, Rajeev. *Windows NT® File System Internals,* OSR Press, Amherst, NH, 2006. ISBN-13: 9780976717515.

Naik, Dilip. *Inside Windows Storage: Server Storage Technologies for Windows 2000, Windows Server 2003, and Beyond,* Addison-Wesley, Boston, MA, 2004. ISBN-13: 9780321126986.

Nottingham, Jason P., Makofsky, Steven, and Tucker, Andrew. *SAMS Teach Yourself Windows® CE Programming in 24 Hours,* Que Corporation, Berkeley, CA, 1999. ISBN-13: 9780672316586.

Ohlund, Jim. *Network Programming for Microsoft® Windows®, Second Edition,* Microsoft Press, Redmond, WA, 2002. ISBN-13: 9780735615793.

Oney, Walter. *Programming the Microsoft® Windows® Driver Model, Second Edition,* Microsoft Press, Redmond, WA, 2003. ISBN-13: 9780735618039.

Petzold, Charles. *Programming Windows®, Fifth Edition,* Microsoft Press, Redmond, WA, 1998. ISBN-13: 9781572319950.

Plauger, P. J. *The Standard C Library,* Prentice Hall, Englewood Cliffs, NJ, 1991. ISBN-13: 9780131315099.

Raymond, Eric S. *The Art of UNIX Programming,* Addison-Wesley, Boston, MA, 2004. ISBN-13: 9780131429017.

Rector, Brent, and Newcomer, Joseph M. *Win32 Programming,* Addison-Wesley, Reading, MA, 1997. ISBN-13: 9780201634921.

Richter, Jeffrey and Nasarre, Christophe. *Windows® via C/C++, Fifth Edition,* Microsoft Press, Redmond, WA, 2007. ISBN-13: 9780735624245.

Richter, Jeffrey, and Clark, Jason. *Programming Server-Side Applications for Microsoft® Windows® 2000,* Microsoft Press, Redmond, WA, 2000. ISBN-13: 9780735607538.

Robbins, Arnold. *UNIX in a Nutshell, Fourth Edition,* O'Reilly Media, Inc., Cambridge, MA, 2008. ISBN-13: 9780596100292.

Russinovich, Mark, Solomon, David, and Ionescu, Alex. *Windows® Internals: Including Windows Server® 2008 and Windows Vista®, Fifth Edition,* Microsoft Press, Redmond, WA, 2009. ISBN-13: 9780735625303.

Schmidt, Douglas, and Pyarali, Irfan. *Strategies for Implementing POSIX Condition Variables in Win32,* www.cs.wustl.edu/~schmidt/win32-cv-1.html.

Sinha, Alok K. *Network Programming in Windows NT*™, Addison-Wesley, Reading, MA, 1996. ISBN-13: 9780201590562.

Smith, Ben, Komar, Brian, and the Microsoft Security Team. *Microsoft® Windows® Security Resource Kit, Second Edition,* Microsoft Press, Redmond, WA, 2005. ISBN-13: 9780735621749.

Stevens, W. Richard, and Rago, Stephen A. *Advanced Programming in the UNIX® Environment, Second Edition,* Addison-Wesley, Boston, MA, 2008. ISBN-13: 9780321525949.

Stevens, W. Richard. *TCP/IP Illustrated, Volume 3: TCP for Transactions, HTTP, NNTP, and the UNIX® Domain Protocols,* Addison-Wesley, Reading, MA, 1996. ISBN-13: 9780201634952.

————. *UNIX Network Programming—Networking APIs: Sockets and XTI, Volume I,* Prentice Hall, Upper Saddle River, NJ, 1998. ISBN-13: 9780134900124.

Tanenbaum, Andrew S. *Modern Operating Systems, Third Edition,* Prentice Hall, Upper Saddle River, NJ, 2008. ISBN-13: 9780136006633.

Unicode Consortium, The. *The Unicode Standard, Version 2.0,* Addison-Wesley, Reading, MA, 1997. ISBN-13: 9780201483451.

Williams, Robert, and Walla, Mark. *The Ultimate Windows Server 2003 System Administrator's Guide,* Addison-Wesley, Boston, MA, 2003. ISBN-13: 9780201791068.

Index

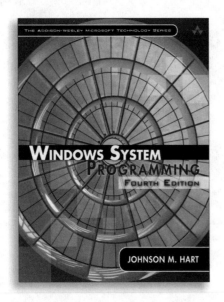

FREE Online Edition

Your purchase of **Windows System Programming, Fourth Edition,** includes access to a free online edition for 45 days through the Safari Books Online subscription service. Nearly every Addison-Wesley Professional book is available online through Safari Books Online, along with more than 5,000 other technical books and videos from publishers such as, Cisco Press, Exam Cram, IBM Press, O'Reilly, Prentice Hall, Que, and Sams.

SAFARI BOOKS ONLINE allows you to search for a specific answer, cut and paste code, download chapters, and stay current with emerging technologies.

Activate your FREE Online Edition at www.informit.com/safarifree

> **STEP 1:** Enter the coupon code: DKCDIWH.

> **STEP 2:** New Safari users, complete the brief registration form.
> Safari subscribers, just log in.

If you have difficulty registering on Safari or accessing the online edition, please e-mail customer-service@safaribooksonline.com